Labor Statistics
Measurement Issues

Studies in Income and Wealth
Volume 60

National Bureau of Economic Research
Conference on Research in Income and Wealth

Labor Statistics
Measurement Issues

Edited by   John Haltiwanger,
Marilyn E. Manser, and
Robert Topel

The University of Chicago Press

Chicago and London

BMC 5593-4/3

JOHN HALTIWANGER is professor of economics at the University of Maryland and chief economist at the Bureau of the Census. MARILYN E.
MANSER is assistant commissioner for employment research and program
development at the Bureau of Labor Statistics, U.S. Department of Labor.
ROBERT TOPEL is the Isidore Brown and Gladys J. Brown Professor in Urban and Labor Economics at the University of Chicago Graduate School
of Business and a research associate of the National Bureau of Economic
Research.

The University of Chicago Press, Chicago 60637
The University of Chicago Press, Ltd., London
© 1998 by the National Bureau of Economic Research
All rights reserved. Published 1998
Printed in the United States of America
07 06 05 04 03 02 01 00 99 98   1 2 3 4 5
ISBN: 0-226-31458-8 (cloth)

Library of Congress Cataloging-in-Publication Data

Labor statistics measurement issues / edited by John Haltiwanger,
    Marilyn E. Manser, and Robert Topel.
        p.   cm.—(NBER studies in income and wealth ; 60)
    Conference proceedings.
    Includes bibliographical references and index.
    ISBN 0-226-31458-8 (cloth : alk. paper)
    1. Labor supply—United States—Statistical methods—Congress.
2. Labor productivity—United States—Statistical methods—
Congress.   3. Work measurement—United States—Congress.
4. Unemployed—United States—Congress.   I. Haltiwanger,
John.   II. Manser, Marilyn.   III. Topel, Robert H.   IV. Series:
Studies in income and wealth ; v. 60.
HC106.3.C714 v. 60
[HD5711 IN PROCESS]
330 s—dc21
[331.1'07'24]   98-22635
                                                            CIP

⊗ The paper used in this publication meets the minimum requirements of
the American National Standard for Information Sciences—Permanence
of Paper for Printed Library Materials, ANSI Z39.48-1992.

Contents

Prefatory Note

This volume contains revised versions of the papers and discussion presented at the Conference on Research in Income and Wealth entitled Labor Statistics Measurement Issues, held in Washington, D.C., on 15–16 December 1994. Conference participants also attended a preconference at the National Bureau of Economic Research in August 1994.

Funds for the Conference on Research in Income and Wealth are provided to the National Bureau of Economic Research by the Bureau of the Census, the Bureau of Economic Analysis, the Bureau of Labor Statistics, the Internal Revenue Service, the National Science Foundation, and Statistics Canada; we are indebted to them for their support. The Labor Statistics Measurement Issues conference was supported under National Science Foundation grant SBR 9410038.

We also thank John Haltiwanger, Marilyn E. Manser, and Robert Topel, who served as conference organizers and editors of this volume.

Volume Editors' Acknowledgments

We are grateful to Katharine Abraham for discussions that helped to shape the conference. We thank Kirsten Foss Davis, Deborah Kiernan, Cristina McFadden, and Elizabeth Gertsch for organizing the conference arrangements and handling the publication. Finally, we thank two anonymous referees for their comments on the manuscript.

Introduction

John Haltiwanger, Marilyn E. Manser, and Robert Topel

Beginning in the 1970s, the American labor market experienced a number of important structural changes. Reversing previous trends, wage and income inequality steadily increased, and the wage premiums commanded by skilled workers rose sharply. While women's wages and labor force participation continued to rise, average wage growth among men stagnated and male labor force participation trended downward, especially among the least skilled. Some observers have argued that employment relations themselves have become less stable, so that the concept of a "lifetime job" no longer applies to American workers.

A variety of explanations have been offered for these changes, including the decline of unions, increased immigration of less skilled labor, and increased competition from foreign manufacturers. While these factors may yet prove important, most current evidence points to technological change as the main driver that has shifted labor demands—and thus changed wages and working conditions—over the past 20 years. Much remains unknown, however. For example, if technical change has raised the value of skilled labor, how have private sector training programs responded? Is it the case, as some allege, that human capital investment by American firms and workers has been inadequate? Is there any prospect that private sector training and other forms of human capital investment will reduce wage inequality in the near future?

Despite the importance of these and other labor market questions, there has been little work on the measurement issues involved. To focus greater profes-

John Haltiwanger is professor of economics at the University of Maryland and chief economist at the Bureau of the Census. Marilyn E. Manser is assistant commissioner for employment research and program development at the Bureau of Labor Statistics, U.S. Department of Labor. Robert Topel is the Isidore Brown and Gladys J. Brown Professor in Urban and Labor Economics at the University of Chicago Graduate School of Business and a research associate of the National Bureau of Economic Research.

sional attention on these measurement issues, we organized a conference to bring together economic researchers, data providers, and policy analysts from academia, government, and the private sector. This conference, sponsored by the National Bureau of Economic Research (NBER) Conference on Research in Income and Wealth (CRIW), was held in Washington, D.C., 15–16 December 1994.

This volume contains 13 papers from the 1994 conference, broadly organized around the issues of measuring employment, unemployment, and wages and evaluating training and workplace practices. Some of the papers involve conceptual issues of what is meant, what is known or can be learned from existing data, and what needs have not been met by available data sources. Other papers make innovative uses of existing data to analyze these topics. Papers examining how answers to important questions are affected by alternative measures used and how these can be reconciled are also included.

Existing Data System and Overall Needs

The volume begins with two overview papers. Marilyn Manser attempts to set the stage for considering needs and possibilities by reviewing existing government data on employment, unemployment, compensation, and other labor market topics and the major current purposes of these data. She analyzes the use of these data for one major purpose, academic research studies. Finally, she discusses recognized additional needs for data and other needs that could be addressed with existing data. Two major themes emerge: the need for microdata to address issues involving labor demand and the related need to provide greater accessibility to the microdata collected and processed by the statistical agencies.

Robert Topel distinguishes between two functions for data, description and the estimation of models of labor market behavior. He argues that empirical research has been very successful in describing labor markets, particularly on the household side, although he points to three areas in need of more data. With respect to model estimation, he argues that empirical research has been much less successful in calibrating economic behavior; what would be needed here is more information on real-world experiments.

Employment and Wages

The second set of papers examines new dimensions in measuring and understanding employment, unemployment, and wages. Three of these provide new perspectives on the topic of labor market turbulence. Steven Davis and John Haltiwanger examine the connection between gross job flows and gross worker flows. It has long been recognized from analysis of household data that the pace of worker flows between labor force states is very high in the United States. However, based solely on household information it has been virtually impossible to gauge the relative contribution of the reallocation of jobs versus the reallocation of workers across a given allocation of jobs. Using longitudinal establishment data, Davis and Haltiwanger develop measures of gross job creation and destruction that characterize the connection between worker and job flows. While considerable progress on measuring job flows has been made in the past decade, Davis and Haltiwanger emphasize that data limitations restrict this type of analysis on a timely, economy-wide basis. They review ongoing developments at statistical agencies to develop economy-wide longitudinal microeconomic databases and argue that development of matched employer-employee longitudinal data would be an especially useful research tool.

Henry Farber shows that existing data can shed considerable light on the durability of employment relations in the United States. Using the Current Population Survey (CPS) for the years 1973–93, he examines the evolution of job tenure of American workers and concludes that the length of the typical employment relationship did not change much over this period. While contrary to popular perception, this is generally in accord with related findings on gross job flows, which do not show an increase in job turnover. Farber, however, does find that job durations have declined for some demographic groups, particularly men with less than a high school education, while they have increased for others, especially women with at least a high school education, who are now more committed to the labor force.

Stephen Jones and Craig Riddell, using Canadian data, expand the usual treatment of worker flows between labor force states (for which official U.S. measures are not available) to examine whether those persons out of the labor force who are "marginally attached" are behaviorally distinct from those counted as unemployed or from the remainder of those persons classified as out of the labor force. While there are some notable differences across demographic groups, they conclude that marginally attached workers are behaviorally distinct from others not in the labor force and are closer in behavioral terms to the unemployed than to other nonworkers.

Anne Polivka and Steven Miller examine the impact of the major 1994 CPS redesign. An important practical contribution of their paper is the calculation of historical adjustment factors that allow researchers to compare pre- and post-redesign labor force series. They conclude that the pre-1994 CPS accurately measured labor force status for the vast majority of individuals who were working or looking for work. There was some mismeasurement for individuals on the "periphery" of the labor market.

As emphasized in the paper by Manser, data limitations mean that relatively little is known about certain aspects of firm behavior and employment and wages in the United States. Robert McGuckin, Sang Nguyen, and Arnold Reznek utilize data from the Census Bureau's Longitudinal Research Database (LRD) and find that ownership change is positively associated with growth in productivity and wages. Focusing on the food-manufacturing industry, they also find that ownership change is associated with employment growth of the firm and the likelihood that a plant survives. Their paper also illustrates many of the measurement difficulties in developing longitudinal establishment data for the investigation of labor market dynamics.

Even where data are available, important dimensions of labor markets may not be well understood. One major question concerns the trend of real wages. Katharine Abraham, James Spletzer, and Jay Stewart describe available wage series and their behavior and explore alternative hypotheses concerning their differing trends. Among other findings, they conclude that it is likely that Current Employment Statistics (CES) weekly earnings have diverged from CPS and National Income and Product Accounts weekly earnings measures because they apply to a different worker population, although this population may not be precisely the production and nonsupervisory group specified by the formal CES definitions.

Looking Inside the Firm

The final set of papers looks inside the firm. Canice Prendergast takes a broad-ranging, nontraditional look at the question of how jobs are defined and when a workplace is well designed in terms of incentives and other factors. He examines the extent to which various types of data are available (quite limited) or might be developed to distinguish among alternative theories in this area. One of his main conclusions is that we need data on individual contracts within firms to understand the nature of incentive and compensation policies and in turn the distribution of wages.

John Abowd and Francis Kramarz utilize data from a large, representative matched firm-worker sample for France to analyze internal and external labor markets. They find that the majority of the firm size–wage differential in France is explained by the tendency of high-wage firms to employ individuals with high external wage opportunities. That is, the wage differential reflects skills, not rents that accrue to workers of large firms. The high quality of the French matched worker-firm data serves as a model for the potential development of analogous databases in the United States.

Kenneth Troske describes the Worker-Establishment Characteristic Database (WECD) that provides information from the 1990 decennial census long form for workers in manufacturing industries that could be matched to establishment data from the LRD. He assesses the quality of the match and provides examples of how these data can be used to increase understanding of the wage determination process. The WECD is one of the few matched employer-employee data sets available for the United States. This paper illustrates the many potential uses of this database but also notes its limitations given that it is based on a single cross section.

Lisa Lynch addresses the conceptual issue of defining both formal and informal training, assesses how analytic results using presently available information are affected by alternative measures, and considers the need for data on training. She provides an excellent overview of available data sources, including a critical review of data limitations in this area. Her evaluation of available data yields one of the common conclusions from this conference: making progress on our understanding of these issues depends on the development of matched employer-employee data. This refrain is especially forceful in this context given the interrelated decisions of workers and firms on investments in training.

Following the theme of the need for matched employer-employee data, Stephen Bronars and Melissa Famulari utilize data from a small, special test of collecting information on worker demographics in the Bureau of Labor Statistics White Collar Pay Survey. They analyze the incidence of employer-provided training programs and the impact of these programs on wage-tenure profiles. In addition, by matching the data to the Compustat database they are able to examine the relationship between firm profitability, investment in capital equipment and R&D, provision of formal training programs, and returns to training.

Concluding Remarks

In conclusion, a wide variety of rich data already exist on labor markets, particularly households, and major new research studies have continued to appear during the past 10 years, as detailed by Manser. The papers in this volume present interesting new findings as well as point to unmet needs. Although U.S. data are generally viewed as very limited for studying the dynamics of labor markets, papers by Davis and Haltiwanger and by Farber both report important new findings in this area based on various existing data sets. Bronars and Famulari and Troske show the importance of new results that can be obtained from the very limited, and less than ideal, matched worker-establishment data sets that exist for the United States, and Abowd and Kramarz demonstrate the importance of such information indirectly by providing informative analytic results using high-quality French data. Other papers explicitly address the great and continuing need for expanded matched worker-establishment data (Topel, Davis and Haltiwanger, and Lynch). Among important topics, needs for additional data on training and on incentives and compensation practices within firms were explicitly addressed by Lynch and Prendergast, respectively. Topel's and Prendergast's papers, as well as Meyer's discussion, point to the potential value of utilizing data other than large-scale government databases, especially personnel records for a few firms, to address topics for which the former are not well suited.

Although the papers in this volume address a wide variety of important measurement issues affecting understanding of labor markets, they by no means address all of them. For example, there has been substantial change over time in the proportion of employee compensation that takes the form of nonwage benefits. The questions of why this has occurred, how understanding of labor markets is affected by the focus on money wages only, and how nonwage compensation is valued by employees are not addressed here. These issues have received surprisingly little attention since being the focus of the 1981 CRIW conference (Triplett 1983).

Another important omitted topic is the role of changes in the degree of outsourcing, contracting out, and the use of temporary help agency workers in the U.S. economy. These issues loom large in our measurement of labor input by sector and in turn our measurement of labor productivity by sector. Further, changes along these dimensions reflect broader changes in the way labor is used to produce goods and services in the economy. While we neglect the specific issues of contracting out and temporary workers, finding ways to measure and understand the underlying broader changes in the structure of U.S. labor markets motivates much of the analysis and discussion in this volume.

Reference

Triplett, Jack E., ed. 1983. *The measurement of labor cost.* NBER Studies in Income and Wealth, vol. 48. Chicago: University of Chicago Press.

I The Need for Expanded Information

1 Existing Labor Market Data: Current and Potential Research Uses

Marilyn E. Manser

Major new research questions and policy issues concerning labor markets have arisen in recent years. An overriding set of issues involves the perception that many jobs have become less secure and newly created jobs may not be "good jobs" on a number of dimensions. Analysis of these issues requires understanding of contingent work and other nontraditional work arrangements, the pattern of individual job changes and career growth, the process of job destruction and creation, the structure of compensation, and policies within firms. At the same time that there appear to have been major changes in the labor market, there has been little change in the concepts used, the types of information collected, the surveys employed, or the way data are processed and made available.

The purpose of this paper is to set the stage for addressing the current needs for labor market information. The first part provides background for the conference by describing existing government data on employment, unemployment, and compensation and the major purposes of these data and by analyzing their uses in recent labor economics research. The second part of the paper is interpretive and more forward looking: it examines other possible uses of the data and problems in responding to changing needs for data.

Marilyn E. Manser is assistant commissioner for employment research and program development at the Bureau of Labor Statistics, U.S. Department of Labor.

The views expressed are those of the author and do not reflect the policies of the Bureau of Labor Statistics (BLS) or views of other BLS staff members. The author is grateful to Charlie Brown, Dan Hamermesh, and a number of BLS staff members for helpful comments and discussions on a previous draft; to Frank Stafford for detailed discussions about his earlier review of data use in labor economics research; and to Karen Kosanovich for expert research assistance on the analysis of the recent economics literature. Any errors are the sole responsibility of the author.

1.1   Existing Data Sets and Usage

The "official" U.S. data on labor markets are produced by the Bureau of Labor Statistics (BLS). BLS data are also used for labor economics research and analysis, along with various data sets produced by other agencies. To provide some historical perspective, table 1.1 lists the BLS's present labor market data programs, in chronological order of introduction.

The BLS predates the Department of Labor, having been established in 1886 after receiving considerable support from the labor reform movement.[1] For instance, Samuel Gompers of the American Federation of Labor testified in Senate hearings during 1883 that a national bureau "would give our legislators an opportunity to know, not from mere conjecture, but actually, the condition of our industries, our production, and our consumption, and what could be done by law to improve both" (quoted in Goldberg and Moye 1985, 3). The initial focus of the bureau was on prices and, in the labor area, on wages for various occupations and industries. What may seem in more recent years like an overemphasis on certain types of workers (production) and on certain industries (manufacturing) probably has its origins in historical concerns about "working class" men and women in what were earlier emerging industries.[2]

Information on the workforce was obtained for the first time by the Census Bureau in decennial censuses of population conducted in the 1800s. Data were obtained based on the "gainful worker" concept, which counted persons aged 10 and over based on their usual occupation; there was no unemployment measure. During 1914–15, the BLS considered and conducted surveys on unemployment in part of New York City. These were not continued, but a new program to measure employment and payrolls in certain establishments began publication in late 1915 with five manufacturing industries. This was the beginning of the Current Employment Statistics survey program. Just after World War I, interest in unemployment heated up again, but no major changes in data collection concerning unemployment occurred for a number of years afterward. Recommendations for expansion of the employment data to cover nonmanufacturing industries, to collect information on hours worked and some characteristics of workers, and to improve statistical aspects of the survey were made as early as 1926.[3] Data collection for some nonmanufacturing industries began in 1928. In response to policy concerns about unemployment and research with sample surveys that attempted to classify the population as employed, unemployed, or out of the workforce, a new conceptual framework was

1. See Goldberg and Moye (1985, 2–3). This section draws heavily on information provided in Goldberg and Moye.
2. A focus on production workers and manufacturing has existed for some other countries as well—e.g., Great Britain. Additional study would be needed to see if this is typical.
3. A committee was formed by President Hoover to study the factors underlying employment and practical measures that could be undertaken to reduce unemployment. The result was a study by the National Bureau of Economic Research, the Russell Sage Foundation, and the American Statistical Association that was published in 1926.

Table 1.1   **BLS Ongoing Labor Surveys**

First Data Collection	Originating Agency	Program	Date Transferred to BLS
1800s	BLS	Occupational pay surveys	
1915	BLS	Current Employment Statistics (CES or 790)	
1935	Department of Labor– Manpower Administration	Unemployment insurance data (ES-202–Universe File)	1972
1940	Work Projects Administration transferred to Bureau of the Census in 1942	Current Population Survey (CPS)	1959
1948	BLS	Collective bargaining	
1966	Department of Labor– Employment and Training Administration	National Longitudinal Surveys of Labor Market Experience (NLS)	1986
1971	BLS	Occupational Employment Statistics (OES) Survey	
1976	BLS	Employment Cost Index (ECI)	
1980	BLS	Employee Benefits Survey (EBS); earlier surveys of benefits were also done	
1981	BLS	Hours at Work Survey	

adopted for the 1940 census.[4] Also in 1940, a new survey—the predecessor of the Current Population Survey—was begun with labor force classification based on an "activity" concept, which included only those persons who were working or seeking work.[5]

Thus, over 50 years ago, a framework of data on employment, unemployment, and wages had been established based on concerns of policymakers, unions, and academics. Numerous specific changes occurred over the years, leading to the configuration of labor market data programs and other useful research data sets that exists today. In order to help inform the discussion about current needs, the next sections provide an overview of these data sources.[6]

1.1.1   BLS Labor Surveys

This section provides a brief discussion of BLS labor data programs.[7] It does not attempt to fully describe all content of a survey or to assess the important

4. Professional economists inside and outside government and organized labor both played important roles in the call for and development of the employment and unemployment series at various points from 1915 through the 1950s.

5. This paragraph is based in part on the National Commission on Employment and Unemployment Statistics (1979, 21–23).

6. The reader may also be interested in Antos's (1983) discussion of concepts for analyzing labor costs and his survey of BLS information relating to labor costs that existed in the 1970s and early 1980s.

7. The Occupational Safety and Health program is excluded from this survey.

issues of survey methodology and data quality. Documentation on all of the BLS series, with the exception of the "special surveys," is provided in Department of Labor (1992).

Household Surveys

Current Population Survey (CPS). Empirical labor market studies probably rely most heavily on the CPS, a monthly survey of about 50,000 households collected by the Census Bureau for the BLS. This survey is extremely timely: information on labor force status—employment, unemployment, out of the labor force—for the week of the 12th of the month is collected the week of the 19th. The official monthly unemployment rate is calculated from this information and is released about three weeks after the reference period, usually on the first Friday of the following month. A key federal economic indicator, this measure is among the measures most watched by the policy and business communities. Tabulations of labor force status for various demographic groups are also regularly provided based on CPS data. Although establishment surveys are understood to yield better quality measures of industry and occupation, the CPS is the primary source for research on employment or wages by occupation or industry whenever demographic information is needed as well.

A major revision of the CPS, begun in 1986 and conducted jointly by the BLS and the Census Bureau, was recently completed; the official estimates have been based on the new survey since January 1994. In addition to updating the sample design based on the 1990 Census of Population and improving collection methodology and processing, this revision improved question wording. There were also conceptual changes in certain measures (discouraged workers, part time) in accord with recommendations of the National Commission on Employment and Unemployment Statistics (1979), often called the Levitan Commission. This revision completed implementation of the commission's recommendations concerning the monthly CPS except for those concerned with longitudinal data (see below).

Many research and analytic studies based on the CPS use data from the March income supplement funded primarily by the Census Bureau, which provides detailed annual income information and recall measures of employment and unemployment over the past year. Various special supplements, including the Displaced Workers Supplement, have also provided important labor market information.

National Longitudinal Surveys of Labor Market Experience (NLS). The NLS provides data over a long period of time for the same individuals for four "original" cohorts begun in the mid- to late 1960s, namely, older men, mature women, young men, and young women, and for the youth cohort (now called NLSY79) begun in 1979. Data collection for the older men and young men was discontinued in the early 1980s, but the older men were reinterviewed in 1990 with funding from the National Institute on Aging. Data for the ongoing original cohorts and the NLSY79 are collected and disseminated under a contract with Ohio State University. Currently, interviews with about 3,100 respondents from the mature women's cohort and 3,400 respondents from the young women's cohort are collected in a combined survey conducted biennially. About 9,000 respondents are still interviewed in each round of the NLSY79, which was conducted annually through 1994 but is now biennial.

The NLS contains a rich body of labor market and related information and permits the analysis of issues that cannot be explored with cross-sectional or short-term longitudinal surveys. The NLSY79 data include comprehensive work history information, measures from the Armed Services Vocational Aptitude Battery, and information on an especially wide variety of special topics. The National Institute for Child Health and Human Development has sponsored collection of a unique body of fertility-related information and a set of assessment instruments administered every other year beginning in 1986 to the children of the female respondents. These assessments provide information on the child's development and the home environment. The Department of Labor's Employment and Training Administration, and now the BLS, have made available NLSY79 data with identifiers and important variables for local areas through special agreements with research institutions.

Among changes in questionnaire content in recent years, the NLSY79 section on employer-provided training was reinstated and expanded. Questions on special topics have also been included; for example, questions relating to internal labor markets, focusing on promotions and job ladders, were asked in 1988–90, and questions on contingent work were included in the 1994 survey. A regular BLS publication with descriptive analyses, *Work and Family,* was initiated to bring important results to the attention of persons beyond the NLS's traditional users in the academic research community.

A fiscal year 1995 budget expansion provided funding for a new youth cohort, NLSY97, with data collection beginning early in 1997 under a contract with the National Opinion Research Center (NORC). Data will be collected annually for a sample of about 10,000 youths aged 12–16 as of 1 January 1997.

Establishment Surveys and Administrative Records Data

Employment and wages covered by unemployment insurance (ES-202 program). The ES-202 program maintains data collected from administrative records covering all employers subject to the unemployment insurance (UI) and unemployment compensation for federal employees (UCFE) programs. This effort is a cooperative endeavor of the BLS and the state employment security agencies. Using quarterly data received about five months after the close of the quarter, the BLS summarizes data on employment and wages and salaries for workers covered by UI and UCFE laws, who account for 98 percent of wage and salary civilian employment.[8] Annual average employment and "wages" (a broad measure of cash earnings per employee) are published for

---

8. Estimates are available initially about four months after receipt of the data. Some minor revisions are made to the data.

virtually all four-digit SICs at the national and state levels. Also, monthly employment and quarterly wage data are now available at the national, state, and county levels. The ES-202 does not provide hours data. It is used as a benchmark for the Current Employment Statistics (see below). In addition, microdata from the ES-202 program are used as the sampling frame for all BLS establishment surveys except the 790.

The program provides information to the Employment and Training Administration and the various state employment security agencies for administering the employment security program. It is used by the Bureau of Economic Analysis as the basis for estimating a large part of the wage and salary component of the national accounts. An effort is under way to develop a longitudinal establishment-level file. There has also been discussion of a proposal to create a wage records database.

Current Employment Statistics (CES or 790) survey. The CES is an establishment survey conducted monthly in cooperation with the state employment security agencies. It provides very timely data for the pay period including the 12th of the month on employment for all employees and women workers and, separately, for production workers in goods-producing industries and nonsupervisory workers in service-producing industries.[9] Preliminary monthly estimates are released along with the CPS estimates, usually on the first Friday of the following month. Data on payrolls and hours paid are collected for production and nonsupervisory workers only (about 81 percent of workers). Information on overtime hours is collected for manufacturing industries. Data are collected from about 390,000 reporting units, permitting publication of current data for the United States as a whole, for all states, and for 275 metropolitan areas, with extensive industry detail.[10]

Together with unemployment data from the CPS, the employment data from the CES are generally the first major economic series to be released each month. The employment estimate is used in the Index of Coincident Economic Indicators, and the manufacturing average weekly hours series is used in the Index of Leading Economic Indicators. The CES data are important to business and policy users who are concerned about current industry conditions because they are the only very timely information available at the detailed in-

9. Although the CES predates the statistical use of the ES-202 data, one can now think of the CES as a survey that "moves" the ES-202 employment data, i.e., provides preliminary estimates that will later be updated by ES-202 data, provides monthly rather than quarterly payroll data, and provides hours information.

10. The CES sample is unique among BLS surveys in not being probability based. Formerly, this was not seen as a problem by the program, given the focus on aggregate estimates, for two reasons. First, the sample size has been extremely large; it was about doubled during the late 1970s and mid-1980s, and now the reporting units include 40 percent of all persons on nonfarm payrolls. Second, the employment data are benchmarked to the ES-202 (although the payroll and hours estimates are not benchmarked). The American Statistical Association Panel (1994) recommended that the BLS implement probability sampling for this survey, and the BLS is currently conducting research in this area.

dustry level. In addition, the CES earnings data are used in preliminary estimates of the national accounts and the hours data are used in estimates of productivity.

The CES payroll and hours data are used to construct an average hourly earnings measure. This measure will be affected by changes in employment of less experienced workers, in occupations, and in differences between full-time and part-time status (to the extent that such workers are paid at different rates) that occur over the cycle or over time, so it may not proxy well movements in the cost of hiring labor; see the description below of the Employment Cost Index, which is designed for this purpose. (For some important purposes, such as analyzing wages received by the typical worker, use of an index that measures the cost of the effective quantity of labor would not be appropriate.) Comparisons of average hourly earnings between goods-producing and service-producing industries are problematic because the concept of workers included differs between these sectors. Finally, benefits are excluded. For all of these reasons, the CES wage data are probably less widely used by researchers and business economists than the employment information, as noted in American Statistical Association Panel (1994, 55–59).[11]

Occupational Employment Statistics (OES) survey. The OES was begun in 1971 in cooperation with the Employment and Training Administration and 15 state employment security agencies to obtain national, state, and area occupational employment estimates by industry. It presently surveys about 725,000 establishments on a three-year cycle. Recently, 15 state employment security agencies began collecting occupational wage distributions. The OES has been used primarily for educational planning. Beginning with the 1996–97 collection cycle, plans are for the OES to expand to survey each industry every year and also to collect wage information.

Compensation surveys. The Employment Cost Index (ECI) was developed in response to the need for a broad measure of the change in wage costs. First published in 1976 for wages and salaries and in 1980 for total employee compensation, it measures the rate of change in employee compensation, which includes wages, salaries, and employers' costs for employee benefits. The ECI is published quarterly, one month after the reference date. The sample comprises about 4,200 establishments in the private sector and 1,000 establishments in state and local government.

As a fixed-weight, Laspeyres index of the change in the price of labor, the ECI provides an important picture of compensation changes that eliminates the effects of employment shifts among industries and occupations. That is, it provides a measure of the change in the "price" or "cost" to the employer of a

---

11. The BLS is currently conducting research on possibilities for also collecting a more comprehensive earnings measure in the CES.

unit of labor. Thus the ECI series is preferable to an average hourly earnings–type measure for many analytic purposes. However, industry and occupational detail are not extensive. The ECI is more comprehensive in terms of benefit costs than are other U.S. series. Since 1987, annual estimates of compensation cost levels have been published; this series is constructed using the ECI cost change data and current weights for industry employment from the 790 and for occupations from the ECI. In addition to its use by economists and policy-making agencies, the ECI is used as an escalator of labor costs. Under the Federal Employees Pay Comparability Act of 1990, one phase of the federal pay-setting process now calls for a general pay increase for all white-collar federal employees that is tied to changes in the ECI.[12]

The present annual Employee Benefits Survey (EBS) began in 1980, in response to the Office of Personnel Management's desire for data on benefits. Expansion of coverage has taken place since then. Presently, data on the incidence and characteristics of employee benefits are collected in odd-numbered years for medium-size and large private establishments and in even-numbered years for small private establishments and state and local governmental units. The sample includes 4,400 establishments in the private sector and 1,300 governmental units. EBS data are used in analyses by various government agencies and business organizations, and in labor negotiations.

Over the years, data on wages for selected occupations and industries have been collected in a variety of occupational pay surveys. The effort was restructured in 1990, with a focus on data collection for Office of Personnel Management use in federal pay setting, where in addition to a general pay change there is a provision for adjustment in pay by area. The Occupational Compensation Survey Program (OCSP) presently collects information on wages in 46 selected occupations, by work level, from about 18,000 establishments in about 160 localities. This survey replaced predecessor surveys—namely, the White Collar Pay Survey, whose predecessor was the Professional, Administrative, Technical, and Clerical survey; the Area Wage Surveys, which provided information for selected occupations in major standard metropolitan statistical areas;[13] and the Industry Wage Surveys, which formerly were conducted in various industries on a three- to five-year cycle. The OCSP data are compatible with the Area Wage Survey data.

It is interesting to note that the primary use of the Industry Wage Surveys and Area Wage Surveys in recent decades was not the same as for most economic statistics, that is, by policymakers and the business community in general, nor was it for research purposes. Instead, the primary users were compensation specialists in firms or unions, who used them for "wage determination purposes." Interestingly, Rees (1993) argues that in practice wage comparisons

---

12. In practice, since 1978 an alternative plan for federal pay has always been substituted for the payment specified by the process using wage data.

13. In addition, special, more limited, area-type wage surveys have been and still are being conducted for, and used by, the Department of Labor's Employment Standards Administration in administering the Service Contract Act of 1965.

are made in both nonunion and union situations and if no suitable survey exists firms will conduct one.[14]

The BLS has begun an effort, called "Comp 2000," which is considering possibilities for integrating the ECI, EBS, and OCSP programs.

Hours at Work Survey. Begun in 1981, this survey of about 5,500 establishments collects quarterly and annual ratios of hours at work to hours paid. It is used to adjust the hours paid by industry information from the CES for use in BLS productivity measures.

Negotiated wage and benefit changes. This program, which was eliminated in 1996 in response to budget cuts, prepared information on current changes in wages and benefits agreed to in collective bargaining. Provisions of agreements were published in *Compensation and Working Conditions.* Monthly listings gave the company, employer association, or governmental unit in which a change had occurred, the union involved, the general wage increase and effective date, and related information on the contract. The BLS prepared series on wage rate changes in major collective bargaining settlements (those covering 1,000 workers or more) and on compensation changes in the largest settlements (those covering 5,000 workers or more in all industries and 1,000 workers or more in construction).

Special surveys. Beginning in the late 1980s, some special establishment surveys and pilot studies have been conducted by the BLS. The first were surveys of contracting-out practices in selected industries. Special surveys of day care and drug testing have also been collected. A pilot survey that collected information on demographic characteristics of a sample of employees within establishments, conducted as part of the White-Collar Pay Survey, is of interest for research purposes (see Bronars and Famulari, chap. 13 in this volume). A pilot survey on job vacancies was also conducted, but a full survey, which would have been quite costly, was not funded.[15] Most recently, two establishment Sur-

14. Rees uses this in arguing for the role of "fairness" in wage determination, but other things could also be responsible, i.e., imperfect information coupled with the desire to set efficiency wages or to avoid the unnecessary costs that would be incurred if information is gained only by observing increased quits.

15. The BLS conducted several special studies of turnover beginning in 1916. Interest in this topic arose from the movement "to promote the more intelligent treatment of laborers" (see Goldberg and Moyes 1985, 98). Various efforts to collect job vacancy statistics were carried out in the 1950s, 1960s, and 1970s. A pilot study for improvement in the late 1970s showed that such an effort would be extremely costly. The then existing labor turnover program was terminated as part of the 1982 budget cut. The Levitan Commission did not recommend the collection of job vacancy statistics. The commission argued that "despite the conceptual appeal of data on job openings, the commission has found job vacancies to be subject to numerous problems of measurement and interpretation, and it doubts that useful data could be obtained at reasonable cost. Aggregate national data would afford little insight beyond what is already provided by other indicators. Vacancy data with occupational, industrial, and area detail would be extremely valuable if combined with similarly detailed data on unemployment and turnover, but the expense of obtaining all these data would be exorbitant" (National Commission on Employment and Unemployment Statistics 1979, 8).

veys of Employer-Provided Training have been conducted. The second survey included interviews with two representative employees from each establishment.

1.1.2 Other Labor Market Information

Labor is a key input into production, and labor income is the major source of personal income. Consequently, it is to be expected that many surveys whose primary focus is not labor markets nonetheless obtain considerable information relevant to them. Major sources of information relating to labor markets collected by other agencies are briefly described in this section.

Household Surveys

Panel Study of Income Dynamics (PSID). The PSID, presently funded by the National Science Foundation and conducted by the University of Michigan Survey Research Center, began in 1968. The initial sample included two subsamples: a probability sample of 2,930 U.S. households and a supplemental sample of 1,872 low-income households taken from the Survey of Economic Opportunity. Individuals from these households have been followed over time with annual interviews. Children born to the sample members become part of the sample. In addition, data have been collected for a supplemental national sample of Latino households beginning in 1990. The PSID has focused primarily on economic well-being and provides a rich body of information including considerable employment-related information. Since the mid-1980s, it has obtained some event history information on employment, income transfers, and demographic states. The PSID also provides detailed information about the neighborhoods (census tracts) in which sample members live.

Survey of Income and Program Participation (SIPP). The SIPP and its predecessor, the Income Survey Development Program data, were developed by the Department of Health and Human Services and the Census Bureau primarily to provide improved and expanded short-term information on participation and turnover in government programs and on sources of income. In the early 1980s, the Census Bureau was given responsibility for the program. SIPP data, collected every four months, provide considerable information on employment and related variables and also on various special topics. There are important differences in concept between the CPS and SIPP unemployment questions, as detailed in Ryscavage and Bregger (1985). A major difference from the CPS is that the SIPP provides the opportunity to examine labor force status *throughout* the month rather than for just the week of the 12th. SIPP data are much less timely than CPS data. SIPP labor force concepts differ from those in the NLS as well. The SIPP has recently undergone a redesign. It will continue with interviews every four months, but now they will continue for four years. In addition, plans call for the Census Bureau to collect data on the 1992–93 SIPP panels annually through 2002. This survey will be called the Survey of Program Dynamics.

Retirement surveys. Among surveys that have supported important work in the labor area are those dealing with retirement-aged individuals. Numerous retirement-related studies were carried out in the past using the NLS older men's survey and the Social Security Administration's Longitudinal Retirement History Survey (LRHS). The LRHS began in 1969 with a sample of household heads aged 58–63. Follow-ups were conducted every two years through 1977. Recognition of the need for new longitudinal information on retirement decisions of older Americans and their well-being after retirement has been widespread; to meet this need, the National Institute on Aging recently began a new Health and Retirement Survey, which is being conducted by the University of Michigan Survey Research Center.

Department of Education longitudinal surveys. Longitudinal studies of young persons sponsored by the Department of Education have been intended to provide information about what occurs at the various levels of education and the major transition phases for students.[16] They have been used for some labor market studies, particularly when detailed information is needed about secondary school(s) attended or about postsecondary schooling of respondents. In particular, the National Longitudinal Study of the Class of 1972 began with interviews of twelfth grade students during the 1971–72 academic year. Follow-ups were conducted in 1973, 1974, 1976, 1979, and 1986. High School and Beyond began in 1980 with high school sophomores as well as seniors. To date, follow-ups have been conducted in 1982, 1984, 1986, and 1992. The National Educational Longitudinal Study of 1988 surveyed eighth grade students; follow-ups were conducted in 1990 and 1992.

Decennial censuses. The decennial Census of Population obtains basic information for the entire U.S. population. Smaller samples of the population have received long-form questionnaires that provide more detailed demographic, socioeconomic, and housing data. The size of the samples has varied over time. Microdata from the decennial censuses are available on various public-use tapes for 1940 and later years. These data have been particularly useful for research studies of immigrants and for studies where a very long time period is of interest, as well as for other purposes where an extremely large sample is needed, such as constructing data for small areas or small demographic groups or for analyses where only weak instruments are available. Planning is under way at the Census Bureau for the 2000 census.

Establishment Surveys

Censuses, annual surveys, and the Longitudinal Research Database (LRD). The Census Bureau conducts a quinquennial Census of Manufactures. The sample for a parallel survey, the Annual Survey of Manufactures (ASM), is

---

16. The samples are two phased: a sample of schools is selected, then a sample of students within each participating school is interviewed.

drawn from the preceding census. The ASM follows a panel of establishments for five years, beginning in years ending in 4 and 9. Additional establishments are added over the life of the panel to capture births and maintain representativeness. Generally speaking, both the census and ASM contain data on firms with five or more employees. Information is collected on revenues, number of products sold, and costs of about 10 broad classes of inputs, including labor. Two types of employment data are available. Data on total employment and on production worker employment are available for the payroll period including 12 March. Data on production worker employment only are available for payroll periods including 12 February, 12 May, 12 August, and 12 November. Data on the average establishment production worker wage are also available. The Census Bureau, since the 1970s, has developed and maintained a longitudinal file, now called the LRD. The LRD file contains census data beginning in 1963 and ASM data for all manufacturing establishments sampled in the ASMs beginning in 1972. The LRD file has been used for many research studies that could not have been done with other types of data. But in addition to the obvious limitation to only the manufacturing sector, an inherent limitation for some long-term analyses is that the establishments that remain in the sample for more than five years greatly overrepresent large establishments.

Data for service industries are more limited. In 1992, all previously uncovered service industries were added to the economic censuses. Not all industries are presently covered in annual surveys, and content varies by industry. Only two of the annual surveys for services (for SICs 42 and 48) collect information on payrolls; none collect information on employment.

County business patterns. This program provides annual information from Internal Revenue Service administrative records. Outside the Census Bureau, information is available on the number of establishments, employment the week including 12 March, and first quarter and annual payroll for states and counties by two-digit SIC and by more detailed SIC where publication or confidentiality rules are met.

1.1.3   Uses in Labor Economics Research

Labor market information has a variety of important purposes and uses, including academic research studies. Stafford (1986) analyzed the character of labor economics research, the usage of various data sets, and their interaction, for the period 1965–83. In this section, I update his analysis to the period 1984–93. I include articles in the six major U.S. journals he considered.[17] In addition to these "general purpose" journals, I also consider, separately, three

17. The six journals are the *American Economic Review, Econometrica, Journal of Political Economy, Quarterly Journal of Economics, Review of Economics and Statistics,* and *International Economic Review.* Following Stafford, I exclude notes, comments, shorter papers, and all articles in the *American Economic Association Proceedings.* Also, separate special supplements are excluded.

major "specialized" journals that focus on labor economics either exclusively or in large part, namely, *Industrial and Labor Relations Review, Journal of Human Resources,* and *Journal of Labor Economics.*

In describing the topics of the published papers, I follow the classification scheme used by Stafford, which was based primarily on the chapter topics in Ashenfelter and Layard (1986). Many articles deal with more than one topic category. In this analysis, as in Stafford, each article is assigned to only one category; the assignment is based on the primary focus of the article. Drawing the line between what to count as a labor economics study and what not to count is far from straightforward. I have followed the rule that articles included should deal with labor issues in large part. Thus, for example, a study of economic growth with some reference to human capital would be excluded, as would a theoretical piece on industrial organization with some reference to labor. To be consistent with Stafford and with Hamermesh's (1993) discussion, I have included general factor demand studies that include estimates of labor demand elasticities or substitution elasticities between labor and other factors of production.[18]

This analysis does not attempt to describe the overall importance of various data sets in research; not only are some economics journals excluded from my survey but also many research uses of some of the data sets described above are excluded.[19] For example, macroeconomic studies not focused on labor markets often use the overall unemployment rate from the CPS or employment figures from the CES, but such studies are not included here. As another type of example, many studies using NLS data are conducted by social scientists other than economists or focus on nonlabor topics. To some extent, the present analysis is backward looking in that it does not consider current usage as would be reflected in, say, a review of working papers. However, the focus on major journals has the advantage of limiting studies considered to those that have particular merit as judged by peer review.

Topics

Table 1.2 presents the percentage distribution of articles by major topic area for the period 1984–93, following Stafford's categorization. For comparative purposes, information for 1965–83 from Stafford is reproduced here. Additional detail is provided in appendix table 1A.1. I have broken out several additional separate subcategories under all but the labor supply category.

The distribution for the general journals that I find for 1984–88 is only somewhat different from that found by Stafford for the immediately preceding period. It is important to note that some portion of the difference across these periods may be due to coding differences rather than to real changes.

18. Hamermesh (1993, 6–7) presents counts of articles in the six journals considered by Stafford for 1984–90 for the labor demand and labor supply categories.

19. In addition, I have not attempted to determine which empirical papers had "meaningful" theoretical sections or to determine which papers were "significant" as Stafford did.

Table 1.2   Percentage Distribution of Articles by Topic, 1965–93

Topic	General Journals						Specialty Journals	
	1965–69	1970–74	1975–79	1980–83	1984–88	1989–93	1984–88	1989–93
Labor supply	25.0	32.0	34.0	26.0	23.1	23.1	20.5	23.2
Labor demand	15.5	9.0	8.0	12.0	11.2	12.0	0.9	2.4
Wage determination and earnings	25.5	37.0	34.0	29.5	24.8	28.9	29.1	26.8
Labor market equilibrium and friction	18.0	17.0	18.0	25.0	27.3	25.3	18.7	20.2
Institutional structures	13.0	5.5	5.5	8.0	13.6	10.7	30.9	27.4

Sources: For 1965–83, Stafford (1986, 392); for 1984–93, author's computations.

Continuing to focus on the general journals, note that labor supply accounted for a slightly lower percentage of articles in 1984–93 than Stafford found for 1980–83, which was notably lower than in the preceding 10 years. The percentage of articles on labor demand, small throughout the 1965–83 period, remained about the same.[20] The fraction of articles on wage determination and earnings fell somewhat in 1984–88 compared to earlier periods but rose again in 1989–93. Compared to preceding periods, the proportions of articles dealing with labor market equilibrium and friction and with institutional structures rose in 1984–88 but fell back in 1989–93.

The distribution of topics covered in the specialty labor journals was very different from that in the general journals. Articles on labor demand accounted for an extremely small proportion of articles in these journals. The proportion of articles on institutional structures was well over twice as high in the specialty journals as in the general journals, and the proportion on labor market equilibrium and friction was somewhat smaller.

It is interesting to note that only seven papers published during 1984–93 (three of them in general journals) were primarily concerned with data measurement issues. Stafford found only one such article in his period. All measurement papers are classified in the present study according to the subject addressed.

Data Usage

Table 1.3 presents information on the use of various types of data in labor economics articles during the period 1965–93.[21] The trend toward an increasing proportion of theoretical articles in the general journals stabilized in the 1984–88 period but declined in 1989–93, the first decline in the entire period considered. The proportion of theoretical articles in the labor journals also declined between 1984–88 and 1989–93 and was much lower than in the general journals in both periods. Another striking result concerns the importance of microdata. The percentage of articles based on microdata in the general journals increased in 1984–88 compared to the two preceding periods and increased even more in 1989–93. Microdata usage was even greater in the specialty journals. Table 1.3 reveals a decline in labor economics articles in general journals based on time-series data between 1984–88 and 1989–93, continuing the long-term decline in the use of this type of data in labor economics research.[22] The proportion of such articles in the specialty journals was

20. Taking a narrower definition, including only articles with a major focus on labor and thereby excluding general factor demand studies, results in considerably smaller shares of articles devoted to labor demand: 6.9 percent of articles in general journals in 1984–88 and 7.0 percent in 1989–93.

21. Articles are counted as theoretical if they presented no empirical analysis, although they might cite a few previously published figures or pick estimates from previous studies for use in an illustrative simulation. This table counts data set usage, not articles; there are 63 articles that used multiple data sets (some of which fall in the same data type category, however).

22. The exclusion of general factor demand studies, most of which are based on time-series data, results in even lower proportions of articles based on time-series data: 12 percent in 1984–88 and 8 percent in 1989–93.

Table 1.3   **Percentage Distribution of Articles by Data Source, 1965–93**

Data Used	General Journals						Specialty Journals	
	1965–69	1970–74	1975–79	1980–83	1984–88	1989–93	1984–88	1989–93
Theory only	14	19	23	29	29	23	17	10
Microdata	11	27	45	46	51	64	70	82
Time series	42	27	18	16	16	12	8	6
Local area cross section	3	2	4	3	4	3	4	5
State	7	6	3	3	2	1	1	1
Other aggregate cross section	14	16	8	4	2	2	2	1
Secondary data analysis	14	3	3	4	2	1	3	3
Laboratory experiments	—[a]	—[a]	—[a]	—[a]	0	1	0	1
Number of articles	106	191	257	205	242	225	327	332

Sources: For 1965–83, Stafford (1986, 392); for 1984–93, author's computations.

[a]Stafford did not have a laboratory experiments category.

much lower. Table 1.3 also shows that the percentages of articles based on secondary data and on local area cross-sectional, state, or other aggregate cross-sectional data continued to be extremely low, as they were for the latter part of Stafford's period.

A breakdown of the percentage distribution of labor articles by more detailed categories of data sources is given in table 1.4 for 1984–93. Household or individual survey microdata accounted for by far the largest share of microdata sources. The percentage of articles based on household microdata increased between 1984–88 and 1989–93 as did the percentage of articles based on establishment microdata. The use of microdata from administrative records (not matched to household survey data) was quite low. Use of microdata on other units, primarily unions or bargaining pairs, was fairly low in the general journals but more substantial in the specialty journals.

The important role of the CPS, NLS, and PSID in empirical research in labor economics found by Stafford continued, with use of the CPS increasing somewhat. The use in the general journals of household data from social experiments, which accounted for only 2 percent in 1975–83, increased to 5.4 percent in 1984–88 and 7.6 percent in 1989–93; usage of these data was fairly similar in the specialized journals.

As pointed out forcefully by Hamermesh (1990), microdata for establishments have been lacking in the United States.[23] However, articles using such data did account for 7.7 percent of articles in the general and specialty journals in 1984–88; this rose to 11.0 percent in 1989–93. The establishment microdata sources used the most frequently in these articles were the Employment Opportunities Pilot Project (EOPP) establishment data, 10 articles; Equal Employment Opportunity data and the BLS's Industry Wage Surveys, 6 articles each; and Compustat data and the LRD, 5 articles each. More articles used firm or establishment microdata obtained by the individual researchers themselves than used any one of the above sources.

Of all these labor articles published in 1984–88, 6.7 percent used data from countries other than the United States. This increased to 8.5 percent of articles in 1989–93.

Discussion

To what extent are empirical studies stimulated by theoretical developments and policy interests, and to what extent are they stimulated by data availability? Stafford argued that "the greater range and quality of our knowledge and theorizing on particular topics does significantly stem from the advent of large-scale micro level datasets. These datasets use individuals and households as the unit of observation and are important in explaining why, during the 1970s,

---

23. As can be seen from references in Hamermesh (1993) to labor demand studies using establishment data from other countries, the United States has lagged behind a number of other countries in use of establishment microdata.

Table 1.4   **Percentage Distribution of Articles by Detailed Data Type, 1984–93**

Data Used	General		Specialty		All Journals	
	1984–88	1989–93	1984–88	1989–93	1984–88	1989–93
Theory only	28.9	22.7	16.8	9.9	22.0	15.1
Household survey microdata	40.9	47.6	49.8	59.6	46.0	54.8
PSID	7.9	7.1	6.7	6.0	7.2	6.5
NLS	4.1	7.1	7.0	7.8	5.8	7.5
CPS	8.7	8.4	11.6	15.4	10.4	12.6
SIPP	0.0	2.2	0.0	0.9	0.0	1.4
Department of Education	0.4	0.0	0.9	1.8	0.7	1.1
Decennial census	1.2	1.8	2.1	2.4	1.8	2.2
Other household data	16.9	20.9	19.6	24.1	18.5	22.8
Other international household data	4.5	2.2	0.9	1.5	2.5	1.8
Other social experiment data	5.4	7.6	4.6	9.0	4.9	8.4
Household/administrative matches	1.7	0.0	1.8	1.2	1.8	0.7
Firm or establishment survey microdata	6.2	9.8	8.9	11.4	7.7	10.8
EOPP (establishment only)	0.4	1.3	0.6	1.2	0.5	1.3
LRD	0.0	1.8	0.0	0.3	0.0	0.9
Other establishment data	5.8	6.7	8.3	9.9	7.2	8.6
Other international establishment data	0.4	0.9	0.6	1.8	0.5	1.4
Microdata from administrative records	1.7	2.7	3.1	2.7	2.5	2.7
Individual microdata	1.7	2.7	1.8	1.2	1.8	1.8

Individual international microdata	0.0	0.0	0.6	0.3	0.4	0.2
Establishment microdata	0.0	0.0	0.6	0.9	0.4	0.5
Establishment international microdata	0.0	0.0	0.0	0.3	0.0	0.2
Other microdata	2.5	3.6	8.0	7.5	5.6	5.9
Other microdata	0.0	0.9	0.3	0.3	0.2	0.5
Other international microdata	0.0	0.0	0.3	0.0	0.2	0.0
Labor contract/strike microdata	2.5	2.7	7.3	7.2	5.3	5.4
BLS Compensation and Working Conditions	1.2	0.9	2.4	3.0	1.9	2.2
Other international contract data	0.4	1.8	1.5	1.8	1.1	1.8
Time series	16.1	11.6	8.3	6.0	11.6	8.3
Time-series data	14.5	8.0	7.6	4.2	10.5	5.7
International time-series data	1.7	3.6	0.6	1.8	1.1	2.5
Local area cross section	3.7	3.1	4.3	5.4	4.0	4.5
Census tract	2.1	3.1	1.2	3.0	1.6	3.1
International census	0.8	0.0	0.3	0.3	0.5	0.2
Other area cross section	0.8	0.0	2.8	2.1	1.9	1.3
State	1.7	0.9	0.9	0.9	1.2	0.9
Other aggregate cross section	2.1	1.8	1.8	1.5	1.9	1.6
Other aggregate cross section	1.2	1.3	1.8	1.2	1.6	1.3
International aggregate cross section	0.8	0.4	0.0	0.3	0.4	0.4
Secondary data analysis	2.1	0.9	3.4	3.0	2.8	2.2
Experimental data	0.4	0.9	0.0	1.2	0.2	1.1
Number of observations	242	225	327	332	569	557

about two-thirds of labor articles in major journals were on the broad subjects of labor supply and wage determination" (1986, 388). Hamermesh (1993) argues that the study of labor demand has been conditioned by the availability of data. At the same time, however, data collection itself necessarily is conditioned by demand for it. While the demand for data is primarily affected by the needs of government policymakers and the business community, it is likely to be indirectly responsive to research developments.

The decline in the share of theoretical articles in 1989–93 in labor economics research does not correspond to the appearance of whole new government data sources. There were not many new sources, and such sources were little used (i.e., SIPP, although all of its use came in the most recent period 1989–93). The Quality of Employment Survey, which interviewed workers in 1972–73 and 1977 but has not been continued, was used in ten papers in 1984–88 and only two in 1989–93. Data from the social experiments that were used most frequently during 1984–93 (notably, the Seattle Income Maintenance Experiment/Denver Income Maintenance Experiment and the EOPP) are becoming outdated; recent experiments have been more specialized, and I expect use of this type of data in labor economics to decline in the near future.

In discussing the large volume of research on labor supply and related issues that was produced over the period 1965–83, Stafford (1986) specifically mentioned the rich microdata that became available for the first time early in that period from the CPS, NLS, and PSID. Stafford expected that continued use of these data sources might be primarily a reworking of the same topics, but that has not been the case. Situations facing workers have changed so that analyses using data for recent years provide additional information far beyond reworking.[24] New uses of the NLS and PSID have arisen since the early 1980s. In an area where research seems to be expanding, both the NLS and the PSID provide excellent opportunities for studies of intergenerational or within-family linkages of welfare dependency and income and employment. Additional topics have been covered in these surveys in recent years, and this expanding or revised content has been important in the most recent 10 years, as Stafford (1986, 404) suggested was the case for his period. In addition, the development of event history data permits examination of new aspects of the labor market experiences of workers in addition to permitting improved analyses of topics previously addressed. The increased use of the CPS is not primarily due to expanding content. CPS content has been expanded or revised largely through additional special supplements. One new supplement, the Displaced Workers Supplement, accounted for just under 1 percent of the labor articles. Increased accessibility of CPS microdata may have been responsible for its increased use.

---

24. The view that analyses can be done with very old data and provide still relevant information often seems implicit in microeconomic research. This is in stark contrast with the business and policy communities, which find anything more than a few years old, or in some cases a few months old, obsolete and uninteresting.

Determining the extent to which theoretical studies and policy interests are stimulated by data availability and vice versa is beyond the scope of this paper. Tabulations presented in table 1.5, which include articles in both the general and specialty journals, are useful in assessing the much more limited question of the extent to which the focus on broad topic areas differed between theoretical and empirical articles during 1984–93. It is interesting to note first that the percentage of articles that are theoretical varies considerably across major topic areas, from a high of 34 percent in the labor market equilibrium and friction category to a low of 10 percent in the wage determination and earnings category. Within some of these topic categories there is also considerable variation in the percentage of articles that are theoretical, most notably in the labor market equilibrium and friction category. Sixty-five percent of the articles on screening, signaling, contracting, and matching are theoretical. In contrast, only 6 percent of articles on career mobility, gross job flows, and other turnover are theoretical.

Among empirical articles, the various types of data are used to very different extents in studying different topics. Household microdata are used in the majority of studies of labor supply and of wage determination and earnings and in 38 percent of the studies of labor market equilibrium and friction (which account for well over half of the empirical articles in this latter topic area). As already noted, time-series data are used far more extensively in analyses of labor demand than in the other areas. Only a small fraction (11 percent) of the use of establishment microdata is in studies of labor demand, a very small category; these data are used in about 17 percent of labor demand studies. In fact, the majority of articles on all the major topics except labor demand use some type of microdata. Use of local area cross-sectional data, state data, other aggregate cross-sectional data, and secondary data is not quantitatively important for any of the topics.

This analysis has shown that empirical economics was alive and well in labor economics research over the 1984–93 period. Unlike the 1969–83 period analyzed by Stafford, this was not primarily due to development of new government survey efforts. Although the improvement of econometric methods played a role in this later period as in the earlier years, and the expanded content of ongoing surveys was also important, the dramatically reduced cost of computing may have played an important role. The reduction in computational costs has not only made the use of complex econometric methods feasible but has also permitted many studies that use great amounts of data (such as many years of CPS microdata) while not exploiting new methods.

The ultimate benefit from empirical research is not the number of articles published but the extent to which understanding of the economy is improved, policy discussions are informed, and programs can be evaluated. Topel's paper (chap. 2) in this volume assesses data needs and success of labor economics studies for two purposes: description and estimation of the parameters of economic models. Section 1.2 of this paper addresses needs for data, including uses other than in research studies.

Table 1.5   Cross-Tabulation of Major Topic by Data Type, 1984–93

Data Used	Labor Supply	Labor Demand	Wage Determination and Earnings	Labor Market Equilibrium and Friction	Institutional Structures	Total
Theory only	36.0	11.0	30.0	85.0	47.0	209
Household microdata	183.5	8.0	185.3	95.5	54.0	526
Establishment microdata	2.0	11.0	28.7	27.5	27.5	97
Administrative microdata	6.0	0.0	8.5	9.0	2.5	26
Other microdata	1.0	0.0	3.5	3.0	52.8	60
Time series	10.5	28.0	19.0	16.3	32.8	107
Local area cross section	6.0	3.0	15.0	2.0	16.0	42
State	3.0	1.0	2.0	2.8	1.5	10
Other aggregate cross section	1.0	3.0	4.0	5.5	3.3	17
Secondary data	3.0	0.0	11.0	4.3	7.0	25
Experimental data	0.0	0.0	1.0	0.0	5.5	7
Total	252	65	308	251	250	1,126
Column Percentages						
Theory only	14.3	16.9	9.7	33.9	18.8	
Household microdata	72.8	12.3	60.2	38.1	21.6	
Establishment microdata	0.8	16.9	9.3	11.0	11.0	
Administrative microdata	2.4	0.0	2.8	3.6	1.0	

Other microdata	0.4	0.0	1.1	1.2	21.1
Time series	4.2	43.1	6.2	6.5	13.1
Local area cross section	2.4	4.6	4.9	0.8	6.4
State	1.2	1.5	0.6	1.1	0.6
Other aggregate cross section	0.4	4.6	1.3	2.2	1.3
Secondary data	1.2	0.0	3.6	1.7	2.8
Experimental data	0.0	0.0	0.3	0.0	2.2
Total	100	100	100	100	100

Row Percentages

Theory only	17.2	5.3	14.4	40.7	22.5	100
Household microdata	34.9	1.5	35.2	18.1	10.3	100
Establishment microdata	2.1	11.4	29.7	28.4	28.4	100
Administrative microdata	23.1	0.0	32.7	34.6	9.6	100
Other microdata	1.7	0.0	5.8	5.0	87.6	100
Time series	9.8	26.3	17.8	15.3	30.8	100
Local area cross section	14.3	7.1	35.7	4.8	38.1	100
State	29.1	9.7	19.4	27.2	14.6	100
Other aggregate cross section	5.9	17.8	23.8	32.7	19.8	100
Secondary data	11.9	0.0	43.5	17.0	27.7	100
Experimental data	0.0	0.0	15.4	0.0	84.6	100

Note: If an article uses n data sets, each use is counted as $(1/n)$th of a data set.

1.2   Other Uses, Needs, and Possibilities

In their examination of the need to improve federal statistical programs, Duncan and Gross suggest that "as the 21st century approaches, it is increasingly clear that our conceptual net, designed for earlier realities, fits our current situation only very imperfectly" (1993, 11). Is this true of labor market data? What seems clear on the surface is that the system is fragmented and certainly is not what would be designed for research or policy purposes if one were starting from scratch in an ideal world. But in a world of limited resources, this is less clear: each survey has users who consider it important. Timeliness, periodicity, and detail differ among surveys, and needs for them differ by purpose.

Of course, a particular measure cannot serve all uses and users. Sometimes a finding that a particular measure is inappropriate for a certain purpose leads to development of a new survey. For instance, the ECI was developed in response to a call for a suitable measure of labor costs. But some of the information collected separately in the past might have been developed instead through a consolidation of programs.

What are the needs and how do we determine them? Ultimately, the demands of economic policymakers and private sector users will influence this, as was certainly the case in the early years of the BLS. But it has been argued by Triplett that "today's research need becomes tomorrow's policy-analytic need" (1990, 343). This suggests a key role for researchers in helping to inform statistical agency concerns. As Triplett points out, historically researchers have had little ability to provide input into agency decisions. In fact, some efforts have been driven by research and policy analytic needs outside of statistical agencies—as the major examples in labor economics, household longitudinal surveys were not begun by statistical agencies, although the NLS and SIPP have been transferred to them. At the beginning of her tenure at the BLS in 1993, Commissioner Abraham announced two major goals: improving access to data, particularly microdata, and expanding survey content. This provides perhaps an unparalleled opportunity for research and researchers to help shape statistical programs.

This part of the paper begins by addressing recognized needs for additional information. Resources for maintaining the statistical system, let alone expanding the data provided, have been restrained over the past decade. In view of this, the paper concludes with a discussion of how to make the system more useful in a situation where resources are very tight.

1.2.1   What Is Missing? Recognized Needs

Content

The discussion of existing programs suggests that new or changed data programs frequently arose from the interests of the day. It does not appear that there have been many concerted calls for additional information that have gone unrecognized over the past 10 or 15 years, at least not for things that would call for whole new programs.

Some emerging issues can be addressed with existing data, although perhaps imperfectly. The major research topics of declining real wages and increasing wage dispersion have perhaps been driven by the recognition of trends in existing data and so far do not appear to call for more data. But there are related concerns as well as other issues for which data do not exist or on which existing data are extremely limited.

Labor supply behavior of youth and retirement decisions. During the mid- to late 1980s it became clear that in spite of the existence of major household surveys there were important gaps in data for analyzing key labor supply phenomena. Because the experience of existing NLS sample members during their youth is not expected to be representative of the experience of today's youth who face very different labor market and family situations, a primary need was for development of a new survey of youth. This need will be satisfied by beginning a new NLS youth cohort; this is probably best viewed as a sample replenishment effort rather than a "new" effort. The other major area of need was for development of data suitable for analyzing the current retirement behavior of Americans. This need has been met by the National Institute on Aging's new Health and Retirement Survey.

Contracting out and contingent work. Since the mid- to late 1980s, there has been recognition of changing types of employment, in terms of the growth of contracting out and of "contingent work." Some information on the former was provided through special surveys. Information on contingent workers is being collected in a special supplement to the CPS and also in the NLS.

Nonwage compensation. Data on compensation as opposed to money wages have been very limited. This may have particularly important implications for understanding labor markets because compensation practices may be continually changing. Even the definition of cash wages is problematic and differs across surveys. In the mid-1980s, there was attention at the BLS to the increasing use of lump-sum payments in lieu of wages and how they should be treated in series that include them. While it had appeared that this trend was stabilizing or declining, conversation with industry specialists and some recent union agreements (e.g., the recent agreement at the Xerox Corporation facility in Webster, New York; *Washington Post,* 9 June 1994) suggest that use of some type of bonuses or payments in lieu of wage increases may be reemerging as a trend, implying a need for broader measures of cash compensation.

Labor demand. Hamermesh (1990, 1993) and others have called for improved data for studying labor demand issues. Hamermesh specifically recommended a relatively small but representative quarterly or monthly survey of establishments with extensive content: employment by major skill category, hours worked by each group of workers, payroll for each type of worker, other labor costs, and total sales and production. This he suggested would be an extension or rationalization of existing information. Hamermesh would ideally also include some key information on worker characteristics through a linked survey. Like Hamermesh, Juster (1983) called for more information relating to the demand for labor but recommended information on hiring practices, on-the-job training, and how firms evaluate worker productivity and decide on promotions, raises, firings, and so forth.

A related point is the recognition by a variety of data users that there has been no detailed establishment information on wages by occupation for all industries. The lack of such information has been noted frequently by analysts, and sometimes by users who would want the microdata together with information on other costs faced by establishments. Thus analyses of wages by occupation and industry typically have been carried out with the CPS, for which there is concern about coding of industry and occupation and which does not provide other establishment information. The planned OES expansion will address this need.

Training and workplace practices. Training and workplace practices and their relation to wages, employment growth, and productivity are issues of considerable current policy concern. Detail on the structure of compensation is needed to test alternative theories about work organization and incentives as well as for completeness to avoid erroneous conclusions about what is happening to employee well-being. Additional information needed includes measures of amount of supervision and worker control over the job, hiring and promotion practices, and various characteristics of the workplace, including use of teams or quality circles. As already noted, a small establishment Survey of Employer-Provided Training with worker information was conducted by the BLS in 1995.

Target Population

It is interesting that in the United Kingdom as well as in the United States early collection of data focused on certain types of workers—"manual" workers in the United Kingdom and production workers in the United States—and on manufacturing industries. Perhaps this was true in most countries. In important instances, U.S. establishment surveys still do not provide complete coverage of workers. In addition to sometimes focusing on only production and nonsupervisory workers, U.S. establishment surveys occasionally exclude workers in small firms and typically exclude the self-employed. This latter omission, as noted by Orchard and Stibbard (1993), affects different sectors of the economy differently; notably, certain service industries will be greatly underrepresented. For understanding the labor market situation, it is critical to have at least some data that cover all of these workers. For instance, major policy issues concern things like whether real earnings are declining and what is happening to low-paid workers relative to the more highly paid. It is important to have complete coverage to satisfactorily address these questions, to make comparisons of wages across industries, and so forth. One advantage of household data is broader coverage.

Household Longitudinal Data

The Levitan Commission pointed to a lack of information on the dynamics of labor market experience. The commission members argued that changes during the 1960s and 1970s gave workers wider choices and that "the data on current labor force status must be supplemented with information on how that status came about and the conditions under which it might change" (National Commission on Employment and Unemployment Statistics 1979, 1). They explicitly recommended the development of publishable gross flow data using the monthly CPS, which would show the numbers of unemployed who remain unemployed, find employment, or leave the labor force in the next month, and similar numbers for those employed or out of the labor force in the first month. Such information has not been published by the BLS because of problems with quality due especially to failure to follow movers and classification error. No adjustment method has been widely agreed to, and there is need for further research. But some argue that such information can help in the interpretation of the monthly labor force situation, despite the measurement problems with existing tabulations (see Barkume and Horvath 1995). If gross flow data could be published, policy interest would likely be high. Currently, the BLS is planning to follow movers in the CPS for one month, which would permit construction of improved gross flow estimates and improved analyses using CPS microdata.

The Levitan Commission also made recommendations for more complete identification of the labor market problems experienced by women and supported special longitudinal studies of women's lifetime work experience. This need is being satisfied by the continuation and aging of the NLS women's data together with the initiation of a new youth cohort. Changes in the labor market such as a decline in labor force participation of middle-aged and older men and worsening job prospects for many young men suggest that long-term studies of labor market experience are now essential for men also.

Establishment Surveys with Demographic Data and
Linked Household-Establishment Surveys

Linked household-establishment surveys, which have rarely been done in the United States, and to my knowledge are not done in the United States on an ongoing basis, could provide extremely rich information for labor market analysis.[25] Such data were recommended by Hamermesh (1990), and Rosen (1990) argues that they are essential for understanding the matching aspects of labor market exchange.[26]

Merged establishment-household data are desirable for reasons other than microdata research needs. As is widely recognized, some information can be collected more accurately from establishment surveys—for instance, the industry and occupation (type of work) of the job. But in the United States, if we want to know anything about the human capital or demographic characteristics of workers in an industry or occupation, we almost always have to turn to household surveys. If some information is available only on household surveys and other information is available on establishment surveys, one can bring them together based on tabulations of data from the two sources—that is, one can use data on earnings in an industry from an establishment survey and data on the educational attainment of workers in that industry from a household survey—but since the industry variables are measured differently such unions are less than ideal. It is possible to collect information from establishments on a limited set of demographic variables, as was done, for instance, in the special demographic supplement to the BLS's White Collar Pay Survey used by Bronars and Famulari (chap. 13 in this volume).[27] But to collect detailed information on human capital, family characteristics, and nonearnings income, it would be necessary to interview workers. It should be noted however that it would be difficult to develop useful longitudinal worker-employer data because of frequent job changes.

There are other ways of obtaining establishment information linked to some information on workers. Both Orchard and Stibbard (1993) and Hostrup-Pedersen (1993) describe establishment data sets that provide some information on persons, for the United Kingdom and Denmark, respectively. Hostrup-Pedersen describes the use by Danmarks Statistics of register-based data to produce employment data. Detailed tabulations by area are possible, and the distribution of employees within an industry by occupation, education, sex, and age is produced, something that in the United States is regularly available only from household interviews. Denmark's use of a register provides a

---

25. There have been special linked surveys. Troske uses matched LRD–Census of Population data (chap. 11 in this volume). The EOPP, a test of a proposed welfare reform option, included collection of data for a sample of households and employers in test and comparison sites in 1980. A second wave of the EOPP employer survey, sponsored by the National Institute of Education and the National Center for Research in Vocational Education, provides data for 1981. The BLS is planning a small test to obtain information from a sample of workers within the approximately 1,200 establishments to be surveyed in a second Survey of Employer-Provided Training.

26. In contrast, Rosen was not enthusiastic about Hamermesh's recommendation for additional high-frequency establishment data for the particular purpose of studying labor demand.

27. That effort showed that some kinds of worker information are much easier to collect in establishment surveys than other kinds. Most notably, reporting of information on the starting wage was very low. However, obtaining retrospective information of any type in establishment or household surveys is problematic, which is why longitudinal information surveys are needed for many purposes.

straightforward method for obtaining linked employer-employee information with a frame that should be of extremely high quality. The United States does not have such a register of persons that is used in this way. But as the Orchard-Stibbard paper shows, it is not necessary to have such an individual register to get this information—it can be obtained by beginning with any administrative data set or sample frame providing information on persons. For example, the U.K. New Earnings Survey contains information from employers' payroll records on earnings, sex, age, occupation, industry, and collective bargaining coverage; occasionally, special questions have been included. An important limitation is that this U.K. source does not cover persons below a certain income tax threshold. It is important to note that microdata from these surveys for Denmark and the United Kingdom are not provided to outsiders for research purposes, and it appears they are not used internally for such purposes either.

Some kinds of information we may want for household-based analyses cannot be obtained directly from households. For instance, information on the amount of fringe benefits paid to particular individuals together with information on household demographics and income sources is not available in the United States, and high-quality information of this type would only be possible with a linked household-establishment survey. Thus, whether beginning from the perspective of looking at establishments or households, there are many reasons why linked establishment-worker data are desirable.

1.2.2   How to Make the Existing System More Useful

Microdata Usage and Linkages

An important need recognized by many researchers is increased microdata availability from both household and establishment surveys. In the case of household surveys, there is considerable demand for small-area data and for matched administrative records data. Both are problematic for statistical agencies because of concerns about privacy (see also the discussion below of confidentiality in the context of establishment surveys). Releasing data with information for very small geographic areas greatly increases the probability that a respondent could be identified.[28] Matching to administrative records can be particularly problematic. For instance, for the 1990 interview of the NLS older men, waiver forms were developed by the Census Bureau to obtain consent from respondents for matching to social security records but they were not approved in the Office of Management and Budget clearance process.

In contrast to the large volume of research using household microdata, there has been relatively little research using establishment microdata. Use of estab-

---

28. The PSID provides census tract information, but the NLS has not done so under its geocode agreement. However, recently the NLS has decided to make available local area information from the NLS youth cohort to researchers working at NORC in Chicago; presumably this could be done at the BLS in Washington, D.C., as well.

lishment microdata, both cross sectional and longitudinal, is essential in order to expand the issues that can be addressed. For instance, using LRD data Davis and Haltiwanger (1990) found important results about expansion and contraction of establishments over the business cycle, results that could never have been obtained with aggregate U.S. statistics as previously conceived. Analyses using establishment microdata are needed also to address topics previously studied using aggregated data. As Caballero (1992) has pointed out, fallacies can arise from application of the representative agent framework to model macroeconomic data; to avoid such fallacies of composition, analyses using firm or establishment microdata are required.

At the BLS, establishment microdata have not been kept in the appropriate form for ready use within the agency. Microdata from some surveys have not been saved at all in some instances. In other instances, some data elements collected have been discarded when they are no longer needed for program purposes. The BLS is currently developing longitudinal microdata from the ES-202 program and is forming a CES-linked longitudinal microdata file of respondents from 1972 forward.

While the Census Bureau has for a number of years supported development of the LRD file for research use within the agency, it has been argued that even Census Bureau support for microdata has been insufficient (see McGuckin 1991). But it must be noted that uses are also very limited as long as no way is established to make these data widely accessible to outside researchers. In fact, my initial view of Hamermesh's (1990) call for a whole new effort on labor demand was that it was hard to see how it could be justified unless some way could be found to improve access to the data.

For the past 10 years or so, outside researchers have been able to access confidential microdata while serving as ASA/NSF fellows at either the Census Bureau or the BLS. Some other researchers have also been able to access the LRD data at the Census Bureau, and a few outside researchers have used confidential microdata at the BLS. The Census Bureau has recently established a regional data center. Considerable thought is now being given at the BLS to making data more accessible while preserving confidentiality. In addition to expanding possibilities for use of these data within the agency by both BLS and outside researchers, another approach might be through use of special agreements, as is done by the BLS for the NLS youth cohort geocode data. An alternative approach, masking data, has been discussed in various contexts for a long time; this is not a promising approach because it seems unlikely that masked data could meet very many needs, given the wide range of interests of researchers and the different econometric issues that are pertinent for each study.

Other countries too have been slow to make available establishment microdata for research purposes. Among microdata that have been used for research are French data used to study investment and labor demand (Mairesse and Dormont 1985) and compensation (Abowd and Kramarz, chap. 10 in this volume).

In Great Britain, there has been one major establishment survey for which microdata are publically available for research, the Workplace Industrial Relations Survey (WIRS), begun in 1980 (see, e.g., Millward 1993 for a discussion). According to Hamermesh, the WIRS, which focuses on the practices of management-employee relations at the workplace, provides "most of the variables one might want for studying labor demand" (1993, 398). It has been collected and processed by a private research organization rather than a government agency, although three government agencies, including the Department of Employment, have been sponsors. Research topics studied using this survey have included the impact of unions of various types on wages and the effects of profit-related pay. Similar surveys have recently begun in Australia and France.

The Census Bureau has increased the number of issues that can be addressed using the LRD file by linking it with other surveys—for instance, the wage data described in the paper by Troske (chap. 11 in this volume). There are gains possible from matching BLS files as well. In the past, limited efforts have been made by researchers within the BLS: Pergamit (1987) matched CES data with the union status variable from the Area Wage Surveys for two states. Ruser (1993) matched Occupational Safety and Health Statistics annual data on injury counts, hours, and employment to CES data on the weekly wage, percentage of production workers, percentage female, and weekly overtime hours. But such efforts have been difficult for a single researcher, and many possibilities have been prevented or made extremely costly by data's not being stored and maintained in a suitable way. In theory, matching at least some historical data is possible fairly readily across all BLS establishment surveys. Unfortunately, such matches (except those with the ES-202) will only yield coverage of large firms since there will be very few matches of smaller firms that are sampled with low probability. Matching "special surveys" to ongoing surveys may also be beneficial if enough matches could be obtained. For instance, matching a special survey of workplace practices, if one were to be conducted, to ECI and EBS data would greatly enhance research possibilities because of the importance of information on compensation structure. It is important to note the problem of sample representativeness when samples are linked over time and when differing surveys are matched, but regression studies can still be performed and statistical work to figure out how to create improved estimates from such matches might be possible.

In our decentralized statistical system, matching confidential data collected by different agencies is not possible at present. Important improvements in knowledge about the U.S. economy would come about through matching the Census Bureau's LRD file with BLS data, for instance, producer price index data or occupational safety and health data. This would necessitate data-sharing legislation or some other mechanism. However, as with matching existing BLS surveys, there would be a problem of few matches except for large establishments.

Developing and maintaining readily accessible longitudinal microdata files seems a minimal part of any effort to improve establishment data for research purposes. Development of matched files across surveys may also be valuable. An advantage is that, at extremely low cost, knowledge can be expanded. It might also be possible to consider changes in the surveys themselves that would improve research uses while continuing to permit historic program uses; such changes may not always be particularly expensive and may even save money. An example is that, starting in 1989, the same establishments have been included in the ECI and EBS. While this was done for cost reasons and the two surveys have not been processed together, the common sample will provide interesting research opportunities. A conference of researchers was held in September 1994 to address possibilities for a microdata file containing both sets of information—among the difficulties in this are differing units of observation, that is, occupation in the ECI and benefit plan in the EBS.

Improving Content

One of Commissioner Abraham's major goals is to expand the content of existing surveys. In the recent past, relatively little new information has been added to or proposed for existing surveys.

The American Statistical Association Panel report (1994, 10, 30) recommended investigating the feasibility of collecting additional data through the CES survey.[29] If a probability sample is implemented, the addition of information to the CES would be an obvious place to begin developing information for analyzing labor demand. For such a huge sample, adding information to only a small subsample of the monthly survey or fielding a special supplement quarterly or annually would provide a basis for numerous analyses. Presumably, it would not be feasible to collect nearly as extensive a set of information as would be ideal for some uses—see Hamermesh (1990, 1993)—because it is not a personal interview survey. In fact, respondent burden would probably be seen as limiting how much desirable information would be collected even in a personal visit survey.

New Uses

In the current budget environment, it appears that not very many major new efforts will be feasible. Therefore, improvements in use of existing data that can be achieved at modest cost are an important focus. Development of gross change measures from both household and establishment data is an important need. As discussed above, Davis and Haltiwanger's work on gross employment change provides major new measures for the United States but refers only to the manufacturing sector. Work at the BLS is just beginning to construct simi-

29. The American Statistical Association Panel report also recommends research on "the development of CES concepts that would more nearly meet the needs of the user community," including "where needed, to investigate the feasibility of changing the set of variables collected . . . to meet users' needs" (1994, 6). The panel recommends consideration of obtaining data on broad occupational breakdowns and on lump-sum payments and employee contributions to thrift savings plans.

lar measures using ES-202 data that will include all industries and be representative of small firms. Also, measures of gross change in payrolls and hours
might be constructed using the CES data. Adding content to existing surveys,
discussed above, is another way of obtaining new information at relatively
low cost.

Current research by Anderson and Meyer (1994) using individual microdata
from UI administrative wage records for eight states for 1978–84 combines
information on individual workers and establishments. The view taken is an
establishment perspective. They divide turnover into temporary separations
and accessions, permanent job position creation and destruction as firms grow
or decline, and job match creation and destruction as individuals move across
continuing positions at different firms. Since little demographic information is
available, and hours data are lacking, these data cannot be used to address
many of the issues that researchers would want to explore using an ideal
matched firm-worker data set. But clearly Anderson and Meyer's analysis extends our knowledge in important ways and suggests additional statistics that
could be produced with existing information. A possible new effort is being
discussed at the BLS to create a wage record microdatabase. If these data could
be linked to CPS microdata, the research payoff could be enormous, both in
terms of assessing the quality of earnings data obtained from both sources and
for providing demographic information for a variety of analytic purposes, including expanding on the type of analyses done by Anderson and Meyer. But
data-sharing legislation would clearly be needed to enable this. NLS youth
cohort data might also be linked to UI data.

Trade-Offs

The focus in this paper has been on research needs, but of course there are
many other major uses for labor statistics. Research needs cannot be addressed
apart from these other needs in a tight budgetary period. There is considerable
interest on the part of a variety of users, including policymakers, the Federal
Reserve Board, macroeconomic forecasters, and financial sector analysts, in
very timely monthly aggregate statistical series.

Another major use of BLS data is in automatic formulas for indexing and
other purposes. In the case of labor measures, ECI data are well suited to use
in escalation where a measure of labor costs is needed. Among such uses, the
Health Care Financing Administration uses the ECI as part of an input price
index for prospective reimbursement of hospital charges under Medicare. Average hourly earnings is also used for escalation purposes in private sector
contracts because of its extensive industry detail. In addition, local-area unemployment statistics (constructed using the CPS and statistical methods) have
been used for allocating funds under the Comprehensive Employment and
Training Act and successor programs.

Another need is for large sample sizes to provide state and area data and
more statistical precision. For instance, there is demand by states for data to

use in forecasting revenues. But there is a trade-off between this need and the need for richer information.[30]

Trade-offs clearly exist between features of programs that serve needs for timely macrodata, indexing or allocating funds, and state and area detail and features of programs that serve research and other policy needs. Trade-offs exist between accuracy, frequency, and detail of information provided. Consideration of these sorts of trade-offs is beyond the scope of this paper.

30. For instance, in discussing Antos's (1983) paper, which described BLS data on compensation, Juster (1983) recognized the desires of others such as states for detailed data but called for a different trade-off. He stated: "I would make the judgment that the BLS program would be better if it collected data from fewer units of observation generally, but measured more variables for those same units. The basic reason is that I would be prepared to live with somewhat more sampling variance, if the benefits were a substantially enhanced analytic potential" (180).

Appendix

Table 1A.1   Percentage Distribution of Articles by Detailed Topic, 1984–93

Topic	General Journals		Specialty Journals		All Journals	
	1984–88	1989–93	1984–88	1989–93	1984–88	1989–93
Labor supply	23.1	23.1	20.5	23.2	21.6	23.2
Population size and structure	2.5	1.3	0.6	0.9	1.4	1.1
Household production	1.2	3.6	0.9	2.4	1.1	2.9
Labor supply of men	0.0	0.9	2.1	0.9	1.2	0.9
Labor supply of women	2.1	2.7	2.1	3.6	2.1	3.2
Other labor supply	9.9	8.4	6.1	9.3	7.7	9.0
Retirement	2.1	1.3	4.9	2.7	3.7	2.2
Education demand	1.7	2.2	1.5	1.5	1.6	1.8
Migration	3.7	2.7	2.1	1.8	2.8	2.2
Labor demand	11.2	12.0	0.9	2.4	5.3	6.3
Basic labor demand	4.5	4.0	0.6	0.9	2.3	2.2
Adjustment and dynamic demand	0.8	2.2	0.3	0.0	0.5	0.9
Minimum wage	1.2	0.4	0.0	1.5	0.5	1.1
Static factor demand	4.1	3.1	0.0	0.0	1.8	1.3
Dynamic factor demand	0.4	2.2	0.0	0.0	0.2	0.9
Wage determination and earnings	24.8	28.9	29.1	26.8	27.2	27.6
Earnings functions	12.0	12.0	8.9	13.3	10.2	12.7
Theoretical lifetime earnings	0.0	0.9	0.3	0.0	0.2	0.4
Compensating wage differentials	2.1	1.3	0.9	0.9	1.4	1.1

(*continued*)

Table 1A.1   (continued)

Topic	General Journals		Specialty Journals		All Journals	
	1984–88	1989–93	1984–88	1989–93	1984–88	1989–93
Discrimination	2.5	2.2	5.8	3.0	4.4	2.7
Earnings inequality	3.3	7.6	5.5	5.7	4.6	6.5
Occupational choice	2.9	0.9	1.5	0.6	2.1	0.7
Training effects	1.2	1.3	2.8	1.5	2.1	1.4
Compensation policy and strategy	0.8	2.7	3.4	1.8	2.3	2.2
Labor market equilibrium and friction	27.3	25.3	18.7	20.2	22.3	22.3
Specific training and turnover	1.2	0.4	0.6	2.1	0.9	1.4
Search	3.7	2.7	3.4	1.8	3.5	2.2
Unemployment structure	9.1	7.1	5.2	3.6	6.9	5.0
Cyclical movements	1.7	1.8	1.5	0.6	1.6	1.1
Screening, signaling, contracting, matching	5.0	4.0	3.4	3.3	4.0	3.6
Career mobility and other turnover	2.1	3.1	1.8	3.0	1.9	3.1
Other internal labor markets	4.1	3.6	1.2	3.6	2.5	3.6
Gross job flows	0.0	0.9	0.0	0.3	0.0	0.5
Safety	0.4	1.8	1.5	1.8	1.1	1.8
Institutional structures	13.6	10.7	30.9	27.4	23.6	20.6
Trade unions and union wage effects	6.2	2.7	15.0	13.0	11.2	8.8
Strikes and collective bargaining	6.2	7.1	10.7	9.9	8.8	8.8
Stratification, segmentation	1.2	0.4	1.5	1.2	1.4	0.9
Public sector labor markets	0.0	0.4	3.7	3.3	2.1	2.2
Total	100.0	100.0	100.0	100.0	100.0	100.0

References

American Statistical Association Panel. 1994. A research agenda to guide and improve the Current Employment Statistics survey. Alexandria, Va.: American Statistical Association, January.

Anderson, Patricia M., and Bruce D. Meyer. 1994. The extent and consequences of job turnover. *Brookings Papers on Economic Activity: Microeconomics,* 177–237.

Antos, Joseph R. 1983. Analysis of labor cost: Data concepts and sources. In *The measurement of labor cost,* ed. J. E. Triplett. Chicago: University of Chicago Press.

Ashenfelter, Orley C., and Richard Layard, eds. 1986. *Handbook of labor economics.* New York: Elsevier.

Barkume, Anthony J., and Francis W. Horvath. 1995. Using gross flows to explore movements in the labor force. *Monthly Labor Review* 118 (April): 28–35.

Caballero, Ricardo J. 1992. A fallacy of composition. *American Economic Review* 82 (December): 1279–92.

Davis, Steven, and John Haltiwanger. 1990. Gross job creation and destruction: Microeconomic evidence and macroeconomic implications. In *NBER macroeconomics annual 1990,* ed. O. J. Blanchard and S. Fischer, 123–86. Cambridge, Mass.: MIT Press.

Duncan, Joseph W., and Andrew C. Gross. 1993. *Statistics for the 21st century.* New York: Dun and Bradstreet.

Goldberg, Joseph P., and William T. Moye. 1985. *The first hundred years of the Bureau of Labor Statistics.* BLS Bulletin no. 2235. Washington, D.C.: U.S. Department of Labor, Bureau of Labor Statistics, September.

Hamermesh, Daniel S. 1990. Data difficulties in labor economics. In ed. E. R. Berndt and J. E. Triplett, 273–95. *Fifty years of economic measurement,* Chicago: University of Chicago Press.

———. 1993. *Labor demand.* Princeton, N.J.: Princeton University Press.

Hostrup-Pedersen, Soren. 1993. Statistics of employment in businesses—Denmark. In *Proceedings of the International Conference on Establishment Surveys,* 309–15. Alexandria, Va.: American Statistical Association.

Juster, F. Thomas. 1983. Comment. In *The measurement of labor cost,* ed. J. E. Triplett. Chicago: University of Chicago Press.

Mairesse, Jacques, and Brigitte Dormont. 1985. Labor and investment demand at the firm level: A comparison of French, German and U.S. manufacturing, 1970–79. *European Economic Review* 28:201–31.

McGuckin, Robert. 1991. Multiple classification systems for economic data: Can a thousand flowers bloom: And should they? In *Proceedings of the 1991 International Conference on the Classification of Economic Activities,* 384–407. Washington, D.C.: U.S. Bureau of the Census.

Millward, Neil. 1993. Establishment surveys in Britain: A boon to labour economists. In *Proceedings of the International Conference on Establishment Surveys,* 266–74. Alexandria, Va.: American Statistical Association.

National Commission on Employment and Unemployment Statistics. 1979. *Counting the labor force.* Washington, D.C.: Government Printing Office, September.

Orchard, Terry, and Peter Stibbard. 1993. Labour income surveys in the United Kingdom. In *Proceedings of the International Conference on Establishment Surveys,* 316–22. Alexandria, Va.: American Statistical Association.

Pergamit, Michael R. 1987. The effects of unions on employment and hours movements in manufacturing establishments. Washington, D.C.: U.S. Department of Labor, Bureau of Labor Statistics. Unpublished paper.

Rees, Albert. 1993. The role of fairness in wage determination. *Journal of Labor Economics* 11 (January): 243–352.

Rosen, Sherwin. 1990. Comment. In *Fifty years of economic measurement,* ed. E. R. Berndt and J. E. Triplett, 295–98. Chicago: University of Chicago Press.

Ruser, John W. 1993. Workers' compensation and the distribution of occupational injuries. *Journal of Human Resources* 28 (3): 593–617.

Ryscavage, Paul M., and John E. Bregger. 1985. New household survey and the CPS: A look at labor force differences. *Monthly Labor Review* 108 (September): 3–12.

Stafford, Frank. 1986. Forestalling the demise of empirical economics: The role of microdata in labor economics research. In *Handbook of labor economics,* ed. Orley C. Ashenfelter and Richard Layard, 1:387–423. New York: Elsevier.

Triplett, Jack E. 1990. Reviving the federal statistical system: A view from within. *American Economic Review* 80 (May): 341–44.

U.S. Department of Labor. Bureau of Labor Statistics. 1992. *BLS handbook of methods.* BLS Bulletin no. 2414. Washington, D.C.: U.S. Department of Labor, Bureau of Labor Statistics, September.

Comment   Charles Brown

Marilyn Manser has given a very useful overview of the many data sets that can be used to study U.S. labor markets, an analysis of data use and main topics in papers appearing in major journals, and some indications of what will and might be done to improve the usefulness of the data. The section on data use in particular is valuable not only as a summary of what labor economists are doing but as framework for thinking about new data and better uses for existing data.

Finding little to complain about, I will instead hope to add a constructive outsider's perspective to three aspects of making the data more useful to researchers: adding content areas, generating matched employer-worker data, and increasing the use of establishment data.

Additional Content

Manser identifies a number of areas where the BLS has recognized a need for additional data collection efforts, either as "permanent" changes to regular programs or occasional studies. No discussant could resist the temptation to add a few more to the list:

Impacts of growing internationalization. While wage and employment data allow one to ask whether industries that export a significant share of output or have significant import penetration fare better or worse than other industries, much less is known at the firm or plant level. Have firms or plants that export

Charles Brown is professor of economics and research scientist at the Institute for Social Research, University of Michigan, and a research associate of the National Bureau of Economic Research.

a significant fraction of their output or import a significant fraction of their intermediate inputs done better than other plants in the same industry? How do wage and employment growth at firms with subsidiaries abroad compare with wholly domestic concerns?

Small businesses? Or new businesses? Despite the increased interest in job growth in small firms, regularly published data by firm size are scarce. And much of what we "know" may be misleading: the job growth attributed to small firms may in large part be growth of new businesses that happen to be small, rather than evidence of the robustness of small firms in general.

What goes on inside the firm? Much of the new theoretical work in labor economics has emphasized the imperfect information that employers have on both the ability of prospective workers and the productivity of those they hire. That has led to interest in how intensively firms collect information prior to hiring, how often less productive workers are discharged or encouraged to leave, the extent of pay variation within job grades (and the extent to which such variation is tied to performance rather than seniority), the importance of promotions in providing incentives, and whether voluntary turnover is concentrated among the most or least productive workers. The BLS has in the past successfully collected data on pay variation within job grades and the importance of performance in progressing through a grade. Significant improvements in our knowledge base here are possible by extending these efforts, even though some of these questions are best answered by an accumulation of firm-level case studies (see Prendergast, chap. 9 in this volume).

Areas dominated by "theory only" papers. Despite the admirable detail that Manser does present, it is difficult to judge from table 1.5 whether the "theory only" papers theorize about topics on which useful data might be collected, require data that realistically cannot be collected, or could (or have) been tested by other researchers with available data. It is worth asking whether a subset of the theory-only papers might help identify a few gaps that could usefully be filled.

Matched Employer-Worker Data

As Manser notes, matched data on workers and their employers has been on the wish list of labor economists for some time. One of the more promising recent data developments is the beginning of progress in assembling such data; indeed, three papers presented at the conference offer examples. The French data used by Abowd and Kramarz (chap. 10) match workers' earnings records (from social insurance administrative files) to longitudinal surveys of their employers. Troske's (chap. 11) data come from matching manufacturing workers' decennial census records to their employers' Census of Manufactures and Annual Survey of Manufactures data. Bronars and Famulari's (chap. 13) data are from a pilot project that used one-stop shopping, asking employers about detailed characteristics of their workers as well as about the establishments themselves.

Another approach is to begin with traditional household surveys, ask respondents to identify their employers, and then either contact the employer directly or locate employer data from an external file. The Health and Retirement Survey, which began in 1992 with in-person interviews of individuals born in 1931–41 and their spouses, obtained the names and addresses of respondents' employers in order to collect matched data on pension plans and health insurance coverage directly from the employers. Preliminary analysis suggests surprisingly high cooperation levels by respondents, success in locating employers, and employer cooperation rates similar to those obtained by the BLS in its surveys of employer benefit practices. Contacting only employers who offered pension plans or health insurance focused our employer surveys on relatively larger, more established employers.

We also have had some modestly encouraging experience with the employer lookup strategy. Starting with workers interviewed as part of a household survey, we asked respondents for employer name and address and attempted to find these employers in the Dun and Bradstreet files. Here we encountered some respondent reluctance, probably increased by the fact that we were obtaining the information by telephone, and some difficulty finding matching employer data, particularly when the address information was incomplete or the employer was a small business (Brown and Medoff 1996).

Taken together, the variety of strategies that have been used to produce matched data are one of the more optimistic developments for empirical labor economists.

Increasing the Use and Usefulness of Establishment Data

For me, the most striking single facts in table 1.4 are the increasing dominance of household survey microdata and the very limited use of data collected from establishments. I see three important reasons for the greater use of household data: household surveys have recognized the power of longitudinal analysis, they tend to have a broad, multipurpose focus and plentiful covariates for multivariate analysis, and they have found it possible to make microdata available to researchers. It is natural to ask whether establishment surveys might be made more useful in these three ways.

Longitudinal analysis. There are two barriers to matching across waves of an establishment survey to create longitudinal data. One is technical: rotation patterns that minimize compliance burdens for small establishments limit the number of periods that such establishments can appear. The other is traditional: because users of the establishment data have analyzed changes in employment, wages, and so forth, aggregated across establishments, the focus on establishment-level changes that would lead to routine creation of longitudinal files has been missing. If other barriers to use of establishment data can be overcome, the traditional use will change quickly in directions that make longitudinal files irresistible; where the rotation pattern is a serious limitation, the possibility of stretching out participation (e.g., the CPS's four months in, eight months out, four months in rotation) will naturally arise once the usefulness of longitudinal analysis is established.

Broader focus. Compared to establishment surveys, household surveys often have fewer observations but more variables. This is particularly true when successive waves of a household survey that feature "one shot" supplements can be linked longitudinally, so that parts of different supplements can be analyzed together even though the data were obtained at different times. In principle, information about individual establishments can be broadened either by matching observations across surveys or by adopting the one-shot supplements as a regular feature of establishment survey programs. In practice, matching across surveys is constrained by institutional limitations that are uniquely American (so that, at present, the boundary that separates the BLS and the Census Bureau has not been overcome) and by the fact that small establishments are sampled with low probabilities in different surveys (so that, by design, few would have answered two different surveys that one might want to match). Still, the option of matching ES-202 data (which is available for virtually all establishments) for several years before *and after* a smaller survey is appealing and hopefully will become common practice. Supplements seem more promising. While there are concerns that longer surveys will jeopardize cooperation, short supplements to *several* waves of a survey can produce the same favorable benefit-burden ratio that one finds in household surveys. (One subtle cost of broadening an establishment survey is that a different "knowledgeable respondent" may be required for the additional information.)

Microdata. Concerns about confidentiality have nearly prevented nongovernment researchers from obtaining access to establishment microdata, and this in turn is largely responsible for labor economists' neglect of such data. A sensible policy on data release ought, however, to begin by recognizing the exceptions to the preceding sentence. Establishment data has, on occasion, been made available to outside researchers, often but not always with top-coding or other ways of blurring the identity of individual establishments. I probably have never gotten the *really* sensitive stuff, whatever that is, but that is my point—that "confidential" but not particularly sensitive data are excellent candidates for wider, if still restricted, availability. Last month's R&D spending is sensitive; employment—which is anyway available from Dun and Bradstreet's for most establishments and firms—is not.

Regional data centers that provide controlled access to such data for selected researchers are a welcome development. An alternative is to make the data available to selected outside users via contracts that specify prohibitive penalties if the data are abused. The contractual approach is particularly helpful to researchers who cannot feasibly relocate to a data center; it has worked well for making detailed geographic identifiers available to users of household surveys.

For some research purposes, observations for individual establishments may not be needed but published tabulations represent an inadequate way of aggregating the data. More creative ways of grouping data can sometimes provide "almost micro" data (minimizing within-group variation) while preventing researchers from identifying individual establishments. For example, define cells according to a rather elaborate cross-tabulation (e.g., industry by region by *very* detailed size class) and then aggregate across adjoining size classes when case counts fall below some cutoff. Within-cell variances would come (almost) free; researchers could work with the means of the logarithms of variables rather than the logarithms of the means. As long as an (incremental) government employee could process one or two such requests per week, the costs would be comparable to one round-trip airfare to a data center.

Grounds for Optimism?

In addition to the explicit content of Manser's paper, I detect an implied theme that is, potentially, very important. The historical mission of many federal surveys was to provide reliable aggregated data for a rather limited (if very important) set of variables. As long as that focus remained, innovations along the lines discussed in her paper and my comment were unlikely. Implicit in Manser's paper is a broader view of what the establishment surveys are meant to do, and that is a critical first step in improving their usefulness, and so increasing their use.

Reference

Brown, Charles, and James Medoff. 1996. Employer characteristics and work environment. *Annales d'Économie et de Statistique,* no. 41/42.

2   Analytical Needs and Empirical Knowledge in Labor Economics

Robert Topel

I was grateful to be able to answer promptly and I did.
I said I didn't know.
—Mark Twain

That would be a large mistake, even for an economist.
—An astrophysicist, commenting on a gross miscalculation
of the location of a galaxy

What types of new data would further our understanding of how labor markets work? My unenviable task is to summarize important analytical issues in empirical labor economics, and how these issues might be resolved through the collection of better data. This is no small assignment since it requires a parallel assessment of the state of empirical knowledge—what we know and what we should know—in the study of income and wealth. This evaluation is bound to be subjective, which may itself be a comment on our current state of knowledge. The type of data that I think should be collected and analyzed depends naturally on what I think it is important to learn about.

The paradigm for my discussion divides empirical research in labor economics into two useful functions. The first is descriptive. Perhaps more than any other scholars, labor economists are walking arsenals of facts. How has wage inequality changed over the past 25 years? How much more do Americans work than Germans? How much more do college graduates earn than high

Robert Topel is the Isidore Brown and Gladys J. Brown Professor in Urban and Labor Economics at the University of Chicago Graduate School of Business and a research associate of the National Bureau of Economic Research.

This work was supported by the National Science Foundation and by the Scaife Foundation. The author is grateful to Gary Becker, Kevin Murphy, Sherwin Rosen, and Canice Prendergast for discussions, as well as to conference participants.

school graduates, and how has that premium changed over time? Which worker types earn more than others? How many times does the typical worker change jobs in his or her career, and when do those changes occur? To answer these questions, labor economists describe a particular market equilibrium or compare equilibrium outcomes over time or space.

For this descriptive function the main data issue is one of detail. How can we get more, and more detailed and accurate, data that allow us to describe the labor market and employment relationships?

The second function, which is at least as important and involves substantially more economics, is to estimate the comparative statics of economic models that apply to the labor market. How does immigration affect the wages of native workers? Do declining wages cause unemployment rates to rise? How would a particular policy intervention (mandated employment benefits, payroll taxes, transfer programs, etc.) affect behavior? Does pay-for-performance improve productivity? For questions like these, the key data requirement is rarely one of detail. Instead, these issues require sources of variation in real-world data and constraints that are capable of identifying behavioral parameters.

My view is that empirical research on labor markets has been remarkably successful in the first, descriptive function. Microdata on individuals and households, which became widely available in the 1970s, have greatly advanced our stock of knowledge about basic empirical facts. There is much left to be learned, but at least the types of data that could be collected are well defined. And, if more data were collected, we can be confident that important factual questions about labor markets and the determinants of income would be answered. In turn, these facts will influence research by labor and other economists—they constrain theories to be within the bounds of what we know to be true or relevant—just as our past accumulation of empirical knowledge has done. And more constraints put on economic theorists would surely be good.

Much less can be said for our knowledge of the behavioral parameters of economic models. The same mass quantities of microdata, which have been analyzed by every labor economist, have not led to consensus on behavioral responses. What are the elasticities of labor supply and demand? The range of credible estimates of these most basic parameters is, as one survey of the labor supply literature put it, "dauntingly large." Years of quantitative research have not done much to narrow our (or at least my) confidence bounds on these effects. This is regrettable because knowledge of behavioral parameters is the foundation of policy evaluation, about which we should have something to say. In this area, perhaps labor (and other) economists should be more willing to follow Twain's example of modesty.

Why the dichotomy between our knowledge of facts and our ability to measure economic behavior? I think there are two reasons. One is that much descriptive research is model free. It describes what is, not why. It is one thing to point out that college enrollment rates and the relative wages of college graduates both increased in the 1980s. It is harder to show that one caused the other. Not all descriptive research is model free, however. I would categorize the ever growing literature on estimating the "true" returns to schooling as descriptive. Yet this literature seeks to identify a particular parameter, with many of the same identification issues that arise in estimating behavioral models.

The second reason is the nature of the data that labor economists analyze. Household data constructed to study income and wealth, like the census, the Current Population Survey (CPS), and the Panel Study of Income Dynamics (PSID), are *meant* to be descriptive. They are not experimental. Behavioral effects can only be teased out of such data through identifying assumptions that are typically open to dispute. "Natural experiments," which seek arguably exogenous variations in incentives in nonexperimental data, are just another name for credible identifying assumptions. Absent true experimental data— which are only rarely available, and even then only for the narrowest of problems—this state of affairs will continue. There are no easy solutions, so progress will remain slow.

The paper is organized as follows. Section 2.1 describes a role for descriptive empirical research, outlines some successes, and discusses some areas where I believe that better data would have high marginal value. I do not propose any general strategy for collecting new data, or new types of data. I follow in section 2.2 with a largely pessimistic review of what we know about magnitudes of behavioral responses in economic models of the labor market, and the prospects for improving the situation with better data. I offer no solutions. Section 2.3 concludes the paper.

2.1 Describing Labor Markets

The growth of empirical labor economics as a field of research coincides with the availability of detailed microdata on firms and especially households. Labor economists today are vastly better informed about the details of relative wages, unemployment rates, and labor force composition than 25 years ago. The wealth of our knowledge, and our continuing efforts to document more facts, is not always counted as a blessing. One of my colleagues, an international economist, disparagingly refers to labor economists as "accountants." Another laments that there is too little *economics* in recent empirical research. Yet the international economist studies the effects of international trade on wage inequality. His own research agenda would be entirely different had labor economists not documented the unprecedented increase in inequality that occurred over the past two decades and postulated that it might have to do with trade (Murphy and Welch 1992; Johnson and Stafford 1993; Borjas, Freeman, and Katz 1992).

This effect is one of the main roles of descriptive economic research. Economic problems are inherently empirical, seeking to explain or predict real-world outcomes and behaviors. Descriptive research then affects theory in two useful ways. First, theories are developed in order to explain prominent facts that arise from data. The observation that wages rise with experience and job tenure, but at decreasing rates, spawned theories of life cycle human capital investment and the distinction between general and specific training (e.g., Ben-Porath 1967), as well as competing models based on search and matching (Jovanovic 1979a, 1979b) and incentives (Lazear 1995).

Second, the "facts" act as a constraint on the class of admissible theories. The observation that real wages are procyclical caused an early rejection of Keynes's original formulation, which predicted a countercyclical wage. The fact that displaced workers suffer substantial and persistent reductions in earning power (e.g., Jacobsen, LaLonde, and Sullivan 1993) gives credence to models that emphasize the importance of specific human capital in employment relationships. Models in which human capital is general are not up to the task. Similarly, the robustness of estimated returns to schooling means that signaling theories of the demand for education are no longer given much credence.

This role for descriptive research helps to define the areas where collection of more, or more detailed, data would have the greatest returns. In what areas of labor market analysis is theory constrained the least by hard empirical facts? Anyone's list of areas where more or better data would be beneficial is long; I will emphasize four that stand out in my own thinking: (i) the economics of personnel and internal labor markets, (ii) the determinants of wage and income inequality, (iii) the activities of low-income individuals, and (iv) the operation of labor markets in developing economies.

2.1.1   Internal Labor Markets

The typical male worker in the U.S. labor market is now employed in a job that will last 18 years (Akerlof and Main 1980). This means that the wages, incomes, and hours of work we observe in survey data are mainly the outcomes of continuing trade between a single employee and a single employer. We know that these durable employment relations evolve from rapid turnover at the beginning of careers, accompanied by substantial wage gains at job transitions (Topel and Ward 1992). We also know that the termination of long-term employment relations typically causes large and persistent reductions in earning power (Jacobson et al. 1993). But we know very little about what happens in between.

This ignorance is a boon to theory. Almost all of the literature on compensation, advancement, and incentives in organizations is based on anecdotal or impressionistic evidence, or just introspection. Examples from universities loom large. The facts impose few constraints, so theories are built with little notion of which factors are important in real-world employment relations and which are not. Among the things worth knowing are the following:

1. What is the relationship between total compensation and wages for workers at different skill levels? Aggregate evidence suggests that much of the

slowdown in aggregate real wage growth during the 1970s and 1980s can be attributed to the growing value of nonwage benefits (Council of Economic Advisers 1987). Collection of detailed data from *firms* on what they pay, and the value of benefits they offer, would give us a more detailed picture of the distribution of well-being. It is likely that the distribution of compensation has become even more unequal than the distribution of income, but we will not know until the data are collected.

2. How do careers develop? Do movements of employees among tasks and levels of firms mirror patterns of mobility between firms? How does within-firm mobility contribute to wage growth? Do raises mainly occur at times of promotion (McCue 1996), or is there substantial growth among workers who remain at a single task? Does within-cohort wage inequality increase, as most theories of learning about talent would imply?

3. Who leaves an organization? Is it the stars, who have risen rapidly, or the poorer performers who may be poorly matched?

4. How is performance evaluated and rewarded? How does evaluated performance vary over a career?

5. Do compensation policies emphasize equity relative to measured performance? To what extent are wages tied to jobs, or tasks, rather than to individuals? Under what circumstances is pay more likely to be individual based, as opposed to job based?

What kinds of data would allow us to answer these questions? Most large organizations that I have encountered maintain detailed personnel histories in computer databases. Analyzing a single company is a research project in itself (for initial attempts, see Lazear 1995; Baker, Gibbs, and Holmstrom 1994). This means that truly generalizable results will be slow in coming. But we know so little now that any information on what goes on inside the "black box" of employment relationships would be useful. It is noteworthy that in other countries—such as Korea, Japan, and France—detailed data are collected from firms on the compensation and characteristics of individual employees. Similar data for the United States would be a major step forward.[1]

2.1.2 Determinants of Wage Inequality

Why do some workers earn more than others? Information on personal characteristics in the typical survey file—like the CPS or PSID—does not go much beyond a respondent's age and years of schooling. These observable dimensions of human capital explain about 30 percent of the variance in wages. The rest is open to theorizing. For example, the fact that some industries or firms pay more than others (Brown and Medoff 1989; Krueger and Summers 1987) is interpreted by some as evidence of economic rents (for a summary, see Katz 1986) and by others as evidence of selection on talents that are unobserved by

---

1. Abowd and Kramarz (1994) analyze the French data, which are longitudinal and cover most of the workforce.

econometricians (Murphy and Topel 1987). Similarly, race and gender differences in wages may reflect market discrimination or premarket differences in unobserved human capital.

Collection of more detailed information on personal characteristics could go some distance toward resolving these puzzles. What types of schools did people attend? What did they study, and how well did they do? An unresolved issue is the role of standardized tests in measuring the talents that are valued in the market. Johnson and Neal (1996), using the National Longitudinal Survey (NLS) youth cohort, find that performance on the Armed Forces Qualifying Test (AFQT), taken in high school, helps to predict subsequent earnings. A 1-standard-deviation increase in AFQT performance raises earnings by about 20 percent. They find that wage differences between young blacks and whites are greatly reduced when AFQT scores are controlled for. These results suggest that market discrimination may be less important than differences in premarket opportunities in determining earnings. More important, they point to an important role for basic premarket skills in affecting earnings. These skills are unmeasured in most sources of survey data.

How important are these skills in affecting inequality? Many have hypothesized that increased income inequality in the United States is driven by an increased price of unobserved skills. Murnane, Levy, and Willet (1995) provide some direct evidence, using cognitive test scores from the National Longitudinal Study of the Class of 1972 data and High School and Beyond. Their results show strong effects of mathematics scores on earnings at age 24, even controlling for years of completed schooling. As important, this effect was stronger in 1986, when the price of skill is expected to be higher, than it was in 1978.

These results indicate a strong role for skills in determining income differences. But test scores are surely poor proxies for the array of talents that are valued in labor markets. (The mathematics test measures only concepts taught before eighth grade.) Other tests, or collection of more detailed data on the skills of individual workers, may get us closer to understanding the important determinants of income differentials.

The early literature on income mobility—the movement of individuals between portions of the wage distribution over time—drew a distinction between inequality of income and inequality of lifetime wealth or utility (Lillard and Willis 1978). If poverty is a transitory state, then it is arguably less worrisome as a social problem. This issue has taken on added import with the steady increase in income inequality over the past 25 years, which most economists believe is driven by a change in the "price" of skill. In this context, the question of income mobility can be phrased in different ways. First, is rising inequality simply a spread in the distribution of pay across a relatively fixed distribution of skill? That is, are those who are at the bottom of the wage distribution in 1994 the same people who would have been at the bottom in 1974? Or has the increase in inequality been partially caused by the movement of people from the middle of the income distribution toward the bottom? This type of "mobility" suggests that previously valuable human capital has become obsolete, as seems to occur when workers are displaced from long-term employment relationships.

The second question is: Once people reach the bottom of the wage distribution, what are their prospects for recovery? If human capital is firm or industry specific, then movements down in the distribution are likely to reflect the obsolescence just mentioned. Then mobility is a one-way street and recovery is unlikely, especially for experienced workers who have lost their previously valuable skills. Poverty is more of an absorbing state in this case, with large effects on lifetime wealth.

These issues have hardly been addressed in the burgeoning literature on wage inequality. (See Gottschalk and Moffitt 1994 for an exception. Topel 1993 contains preliminary calculations.) In part this is because the two main sources of panel data, the PSID and the NLS, are fairly small, so that movements between portions of the wage distribution are difficult to gauge accurately. The only solution is to obtain larger longitudinal data sets. For example, in Sweden it is possible to obtain longitudinal data on tax returns *for the entire population*. That is a data set up to the task of measuring income mobility. Concerns about confidentiality are greater in the United States, so the likelihood of obtaining such data is small. An alternative that could go some of the way there would be to match *individuals* (not households) from one census year to another, or at least to ask about earnings histories in standard cross-sectional surveys. Data like the Displaced Workers Supplements of the January CPS have proved useful in this regard, but they are limited to workers who have lost a job in a five-year window.

2.1.3   Activities of Low-Income Individuals

The low-income "underclass" is one of the most serious social problems of our day. Reported incomes of persons at the bottom of the U.S. income distribution are grindingly low, having fallen by nearly a third since the early 1970s (Juhn, Murphy, and Pierce 1993). Aggregate statistics tell us that declining earning power is associated with rising rates of labor force withdrawal among prime-aged men (Juhn, Murphy, and Topel 1991; Juhn 1992). How do these people survive? Do they rely on families and friends, or are there other sources of income that are not reported in survey data? What role is played by the underground economy?

These questions are important if we are to understand the causes and consequences of poverty, and the workings of low-wage labor markets generally. Yet economists rarely touch these issues. Sociologists have played a much more active role (e.g., Wilson 1987) by collecting their own data instead of relying on government sources alone. Recent efforts to interview individuals in inner city labor markets, part of the NBER's project on unemployment, are a step in the right direction.

2.1.4   Labor Markets in Developing Countries

The recent resurgence of interest by macroeconomists in economic growth has emphasized the role of human capital as an "engine" of growth (e.g., Lucas 1988). At a descriptive empirical level, the growth accounting exercises of Young (1992, 1994) have stressed the contribution of human capital accumulation to the growth "miracles" of Korea, Singapore, Taiwan, and Hong Kong. In these countries, the labor force has been transformed—over a relatively brief period—from a predominantly rural, unskilled, and agricultural base to being relatively skilled, urban, and industrial. In these countries, productivity and real wages more than tripled in the space of two decades.

What is the role of the labor market in the development process? What forces drive the industrial migration of labor? Does industrial expansion require rising educational attainment? Do changing factor proportions, caused by rising average schooling levels, change relative wages? These are basic and answerable questions about what happens during the growth process. Aside from a few country-specific studies, however, little is known about their answers.

What kinds of data would help? Collecting new data would help us to understand the role of the labor market during future episodes of growth, and so one might wish that governments or international agencies collected data on the model of the American CPS. Many governments do, but there is no centralized agency—say, the World Bank—that serves as a repository for the data. Perhaps greater progress could be made if *existing* data were made available to economic researchers. In Japan and Korea, for example, ministries of labor collect detailed individual data on random samples of employees for all firms with more than 10 workers. While tabulations of these data are published, the raw data—which exist in tape form—are generally not available to outside users. Much can be learned from these data, but they have to be pried from the fingers of bureaucracies.

2.2   Parametric Models: Gauging Behavioral Responses

Most of economics is about incentives and behavioral responses to varying constraints. One of the main functions of an empirical economist is to be knowledgeable about these responses, which may range from simple supply and demand elasticities to the parameters of value functions in models of dynamic optimization. Yet in spite of the increased sophistication of econometric methods, we remain largely ignorant about the magnitudes of even the simplest behavioral responses, such as the elasticities of labor demand and supply for particular types of workers. Our knowledge of other behavioral responses—such as how changes in a firm's compensation policy affect the effort and performance of employees, or how rising educational wage premiums affect investment in human capital—is weaker still.

Supply and demand responses remain at the center of current debate in labor economics, and they are essential for even the most simple problems of policy evaluation. Consider the following issues that have attracted substantial research and policy attention but remain unresolved.

Immigration and wages. How does an increase in immigration, particularly the immigration of less skilled workers, affect the wages and welfare of natives? A number of papers have found small or negligible effects (Borjas 1987; LaLonde and Topel 1991; Altonji and Card 1991; Card 1990; Hunt 1992). The magnitude of these effects depends inversely on demand elasticities. In spite of negative results from previous research, many economists are convinced that substantial effects are being missed. More recent evidence suggests that the effects of immigration of less skilled Hispanics and Asians to California may have substantially reduced the wages of less skilled natives. Wage inequality increased more in California than in any other region of the country (Topel 1994).

Welfare states and income transfers. In many contexts, the distortionary effects of income transfer programs depend on elasticities of labor supply. The NBER's recent project on Sweden sought to evaluate many of these effects in the context of the world's most aggressive welfare state (Freeman, Topel, and Swedenborg 1997). Has the growth of the public sector affected women's employment? How distortionary is state-provided child care? Have policies that compress the Swedish wage distribution affected incentives to invest in education and human capital? All of these questions depend on supply elasticities, about which there is substantial uncertainty (Aronsson and Walker 1997). Proponents of redistribution policies will argue that the effects are small, while opponents predictably argue that they are large (Lindbeck 1993; Lindbeck et al. 1994).

Education and relative wages. Changes in the educational composition of the workforce shift factor ratios, which change relative wages in inverse proportion to demand elasticities and elasticities of substitution (e.g., Freeman 1976; Welch 1979). The general pattern of these effects has been confirmed in the United States (Murphy and Katz 1992), Sweden (Edin and Holmlund 1995), Korea (Kim and Topel 1995), and Taiwan (Lu 1993). Magnitudes are not consistent across countries, however. For example, growth in the supply of more educated labor was accompanied by a greater reduction in the college wage premium in Sweden than in the United States. Is the elasticity of substitution smaller in Sweden, or were factors other than relative supply acting to narrow the Swedish wage distribution?

Cyclical fluctuations in employment. Much of what is done in economics is a result of our ignorance about behavioral parameters. Nowhere is this more apparent than in macroeconomics, where the labor market plays a central role. Since Keynes, the welfare implications of economic fluctuations have been a central issue in traditional macroeconomics. Keynesians and neo-Keynesians typically treat economic fluctuations as market failures in which labor markets fail to clear. Activist government policies can then be welfare improving. In contrast, "real business cycle" (RBC) models treat economic fluctuations as efficient responses to real shocks. Labor and other markets operate smoothly, and all gains from trade are realized. As one RBC proponent characterized cyclical contractions: "You don't have to be out of equilibrium to suffer."

At its core, the Keynesian-RBC debate is founded on divergent views about the validity of the intertemporal substitution hypothesis (ISH) in labor supply. If intertemporal substitution of work effort is "small," then it is difficult to reconcile the magnitudes of economic fluctuations in employment with the observed behavior of wages and productivity. Labor supply is insufficiently elastic to reconcile large fluctuations in employment with relatively small changes in wages. In contrast, if intertemporal substitution is "large," then contractions of employment and hours might be market-clearing responses to real productivity shocks. The remarkable state of our empirical knowledge is that these opposing views can coexist, and not just for a short while. In spite of empirical research carried out over a period of *decades,* most economists remain unconvinced by empirical research on the ISH. It is fair to say that many give greater weight to their own priors about the intertemporal elasticity of labor supply, and perhaps properly so.[2] A final issue serves as a useful example to frame the remaining discussion.

2.2.1   An Example: Policy Evaluation and Employer Mandates

Recent proposals to extend health insurance coverage to the uninsured relied heavily on "employer mandates." Under these proposals, employers that do not now provide health insurance coverage for their workers would be required to do so. Most economists would recognize that mandated benefits act as an implicit tax on employment that will distort hiring and labor supply decisions. If we concentrate on the market for a particular labor type that does not now receive employer-provided benefits—so benefits have less private value than wages, at the margin—the distortionary effects of the tax are proportional to the induced reduction in employment. This reduction is given by

$$(1) \qquad\qquad d \ln N = \frac{E_S E_D}{E_S E_D} \cdot \frac{\tau}{w}.$$

2. For reviews of the empirical literature, see Pencavel (1986) and MaCurdy (1985). Pencavel suggests that further research on the topic "should not proceed without some assessment of whether this extraordinary effort and expense will yield sufficiently high returns." Mulligan (1995) offers evidence from a variety of sources that supports the ISH. His evidence suggests that an intertemporal labor supply elasticity of about 2.0 is consistent with the data events that he studies.

In equation (1), E_D and E_S are the elasticities of demand and supply for the type of labor in question, and τ/w is the implicit tax as a proportion of the wage.[3] Either explicitly or implicitly, equation (1) was at the center of policy debates over the effects of employer mandates. Policymakers were interested in how many "jobs" would be lost, and the expertise of labor economists was sought. Supporters of mandates looked for economists who could attest that one or the other of the elasticities in equation (1) is small (zero would do nicely). Opponents sought the opposite view. It should come as no surprise that both opinions were in ample supply. Reputable economists could cite research that would support either small or large effects of this particular policy because the economics profession has achieved no consensus on the parameters of equation (1). What is the state of knowledge about these parameters?

2.2.2 Supply Elasticities

Consider the elasticity of labor supply. No other parameter in all of economics has attracted more research time and money than this one. Potential distortions in equation (1) would be most relevant in markets for less skilled workers, who currently have the lowest health insurance coverage. What value might we assign to E_S for these workers? The most widely cited survey articles on labor supply, by Pencavel (1986) and Heckman and Killingsworth (1986), make no mention of how responses might vary across skill groups. Even so, they provide the most exhaustive reviews of the profession's state of knowledge about labor supply responses.

For women, Heckman and Killingsworth note that most studies find large and positive labor supply responses, yet "the range of estimates of the uncompensated elasticity of annual hours is dauntingly large."[4] The studies they review report uncompensated supply elasticities ranging from -0.30 up to $+14.0$. What they call a "reasonable guesstimate" of the elasticity of women's labor supply is probably positive, but it has a huge standard error (much larger than reported in any of the cited papers). A value of $E_S = 0.5$ might be reasonable (e.g., Hausman 1981), but elasticities well above 2.0 (e.g., Heckman 1976, 1980) are just as likely on the basis of current evidence. If we wish to apply equation (1) to women, then, our "guesstimate" might be off by a factor of 5 or more.[5]

Econometric estimates of labor supply elasticities for men have a much smaller range. At the end of an extraordinarily careful review of the literature on male labor supply, Pencavel (1986) concludes that "the vast proportion of

---

3. If $m < 1$ is the value of \$1 in insurance benefits to workers, then $\tau = 1 - m$. Then equation (1) says that there is no distortion if workers are indifferent between mandated benefits and wages.

4. The uncompensated elasticity is appropriate here because real incomes are not held constant for the group in question.

5. Rosen (1997) applies a value of $E_S = 2.0$ in his welfare calculations for Sweden, yielding large distortions from child care subsidies.

[empirical work on men's labor supply]—both that based on the static model and that based on the life-cycle model—indicates that the elasticities of hours of work with respect to wages are very small. In other words, the focus of most economists' research has been on behavioral responses that for men appear to be of a relatively small order of magnitude." Indeed, in Pencavel's review, 19 of 22 reported estimates of the uncompensated elasticity of labor supply from nonexperimental data are *negative*, while the largest estimate from eight studies based on negative income tax experiments is 0.2. The average estimated elasticity over all cited studies is −0.08. If we take this as a "consensus" estimate of the elasticity of male labor supply, the evidence is that time worked is completely unresponsive to changes in wages. For men, the existing literature suggests that the employment change in equation (1) is likely to be negligible.

I do not think there is consensus, however. Economists' objections to the canonical model of labor supply, applied to cross-sectional data, are numerous and well known. (Most workers are engaged in long-term employment relationships, where the current wage is not a summary statistic for the terms of trade. Wages are measured with substantial error in the microdata sets used to estimate labor supply, and valid instrumental variables are hard to come by. And so on.) In contrast to the evidence produced by the labor supply literature, my guess is that most economists *believe* that the true elasticity of male labor supply is positive, at least among men who earn low wages. That is, most economists think that the policies underlying equation (1) will have some distortionary effect.

In support of this view, figure 2.1 shows the relationship between weeks worked per year and hourly wages of prime-aged men for the 20-year period 1970–89. The data are from the March CPS, as described in Juhn et al. (1991). The figure shows that those who earn more typically work more too. In fact, the curve looks suspiciously like the labor supply curves we are accustomed to drawing in class. Of course, the displayed relationship between wages and weeks worked does not mean that a reduction in the wages of low-wage workers would cause them to work less. In fact, the "consensus" estimates from the male labor supply literature predict that their hours would remain roughly unchanged.

An experiment of this type has occurred in the United States during the past 25 years. Widening inequality has reduced the real wages of workers at the bottom of the wage distribution by as much as 30 percent since 1970. This widely documented change in real wages is surely demand driven (Katz and Murphy 1992; Bound and Johnson 1992), which allows us to test the prediction that working time will not fall with wages. Figure 2.2 compares the distributions of changes in real wages and changes in annual time worked across deciles of the wage distribution, based on calculations in Juhn et al. (1991). The figure demonstrates that both dimensions of nonwork—nonparticipation and unemployment—increased over this period. More important, declining em-

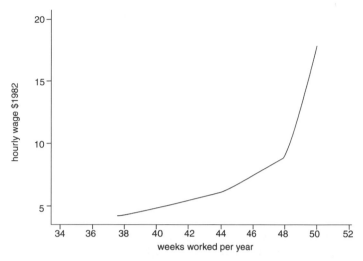

Figure 2.1   Relationship between hourly wages and weeks worked for prime-aged men, 1970–89

Source: Calculated from March Current Population Survey files, 1968–90. See Juhn, Murphy, and Topel (1991) for a description of the data.

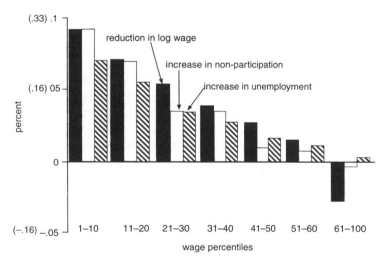

Fig. 2.2   Changes in log wages, unemployment, and nonparticipation by wage percentile, 1967–69 to 1987–89

Table 2.1   **Elasticities of Labor Supply and Changes in Weeks Worked across Percentiles of Wage Distribution**

	Percentiles of Wage Distribution				
	1–10	11–20	21–40	41–60	61–100
Elasticity of supply					
From figure 2.1	.42	.29	.21	.15	.07
From regional variation[a]	.49	.31	.17	.07	.08
	(4.31)	(4.53)	(3.56)	(1.60)	(2.02)
Change in weeks worked, 1972–89					
Actual	4.83	2.54	1.66	.41	.10
Predicted from supply elasticity	4.58	2.96	1.71	.78	.05

Note: See text and figure 2.1.
[a]Numbers in parentheses are *t*-ratios.

ployment was concentrated among workers whose earning power was also falling. Among workers above the median of the wage distribution there was no change in labor supply behavior.

These calculations suggest that labor supply did respond to changes in wages over this period. To test this idea, we used regional data on wages and employment rates to estimate

$$(2) \qquad e_{irt} = A_{it} + B_{ir} + C_i w_{irt} + \varepsilon_{irt}.$$

In equation (2), e_{irt} is the employment rate of workers from interval i of the wage distribution in region r and year t, and w_{irt} is the average log wage for that group. Estimated uncompensated "labor supply elasticities" from equation (2) are shown in table 2.1. I also show the elasticities implied for each interval from the curve in figure 2.1. The correspondence is fairly remarkable: actual changes in working time, generated by time-series changes within regional labor markets, are not much different from what the cross-sectional relationship of wages to work would imply. These estimates also do well in predicting the distribution of changes in labor supply across intervals of the wage distribution, as shown at the bottom of table 2.1.

The "labor supply elasticities" shown in table 2.1 are far above the consensus estimates one might draw from the existing literature. For the workers at the bottom of the distribution our estimates imply an elasticity of weeks worked with respect to wages in excess of 0.40. It is worth noting that much of this effect is driven by labor force withdrawals among unskilled men, whose wages fell. This margin is often ignored in male labor supply studies, but it is surely relevant for our example, or any other welfare calculation.

Does this evidence mean that male labor supply really *is* responsive to changes in wages? Perhaps not. Perhaps other factors also changed over this period, and they coincidentally caused men with declining wages to work less. But the conceptual experiment—do people work less when wages fall?—

is surely appealing as identifying leverage for estimating labor supply responses. At the least, this evidence makes me unsure of any prediction based on small estimated elasticities of supply, especially as it may apply to low-wage markets.

Labor supply responses play a central role in policy evaluation, yet labor supply studies seem to have gone out of vogue in empirical labor economics. Most studies that underlie our working knowledge of labor supply are based on a small number of data sets that were collected in the 1960s and early 1970s. Labor markets have changed dramatically since then, and most would argue that changing relative demands for different worker types have been the major driving force. These forces provide a potentially useful environment in which to study labor supply. Given the importance of these issues, and the weak state of our current knowledge, I believe that a reassessment is warranted.

2.2.3   Demand Elasticities

The best source of evidence on labor demand is Hamermesh (1993). His survey of studies that estimate the effect of wages on employment concludes that the output-constant, long-run elasticity of labor demand (i) is bounded by zero and 1.0 for most firms, with a likely confidence interval from 0.15 to 0.75, and (ii) is larger among less skilled workers than more skilled ones. We might inflate these bounds a bit to reflect scale effects and additional opportunities for substitution at the market level of aggregation, and larger elasticities for the less skilled. If applied to equation (1), this range of estimates might yield a range of several hundred thousand jobs.

But even Hamermesh's rather wide confidence interval is probably optimistic. Studies of inverse demand systems—where factor supplies are allowed to affect wages—typically find only small effects. For example, Welch (1979) and Berger (1989) find elasticities of wages with respect to cohort size that are smaller than 0.2. LaLonde and Topel (1991), Card (1990), and Hunt (1992) find negligible effects of increases in the supply of immigrants on the wages of other immigrants and of similarly skilled natives. The implication of these studies is that marketwide, own-price demand elasticities for less skilled labor are fairly large, vastly above Hamermesh's upper bound of 0.75 for direct estimates. At the other extreme, recent studies of the impact of minimum wages in less skilled markets attempt to make the case that the own-price elasticity of demand for low-wage labor is virtually zero (Card and Krueger 1992).

Unlike the literature on labor supply, most of the demand studies just cited did not have the goal of estimating a demand elasticity per se. Instead, they are case studies that apply a labor demand framework to a particular problem. They provide useful answers to the problem at hand—did immigration have a discernible effect on natives' wages?—but they are wildly inconsistent with each other, at least within the context of a labor demand model. The results cannot be generalized in any obvious way. Indeed, the fact that we undertake so many case studies is evidence of our uncertainty about (a) the model itself when applied in any particular context and (b) the parameters of the model, even when appropriately applied. The combination of these leaves me with an extraordinarily wide confidence interval for demand elasticities in low-wage markets. A value of 0.3 does not seem unreasonable, but neither does 1.3.

2.2.4 Data Needs for Parametric Models

My assessment of the state of our knowledge about supply and demand elasticities in the labor market is pessimistic, but I do not think excessively so. Even less is known about other important behavioral effects. How do skill differentials in wages affect human capital investment decisions? Does performance pay improve work effort? How does geographic mobility respond to interarea wage differentials? Theory and common sense tell us the sign of these effects, and perhaps some values that would be utterly unreasonable, but that is about all.

What can be done to obtain better estimates of behavioral effects? In the absence of experimental data, the obvious answer is to study real-world conceptual experiments in which the identifying assumptions of econometric models are convincingly satisfied. There is nothing new in that statement. But the cause of our uncertainty about key parameters is that such conceptual experiments are few and far between, not that economists have ignored them when they occur. The identification problem is difficult enough in the case of descriptive models that estimate, say, the returns to schooling. It is much harder in behavioral models that try to isolate the adjustments of agents to differences or changes in market equilibria. Uncertainty about behavioral effects may be the nature of things.

More data can only help if we believe that there are real-world experiments for which too little information is now collected. Most empirical economists can think of plausible examples where this is the case. Is it important to understand whether incentive pay affects employee performance, which is the foundation of agency literature on employment relations? Then we need to observe cases where performance is measurable and firms changed their compensation policies. Examples like this one are obvious. A long list could be drawn up. Beyond them, I cannot offer concrete proposals or an agenda for data collection that will reduce our uncertainty about behavioral effects in the labor market.

2.3 Conclusions

Empirical research in labor economics has been remarkably successful in describing labor market outcomes. For the most part, this knowledge has been fueled by the availability of large-scale microdata sets that are publicly collected or funded. These data have vastly improved our understanding of how labor markets work and the magnitudes of social problems, and they have greatly influenced the direction of economic research (Stafford 1986). Use of these data also points to feasible areas where more information is needed, and where the payoffs in terms of hard empirical knowledge are likely to be large. I described above some areas that I think are important.

Empirical research has been less successful in calibrating economic behavior. Despite substantial efforts to estimate behavioral responses, our confidence intervals for these effects remain embarrassingly large. For policy evaluations that depend on these effects, it is often the case that the state of our empirical knowledge hardly crosses the threshold of being useful. In part, this is the nature of the beast. Real-world conceptual experiments that allow us to isolate relevant parameters are rare, and even when they occur it is not clear that the results are easily generalizable to other contexts and problems. It is hard to be optimistic that progress will come quickly on these issues.

There is irony in this. The power of economic analysis comes from its ability to model human behavior in a systematic way. Economics has something to say about behavior, but empirical economics is a long way from accurately measuring it.

References

Abowd, John M., and Francis Kramarz. 1994. The entry and exit of workers and the growth of employment. NBER Working Paper no. 5551. Cambridge, Mass.: National Bureau of Economic Research.

Akerlof, George A., and Brian G. M. Main. 1980. Unemployment spells and unemployment experience. *American Economic Review* 70 (December): 885–93.

Altonji, Joseph, and David Card. 1991. The effects of immigration on the labor market outcomes of less skilled natives. In *Immigration, trade, and the labor market,* ed. John M. Abowd and Richard B. Freeman. Chicago: University of Chicago Press.

Aronsson, Thomas, and James R. Walker. 1997. The effects of Sweden's welfare state on labor supply incentives. In *The welfare state in transition: Reforming the Swedish model,* ed. Richard B. Freeman, Robert Topel, and Birgitta Swedenborg. Chicago: University of Chicago Press.

Baker, George, Michael Gibbs, and Bengt Holmstrom. 1994. The internal economics of the firm: Evidence from personnel data. *Quarterly Journal of Economics* 109 (November): 881–920.

Ben-Porath, Yoram. 1967. The production of human capital and the life cycle model of labor supply [earnings]. *Journal of Political Economy* 75 (August): 352–65.

Berger, Mark C. 1989. Demographic cycles, cohort size, and earnings. *Demography* 26:311–21.

Borjas, George. 1987. Immigrants, minorities, and labor market competition. *Industrial and Labor Relations Review* 40:382–92.

Borjas, George, Richard B. Freeman, and Lawrence Katz. 1992. On the labor market effects of immigration and trade. In *Immigration and the work force: Economic consequences for the United States and source areas,* ed. George Borjas and Richard B. Freeman. Chicago: University of Chicago Press.

Bound, John, and George Johnson. 1992. Changes in the structure of wages during the 1980s: An evaluation of alternative explanations. *American Economic Review* 82 (June): 371–92.

Brown, Charles, and James Medoff. 1989. The employer size-wage effect. *Journal of Political Economy* 97 (October): 1027–59.

Card, David. 1990. The impact of the Mariel boatlift on the Miami labor market. *Industrial and Labor Relations Review* 40 (April): 382–93.

Card, David, and Alan B. Krueger. 1992. School quality and black-white relative earnings: A direct assessment. *Quarterly Journal of Economics* 107 (February): 151–200.

Council of Economic Advisers. 1987. *Economic report of the president 1986.* Washington, D.C.: Government Printing Office.

Edin, Per-Anders, and Bertil Holmlund. 1995. The Swedish wage structure: The rise and fall of solidarity wage policy? In *Differences and changes in wage structures,* ed. Richard B. Freeman and Lawrence F. Katz. Chicago: University of Chicago Press.

Freeman, Richard B. 1976. *The overeducated American.* New York: Academic Press.

Freeman, Richard B., Robert Topel, and Birgitta Swedenborg, eds. 1997. *The welfare state in transition: Reforming the Swedish model.* Chicago: University of Chicago Press.

Gottschalk, Peter, and Robert Moffitt. 1994. The growth of earnings instability in the U.S. labor market. *Brookings Papers on Economic Activity,* no. 2:217–54.

Hamermesh, Daniel S. 1993. *Labor demand.* Princeton, N.J.: Princeton University Press.

Hausman, Jerry. 1981. Labor supply. In *How taxes affect economic behavior,* ed. H. Aaron and J. Pechman. Washington, D.C.: Brookings Institution.

Heckman, James J. 1976. The common structure of statistical models of truncation, sample selection, and limited dependent variables and a simple estimator for such models. *Annals of Economic and Social Measurement* 5 (fall): 475–92.

———. 1980. Sample selection bias as a specification error. In *Female labor supply,* ed. J. Smith, 206–48. Princeton, N.J.: Princeton University Press.

Heckman, James J., and Mark Killingsworth. 1986. Female labor supply: A survey. In *Handbook of labor economics,* ed. O. Ashenfelter and R. Layard. Amsterdam: North-Holland.

Hunt, Jennifer. 1992. The impact of the 1962 repatriates from Algeria on the French labor market. *Industrial and Labor Relations Review* 45 (April): 556–72.

Jacobson, Louis, Robert J. LaLonde, and Daniel Sullivan. 1993. *Earnings losses of displaced workers.* Kalamazoo, Mich.: W. E. Upjohn Institute for Employment Research.

Johnson, George E., and Frank P. Stafford. 1993. International competition and real wages. *American Economic Review* 83 (May): 127–30.

Johnson, William, and Derek Neal. 1996. The role of premarket factors in black-white wage differentials. *Journal of Political Economy* 104 (October): 869–95.

Jovanovic, Boyan. 1979a. Firm-specific capital and turnover. *Journal of Political Economy* 87 (December): 1246–60.

———. 1979b. Job matching and the theory of turnover. *Journal of Political Economy* 87 (October): 972–90.

Juhn, Chinhui. 1992. Decline of male labor market participation: The role of declining market opportunities. *Quarterly Journal of Economics* 107 (February): 79–122.

Juhn, Chinhui, Kevin M. Murphy, and Brooks Pierce. 1993. Wage inequality and the rise in returns to skill. *Journal of Political Economy* 101 (June): 410–42.

Juhn, Chinhui, Kevin M. Murphy, and Robert H. Topel. 1991. Why has the natural rate of unemployment increased over time? *Brookings Papers on Economic Activity,* no. 2:75–142.

Katz, Lawrence F. 1986. Efficiency wage theories: A partial evaluation. In *NBER mac-*

roeconomics annual 1986, ed. Stanley Fischer, 235–75. Cambridge, Mass.: MIT Press.

Katz, Lawrence F., and Kevin M. Murphy. 1992. Changes in relative wages, 1963–87: Supply and demand factors. *Quarterly Journal of Economics* 107 (February): 35–78.

Kim, Dae-Il, and Robert H. Topel. 1995. Labor markets and economic growth: Lessons from Korea's industrialization, 1970–1990. In *Differences and changes in wage structures,* ed. Richard B. Freeman and Lawrence F. Katz. Chicago: University of Chicago Press.

Krueger, Alan B., and Lawrence H. Summers. 1987. Reflections on the inter-industry wage structure. In *Unemployment and the structure of labor markets,* ed. Kevin Lang and Jonathan S. Leonard, 17–47. New York: Blackwell.

LaLonde, Robert J., and Robert H. Topel. 1991. Labor market adjustments to increased immigration. In *Immigration, trade, and the labor market,* ed. John M. Abowd and Richard B. Freeman. Chicago: University of Chicago Press.

Lazear, Edward P. 1995. A jobs-based analysis of labor markets. *American Economic Review* 85 (May): 260–65.

Lillard, Lee A., and Robert Willis. 1978. Dynamic aspects of earnings mobility. *Econometrica* 46 (September): 985–1012.

Lindbeck, Assar. 1993. *The welfare state.* Brookfield, Vt.: Elgar.

Lindbeck, Assar, Per Molander, Torsten Persson, Olof Petersson, Agnar Sandmo, Birgitta Swedenborg, and Niels Thygesen. 1994. *Turning Sweden around.* Cambridge, Mass.: MIT Press.

Lu, Hsin Chang. 1993. The structure of wages in Taiwan: The roles of female labor force participation and international competition. Ph.D. dissertation, Department of Economics, University of Chicago.

Lucas, Robert. 1988. On the mechanics of economic development. *Journal of Monetary Economics* 22:3–42.

MaCurdy, Thomas E. 1985. Interpreting empirical models of labor supply in an intertemporal framework with uncertainty. In *Longitudinal analysis of labor market data,* ed. J. Heckman and B. Singer, 111–55. Cambridge: Cambridge University Press.

McCue, Kristin. 1996. Promotions and wage growth. *Journal of Labor Economics* 14 (April): 175–209.

Mulligan, Casey B. 1995. The intertemporal substitution of work: What does the evidence say? Working paper, Department of Economics, University of Chicago, June.

Murnane, Richard, Frank Levy, and John Willet. 1995. The growing importance of cognitive skills in wage determination. *Review of Economics and Statistics* 77 (2): 251–66.

Murphy, Kevin M., and Lawrence F. Katz. 1992. Changes in relative wages, 1963–1987: Supply and demand factors. *Quarterly Journal of Economics* 107 (February): 35–78.

Murphy, Kevin M., and Robert H. Topel. 1987. The evolution of unemployment in the United States: 1968–1985. In *NBER microeconomics annual 1987,* ed. Stanley Fischer, 2:7–58. Cambridge, Mass.: MIT Press.

Murphy, Kevin M., and Finis Welch. 1991. Wage differentials in the 1980s: The role of international trade. In *Workers and their wages: Changing patterns in the United States,* ed. Marvin Kosters, 39–69. Washington, D.C.: American Enterprise Institute.

———. 1992. The structure of wages. *Quarterly Journal of Economics* 107 (February): 285–326.

Pencavel, John. 1986. Labor supply of men: A survey. In *Handbook of labor economics,* ed. O. Ashenfelter and R. Layard, 2–102. Amsterdam: North-Holland.

Rosen, Sherwin. 1997. Public employment, taxes, and the welfare state in Sweden. In *The welfare state in transition: Reforming the Swedish model,* ed. Richard B. Freeman, Robert Topel, and Birgitta Swedenborg. Chicago: University of Chicago Press.

Stafford, Frank. 1986. Forestalling the demise of empirical economics: The role of microdata in labor economics research. In *Handbook of labor economics,* ed. O. Ashenfelter and R. Layard, vol. 1. Amsterdam: North-Holland.

Topel, Robert H. 1993. What have we learned from empirical studies of unemployment and turnover? *American Economics Review Papers and Proceedings* 83 (May): 110–15.

———. 1994. Regional labor markets and the determinants of wage inequality. *American Economic Review Papers and Proceedings* 84 (May): 17–22.

Topel, Robert H., and Michael Ward. 1992. Job mobility and the careers of young men. *Quarterly Journal of Economics* 107 (May): 441–79.

Welch, Finis. 1979. Effects of cohort size on earnings: The baby boom babies' financial bust. *Journal of Political Economy* 87: S67–S98.

Wilson, William Julius. 1987. *The truly disadvantaged.* Chicago: University of Chicago Press.

Young, Alwyn. 1992. A tale of two cities: Factor accumulation and technical change in Hong Kong and Singapore. In *NBER Macroeconomics Annual,* ed. Olivier J. Blanchard and Stanley Fischer. Cambridge, Mass.: MIT Press.

———. 1994. Lessons from the East Asian NIC's: A contrarian view. *European Economic Review* 38:964–73.

Comment   Frank P. Stafford

Several years ago at a conference of this nature Al Rees made a remark along the lines of the Mark Twain quote. He said that labor economics was different from other fields in economics and from the rest of the social sciences. Labor economists know what it is they don't know. If anything, this remark has become more applicable in recent years. Labor economists have led the way in published work addressing the issues of measurement and data quality. Some of this has been disheartening. In one sense we can say that we know what we don't know, and every day we add to our knowledge!

Based on numerous studies there is the sense that the gap between perceived ex ante data quality and actual data quality has often been large. For example, the research interest in fixed effects models has shown up the extent to which wage measures based on respondent reports of hours and earnings are subject to large doses of measurement error (Björklund 1989; Hamermesh 1989). On the other hand, some studies have shown that external records from an employer can be extremely useful (Stafford and Sundström 1996). Even if such external records are not available, we can proceed as long as the character of the data errors is known.

The main thesis in Topel's paper is that data and estimation and the development of economic theory *should* be interactive. Theory shapes the questions to be addressed empirically, but theory is stimulated by observing puzzles, either in the data or in casual observation. Labor economics has become distinct from

Frank P. Stafford is professor of economics and a research scientist at the Institute for Social Research, University of Michigan.

other fields in economics by the extent to which the empirical side of the ledger is given attention, undue attention in the minds of some of our colleagues in fields such as industrial organization or economic theory per se. Only in labor economics are studies that are "purely descriptive" deemed to be professionally respectable, or at least unlikely to bring on a revocation of tenure! In fact, however, much of the descriptive work is motivated by the discovery that facts implied by prevailing theory and facts turned up empirically are often difficult to reconcile.

A classic example of data leading theory has to be the apparent wage slowdown and decline in the per capita earning power or real wage in the United States during the past 25 years. Either our theories are bad or our data are bad, or both! Wages should not stall out when investment (broadly defined to include human and physical components) increases, trade expands rapidly, and significant new information technology pervades the society! As pointed out in the paper on divergent trends in alternative real wage series (Abraham, Spletzer, and Stewart, chap. 8 in this volume), a good part of the problem seems to be that hours of market work are not well measured either by employer reports of hours paid for or by respondent reports of hours of market work in household surveys.

The latter problem of household survey estimates of market hours is underscored by comparisons with data from time diaries. Quite an extensive set of methodological studies show that diaries provide unbiased estimates of market work and other activities and are designed by construction to "add up" to the constraint of 24 hours per day. It has long been known that time diaries show a stronger trend toward reduced hours of market work in postwar industrial economies, in comparison to such trends estimated from conventional hours reports by respondents. This can be shown for the United States and Japan over the period 1965–80 (Stafford and Duncan 1985). A recent methodological comparison suggests that for adult men in the United States, weekly hours of work beyond 40 from respondent reports are virtually all exaggeration (Robinson and Bostrom 1994). If proper measures of real wage growth (based on hours estimates from diaries) were to show somewhat greater growth, there would be more credibility to our prevailing theories as well as an opportunity to support or refute the innovative new variants of growth theory.

To what extent is it possible to use even ideally error-free data to test hypotheses and estimate theoretically relevant relationships? How often does nature give us the equivalent of experiments? These concerns have motivated the era of social experiments (Hausman and Wise 1985). The impact of these experiments on the research community has been quite small, at least judging from the extent to which they led to published papers, even during the era when the data were collected (Manser, chap. 1 in this volume). Instead, the use of nonexperimental data has come to the fore with microdata sets, notably the NLS, PSID, and CPS, having a remarkably high share of the research publications in labor economics. Further, the research uses of the NLS and the PSID are branching out into related social sciences (in the area of intergenerational mobility, child development, and early human capital formation) and into macroeconomic areas (based on income dynamics and asset accumulation).

Microdata scts have been applied in "natural experiments" across different market economies (Kim and Topel 1995; Blank 1994) and have turned up not so much clean tests of the "experimental" variety but much deeper insight into the variety of ways in which market economies and their related social institutions accomplish economic functions. On the experimental side, there have been some interesting "tests" too. The recent tax reform in Sweden has apparently had only small short-run effects on labor supply. Panel respondents were placed into three groups: substantially lower taxes, substantially higher taxes, and no significant change in taxes. Preliminary results indicate no significant differences in behavior between the lower tax and higher tax groups (Klevmarken 1994). Perhaps a difference will emerge through time, or perhaps the prior tax reforms had already muted the incentive effects of tax changes in Sweden. In any event this is an interesting case to study since many of the tax changes can be regarded as income compensated. After-tax wage rates rose, but "fixed" taxes on fuel and other items were raised to preserve overall macroeconomic budget balance.

Before becoming too pessimistic about what can be learned, we should reflect occasionally on our successes. Application of microdata has had some dramatic successes both within labor economics and in other fields. The first big success story with microdata was in the area of consumer behavior. The theories of the permanent income hypothesis and the life cycle hypothesis were tested, as well as the simple Keynesian consumption function. My impression is that the work in that area has been remarkably successful. In the area of the permanent income hypothesis, use of microeconomic panel data established the robustness of both the short-run consumption function and the longer run function, including disaggregation of family income into various components (Holbrook and Stafford 1971).

The life cycle consumption hypothesis has not been such an apparent success, but it is harder to test since it implies smoothing over a much longer time period. This longer time period gives rise to much more complex issues of income and asset uncertainty, information, and changing family and household composition through time. Work with the PSID has shown that liquidity constraints lead younger workers to desire *more hours of work* in light of a wage decline rather than fewer (Dau-Schmidt 1984). If so, the life cycle consumption hypothesis should be merged with labor supply under uncertainty and could be useful in explaining the inability of wage changes to clear the labor market entirely when demand declines: if constrained workers seek more hours (and recent data show how little most workers, even in preretirement years, have in the way of liquid assets), then when labor demand shifts inward, labor supply shifts outward, placing an extreme burden on wages as the sole clearing mechanism, particularly in light of our theories of labor contracting.

The discussion by Topel on the lack of clear results from the studies of labor supply elasticities is illuminating if disheartening. To a range of theoretical concerns about the excessive simplicity of the modeling as it applies to individuals (who may be working under a long-term arrangement) one must add a host of data problems. Progress seems possible if the right "experiment" comes along. One pointed to is the sharp fall in the wage of less skilled workers in the past two decades. There is some evidence from the CPS that these workers have responded by *increasing* their hours of work (Bosworth and Burtless 1992). In contrast, other evidence (Juhn, Topel, and Murphy 1991) suggests that these workers have responded by *reducing* their hours of work.

It is anxiety creating to have well-known empirical researchers reporting such different results. A closer look suggests that the differences likely stem, at least partly, from alternative conceptual approaches. In the Bosworth-Burtless paper, the analysis adjusts for cyclical unemployment and looks at (increasing) hours supplied as the wages of less skilled workers have declined through time. The implication is that income effects have induced more (desired) hours. The Juhn-Topel-Murphy paper treats long-term shifts into unemployment and out of the labor force as part of labor supply and implies that hours of market work have declined via substitution effects. The matter here is heavily one of theoretical approach to analysis of the data rather than data gaps or problems. Other areas of labor supply research are clouded by both data problems and differences in conceptualization.

If we define success by a better consensus concerning the empirical regularities highlighted by theory, a leading candidate for the designation of "success" has to be the life cycle human capital theory. It seems to me that while this is not the whole wage story, the basic elements are supported and appear to be better supported the better the measures are. For example, virtually any disaggregation of work history into work experience of different types of spells out of the labor force "works" in the sense that earnings variation is better explained. The success of these partial equilibrium models may not carry over to studies that consider the overall labor market as a set of interconnected markets. This demand side of the market and a topic discussed by Topel, internal labor markets, will require that far better data be available on the employer side of the market, for one thing.

Recent progress in merging establishment data with individual data (Abowd and Kramarz, chap. 10 in this volume) appears promising. On the other hand, "employment units" are inherently more difficult to survey than "household units." Individuals can be followed, and they attach to new families and firms. Large firms change quite a lot, and small firms are always changing. It is also hard to know who is actually making decisions in a firm, so that verbal corroboration of the rationale for some critical observed behavior is not available to the extent it is in households. On the other hand, I draw a fairly strong conclusion from the results reported by Marilyn Manser (chap. 1 in this volume). The establishment of an interactive process to receive input from the larger research community is important for success in the design and use of such a database. Large projects directed from within government agencies without research community involvement and guidance from conceptual models are unlikely to contribute much to our knowledge.

References

Björklund, Anders. 1989. Potentials and pitfalls of panel data. *European Economic Review* 33: 537–46.

Blank, Rebecca, ed. 1994. *Social protection and economic flexibility: Is there a trade-off?* Chicago: University of Chicago Press.

Bosworth, Barry, and Gary Burtless. 1992. Effects of tax reform on labor supply, investment and saving. *Journal of Economic Perspectives* 6 (1): 3–25.

Dau-Schmidt, Kenneth. 1984. The effect of consumption commitments on labor supply. Ph.D. diss., Department of Economics, University of Michigan, Ann Arbor.

Hamermesh, Daniel. 1989. Why do individual effects models perform so poorly? *Southern Economic Journal* 56: 39–45.

Hausman, Jerry, and David Wise, eds. 1985. *Social experimentation.* Chicago: University of Chicago Press.

Holbrook, Robert, and Frank P. Stafford. 1971. The propensity to consume separate types of income: A generalized permanent income hypothesis. *Econometrica* 39 (January): 1–21.

Johnson, George E., and Frank P. Stafford. 1995. Occupational exclusion and the distribution of earnings. Ann Arbor: University of Michigan, Department of Economics, January. Manuscript.

Juhn, Chinhui, Robert H. Topel, and Kevin M. Murphy. 1991. Why has the natural rate of unemployment increased over time? *Brookings Papers on Economic Activity,* no. 2: 75–142.

Kim, Dae-Il, and Robert H. Topel. 1995. Labor markets and economic growth: Lessons from Korea's industrialization, 1970–1990. In *Differences and changes in wage structures,* ed. Richard B. Freeman and Lawrence F. Katz. Chicago: University of Chicago Press.

Klevmarken, N. Anders. 1994. A statistical analysis of the effects of income tax changes on hours worked in Sweden, 1985–1990. Uppsala: Uppsala University, Department of Economics, July. Manuscript.

Robinson, John, and Ann Bostrom. 1994. The overestimated work week? What time diary measures suggest. *Monthly Labor Review* 117 (8): 11–23.

Stafford, Frank P., and Greg Duncan. 1985. The use of time and technology by households in the United States. In *Time goods and well-being,* ed. F. Thomas Juster and Frank P. Stafford. Ann Arbor: University of Michigan, Institute for Social Research.

Stafford, Frank P., and Marianne Sundström. 1996. Time out for childcare: Signalling and earnings rebound effects for men and women. *Labour* 10 (3): 609–29.

II The Measurement of Employment and Unemployment: New Dimensions

3   Measuring Gross Worker and Job Flows

Steven J. Davis and John Haltiwanger

3.1 Introduction

Market economies exhibit high rates of worker flows from one job to another and between employment and joblessness. The myriad forces that drive these flows fall into two broad categories: one associated with events or circumstances that induce workers to reallocate themselves among a given set of jobs and establishments and a second associated with events that alter the distribution of available jobs among establishments.

The first category encompasses job-to-job movements for reasons of career advancement, family relocation, job satisfaction, and quality of the worker-job match. It also encompasses labor force entry and exit for reasons of health, schooling, child rearing, family relocation, and retirement. The second category encompasses the many forces that impinge on the spatial distribution of labor demand such as the growth and decline of markets, the restructuring of firms and industries, changing patterns of domestic and foreign competition, and local changes in costs and the business environment. These forces drive establishment-level job creation and destruction, which in turn cause workers to change employers and shuffle between employment and joblessness. In this way, the second category of forces gives rise to both job and worker flows.

Steven J. Davis is professor of economics at the University of Chicago Graduate School of Business. John Haltiwanger is professor of economics at the University of Maryland. Both authors are research associates of the National Bureau of Economic Research and the Center for Economic Studies of the U.S. Bureau of the Census.

The views expressed in this paper are those of the authors and do not reflect the views of the Bureau of the Census. The authors thank Bruce Meyer for many helpful comments on a previous draft. Catherine Buffington, Andrew Figura, and Lucia Foster provided excellent research assistance. The authors gratefully acknowledge research support provided by the National Science Foundation.

This paper quantifies the magnitudes of job and worker flows, assesses the relative importance of the two broad categories of driving forces behind worker reallocation, and describes several key empirical regularities in the behavior of worker and job flows. We draw heavily on previous research to compile the empirical evidence, and we develop new evidence related to cyclical patterns in job and worker flows. Our treatment of evidence and data focuses almost exclusively on the United States.[1]

Previous studies use a variety of household, worker, establishment, and firm data sets to examine specific aspects of worker and job flows. Because there is no comprehensive source of information on worker and job flows in the U.S. economy, it is necessary to draw upon several different studies and data sets to assemble a fuller, more accurate picture of labor market flows. Available data sets differ, often greatly, in terms of sampling frequency, sampling unit, time period, and extent of regional and industrial coverage. We discuss these differences and assess the relative strengths and weaknesses of the available data sets. The worker and job flow concepts that can be measured also differ greatly among available data sets, sometimes in subtle ways. To clarify these differences, we spell out the relationships among alternative measures that appear in the literature.

In the concluding section, we discuss prospects for the development of new longitudinal employer-level data sets that would permit timely, detailed, and comprehensive measures of gross job flows. In this regard, we consider two sources of administrative records maintained by the U.S. government. Since these administrative records are already in place and are collected on an ongoing basis, they offer a relatively low cost vehicle for the construction of gross job flow statistics. We also discuss a third source of administrative records that holds open the promise of comprehensive, linked statistics on job flows *and* worker flows.

A few additional road signs to the organization of the paper may be helpful. Section 3.2 outlines several reasons to measure and study gross worker and job flows. Section 3.3 defines worker and job flow measures used in previous studies, spelling out the relationships among them. Section 3.4 describes the main U.S. sources of data on the various measures of worker flows and job flows. Section 3.5 compiles the evidence and synthesizes much of what we know about the empirical behavior of U.S. worker flows and job flows. Section 3.6 summarizes this synthesis in a bare-bones recital of facts and empirical regularities. Section 3.7 describes prospects for new sources of data on U.S. worker flows and job flows.

---

1. For evidence and references related to gross worker and job flows in other countries, see table 2.2 in Davis, Haltiwanger, and Schuh (1996), the January/June 1996 volume of *Annales d'Economie et de Statistique,* and Organization for Economic Cooperation and Development (1994, 1996).

3.2   Why Measure and Study Gross Worker and Job Flows?

There are many reasons to measure gross worker and job flows and to study their behavior. We sketch out a dozen reasons here. As a by-product, we draw attention to areas of research that exploit or have been stimulated by gross flow statistics, and we identify other potentially fruitful applications of data on labor market flows.

Reasons for worker mobility. The two broad categories of driving forces behind gross worker flows identified in the introduction lead to different theories of worker mobility. The first category leads to a focus on job shopping, match quality, and events that affect preferences regarding work. The second category leads to a focus on demand-side disturbances that induce shifts in the distribution of job opportunities across locations. Quantifying the relative importance of each set of reasons for worker flows—and measuring how the relative importance differs among groups of workers, among types of employers, and over time—helps to direct theorizing and policy making about worker mobility behavior and related phenomena.

Unemployment and wage determination. The magnitude of gross worker and job flows sheds light on the plausibility of alternative theories of unemployment and wage determination. For example, the large magnitude of gross job flows documented in previous studies underscores the empirical relevance of theories that model unemployment as a frictional phenomenon, that is, as a consequence of continual shifts in the structure of labor demand. By the same token, high rates of worker and job flows in all market economies and almost every industry and type of firm diminish the empirical relevance of theories that stress conflicts between static groups of employed insiders and jobless outsiders.

Worker sorting and job assignment. Many economic theories deal with assignment problems that arise when workers are imperfect substitutes in production, or when they differ in their ability or desire to work with cooperating factors. Assignment models underlie the analysis of several important topics in labor economics, including dual labor markets, equalizing differences in wage payments, labor market sorting based on comparative and absolute advantage, and the organization of workers into teams and hierarchies (see Sattinger 1993). Worker and job flows across locations are among the most important mechanisms by which the economy continually adjusts the assignment of workers to each other and to cooperating factors of production.

Job tenure differences. Job flow statistics shed light on the reasons for differences in job tenure distributions across industries, among different types of firms, and over time. For example, pronounced differences in job destruction rates probably account for much of the differences in job tenure distributions by size of employer. Linked measures of worker and job flows would be especially useful for understanding why tenure distributions differ among groups of workers and how these differences relate to interactions between individual and employer characteristics.

Local labor market spillovers. Data on the geographic incidence and concentration of gross job flows greatly facilitate the study of wage and employment spillovers in local labor markets. Such data could be combined with information on defense contract awards, for example, to identify job creation and destruction events that are exogenous to local labor markets. One could then examine the impact of job creation and destruction events on wages, employment, gross worker flows, population, and the tax base in nearby and more distant labor markets.

Employer life cycle dynamics. Cross-sectional evidence on gross job flows sheds light on the life cycle dynamics of establishment-level and firm-level employment. For example, Davis and Haltiwanger (1992) find a strong, pervasive pattern of higher gross job flow rates at younger plants. This ubiquitous pattern highlights the connection between employer age and heterogeneity, and it provides strong support for the importance of selection effects in the evolution of industries and plants (Jovanovic 1982).

Reallocation and productivity growth. Recent studies by Baily, Hulten, and Campbell (1992), Baily, Bartelsman, and Haltiwanger (1996), and Olley and Pakes (1996) find that the reallocation of jobs and factor inputs from less efficient to more efficient plants accounts for a large fraction of industry-level productivity gains. More generally, data on gross job flows provide a tool for studying the connection between the reallocation process and the growth of productivity and wages.

Reallocation and business cycles. Time-series data on gross flows shed new light on the nature of business cycles and provide a window into the connection between recessions and the reallocation of workers and jobs. For example, evidence presented below for the U.S. manufacturing sector indicates that recessions are characterized by sharp jumps in job destruction rates but little change in job creation rates. This pattern holds in the U.S. manufacturing sector for every recession since 1937.[2]

Search theories. Evidence on the time-series properties of gross job flows has helped stimulate and guide a resurgence of research on dynamic equilibrium

---

2. As yet, available evidence is too sparse to confidently judge the prevalence of this pattern across industries and countries.

search theories and the role of search in aggregate fluctuations. Prominent examples include work by Andolfatto (1996), Blanchard and Diamond (1990), Caballero and Hammour (1994), Mortensen (1994a), and Mortensen and Pissarides (1993).

Identification in time-series analysis. Time-series data on gross job flows provide a new source of leverage for drawing inferences about the driving forces behind aggregate economic fluctuations. See, for example, Davis and Haltiwanger (1996) and Caballero, Engel, and Haltiwanger (1997).

Lumpiness, heterogeneity, and aggregation. The pervasiveness and magnitude of large-scale gross job flows underscore the dangers of reasoning about aggregate and industry-level dynamics from representative employer models. Large-scale heterogeneity among employers implies considerable scope for aggregation to smooth away even pronounced nonlinearities and asymmetries in firm-level and establishment-level employment dynamics. See Caballero (1992) and Hamermesh (1993, chap. 7). Furthermore, gross job flow data point to considerable lumpiness in establishment-level employment changes. Lumpiness and heterogeneity imply that aggregate employment dynamics are closely intertwined with the evolution of the cross-sectional distribution of establishment-level employment changes. See, for example, Caballero and Engel (1993).

Quantitative theoretical analyses. Data on gross job and worker flows have proved useful as inputs into quantitative theoretical analyses of firing costs (Hopenhayn and Rogerson 1993), the welfare implications of aggregate business cycles (Caballero and Hammour 1996), the efficiency of the reallocation process (Mortensen 1994b), and the asset value of a worker (Yashiv 1996).

3.3   Concepts and Definitions

Section 3.2 offers motivation for measuring and studying gross worker and job flows. In this section, we define several measures that have been adopted in previous work, and we spell out the relationships among them.

3.3.1   Worker Flow Measures

We begin by defining a measure of gross worker reallocation:

Gross worker reallocation at time t equals the number of persons whose place of employment or employment status differs between t − 1 and t.

A change in employment status means a transition from employment to nonemployment, or vice versa. Gross worker reallocation can be measured by counting the number of persons who have either a different employment status or a different place of employment between two points in time.

It is important to distinguish this concept of gross worker reallocation from a widely used measure of worker turnover:

Total turnover at time t equals the number of accessions plus the number of separations that occur during the interval from t − 1 to t.

Total turnover measures the gross number of labor market transitions, whereas gross worker reallocation measures the number of persons who participate in transitions. Differences between these two measures of labor market flows arise for two reasons. First, job-to-job movements induce twice as much total turnover as worker reallocation. To see this point, consider the example of two workers who exchange jobs and employers. Under the total turnover measure, this example involves four transitions: two separations and two accessions. Under the gross worker reallocation measure, two workers participate in the transitions. Other patterns of labor market flows induce equal-sized increments to total turnover and worker reallocation. For example, consider an unemployed and an employed worker who switch positions. This event involves two transitions—one separation and one accession—but it also involves two individuals.

A second difference arises from the different sampling methods that are often used to measure these two concepts of labor market flows. Some total turnover measures—for example, the well-known Bureau of Labor Statistics (BLS) turnover series—encompass all separations and accessions that occur during an interval of time. For example, if an individual is employed at the beginning of the time interval but undergoes a completed spell of temporary layoff and recall during the interval, that worker contributes two transitions to the total turnover measure: one separation and one accession.[3] In contrast, gross worker reallocation measures are typically based on changes in employment status and place of employment between two discrete points in time. Hence, the worker in the previous example contributes nothing to the measure of gross worker reallocation because he holds the same employment position at the beginning and end of the sampling interval.

The conceptual differences between gross worker reallocation and total turnover appear not to have been fully appreciated in the recent literature. Anderson and Meyer (1994) and Lane, Isaac, and Stevens (1993) construct total turnover measures, but they treat their measures as analogous to the measure of gross worker reallocation calculated by Davis and Haltiwanger (1992). The

---

3. The definition of total turnover stated in the text corresponds precisely to the sum of separations plus accessions as measured in the BLS turnover data, but it corresponds imperfectly to some other measures that appear in the literature under the name of turnover or job turnover. E.g., Anderson and Meyer (1994) use a measure of turnover that picks up some, but not all, of the layoff-recall events that are completed within the sampling interval. The turnover measure used by Lane, Isaac, and Stevens (1993) does not include any layoffs that are reversed within the sampling interval.

preceding remarks make clear that total turnover and gross worker reallocation are not analogous.

However, there is something to be learned by comparing the two quantities. To the extent that one can ignore or delete accessions and separations that are reversed within the sampling interval, the difference between total turnover and gross worker reallocation equals the number of job-to-job transitions that occur during the sampling interval. One can imagine using data on temporary layoffs and recalls to "correct" total turnover for the accessions and separations that are reversed within the interval.[4] Absent such a correction, one can still interpret the difference between total turnover and worker reallocation as an upper bound on the number of job-to-job transitions that occur during the interval.

3.3.2   Job Flow Measures

Much of this paper decomposes worker flows along a different line. As suggested in the introduction, there are two broad sets of driving forces behind gross worker reallocation—one associated with job reallocation and one associated with worker reallocation among a fixed set of jobs. To develop this decomposition, we begin by defining measures of gross job flows:

> *Gross job creation at time t equals employment gains summed over all establishments that expand or start up between t − 1 and t.*
> *Gross job destruction at time t equals employment losses summed over all establishments that contract or shut down between t − 1 and t.*
> *Gross job reallocation at time t equals the sum of all establishment-level employment gains and losses that occur between t − 1 and t. It equals the sum of job creation and destruction.*

Because they are cumulated from net establishment-level employment changes, these job flow measures omit job reallocation that takes the form of changes in the mix of employment positions within establishments.[5] In this respect, the job flow measures share a feature of the gross worker reallocation and total turnover measures, neither of which directly encompass internal labor mobility. Hence, all of the labor flow measures considered in this paper can be viewed as lower bounds on conceptually similar, but broader and more encompassing measures.

---

4. Temporary layoffs and recalls are likely to be the main source of separations and accessions that are reversed within the sampling interval.

5. Two recent studies provide some evidence on the magnitude of job reallocation within firms and plants. Based on a two-way classification into production and nonproduction positions, Dunne, Haltiwanger, and Troske (1997) find that intraplant job reallocation amounts to 12 percent of interplant job reallocation in the U.S. manufacturing sector over the 1972–88 period. Based on firms' responses to the question "How many employees changed functions and/or changed departments within the organization?" Hamermesh, Hassink, and Van Ours (1996) find that intrafirm job reallocation amounts to 13 percent of interfirm job reallocation in a sample of Dutch firms in 1990.

However, at least some changes in the mix of jobs within establishments are likely to induce separations and accessions that enter into the measures of total turnover and gross worker reallocation. In this respect, the worker reallocation and total turnover measures are more inclusive than the job flow measures. Put another way, the gross job flow measures miss a portion of the changes in the structure of labor demand that underlie the demand-driven component of measured worker reallocation and total turnover. This matter seems minor, and we ignore it in the remainder of the paper.

3.3.3   Quantifying the Connection between Worker Flows and Job Flows

Given data that match workers to their employers and follow each over time, one can directly quantify the connection between worker flows and job flows. For example, one can calculate the fraction of worker accessions accounted for by job creation and the fraction of worker separations accounted for by job destruction. To the extent that such data encompass the entire economy—thereby precluding worker transitions into or out of the covered sector—one can directly calculate the fraction of gross worker reallocation accounted for by job reallocation. Lane et al. (1993) and Anderson and Meyer (1994) carry out such calculations using data for particular states, and Albaek and Sorensen (1995) do so using Danish data. While the data requirements are demanding, matched worker-employer longitudinal data make it feasible to precisely characterize the relationship between worker flows and job flows and to study changes over time and differences in this relationship among groups of workers and employers. As we discuss below in section 3.7, there are prospects for constructing comprehensive matched worker-employer data for the United States.

In the absence of suitable matched worker-employer data, one can place bounds on the amount of worker reallocation induced by the reshuffling of job opportunities as follows. Job reallocation equals the maximum amount of worker reallocation directly induced by the reshuffling of employment opportunities across locations. We say the "maximum amount" because some job-losing workers move from a shrinking establishment to a new job at a growing establishment within the sampling interval. Such workers are counted twice in the job reallocation measure—once in the job destruction column and once in the job creation column. To eliminate any possibility of double counting in quantifying the link between job and worker reallocation, we use the following measure:

> *Minimum worker reallocation equals the larger of job creation or job destruction. It represents a lower bound on the amount of worker reallocation required to accommodate job reallocation.*

We can also obtain bounds on the number of workers who engage in reallocation among a given set of jobs. In particular, subtracting job reallocation (minimum worker reallocation) from the gross worker reallocation measure yields a lower bound (upper bound) on the number of workers who engage in transitions among a given set of jobs.[6]

In short, we can assess the relative importance of the two broad categories of driving forces behind worker reallocation by combining independent data on worker flows and job flows. Data on worker flows provide a count of the number of workers who make labor market transitions; data on job flows provide bounds on the number of such transitions that occur because of changes in the spatial structure of labor demand.

To accurately assess the relative magnitude of the driving forces behind these transitions, it is essential to measure worker flows and job flows in comparable ways. The worker reallocation and gross job flow measures defined above involve changes in employment status, place of employment, or number of employees between two discrete points in time. In practice, we compare worker flows and job flows computed over sampling intervals of equal length.

This discussion should also make clear that comparisons between total worker turnover and job reallocation are *not* directly informative about the number of workers who make transitions because of job reallocation. Total turnover does not measure the number of workers involved in labor market transitions during an interval of time because it double counts job-to-job transitions. In addition, many turnover measures include transitions that are reversed within the sampling interval, but gross job flow measures do not include establishment-level employment changes that are reversed within the interval.

3.3.4 A Summary of Relationships among the Measures

We summarize the relationships among the various measures in a few declarative statements:

- Total turnover is the number of labor market transitions, that is, the sum of separations and accessions.
- Worker reallocation is the number of workers who make transitions.
- Job reallocation equals job creation plus job destruction.
- Job reallocation is an upper bound on the number of workers who participate in transitions that occur because of changes in the location of employment opportunities.
- Minimum worker reallocation, the larger of job creation and job destruction, is a lower bound on the number of workers who participate in transitions that occur because of changes in the location of employment opportunities.
- Job reallocation is a lower bound on the number of worker transitions (i.e.,

---

6. We recognize that not all job flows cleanly reflect changes in the spatial structure of labor demand. Suppose, e.g., that a well-matched worker quits because of a change in personal circumstances and that the employer chooses not to replace the worker because the expected net return from a new match is too low. In this scenario, the job flow event triggered by the quit reflects elements of both job matching and job reallocation. In practice, we count such events as worker reallocation induced by job reallocation.

total turnover) that occur because of changes in the location of employment opportunities.
* Total turnover minus worker reallocation is an upper bound on the number of job-to-job transitions.
* Total turnover, exclusive of separations and accessions reversed within the sampling interval, minus worker reallocation equals the number of job-to-job transitions.

3.4   Sources of Data on Worker and Job Flows

3.4.1   CPS Gross Worker Flows

Many studies use gross worker flows tabulated from Current Population Survey (CPS) data on labor market status (employed, unemployed, or not in the labor force; see, e.g., Clark and Summers 1979; Abowd and Zellner 1985; Poterba and Summers 1986; Blanchard and Diamond 1989, 1990; Davis and Haltiwanger 1992; Davis et al. 1996). The gross worker flows are tabulated from matched monthly household surveys by counting persons who change labor market status between survey dates. These worker flow statistics are based on a comprehensive, national probability sample and are available at high frequency for a long time span (beginning in 1948), two very attractive features of the data.

Unfortunately, CPS-based statistics on gross worker flows suffer from important measurement-related problems. The misclassification of individual employment status generates large spurious gross flows between states. This problem is most serious for transitions between unemployment and out of the labor force, but it is also important for part-time workers, temporary workers, and workers on temporary layoff awaiting recall. Missing observations that are correlated with labor market status present another problem. Several studies develop adjustments to the published data for classification and other measurement error problems (e.g., Abowd and Zellner 1985; Poterba and Summers 1986). Adjustments for classification error are based on information contained in CPS reinterview surveys. Missing observations are allocated to labor market states by matching the time-series behavior of CPS data on stocks with the changes in stocks implied by the measured gross flows.

In addition to measurement problems, the data have other important limitations as well. First, the published CPS gross flow data contain limited information on worker characteristics and the reasons for worker flows. Second, the rotating nature of the CPS panel makes it impossible to follow individuals for more than four consecutive observations at monthly intervals or two consecutive observations at 12-month intervals. This aspect of the CPS sampling scheme precludes analysis of longer term worker mobility dynamics of the sort that can be carried out with other, smaller panel data sets (see, e.g., Loungani and Rogerson 1989). Third, the CPS has virtually no information on employer characteristics. Finally, it is impossible to measure direct job-to-job transitions.

3.4.2   Unemployment Insurance Administrative Data

Administrative data on individual worker and employer histories maintained by the unemployment insurance (UI) system have been used to measure both worker flows and job flows. Some studies use administrative data on employers in particular states to measure gross job flows (see, e.g., Brown et al. 1990; Leonard 1987; Troske 1993; Spletzer 1995). More recently, Anderson and Meyer (1994) measure both worker and job flows using the Continuous Wage and Benefit History (CWBH) database, which draws on UI administrative data for individual workers. The CWBH includes information on firm size and other employer characteristics in the individual worker records. In a similar fashion, Lane et al. (1993) have linked individual worker records with firm records for the state of Maryland to measure gross worker and job flows.

UI administrative data have several attractive features. First, they provide extensive coverage of the business and worker populations. Self-employed persons are the only important sector of the private economy outside the scope of the UI system. Second, the data are available at high frequency—monthly employment observations and quarterly payroll information. Third, and perhaps most important, the UI data offer the great advantage of being able to simultaneously measure gross worker flows and gross job flows and to link the two types of flows at the level of individual employers.

UI data on individual workers and employers are not in the public domain, which hampers their widespread use as a research tool, but several researchers have obtained data for particular states through various licensing arrangements. The UI data also present other difficulties and limitations, primarily involving historical records prior to 1992. Since several studies use these historical records and they remain an important research tool, it is worthwhile to briefly discuss weaknesses in these data.

The main problems arise from the ambiguous nature of a UI reporting unit in the pre-1992 data. In these data, the UI reporting unit may represent an entire firm, part of a firm (e.g., all activity within a particular industry in the state or county), or an individual establishment. In some cases, firms could and did alter the level of aggregation at which they reported information to the UI offices. Nonlinearities and experience rating in the UI tax schedule sometimes gave firms an incentive to change their reporting practices over time. As a related problem, because the employer identifier in the UI files could change as a result of corporate restructuring or a change in a firm's reporting practices, there are difficulties in creating longitudinal employer histories. The severity and exact nature of these problems vary among states and over time within states.

One approach to longitudinal linkage problems in UI data relies on the federal employer identification number (FEIN), which typically occupies a field on employer UI records. Unfortunately, FEIN identifiers suffer from many of the same problems as UI account numbers. That is, FEINs change with changes in corporate structure. Further, firms can and do have multiple FEINs (both within and between states). Based on tabulations from the Bureau of the Census's Standard Statistical Establishment List and Company Organization Survey, among firms with more than one location, there are approximately 1.8 million establishments, 300,000 unique FEINs, and 200,000 firms.

The preceding remarks suggest two points to keep in mind about gross flow studies based on historical UI data. First, to the extent that longitudinal linkage problems are present, UI-based data overstate the magnitude of gross job flows and, perhaps, distort their timing. The seriousness of this problem varies among the states and probably diminished over time, but we are unaware of studies that quantify the extent or pattern of this source of measurement error. Second, job creation and destruction statistics constructed from historical UI data do not reflect purely establishment-level or purely firm-level employment changes, but a mixture of the two. Again, we are unaware of studies that carefully quantify this matter. (For further discussion, see Armington 1991, 1994; Brown et al. 1990; Spletzer 1995; Troske 1993.)

The state UI agencies and the BLS initiated a major effort to improve the UI business establishment list in 1990 and 1991. As of 1992, all states require multiestablishment employers with 10 or more employees at secondary work sites to file UI reports at the establishment level. The discussion in Spletzer (1995) suggests that compliance with the multiple work site reporting requirement is high and improving over time.[7] Spletzer also remarks on ongoing BLS-funded efforts to improve the quality of longitudinal linkages in UI data sets.

3.4.3   BLS Manufacturing Turnover Data

The BLS manufacturing turnover data (MTD) was once a major source of information on worker and job flows. Based on a monthly survey of manufacturing employers, the MTD yielded monthly rates of accessions and separations including a decomposition of accessions into new hires, recalls, and other accessions and a decomposition of separations into layoffs, quits, and other separations. The data are available from 1930 through 1981. The survey was terminated in 1981, apparently because of budgetary pressures and perceived problems with the survey.

These data have been a key source of information on job and worker flows for important studies by Woytinsky (1942), Lilien (1980), Akerlof, Rose, and Yellen (1988), Blanchard and Diamond (1989, 1990), and others. Despite the termination of the MTD survey, the data remain an important research tool because they allow time-series analysis of total worker turnover and its components. Blanchard and Diamond (1990) develop a methodology for using these series to estimate and study the cyclical behavior of job creation and job destruction. Below, we apply their methodology to the MTD to characterize the

7. Spletzer states that multiestablishment employers who filed as single units in 1993 (because of either noncompliance or small secondary work sites) account for 1.4 percent of all employer records. He does not report a corresponding employment percentage.

relationship between total turnover and job reallocation over the 1930–81 period.

While the MTD are valuable and informative, they have important limitations. First, they are restricted to manufacturing. Second, the survey was voluntary, and the sample overrepresented large manufacturing employers. Third, the MTD survey did not produce a longitudinal file of individual employers, and as a consequence, the data do not provide information about the persistence of the establishment-level employment movements that underlie the aggregated turnover statistics. Finally, and quite important at this point, the data terminate in 1981. For further discussion of these data, see Hall and Lilien (1979).

3.4.4   Unemployment Flows Based on CPS Incidence and Duration Data

Many studies use CPS data on the incidence and duration of unemployment to measure flows into and out of unemployment (see, e.g., Davis 1987; Darby, Haltiwanger, and Plant 1985, 1986; Murphy and Topel 1987; Juhn, Murphy, and Topel 1991; Davis et al. 1996). Since the survey is conducted monthly, the flow into unemployment can be measured as the number of individuals who report an unemployment spell that has been ongoing for less than five weeks. The flow out of unemployment can be measured as the number of unemployed persons in the previous month minus the number of currently unemployed persons who report an unemployment duration of greater than five weeks.

This method has some advantages over the CPS gross worker flow data described above. The duration-based method generates unemployment flows that correspond to movements in the official unemployment rate because it uses the entire CPS sample. In addition, the duration-based method permits easy cross-tabulation of unemployment flows with individual demographic characteristics and reason for unemployment (temporary layoff, permanent layoff, quit, or entrant). In principle, one could construct the same cross-tabulations in the CPS gross worker flow data, but detailed tabulations are unavailable in the published data, and their construction requires individual-level data to be longitudinally linked across monthly surveys.

There are also important problems and limitations associated with the duration-based measures of unemployment flows. Imperfect recall and other sources of error in the reported duration of ongoing unemployment spells cause mismeasurement of flows into and out of unemployment. Another issue arises when using data on the classification of unemployment by reason. These data reflect responses to questions about prospects for recall during an ongoing unemployment spell. As emphasized by Katz and Meyer (1990), it is important to distinguish between ex ante temporary layoffs (worker expects to be recalled at the time of layoff) and ex post temporary layoffs (worker is recalled). The CPS-based data on unemployment by reason provide neither purely ex ante nor purely ex post measures of temporary layoff unemployment. As a consequence, changes over time in the CPS measure of workers on temporary layoff partly reflect variations in the recall expectations of individual workers over the course of ongoing unemployment spells.

It is natural to ask how duration-based measures of unemployment flows compare to measures that rely on counting changes in employment status in longitudinally linked CPS files. Davis et al. (1996, chap. 6) shed some light on this matter by plotting quarterly data on unemployment inflows and outflows from 1968 to 1986 based on both measurement methods. For the latter method, they use the Abowd-Zellner adjusted gross worker flow data. The duration-based measures show a smaller variance over time and unemployment flow rates that are typically 10 to 20 percent higher than corresponding rates in the Abowd-Zellner data. The simple correlation between the two measures of unemployment inflow (outflow) rates is .92 (.93). Both sets of unemployment flow measures show pronounced seasonality.

3.4.5   Dun and Bradstreet Data

Many early studies of job creation and job destruction are based on the Dun and Bradstreet Market Identifier (DMI) files (see, e.g., Birch 1979, 1987; Small Business Administration 1983, 1987, 1988, 1991). In principle, the DMI file represents a longitudinal database on individual employers that can be used to measure job creation and destruction on an annual basis for virtually all sectors of the U.S. economy. Unfortunately, while the Dun and Bradstreet database has many impressive attributes and represents an unparalleled source of information for many commercial purposes, it is not designed or maintained as a tool for statistical analysis of job creation and job destruction. Numerous studies have highlighted severe problems with the DMI files as a tool for measuring job creation and destruction or business births and deaths (see Armington and Odle 1982; Birch and McCracken 1983; Birley 1984; Howland 1988, chap. 2; Evans 1987; Aldrich et al. 1988; Small Business Administration 1983, 1987, 1988, 1991).

For the purpose of investigating the job creation process, the DMI files suffer from two key problems. First, there is an enormous discrepancy between U.S. total employment as tabulated from the DMI files and the corresponding employment figures produced by the BLS or the Bureau of the Census. In 1986, for example, total employment tabulated from the DMI files exceeds the corresponding BLS and Census Bureau figures by nine million persons (see Bureau of the Census 1986, 514). In an economy with roughly 110 million employees, a discrepancy of this magnitude raises serious doubts about the accuracy of any statistical portrait generated from the DMI files.

Second, the DMI files do not accurately track business births and deaths or other important employment events. The U.S. General Accounting Office (GAO) has analyzed the accuracy of the DMI files in accounting for mass layoffs, with particular emphasis on layoffs due to plant closures. The Small Business Administration provided the GAO with a sample of mass layoffs and plant closures from the DMI files for the 1982–84 period.[8] The GAO study found that 81 percent of the mass layoff events in the DMI files were mistakenly identified. In reality, these 81 percent represented some other event, such as a change in ownership structure, not a mass layoff or plant closure.

The DMI files also inaccurately identify plant births. A study by Birley (1984) compares three alternative sources of data for identifying new firms: the DMI file, the ES-202 data generated from administrative records maintained by state unemployment insurance agencies, and the telephone directory. She finds that the DMI files failed to identify 96 percent of the new firms found in the ES-202 data. Using a similar methodology, Aldrich et al. (1988) find that the DMI files missed 95 percent of apparently new businesses in the ES-202 data and 97 percent of those in the telephone directory.

In short, previous research indicates that the DMI files are unsuitable for generating accurate job creation and destruction figures. Identifying plant births and deaths and tracking businesses over time is most difficult in the case of small employers.[9]

3.4.6 Longitudinal Research Database

The Longitudinal Research Database (LRD), housed at the Center for Economic Studies at the Bureau of the Census, has been the source of several recent studies of gross job flows.[10] The LRD links plant-level data from the Census of Manufactures and Annual Survey of Manufactures (ASM) for the years 1963, 1967, and 1972–91. The data contain a wealth of information on firm and plant characteristics and permit construction of annual and quarterly measures of job creation and destruction for the U.S. manufacturing sector.

The LRD offers several key advantages relative to other data sets that have been used to measure U.S. job flows: a comprehensive sampling frame for a major sector of the U.S. economy, large probability-based samples that minimize sampling error, the incorporation of births into ongoing panels, a careful distinction between firms and establishments, and a careful distinction between ownership transfers and births and deaths of establishments. Through its economic censuses and the Company Organization Survey, the Bureau of the Census assigns individual establishments unique, time-invariant identifiers that enable accurate tracking of the activity at individual establishments over an extended period of time.

Another key advantage of the LRD is that the ASM (and other Census

---

8. The GAO defined a mass layoff as the dismissal of at least 20 percent of a plant's permanent workforce.

9. Since it is particularly ill suited for the study of small employers, it is ironic that the DMI files have been the source of many of the claims for the job-creating prowess of small businesses. See Davis et al. (1994, 1996) for further discussion of these issues.

10. See, e.g., Dunne, Roberts, and Samuelson (1989), Davis and Haltiwanger (1990, 1992, 1996), and Davis et al. (1996). Chapter 1 and the technical appendix in Davis et al. (1996) describe the LRD in detail.

Bureau surveys that can be linked to the ASM) contains a wealth of information about the characteristics of plants and firms, including industry, location, size, age, capital intensity, energy intensity, productivity, and wages. These employer characteristics can be cross-tabulated with measures of gross job flows. Thus the LRD can be used to provide a wide range of information about the characteristics of the employers that create and destroy jobs.

The LRD also has important limitations. Like the UI-based data sets, LRD data are not in the public domain. Currently, use is restricted to studies conducted at the Center for Economic Studies in Suitland, Maryland, or at the Research Data Center in the Census Regional Office in Boston. Second, the data are currently restricted to manufacturing establishments. (As discussed below in section 3.7, the LRD could be extended to nonmanufacturing sectors.) Third, the LRD excludes very small establishments that account for about 4 percent of manufacturing employment.[11] Fourth, the LRD contains very limited information about workers and worker characteristics, and it does not permit simultaneous measurement of worker and job flows.

3.5   An Overview of What We Know about Gross Worker and Job Flows

3.5.1   Magnitudes

Table 3.1 presents estimated average rates of total turnover, gross worker reallocation, gross job reallocation, and minimum worker reallocation. The various estimates draw on different data sets, different sectors, different states, and different time periods, so that considerable care must be used in comparing and interpreting the results. All reported rates in table 3.1 are measured as percentages of employment. Annual rates reflect changes over twelve-month intervals, while quarterly rates mostly reflect changes over three-month intervals.[12] Since the MTD include no direct measures of job creation and destruction, we follow Blanchard and Diamond (1990) and estimate creation and destruction rates from information on separations and accessions.[13]

The annual worker reallocation measure in table 3.1 is drawn from Davis and Haltiwanger (1992).[14] We constructed this measure using two different

11. The precise size cutoff varies among industries and over time, but a reasonable rule of thumb is that the LRD sampling frame excludes establishments with four or fewer employees. Using UI data for West Virginia over the period 1990–94, Spletzer (1995) reports that including establishments with fewer than five employees raises the annual job creation (destruction) rate in manufacturing from 4.38 (5.00) percent to 4.45 (5.07) percent.

12. The quarterly MTD figures are cumulated from monthly rates. The CWBH figures designated "total" include employment transitions that are reversed within the quarter, as discussed below.

13. We describe the methodology in section 3.5.3 below.

14. Table 3.2 below presents decompositions of quarterly worker reallocation. However, the measures of worker reallocation used for that purpose are obtained by adjusting total turnover figures for direct job-to-job transitions.

Table 3.1   **Estimated Average Rates of Worker and Job Flows (percentages of employment)**

Data Set	Sectoral Coverage	Annual	Quarterly
Worker Reallocation			
CPS	All	36.8	
Several	All		26.2
Total Turnover			
CWBH	All—Total		43.6
CWBH	Manufacturing—Total		49.3
CWBH	All—Permanent		31.6
CWBH	Manufacturing—Permanent		26.3
UI-MD	All		34.3
UI-MD	Manufacturing		22.8
MTD	Manufacturing		20.9
Job Reallocation			
LRD	Manufacturing	19.4	10.7
CWBH	All—Permanent	21.2	13.4
CWBH	Manufacturing—Permanent	21.6	12.0
UI-MD	All		12.0
UI-MD	Manufacturing		10.0
MTD	Manufacturing		11.1
Minimum Worker Reallocation Required to Accommodate Job Reallocation			
LRD	Manufacturing	11.7	6.2
CWBH	All—Permanent	11.3	8.1
MTD	Manufacturing		6.5

Sources: CPS, based on tabulations from the Current Population Survey reported in Hall (1982) for 1978 and in Davis and Haltiwanger (1992) for the period 1968–87; see the text for details. CWBH, tabulations from the Continuous Wage and Benefit History files reported in Anderson and Meyer (1994) for the period 1979–83. UI-MD, tabulations of Unemployment Insurance administrative data for the state of Maryland reported in Lane, Isaac, and Stevens (1993) for the period 1986–91. LRD, tabulations from the Longitudinal Research Database reported in Davis, Haltiwanger, and Schuh (1996) for the period 1972–88. MTD, authors' calculations based on BLS manufacturing turnover data for 1972–81; see the text for an explanation of how these data are used to calculate job reallocation figures. See the text for an explanation of how the quarterly worker reallocation rate is calculated.

pieces of information available from the CPS. First, Hall (1982) reports that 28.2 percent of employment in 1978 represents workers with job tenure of 12 months or less. Second, our tabulations of March-March matched CPS files in Davis and Haltiwanger (1992) find that the number of currently jobless persons who were employed 12 months earlier averages 8.6 percent of employment over the 1968–87 period. Summing these two pieces, the total number of persons who currently have a different job or employment status than they had 12 months earlier equals 37 percent of employment.

Several measures of total turnover are available on a quarterly basis. Anderson and Meyer (1994) report two different measures constructed from the CWBH. Their "total" measure of quarterly turnover includes workers who were temporarily laid off and recalled within the same quarter, if they can detect such transitions from the payment of unemployment benefits. As such, their measure of quarterly total turnover includes some layoff-recall events that transpire within the quarter. This feature of their total measure complicates comparisons to worker and job flow measures based on changes between discrete points in time. However, Anderson and Meyer also report a "permanent" turnover measure that excludes turnover associated with layoff spells that end in recall. Since their definition of temporary turnover includes layoff spells that end in recall within the quarter *and* some layoff-recall spells that overlap more than one quarterly interval, their permanent turnover measure omits some turnover events that are included in measures from, say, the Maryland UI data. Nonetheless, the permanent total turnover estimates from Anderson and Meyer more closely correspond to the total turnover estimates from Lane et al. (1993). This similarity suggests that much of the temporary turnover measured by Anderson and Meyer actually occurs within the quarter.[15]

In any case, total turnover is quite large even when temporary turnover is excluded. According to table 3.1, total turnover amounts to about 33 percent of employment per quarter, taking the simple mean of the UI-MD and (permanent) CWBH rates for the private sector. Total turnover rates are lower in manufacturing than in the rest of the economy. Using this total turnover figure, a crude estimate of quarterly worker reallocation can be generated by considering the evidence on direct job-to-job transitions in Akerlof et al. (1988) and Blanchard and Diamond (1990). They estimate that between 30 and 50 percent of all separations (and accessions) are associated with direct job-to-job movements. Taking the midpoint of this range, 40 percent of total turnover reflects direct job-to-job transitions, which in turn implies that the total turnover rate of 33 percent translates into a worker reallocation rate of about 26 percent.[16] That is, roughly one worker in four experiences a change in employer or employment status each quarter. By comparing the annual and quarterly worker reallocation figures, it is clear that many workers experience repeated transitions during the year or transitions that are reversed within the year.

The third panel of table 3.1 reports estimates of the job reallocation component of worker flows. Annual job reallocation rates range from 20 to 30 percent, and quarterly rates range from 10 to 13 percent. The manufacturing sector appears to have lower rates of job reallocation than other sectors, but the differences are not dramatic. In this regard, there is less variation between manufacturing and nonmanufacturing in job reallocation rates than in total turnover rates. It follows that worker reallocation activity for reasons other than job creation and destruction plays the dominant role in explaining differences in total turnover rates. Finally, comparing the quarterly job reallocation rates to

15. Aside from differences in measurement procedures, differences in sample selection criteria between the two studies make us reluctant to give too much weight to this sort of comparison.

16. We arrive at this figure by calculating $.33[1 - (1/2)(.40)] = .264$. This calculation adjusts for the fact that each person who experiences a job-to-job transition is counted twice in the turnover measure, once as a separation and once as an accession. See section 3.3.

Table 3.2   **Decompositions of Total Turnover and Worker Reallocation**

Total Turnover (Number of Worker Transitions) Accounted for by Job Reallocation (%)

Data Set	Sectoral Coverage	Annual	Quarterly
CWBH	All—Permanent		42
CWBH	Manufacturing—Permanent		46
UI-MD	All		35
UI-MD	Manufacturing		44
LRD/MTD[a]	Manufacturing		53 (lower bound)

Worker Reallocation (Number of Workers Engaged in Transitions)
Accounted for by Job Reallocation (%)

		Annual		Quarterly	
Data Set	Sectoral Coverage	Lower Bound	Upper Bound	Lower Bound	Upper Bound
CWBH	All—Permanent	31	58	32	53
CWBH	Manufacturing—Permanent		59		57
UI-MD	All				55
MTD	Manufacturing			37	66
LRD	Manufacturing	32	53	37	66

Sources: See sources for table 3.1.

Notes: All annual decompositions of worker reallocation use the CPS-based figure for worker reallocation reported in table 3.1. All quarterly decompositions of worker reallocation are based on assuming that 40 percent of all separations are direct job-to-job transitions. This assumption yields an estimate of worker reallocation equal to four-fifths of total turnover.

[a]The LRD/MTD-based decomposition of quarterly total turnover uses the MTD figure for total turnover and the LRD figure for job reallocation.

the annual rates indicates that a significant fraction of quarterly job reallocation reflects establishment-level employment changes that are reversed within the year. We return to this matter below.

3.5.2   The Contribution of Job Reallocation to Total Turnover and Worker Reallocation

Table 3.2 reports decompositions of total turnover and worker reallocation. The table entries show the percentage of worker transitions and the percentage of workers involved in transitions accounted for by job creation and destruction activity.[17] Since the LRD does not yield an estimate of total turnover, the LRD/MTD entry in the top panel relies on estimates of total turnover from the MTD. Since the MTD turnover measure includes layoff spells that end in recall within the quarter, the LRD/MTD entry should be interpreted as a lower bound on the

---

17. Table 3.2 uses Anderson and Meyer's "permanent" total turnover measure because it is more suitable for comparison with job reallocation statistics based on establishment-level employment changes between two discrete points in time.

percentage of worker transitions in the manufacturing sector that occur because of shifts in the location of employment opportunities (i.e., because of job reallocation activity).

Depending on the data source and sectoral coverage, job reallocation accounts for 35 to 46 percent or more of quarterly total turnover. Although job reallocation rates tend to be lower than average in manufacturing, job reallocation accounts for a higher fraction of total turnover in manufacturing. Thus, as we inferred above, the other forces driving total turnover play a smaller role in the manufacturing sector.[18]

Our decomposition of worker reallocation takes into account the fact that job reallocation represents an upper bound on the number of workers induced to change employers or employment status by job reallocation. Thus both the upper bound and lower bound decompositions described in section 3.3 are reported. For the annual decompositions, all reported estimates are based on the CPS figure for worker reallocation. For the quarterly decompositions, the reported estimates are based on constructing worker reallocation estimates from the total turnover figures under the assumption that 40 percent of all separations and accessions reflect direct job-to-job transitions.

The various data sets yield a consistent picture of the contribution of job reallocation to worker reallocation. The lower bound estimates are all around one-third. The upper bound estimates are between one-half and two-thirds. Simply put, job reallocation accounts for between one-third and two-thirds of total worker reallocation.

Two observations provide further perspective on the magnitude of job reallocation's contribution to worker reallocation. First, the preceding calculation neglects secondary waves of worker reallocation initiated by job creation and destruction. For example, a person who quits an old job in favor of a newly created job potentially creates a chain of further quits as other workers reshuffle across the set of available job openings. It follows that the direct plus indirect contribution of job reallocation to worker reallocation exceeds the one-third to two-thirds figure derived above.[19]

18. Anderson and Meyer (1994) draw a different inference when they use their estimate of total turnover including temporary turnover. Temporary turnover as they define it is disproportionately important in manufacturing. Accordingly, they find that permanent job reallocation accounts for a smaller fraction of total turnover (including temporary turnover) in manufacturing than in other sectors. We find it somewhat difficult to interpret this calculation when it is based on job and worker transitions measured under different sampling procedures. I.e., the job reallocation estimate only reflects changes in employment that occur from one point in time to another three months later, but their estimate of total turnover includes temporary transitions that reverse themselves within the three-month interval.

19. Hall (1995) pursues the implications of this idea for unemployment rate dynamics over the business cycle. He argues that the burst of permanent job destruction at the onset of recessions begets further waves of accessions and separations, since workers whose jobs are destroyed seek new matches, and new matches are subject to higher termination rates than the typical existing match. He presents supporting evidence that the observed persistence in unemployment rate dynamics is closely linked to the slow rebuilding of employment relationships after the sharp episodes of primary job loss at the onset of recessions.

Second, a certain amount of worker reallocation inevitably arises from life cycle considerations as old workers retire and young workers enter the workforce. If the typical person works 45 years, then retirement and initial labor force entry directly cause transitions between employment and nonemployment equal to about 4.4 percent of the workforce in a typical year. It follows from our figure for annual worker reallocation that simple life cycle effects account for roughly 12 percent of annual worker reallocation. After accounting for job reallocation and life cycle effects, the residual amount of worker reallocation equals 13 to 21 percent of employment, or 35 to 56 percent of annual worker reallocation (using the LRD estimates of job reallocation). This component of worker reallocation reflects temporary exits from the workforce and the sorting and resorting of workers across existing jobs for a variety of reasons. Thus, according to our estimates, these supply-side reasons for worker reallocation are neither more nor less important than shifts over time in the locational distribution of job opportunities.

3.5.3 Cyclicality

In this subsection, we briefly characterize the cyclical behavior of job creation, job destruction, and total turnover. We also decompose the cyclical variation in total turnover into a component due to job reallocation and a component due to other factors. We focus on the cyclicality of total turnover rather than worker reallocation because the BLS MTD provide high-frequency observations on total turnover for an extended period of time. Comparable time-series data on U.S. worker reallocation rates are not available. Because of limited time-series data for other sectors, we restrict our attention to the manufacturing sector.

Figure 3.1 depicts total turnover and net employment growth for the U.S. manufacturing sector from 1930:1 to 1981:1.[20] Total turnover was higher in the 1930s than in the post–World War II period, but turnover was even higher during World War II. The correlation between the rates of total turnover and net employment growth equals .31 over the sample period, but the cyclical relationship between these two variables does not appear stable over time, an issue we address further below.

As we noted above, the BLS MTD do not yield direct estimates of job creation and destruction. The MTD-based figure for job reallocation that appears in table 3.1 relies on a procedure suggested by Blanchard and Diamond (1990). Their methodology requires an estimate for the fraction of quits that are replaced. Given such an estimate, one computes gross job destruction as the sum

---

20. MTD accession and separation data exhibit pronounced seasonality, and the nature of the seasonality varies over time. Thus, following Blanchard and Diamond (1990), we used the Census X11 seasonal adjustment procedure on these series to allow for time variation in the nature of the seasonality. To aid in the comparison of the job creation and destruction estimates from the MTD and the LRD, we also seasonally adjusted the LRD-based figures for job creation and destruction using the X11 procedure for the analysis in this section.

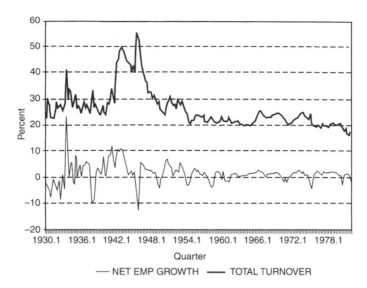

Fig. 3.1   Total turnover and net employment growth rates in U.S. manufacturing sector, quarterly, 1930–81
Source: Authors' tabulations of the BLS manufacturing turnover data.

of layoffs and (1 minus the quit replacement rate) times the number of quits. One computes gross job creation as new hires plus recalls minus the quit replacement rate times the number of quits.[21]

Based on a one-time BLS survey in 1972, Blanchard and Diamond assume that 85 percent of quits are replaced. While this estimate seems reasonable, no direct evidence on time variation in the quit replacement rate is available. Lacking such evidence, we assume a constant 85 percent quit replacement rate to generate job creation and destruction rates over the entire MTD sample period. If the true replacement rate is procyclical (a plausible conjecture), the 85 percent assumption leads us to understate the increase in job destruction in recessions and to overstate the increase in job creation in booms. It also leads us to understate the relative amplitude of fluctuations in job destruction.[22]

To gauge the accuracy of MTD-based estimates of job creation and destruction rates, figure 3.2 reports the quarterly job creation and destruction figures

21. Unlike Blanchard and Diamond, we do not make an adjustment for changes in the number of vacancies in our measure of job creation. Instead, as in most other studies, we define job creation as the creation of newly filled employment positions. In contrast, Blanchard and Diamond (1990) attempt to measure the creation of new employment positions, whether filled or not. Elsewhere, we have examined the behavior of job creation with the vacancy adjustment over the period 1951–81 (see Davis et al. 1996, fig. 5.6). The vacancy adjustment does not change the basic properties of the job creation series.

22. To see these points, assume that the MTD measure layoffs, new hires, recalls, and quits without error. Then the true destruction rate is related to the MTD-based measure according to

$$D = \tilde{D} + (\tilde{\theta} - \theta)Q,$$

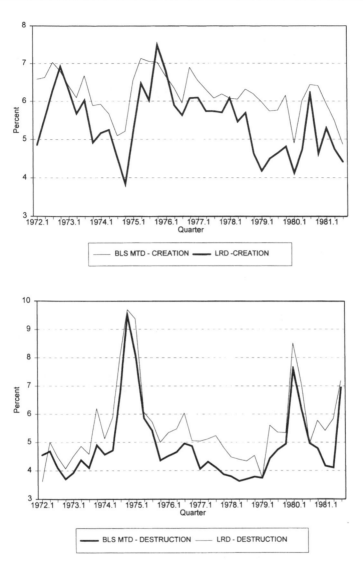

Fig. 3.2   Gross job creation and job destruction rates in U.S. manufacturing sector, quarterly, 1972:2–81:1
Source: Authors' calculations from the BLS manufacturing turnover data (MTD) and Longitudinal Research Database (LRD) tabulations in Davis, Haltiwanger, and Schuh (1996).

---

where θ denotes the true quit replacement rate, Q denotes the quit rate, and a tilde indicates a measured quantity. Likewise, the true and measured creation rates satisfy

$$C = \tilde{C} + (\tilde{\theta} - \theta)Q.$$

If we specify a constant value for $\tilde{\theta}$ when the true quit replacement rate is procyclical, the statements in the text about cyclical measurement error follow immediately.

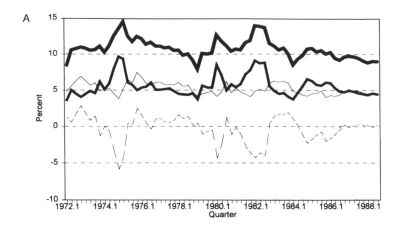

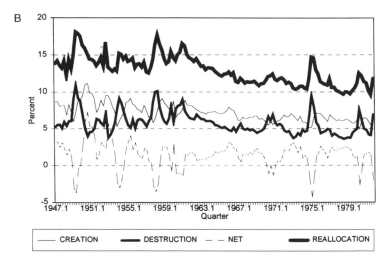

CREATION   DESTRUCTION   — — NET   REALLOCATION

Fig. 3.3   Gross and net job flow rates in U.S. manufacturing sector, quarterly, 1930–81

Source: Authors' calculations from the BLS manufacturing turnover data (MTD) and Longitudinal Research Database (LRD) tabulations in Davis, Haltiwanger, and Schuh (1996).

Note: (A) LRD data; (B), (C) MTD data.

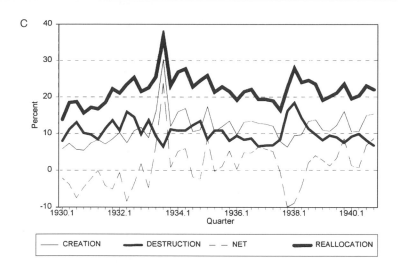

for the 1972–81 period of overlap between the MTD and LRD. Aside from an incorrect assumption about the quit replacement rate, three other factors lead to differences between LRD-based and MTD-based figures for job creation and destruction. First, the quarterly LRD estimates reflect changes over three-month intervals in point-in-time measures of employment levels, whereas the MTD figures reflect cumulative monthly flows over the quarter. Second, the MTD figures include temporary layoff spells that ended in recall within the month. Third, the sample frames for the MTD and the LRD differ.

Despite these differences, the job creation rates and, especially, the job destruction rates computed from the two different data sources exhibit similar levels and similar patterns of time variation. The correlation between the two job creation (destruction) rates is .76 (.95). Thus figure 3.2 suggests that we can use the MTD to characterize the behavior of job creation and destruction rates over a long time period that predates the LRD sample period.

Figure 3.3A displays LRD-based quarterly rates of job creation, job destruction, job reallocation, and net employment growth in the manufacturing sector for the 1972–88 period. Figures 3.3B and 3.3C display MTD-based figures for the 1947–81 and 1930–40 periods. Table 3.3 reports summary statistics on correlations and time variability for turnover and job flow rates.

As emphasized by Davis and Haltiwanger (1990, 1992), figure 3.3A and table 3.3 show that over the 1970s and 1980s job creation and job destruction are negatively correlated, job destruction varies much more over the cycle than job creation, and job reallocation varies countercyclically. (Here, we take the net employment growth rate as the indicator of the business cycle.) Figure 3.3B and the statistics in table 3.3 indicate that these basic patterns hold for the U.S.

Table 3.3 Cyclical Properties of Gross Flows in Manufacturing Sector

Data Set	Time Period	Correlation of Creation and Destruction	Variance Ratio of Destruction to Creation	Correlation of Net Employment Growth and Reallocation	Correlation of Net Employment Growth and Total Turnover	Correlation of Net Employment Growth and Other Turnover
LRD	1972:2–88:4	−.35	2.96	−.52		
LRD	1972:1–81:4	−.47	2.73	−.51		
MTD	1930:1–81:4	.22	.68	.19	.31	.22
MTD	1972:1–81:4	−.43	5.27	−.72	.03	.38
MTD	1947:1–81:4	.09	1.35	−.15	.29	.40
MTD	1930:1–40:4	−.45	.43	.44	.46	−.07

Sources: See sources for table 3.1.

manufacturing sector over the entire post–World War II period, but the patterns are less pronounced in the earlier period. In particular, figure 3.3 makes clear that job creation was more volatile in the 1950s than in later periods.

The 1930s offer what at first glance appears to be a very different picture. Based on the correlations reported in table 3.3 for the 1930s, job creation and job destruction are positively correlated, job creation varies more over the cycle than job destruction, and job reallocation is procyclical. However, careful examination of figure 3.3C reveals that these different patterns are largely driven by the extremely sharp rise in job creation in the summer of 1933. Figure 3.1 makes clear that this quarter yielded by far the highest net employment growth rate over the 1930–81 period. As emphasized by Woytinsky (1942, esp. 48, diagram VIII), the remarkably high employment growth rate in the summer of 1933 must be interpreted in the context of the behavior of employment over the previous four years. By spring 1933, employment in manufacturing had fallen to 60 percent of its 1929 level. The sharp increase in employment in summer 1933 brought employment up to slightly more than 70 percent of its 1929 level. Employment in manufacturing did not return to its 1929 level until 1937. While this extreme episode can hardly be dismissed, we note that the recession in 1937–38 exhibits the typical post–World War II pattern: a sharp increase in job destruction that coincides with a comparatively mild decline in job creation.

We now use the MTD measures to decompose the time variation in total turnover into a component due to job reallocation and a component due to other factors. Figure 3.4 depicts job reallocation, other turnover (measured as the difference between total turnover and job reallocation), and net employment growth in the manufacturing sector for the 1947–81 period.[23] Table 3.3 reports correlations involving these series over alternative time periods.[24]

Figure 3.4 and table 3.3 suggest the following characterization of the cyclical variation in the components of total turnover. Job reallocation is countercyclical: during recessions the economy intensifies the pace at which it reallocates employment positions among establishments. The number of worker transitions induced by job reallocation activity rises during recessions and declines during expansions. In contrast, the number of worker transitions (between employers and between employment and joblessness) induced by other factors fluctuates procyclically. In short, these two conceptually distinct com-

23. Fig. 3.4 focuses attention on the post–World War II time period because we are less comfortable with our constant quit replacement rate assumption over the earlier period.

24. Close inspection of fig. 3.4 reveals that there is a mild downward trend in both job reallocation and job creation over the post–World War II period. Thus the simple correlations reported in table 3.3 in part reflect this low frequency variation. Davis and Haltiwanger (1996) examine the impact of trends on such simple correlations using similarly constructed job creation and destruction data for the 1947:1–88:4 period. After linear detrending, they find that the correlation between net employment growth and job reallocation is −.52 for the 1947:1–88:4 period and −.65 for the 1972:2–88:4 period. These findings suggest that the countercyclical pattern of job reallocation in U.S. manufacturing is pervasive for the entire post–World War II period.

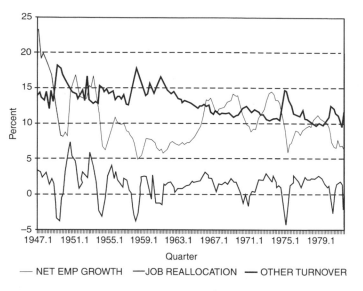

Fig. 3.4   Job reallocations, other worker turnover, and net employment growth in U.S. manufacturing sector, quarterly, 1947:1–81:1
Source: Authors' calculations from the BLS manufacturing turnover data.

ponents of total turnover exhibit sharply different cyclical behavior. Having drawn this conclusion, we wish to remind the reader that job reallocation provides a lower bound on the number of worker transitions that occur because of changes in the location of employment opportunities. (See section 3.3.) Thus our inferences about the cyclical variation in the decomposition of total turnover rest on the assumption that the tightness of the bound does not vary too much over the cycle.

Interestingly, manufacturing job reallocation has become increasingly countercyclical during the post–World War II period. In contrast, manufacturing turnover due to other forces has maintained the same degree of procyclicality over this period. Consequently, total manufacturing turnover has become less procyclical over the post–World War II period and by the 1970s is essentially acyclical (the correlation of total turnover and net employment in the 1970s is .03).

3.5.4   More on the Connection between Job Flows and Worker Flows

The preceding sections develop several facts about the connection between worker flows and job flows, but they also leave many gaps in our statistical portrait. This subsection looks at the connection along several dimensions in order to fill in some of the gaps. We examine the persistence and concentration of job flows and the associated implications for worker flows. We also consider

Table 3.4   **Average Persistence Rates for Job Creation and Destruction in Manufacturing Sector**

	Annual Measures, 1972–88		Quarterly Measures, 1972:2–88:4	
Horizon	Creation	Destruction	Creation	Destruction
One quarter			67.8	72.3
Two quarters			50.4	58.9
One year	70.2	82.3	37.7	59.2
Two years	54.4	73.6	22.6	38.4

Source: Tabulations from the Longitudinal Research Database reported in Davis, Haltiwanger, and Schuh (1996).

the connection between job flows and unemployment flows.[25] Data limitations restrict much of our discussion in this section to the manufacturing sector.

Persistence of Job Flows

How persistent are the plant-level employment changes that underlie the job creation and destruction figures? The persistence of plant-level employment changes bears directly on the nature of the worker reallocation associated with job reallocation. To the extent that job creation and destruction represent short-lived employment changes, the changes can be implemented largely through temporary layoffs and recalls. To the extent that plant-level employment changes are persistent, they must be associated with long-term joblessness or worker reallocation across plants.

In thinking about how to measure persistence, we stress that our focus is on the persistence of the typical newly created or newly destroyed job. This focus is distinct from a focus on the persistence of the typical existing job or the persistence of establishment size. In line with our focus, we measure persistence according to the following definitions:

> *The N-period persistence of job creation is the percentage of newly created jobs at time t that remain filled at each subsequent sampling date through time t + N.*
>
> *The N-period persistence of job destruction is the percentage of newly destroyed jobs at time t that do not reappear at any subsequent sampling date through time t + N.*

Table 3.4 summarizes the persistence properties of job creation and destruction over various horizons based on the LRD. In the annual data, roughly seven in ten newly created jobs survive for at least one year, and roughly eight in ten newly destroyed jobs fail to reappear one year later. After two years, the

25. Davis et al. (1996) provide a more thorough treatment of these topics.

persistence of annual job creation and destruction falls to 54 and 74 percent, respectively. The most important aspect of these results is that the annual job creation and destruction figures largely reflect persistent plant-level employment changes.

The quarterly job flow figures show much smaller persistence rates than the annual figures. There are two reasons for this discrepancy. First, transitory plant-level employment movements, including seasonal movements, are much more likely to enter into the calculation of gross job flows over three-month, as opposed to twelve-month, intervals. Second, over any given horizon, there are fewer sampling dates in the annual data than in the quarterly data. Thus newly destroyed and newly created jobs must meet more stringent criteria in the quarterly data to satisfy the concept of persistence specified in the definitions above.

These remarks also reconcile the high persistence of annual job creation and destruction with some well-known facts about the importance of temporary layoffs in the U.S. manufacturing sector. For example, Lilien (1980, table III) uses the MTD to calculate that 60 to 78 percent of all manufacturing layoffs ended in recall during the years 1965–76. He also reports that 92 percent of manufacturing unemployment spells ending in recall last three months or less. Most of these short-duration temporary layoffs are not captured by annual job creation and destruction measures.

Concentration of Job Flows

What role do plant births and deaths play in the creation and destruction of jobs? More generally, how are job creation and destruction distributed by plant-level employment growth rates? Do job creation and destruction primarily involve mild expansions and contractions spread among a large number of plants, or wrenching and dramatic changes at a few plants? The consequences of job creation and destruction for workers and for the local communities in which they reside depend, in large part, on the answers to these questions.

Based on the LRD, figure 3.5 displays simple pie charts that condense information on the distribution of annual and quarterly job creation and destruction into a small number of growth rate intervals. Figure 3.5 reveals that shutdowns account for 23 percent of annual job destruction, while start-ups account for 16 percent of annual job creation.[26] The message is plain: much job creation and destruction in the manufacturing sector involve dramatic events such as the start-up of a new plant or the death of an old plant.

To elaborate on this point, figure 3.5 also shows that two-thirds of annual job creation and destruction occur at start-ups, shutdowns, and continuing

26. Shutdowns and start-ups account for smaller fractions in the quarterly data for two reasons: (1) these events may require more than a single quarter to complete, and (2) transitory plant-level employment movements account for larger fractions of job creation and destruction in the quarterly data, as shown in the preceding sections. These transitory events are unlikely to involve complete plant shutdowns.

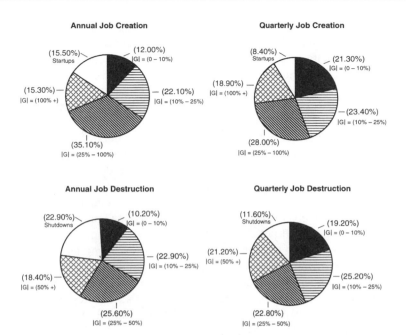

Fig. 3.5   Concentration of job creation and job destruction in U.S. manufacturing sector, 1973–88

Source: Tabulations from the Longitudinal Research Database as reported in Davis, Haltiwanger, and Schuh (1996, fig. 2.3).

Note: The pie charts summarize the distributions of creation and destruction by plant-level growth rates. The numbers in parentheses indicate share of the total. The growth rates in the figure (*G*) are the conventional measure.

plants that expand or contract by at least a quarter of their initial workforce. The dramatic, highly publicized character of much job creation and destruction activity in the manufacturing sector also reflects the concentration of manufacturing employment at large plants. In 1986, the average manufacturing employee worked at a facility that had nearly 1,600 workers (Davis and Haltiwanger 1991, fig. 4.B).[27] Thus manufacturing employment is concentrated at large plants, and manufacturing job creation and destruction are concentrated at plants that experience large percentage changes in employment.

These two facts about concentration explain why job creation and destruction at manufacturing plants often have important effects on nearby communities. A dramatic employment reduction at a single large plant can flood the local labor market, which increases the economic hardship that falls on each

27. Davis (1990) provides summary statistics on the distribution of employees by establishment size for about 20 manufacturing and 60 nonmanufacturing industries that cover the nonfarm private sector of the U.S. economy. These statistics confirm that employment at large establishments is more important in manufacturing industries than in most nonmanufacturing industries.

job loser (see, e.g., Carrington 1993). Conversely, a sharp employment increase at a single plant can induce an in-migration of workers and their families that strains the capacity of the local community to provide certain public and private goods such as schooling, housing, roads, and sewers.

The facts on the concentration and persistence of gross job flows also shed light on the connection between job reallocation and worker reallocation. Since only one-third of job destruction is accounted for by establishments that shrink by less than 25 percent over the span of a year, the bulk of job destruction cannot be accommodated by normal rates of worker attrition resulting from retirements and quits. In other words, most of the job destruction represents job loss from the point of view of workers. Since annual job creation and destruction primarily reflect persistent establishment-level employment changes, the bulk of annual job creation and destruction cannot be implemented by temporary layoff and recall policies. Hence, most of the job destruction reflects permanent job loss that leads to a change in employer, a long-term unemployment spell, exit from the labor force, or some combination of these events. These inferences about the connection between job reallocation and worker reallocation reflect evidence for the manufacturing sector only; the extent to which similar characterizations hold for nonmanufacturing sectors of the U.S. economy is a largely unaddressed question.

Connection to Unemployment

Figure 3.6 provides information about the cyclical variation in unemployment flows and gross job flows. The unemployment flows are based on the CPS unemployment incidence and duration data, and the job flows are based on the LRD.[28] These time-series patterns show that unemployment inflows account for most of the cyclical variation in unemployment. During recessions, unemployment inflows rise dramatically. Unemployment outflows also rise during recessions, but by less than their counterparts and not until later in a recession.

Figure 3.6 shows that the connection between job destruction and worker flows is stronger than that between job creation and worker flows. Job destruction and unemployment inflows rise sharply during recessions, and they exhibit a high contemporaneous correlation (.71). Looking at the other side of the flows, unemployment outflows show only weak positive correlation with job creation (.16).

The figure illustrates the mirror-image quality of unemployment flow dy-

28. This figure combines information on CPS-based unemployment flows for the aggregate economy with the LRD-based job creation and destruction measures for the manufacturing sector. The difference in sectoral coverage naturally raises concerns about comparability. On this matter, the correlation between the aggregate unemployment rate and the manufacturing unemployment rate is .92, where the manufacturing unemployment rate equals the number of unemployed persons who previously worked in the manufacturing sector divided by the sum of that number and manufacturing employment. The close relationship between aggregate unemployment and manufacturing unemployment mitigates concerns that arise from using worker and job flow statistics that differ in scope of sectoral coverage.

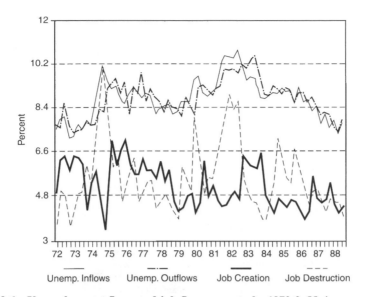

Fig. 3.6   Unemployment flows and job flows, quarterly, 1972:2–88:4

Sources: Authors' calculations of unemployment flows for the entire U.S. economy from the Current Population Survey. Longitudinal Research Database tabulations of job creation and destruction for the U.S. manufacturing sector from Davis, Haltiwanger, and Schuh (1996).

Note: Job creation and destruction are measured as percentages of employment; unemployment flows are measured as percentages of the labor force.

namics and job flow dynamics. We have already seen that job destruction rises sharply in recessions, whereas job creation displays much more modest variation over the business cycle. In a similar manner, the unemployment inflows rise sharply in recessions. But the component most closely related to job creation—unemployment outflows—changes relatively little over the business cycle.

This picture of a tight connection between job flows and unemployment flows is further enhanced by consideration of the evidence on unemployment flows by reason of unemployment (table 3.5) and by demographic characteristics. We do not present a detailed analysis of the evidence here, but findings presented elsewhere suggest the following characterization.[29] During good times, unemployment is dominated by entrants, quitters, and young people. These workers transit across states of the labor market to accommodate life cycle entry and exit and normal search for a suitable job match. During recessions, increases in unemployment are dominated by permanent and temporary layoffs as firms restructure their employment positions. These layoffs are accompanied by an increase in the share of unemployment of prime-aged work-

29. Chap. 6 of Davis, Haltiwanger, and Schuh (1996) presents an in-depth analysis of the connection between job flows and unemployment by reason and by demographic characteristics.

Table 3.5   Cyclical Changes in Unemployment by Reason for All Workers

	Fraction of Change in Unemployment Due to Reason	
Reason	Trough to Peak	Peak to Trough
	Average for 1970:11–92:12	
Temporary layoffs	0.58	0.32
Permanent layoffs	0.33	0.46
Quits	−0.06	0.02
Entrants	0.14	0.21
Change in unemployment	−2.7	2.8
	1970:11–75:3	
	1970:11–73:11	*1973:11–75.3*
Temporary layoffs	0.50	0.44
Permanent layoffs	0.29	0.40
Quits	−0.18	0.00
Entrants	0.38	0.16
Change in unemployment	−1.0	4.6
	1975:3–80:7	
	1975:3–80:1	*1980:1–80:7*
Temporary layoffs	0.44	0.19
Permanent layoffs	0.42	0.26
Quits	0.03	0.05
Entrants	0.11	0.50
Change in unemployment	−2.3	1.0
	1980:7–82:11	
	1980:7–81:7	*1981:7–82:11*
Temporary layoffs	1.11	0.32
Permanent layoffs	0.08	0.65
Quits	−0.05	−0.05
Entrants	0.14	0.09
Change in unemployment	−0.5	3.0
	1982:11–91:3	
	1982:11–90:7	*1990:7–91:3*
Temporary layoffs	0.28	0.46
Permanent layoffs	0.54	0.67
Quits	−0.03	−0.02
Entrants	0.21	−0.11
Change in unemployment	−4.9	1.6

Source: Tabulations from the Current Population Survey reported in Davis, Haltiwanger, and Schuh (1996).

ers (especially men), most of whom have considerable work experience and strong attachment to the labor force.[30]

This interpretation of unemployment rate dynamics offers an interesting parallel to the details of job flow dynamics documented in Davis et al. (1996). Job

30. Young workers also face increased layoffs in recessions. However, unemployment and unemployment inflows of prime-aged workers rise disproportionately.

flows in good times are dominated by the creation and destruction of jobs among relatively young and small plants. These younger and smaller plants are, like young workers, trying to determine whether and where they fit into the marketplace. During recessions, older and larger plants experience sharply higher job destruction rates, so that their contribution to the job and worker reallocation process rises. This time of intense job destruction by older and larger plants coincides with the rise in layoff unemployment, especially among prime-aged workers.[31]

3.6   A Collection of Facts about Worker Flows and Job Flows

This brief section lists several empirical findings related to the behavior of U.S. worker flows and job flows. The list offered below simply collects and restates, sans qualifications and caveats, the main empirical results developed in the preceding section. The symbol "(M)" designates findings drawn from data limited to the manufacturing sector.

- Total worker turnover, the sum of accessions and separations, amounts to about one-third of employment per quarter.
- Roughly one worker in four experiences a change in employer or employment status (employed vs. not employed) each quarter.
- The number of persons who change employer or employment status in a typical year amounts to about 37 percent of employment.
- Average annual job reallocation rates (sum of creation and destruction rates) range from 20 to 30 percent of employment depending on industrial sector, region, and time period.
- Average quarterly job reallocation rates range from 10 to 13 percent of employment.
- Annual job creation and destruction figures largely reflect persistent plant-level employment changes. For example, roughly seven in ten newly created jobs survive for at least one year, and roughly eight in ten newly destroyed jobs fail to reappear one year later. (M)
- Job flows are spatially concentrated: Two-thirds of annual job creation and destruction occur at start-ups, shutdowns, and continuing plants that expand or contract by at least a quarter of their initial workforce. Shutdowns alone account for nearly one-quarter of job destruction. (M)
- Job reallocation accounts for 35 to 46 percent or more of total turnover (number of worker transitions) in quarterly data.
- The rate of job reallocation is moderately smaller but accounts for a much larger fraction of total turnover in the manufacturing sector.
- Job reallocation accounts for between one-third and two-thirds of all persons

---

31. We believe that older plants disproportionately employ older workers, but we know of no direct evidence on this matter.

who change employer or employment status over both three-month and twelve-month intervals.

• The simple correlation between quarterly rates of total turnover and net employment growth equals .31 over the 1930–80 period, but the cyclical behavior of turnover is not stable over this time period. (M)

• Job creation and destruction are negatively correlated, and job destruction varies more over the cycle than job creation. These patterns hold for the entire postwar period but are less pronounced in the 1950s and 1960s. (M)

• The number of worker transitions induced by job reallocation activity rises during recessions and declines during expansions. (M)

• In contrast, the number of worker transitions induced by other factors fluctuates procyclically. (M)

• Job destruction and unemployment inflows rise sharply during recessions, and they exhibit a high contemporaneous correlation (.71). Looking at the other side of the flows, unemployment outflows show only a weak positive correlation (.16) with job creation. (M)

• During expansions, unemployment is dominated by entrants, quitters, and young persons.

• During recessions, increases in unemployment are dominated by permanent and temporary layoffs. These layoffs are accompanied by an increase in the share of unemployment accounted for by prime-aged workers (especially men), most of whom exhibit strong attachment to the labor force.

• During expansions, gross job flows are dominated by the creation and destruction of jobs among relatively young and small plants. (M)

• During recessions, older and larger plants experience sharply higher job destruction rates, so that their contribution to the job and worker reallocation process rises. (M)

3.7   New Sources of Data on Gross Job and Worker Flows

In the preceding sections, we have synthesized and summarized much of what we know about the dynamics of worker flows and job flows, drawing on various data sets and studies. While we have learned a great deal about the dynamics of the labor market from existing data, our understanding is clearly incomplete. U.S. statistical agencies do not currently produce timely, comprehensive worker and job flow statistics for the U.S. economy. The economic and policy importance of the dynamics of the labor market constitute a prima facie argument for developing longitudinal business-level and worker-level databases that permit more timely, comprehensive, and detailed measures of worker and job flows. This section discusses possible paths toward that objective.[32]

In the ensuing discussion, we limit attention to the potential uses of existing administrative record databases, because they offer an inexpensive means of

32. This section draws heavily on chap. 8 of Davis et al. (1996).

constructing statistics on gross job and worker flows. Within that constraint, our discussion ranges from general remarks about methods for measuring gross flows to specific remarks about the advantages and disadvantages of particular data sources. The specific remarks serve to delineate reasonable objectives for data construction and to highlight some of the issues that must be confronted in developing longitudinal business-level databases.

3.7.1 Standard Statistical Establishment List

The Standard Statistical Establishment List (SSEL) merits serious consideration as a comprehensive source of statistics on annual gross job flows. The SSEL is a master establishment list of all businesses with at least one employee in the United States. The Bureau of the Census maintains the SSEL using Internal Revenue Service administrative records and drawing heavily on information contained in the bureau's annual Company Organization Survey (COS). Currently, the Bureau of the Census uses the SSEL to define the statistical sampling frame for its many economic censuses and surveys of individual businesses.[33] Initial efforts to construct gross job flow statistics from the SSEL have been under way at the Bureau of the Census since 1993.

The SSEL offers important advantages as a potential source of job creation and destruction statistics. First, as with the LRD, establishments (i.e., physical locations) constitute the observational units. Second, the SSEL is suitable for tracking individual establishments over time in a way that correctly treats mergers, births and deaths, and transfers of ownership and control. These strengths of the SSEL stem in large part from its reliance on the COS.

The COS provides information about the ownership and operational control of production and nonproduction facilities, information that enables the Census Bureau to distinguish between establishments and enterprises. In the SSEL, as in the LRD, an enterprise is either a single establishment owned and operated by a single-unit firm or the set of establishments under the ownership and operational control of the same firm.[34] Thus the SSEL offers the promise of circumventing the spurious linkage problems that potentially compromise efforts to track individual establishments through time, to distinguish between establishments and enterprises, and to accurately measure gross job flows.[35]

---

33. Bureau of the Census (1979) describes the use of the SSEL as a sampling frame for Census Bureau surveys.

34. During intercensal years the sample frame of the COS is the set of multiunit companies with at least 50 employees in the previous economic census. Consequently, new establishments born in an intercensal year and affiliated with establishments classified as single-unit establishments in the previous census will not be properly linked to their parent firms until the subsequent census. Similarly, new establishments affiliated with companies that had fewer than 50 employees in the previous census will not be properly linked to their parent firms until the subsequent census. This feature of the COS does not affect the quality of the longitudinal establishment linkages in the SSEL, but it does affect the quality of the enterprise identifiers. As such, it affects, e.g., the ability to track employment growth by enterprise size (as opposed to establishment size). See Bureau of the Census (1979) for further discussion of how the COS is used to maintain the SSEL.

35. The SSEL contains a variety of establishment and enterprise identifiers (e.g., the Census Bureau identification number, the federal taxpayer identification number, and the permanent plant

Spurious job flows can arise when longitudinal links are incorrectly broken because of simple processing errors or because of changes in ownership, corporate status, business name or address, or employer taxpayer identification number.

The SSEL contains annual data on employment and payroll plus information on location, industry, and establishment age. The SSEL for any given year becomes available in the subsequent year, so that gross job flow statistics by detailed industry, state, local area, establishment and enterprise size, establishment and enterprise wage level, and establishment age could be made available on a yearly basis with a lag of approximately nine to twelve months. In addition, the SSEL could be linked to the many business censuses and surveys conducted by the Bureau of the Census. In this way, it would be feasible to provide gross job flow statistics broken down by a wealth of other establishment and enterprise characteristics including sales, investment, input usage, inventories, international trade involvement, and technology usage.

3.7.2   Bureau of Labor Statistics ES-202 Data Set

The BLS ES-202 data set also merits serious consideration as a comprehensive source of gross job flow statistics for the U.S. economy. This data set reflects quarterly reports on monthly employment and quarterly payroll for all employers covered by either state UI laws or the unemployment compensation program for civilian federal employees. According to Department of Labor (1995), the ES-202 data cover 98 percent of U.S. civilian employees. The only large sectors excluded from the ES-202 universe are the self-employed and the armed forces.

The ES-202 data set closely parallels the SSEL in scope, content, and use as a sample frame. (The ES-202 data set serves as the statistical sampling frame for most BLS establishment surveys, just as the SSEL serves as the sampling frame for most Census Bureau establishment surveys.) As we discussed in sections 3.4 and 3.5, several researchers have already used the UI component of the ES-202 data set to create longitudinal files and analyze job flow behavior in selected states. We also discussed several important features of UI data in section 3.4.2 that are pertinent to the discussion here, but which we do not repeat.

Two important advantages of the BLS ES-202 data set, relative to the SSEL, are its greater timeliness and frequency. Employment and payroll information become available approximately five months after the end of each calendar quarter (Manser, chap. 1 in this volume). Thus gross job flow statistics computed from ES-202 data could be released on a quarterly rather than yearly basis and with a shorter time lag than statistics calculated from the SSEL. Unlike the SSEL, the ES-202 data provide the grist for monthly statistics on

number) that facilitate longitudinal and cross-sectional linkages. Other information in the SSEL such as company and establishment names, street address, and detailed industry and location codes can be used to verify the linkages and enhance their quality. See Bureau of the Census (1979) for a discussion of how the various identifiers in the SSEL are created.

gross job flows. In sum, the ES-202 data could be used to generate monthly gross flows on a comprehensive, nearly real-time basis broken down by industry, geographic area, and employer size. For policymakers (e.g., the monetary authorities) and business forecasters who rely heavily on high-frequency, real-time economic indicators, monthly gross job flow statistics with a short reporting lag would be of great interest. Monthly job flow data would also be useful in research on business cycles and other topics. Finally, job flow data generated from the ES-202 data could be linked to BLS surveys that provide employer-level information on occupational structure, wages, and employee benefits.

3.7.3   A National Wage Records Database

A key advantage of UI-based data involves prospects for simultaneously measuring worker and job flows from a longitudinal employer-worker database that links workers to employers. In addition to the employer records that enter into the BLS ES-202 data set, the individual states maintain quarterly earnings records for individuals at UI-covered firms to assess eligibility and compute benefit amounts for UI claimants.[36] These records contain information suitable for following individuals over time and for identifying their employers. A current BLS initiative is considering how these records might be combined into a national wage records database (NWRD) that would be useful for measuring job flows, worker flows, and related concepts.[37]

Unlike the SSEL and the BLS ES-202 data, the NWRD offers the prospect of comprehensive statistics on job flows *and* worker flows. Because individual workers could be linked to individual employers, this database also offers much greater scope for describing and analyzing the connection between worker and job flows.[38] In addition, a wealth of information in the many BLS employer surveys could be linked to the NWRD and used to gain additional insight into the behavior of worker flows and job flows.[39]

The NWRD would be constructed from the same data collection system as the UI component of the BLS ES-202 data. Consequently, it would be subject to the same cross-sectional and longitudinal linkage problems as the ES-202 data. Relative to its enormous value as a tool for research and policy analysis, however, these shortcomings of a UI-based longitudinal employer-worker data set are minor.

---

36. The states also maintain individual-level files that track UI claims and benefit payments.

37. This initiative was the focus of an April 1994 BLS conference held in Washington, D.C.

38. As discussed in section 3.4, two research teams have already used the type of data envisaged for the NWRD to simultaneously measure worker and job flows. See Lane et al. (1993) and Anderson and Meyer (1994). Both studies expand our knowledge of labor market dynamics, and they demonstrate the feasibility and value of using a UI-based linked employer-worker database as a research tool. Jacobson, LaLonde, and Sullivan (1993) use NWRD-type data to examine the costs of job loss.

39. Manser (chap. 1 in this volume) summarizes the many surveys of labor market behavior carried out by the BLS.

3.7.4 Possibilities and Practicalities

The preceding discussion makes clear that administrative data already exist at both the Bureau of the Census and the BLS that could be used to measure gross job flows in a timely, comprehensive, and detailed manner. Converting these administrative records into operational longitudinal data files would require considerable effort and resources, but the costs would be small relative to alternative approaches that require major new surveys or other data sources.

The administrative records data at the BLS and Census Bureau offer distinct advantages and disadvantages that reflect differences in the history and mission of the two bureaus. Data at the Bureau of the Census offer greater scope for spelling out the connection between job flows and employer characteristics. Data at the BLS offer the prospect of directly linking job flows to worker flows and worker characteristics.

Ideally, data from both bureaus would be combined so as to simultaneously link job flows to employer characteristics, worker flows, and worker characteristics. Although the current institutional structure of the statistical bureaus stands in the way of efforts to pool data resources, we strongly advocate cooperative agreements and mechanisms that facilitate the sharing of survey and administrative record data on individual businesses. Such data-sharing arrangements would greatly enhance the value of both Census Bureau and BLS data as tools for economic research and policy evaluation. By providing each bureau with an alternative business universe, data-sharing arrangements would also facilitate the identification of problems with existing statistical sampling frames and, over time, lead to improvements in the accuracy of published statistics.[40]

References

Abowd, John, and Arnold Zellner. 1985. Estimating gross labor force flows. *Journal of Economic and Business Statistics* 3 (3): 254–83.
Akerlof, George, Andrew Rose, and Janet Yellen. 1988. Job switching and job satisfaction in the U.S. labor market. *Brookings Papers on Economic Activity,* no. 2: 495–582.
Albaek, Karsten, and Bent E. Sorensen. 1995. Worker flows and job flows in Danish manufacturing, 1980–91. Providence, R.I.: Brown University. Mimeograph.
Aldrich, Howard, Arne Kallenberg, Peter Marsden, and James Cassell. 1988. In pursuit of evidence: Five sampling procedures for locating new businesses. Paper prepared for Babson College entrepreneurship conference, Babson Park, Mass.
Anderson, Patricia M., and Bruce D. Meyer. 1994. The nature and extent of turnover. *Brookings Papers on Economic Activity: Microeconomics,* 177–237.
Andolfatto, David. 1996. Business cycles and labor market search. *American Economic Review* 86 (1): 112–32.
Annales d'Economie et de Statistique. 1996. 41/42 (January/June).

---

40. Manser (chap. 1 in this volume) also remarks on the potential benefits of data-sharing arrangements between the Census Bureau and BLS.

Armington, Catherine. 1991. Firm linkage of the 1989 universe data base. Final report on Department of Labor Contract no. J-9-J-9-0091. Washington, D.C.: U.S. Department of Labor.

—. 1994. Proposed structure and content for BLS' longitudinal establishment and firm database. Washington, D.C.: U.S. Department of Labor, Bureau of Labor Statistics. Mimeograph.

Armington, Catherine, and Marjorie Odle. 1982. Sources of employment growth, 1978–80. Washington, D.C.: Brookings Institution. Unpublished report.

Baily, Martin Neil, Eric J. Bartelsman, and John Haltiwanger. 1996. Downsizing and productivity growth: Myth or reality? *Small Business Economics* 8 (4): 259–78.

Baily, Martin Neil, Charles Hulten, and David Campbell. 1992. Productivity dynamics in manufacturing plants. *Brookings Papers on Economic Activity: Microeconomics,* 187–249.

Birch, David L. 1979. *The job generation process.* Cambridge, Mass.: MIT Program on Neighborhood and Regional Change.

—. 1987. *Job creation in America: How our smallest companies put the most people to work.* New York: Free Press.

Birch, David L., and Susan McCracken. 1983. The small business share of job creation: Lessons learned from the use of a longitudinal file. Cambridge, Mass.: MIT Program on Neighborhood and Regional Change. Unpublished report.

Birley, Susan. 1984. Finding the new firm. *Proceedings of the Academy of Management Meetings* 47:64–68.

Blanchard, Olivier, and Peter Diamond. 1989. The Beveridge curve. *Brookings Papers on Economic Activity,* no. 1: 1–60.

—. 1990. The cyclical behavior of gross flows of workers in the U.S. *Brookings Papers on Economic Activity,* no. 2: 85–155.

Brown, Charles, Judith Connor, Steven Heeringa, and John Jackson. 1990. Studying (small) businesses with the Michigan Employment Security Commission longitudinal database. *Small Business Economics* 2 (4): 261–77.

Caballero, Ricardo. 1992. A fallacy of composition. *American Economic Review* 82 (5): 1279–92.

Caballero, Ricardo, and Eduardo Engel. 1993. Microeconomic adjustment hazards and aggregate dynamics. *Quarterly Journal of Economics* 108 (2): 313–58.

Caballero, Ricardo, Eduardo Engel, and John Haltiwanger. 1997. Aggregate employment dynamics: Building from microeconomic evidence. *American Economic Review* 87 (1): 115–37.

Caballero, Ricardo, and Mohamad Hammour. 1994. The cleansing effect of recessions. *American Economic Review* 84:1350–68.

—. 1996. On the timing and efficiency of creative destruction. *Quarterly Journal of Economics* 111 (3): 805–52.

Carrington, William J. 1993. Wage losses for displaced workers. *Journal of Human Resources* 28 (3): 435–62.

Clark, Kim, and Lawrence Summers. 1979. Labor market dynamics and unemployment: A reconsideration. *Brookings Papers on Economic Activity,* no. 2: 13–60.

Darby, Michael, John Haltiwanger, and Mark Plant. 1985. Unemployment rate dynamics and persistent unemployment under rational expectations. *American Economic Review* 75 (4): 614–37.

—. 1986. The ins and outs of unemployment: The ins win. NBER Working Paper no. 1997. Cambridge, Mass.: National Bureau of Economic Research.

Davis, Steven J. 1987. Fluctuations in the pace of labor reallocation. *Carnegie-Rochester Conference Series on Public Policy* 27:335–402.

—. 1990. Size distribution statistics from county business patterns data. Chicago: University of Chicago. Mimeograph.

Davis, Steven J., and John Haltiwanger. 1990. Gross job creation and destruction: Microeconomic evidence and macroeconomic implications. *NBER Macroeconomics Annual* 5:123–68.

———. 1991. Wage dispersion between and within U.S. manufacturing plants, 1963–86. *Brookings Papers on Economic Activity: Microeconomics,* 115–200.

———. 1992. Gross job creation, gross job destruction, and employment reallocation. *Quarterly Journal of Economics* 107 (3): 819–63.

———. 1996. Driving forces and employment fluctuations. NBER Working Paper no. 5775. Cambridge, Mass.: National Bureau of Economic Research, September.

Davis, Stephen J., John Haltiwanger, and Scott Schuh. 1994. Small business and job creation: Dissecting the myth and reassessing the facts. In *Labor markets, employment policy, and job creation,* ed. Lewis C. Solmon and Alec R. Levenson. Boulder, Colo.: Westview.

———. 1996. *Job creation and destruction.* Cambridge, Mass.: MIT Press.

Dunne, Timothy, John Haltiwanger, and Ken Troske. 1997. Technology and jobs: Secular changes and cyclical dynamics. *Carnegie-Rochester Conference Series on Public Policy* 46 (June): 107–78.

Dunne, Timothy, Mark Roberts, and Larry Samuelson. 1989. Plant turnover and gross employment flows in the U.S. manufacturing sector. *Journal of Labor Economics* 7 (1): 48–71.

Evans, David. 1987. The relationship between firm growth, size and age: Estimates for 100 manufacturing industries. *Journal of Industrial Economics* 35 (4): 567–81.

Hall, Robert E. 1982. The importance of lifetime jobs in the U.S. economy. *American Economic Review* 72 (4): 716–24.

———. 1995. Lost jobs. *Brookings Papers on Economic Activity,* no. 1: 221–73.

Hall, Robert E., and David Lilien. 1979. The measurement and significance of labor turnover. Background Paper no. 27. Washington, D.C.: National Commission on Employment and Unemployment, April.

Hamermesh, Daniel S. 1993. *Labor demand.* Princeton, N.J.: Princeton University Press.

Hamermesh, Daniel S., Wolter H. J. Hassink, and Jan C. Van Ours. 1996. Job turnover and labor turnover: A taxonomy of employment dynamics. *Annales d'Economie et de Statistique* 41/42 (January/June): 21–40.

Hopenhayn, Hugo, and Richard Rogerson. 1993. Job turnover and policy evaluation: A general equilibrium analysis. *Journal of Political Economy* 101 (5): 915–38.

Howland, Marie. 1988. *Plant closings and worker displacements: The regional issues.* Kalamazoo, Mich.: W. E. Upjohn Institute for Employment Research.

Jacobson, Louis, Robert LaLonde, and Daniel Sullivan. 1993. *The costs of worker dislocation.* Kalamazoo, Mich.: W. E. Upjohn Institute for Employment Research.

Jovanovic, Boyan. 1982. Selection and the evolution of industry. *Econometrica* 50 (3): 649–70.

Juhn, Chinhui, Kevin M. Murphy, and Robert H. Topel. 1991. Why has the natural rate of unemployment increased over time? *Brookings Papers on Economic Activity,* no. 2: 75–142.

Katz, Lawrence F., and Bruce D. Meyer. 1990. Unemployment insurance, recall expectations, and unemployment outcomes. *Quarterly Journal of Economics* 105 (4): 973–1002.

Lane, Julia, Alan Isaac, and David Stevens. 1993. How do firms treat workers? Worker turnover at the firm level. Washington, D.C.: American University. Mimeograph.

Leonard, Jonathan S. 1987. In the wrong place at the wrong time: The extent of frictional and structural unemployment. In *Unemployment and the structure of labor markets,* ed. Kevin Lang and J. Leonard. New York: Blackwell.

Lilien, David. 1980. The cyclical pattern of temporary layoffs in United States manufacturing. *Review of Economics and Statistics* 62 (1): 24–31.

Loungani, Prakash, and Richard Rogerson. 1989. Cyclical fluctuations and the sectoral reallocation of labor: Evidence from the PSID. *Journal of Monetary Economics* 23: 259–73.

Mortensen, Dale T. 1994a. The cyclical behavior of job and worker flows. *Journal of Economic Dynamics and Control* 18 (November): 1121–42.

———. 1994b. Reducing supply-side disincentives to job creation. Evanston, Ill.: Northwestern University. Mimeograph.

Mortensen, Dale T., and Christopher A. Pissarides. 1993. The cyclical behavior of job creation and job destruction. In *Labor demand and equilibrium wage formation,* ed. Jan C. Van Ours, Gerard A. Pfann, and Geert Ridder. Amsterdam: North-Holland.

Murphy, Kevin, and Robert Topel. 1987. The evolution of unemployment in the United States: 1968–1985. *NBER Macroeconomics Annual* 3:11–58.

Olley, G. Steven, and Ariel Pakes. 1996. The dynamics of productivity in the telecommunications equipment industry. *Econometrica* 64 (6): 1263–97.

Organization for Economic Cooperation and Development. 1994. *Employment outlook.* Paris: Organization for Economic Cooperation and Development.

———. 1996. *Job creation and loss: Analysis, policy, and data development.* Paris: Organization for Economic Cooperation and Development.

Poterba, James, and Lawrence Summers. 1986. Reporting errors and labor market dynamics. *Econometrica* 54 (6): 1319–38.

Sattinger, Michael. 1993. Assignment models of the distribution of earnings. *Journal of Economic Literature* 31 (2): 831–80.

Small Business Administration. 1983, 1987, 1988, 1991. *The state of small business: A report of the president.* Washington, D.C.: Government Printing Office.

Spletzer, James R. 1995. The contribution of establishment births and deaths to Employment growth. Paper presented at the January 1996 meetings of the Econometric Society, San Francisco.

Troske, Kenneth. 1993. The dynamic adjustment process of firm entry and exit in manufacturing and finance, insurance, and real estate. Washington, D.C.: U.S. Bureau of the Census, Center for Economic Studies. Mimeograph.

U.S. Bureau of the Census. 1979. The Standard Statistical Establishment List program. Bureau of the Census Technical Paper no. 44. Report prepared by the Economic Surveys Division. Washington, D.C.: U.S. Bureau of the Census, January.

———. 1986. *Statistical abstract of the United States.* Washington, D.C.: U.S. Department of Commerce.

U.S. Department of Labor. Bureau of Labor Statistics. 1995. *Employment and wages, annual averages, 1994.* Washington, D.C.: Government Printing Office.

Woytinsky, Wladimir S. 1942. *Three aspects of labor dynamics.* Washington, D.C.: Committee on Social Security, Social Science Council.

Yashiv, Eran. 1996. Explaining the flow of hiring: An asset pricing approach. Tel Aviv: Tel Aviv University, August.

Comment   Bruce D. Meyer

This chapter provides a nice summary of many dimensions of the recent research on worker and job flows. The authors are the central pioneers and popularizers of this area of research. The chapter will be a classic reference, particu-

Bruce D. Meyer is professor of economics and research fellow of the Institute for Policy Research, Northwestern University, and a research associate of the National Bureau of Economic Research.

larly for the five topics that the authors summarize: (1) reasons for studying worker and job flows, (2) concepts and definitions, (3) current data sources, (4) current knowledge, and (5) new data sources. The chapter clarifies many concepts and provides a wealth of facts. It also provides many insights about what future research could examine.

While I will comment on each of the five topics in order, my principal concern is that the concepts and definitions used throughout the chapter are partly driven by the characteristics of the data source with which the authors are most familiar, the Longitudinal Research Datafile (LRD). Their choices are quite natural in their context but may differ from ideal ones, and in other data sets different definitions will be more appropriate. This distinction should be kept in mind when reading the chapter.

In the first section of the chapter the list of reasons provided for why we should study worker and job flows will undoubtedly lengthen as research progresses. For example, several new areas of study would be possible with individual wage records that would be part of a proposed national wage records database. We have begun to see some of these types of analyses done for single states or groups of states. Such data would allow the examination of the costs of job displacement as has been done for Pennsylvania by Jacobson, LaLonde, and Sullivan (1993). They would also allow an examination of the returns to tenure and mobility (Topel and Ward 1992; Altonji and Shakotko 1987), the effects of job destruction on geographic and industry mobility of workers, and other issues.

The section on concepts and definitions is very useful because it defines and discusses various turnover and worker reallocation concepts. One of the main motivations for these concepts seems to be that decreases in employment at the establishment level are a good measure of jobs destroyed as a result of demand changes, while increases in employment at the establishment level are a good measure of jobs created as a result of demand changes. It should be clear that this relationship is only an approximation. Jobs can be created and destroyed within an establishment with constant employment. Technological change may involve a change in the composition of the workforce but not its size. In addition, declines in employment are due to factors besides demand changes, such as quits from small establishments or exits by groups of people from professional practices to establish their own practices. Last, some movements of workers between nearby establishments within a firm may have little to do with total employment or unemployment and should not be called job creation or destruction.

Many of the necessary complications in the concepts and definitions emphasized in the chapter come from the distinction between counting workers and counting jobs. This distinction leads to great effort by the authors to calculate the fraction of workers changing jobs who change jobs as a result of job creation or destruction. Emphasizing this number raises several concerns. First, this number is not nearly as interesting as its components, that is, what fraction of people who leave or lose their jobs do so because of job destruction and what fraction of those who find new jobs get newly created jobs. When one combines jobs lost and jobs gained, one is, in many situations, combining very different things. Since jobs are often lost for different reasons than they are gained, it is often better to analyze the two separately. Second, suppose 100 people separate from jobs: 50 lose jobs when plants shut down, while the other 50 quit. Also suppose that all workers find new jobs, one-half in new plants and one-half in the jobs vacated by those that quit. *The fraction of people who change jobs as a result of job creation or destruction depends on which workers take the jobs in the new plants.* The fraction could be anywhere between .5 and 1.0 in this example. It is not intuitive that we should care about which workers find jobs in which plants. We are better off knowing that one-half of separations are due to job destruction and one-half of new hires are due to job creation. This anomaly adds to my suspicion that the combined number is not that important. Finally, we cannot measure the concept very well, as I discuss below.

In the discussion of temporary separations, it is not clear to me that temporary layoffs between time $t - 1$ and t should be ignored. Most data examined by the authors do not measure temporary layoffs. The authors deal with temporary changes by looking at the persistence of job creation and destruction, that is, the extent to which employment does not return to its old level. This approach is only indirect, because in large part we care about flows of workers. The time periods for persistence examined by the authors, one to three years, may be short from the perspective of a firm, but if a decline in employment lasts six months it may mean that workers must move on to new permanent jobs at a different firms if they cannot be without jobs for six months. We care about whether the same workers are able to return to their old jobs; this is a more natural measure of permanence. Using matched data on firms and workers, such as unemployment insurance data, one can directly examine if changes in employment lead to permanent job loss for workers.

The authors emphasize changes between discrete times rather than flows over an interval in their concepts and definitions. This choice misses many separations, though it may focus attention on events (separations, employment declines) that are more important, that is, those that are permanent and involve greater losses in investment. However, if one is studying the costs of separations, such as hiring and training costs, one may prefer flow measures that include all job separations rather than changes between discrete times.

The section on current sources of data is extremely useful, and I only have a few comments. The authors are too kind when discussing the accuracy of the CPS gross flow and length of employment and unemployment data. The authors acknowledge large problems with measurement error and missing observations in the gross flow data and note that adjustment methods have been proposed to correct these problems. While the methods that have been proposed are clear improvements (Abowd and Zellner 1985; Poterba and Summers 1986; Fuller and Chua 1985), they are approximations, and the different methods yield very different numbers. As for CPS spell measures, Poterba and

Summers (1984) find an enormous amount of measurement error in CPS unemployment spell lengths. On the other hand, concerning the discussion of unemployment insurance records, the evidence that we have on spurious federal employer identification number changes indicates that they are not a major problem. An upper bound on the extent of spurious changes is obtained in Anderson and Meyer (1994) by looking at the fraction of people who separate but do not have an SIC change or big employment change. This fraction is small.

The next section examines what we know about worker and job flows. This section is a wonderful summary and synthesis of the literature. My only comment is related to my qualms mentioned above about the emphasis given to measuring the fraction of worker reallocation due to job reallocation. We cannot measure this number with much precision, as the estimates provided here indicate that the fraction is between 35 and 56 percent. Even this calculation requires merging data with different industry coverage, timing, and definitions. The imprecision in measuring this concept makes me further doubt its utility. On the other hand, we can precisely measure the fraction of separations due to job destruction and the fraction of new hires due to job creation in matched firm and worker data such as unemployment insurance records.

The final section on new data sources is very instructive on the new research that could be done with existing administrative databases. This section is an exciting list of research areas that may expand in the future. I might also add that some questions might be answered by good personnel records and organization charts for a few firms. I would put in this category information on the importance of changes in the mix of jobs within establishments, the implications of temporary changes in employment of different durations for permanent worker separation from a firm, and the importance of movements of personnel between establishments within a given firm.

References

Abowd, John, and Arnold Zellner. 1985. Estimating gross labor-force flows. *Journal of Business and Economic Statistics* 3:254–83.
Altonji, J. G., and R. A. Shakotko. 1987. Do wages rise with job seniority? *Review of Economic Studies* 54:437–59.
Anderson, Patricia M., and Bruce D. Meyer. 1994. The extent and consequences of job turnover. *Brookings Papers on Economic Activity: Microeconomics,* 177–248.
Fuller, Wayne A., and Tin Chiu Chua. 1985. Gross change estimation in the presence of response error. In *Proceedings of the Conference on Gross Flows in Labor Force Statistics.* Washington, D.C.: U.S. Department of Commerce.
Jacobson, Louis, Robert LaLonde, and Daniel Sullivan. 1993. Earnings losses of displaced workers. *American Economic Review* 83:685–709.
Poterba, James, and Lawrence Summers. 1984. Survey response variation in the Current Population Survey. *Monthly Labor Review* 107:31–37.
———. 1986. Reporting errors and labor market dynamics. *Econometrica* 54:1319–88.
Topel, Robert H., and Michael P. Ward. 1992. Job mobility and the careers of young men. *Quarterly Journal of Economics* 107:439–80.

4   Unemployment and Labor Force Attachment: A Multistate Analysis of Nonemployment

Stephen R. G. Jones and W. Craig Riddell

Few official statistics are more closely monitored than the rate of unemployment, yet its definition and measurement remain controversial. In most countries, the population is divided into three labor force categories—employment (E), unemployment (U), and out of the labor force (O)—based on the results of household surveys. While employment versus nonemployment is relatively clear-cut, drawing the line between state U and state O is often difficult in practice. Although this latter distinction is usually based on some definition of job search,[1] such a separation does not necessarily correspond well to an economic frame of analysis. The search requirement is typically not defined in terms of either time or monetary inputs and also makes little or no reference to the set of job characteristics, especially the wage, that would make the job acceptable. Missing is some concept of whether a particular type of job search is appropriate for the person concerned; without something of this sort, the distinction between state U and state O might be based on survey responses that contain little or no behavioral content.[2]

Relatedly, there is undoubtedly considerable heterogeneity in the group of people currently classified in state O. Some might be thought close to the unemployed category because of a fairly recent job search or because of an ex-

Stephen R. G. Jones is professor of economics at McMaster University. W. Craig Riddell is professor of economics at the University of British Columbia and an associate of the Canadian Institute of Advanced Research.

The authors are grateful to Arthur Sweetman for excellent research assistance, to the SSHRC for research support, and to Ian Macredie, Scott Murray, and Ray Ryan of Statistics Canada for their assistance in providing access to the data used in this study. They also thank Tom Lemieux, John Beggar, and conference participants for useful comments.

1. The principal exceptions to this rule are for persons awaiting recall to a former job and persons with a future job start at a definite date in the (near) future.

2. See Lucas and Rapping (1969) for a statement of this type.

pressed desire for employment.[3] Others have been detached from the labor force for long periods and have few marketable skills or little desire to participate. One group classified as state O for whom there is some detailed information consists of "discouraged workers," persons who state that they desire work but who did not search because they believed no work to be available. More generally, the O category includes "persons on the margin of the labor force," defined as individuals who indicate that they want work but are not engaging in job search for "personal" or "economic" reasons.[4] There is considerable debate over whether this marginal attachment group should be included among the unemployed[5] or, as is current procedure, treated as out of the labor force.[6]

There are a number of reasons why these definitional questions are important. First, Canadian evidence suggests that the group of persons on the margin of the labor force may number up to one-third the total currently counted as unemployed (Akyeampong 1987).[7] Second, the size of this potentially substantial marginal attachment group may vary cyclically or secularly, which could affect conclusions about the time-series behavior of unemployment.[8] Third, the relative importance of the marginal attachment category will likely vary regionally or by demographic group; this variation could be important for assessment of relative unemployment experiences across regions or demographic groups. Fourth, consideration of unemployment and marginal attachment may be important for the analysis of jobless durations and for an understanding of duration dependence. If these two states are behaviorally equivalent, a period in which there is a spell of marginal attachment in the middle of two spells of unemployment might well be counted as one long spell of unemployment, broadly defined, rather than as three comparatively short spells (U, O, and U,

3. Note, though, that this desire for work is subject to the same qualifications as the job search requirement, in that job characteristics such as the wage are not considered in the survey response.

4. One interpretation of this description is that such marginally attached persons would work at the "going wage" if a job presented itself but their benefit from so doing is not great enough to warrant the time and monetary costs of job search. Strictly speaking, though, the questionnaire definition—like that of job search itself—makes no reference to a "going wage" or other job characteristics.

5. An illustration of this debate is the fact that discouraged workers were in principle included among the unemployed in the United States and Canada in previous versions of the Current Population Survey and Labour Force Survey. E.g., prior to 1967 the Current Population Survey included among the unemployed those who would have been looking for work except that they believed no jobs were available in their line of work or in their community. However, this information was recorded only if it was volunteered by the respondent. Thus the number of discouraged workers actually included among the unemployed was probably undercounted relative to more recent counts based on an explicit question about desire for work and reasons for not searching.

6. Examples of this literature are Akyeampong (1987), Cain (1980), Cohen (1991), Devereaux (1992), Gower (1990), Jackson (1987), Norwood (1988), Organization for Economic Cooperation and Development (OECD 1987), and Stratton (n.d.).

7. As U.S. evidence on the number of discouraged workers, the number of "persons who desire work but think they cannot get jobs" was 12 percent of the total unemployed in 1992 (Department of Labor 1993).

8. Some evidence of a secular decline in the proportion of "discouraged workers" in Canada in the early 1990s is provided in Akyeampong (1992).

respectively). More generally, a period of "waiting" in the marginal attachment state may be as productive (in terms of future employment) as a period of actual job search (cf. Hall 1983). Furthermore, it is likely that this issue of behavioral equivalence may vary by age, sex, and region. Finally, and more generally, Card and Riddell (1993) found that most of the divergence in Canadian-U.S. unemployment rates in the 1980s could be attributed to differences in the probability that a nonemployed person was counted as unemployed, although the reasons for this difference were not identified. Further work on the nature of nonemployment and specifically on the mechanics of its division into unemployment and nonparticipation is clearly warranted.

To date, most discussion of these labor market categorization issues has been a priori in nature (e.g., OECD 1987), although Stratton (n.d.) examined the past labor market behavior and current demographic characteristics of U.S. discouraged workers, relative to those of the unemployed, and concluded that these two groups appear different in this retrospective sense. Our goal in this paper is to extend this debate by using a framework that enables the appropriate survey criteria to be determined on empirical grounds rather than a priori. This framework involves examining whether different labor force groups differ in terms of their transition probabilities among labor force states. In particular, we assess whether the marginally attached are behaviorally distinct from those counted as unemployed. We also evaluate whether members of the marginal attachment group differ behaviorally from the balance of those classified as out of the labor force.

Our approach for this evaluation of behavioral equivalence extends the procedure proposed by Flinn and Heckman (1982, 1983), who tested (and rejected) Clark and Summers's (1979) idea that unemployment and out of the labor force are not distinct states for white male high school graduates.[9] In turn, this issue was further analysed by Gönül (1992), who employed a broader sample of male and female youth. It should be noted that these authors used the National Longitudinal Survey youth data, in which only the states E, U, and O are observed.[10] In the population as a whole, however, the O category must include many persons with very little genuine labor force attachment (e.g., full-time students and the retired). The behavior of many such unattached persons is surely distinct from that of the unemployed. For both measurement and policy purposes, a more important question is whether the marginal attachment subset of O is distinct from U or the rest of those in O. Equivalently, this issue amounts to whether unemployment should be defined by some sort of

9. Three-state models (i.e., with states E, U, and O) are employed by Blau and Robins (1986), Burdett et al. (1984), Tano (1991), and Van den Berg (1990).

10. Note also that the existing work must grapple with the serious problem that in the National Longitudinal Survey youth data, individual nonemployment spells (rather than proportions of time) are not identified. Flinn and Heckman exclude from their sample all nonemployment spells that are partially spent in unemployment, while Gönül allows for all possible cases in a combinatorial fashion, given some maintained assumptions.

job search requirement or perhaps by a weaker requirement such as an expressed desire for work. Clearly, to address this question empirically requires data that identify marginal attachment to the labor force.

This paper builds on the testing framework established in Jones and Riddell (in press), which examined only aggregate data. The present focus is rather on the demographic and regional components of these labor market categorization issues and on how these components vary through time.

4.1   Statistical Framework

The framework for analysis is a Markov model of transitions among various labor force states. We consider four states: employment (E), unemployment (U), marginal attachment (M), and not in (and not marginally attached to) the labor force (N). Both employment and unemployment correspond to those conventionally measured in the Labour Force Survey but the latter two states, M and N, arise from separating the usual "out of the labor force" category O into two components, according to marginal attachment status. In this paper, such marginal attachment status represents individuals who did not engage in job search in the reference period but who nonetheless report that they desired work. The balance of the population then falls in the "not attached" state (N) that consists of nonemployed individuals who *neither* searched for *nor* desired work.

The dynamic structure is summarized by a four-by-four transition matrix P, where the ij element p_{ij} gives the probability of an individual's being in state j in the next period given that the individual is in state i in the current period:

$$(1) \qquad P = \begin{pmatrix} pEE & pEU & pEM & pEN \\ pUE & pUU & pUM & pUN \\ pME & pMU & pMM & pMN \\ pNE & pNU & pNM & pNN \end{pmatrix}.$$

Given this Markovian structure, a necessary and sufficient condition for the states of marginal attachment (M) and not attached (N) to be behaviorally identical is that the probability of a transition from M to E equals that of a transition from N to E *and* the probability of a transition from M to U equals that of a transition from N to U:

$$(2) \qquad \begin{aligned} pME &= pNE, \\ pMU &= pNU. \end{aligned}$$

If this condition holds, the four-state model is equivalent to a three-state model where the conventional categorization (E, U, and O) is appropriate. Given equation (2), the desire-for-work question would convey no information regarding labor force status.

Another polar case would obtain if, given the desire-for-work question, information on job search itself conveyed no further information about labor force status. This would correspond to the idea that those in the marginal attachment group are not behaviorally distinct from the unemployed, a view that would suggest that the conventional job search requirement for unemployment is too narrow, and would hold if

(3)
$$pUE = pME,$$
$$pUN = pMN.$$

If conditions (2) and (3) were to both fail, one might well expect some ordering of attachment such as

(4)
$$pUE > pME > pNE,$$

which would suggest use of a four-state model and would provide a reason for the reporting of unemployment, marginal attachment, and nonattachment to the labor force as distinct labor force states. From the perspective of data collection, a finding that pME substantially exceeds pNE would suggest considerable value in the inclusion of a desire-for-work question.

4.2   Data Collection and Construction

The data we employ are drawn from the Survey of Job Opportunities (SJO), an annual supplement to the monthly Canadian Labour Force Survey (LFS). The SJO provides information on the desire for work among those who did not engage in job search during the reference period; it also collects self-reported reasons for not searching. We use the 13 SJO files that cover March for the years 1979–92 (in March 1990, the survey was not administered).[11]

For the present longitudinal analysis, we then *match* these SJO files on an individual basis with the subsequent month of the LFS itself. Since the LFS rotation group structure has a respondent being surveyed for six consecutive months and then dropped, it follows that (approximately) five-sixths of the respondents to the SJO will also be present in the LFS in the subsequent month.[12] Our data file contains the complete SJO information for each March together with the LFS labor force status (E, U, or O) for the following April. Accordingly, the *empirical* transition matrix from the three SJO nonemployment states to the three LFS states is given by

---

11. The SJO was also administered in September of 1981 and 1984, which gives some slight insight into the seasonal patterns of marginal attachment, but we do not use those two files in the current analysis. However, it is worth noting that the broad pattern of our results below also holds for those two data sets.

12. In the old U.S. Current Population Survey, discouraged worker questions were asked only of members of the two outgoing rotation groups, which would preclude the longitudinal matching we shall undertake. In future work, however, we plan to exploit the monthly discouraged worker questions in the new Current Population Survey (beginning January 1994) to study the dynamics of this marginal attachment.

$$(5) \qquad P_{SJO \to LFS} = \begin{pmatrix} pUE & pUU & pUO \\ pME & pMU & pMO \\ pNE & pNU & pNO \end{pmatrix}.$$

Since we do not observe the full transition matrix corresponding to matrix (1), the data evidently set some limits on the tests we can perform. In particular, while condition (2) can be tested with these data (essentially since both destination states E and U are observed unambiguously in the LFS), we are unable to test the latter part of condition (3), that $pUN = pMN$, because O (which is just M + N) and not N is observed in the destination month. Testing of condition (3) must then be partial, assessing only the first equation that governs transitions into employment.

We should also comment briefly on the fact that our work is based on linked record data and is accordingly subject to the problems of missing data and classification error (see, e.g., Abowd and Zellner 1985; Meyer 1988; Poterba and Summers 1986; Romeo 1992a, 1992b; Stasny 1988).[13] Missing data can arise, for example, when persons in the March sample move before the April survey, and a major concern is that such moves may be correlated with labor force status (such as when an individual moves to take a job), so that data are missing on a nonrandom basis. Classification errors occur when an individual's labor force status is incorrectly classified, such as when someone who is in fact employed is counted as unemployed. These errors can occur because of incorrect responses to questions (perhaps associated with proxy responses), misunderstandings by the interviewer, or errors that occur in the data capture process. If random, these errors tend to be offsetting in cross-sectional samples. However, classification error can bias results based on gross flow data even if the errors are random because a single misclassification can give rise to two incorrectly recorded transitions. In the present context we note that the battery of supplemental SJO questions asked in the March survey (which pertain to particular labor force states) means that the problem of classification error is likely to be chiefly associated with the April LFS data.[14] We do not have access to LFS reinterview data that could serve to check the accuracy of these April figures, however.[15]

In practice, we should note that the distinction between unemployment and nonparticipation typically depends on more than job search. For persons on temporary layoff and for those with a job to start at some definite date in the future, job search is not required in order for the respondent to be categorized

13. In part because of these problems, Statistics Canada does not regularly publish the gross flow data created by linking adjacent LFSs. However, these data are available on request and have been used in a number of studies.

14. Compare the analysis of Poterba and Summers (1995).

15. Using Canadian data on gross flows of labor, LeMaître (n.d.) questions the assumption of serially independent classification errors that underlie standard correction procedures based on reinterview data. Singh and Rao (1991) report classification error estimates that are based on re-interview data but that do not rely on independence of classification error.

as unemployed and the key criterion is rather that of current availability for work.[16] Thus our methodology could be employed for two related purposes: first, to examine whether the criteria for determining the status of "temporary layoffs" and "future job starts" are appropriate and, second, to examine whether availability for work is the best criterion for distinguishing between unemployment and out of the labor force for these individuals.

The data that we use in this paper represent a subset of the full SJO-LFS match, in that we only use part of the full nonemployed group, and it is important to explain the nature of the data carefully before proceeding. For employment, we follow the LFS so that respondents are classified as employed if they worked in the reference week (the week prior to the survey, usually the week containing the 15th of the month) or if they had a job but did not work for reasons such as illness, family responsibilities, bad weather, and vacation.[17] For the nonemployed, there are four circumstances to address: "no job attachment," "future job starts," "temporary layoffs," and "permanently unable to work."

"No job attachment" refers to persons without a job in the reference week (including a job from which the individual was temporarily laid off) who did not have a job scheduled to start at a definite date in the future. For these individuals, the distinction between state U and state O is based on job search, specifically on whether the respondent searched for work at least once in the previous four weeks. "Future job starts" refers to persons who were nonemployed in the reference week but who have a job to start at a definite date in the future: there is a subdivision into short-term and long-term future starts according to whether the new job start is one to four weeks away or more than four weeks away. "Temporary layoffs" refers to those who report that they did not work last week because of a temporary layoff from a job to which they expect to be recalled. Short-term future job starts and temporary layoffs are classified as state U or O depending on availability for work in the reference week, and job search is not required for individuals in these two categories to be classified as unemployed.[18] In contrast, long-term future starts are treated

16. As described in more detail later, availability for work is used to distinguish state U from state O for those with a job to start within four weeks ("short-term future starts"), while job search is employed for those with a job to start in more than four weeks ("long-term future starts").

17. See Statistics Canada (1992) on the details of the LFS questionnaire.

18. The determination of availability for work in the reference week is based on responses to question 63 on the LFS: "Was there any reason . . . could not take a job last week?" Persons who answer no are classified as unemployed, as are those who answer yes because of "own illness or disability," "personal or family responsibilities," or "already has a job." (Individuals answering yes for these reasons are considered available for work even though they may have been temporarily unavailable during the reference week.) On the other hand, those who answer yes to question 63 because they are "going to school" or "other" reasons are regarded as unavailable and are hence classified as out of the labor force, even if they are categorized as temporary layoffs or short-term future job starts.

The one exception to this occurs for full-time students looking for full-time work, who are classified as not in the labor force, even though they may (also) be temporary layoffs, short-term future job starts, or unattached job seekers.

similarly to the no job attachment group in the LFS in that the distinction between state U and state O is based on job search.

The SJO provides information about expressed desire for work and reasons for not searching for work. The coverage of the SJO is restricted to nonemployed persons who are not seeking work or on temporary layoff. That is, within the group of those not seeking work, the SJO solicits information from future job starts (short term and long term) and those with no job attachment. Appendix table 4A.1 details the groups surveyed.[19]

The focus of the paper is on the no job attachment group; the question of whether labor force activity should be classified in terms of job search or in terms of desire for work is clearly most relevant for this group. Over our sample period as a whole, the no job attachment category represents the bulk of both unemployment (85 to 90 percent) and not in the labor force (93 to 94 percent). Future job starts represent 4 to 6 percent of U and less than 1 percent of O; there are too few such individuals to permit the analysis carried out in this paper.

Our particular use of the SJO data is its information on the marginal attachment group, which is based on the response to the SJO question "Did . . . want a job last week?" Persons who respond yes to this question (and who are classified by the LFS as O)[20] are placed in the M category; the remainder are treated as not attached (N). Additionally, the N category also includes those who are classified as O by the LFS and who did not respond to the SJO (i.e., those permanently unable to work and temporary layoffs classified as O). Appendix table 4A.1 gives the details for each case.

4.3   Transition Rates

We first examine the properties of the observed transition rates from the empirical matrix (5). Consistent with our interest in the demographic breakdown of these rates, we address the differences by age, sex, and region. In each case, as discussed above, we focus on the no job attachment group, which excludes those on temporary layoff and those classified as being future job starts. Analysis of the future job starts group within each demographic and regional subsample is precluded by considerations of sample size.

4.3.1   Age

Figures 4.1, 4.2, and 4.3 present the nine transition rates for "youths" (those aged 15 to 24) and "adults" (those aged 25 or over) graphed for each year of

19. The employed and the nonemployed on temporary layoff or permanently unable to work do not respond to the SJO, while job seekers do not complete the majority of the form, ending at question 11 of the survey.

20. However, note that persons who are classified by the LFS as U and who respond to the SJO naturally remain in the U category for the purposes of our empirical analysis.

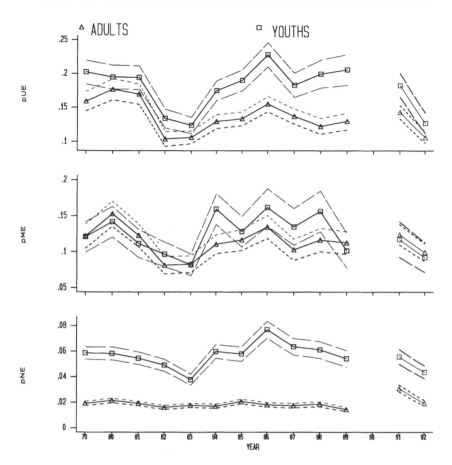

Fig. 4.1 Transitions into employment by age

Note: To accommodate a maximal amount of information, the vertical scales on these graphs (and those in subsequent figures) are not uniform and do not necessarily start at zero. The long- and short-dashed lines represent 95 percent confidence intervals.

the SJO-LFS sample.[21] The transitions into employment in figure 4.1 show a hazard from unemployment for youths that is often significantly higher than that for adults, especially for the later part of the 1980s. The transition rate from marginal attachment is less clearly different by age group, although the youth group point estimate is usually higher, while the hazard from N is roughly three times as large for youths as for adults. All three series display

21. Throughout the paper we use the LFS weights in calculating transition rates. Thus the *pUE* hazard is the fraction of the weighted number of unemployed in March who are employed in April.

The division between youths and adults at age 25 matches that available in the Canadian monthly gross flow data.

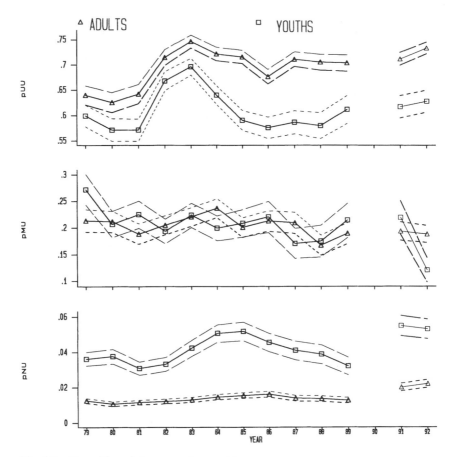

Fig. 4.2   Transitions into unemployment by age

some temporal stability, subject to the influence of the recessions in 1981–82 (from which recovery was particularly slow in Canada) and the early 1990s.

The hazards into unemployment in figure 4.2 exhibit analogous variations by age. The probability of remaining in unemployment is always significantly lower for youths than for adults, especially after 1983, while there is little difference in the transition rate from marginal attachment into unemployment. Finally, the hazard from N into unemployment, like that from N into employment, is significantly higher for youths. From figure 4.3, we can relatedly see that the hazard from U to O is also higher for youths, reflecting a lower degree of labor force attachment, while again there is very little difference by age in the hazard out of M into O. The hazard from N to O is high and relatively stable for both age groups but is significantly higher for the adult group.

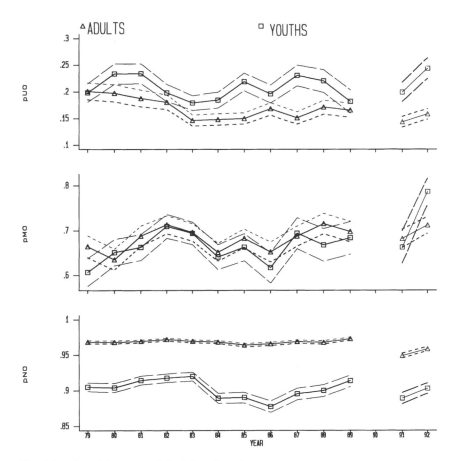

Fig. 4.3   Transitions out of the labor force by age

4.3.2   Sex

Figures 4.4, 4.5, and 4.6 present the nine empirical hazards for the 13 SJO-LFS samples broken down by sex. The hazards into employment in figure 4.4 are all somewhat higher for men than for women, this being especially true for the transition rate from N, and cyclical patterns are strong in all three series. The rates into unemployment in figure 4.5 are also higher for men, although there is some sign of convergence in the probability of remaining unemployed in the later part of the sample. Analogously, the hazards into O in figure 4.6 are higher for women for each origin state, with the difference from unemployment being proportionately greatest. Interestingly, in view of the close similarity of the hazards from marginal attachment for youths and adults, all of the hazards from marginal attachment are different by sex, with men more likely to transit into employment or unemployment and with women significantly more likely to transit into nonparticipation.

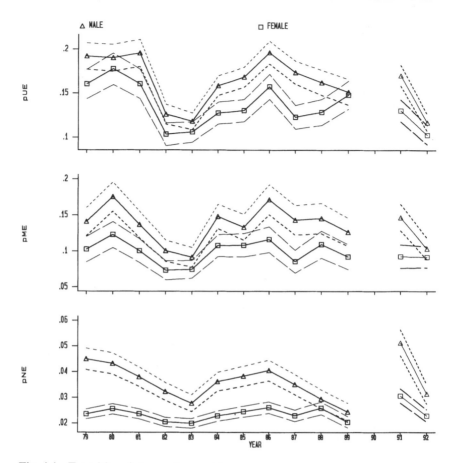

Fig. 4.4   Transitions into employment by sex

4.3.3   Region

The nine hazards disaggregated by region for each year of the SJO-LFS sample are presented in figures 4.7, 4.8, and 4.9. The hazards into employment in figure 4.7 display considerable regional variation, varying by as much as 100 percent from lowest to highest region in a given year. The Prairies tend to have high transition rates (from all three origin states), while those in Quebec tend to be among the lowest. Figures 4.8 and 4.9 give the hazards into unemployment and nonparticipation, respectively, a notable feature being the uniform rise in the probability of remaining unemployed in the early 1980s, together with the relatively uniform failure of this probability to improve much throughout the rest of the decade. Also, the widening of the diversity of regional experience during the 1980s for the hazard from U into O is remarkable, with Ontario, Quebec, and the Atlantic provinces having by 1989 transition rates double those of the Prairies and British Columbia.

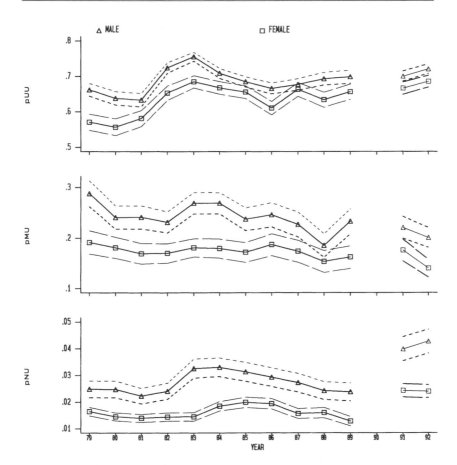

Fig. 4.5   Transitions into unemployment by sex

4.3.4   Behavior of Nonparticipants

In each of these nine graphs, we should note an issue that arises with the final two years of these SJO-LFS data, which is that there is some sign of temporal instability compared with the levels and trends from the late 1980s. This phenomenon is most clear for *pNU* by age (fig. 4.2), for *pNE* and *pNU* by sex (figs. 4.4 and 4.5), and for *pNE*, *pNU*, and *pNO* (figs. 4.7, 4.8, and 4.9) for the regional analysis. We suspect that these apparent disjunctions reflect the changing nature of nonparticipants in the early 1990s. In particular, an especially sharp decline in labor force participation was experienced during the 1990–92 recession. For example, the overall participation rate fell by 1.4 percentage points from November 1989 to November 1992, with the analogous figure for youth being a drop of 5.9 percentage points (Sunter 1993). Furthermore, during the subsequent weak recovery, participation rates—including those for adult women—failed to resume their pre-1990 trends. Clearly, the

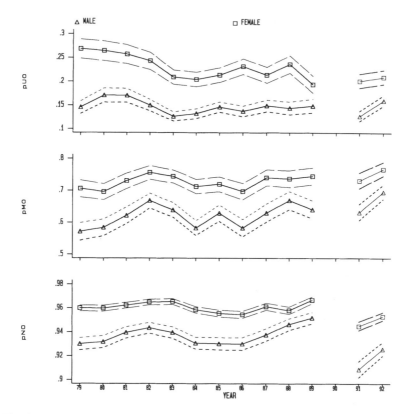

Fig. 4.6   Transitions out of the labor force by sex

unfortunate fact that the SJO was not administered in 1990 makes further analysis of these issues difficult with the present SJO-LFS data.

4.3.5   Comparison of Unemployment and Marginal Attachment Origin States

The preceding figures and associated discussion suggest that there are few differences by age or sex in the hazards out of the marginal attachment category. A related question that is less easy to answer in those figures is whether, within each age or sex grouping, the transition rates out of unemployment differ from those out of marginal attachment. In order to address this issue, the *pUE* and *pME* hazards and associated 95 percent confidence bands are presented by age in figure 4.10 and by sex in figure 4.11.[22]

For both the adult and youth age groups, the point estimate of *pUE* exceeds

22. The estimates and confidence bands are calculated from each individual SJO or LFS sample rather than by pooling the samples.

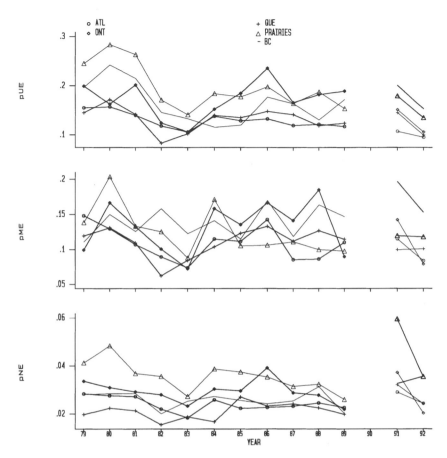

Fig. 4.7   Transitions into employment by region

that of *pME* in each year. However, the two series move closely together over the cycle, and their point estimates are quite close. For adults, the *pUE* and *pME* 95 percent confidence intervals overlap in every year, although, for youths, *pUE* significantly exceeds *pME* except in the 1983–84 aftermath of the recession. On this unconditional basis, then, it appears that the marginal attachment state is behaviorally closer to unemployment for the over age 25 group than for those 15 to 24 years of age.

The closeness of *pUE* and *pME* is also apparent in figure 4.11 for men, with the *pUE* > *pME* ordering again accompanied by close comovement over the cycle and by confidence intervals that overlap in most years. For women, the ranking is rather more marked, with *pME* being only two-thirds the value of *pUE* early in the sample and with a distinct separation between the two confidence bands for most years. Thus, while men in the marginal attachment cate-

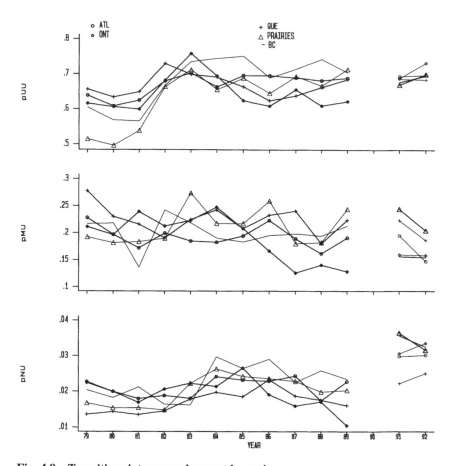

Fig. 4.8   Transitions into unemployment by region

gory look very similar to unemployed men in terms of their future labor market transitions, there is somewhat more difference between the two states for women.

4.4   Econometric Results

Although the properties of the unconditional transition rates from various origin states are informative, each transition rate summarizes the average behavior of a heterogeneous group of individuals. To assess whether there is equivalence of two origin states conditional on observable characteristics such as sex, age, marital status, region, and education level, we must estimate a model of the determinants of transitions among various states and test whether the same model holds from the two origin states under consideration. This

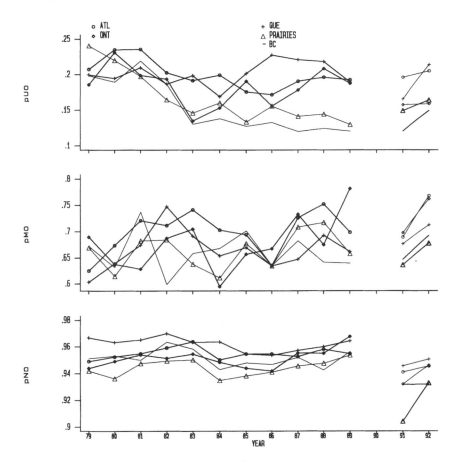

Fig. 4.9   Transitions out of the labor force by region

amounts to estimation of the conditional versions of equations (2) and (3) above.

In practice, as noted above, we are able to conduct the full test of equivalence of origin states only between M and N. We adopt a multinomial logit specification of the movement from an origin state into employment, unemployment, or out of the labor force, and since this model requires a normalization, we treat O as the omitted group.[23] Hence, we estimate three multinomial logit models, one from the marginal attachment state M, one from the not

23. Note that the multinomial logit model implicitly imposes the independence of irrelevant alternatives; in this case, the relative probabilities of transits into E and U, e.g., would be left unaltered by the removal of the (irrelevant) alternative of transiting into O. Below, we report estimates from both multinomial and binary logits—models that make the polar opposite assumptions of independence and perfect correlation, respectively—and we find results that seem fairly robust across these opposite specifications. We thank Tom Lemieux for this interpretation of our results.

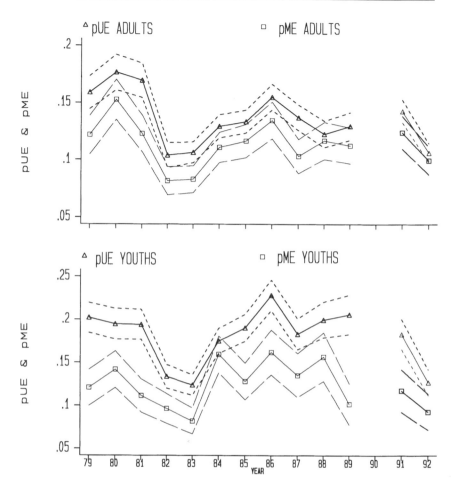

Fig. 4.10   Comparing *pUE* and *pME* by age

attached state N, and one from the two states pooled, and we employ a likelihood ratio test to determine whether we can reject the pooling.[24]

For the other two tests of interest, (i) the equivalence of U and M and (ii) the equivalence of U and N, we do not observe the necessary destination states in the SJO-LFS data. In each case, we observe destination states E and O, although our tests would respectively require that we observe (i) E and N and (ii) E and M. Since O is made up of M and N, we can only estimate part of condition (2) (or the analogous condition for testing U = N). Accordingly, we have estimated a binary logit model of the determinants of the transition into

24. Our data are weighted, so in order to attain the correct likelihood overall and in each subcase, we actually estimate the (equivalent) fully interacted model in which each explanatory variable is interacted with the origin state dummy.

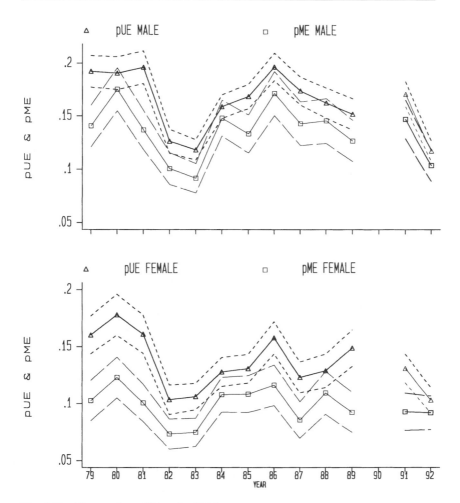

Fig. 4.11   Comparing *pUE* and *pME* by sex

employment for these two tests. Clearly, though, we could incorrectly fail to reject U = M if we have *pUE = pME* but *pUN ≠ pMN*. Thus the restrictions we test are necessary but not sufficient for the equivalence of U and M and U and N.

The results of these likelihood ratio tests for the pairwise equivalence of the U, M, and N states are given in tables 4.1, 4.2, and 4.3. In each case, we present the *p*-value of the test for each year of the SJO-LFS sample and for each demographic group or region in question. For both youths and adults in table 4.1, we decisively reject M = N and U = N in every year, though the equivalence of U and M is not rejected at the 5 percent level in three of the thirteen years for youths and in five of these years for adults. Similarly, the results for men

Table 4.1   **Probability Values for Binary and Multinomial Logit Tests of Equivalence of Labor Market States: By Age**

	Youth			Adult		
Year	U = M	M = N	U = N	U = M	M = N	U = N
1979	.00	.00	.00	.02	.00	.00
1980	.01	.00	.00	.00	.00	.00
1981	.00	.00	.00	.41	.00	.00
1982	.14	.00	.00	.02	.00	.00
1983	.01	.00	.00	.08	.00	.00
1984	.42	.00	.00	.10	.00	.00
1985	.00	.00	.00	.35	.00	.00
1986	.00	.00	.00	.01	.00	.00
1987	.02	.00	.00	.00	.00	.00
1988	.00	.00	.00	.08	.00	.00
1989	.00	.00	.00	.00	.00	.00
1991	.00	.00	.00	.00	.00	.00
1992	.17	.00	.00	.43	.00	.00

Notes: U is unemployed, M is marginally attached, and N is out of the labor force and not marginally attached. Likelihood ratio tests based on binary logit are used for U = M and U = N, multinomial logit for M = N. Explanatory variables are female, marital status (currently married or not), education (postsecondary certificate or higher, or not), and regions (Atlantic, Quebec, Ontario, Prairies, or British Columbia). All for no job attachment group.

Table 4.2   **Probability Values for Binary and Multinomial Logit Tests of Equivalence of Labor Market States: By Sex**

	Male			Female		
Year	U = M	M = N	U = N	U = M	M = N	U = N
1979	.01	.00	.00	.00	.00	.00
1980	.02	.00	.00	.00	.00	.00
1981	.03	.00	.00	.00	.00	.00
1982	.14	.00	.00	.00	.00	.00
1983	.04	.00	.00	.10	.00	.00
1984	.10	.00	.00	.00	.00	.00
1985	.02	.00	.00	.19	.00	.00
1986	.06	.00	.00	.00	.00	.00
1987	.00	.00	.00	.46	.00	.00
1988	.10	.00	.00	.02	.00	.00
1989	.00	.00	.00	.00	.00	.00
1991	.01	.00	.00	.01	.00	.00
1992	.20	.00	.00	.01	.00	.00

Notes: U is unemployed, M is marginally attached, and N is out of the labor force and not marginally attached. Likelihood ratio tests based on binary logit are used for U = M and U = N, multinomial logit for M = N. Explanatory variables are age groups (15–24, 25–34, 35–54, 55+), marital status (currently married or not), education (postsecondary certificate or higher, or not), and regions (Atlantic, Quebec, Ontario, Prairies, or British Columbia). All for no job attachment group.

Table 4.3   Probability Values for Binary and Multinomial Logit Tests of Equivalence of Labor Market States: By Region

Year	Atlantic			Quebec			Ontario			Prairies			British Columbia		
	U = M	M = N	U = N	U = M	M = N	U = N	U = M	M = N	U = N	U = M	M = N	U = N	U = M	M = N	U = N
1979	.06	.00	.00	.06	.00	.00	.01	.00	.00	.00	.00	.00	.00	.00	.00
1980	.36	.00	.00	.04	.00	.00	.69	.00	.00	.11	.00	.00	.05	.00	.00
1981	.05	.00	.00	.64	.00	.00	.10	.00	.00	.00	.00	.00	.10	.00	.00
1982	.00	.00	.00	.22	.00	.00	.99	.00	.00	.09	.00	.00	.77	.00	.00
1983	.01	.00	.00	.06	.00	.00	.61	.00	.00	.15	.00	.00	.25	.00	.00
1984	.08	.00	.00	.15	.00	.00	.27	.00	.00	.73	.00	.00	.86	.00	.00
1985	.02	.00	.00	.25	.00	.00	.09	.00	.00	.06	.00	.00	.03	.00	.00
1986	.32	.00	.00	.45	.00	.00	.01	.00	.00	.00	.00	.00	.59	.00	.00
1987	.03	.00	.00	.21	.00	.00	.06	.00	.00	.01	.00	.00	.26	.00	.00
1988	.04	.00	.00	.10	.00	.00	.04	.00	.00	.00	.00	.00	.41	.00	.00
1989	.03	.00	.00	.00	.00	.00	.00	.00	.00	.19	.00	.00	.00	.00	.00
1991	.09	.00	.00	.01	.00	.00	.13	.00	.00	.38	.00	.00	.07	.00	.00
1992	.14	.00	.00	.00	.00	.00	.57	.00	.00	.59	.00	.00	.13	.00	.00

Notes: U is unemployed, M is marginally attached, and N is out of the labor force and not marginally attached. Likelihood ratio tests based on binary logit are used for U = M and U = N, multinomial logit for M = N. Explanatory variables are female, age groups (15–24, 25–44, 45+), marital status (currently married or not), education (postsecondary certificate or higher, or not). All for no job attachment group.

and women in table 4.2 always reject M = N and U = N but fail to reject U = M five times for men and three times for women. Finally, the regional results in table 4.3, based on slightly coarser definitions of the underlying explanatory variables,[25] again reject M = N and U = N for every region and in every year. For the testing of U = M, these regional results fail to reject (at the 5 percent level) seven times in the Atlantic provinces, nine times in Quebec, nine times in Ontario, eight times in the Prairies, and ten times in British Columbia, all out of a total of thirteen tests.

These results give strong support to the idea that the marginal attachment group is behaviorally distinct from the not attached group, based on the full multinomial model, as well as rejecting the hypothesis that unemployment and out of the labor force are equivalent (which was probably much less likely on a priori grounds). The fact that these sets of results hold across our age, sex, and region groupings and hold for every year of the SJO-LFS data is a striking regularity. The results on the U = M hypothesis are less clear-cut, and the failure to reject in many cases gives greater grounds for suggesting that these two states may be "close" behaviorally, at least in some years and for some groups in the overall sample.[26]

Two issues arise from this set of results. First, while U = N might be intu- itively unappealing (given our likely ranking as in eq. [4]), both U = M and M = N might seem plausible hypotheses. However, the nature of our data forces a *binary* logit partial testing of U = M but permits a *multinomial* logit testing of M = N, so we have some concern that the evident regularities in our results could derive in part from this difference in testing procedures. While we cannot apply the multinomial approach to the U = M hypothesis, we can apply the binary model to the M = N null, testing separately whether $pME = pNE$ and whether $pMO = pNO$. We have conducted these separate binary tests for each year by age, sex, and region. In every case, both binary tests reject equivalence, lending considerable support to the view that the uniform pattern of rejection found in the multinomial testing is a reflection of the true nature of these data rather than an artifact of the nature of the hypothesis testing.

Second, we are interested in understanding further the reasons why in many cases we cannot reject the equivalence of unemployment and marginal attach- ment. Persons who indicate that they desire work but are not searching are categorized by the SJO according to the reason(s) given for not searching, the potential reasons being as follows:

1. Own illness or disability
2. Personal or family responsibilities

25. The slight regrouping of the explanatory variables in all of the regional analyses was necessi- tated by some of the small cell sizes in the demographic breakdown of the regional data; the notes to the tables detail the exact variable definitions employed.

26. The equivalent tests for the full sample are broadly similar to these results by age, sex, and region. We reject the equivalence of U and M in all but three sample years and consistently reject equivalence of U and N and M and N (Jones and Riddell, in press).

3. Going to school
4. No longer interested in finding work
5. Waiting for recall (to former job)
6. Has found new job
7. Waiting for replies from employers
8. Believes no work available (in area or suited to skills)
9. No reason given
0. Other

We group these codes into two subcategories, waiting (codes 5, 6, and 7) and nonwaiting (codes 1 through 4 and codes 8, 9, and 0).[27] We investigate the transition rates out of the marginal waiting category (MW) and the marginal nonwaiting category (MNW), comparing these rates with hazards out of employment.

Figure 4.12 gives the three hazards, pUE, $p(MW)E$, and $p(MNW)E$, for the adult and youth groups in our population; figure 4.13 gives the analogous hazards for the male and female samples. The levels of these unconditional hazards are striking, with the $p(MW)E$ hazard being *higher* than that out of unemployment for every year for adults and for men and women. For youths, the hazards are equal in one year and this ordering is reversed in one year, but the same overall pattern obtains in the rest of the years. Thus persons waiting for recall, waiting for a job start, or waiting for replies from employers have higher hazards into employment than those usually counted as unemployed.[28] Note that all of these persons are currently counted as nonparticipants according to the LFS, even though they have high average transition rates into employment. We believe this to be the result of two LFS procedures: first, that persons awaiting recall to a seasonal job are counted as out of the labor force unless they engage in job search and, second, that future job starts who lack a definite date for the job start are similarly categorized as nonparticipants in the absence of job search.

We have further investigated these issues by testing for equivalence between unemployment and these two subcategories of the marginally attached. These results, all based on binary logits, are presented in the final three tables.[29] The p-values for the likelihood ratio tests by age are presented in table 4.4. For both youths and adults, we reject the hypothesis that unemployment and the *non*waiting subcategory of M are behaviorally equivalent, although the pattern

---

27. Discouraged workers correspond to code 8, while codes 1 through 4 are usually categorized as "personal" reasons for not searching.

28. We believe, based on aggregate work with these data (Jones and Riddell, in press), that these results for the MW group derive chiefly from the recall and found new job codes (5 and 6), rather than from the waiting for replies code (7).

29. Note, though, that the ordering of the hazards in figs. 4.12 and 4.13 might lead to a rejection of the equivalence of MW and U because the unemployed have transition rates into employment that are too low, not too high. I.e., these results violate the ordering (4) at which we speculated above.

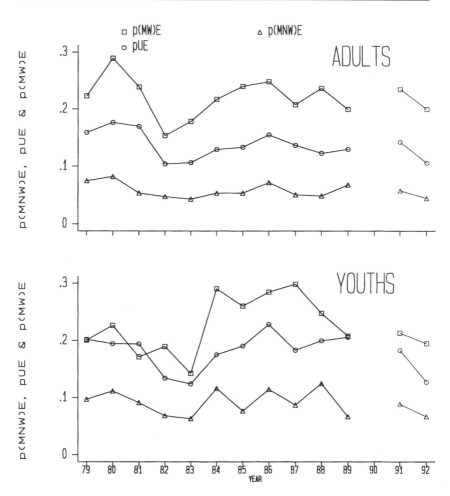

Fig. 4.12   Transitions into employment by initial state and age

for the waiting group varies more by age. For youths, results for four out of thirteen years fail to reject equivalence of unemployment and the waiting sub-category of the marginal attachment group, though this failure to reject only occurs in the first year of our sample for adults. By sex, the table 4.5 results are more clear-cut, with equivalence between unemployment and either the waiting or the nonwaiting marginal attachment category being rejected in almost every case; the one exception is a failure to reject U = MW for women in 1979. Finally, the regional test statistics in table 4.6 are rather more mixed, perhaps as a reflection of sample sizes. The hypothesis that the waiting subcategory of the marginal attachment group is behaviorally equivalent to the unemployed is not rejected three to six times (out of thirteen years), depending on the region, with the most frequent rejections being in the Atlantic provinces.

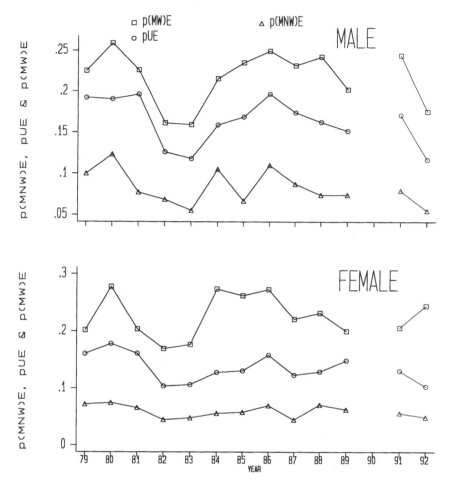

Fig. 4.13   Transitions into employment by initial state and sex

The test of U = MNW is rejected more commonly than that of U = MW, and again the pattern is one with the strongest rejections being in the Atlantic provinces.

4.5   Conclusions

There are four significant conclusions that follow from this analysis. First, the demographics do matter. Both the unconditional hazards and the econometric results suggest that there are important differences by age, sex, and region in the level and the determinants of many labor force transitions. Second, members of the marginal attachment group are behaviorally distinct from the not attached (the remainder of those classified as not in the labor force) across

Table 4.4   **Probability Values for Binary Logit Tests of Equivalence of Labor Market States: Waiting Subgroups by Age**

	Youth		Adult	
Year	U = MW	U = MNW	U = MW	U = MNW
1979	.46	.00	.12	.00
1980	.04	.00	.00	.00
1981	.02	.00	.00	.00
1982	.04	.00	.00	.00
1983	.56	.00	.00	.00
1984	.00	.00	.00	.00
1985	.00	.00	.00	.00
1986	.00	.00	.00	.00
1987	.00	.00	.00	.00
1988	.42	.00	.00	.00
1989	.05	.00	.00	.01
1991	.58	.00	.00	.00
1992	.01	.00	.00	.00

Notes: U is unemployed, MW is the waiting subcategory of marginal attachment, and MNW is the nonwaiting subcategory of marginal attachment. Likelihood ratio tests are based on binary logits. Explanatory variables are female, marital status (currently married or not), education (postsecondary certificate or higher, or not), and regions (Atlantic, Quebec, Ontario, Prairies, or British Columbia). All for no job attachment group.

Table 4.5   **Probability Values for Binary Logit Tests of Equivalence of Labor Market States: Waiting Subgroups by Sex**

	Male		Female	
Year	U = MW	U = MNW	U = MW	U = MNW
1979	.03	.00	.27	.00
1980	.00	.00	.00	.00
1981	.00	.00	.07	.00
1982	.00	.00	.00	.00
1983	.00	.00	.04	.00
1984	.00	.00	.00	.00
1985	.00	.00	.00	.00
1986	.00	.00	.00	.00
1987	.00	.00	.00	.00
1988	.00	.00	.00	.00
1989	.00	.00	.00	.00
1991	.00	.00	.00	.00
1992	.00	.00	.00	.00

Notes: U is unemployed, MW is the waiting subcategory of marginal attachment, and MNW is the nonwaiting subcategory of marginal attachment. Likelihood ratio tests are based on binary logits. Explanatory variables are age groups (15–24, 25–34, 35–54, 55+), marital status (currently married or not), education (postsecondary certificate or higher, or not), and regions (Atlantic, Quebec, Ontario, Prairies, or British Columbia). All for no job attachment group.

Table 4.6   Probability Values for Binary Logit Tests of Equivalence of Labor Market States: Waiting Subgroups by Region

Year	Atlantic		Quebec		Ontario		Prairies		British Columbia	
	U = MW	U = MNW	U = MW	U = MNW	U = MW	U = MNW	U = MW	U = MNW	U = MW	U = MNW
1979	.00	.00	.16	.02	.15	.00	.04	.00	.12	.00
1980	.10	.00	.04	.29	.00	.10	.59	.05	.52	.00
1981	.02	.00	.14	.00	.05	.00	.02	.00	.59	.02
1982	.02	.00	.71	.02	.12	.30	.01	.00	.29	.53
1983	.16	.00	.02	.01	.77	.11	.01	.00	.02	.00
1984	.00	.00	.04	.00	.00	.07	.24	.50	.02	.09
1985	.00	.00	.00	.00	.04	.00	.45	.01	.00	.01
1986	.00	.00	.05	.11	.00	.00	.55	.00	.00	.41
1987	.02	.00	.00	.00	.11	.06	.00	.00	.02	.09
1988	.08	.00	.01	.00	.00	.33	.13	.00	.01	.41
1989	.00	.06	.00	.00	.01	.00	.02	.02	.00	.01
1991	.00	.00	.08	.00	.00	.01	.65	.04	.03	.20
1992	.00	.00	.00	.00	.00	.00	.00	.00	.12	.18

Notes: U is unemployed, MW is the waiting subcategory of marginal attachment, and MNW is the nonwaiting subcategory of marginal attachment. Likelihood ratio tests based on binary logits. Explanatory variables are female, age groups (15–24, 25–44, 45+), marital status (currently married or not), education (postsecondary certificate or higher, or not). All for no job attachment group.

almost all demographic groups and regions. This gives justification for the collection and publication of information on "persons on the margin of the labor force" or the "marginally attached"—those who desire work but are not searching for work. Third, the marginally attached are typically closer in behavioral terms to the unemployed, especially for men and for those aged 25 or over, although the data do sometimes reject the hypothesis that marginal attachment and unemployment are equivalent. Finally, both the unconditional hazards and the tests of behavioral equivalence suggest that there is a significant degree of heterogeneity within the marginal attachment group itself, most notably according to whether the individual is "waiting" or not. Our results suggest that existing criteria for counting temporary layoffs and future job starts as unemployed—which exclude those in the waiting group of the marginally attached—may be too stringent on behavioral grounds.

Appendix

Table 4A.1   Assignment of Labor Force States

Category	Status Assigned by Labour Force Survey	Survey of Job Opportunities Response	Desire Work?	Available for Work?	Status Assigned in This Paper
Employed	E	None	n.a.	n.a.	E
Permanently unable to work	O	None	n.a.	n.a.	N
Temporary layoff	U	None	n.a.	Yes	U
	O	None	n.a.	No	N
Short-term future start, seeking work	U	Part	n.a.	Yes	U
	O	Part	n.a.	No	N
Short-term future start, not seeking work	U	Full	n.a.	Yes	U
	O	Full	Yes	No	M
	O	Full	No	No	N
Long-term future start, seeking work	U	Part	n.a.	Yes	U
	O	Part	n.a.	No	N
Long-term future start, not seeking work	O	Full	Yes		M
	O	Full	No		N
No job attachment, seeking work	U	Part	n.a.	Yes	U
	O	Part	n.a.	No	N
No job attachment, not seeking work	O	Full	Yes		M
	O	Full	No		N

References

Abowd, John M., and Arnold Zellner. 1985. Estimating gross labor force flows. *Journal of Business and Economic Statistics* 3:254–83.

Akyeampong, E. B. 1987. Persons on the margins of the labour force. *Labour Force* 43 (April): 85–142.

———. 1992. Discouraged workers: Where have they gone? *Perspectives on Labour and Income* 4 (autumn): 38–44.

Blau, D. M., and P. K. Robins. 1986. Labor supply response to welfare programs: A dynamic analysis. *Journal of Labor Economics* 4:82–104.

Burdett, K., N. Kiefer, D. Mortensen, and G. Neumann. 1984. Earnings, unemployment, and the allocation of time over time. *Review of Economic Studies* 51:559–78.

Cain, G. 1980. Labor force concepts and definitions in view of their purposes. In *Concepts and data needs,* appendix vol. 1, Washington, D.C.: National Commission on Employment and Unemployment Statistics.

Card, D., and W. C. Riddell. 1993. A comparative analysis of unemployment in Canada and the United States. In *Small differences that matter: Labor markets and income maintenance in Canada and the United States,* ed. D. Card and R. B. Freeman. Chicago: University of Chicago Press.

Clark, K., and L. H. Summers. 1979. Labor market dynamics and unemployment: A reconsideration. *Brookings Papers on Economic Activity,* no. 1: 13–60.

Cohen, G. L. 1991. Then and now: The changing face of unemployment. *Perspectives on Labour and Income* 3 (spring): 37–45.

Devereaux, M. S. 1992. Alternative measures of unemployment. *Perspectives on Labour and Income* 4 (winter): 35–43.

Flinn, C. J., and J. J. Heckman. 1982. Models for the analysis of labor force dynamics. In *Advances in econometrics,* vol. 1, ed. R. Basmann and G. Rhodes, 35–95. Greenwich, Conn.: JAI.

———. 1983. Are unemployment and out of the labor force behaviorally distinct labor force states? *Journal of Labor Economics* 1 (January): 28–42.

Gönül, F. 1992. New evidence on whether unemployment and out of the labor force are distinct states. *Journal of Human Resources* 27 (spring): 329–61.

Gower, D. 1990. Time lost: An alternative view of unemployment. *Perspectives on Labour and Income* 2 (spring): 73–77.

Hall, Robert E. 1983. Is unemployment a macroeconomic problem? *American Economic Review Papers and Proceedings* 73 (May): 219–22.

Jackson, G. 1987. Alternative concepts and measures of unemployment. *Labour Force* 43 (February): 85–120.

Jones, S. R. G., and W. C. Riddell. In press. The measurement of unemployment: An empirical approach. *Econometrica.*

Lemaître, Georges. n.d. The measurement and analysis of gross flows. Ottawa: Statistics Canada. Mimeograph.

Lucas, Robert E., Jr., and Leonard A. Rapping. 1969. Real wages, employment and inflation. *Journal of Political Economy* 77 (September/October): 721–54.

Meyer, Bruce D. 1988. Classification-error models and labor-market dynamics. *Journal of Business and Economic Statistics* 6:385–90.

Norwood, J. L. 1988. The measurement of unemployment. *American Economic Review* 78 (May): 284–88.

Organization for Economic Cooperation and Development (OECD). 1987. On the margin of the labour force: An analysis of discouraged workers and other nonparticipants. In *Employment Outlook 1987,* 142–70. Paris: Organization for Economic Cooperation and Development, September.

Poterba, James M., and Lawrence H. Summers. 1986. Reporting errors and labor market dynamics. *Econometrica* 54:1319–38.

———. 1995. Unemployment benefits and labor market transitions: A multinomial logit model with errors in classification. *Review of Economics and Statistics* 77 (May): 207–16.

Romeo, Charles J. 1992a. A longitudinal evaluation of the truth content of the CPS reinterview data. Working Paper no. 92-11. New Brunswick, N.J.: Rutgers University, Department of Economics, October.

———. 1992b. A unified framework for resolving inconsistencies in reported unemployment duration data in a panel of monthly CPS data: Theory. Working Paper no. 92-10. New Brunswick, N.J.: Rutgers University, Department of Economics, July.

Singh, A. C., and J. N. K. Rao. 1991. Classification error adjustments for gross flow estimates. Working Paper no. SSMD-91-013 E. Ottawa: Statistics Canada, Social Survey Methods Division, Methodology Branch, June.

Stasny, Elizabeth A. 1988. Modeling nonignorable nonresponse in categorical panel data with an example in estimating gross labor-force flows. *Journal of Business and Economic Statistics* 6:207–19.

Statistics Canada. 1992. *Guide to labour force survey data.* Ottawa: Statistics Canada.

Stratton, Leslie S. n.d. Identifying discouraged workers and their relative attachment to the labor market. Tucson: University of Arizona. Mimeograph.

Sunter, Deborah. 1993. Persons not in the labour force. *Labour Force* 49 (April): C2–C23.

Tano, Doki K. 1991. Are unemployment and out of the labor force behaviorally distinct labor force states? *Economics Letters* 36:113–17.

U.S. Department of Labor. Bureau of Labor Statistics. 1993. *Employment and Earnings* 40, no. 1 (January).

Van den Berg, G. J. 1990. Search behaviour, transitions to nonparticipation and the duration of unemployment. *Economic Journal* 100:842–65.

Comment   Thomas Lemieux

This paper uses a series of supplements to the Canadian Labour Force Survey (LFS) to present evidence on transition probabilities among detailed labor market states. These labor market states are based on the usual questions about employment status and search behavior, as well as on questions about willingness to accept employment. The set of labor market states is broader than the usual classification into employment, unemployment, and out of the labor force. This enables the authors to determine whether the transition probabilities of workers are homogeneous within the three usual categories or whether a different aggregation scheme would be more appropriate. This bears directly on the issue of how labor market states such as unemployment should be defined in practice and which questions should be asked to determine these la-

Thomas Lemieux is associate professor of economics at the Université de Montréal, a faculty research fellow of the National Bureau of Economic Research, and a research associate of CIRANO and CRDE.

bor market states in surveys like the Current Population Survey and the Canadian LFS.

The authors find that the transition probabilities into employment of several groups usually classified as out of the labor force are closer to those of the unemployed than other out of the labor force. This is particularly true for discouraged workers who have stopped searching but would like to work and for workers who will start a job in the near future, want to work, but are not currently available for work. One interpretation the authors draw from this finding is that the definition of unemployment should be broadened to include people who are marginally attached to the labor force.

The data used in this paper are unique, and the basic findings about transition probabilities are robust to the estimation procedure used. These findings are quite believable, and the estimation procedure is generally appropriate. My only comment about the estimation procedure is a technical point about the use of multinomial logit models to test whether marginal attachment (M) and not in the labor force (N) are similar states. These multinomial logits rely on a strong assumption of independence between the three possible outcomes (remain in the same state, transit into unemployment, and transit into employment). One implication of this assumption is that relative transition rates into employment and unemployment would remain the same even if the possibility of going back to the original state was eliminated (independence of irrelevant alternatives). This seems unrealistic since unemployment is in one sense closer to being out of the labor force than employment is. An ordered logit would probably be more appropriate for this particular application.

The authors argue for a definition of unemployment based on behavior (do people get jobs or not) instead of a priori criteria like search behavior on which the traditional definition of unemployment is based. My remaining comments focus on the distinction between this behavioral measure of unemployment and the traditional measure of unemployment and on the reasons why one measure should be preferred to the other. In one sense, the way the term "behavior" is used in this paper is a bit confusing. After all, the traditional measure of unemployment is also behavioral since it is based on search behavior. When the authors talk of a behavioral measure of unemployment, what they really mean is an outcome-based measure of unemployment (do people get jobs or not?). Whether the outcome-based measure is preferable to the standard search-based measure is intimately related to what the unemployment rate is supposed to measure. The outcome-based measure is of course appropriate when the unemployment rate is meant to measure how many people are likely to get jobs in the next time period. By contrast, the search-based measure is well suited for measuring how much "mismatch" there is in the labor market and how much time people must allocate to finding a good match. The search-based measure may also be useful for forecasting future economic activity since search behavior likely depends on expectations people have about the future. What matters here is the phenomenon we want to assess with the unemployment rate and not whether this measure of unemployment is or is not based on behavior.

Leaving aside the true meaning of the word "behavior," one important advantage of an outcome-based measure of unemployment is that it relies on what people actually do (find a job or not) instead of what they say they do (look for a job or not). This approach to the measurement of unemployment is very much in the tradition of positive economics, where the usefulness of economic models depends on how well they predict what agents actually do, irrespective of what they say they do. Viewed from this angle, the outcome-based measure of unemployment may be more stable in a structural sense than the traditional search-based measure. For instance, unemployment insurance may induce people to engage in some search activities just to receive benefits even if they know it will not affect their chances of getting a job. This would artificially increase the search-based measure of unemployment with no effects on underlying economic variables such as employment and output. The authors point to the well-known U.S.-Canada divergence in unemployment rates as a case in which an outcome-based measure could depict a very different picture of the divergence than the standard search-based measure does. This is potentially the strongest case for using an outcome-based instead of a search-based measure of unemployment. Note that, under these circumstances, the search-based measure would even be problematic for measuring mismatch or predicting future economic conditions.

The distinction between outcome-based and search-based measures of unemployment can finally be analyzed from a program evaluation perspective. A variety of programs can be implemented to change the behavior of people out of work to increase their chances of finding a job. The relevant question here is whether it is possible to increase the chances of getting a job by moving people from nonemployment to unemployment. This is a causal interpretation of the behavioral definition of unemployment in which a change in labor market state "causes" a change in transition probabilities. This causal interpretation would not hold if labor market states and transition probabilities were jointly determined by some other (omitted) factors, in which case the labor market state would be endogenous. Viewed from this angle, if the outcome-based measure was an exogenous determinant of transition probabilities while the search-based measure was endogenous, the former measure should be preferred to the latter.

However, neither the outcome-based nor the search-based measure of unemployment are likely to be exogenous. The basic problem is that, in presence of duration dependence, neither of these measures take account of the elapsed duration of the unemployment spell. If, as indicated in several empirical studies, there was some duration dependence in the conditional probability of exiting nonemployment, duration would likely affect both the labor market state and transition probabilities. In the most extreme case, labor market states (unemployment, marginally attached, or out of the labor force) would be simple proxies for duration and would have no independent effect on transition probabilities. In this case, neither the outcome-based nor the search-based measure of unemployment would be meaningful behavioral concepts from a causal inference perspective.

This issue could be analyzed in more detail by going beyond the simple binary logits presented in this paper and estimating hazard models. These models would indicate the independent effect of being in a particular state on the transition probability into employment once duration is controlled for. Estimating these models would strengthen the behavioral content of the distinction between unemployment and out of the labor force.

These comments aside, the paper makes an important contribution by showing the importance of disaggregating the relatively heterogeneous group of people out of the labor force on the basis of whether they are willing to work. Although it remains to be seen whether this group should be included in the official definition of unemployment, the paper makes a convincing case for reporting statistics on this group on a regular basis.

5   Are Lifetime Jobs Disappearing? Job Duration in the United States, 1973–1993

Henry S. Farber

5.1 Introduction

The public perception is that there has been a fundamental deterioration of job security in the United States. It is not unusual to see reports in the media to this effect. Headlines such as "Jobs in an Age of Insecurity" are not uncommon. Neither are statements like "Thirty months into recovery, Americans are realizing that the Great American Job is gone" (*Time*, 22 November 1993, p. 32). The same article in *Time* reports survey results finding that "two-thirds believed that job security has deteriorated over the past two years, although those years have seen continuous economic growth." These stories may not only reflect but also help shape the generally reported view that job security is declining.

Job security is not a precisely defined concept and has several dimensions. One dimension is the subjective perception of how secure one's job is. This depends both on how likely it is that the worker will be terminated involuntarily from his or her job and on how valuable that job is to the worker. If the job can be replaced easily (at low pecuniary and nonpecuniary cost) with an equivalent job, then the worker may not feel terribly insecure regardless of the likelihood of losing the current job. On the other hand, if replacing the job is difficult, then even low probabilities of losing the job may engender feelings of insecurity. On this basis, one way to investigate changes in job security is to measure changes in the likelihood and costs of job loss. Some of my earlier work through 1993 from the Displaced Workers Supplements to the Current

Henry S. Farber is the Hughes-Rogers Professor of Economics at Princeton University and a research associate of the National Bureau of Economic Research.

The author thanks David Card, Joanne Gowa, Derek Neal, conference participants, and seminar participants at Cornell, MIT, Michigan, Princeton, and Texas A&M for helpful comments. Financial support for this research was provided by the Center for Economic Policy Studies and the Industrial Relations Section, both at Princeton University.

Population Survey provides evidence that the costs of job loss in terms of post-displacement employment probabilities and earnings are substantial but have not increased since the early 1980s, when the Displaced Workers Supplement was initiated (Farber 1993, 1997). My analysis of the same data shows a small increase in the likelihood of job loss, particularly for more educated workers. It is difficult to find strong evidence in these data of more job insecurity.

An alternative, complementary, and perhaps longer run view of job security is based on the idea that stable long-run employment relationships are an important component of job security for workers, and it is this concept of job security that shapes my analysis. I examine evidence on job durations in order to determine if, in fact, a systematic change in the likelihood of long-term employment occurred between 1973 and 1993.

There is relatively long-standing concern that the basic nature of the employment relationship in the United States is changing from one based on long-term full-time employment to one based on more short-term and casual employment. There has been concern that employers are moving toward greater reliance on temporary workers, on subcontractors, and on part-time workers. Potential reasons for employers to implement such changes range from a need for added flexibility in the face of greater uncertainty regarding product demand to avoidance of increasingly expensive fringe benefits and long-term obligations to workers. The public's concern arises from the belief that these changes result in lower quality (lower paying and less secure) jobs for the average worker.

The analysis in this paper is based on evidence regarding the duration of jobs in progress from supplements to the Current Population Survey with relevant information for selected years from 1973 to 1993. In order to measure changes in the distribution of job durations, I examine changes in selected quantiles (the median and the .9 quantile) of the distribution of duration of jobs in progress. I also examine selected points in the cumulative distribution function including the fraction of workers who have been with their employers (1) no more than 1 year, (2) more than 10 years, and (3) more than 20 years. These data and the distributional measures used are described in more detail in section 5.2.

The central findings, presented in sections 5.3 and 5.4, are clear. No systematic change has occurred in various measures of the overall distribution of job duration over the past two decades. However, the overall figures mask two important, though perhaps unsurprising, changes in the job durations of particular groups of workers. First, individuals, particularly men, with little education (less than 12 years) are less likely to be in jobs of long duration today than they were 20 years ago. This is consistent with the declining real earnings (both relative and absolute) of the least educated workers in the U.S. economy, and it may be part of the mechanism of this decline. Second, women with at least a high school education are substantially more likely to be in long-term jobs today than they were 20 years ago. This is likely a natural result of the declining frequency with which women withdraw from the labor market for periods of time. The increased job durations for women may also help explain the decline in the male-female wage gap in the 1980s (Wellington 1992).

5.2 Data and Measurement Issues

5.2.1 Current Population Survey Data on Job Duration

At irregular intervals, the Census Bureau has appended mobility supplements to the January Current Population Survey (CPS). The years in which it did so include 1951, 1963, 1966, 1968, 1973, 1978, 1981, 1983, 1987, and 1991.[1] These supplements contain information on how long workers have been continuously employed by their current employers. However, only the supplements since 1973 are available in machine-readable form.[2] Information on job duration is also available in pension and benefit supplements to the CPS in May 1979, 1983, and 1988 and in April 1993.

Others have used these data to analyze job duration. An important early paper is by Hall (1982), who used published tabulations from some of the January mobility supplements to compute contemporaneous retention rates. Hall found that, while any particular new job is unlikely to last a long time, a job that has already lasted 5 years has a substantial probability of lasting 20 years. He also finds that a substantial fraction of workers will be on a "lifetime" job (defined as lasting at least 20 years) at some point in their lives. Ureta (1992) used the January 1978, 1981, and 1983 mobility supplements to recompute retention rates using artificial cohorts rather than contemporaneous retention rates.

Two recent papers have examined changes in employment stability using data from the mobility and pension supplements to the CPS. Swinnerton and Wial (1995), using data from 1979–91, analyze job retention rates computed from artificial cohorts and conclude that there was a secular decline in job stability in the 1980s. In contrast, Diebold, Neumark, and Polsky (1994), using data from 1973–91 to compute retention rates for artificial cohorts, find that aggregate retention rates were fairly stable over the 1980s but retention rates declined for high school dropouts and for high school graduates relative to college graduates over this period.

In my analysis, I use data from the mobility supplements to the January 1973, 1978, 1981, 1983, 1987, and 1991 CPS and from the pension and benefit supplements to the May 1979 and April 1993 CPS.[3] These surveys cover 8 years over the 20-year period from 1973 to 1993. One feature that will distin-

---

1. There was also a mobility supplement to the February 1996 CPS, but it was not available at the time this analysis was performed.

2. Only summary tables are available for the 1951, 1963, 1966, and 1968 surveys.

3. There are two pension and benefit supplements that I did not use for different reasons. I did not use the May 1983 supplement because I already have data for 1983 in the January mobility supplement. I did not use the May 1988 supplement because it did not have data on duration for self-employed workers.

guish my analysis is that it uses more recent data (April 1993) than even the newest of the earlier work.

A question of comparability of the data over time arises because of substantial changes in the wording of the central question about job duration. The early January supplements (1951–81) asked workers what year they started working for their current employers (the early question). In later January supplements (1983–91) and in all of the pension and benefit supplements (1979–93), workers were asked how many years they had worked for their current employers (the later question). If the respondents were perfectly literal and accurate in their responses (a strong and unreasonable assumption), these two questions would yield identical information (up to the error due to the fact that calendar years may not be perfectly aligned with the count of years since the worker started with his or her current employer). But responses are not completely accurate, and this is best illustrated by the heaping of responses at round numbers. The empirical distribution function has spikes at 5-year intervals, and there are even larger spikes at 10-year intervals.[4] In the early question, the spikes occur at round calendar years (1960, 1965, etc.). Later, the spikes occur at round counts of years (5, 10, 15, etc.). The two questions may also evoke systematically different responses. Although I do not deal with the comparability problem directly, a preliminary comparison of quantiles of the 1979 distribution of job durations (based on the new question) with quantiles of the 1978 and 1981 distributions of job durations (based on the old question) does not show any systematic difference.

With the exception of jobs of less than one year, the data on job duration are collected in integer form (what year started or how many years employed). This raises questions of interpretation that are particularly serious in examining movements in quantiles. Interpreting the integer responses requires some arbitrary decisions. First consider the early question, which asked what year the worker started working for the current employer. For a survey conducted in January of year T_S, a response of year T_0 to the question of when the job was started was interpreted as a job duration of $D = \max(T_S - T_0, 1)$. Thus a duration of D years computed this way represents a "true" duration (D_T) that is (approximately) in the interval $D - 1 < D_T \leq D$. If there were a uniform distribution of job durations within intervals, D would overstate D_T by one-half year on average. Now consider the later question, which asked how many years the worker has been with the current employer. Call this response Y. If a worker has been with the employer less than one year, he or she is asked the number of months with the employer. I ignore the information on months for these workers and interpret the job duration as $D = \min(Y, 1)$. Thus all workers with durations less than or equal to one year are coded as having durations of one year. The interpretation of workers with reported durations of one year or

---

4. Ureta (1992) accounts for these spikes explicitly in her estimation procedure. Swinnerton and Wial (1995) work around these spikes in selecting intervals over which to compute retention rates.

longer depends on the rounding rules used by the respondents. One reasonable rule would be rounding to the nearest integer so that a response of Y would represent durations in the range from $Y - .5$ to $Y + .5$. Another reasonable rule would be for the respondent to perform the calculation of current year minus starting year and report the difference. This rule seems more reasonable for longer term jobs, and it yields a result equivalent to the procedure I use for the early question. The result is again to overstate job duration by one-half year on average.

There is no way to get direct evidence about how respondents interpret the later-style duration question. However, as noted above, a comparison of the distribution of responses to the 1979 question (later style) with the distributions of responses to the 1978 and 1981 questions (early style) does not show any systematic bias.[5] I proceed assuming that respondents answer the later question as if they report the difference in calendar years between the current date and the job start date. Thus a measured duration of D is interpreted throughout as representing a true duration in the interval $D - 1 < D_T \leq D$.

5.2.2   Interpolated Quantiles

Because job duration data are available in integer form with substantial fractions of the data at particular values, it is difficult to examine movements in quantiles. For example, the median job duration for a specific group of workers might be five years, and it might be the case that 10 percent of the sample reports job durations of five years. Ten years later, the distribution of job durations might have shifted to the right fairly substantially, but the median job duration might still be five years. The problem is that the cumulative distribution function for the integer data is a step function, and the movement "along" a step will not change the quantile unless the next step is reached.

As a result, I use *interpolated quantiles,* defined as

$$(1) \qquad \theta_\tau = (1 - \lambda)D_k + \lambda D_{k+1},$$

where θ_τ is the τth interpolated quantile of the distribution of job durations, D_k is the largest job duration such that $\Pr(D \leq D_k) < \tau$, and D_{k+1} is the smallest job duration such that $\Pr(D \leq D_{k+1}) > \tau$. In this case, the true τth quantile is D_{k+1}, and the τth interpolated quantile is simply a weighted average of the τth quantile and the next smaller observed value of job duration. The weight, λ, is,

$$(2) \qquad \lambda = (\tau - P_k)/(P_{k+1} - P_k),$$

where $P_k = \Pr(D < D_k)$ and $P_{k+1} = \Pr(D < D_{k+1})$. In effect, this calculation assumes that job durations are uniformly distributed within each interval. It is straightforward to use the delta method to compute sampling variances for

---

5. The lack of systematic bias can be examined in the tables and figures presented below. Of course, this evidence is indirect, and it is possible that there is bias but a temporary increase in the 1979 job durations is masking the bias.

these interpolated quantiles under the assumption that the value of the interpolated quantile does not move to a different interval. All quantile results shown below are interpolated quantiles as I define them here. I refer to them simply as quantiles.

5.2.3   Fractions of Workers in Short-Term and Long-Term Jobs

I also examine the fractions of workers who fall into different intervals in the job duration distribution. These are effectively selected points on the cumulative distribution function of job duration and the inverse function of the quantiles. I examine variation in the fractions of workers who report having been with their employers (1) no more than 1 year, (2) more than 10 years, and (3) more than 20 years. These points on the distribution give a clear picture of what has happened to the incidence of very short term jobs and long-term or near lifetime jobs. It is straightforward (indeed more straightforward than computation of the interpolated quantiles) to compute these fractions using the same interpretations of the job duration information that I discussed above.

5.2.4   Employment-Based and Population-Based
Distributions of Job Durations

Cyclical changes in the composition of the sample raise another important measurement issue. It is clear that workers with little seniority are more likely to lose their jobs in downturns (Abraham and Medoff 1984). Thus we would expect quantiles of the distribution of job durations to be countercyclical; tight labor markets will lead the distribution of job durations to lie to the left of the distribution in slack labor markets. Since secular rather than cyclical changes are of interest here, an alternative measure of the distribution that is relatively free of cyclical movements would be useful.

In the standard analysis, we use employed individuals in a given category (e.g., workers in a particular age range) as the base group when computing distributional measures. I call quantiles computed this way *employment-based quantiles,* and I call probabilities of having job duration in a particular category (up to 1 year, more than 10 years, and more than 20 years) *employment-based probabilities.* Cyclical fluctuations in employment add or subtract individuals from the base group for the employment-based measures. A reasonable alternative would be to use the entire population in a given category (e.g., individuals in a given age range) regardless of employment status to compute the measures assuming that those not employed have zero job duration. I call these *population-based measures.*

The employment-based and population-based measures clearly measure different distributions, but both have straightforward interpretations. For example, the median computed on an employment basis is the median duration of jobs in existence at a point in time. In contrast, the median computed on a population basis is the median length of time an individual has been employed (counting as zero the duration of those not employed). As such, the population-based median will be zero if less than half of the relevant group is not working. The contrast between the employment-based and the population-based probabilities is interpreted similarly. For example, the employment-based probability of being on a job more than 10 years is the fraction of workers who have been on their jobs more than 10 years. In contrast, the population-based probability of being on a job more than 10 years is the fraction of all individuals (employed or not) who have been on their jobs more than 10 years.[6]

The population-based measures yield information about the structure of jobs that a given group of individuals hold; the employment-based measures supply information about the structure of jobs that a given group of workers hold.

The population-based measures are not without problems of interpretation. While holding the base group of individuals fixed avoids cyclical problems of movement in and out of employment, secular changes in labor supply directly affect the population-based measures. If a group has increased its labor supply over time (e.g., as women have done), the population-based measures for that group are likely to show an increase. Similarly, if a group has decreased its labor supply over time (e.g., as older men have done), the population-based measures for that group are likely to show a decrease. Changes in population-based measures due to shifts in labor supply do not reflect changes in the underlying structure of jobs. In what follows, I present statistical results on both an employment and a population basis.

5.3   Changes in Interpolated Quantiles, 1973–93

Because the age distribution of the population has changed over time and because job durations are strongly related to age, it is important to control for age when examining the distribution of job durations over time. A visual representation of changes in the distribution of job durations over time is given in figure 5.1. This figure contains plots of four weighted (by CPS sampling weights) interpolated quantiles (.25, .5, .75, .9) of the employment-based tenure distribution by year overall and broken down by sex and four 10-year age categories. This and succeeding figures do not show sampling errors. Sampling errors for these interpolated quantiles, calculated using the delta method, are generally about 0.15 years. Thus statistical significance requires differences across calendar years of about 0.4 years.

Not surprisingly, all four employment-based quantiles in figure 5.1 rise systematically with age. The plots for males look quite flat, with perhaps a slight decline for the upper quantiles of the oldest age category. The plots for females show some upward movement over time. The combined plots (no distinction by sex) look very flat. Analogous plots of population-based quantiles are con-

6. Note that the population-based fraction of individuals on a job less than or equal to one year includes those not employed in both the numerator and the denominator. This is clear from the coding of job durations of those not employed as zero. The resulting probability has a natural interpretation.

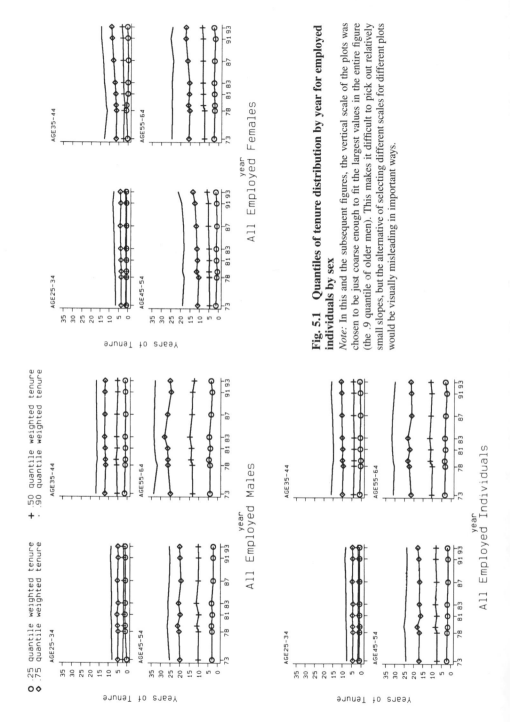

Fig. 5.1 Quantiles of tenure distribution by year for employed individuals by sex

Note: In this and the subsequent figures, the vertical scale of the plots was chosen to be just coarse enough to fit the largest values in the entire figure (the .9 quantile of older men). This makes it difficult to pick out relatively small slopes, but the alternative of selecting different scales for different plots would be visually misleading in important ways.

tained in figure 5.2. These look much like the employment-based quantiles in figure 5.1 with these exceptions: (1) there is fairly substantial upward movement in the population-based quantiles for women, and (2) there is somewhat more decline in the quantiles for older males. These changes largely represent systematic changes in labor force participation. The decrease in the frequency with which women withdraw from the labor force is doubtless an important factor in their increased job duration. The move toward earlier retirement underlies an important part of the decline in population-based measures of job duration among men aged 55–64.

Appendix tables 5A.1 through 5A.4 contain the raw data underlying the median and .9 quantiles for figures 5.1 and 5.2. Table 5A.1, which contains employment-based medians, also includes tabulations of medians by sex and age category based on the January mobility supplements for 1951, 1963, 1966, and 1968.[7] Aside from the fact that age-adjusted medians in 1951 were much lower than later, probably because many workers had to "restart" after returning from World War II, long-term trends using this longer time series are difficult to discern.

Figures 5.3, 5.4, and 5.5 contain plots of the four employment-based quantiles broken down by age and education. Figure 5.3 makes no distinction between sexes. It shows a substantial decline in job duration for workers in the lowest educational category (less than 12 years). Not much change is evident in the overall quantiles in the higher educational categories. Figure 5.4 replicates these plots for males. The substantial changes here are a decline in job duration for the least educated men and some decline for the oldest highly educated men (16 years or more). Figure 5.5 replicates these plots for females. It is interesting that there does not seem to be much decline in job duration for the least educated women. The plots also suggest that there is a fairly systematic increase in job duration for women in the three higher educational categories. This is a consequence of the decreased frequency with which women withdraw from the labor force, and it suggests that there is an increased incidence of long-term stable employment for women.

Figures 5.6, 5.7, and 5.8 replicate these plots using population-based quantiles. Here the results are more striking. There is a sharp drop in the population-based quantiles for the least educated individuals. This is attributable to a decline in job duration among men (fig. 5.7). Thus the well-known deterioration in labor market conditions for poorly educated men resulted not only in shorter jobs but also in a scarcity of jobs themselves. The quantiles of the employment-based job duration distributions for more highly educated men look fairly stable. There is also a sharp increase in job duration for women in the top three educational categories (fig. 5.8). Once again, this largely reflects the decreased frequency with which women withdraw from the labor force.

In order to provide a clearer statistical summary of changes over time in the

---

7. The sources for these published tabulations are Department of Labor (1963, 1967, 1969).

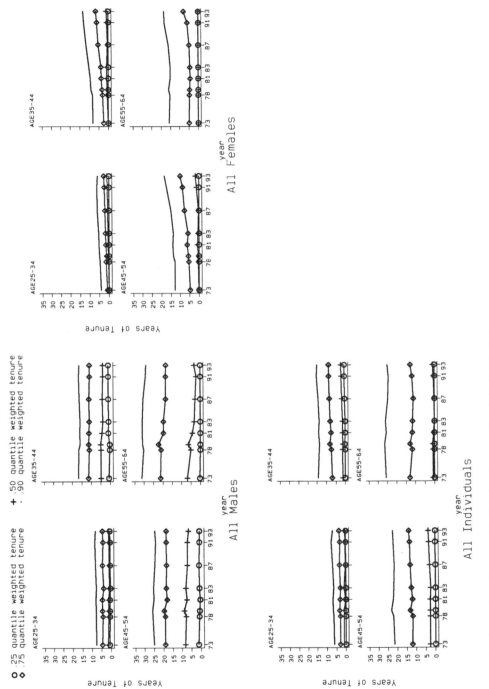

Fig. 5.2 Quantiles of tenure distribution by year for all individuals by sex

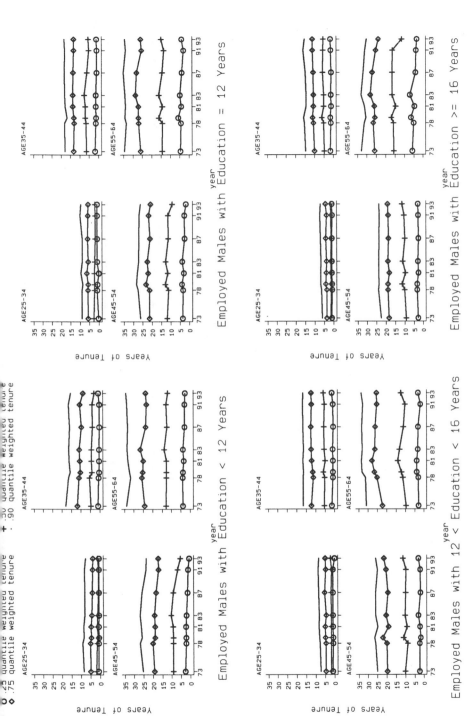

Fig. 5.3 Quantiles of tenure distribution by year for all employed individuals by education

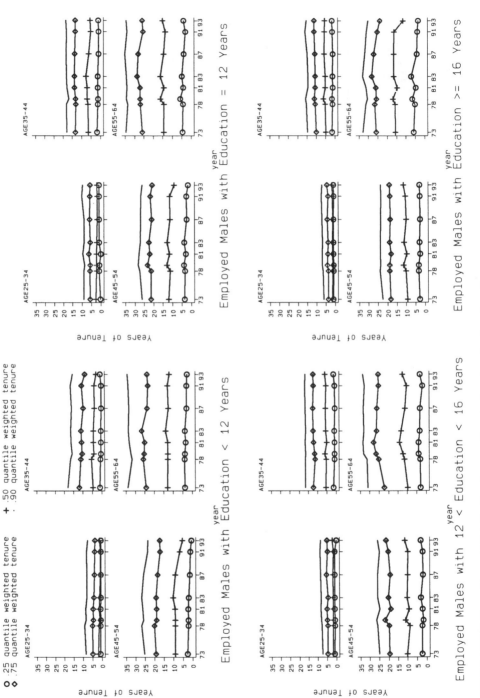

Fig. 5.1 Quantiles of tenure distribution by year for employed males by education

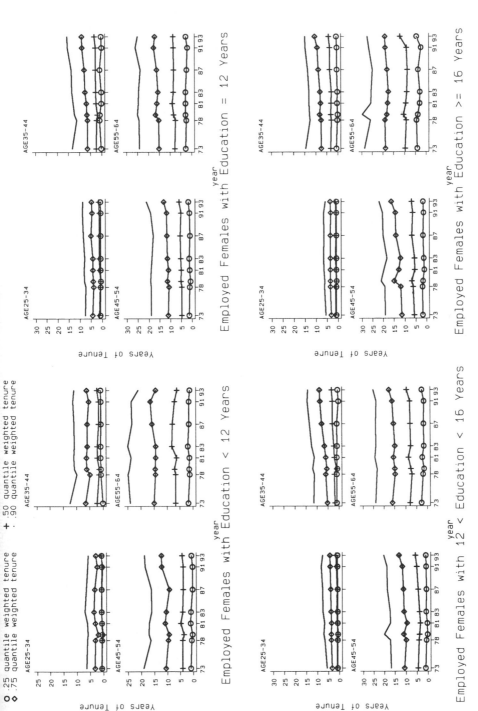

Fig. 5.5 Quantiles of tenure distribution by year for employed females by education

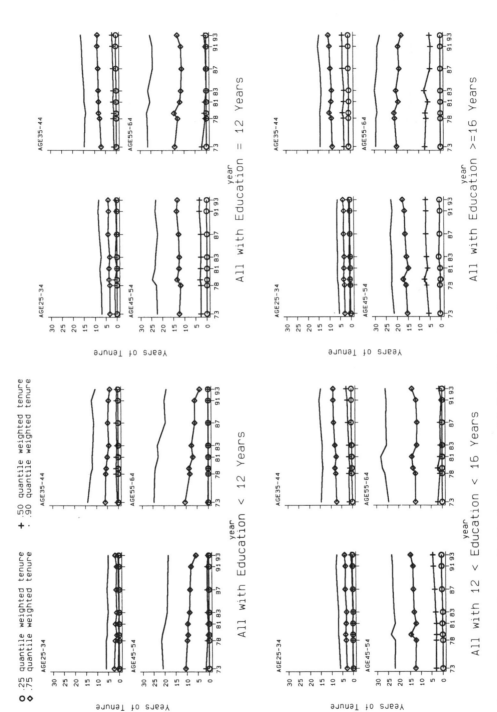

Fig. 5.6 Quantiles of tenure distribution by year for all individuals by education

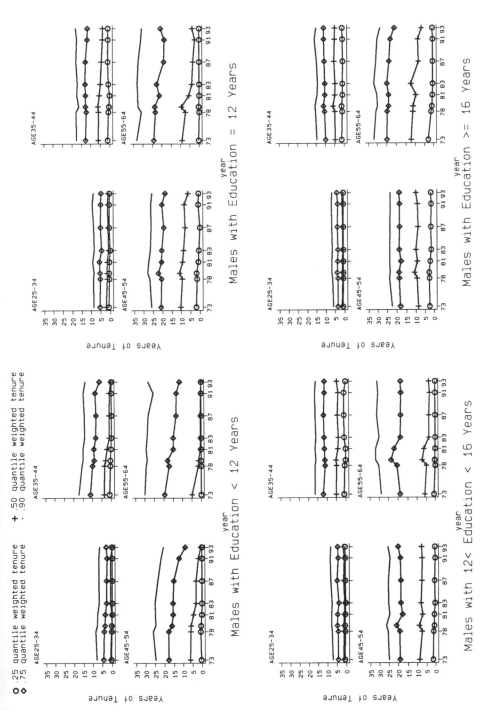

Fig. 5.7 Quantiles of tenure distribution by year for all males by education

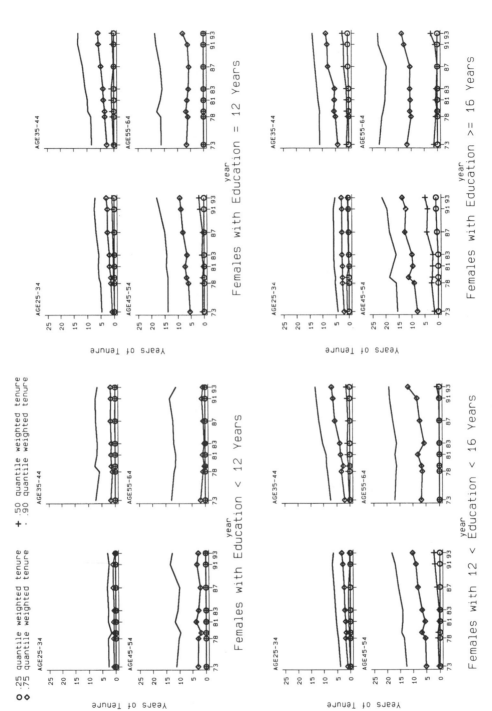

Fig. 5.8 Quantiles of tenure distribution by year for all females by education

quantiles of the distribution of job tenures, tables 5.1, 5.2, and 5.3 contain cell-based regressions of the employment-based quantiles. I compute weighted employment-based medians for cells defined by nine five-year age categories (from age 21 through age 65), four educational categories (less than 12 years, 12 years, between 12 and 16 years, and 16 years or more), and eight calendar years. I do this separately for three samples (employed individuals, employed males, and employed females). The procedure is to specify a linear model that determines the cell quantiles as a function of a set of observable characteristics of the cells.[8] Such a model for the τth quantile of observations in cell j would be

$$(3) \qquad \theta_{\tau j} = X_j \beta + \varepsilon_{\tau j},$$

where $\theta_{\tau j}$ is the τth quantile of observations in cell j, X_j is a vector of observable characteristics for cell j, β is a vector of parameters, and $\varepsilon_{\tau j}$ is an unobserved component. This parameters of this model can be estimated using weighted least squares. One choice of weights is to use the estimated variances of cell quantiles as weights. Another choice is simply to use the number of observations in each cell as weights. Chamberlain (1994) suggests that it may be better to use the cell sizes as weights if it is possible that the model is misspecified. Since I am maintaining the specification for the cell quantiles in equation (3), I weight by cell size.

The X_j vector in tables 5.1 and 5.2 contains eight dummy variables for the age categories, three dummy variables for the educational categories, and one of two specifications of calendar year. One specification (in the odd-numbered columns) contains a complete set of eight calendar year dummy variables (and hence no constant). The other (in the even-numbered columns) contains a linear time trend (calendar year itself) and a constant. I do not present the estimates of the age effects. Not surprisingly, they have a great deal of explanatory power, with older workers having longer job durations. I focus here on the year effects.

In most cases, it is not possible to reject the single variable representation of year effects in the form of a time trend against the unconstrained dummy variable model. As such, most of the subsequent discussion will focus on models with time trends. It is also worth noting that variation in the quantiles across cells is fairly well explained by the main effects specifications used in that the R^2 of these regressions are quite large (over .95).

The estimates in columns (1) and (2) of table 5.1 show no significant relationship between employment-based median job duration and calendar year, either in the unconstrained dummy variable specification or with a single time trend. The estimates in columns (3) and (4) show a marginally significant small negative time trend in median job duration for males only. In contrast, the estimates in columns (5) and (6) show a larger positive time trend in median job duration for females only. These point estimates suggest an average overall

---

8. Chamberlain (1994) developed this technique for estimating quantiles.

Table 5.1   **Median Regression of Job Duration for Employed Individuals Aged 21–64**

	All		Males		Females	
Variable	(1)	(2)	(3)	(4)	(5)	(6)
Constant		.450		2.63		−2.12
		(.537)		(.794)		(.460)
Year		.00240		−.0179		.0332
		(.00639)		(.00941)		(.0055)
1973	.689		1.16		.502	
	(.156)		(.230)		(.131)	
1978	.539		1.11		.342	
	(.150)		(.223)		(.123)	
1979	.731		1.55		.414	
	(.189)		(.279)		(.157)	
1981	.585		1.13		.541	
	(.146)		(.219)		(.118)	
1983	.761		1.52		.639	
	(.151)		(.226)		(.122)	
1987	.633		1.06		.794	
	(.606)		(.226)		(.122)	
1991	.606		.831		.808	
	(.154)		(.232)		(.125)	
1993	.829		.870		1.26	
	(.192)		(.289)		(.155)	
Ed < 12	−.732	−.732	−1.69	−1.70	−.852	−1.54
	(.111)	(.111)	(.159)	(.161)	(.0972)	(.266)
12 < Ed < 16	−.230	−.229	−.863	−.861	−.211	−.649
	(.100)	(.100)	(.150)	(.152)	(.0816)	(.238)
Ed ≥ 16	.570	.571	−.621	−.614	.515	.514
	(.0999)	(.0997)	(.145)	(.147)	(.0851)	(.0864)
p-Value equality of year effects	.646		.0233		<.00005	
p-Value year effects equal trend		.548		.0492		.0273
No. of cells	288	288	288	288	288	288
No. of observations	378,890	378,890	214,210	214,210	164,680	164,680
R^2	.970	.969	.964	.963	.959	.957

Notes: Numbers in parentheses are standard errors. The dependent variable is computed as cell quantile for nine age categories, four educational categories, two sex categories (in col. 3–6), and eight years. Only observations with nonzero quantiles (employed) are included. All observations are weighted by the cell size.

decrease over the 20-year period studied of about 0.35 years in the median for men and an average overall increase of about 0.7 years in the median for women over the same period.

    The estimates in table 5.2 for the .9 quantile of the employment-based distribution of job durations show a similar pattern. There is no significant relationship between year and the .9 quantile of job duration when no sex distinction is made, and there is actually a small *increase* on average in the .9 quantile for

Table 5.2 .9 Quantile Regression of Job Duration for Employed Individuals Aged 21–64

	All		Males		Females	
Variable	(1)	(2)	(3)	(4)	(5)	(6)
Constant		3.03		2.88		−2.76
		(.587)		(.549)		(1.02)
Year		.00839		.0138		.0734
		(.00698)		(.00651)		(.0122)
1973	3.66		3.83		3.19	
	(.172)		(.162)		(.287)	
1978	3.63		3.98		2.62	
	(.164)		(.157)		(.270)	
1979	3.63		3.93		3.12	
	(.208)		(.197)		(.344)	
1981	3.80		4.08		3.15	
	(.160)		(.154)		(.260)	
1983	3.70		4.00		3.16	
	(.165)		(.159)		(.268)	
1987	3.71		4.07		3.35	
	(.165)		(.159)		(.267)	
1991	3.85		4.17		4.21	
	(.169)		(.164)		(.274)	
1993	3.76		4.03		4.40	
	(.211)		(.204)		(.341)	
Ed < 12	−1.13	−1.13	−1.06	−1.06	−1.75	−1.74
	(.122)	(.121)	(.112)	(.111)	(.213)	(.219)
12 < Ed < 16	−.965	−.966	−1.16	−1.16	−.763	−.763
	(.110)	(.109)	(.106)	(.105)	(.179)	(.183)
Ed ≥ 16	−2.07	−2.07	−2.88	−2.88	−.564	.560
	(.110)	(.109)	(.102)	(.102)	(.187)	(.191)
p-Value equality of year effects	.873		.486		<.00005	
p-Value year effects equal trend		.945		.914		.0043
No. of cells	288	288	288	288	288	288
No. of observations	378,890	378,890	214,210	214,210	164,680	164,680
R^2	.995	.995	.996	.996	.974	.972

Notes: Numbers in parentheses are standard errors. The dependent variable is computed as cell quantiles for nine age categories, four educational categories, two sex categories (in col. 3–6), and eight years. Only observations with nonzero quantiles (employed) are included. All observations are weighted by the cell size.

males (about 0.3 years over the 20-year period). The rate of increase in the .9 quantile of job duration for females (about 1.5 years over the 20-year period) is substantially larger than the rate of increase in the women's median.

Important differences in time trends of job duration by educational category were apparent in the figures, particularly for men, and the specification in the first two tables does not allow for these differences. In order to address this problem directly, I reestimated the models with time trends in tables 5.1 and 5.2 with the time trend interacted with the four educational categories. Table 5.3 contains estimates of the relevant parameters. These results are quite clear-cut, and they support and sharpen the visual impression from the figures. Workers with less than 12 years of education suffered a decline in median job duration of over 0.5 years on average over the 20-year period. This seems almost entirely accounted for by less educated males, who suffered a decline in median job duration of almost one full year on average over this period. Men with less than 12 years of education and men with exactly 12 years of education shared this decline. Among workers with more than a high school education, job duration increased on average. There was no significant increase in medians for more educated males (more than 12 years) on average, but the .9 quantile of the job duration distribution did increase significantly for more educated men (about 0.5 years over the 20-year period). In contrast, both quantiles increased substantially for women with at least a high school education. Depending on education level, the increase in the medians over the 20-year period range from about 0.5 years to about 1 year. The increase in the .9 quantiles for women over this period was even larger, ranging from 1.5 years to over 2 years.

Tables 5.4, 5.5, and 5.6 repeat the entire cell quantile regression analysis using population-based quantiles. Recall that these quantiles ought to be less affected by cyclical fluctuations but more affected by secular changes in labor supply. The cell quantile regression model is particularly well suited for this analysis because it allows a natural treatment of those not employed, all of whom are coded as having zero job duration. Effectively, these are censored observations, and any cell for which the particular quantile of the job duration distribution being studied is zero (i.e., is represented by a nonemployed individual) contains no information about the process that generates the cell quantiles.[9]

The results for the population-based quantiles are roughly similar to those for the employment-based quantiles, but there are some differences. Most striking is the substantial decline in the population-based median for males (about 1.6 years over the 20-year period), shown in column (4) of table 5.4. There is also a larger increase in the population-based .9 quantile for females (about 2.5 years over the 20-year period), shown in column (6) of table 5.5. The sources of these substantial trends become clearer with separate year effects by education in table 5.6. The large decrease in the median for males seems to be due almost entirely to individuals with at most a high school education. These individuals have median durations that declined by 2.2 to 3.2 years over the 20-year period. There was no significant change in median job duration for males with more than a high school education. The median job duration for

---

9. Chamberlain (1994) shows that it is appropriate to estimate the cell quantile regression model using only observations for which the cell quantile is not censored, and I follow this procedure.

Table 5.3 Quantile Regression of Job Duration for Employed Individuals Aged 21–64 (year by education interaction)

	All		Males		Females	
Variable	Median (1)	.9 Quantile (2)	Median (3)	.9 Quantile (4)	Median (5)	.9 Quantile (6)
Constant	.902 (.854)	2.36 (.911)	4.70 (1.30)	2.75 (.904)	-1.70 (.697)	-3.89 (1.52)
Ed < 12	1.35 (1.52)	5.06 (1.63)	-1.60 (2.19)	1.89 (1.52)	.852 (1.36)	8.12 (2.98)
12 < Ed < 16	-2.30 (1.40)	-2.19 (1.49)	-5.06 (2.10)	-1.87 (1.45)	-2.54 (1.17)	-2.88 (2.57)
Ed ≥ 16	-.900 (1.40)	-2.45 (1.49)	-5.40 (2.04)	-3.94 (1.42)	-.117 (1.23)	.401 (2.68)
(Ed < 12)*Year	-.0288 (.0156)	-.0595 (.0166)	-.0446 (.0218)	-.0210 (.0151)	.0072 (.0144)	-.0337 (.0314)
(Ed = 12)*Year	-.0029 (.103)	.0167 (.109)	-.0428 (.0157)	.0155 (.0109)	.0283 (.0084)	.0873 (.0183)
(12 < Ed < 16)*Year	.0219 (.0133)	.0312 (.0142)	.0079 (.0198)	.0239 (.0137)	.0560 (.0112)	.112 (.0246)
(Ed ≥ 16)*Year	.0147 (.0133)	.0212 (.0142)	.0149 (.0189)	.0283 (.0131)	.0359 (.0120)	.0756 (.0262)
p-Value equality of year effects	.0656	.0002	.0352	.0722	.0529	.0025
No. of cells	288	288	288	288	288	288
No. of observations	378,890	378,890	214,210	214,210	164,680	164,680
R^2	.970	.995	.964	.996	.958	.974

Notes: Numbers in parentheses are standard errors. The dependent variable is computed as cell quantile for nine age categories, four educational categories, two sex categories (in cols. 3–6), and eight years. Only observations with nonzero quantiles (employed) are included. All observations are weighted by the cell size. All specifications include eight dummy variables for age categories.

Table 5.4 Median Regression of Job Duration for All Individuals Aged 21–64

Variable	All		Males		Females	
	(1)	(2)	(3)	(4)	(5)	(6)
Constant		−1.32	2.02	7.84	−.0393	−2.90
		(.851)	(.325)	(1.13)	(.179)	(.604)
Year		.0201		−.0819		.0387
		(.0102)		(.0134)		(.0073)
1973	.337		1.40		.206	
	(.241)		(.314)		(.155)	
1978	.259		1.92		.174	
	(.234)		(.396)		(.195)	
1979	.352		1.13		.212	
	(.295)		(.305)		(.151)	
1981	.174		.722		.223	
	(.232)		(.312)		(.155)	
1983	.158		.699		.421	
	(.239)		(.317)		(.155)	
1987	.409		.522		.643	
	(.239)		(.323)		(.158)	
1991	.589		.431		.829	
	(.246)		(.402)		(.196)	
1993	.792					
	(.302)					
Ed < 12	−1.28	−1.26	−2.82	−2.81	−.721	−.719
	(.174)	(.174)	(.225)	(.225)	(.444)	(.437)
12 < Ed < 16	.264	.263	−.506	−.504	.177	.176
	(.159)	(.159)	(.214)	(.215)	(.100)	(.0988)
Ed ≥ 16	1.76	1.76	.553	.552	.811	.811
	(.165)	(.165)	(.214)	(.214)	(.108)	(.107)
p-Value equality of year effects	.465		<.00005		<.00005	
p-Value year effects equal trend		.605		.269		.624
No. of cells	262	262	282	282	189	189
No. of observations	502,600	502,600	253,860	253,860	204,050	204,050
R^2	.689	.680	.849	.845	.454	.447

Notes: Numbers in parentheses are standard errors. The dependent variable is computed as cell quantiles for nine age categories, four educational categories, two sex categories (in cols. [3]–[6]), and eight years. Only observations with nonzero quantiles (employed) are included. All observations are weighted by the cell size.

Table 5.5   .9 Quantile Regression of Job Duration for All Individuals Aged 21–64

Variable	All (1)	All (2)	Males (3)	Males (4)	Females (5)	Females (6)
Constant		3.98		6.11		−7.89
		(.985)		(.874)		(1.12)
Year		−.0117		−.0298		.126
		(.0117)		(.0104)		(.0134)
1973	3.17		3.90		1.69	
	(.284)		(.255)		(.318)	
1978	3.13		3.82		1.70	
	(.274)		(.246)		(.309)	
1979	3.31		3.74		2.18	
	(.344)		(.311)		(.384)	
1981	3.01		3.78		2.25	
	(.267)		(.239)		(.300)	
1983	2.80		3.50		2.29	
	(.273)		(.245)		(.308)	
1987	2.77		3.53		2.91	
	(.278)		(.249)		(.313)	
1991	3.05		3.44		3.85	
	(.284)		(.254)		(.320)	
1993	3.08		3.28		3.99	
	(.352)		(.315)		(.397)	
Ed < 12	−2.80	−2.80	−2.29	−2.29	−3.71	−3.70
	(.188)	(.188)	(.171)	(.170)	(.210)	(.211)
12 < Ed < 16	−.484	−.481	−1.11	−1.11	−.0953	−.0946
	(.188)	(.187)	(.169)	(.168)	(.211)	(.212)
Ed ≥ 16	−.710	−.710	−2.45	−2.45	1.08	1.08
	(.195)	(.195)	(.169)	(.167)	(.232)	(.233)
p-Value equality of year effects	.595		.229		<.00005	
p-Value year effects equal trend		.605		.972		.173
No. of cells	288	288	288	288	288	288
No. of observations	550,940	550,940	260,360	260,360	290,580	290,580
R^2	.981	.981	.990	.989	.941	.939

Notes: Numbers in parentheses are standard errors. The dependent variable is computed as cell quantiles for nine age categories, four educational categories, two sex categories (in cols. [3]–[6]), and eight years. Only observations with nonzero quantiles (employed) are included. All observations are weighted by the cell size.

Table 5.6   Quantile Regression of Job Duration for All Individuals Aged 21–64 (year by education interaction)

	All		Males		Females	
Variable	Median (1)	.9 Quantile (2)	Median (3)	.9 Quantile (4)	Median (5)	.9 Quantile (6)
Constant	-1.12	1.47	10.7	4.70	-1.98	-10.3
	(1.35)	(1.47)	(1.83)	(1.36)	(.855)	(1.67)
Ed < 12	.164	11.1	.835	9.33	1.46	7.13
	(2.40)	(2.41)	(2.99)	(2.16)	(7.52)	(2.84)
12 < Ed < 16	-.682	-1.83	-8.14	-3.25	-.644	-1.51
	(2.22)	(2.44)	(2.92)	(2.18)	(1.44)	(2.90)
Ed ≥ 16	.883	-1.81	-7.66	-5.42	-2.31	3.53
	(2.31)	(2.56)	(2.93)	(2.18)	(1.53)	(3.21)
(Ed < 12)*Year	-.0041	-.151	-.161	-.155	.0033	.0225
	(.0246)	(.0236)	(.0292)	(.0206)	(.0856)	(.0282)
(Ed = 12)*Year	.0178	.0190	-.116	-.0124	.0277	.155
	(.0162)	(.0176)	(.0219)	(.0163)	(.0103)	(.0201)
(12 < Ed < 16)*Year	.0291	.0348	-.0238	.0131	.0376	.172
	(.0212)	(.0234)	(.0274)	(.0204)	(.0138)	(.0283)
(Ed ≥ 16)*Year	.0282	.0318	-.0169	.0231	.0650	.126
	(.0225)	(.0251)	(.0274)	(.0204)	(.0151)	(.0326)
p-Value equality of year effects	.860	<.0001	.0004	<.0001	.0058	.0005
No. of cells	262	288	282	288	189	288
No. of observations	502,600	550,940	253,860	260,360	204,050	290,580
R²	.681	.984	.855	.991	.460	.943

Notes: Numbers in parentheses are standard errors. The dependent variable is computed as cell quantile for nine age categories, four educational categories, two sex categories (in cols. [3]–[6]), and eight years. Only observations with nonzero quantiles (employed) are included. All observations are weighted by the cell size. All specifications include eight dummy variables for age categories.

women increases monotonically with educational category, rising from zero for women with less than a high school education to an increase of about 1.3 years over the 20-year period for women with at least 16 years of education. The large increase in the .9 quantile for women was shared across all but the lowest educational category.

Overall, the results in this section show a clear pattern. There has not been much change in the quantiles of the overall distribution of job durations that I studied. However, important changes have taken place in the distribution of job durations for particular subgroups. There are two striking changes: (1) the quantiles of the job duration distribution for the least educated workers, and especially the least educated men, have declined substantially, and (2) the quantiles of the job duration distribution for women, and especially women with more education, have increased substantially.

5.4   Changes in Probabilities of Short-Term and Long-Term Jobs, 1973–93

It is useful to examine specific points of the cumulative distribution function of job durations in order to determine if the same changes found in the quantiles can be measured there. In particular, I examine (1) the fraction of job durations less than or equal to 1 year, (2) the fraction of job durations greater than 10 years, and (3) the fraction of job durations greater than 20 years. Based on the results reported above, it is reasonable to expect that the fraction of short-term jobs (up to 1 year) has grown for the least educated workers (especially for the least educated males) and declined among females (especially those with more than a high school education). Analogously, the fraction of long-term jobs (more than 10 years and more than 20 years) has declined among the least educated male workers and increased among more highly educated females. Given the lack of a pattern in the non-sex-specific quantiles over time, no clear change in the aggregate fractions in these categories is expected.

5.4.1   Employment-Based Probabilities

Appendix tables 5A.5, 5A.6, and 5A.7 present information on the employment-based fraction of workers with job durations in the specified intervals broken down by crude age category, sex, and year. It is difficult to pick out clear trends in these data other than to note that employed females have become less likely to have been in their jobs a short time and have become more likely to have been in their jobs for a substantial length of time.

These tables also show that the probability of being in a new job and the probability of having been on the job for a substantial length of time increase with age. This is so because it is virtually impossible for very young workers to have been on their job for more than 10 or 20 years. While the logit analysis that follows includes detailed controls for age, it makes sense to (1) estimate the logit model of the probability of job duration of more than 10 years on the sample of workers who are at least 35 years old and (2) estimate the logit model of the probability of job duration of more than 20 years on the sample of workers who are at least 45 years old.

Tables 5.7, 5.8, and 5.9 contain estimates of logit models of the employment-based probabilities. The aim of this analysis is to provide summary measures of time trends in the probabilities and to examine variation in these trends across educational categories.

Table 5.7 contains estimates of logit models of the employment-based probability that a worker has been on his or her job no more than one year. The estimates in the odd-numbered columns are for models that contain a linear time trend (calendar year), eight dummy variables for age categories, four dummy variables for educational categories, and a constant. The estimates in the even-numbered columns are for models that include the same variables but allow for a separate time trend for each of the four educational categories. When no distinction is made by sex, there is a slight but significant upward trend in the probability that a job is no more than one year old. Over the 20-year period, the employment-based probability that a job is no more than one year old is predicted to have increased by about 1.3 percentage points.[10] This aggregate figure masks a larger increase for men over the 20-year period of about 3 percentage points and a small decrease for women over the 20-year period of about 1.6 percentage points.

With separate time trends by educational category, a much sharper picture emerges. The hypothesis that the time trends are the same across educational categories can be rejected in all cases. The results suggest that the overall increase in the probability of short durations is due entirely to the two lowest educational categories. The probability of a worker with less than a high school education being in a short-term job is predicted to be about 6 percentage points higher in 1993 than in 1973. This is a substantial change given that the overall probability of being in a short-term job is about .25.

An analysis of the trends separately for men and women suggests that this result is driven by a large increase in the short-term job probability for men with no more than a high school education. Men with less than a high school education have a probability of being in a short-term job that is predicted to be about 8.5 percentage points higher in 1993 than in 1973. The change is somewhat smaller but still quite substantial for men with exactly a high school education (an increase of 5 percentage points).

There has been some decrease in the short-term job probability in the higher

10. The logit coefficient of 0.0034 must be multiplied by some estimate of $p(1 - p)$ when one is computing the derivative of the probability with respect to year. A reasonable mean estimate of $p(1 - p)$ is 0.2. Thus, over the 20-year period, the probability that a worker was in his or her job for no more than one year is predicted to have increased by about 1.4 percentage points ($0.0034 \times 0.2 \times 20 \times 100$). The value of 0.2 for $p(1 - p)$ is used in what follows to adjust the logit coefficient for the employment-based models. A cautionary note is that the underlying probabilities (and hence the appropriate $p(1 - p)$) vary, and the percentage point changes mentioned in the text are, of necessity, approximations.

Table 5.7   **Logit Analysis of Probability of Job Duration One Year or Less for Employed Individuals Aged 21–64 (year by education interaction)**

	All		Males		Females	
Variable	(1)	(2)	(3)	(4)	(5)	(6)
Constant	-2.66	-2.91	-3.16	-3.56	-1.90	-2.22
	(.0587)	(.0910)	(.0806)	(.130)	(.0864)	(.128)
Ed < 12	.293	-.427	.340	-.339	.323	-.0849
	(.0120)	(.155)	(.0163)	(.209)	(.0183)	(.238)
12 < Ed < 16	.0686	1.07	.100	1.40	.0668	1.11
	(.0104)	(.138)	(.0147)	(.194)	(.0147)	(.198)
Ed ≥ 16	.0068	.613	.0904	1.03	-.0176	.596
	(.0107)	(.143)	(.0148)	(.196)	(.0156)	(.212)
Year	.0034		.0080		-.0043	
	(.0006)		(.00087)		(.0009)	
(Ed < 12)*Year		.0153		.0212		.0046
		(.0016)		(.0020)		(.0025)
(Ed = 12)*Year		.0065		.0128		-.0004
		(.0010)		(.0015)		(.0015)
(12 < Ed < 16)*Year		-.0053		-.0026		-.0127
		(.0013)		(.0017)		(.0018)
(Ed ≥ 16)*Year		-.0006		.0016		-.0077
		(.0013)		(.0018)		(.0020)
p-Value equality of time trends	<.0001		<.0001		<.0001	
No. of observations	378,892	378,892	214,211	214,211	164,681	164,681
Log L	-194,019.8	-193,957.1	-102,785.3	-102,734.3	-90,374.8	-90,352.9

Notes: Numbers in parentheses are asymptotic standard errors. The dependent variable is a dummy variable equaling one if job duration is less than or equal to one year. All models include controls for education (three dummy variables for four categories) and age (eight dummy variables for nine categories). The analysis is weighted using CPS sampling weights. The included age range is 21–64.

educational categories. This is driven by a decrease in this probability for highly educated women of about 4 percentage points between 1973 and 1993. There was no significant change in the short-term job probability for highly educated men over this period.

Tables 5.8 and 5.9 contain estimates of logit models of the employment-based long-term employment probabilities (job durations greater than 10 or 20 years).[11] These tables show patterns generally consistent with the results for the short-term job probabilities in table 5.7.[12]

Consider first the estimates for the 10-year probabilities in table 5.8. There is no significant overall trend, but there has been a statistically significant small decrease in this probability for men (about 2.8 percentage points over the 20-year period) and a larger significant increase for women (about 6.5 percentage points over the 20-year period). As before, the change for men is concentrated in the lower educational categories, where there has been a substantial decline in the 10-year probability of about 5 percentage points over the 20-year period. And, aside from the lowest educational category, there has been an even more substantial increase in the 10-year probability for women over time (about 8 percentage points over the 20-year period).

Now consider the estimates for the 20-year probabilities in table 5.9. There is a small significant overall decrease in this probability, which once again, is driven by a decrease in the probability for males and partially offset by an increase in the probability of long-term employment for females. The increase for females (about 3 percentage points over the 20-year period) is particularly noteworthy given the fact that the sample for this analysis consists of women from less recent cohorts.

The breakdown by educational category in the 20-year probabilities is as before. The least educated men have 20-year probabilities that have declined substantially between 1973 and 1993 (by about 8 percentage points). The 20-year probabilities for highly educated women increased over the same period (by about 5 percentage points).[13]

5.4.2   Population-Based Probabilities

Appendix tables 5A.8, 5A.9, and 5A.10 contain population-based sample fractions in the various duration categories broken down by age, sex, and year. The short-term job fractions in table 5A.8 show a substantial (though nonmonotonic) increase over time for men, particularly in the older age categories.[14]

---

11. Recall that the sample for the 10-year probability is restricted to workers aged 35–64 and that the sample for the 20-year probability is restricted to workers aged 45–64.

12. Of course, it does not have to be the case that movements in the probability that jobs last less than one year will be reflected in concomitant movements in the probabilities of long-term job durations.

13. The latter percentage change is computed using a $p(1 - p)$ value of 0.11 rather than the 0.2 applied to all earlier estimates. This lower value is used because the fraction of females who report job durations of more than 20 years is much smaller. See table 5A.7.

14. At least part of this reflects earlier retirement behavior by men.

Table 5.8 Logit Analysis of Probability of Job Duration More Than 10 Years for Employed Individuals Aged 35–64 (year by education interaction)

	All		Males		Females	
Variable	(1)	(2)	(3)	(4)	(5)	(6)
Constant	.383	.364	1.15	1.48	-1.35	-1.39
	(.0611)	(.0967)	(.0792)	(.132)	(.101)	(.149)
Ed < 12	-.178	.658	-.303	-.0159	-.240	.930
	(.0125)	(.162)	(.0162)	(.209)	(.0212)	(.276)
12 < Ed < 16	-.0570	-.642	-.136	-1.06	-.0721	-.984
	(.0127)	(.167)	(.0169)	(.219)	(.0201)	(.275)
Ed ≥ 16	.111	-.0487	-.133	-.972	.237	.271
	(.0120)	(.159)	(.0154)	(.203)	(.0201)	(.275)
Year	-.0012		-.0069		.0161	
	(.0007)		(.0009)		(.0012)	
(Ed < 12)*Year		-.0112		-.0144		.0023
		(.0016)		(.0020)		(.0028)
(Ed = 12)*Year		.0001		-.0107		.0166
		(.0011)		(.0016)		(.0018)
(12 < Ed < 16)*Year		.0059		.00002		.0272
		(.0016)		(.0021)		(.0027)
(Ed ≥ 16) * Year		.0009		-.0008		.0162
		(.0015)		(.0018)		(.0027)
p-Value equality of time trends		<.0001		<.0001		<.0001
No. of observations	218,491	218,491	125,300	125,300	93,191	93,191
log L	-141,041.5	-141,011.1	-82,990.6	-82,969.0	-54,383.7	-54,363.2

Notes: Numbers in parentheses are asymptotic standard errors. The dependent variable is a dummy variable equaling one if job duration is more than 10 years. All models include controls for education (three dummy variables for four categories) and age (five dummy variables for six categories). The analysis is weighted using CPS sampling weights. The included age range is 35–64.

Table 5.9   Logit Analysis of Probability of Job Duration More than 20 Years for Employed Individuals Aged 45–64 (year by education interacton)

Variable	All		Males		Females	
	(1)	(2)	(3)	(4)	(5)	(6)
Constant	-.0733	-.0732	.407	.551	-1.96	-1.92
	(.0900)	(.132)	(.109)	(.178)	(.177)	(.263)
Ed < 12	-.144	.830	-.312	.456	-.213	1.17
	(.0176)	(.231)	(.0211)	(.277)	(.0360)	(.472)
12 < Ed < 16	-.0558	-.819	-.143	-1.45	-.0891	-.701
	(.0199)	(.258)	(.0243)	(.314)	(.0379)	(.507)
Ed ≥ 16	.103	-.345	-.194	-.682	.296	-.794
	(.0185)	(.242)	(.0221)	(.290)	(.0365)	(.490)
Year	-.0079		-.0082		.0074	
	(.0011)		(.0013)		(.0021)	
(Ed < 12)*Year		-.0199		-.0195		-.0099
		(.0022)		(.0026)		(.0048)
(Ed = 12)*Year		-.0079		-.0099		.0070
		(.0017)		(.0021)		(.0031)
(12 < Ed < 16)*Year		.0011		.0056		.0142
		(.0025)		(.0031)		(.0051)
(Ed ≥ 16)*Year		-.0026		-.0041		.0197
		(.0026)		(.0027)		(.0048)
p-Value equality of time trends		<.0001		<.0001		<.0001
No. of observations	122,849	122,849	71,409	71,409	51,440	51,440
log L	-66,675.9	-66,652.6	-43,954.4	-43,933.4	-19,432.2	-19,421.4

Notes: Numbers in parentheses are asymptotic standard errors. The dependent variable is a dummy variable equaling one if job duration is more than 20 years. All models include controls for education (three dummy variables for four categories) and age (three dummy variables for four categories). The analysis is weighted using CPS sampling weights. The included age range is 45–64.

The short-term job fractions for women show a dramatic decline over time, reflecting women's increased employment rates. The long-term job fractions in tables 5A.9 and 5A.10 show analogous patterns.[15] There is an aggregate increase in the 10-year probability for all but the oldest age category, but this is not reflected in the 20-year probability. Both the 10- and 20-year probabilities have declined somewhat for men. This is in contrast to the quite dramatic increase in 10-year probabilities for women, although this is somewhat weaker among women 55–64 years old. There has also been a substantial increase in the 20-year probability for women 45–54 years old, with most of this coming in the past few years. There is no strong trend apparent in the 20-year probability for women 55–64 years old.

Tables 5.10, 5.11, and 5.12 contain estimates of logit models of the population-based probabilities analogous to the employment-based estimates in tables 5.7, 5.8, and 5.9. As before, this analysis provides summary measures of time trends and examines variation in these trends across educational categories. The structure of these tables is the same as in tables 5.7, 5.8, and 5.9. They also include the same control variables.

Table 5.10 contains estimates of logit models of the population-based probability that a worker has been on his or her job no more than one year. When no distinction is made by sex, there is a slight but significant downward trend in the short-term job probability. This small aggregate figure masks large opposing movements of approximately equal magnitudes for males and females (about 8 percentage points each over this period).[16] Once again, separate time trends by educational category allow a much sharper picture to emerge.[17]

The specific results suggest that the overall increase in the probability of short durations is due entirely to the lowest educational category. The probability of a worker with less than a high school education being in a short-term job is predicted to be about 7 percentage points higher in 1993 than in 1973. The estimates show that the time trends in the three higher educational categories were significantly negative, suggesting a lower short-term job probability over time.

Examining the trends separately for men and women suggests that low-education results are driven by large increases in the short-term job probabilities for men in the two lowest educational categories. Men with less than a high school education have a probability of being in a short-term job that is predicted to be fully 16 percentage points higher in 1993 than in 1973. The

---

15. Remember that the 25–34 age column in table 5A.9 is not particularly relevant because many workers that young have not had time to accumulate much job tenure. Neither the 25–34 nor the 35–44 age columns in table 5A.10 are very interesting for the same reason.

16. The calculations of changes in probabilities over the 20-year period in this subsection are again calculated using a $p(1 - p)$ value of 0.2. While this is not far off on average, the same caution noted above applies. The specific percentage changes mentioned in the text are, of necessity, approximations.

17. As with the employment-based probabilities, the hypothesis that the time trends are the same across educational categories can be rejected in all cases.

Table 5.10   Logit Analysis of Probability of Job Duration One Year or Less for All Individuals Aged 21–64 (year by education interaction)

Variable	All		Males		Females	
	(1)	(2)	(3)	(4)	(5)	(6)
Constant	.487	.713	−2.00	−2.45	2.48	2.50
	(.0386)	(.0605)	(.0598)	(.101)	(.0539)	(.128)
Ed < 12	.535	−1.37	.611	−.469	.682	−1.08
	(.0077)	(.0996)	(.0119)	(.154)	(.0110)	(.144)
12 < Ed < 16	−.104	.567	.0640	1.74	−.126	.907
	(.0075)	(.0991)	(.0117)	(.156)	(.0102)	(.136)
Ed ≥ 16	−.450	−.253	−.203	1.49	−.438	.0013
	(.0080)	(.107)	(.0122)	(.163)	(.0112)	(.150)
Year	−.0023		.0206		−.0210	
	(.0004)		(.0007)		(.0006)	
(Ed < 12)*Year		.0182		.0393		.0001
		(.0010)		(.0014)		(.0015)
(Ed = 12)*Year		−.0050		.0261		−.0213
		(.0007)		(.0012)		(.0009)
(12 < Ed < 16)*Year		−.0128		.0062		−.0335
		(.0009)		(.0014)		(.0013)
(Ed ≥ 16)*Year		−.0073		.0060		−.0265
		(.0010)		(.0015)		(.0015)
p-Value equality of time trends		<.0001		<.0001		<.0001
No. of observations	550,552	550,552	260,129	260,129	290,423	290,423
log L	−362,625.5	−362,320.8	−156,831.9	−156,637.3	−189,164.4	−189,006.7

Notes: Numbers in parentheses are asymptotic standard errors. The dependent variable is a dummy variable equaling one if job duration is less than or equal to one year. All models include controls for education (three dummy variables for four categories) and age (eight dummy variables for nine categories). The analysis is weighted using CPS sampling weights. Not-employed workers are classified as having job duration less than one year. The included age range is 21–64.

change is somewhat smaller but still quite substantial for men with exactly a high school education (an increase of 10 percentage points). That these changes are larger than the employment-based changes reflects declines in employment rates over the 1973–93 period for less educated men.

The decrease in short-term job probabilities at higher educational levels is the result of substantial declines in these probabilities for women (a decline of 10 to 12 percentage points between 1973 and 1993). Once again, these changes are larger than those found on an employment basis, and this reflects the increased employment rates of women over the sample period.

Tables 5.11 and 5.12 contain estimates of logit models of the population-based long-term employment probabilities (job durations greater than 10 years and greater than 20 years). These tables show patterns generally consistent with the results for the short-term job probability in table 5.10.

There is a very small decrease in the both aggregate long-term job probabilities over the 1973–93 period (less than 1 percentage point overall). But, as with the short-term job probability, this apparent aggregate stability masks roughly offsetting changes for males and females of about 8 to 10 percentage points over the period. Declines in long-term job probabilities for males were offset by approximately equal increases for females. As before, the decline for men is concentrated in the lowest educational categories, where there has been a substantial decline in both long-term job probabilities of about 8 to 12 percentage points over the 20-year period. For females outside the lowest educational category, there has been an even more substantial increase in both long-term job probabilities over time (ranging from 10 to 16 percentage points for the 10-year probability and somewhat less for the 20-year probability).

Overall, the population-based estimates show the same general patterns as the employment-based estimates. The same patterns exist in both series, though they are generally more substantial in the population-based numbers. This is largely due to the fact that changes in employment rates (both supply and demand induced) that are central to the population-based numbers reinforced the changes apparent in the employment-based numbers.

5.5   Concluding Remarks

The results of my analysis are clear and consistent using several measures of job duration. Simply put, no evidence presented here supports the popular view that long-term jobs are becoming less common in the United States. It is true that long-term jobs are now allocated somewhat differently across the population than they were 20 years ago. Long-term jobs have become more scarce for the least educated (particularly men). This is consistent with other evidence that the economic position of the least educated workers has deteriorated in the past 15 to 20 years (Katz and Murphy 1992). It is worth investigating how much of this deterioration is related to job instability.

Long-term jobs used to be almost exclusively the province of men. The

Table 5.11   **Logit Analysis of Probability of Job Duration More Than 10 Years for All Individuals Aged 35-64 (year by education interaction)**

Variable	All		Males		Females	
	(1)	(2)	(3)	(4)	(5)	(6)
Constant	−.946	−1.20	.979	1.27	−3.56	−3.66
	(.0542)	(.0856)	(.0726)	(.121)	(.0897)	(.133)
Ed < 12	−.390	1.43	−.498	.455	−.564	1.48
	(.0108)	(.141)	(.0144)	(.188)	(.0184)	(.242)
12 < Ed < 16	.0638	−.612	−.0730	−1.25	.0469	−1.19
	(.0114)	(.150)	(.0156)	(.205)	(.0181)	(.247)
Ed > 16	.388	.319	−.0548	−1.24	.454	.187
	(.0109)	(.145)	(.0145)	(.191)	(.0181)	(.247)
Year	−.0013		−.0173		.0240	
	(.0006)		(.0008)		(.0010)	
(Ed < 12)*Year		−.0204		−.0326		.0005
		(.0014)		(.0018)		(.0025)
(Ed = 12)*Year		.0018		−.0208		.0252
		(.0010)		(.0014)		(.0016)
(12 < Ed < 16)*Year		.0097		−.0069		.0396
		(.0015)		(.0019)		(.0024)
(Ed ≥ 16)*Year		.0025		−.0055		.0283
		(.0014)		(.0017)		(.0024)
p-Value equality of time trends		<.0001		<.0001		<.0001
No. of observations	324,121	324,121	152,987	152,987	171,134	171,134
log L	−185,951.4	−185,817.8	−99,287.6	−99,209.7	−75,469.0	−75,400.1

Notes: Numbers in parentheses are asymptotic standard errors. The dependent variable is a dummy variable equaling one if job duration is more than 10 years. All models include controls for education (three dummy variables for four categories) and age (five dummy variables for six categories). The analysis is weighted using CPS sampling weights. Not-employed individuals are classified as having job duration less than one year. The included age range is 35–64.

Table 5.12   Logit Analysis of Probability of Job Duration More Than 20 Years for All Individuals Aged 45–64 (year by education interaction)

Variable	All		Males		Females	
	(1)	(2)	(3)	(4)	(5)	(6)
Constant	−.955	−1.13	.488	.614	−3.71	−3.72
	(.0845)	(.133)	(.103)	(.169)	(.169)	(.251)
Ed < 12	−.351	1.47	−.494	.833	−.539	1.64
	(.0162)	(.216)	(.0197)	(.261)	(.0338)	(.449)
12 < Ed < 16	.0468	−.894	−.100	−1.62	.0195	−1.06
	(.0186)	(.244)	(.0230)	(.300)	(.0360)	(.485)
Ed ≥ 16	.376	−.114	−.0193	−.990	.527	−.761
	(.0174)	(.229)	(.0212)	(.278)	(.0345)	(.467)
Year	−.0097		−.0185		.0139	
	(.0010)		(.0012)		(.0020)	
(Ed < 12)*Year		−.0300		−.0365		−.0126
		(.0021)		(.0025)		(.0046)
(Ed = 12)*Year		−.0076		−.0200		.0140
		(.0016)		(.0020)		(.0030)
(12 < Ed < 16)*Year		.0036		−.0020		.0266
		(.0024)		(.0029)		(.0048)
(Ed ≥ 16)*Year		−.0018		−.0085		.0290
		(.0022)		(.0026)		(.0046)
p-Value equality of time trends		<.0001		<.0001		<.0001
No. of observations	197,872	197,872	92,838	92,838	105,034	105,034
log L	−83,594.0	−83,523.8	−51,275.6	−51,225.1	−25,048.5	−25,022.4

Notes: Numbers in parentheses are asymptotic standard errors. The dependent variable is a dummy variable equaling one if job duration is more than 20 years. All models include controls for education (three dummy variables for four categories) and age (three dummy variables for four categories). The analysis is weighted using CPS sampling weights. Not-employed individuals are classified as not having job duration more than 10 years. The included age range is 45–64.

largest secular change in the data is the dramatically increased probability of long-term employment for women. However, it remains unclear whether these long-term jobs for women are of equal quality to long-term jobs held by men. It is therefore worth investigating how much of the decline in the male-female wage gap in the 1980s is related to increases in job duration (Wellington 1992). In the final analysis, to paraphrase Mark Twain, reports of the death of "the Great American Job" are greatly exaggerated.

Appendix

Table 5A.1   **Median Job Duration by Age, Year, and Sex for Employed Individuals**

Year	Age Category			
	25–34	35–44	45–54	55–64
Employed Individuals				
1951	2.6	3.2	6.3	8.0
1963	3.0	6.0	9.0	11.8
1966	2.7	6.0	8.8	13.0
1968	2.5	5.2	8.6	12.3
1973	2.8	5.2	8.4	11.4
1978	2.5	4.9	8.3	11.1
1979	2.8	5.4	9.7	12.7
1981	3.1	5.1	9.1	12.1
1983	3.0	5.3	9.7	13.0
1987	3.0	5.6	9.2	12.2
1991	3.0	5.5	9.5	11.9
1993	3.2	5.8	9.5	12.4
Employed Males				
1951	2.8	4.5	7.6	9.3
1963	3.5	7.6	11.4	14.7
1966	3.2	7.8	11.5	15.8
1968	2.8	6.9	10.2	14.8
1973	3.1	6.5	11.3	14.4
1978	2.8	6.8	11.1	14.6
1979	3.3	7.6	12.5	15.8
1981	3.1	7.1	11.1	15.1
1983	3.3	7.3	12.7	16.4
1987	3.2	7.1	11.8	15.1
1991	3.2	6.8	11.6	15.0
1993	3.5	6.9	11.7	14.0
Employed Females				
1951	1.8	3.1	4.0	4.5
1963	2.0	3.6	6.1	7.8
1966	1.9	3.5	5.1	9.0
1968	1.6	2.9	5.1	8.7
1973	2.2	3.4	5.7	8.5
1978	2.0	3.3	5.8	8.6
1979	2.2	3.3	6.4	9.6
1981	3.0	4.1	6.1	10.1
1983	2.7	4.1	6.4	9.9
1987	2.6	4.4	6.9	9.9
1991	2.7	4.5	6.8	9.8
1993	3.0	5.0	7.6	10.3

Sources: Statistics for 1951–68 taken from BLS publications and based on supplements to the Current Population Survey in January of the relevant year (Bureau of the Census 1951; Department of Labor 1963, 1967, 1969). Statistics for 1973–93 based on author's calculations of weighted interpolated medians using data from supplements to the Current Population Survey in January 1973, 1978, 1981, 1983, 1987, and 1991; in May 1979; and in April 1993.

Table 5A.2   **.9 Quantile Job Duration by Age, Year, and Sex for Employed Individuals**

		Age Category		
Year	25–34	35–44	45–54	55–64
Employed Individuals				
1973	8.6	17.1	25.3	32.0
1978	8.7	16.4	25.6	31.5
1979	9.3	16.4	26.7	32.5
1981	9.1	16.1	26.1	33.1
1983	9.5	16.6	25.7	33.3
1987	9.7	17.0	25.2	32.8
1991	10.1	17.7	25.1	32.0
1993	9.7	17.5	25.2	31.5
Employed Males				
1973	9.0	18.0	26.4	34.9
1978	9.4	17.8	27.4	32.9
1979	9.7	17.8	28.0	34.3
1981	10.1	18.1	28.0	35.1
1983	9.8	17.9	27.6	35.0
1987	10.0	18.1	27.0	35.0
1991	10.3	18.4	26.6	34.6
1993	10.1	18.3	26.8	34.5
Employed Females				
1973	7.5	13.8	19.9	25.5
1978	7.8	12.4	19.0	25.5
1979	8.6	13.4	20.4	26.3
1981	9.0	14.1	20.1	26.1
1983	8.8	14.4	19.7	26.2
1987	9.1	14.9	19.8	25.4
1991	9.7	16.2	20.8	26.8
1993	9.1	16.1	22.8	25.8

Sources: Statistics for 1973–93 based on author's calculations of weighted interpolated quantiles using data from supplements to the Current Population Survey in January 1973, 1978, 1981, 1983, 1987, and 1991; in May 1979; and in April 1993.

| Table 5A.3 | | Median Job Duration by Age, Year, and Sex for All Individuals | | |

		Age Category		
Year	25–34	35–44	45–54	55–64
		All Individuals		
1973	1.0	2.3	3.7	1.7
1978	1.0	2.4	3.7	0.7
1979	1.4	2.8	4.2	1.1
1981	2.0	3.1	4.1	0.3
1983	1.5	2.9	3.8	0.0
1987	1.7	3.4	4.4	0.2
1991	1.8	3.6	5.0	0.7
1993	2.1	3.8	5.2	1.3
		All Males		
1973	2.7	5.8	9.6	7.9
1978	2.2	5.9	9.0	6.1
1979	2.8	6.6	10.4	8.0
1981	3.1	6.1	9.1	6.1
1983	2.3	5.3	9.6	4.7
1987	2.5	5.7	8.6	4.1
1991	2.5	5.4	8.7	3.6
1993	2.8	5.4	8.2	4.6
		All Females		
1973	0.0	0.05	0.04	0.0
1978	0.2	0.4	0.4	0.0
1979	0.5	0.8	0.5	0.0
1981	0.4	0.7	0.8	0.0
1983	0.5	1.2	0.7	0.0
1987	0.9	1.8	1.8	0.0
1991	1.1	2.3	2.8	0.0
1993	1.4	2.5	3.4	0.0

Sources: Statistics for 1973–93 based on author's calculations of weighted interpolated quantiles using data from supplements to the Current Population Survey in January 1973, 1978, 1981, 1983, 1987, and 1991; in May 1979; and in April 1993. Individuals who are not employed are counted as having zero job duration.

Table 5A.4 **.9 Quantile Job Duration by Age, Year, and Sex for All Individuals**

Year	25–34	35–44	45–54	55–64
		Age Category		
	All Individuals			
1973	7.4	15.5	22.6	26.9
1978	7.6	14.8	23.2	27.3
1979	8.3	15.2	24.8	27.9
1981	8.1	15.1	24.1	27.1
1983	8.1	15.3	23.5	27.6
1987	8.6	15.8	23.1	26.2
1991	9.3	16.7	23.8	25.9
1993	8.7	16.3	24.0	26.5
	All Males			
1973	8.8	17.7	26.0	32.2
1978	8.9	17.5	26.8	31.3
1979	9.4	17.4	27.5	32.3
1981	10.0	17.1	27.0	32.1
1983	9.2	17.2	26.8	32.4
1987	9.6	17.8	26.0	32.0
1991	10.0	18.0	25.7	30.7
1993	9.7	17.7	26.2	30.5
	All Females			
1973	5.2	9.2	14.0	16.7
1978	5.8	9.3	14.0	16.2
1979	6.5	10.7	15.3	17.5
1981	7.1	11.1	16.1	17.0
1983	7.0	11.7	15.2	16.6
1987	7.6	13.1	16.6	17.6
1991	7.8	14.3	18.9	19.7
1993	7.5	14.7	20.1	19.8

Sources: Statistics for 1973–93 based on author's calculations of weighted interpolated quantiles using data from supplements to the Current Population Survey in January 1973, 1978, 1981, 1983, 1987, and 1991; in May 1979; and in April 1993. Individuals who are not employed are counted as having zero job duration.

Table 5A.5 **Fraction with Job Duration of One Year or Less for Employed Individuals**

Year	Age Category			
	25–34	35–44	45–54	55–64
Employed Individuals				
1973	.277	.169	.112	.080
1978	.311	.203	.136	.106
1979	.345	.226	.143	.105
1981	.300	.200	.135	.101
1983	.300	.200	.130	.097
1987	.309	.206	.147	.106
1991	.303	.196	.145	.113
1993	.280	.182	.133	.100
Employed Males				
1973	.249	.137	.097	.070
1978	.283	.166	.110	.095
1979	.309	.173	.113	.089
1981	.267	.172	.111	.094
1983	.276	.168	.112	.089
1987	.282	.174	.127	.096
1991	.280	.167	.129	.106
1993	.268	.161	.130	.099
Employed Females				
1973	.328	.223	.137	.096
1978	.351	.259	.176	.123
1979	.398	.301	.190	.131
1981	.345	.237	.167	.112
1983	.331	.242	.155	.108
1987	.343	.245	.172	.121
1991	.331	.229	.164	.122
1993	.294	.207	.137	.100

Sources: Statistics for 1973–93 based on author's weighted counts using data from supplements to the Current Population Survey in January 1973, 1978, 1981, 1983, 1987, and 1991; in May 1979; and in April 1993.

Table 5A.6   **Fraction with Job Duration of More Than 10 Years for Employed Individuals**

| | | Age Category | | |
Year	25–34	35–44	45–54	55–64
		Employed Individuals		
1973	.066	.288	.451	.546
1978	.063	.274	.443	.535
1979	.057	.284	.465	.561
1981	.076	.286	.453	.566
1983	.059	.283	.459	.562
1987	.066	.282	.438	.536
1991	.083	.297	.446	.531
1993	.074	.300	.456	.538
		Employed Males		
1973	.075	.356	.537	.603
1978	.076	.356	.532	.602
1979	.066	.363	.558	.629
1981	.090	.364	.541	.625
1983	.066	.360	.556	.637
1987	.075	.345	.523	.590
1991	.094	.346	.526	.584
1993	.084	.341	.519	.574
		Employed Females		
1973	.050	.173	.310	.451
1978	.042	.153	.307	.430
1979	.043	.171	.318	.451
1981	.057	.181	.331	.476
1983	.050	.183	.325	.458
1987	.055	.205	.329	.460
1991	.070	.239	.352	.462
1993	.062	.252	.384	.491

Sources: Statistics for 1973–93 based on author's weighted counts using data from supplements to the Current Population Survey in January 1973, 1978, 1981, 1983, 1987, and 1991; in May 1979; and in April 1993.

Table 5A.7 **Fraction with Job Duration of More Than 20 Years for Employed Individuals**

| | | Age Category | | |
	Year	25–34	35–44	45–54	55–64
		Employed Individuals			
	1973	.001	.050	.213	.309
	1978	.000	.042	.209	.314
	1979	.001	.032	.218	.323
	1981	.000	.043	.198	.311
	1983	.000	.030	.194	.307
	1987	.000	.027	.179	.282
	1991	.000	.038	.193	.292
	1993	.000	.036	.206	.287
		Employed Males			
	1973	.001	.060	.283	.388
	1978	.000	.057	.288	.398
	1979	.001	.043	.296	.410
	1981	.001	.058	.271	.394
	1983	.001	.041	.279	.403
	1987	.000	.039	.256	.365
	1991	.000	.047	.268	.367
	1993	.000	.041	.271	.360
		Employed Females			
	1973	.000	.033	.097	.177
	1978	.000	.021	.090	.183
	1979	.000	.018	.097	.181
	1981	.000	.022	.096	.183
	1983	.000	.016	.078	.172
	1987	.000	.013	.081	.164
	1991	.000	.028	.106	.194
	1993	.000	.030	.132	.191

Sources: Statistics for 1973–93 based on author's weighted counts using data from supplements to the Current Population Survey in January 1973, 1978, 1981, 1983, 1987, and 1991; in May 1979; and in April 1993.

Table 5A.8   **Fraction with Job Duration of One Year or Less for All Individuals**

Year	Age Category			
	25–34	35–44	45–54	55–64
All Individuals				
1973	.511	.409	.382	.473
1978	.502	.407	.390	.516
1979	.509	.412	.393	.511
1981	.489	.399	.380	.532
1983	.505	.408	.404	.549
1987	.478	.371	.374	.546
1991	.463	.352	.346	.530
1993	.441	.346	.336	.506
All Males				
1973	.317	.194	.186	.291
1978	.361	.227	.213	.367
1979	.365	.235	.211	.357
1981	.364	.254	.231	.392
1983	.411	.283	.263	.426
1987	.381	.261	.254	.423
1991	.379	.259	.260	.429
1993	.364	.262	.266	.415
All Females				
1973	.691	.607	.563	.635
1978	.635	.574	.554	.649
1979	.645	.578	.566	.654
1981	.606	.533	.518	.657
1983	.594	.525	.533	.655
1987	.570	.475	.485	.654
1991	.544	.441	.427	.620
1993	.515	.427	.401	.590

Sources: Statistics for 1973–93 based on author's weighted counts using data from supplements to the Current Population Survey in January 1973, 1978, 1981, 1983, 1987, and 1991; in May 1979; and in April 1993. Individuals who are not employed are counted as having zero duration.

Table 5A.9   **Fraction with Job Duration of More Than 10 Years for All Individuals**

		Age Category		
Year	25–34	35–44	45–54	55–64
All Individuals				
1973	.045	.205	.313	.312
1978	.045	.204	.313	.289
1979	.042	.216	.329	.306
1981	.056	.215	.325	.294
1983	.042	.209	.314	.281
1987	.050	.223	.321	.272
1991	.064	.239	.341	.282
1993	.058	.240	.350	.294
All Males				
1973	.068	.332	.484	.460
1978	.068	.330	.471	.421
1979	.060	.336	.497	.444
1981	.078	.328	.469	.419
1983	.054	.310	.462	.401
1987	.064	.309	.447	.376
1991	.081	.308	.448	.373
1993	.073	.300	.438	.373
All Females				
1973	.023	.088	.157	.182
1978	.024	.088	.166	.172
1979	.025	.103	.170	.180
1981	.035	.111	.191	.184
1983	.031	.115	.179	.177
1987	.036	.142	.204	.181
1991	.047	.173	.241	.200
1993	.043	.182	.267	.224

Sources: Statistics for 1973–93 based on author's weighted counts using data from supplements to the Current Population Survey in January 1973, 1978, 1981, 1983, 1987, and 1991; in May 1979; and in April 1993. Individuals who are not employed are counted as having zero job duration.

Table 5A.10   **Fraction with Job Duration of More Than 20 Years for All Individuals**

		Age Category		
Year	25–34	35–44	45–54	55–64
		All Individuals		
1973	.000	.035	.148	.177
1978	.000	.032	.148	.170
1979	.000	.025	.154	.176
1981	.000	.032	.142	.162
1983	.000	.022	.133	.153
1987	.000	.021	.132	.143
1991	.000	.031	.148	.155
1993	.000	.029	.158	.157
		All Males		
1973	.000	.056	.256	.296
1978	.000	.053	.254	.278
1979	.000	.039	.263	.290
1981	.000	.052	.234	.265
1983	.000	.035	.231	.254
1987	.000	.035	.220	.233
1991	.000	.042	.228	.234
1993	.000	.036	.228	.234
		All Females		
1973	.000	.017	.049	.072
1978	.000	.012	.048	.073
1979	.000	.011	.052	.072
1981	.000	.013	.055	.071
1983	.000	.010	.043	.067
1987	.000	.008	.050	.065
1991	.000	.020	.073	.084
1993	.000	.022	.092	.087

Sources: Statistics for 1973–93 based on author's weighted counts using data from supplements to the Current Population Survey in January 1973, 1978, 1981, 1983, 1987, and 1991; in May 1979; and in April 1993. Individuals who are not employed are counted as having zero job duration.

References

Abraham, Katharine G., and James L. Medoff. 1984. Length of service and layoffs in union and nonunion work groups. *Industrial and Labor Relations Review* 38 (October): 87–97.

Chamberlain, Gary. 1994. Quantile regression, censoring, and the structure of wages. In *Proceedings of the Sixth World Congress of the Econometric Society,* ed. Christopher Sims. New York: Cambridge University Press.

Diebold, Francis X., David Neumark, and Daniel Polsky. 1994. Job stability in the United States. NBER Working Paper no. 4859. Cambridge, Mass.: National Bureau of Economic Research, September.

Farber, Henry S. 1993. The incidence and costs of job loss: 1982–91. *Brookings Papers on Economic Activity: Microeconomics,* 73–119.

———. 1997. The changing face of job loss in the United States, 1981–1995. *Brookings Papers on Economic Activity: Microeconomics,* 55–128.

Hall, Robert E. 1982. The importance of lifetime jobs in the U.S. economy. *American Economic Review* 72 (September): 716–24.

Katz, Lawrence F., and Kevin M. Murphy. 1992. Changes in relative wages, 1963–1987: Supply and demand factors. *Quarterly Journal of Economics* 106 (February): 35–78.

Swinnerton, Kenneth, and Howard Wial. 1995. Is job stability declining in the U.S. economy? *Industrial and Labor Relations Review* 48 (January): 293–304.

Ureta, Manuelita. 1992. The importance of lifetime jobs in the U.S. economy, revisited. *American Economic Review* 82 (March): 322–35.

U.S. Bureau of the Census. 1951. *Current population reports: Labor force,* Series P-50, no. 36. Washington, D.C.: U.S. Bureau of the Census, 5 November.

U.S. Department of Labor. Bureau of Labor Statistics. 1963. *Job tenure of American workers.* Special Labor Force Report no. 36. Washington, D.C.: Government Printing Office.

———. 1967. *Job tenure of workers.* Special Labor Force Report no. 77. Washington, D.C.: Government Printing Office.

———. 1969. *Job tenure of workers.* Special Labor Force Report no. 112. Washington, D.C.: Government Printing Office.

Wellington, Alison J. 1992. Changes in the male/female wage gap, 1976–1985. *Journal of Human Resources* 28:385–411.

Comment   Derek Neal

In the introduction to this paper, the author correctly notes that recent reports by media and government either state or imply that the typical worker in the United States has recently experienced a significant loss of job security. In the conclusion, the author argues that these reports have likely overstated their

Derek Neal is associate professor of economics at the University of Chicago, a faculty research fellow of the National Bureau of Economic Research, and a faculty affiliate of the Joint Center for Poverty Research at Northwestern University and the University of Chicago.

case. In between, he uses data from the Current Population Survey to provide a careful and thorough description of changes in the distribution of existing job tenure over the period 1973–93.[1]

I want to commend the author for providing a great deal of information that speaks to an important and timely question. Further, I am inclined to agree generally with his conclusions. However, I would like to raise a few issues that I feel the author should have explored further.

My concerns arise from the fact that Current Population Survey data on job tenure do not speak directly to the issue of job security. Tenure data do not provide direct evidence about separation rates, and I will argue later that even with good information about separation rates, we cannot not make clear inferences about job security.

The results in tables 5.1 and 5.4 demonstrate that trends in median tenure among men are quite different depending on whether the estimates are employment based or population based. Both sets of analyses show that median job tenure has declined among less educated men. However, the magnitude of the decline is much greater in the population-based results. The author motivates the presentation of the population-based results by arguing that the employment-based results may be contaminated by business cycle effects because those with the least tenure are laid off during recessions. However, it is possible that male workers with little education spend more time "between jobs" than they did 20 years ago. This would explain the observed pattern of results, and it might occur either because separation rates are now higher among this group or because exit rates from unemployment are lower or both.

Without direct evidence concerning separation rates, it is hard to make strong inferences about secular changes in job security. Further, even if future studies do document how separation rates have changed or not changed within various groups, the implications for changes in job security will not be transparent. Workers leave employment matches either because they receive bad information about their current match or because they receive good information about potential alternatives. When press accounts describe workers as concerned about their job security, I interpret this as a statement that workers are worried about future separations that might arise from sudden negative changes in the expected value of their existing matches. Workers rarely lose sleep over the prospects of leaving their current jobs for better ones.

In recent work on displacement, the author notes that, within several groups, the probability of displacement by layoff or plant closing has changed substantially since the early 1980s (Farber 1993). However, the author also notes that even displacement data give an incomplete picture of job security. Workers may voluntarily leave firms that suffer adverse shocks because shocks cause them to update their forecasts of future wages. Such separations could be

---

1. The author not only examines various conditional quantiles of the tenure distribution, he also examines the cumulative distribution function at 1 year, 10 years, and 20 years of tenure.

traced to exogenous declines in the value of specific employment matches, but they would not appear in the data as displacements.

In short, it may be quite difficult to document trends in job security. We all have a sense of what we mean when we use the term, but we do not have a precise definition that lends itself directly to empirical measurement. In this context, it is interesting to note that both the employment-based and population-based analyses show that median job tenure has risen substantially among women. Should we interpret this as evidence that job security among women has increased over the past two decades, or could the trend in observed job tenure be driven entirely by the increased commitment of women to the labor force? Women are now less likely to leave their jobs when their children are young. This implies that in both the workforce and the population as a whole we should see an increase in median job tenure among women. We might expect that this increased attachment to market work should also increase the value of job-specific matches between women and their employers, thus making women more secure in their jobs. However, I know of no direct evidence that this is the case.

Further, changes in retirement behavior over the past 20 years also raise questions about the interpretation of changes in the distribution of job tenure. I noted earlier that, among men, population-based measures imply larger declines in median tenure than do employment-based measures. A comparison of tables 5A.1 and 5A.3 shows that the largest differences between employment- and population-based estimates of the secular changes in median job tenure come from the analyses of older men. The difference is particularly striking among men aged 55–64.

Are older men simply consuming more leisure, or are they spending more time searching for employment? Hurd (1990) reports that retirement ages have fallen significantly over the past several decades. On the other hand, the author's own work shows that, between the recessions of the early 1980s and early 1990s, displacement became more common among older men (Farber 1993).

It is likely that older workers are retiring earlier primarily because they are wealthier than previous cohorts. However, if workers become less secure in their current employment, they may become more willing to choose early retirement. Workers who view future displacement as a likely outcome may be quite willing to accept early retirement plans and then go back to work if a good opportunity comes along.

In general, it would be interesting to expand the analyses in this paper by estimating each specification separately by age group. Of particular interest is whether the decline in median tenure among less educated men is being driven by the employment patterns of the young, the old, or both. If the decline is being driven by older workers, the issue of retirement decisions becomes crucial. If older males are retiring earlier or shifting from full-time to part-time employment simply because they are wealthier than previous cohorts, the author's results may actually overstate losses of job security among less educated males.[2]

I want to end as I began by stating that this paper is basically a success. Against a backdrop of considerable discussion among both policymakers and the media about the need to address the drastic loss of job security suffered by American workers, the author presents a thorough documentation of recent changes in the distribution of job tenure. He correctly argues that since the overall distribution of tenure has been relatively stable for the past two decades, it is hard to claim that long-term jobs are becoming less common in the United States, and he clearly places the burden of proof on those who contend that declining job security is a pervasive problem.

However, I feel the paper would have been even more interesting if the author had devoted a portion of his efforts to the tasks of defining job security and discussing how one might measure it directly. Popular discussions of job security usually proceed without a clear definition of the term. Although job security is a common topic in policy debates, economists have not thought carefully about how to define it or how to measure it. These problems remain for future research.

References

Farber, Henry S. 1993. The incidence and costs of job loss: 1982–91. *Brookings Papers on Economic Activity: Microeconomics,* 73–119.
Hurd, Michael D. 1990. Research on the elderly: Economic status, retirement, and consumption, and saving. *Journal of Economic Literature* 28:565–637.

2. Furthermore, the interaction between age and educational level raises an important measurement issue. The author uses schooling as a proxy for worker skill, but it is not clear that the relationship between schooling and skill is the same across cohorts. If schooling understates the relative skill of older workers and if the decline in median tenure among the less educated has been particularly dramatic among the old, we may not want to think of the decline as primarily affecting unskilled workers. I thank Bob Topel for raising this point during the discussion.

6   On Measuring the Impact of Ownership Change on Labor: Evidence from U.S. Food-Manufacturing Plant-Level Data

Robert H. McGuckin, Sang V. Nguyen,
and Arnold P. Reznek

6.1   Introduction

Despite strong opposition from labor unions and widespread, often negative, press reports on ownership changes through mergers and acquisitions, there have been few studies of the impact of ownership change on labor. To our knowledge, there are only two published studies on this issue. The first, by Brown and Medoff (1988), uses a sample of mostly small firms from one state, Michigan. They find that, except for divestitures, ownership changes have little impact on either employment or the average wage.

The second study, by Lichtenberg and Siegel (1992b), examines the impact of ownership change on wages and employment in both auxiliary (central office) and production establishments. They find ownership change to be associated with reductions in both wages and employment in central offices but to have little effect at production plants. Since the chief operating officer's salary is a large component of the average wage in small firms, the Brown and Medoff results appear consistent with those of Lichtenberg and Siegel. These studies suggest that managers and white-collar workers suffer the most following ownership change, but overall, the effects on labor, particularly production workers, appear to be relatively small.

While the Brown-Medoff and Lichtenberg-Siegel studies certainly make significant contributions to the empirical literature on the impact of ownership

Robert H. McGuckin is director of economic research at The Conference Board and a research associate of the Center for Economic Studies, U.S. Bureau of the Census. Sang V. Nguyen and Arnold P. Reznek are economists at the Center for Economic Studies, U.S. Bureau of the Census.

The judgments and conclusions herein are those of the authors and do not necessarily reflect those of the Bureau of the Census. The authors thank Ed Dean, Mark Doms, Kathy Friedman, John Haltiwanger, Frank Lichtenberg, Ken Troske, two anonymous referees, the editors, and conference participants for their helpful comments. Becky Turner provided excellent preparation of the manuscript.

changes on labor, several important issues need to be addressed. These include the representativeness of their samples, the measurement and identification of ownership change, and the appropriate unit of analysis (firms vs. plants). For example, the data set used by Brown and Medoff is for a single state, and most of the firms in their sample are small. Moreover, their sample excludes establishments located outside Michigan even when they are owned by Michigan firms.

The sample used by Lichtenberg and Siegel is much broader, covering the entire U.S. manufacturing sector. However, their sample includes only large, surviving plants in the 1972–81 period. Smaller surviving plants and exiting plants of all sizes are excluded. Restriction of the sample to survivors prevents Lichtenberg and Siegel from analyzing the effects of ownership changes on plant closing.

In this study, we examine these and other data problems and measurement issues in the estimation of the impacts of ownership change on labor. For this purpose, we created an unbalanced panel of more than 28,000 manufacturing establishments from the Census Bureau's Longitudinal Research Database (LRD). It covers the entire population of the U.S. food-producing industry (SIC 20) in 1977. We choose the food-manufacturing industry because it exhibits a substantial number of ownership changes that involve a significant portion of total industry shipments during the period under study. At the same time, it provides a large, tractable set of firms and plants for empirical work. Most important, the data set is comprehensive, covering plants of all sizes.[1]

These data allow us to construct a data set that contains firms undergoing ownership changes involving control[2] and a comparable group of firms not experiencing such changes. They also enable us to keep track of the activities of all food-producing firms and their components (i.e., plants) at discrete five-year intervals through 1987. Specifically, these data allow categorization of firms at the beginning of a period into those that operate continuously, those that close, and those that are sold to other firms. Similarly, the plants of a particular firm at the end of the period can be broken down into those the firm originally owned, those it acquired from other firms, and those that are newly constructed.

Our analysis leads to the following principal findings for the food industry. First, the growth rates of wages, employment, and labor productivity for the typical acquired plant (and originally owned plant of an acquiring firm) are higher than those for the typical plant of a nonacquiring firm in the postacquisition period. Second, to a lesser extent, the typical worker in both types of acquiring firms' plants also enjoyed higher growth rates of wages, employment, and productivity after an acquisition. Third, plants that *changed* owners

---

1. Also, data for this industry at both the plant and firm level are "cleaned" ready for this particular analysis.

2. See section 6.3.2 for a discussion of the measurement issues involved in relating ownership change and control.

show a greater likelihood of survival than those that did not. These three find-ings strongly reject the hypothesis that ownership changes through mergers and acquisitions cut wages and employment and reduce labor productivity. None of the findings are obtained using firm-level data, which suggests that plant-level data are more appropriate than firm-level data for studying the ef-fects of ownership changes on the structure and performance of the firm.

We discuss the relationships among ownership change, productivity, wages, and employment in section 6.2. In section 6.3, we describe the data. In particu-lar, we discuss how the LRD data were used to identify ownership change in our sample. In section 6.4, we report some simple statistics describing the characteristics of firms and plants that experienced ownership change. Our re-gression analysis is discussed in section 6.5. Section 6.6 reports the regression results. Discussions of the results are presented in section 6.7. The last section proposes directions for future research and concludes the paper.

6.2   Ownership Change and Labor

Brown and Medoff (1988) suggest that much of the press and labor union concern with ownership change might stem from extensive media coverage of a small and highly selective group of transactions. There are several issues involved here. Changing ownership itself need not be associated with other changes in the operation of the firm; but ownership changes involving "con-trol"—the type of transaction examined here—typically lead to operational changes.[3] Some ownership changes involving control—hostile takeovers, for example—derive their notoriety from the wholesale upheavals that may ac-company them: management dismissal, plant closures, abrogation of pension benefits, and wage reduction. Even though hostile takeovers are not typical of ownership change transactions, other forms of ownership change, such as friendly mergers, also lead to significant operational changes. But even assum-ing control changes and operations are affected, does economic theory offer clear guidance as to the impact of ownership changes on labor?

In fact, there are not clear theoretical links between ownership change and labor market outcomes. For example, at first glance the consequences for em-ployment of ownership changes to create market power appear clear: market power is exercised by reducing output and raising prices, and reduced output will unfavorably affect employment. But this is not the whole story. A strong union might reasonably be expected to share in the monopoly rents.

As another example, many have argued that the dominant incentive during the conglomerate merger wave of the late 1960s to early 1970s was empire building by managers who were not operating in shareholders' interests (Mueller 1969, 1993; Shleifer and Vishny 1989). The merger wave of the

---

3. E.g., in the case of a public firm, ownership is constantly changing as shareholders buy and sell shares, but most of such changes bear little relationship to day-to-day operations of the firm.

1980s has been viewed as a response to the managerial excesses of the conglomerate merger wave in the early period. In this view, the acquisitions of the 1980s were motivated by the gains available from replacement of inefficient managers of poorly performing firms (Jensen and Ruback 1983; Lichtenberg 1992; Jensen 1993). Arguably, the net effect of such shifts on aggregate productivity (and thus wages) and jobs is relatively small.

The foregoing discussion offers an a priori reason for skepticism concerning the aggregate net effects of ownership changes on labor markets. However, even if the aggregate net effects of ownership changes are small, the relocation of jobs and workers associated with them can be substantial. Relocation of jobs is an important ingredient in the shifting of resources from lower to higher valued uses and is extremely important to aggregate productivity growth (e.g., see Baily, Bartelsman, and Haltiwanger 1994; Baily, Campbell, and Hulten 1992).

Recent studies also find ownership change associated with productivity growth. Using longitudinally linked firm-establishment data in the LRD, Lichtenberg and Siegel (1992a) and McGuckin and Nguyen (1994) conclude that ownership changes are positively associated with productivity growth in the U.S. manufacturing sector for the 1980s merger wave. Baldwin (1995) obtains a similar result using Canadian establishment data.[4]

The positive association between productivity growth and ownership change is consistent with most merger theories.[5] A key issue is the source of the gains. For example, one leading hypothesis is that ownership changes are undertaken for managerial discipline reasons. Managerial discipline takeovers are generally associated with poorly performing businesses that can be reorganized and restructured to make them more productive. The importance of this motive for ownership change is supported empirically by Lichtenberg (1992). In addition, Lichtenberg and Siegel (1992b) find evidence supporting the hypothesis that ownership changes lead to the elimination of jobs: downsizing and lower wages for central offices in firms undergoing ownership changes. But Lichtenberg and Siegel find little in the way of employment effects at production plants. Thus they do not find that ownership change is associated with loss of manufacturing jobs.

McGuckin and Nguyen (1994) reject the managerial discipline theory as a broad-based explanation of most ownership change. They reach this conclusion because their data show that it is high, not low, productivity establishments that are most likely to experience ownership change. Matsusaka (1993b)

---

4. These results are in sharp contrast with those found by previous researchers whose samples typically consisted of data only for large firms. E.g., most industrial organization studies have not found gains associated with ownership change (e.g., Ravenscraft and Scherer 1987). As discussed in more detail below, the new microdata appear to have uncovered relationships "hidden" in the more aggregative firm data.

5. Finding productivity gains positively related to ownership change does not fit well with any of the managerial excesses or empire-building arguments.

and Ravenscraft and Scherer (1987) report similar results: corporate acquirers generally purchase good businesses (productive plants) rather than bad businesses. This suggests that the gains in most ownership changes are associated with efficiencies generated by synergies, which result from combining operations.

For a subset of large establishments, McGuckin and Nguyen (1994) find—consistent with Lichtenberg and Siegel (1992a), whose sample consists primarily of larger plants—that establishments changing owners have low initial productivity and improve following the ownership change. Thus, for very large establishments, the results are consistent with managerial discipline motives for ownership change. Matsusaka (1993a) draws a similar conclusion for the 1960s and 1970s using firm-level data and a somewhat different test.

Despite the new evidence that a substantial proportion of the observed ownership changes represent combinations of efficient operations and subsequent improvements in productivity performance, the impact of ownership change on employment cannot be distinguished on theoretical grounds alone. It is possible for the positive association between ownership change and productivity growth to arise in ways that will, on net, have little effect on total employment of the firm. Productivity improvements could come from efficiencies leading to growth, upsizing the firm and increasing employment, rather than from downsizing. But even when synergies are the dominant motive for the ownership change, downsizing is possible. Similarly, one can expect either increases or decreases in wages following ownership changes. Ownership changes leading to productivity increases will tend to increase wages unless all of the rents from the ownership reorganization accrue to management. The relatively small gains to acquiring firms' shareholders found in finance studies are consistent with the view that all the rents do not accrue to acquiring firms. On the other hand, the large premiums paid to acquired firms' shareholders suggest that labor is not a primary recipient of ownership reorganization rents. Even in the absence of rents to labor, however, the average wage could increase if ownership change is associated with shifts to higher levels of worker skills.

To sort out these issues, we turn to a plant-level data set that covers both acquiring and nonacquiring firms and examine the relationships among ownership change, productivity, wages, and employment at both the firm and establishment levels.

6.3 Data and Measurement Issues

In this section, we focus our discussion on the data used and measurement issues associated with this type of research. First, we describe our data set and the details of its construction. Second, we discuss the concept of ownership change, report our techniques for identifying ownership change, and compare our concepts and techniques with those used by Lichtenberg and Siegel and by Brown and Medoff. Third, we discuss the issue of unit of analysis and point out how this can affect empirical results. Finally, we compare our data to those used in previous studies.

6.3.1 Data and Sample Design

Data Source

Our data are taken from the LRD, which contains data on output, employment, and costs for individual U.S. manufacturing establishments. The output data include total value of shipments and value added. Data on costs include information on capital, labor, energy, materials, and selected purchased services. The employment data contain total and production workers, and their wages, as well as worked hours for production workers.

An important feature of the LRD is its plant classification and identification information, including firm affiliation, location, product and industry, and various status codes that identify, among other things, birth, death, and ownership changes. These identifying codes are used in developing both the longitudinal plant linkages and ownership linkages among plants.[6]

Sample Design and Coverage

We first identified each food-manufacturing plant operating in 1977 using the Census Bureau's SIC codes. Because 1977 is a census year, the entire population of food-manufacturing plants and firms is available. We then identified plants that had ownership change during the periods 1977–82 and 1982–87 (see section 6.3.2 for detailed discussion of identifying ownership change). After identifying all plants that experienced ownership change in these periods, we use each plant's 1977 and 1987 census firm identification number (ID) to identify sellers (acquired firms), buyers (acquiring firms—i.e., firms that acquired at least one food-manufacturing plant during the period), and firms that did not have any plant experiencing ownership change. Finally, we grouped all plants under common ownership in the beginning year (1977) of the study period into three categories: (1) surviving own plants—owned by the firm in 1977 and surviving through 1987; (2) closed plants—existed in 1977 but closed by 1987; and (3) sold plants—owned in 1977 but sold to other firms by 1987. Using a similar classification for 1987 gives three categories for acquiring firms: (1) surviving own plants, (2) acquired plants, and (3) new plants. Nonacquiring firms include only categories 1 and 3. These categories allow us to examine shifts in the composition of the firm over time.

We identify ownership changes occurring during the periods 1977–82 and 1982–87. Each period encompasses two Census of Manufactures years so that we are confident of correctly identifying all ownership changes. In noncensus years information is available only for a sample of plants. The full period 1977–87 includes the beginning and ending years of the latest merger move-

6. A more complete description of the LRD is given in McGuckin and Pascoe (1988).

ment, which extended until 1986 or 1987. Our primary focus is on ownership changes between 1977 and 1982. This allows us to evaluate performance five to nine years after an ownership change transaction. This provides plenty of time for the acquiring firm to integrate acquisitions into the firm, or to dispose of them. Using 1977–87 as the measurement interval for our performance measures also avoids the influence of the 1982 recession.

For the period 1977–82, we identified 733 firms that sold at least one food-manufacturing plant. These 733 firms sold in total 2,111 plants (including 1,573 food plants and 538 nonfood plants) to 732 acquiring firms. As shown in table 6.1, the 732 acquiring firms consisted of 93 single-unit firms, 284 new multiunit firms, and 355 multiunit firms. Of the 284 new multiunit firms, 134 entered manufacturing by acquiring only one manufacturing food plant. Each of the remaining 150 nonmanufacturing firms acquired at least two or more plants. The 355 multiunit manufacturing firms that operated in the food industry in 1977 had the biggest role in the 1977–82 acquisition movement. Together, they acquired 1,455 of the 2,111 transferred plants (68.9 percent) and accounted for $37,435 of the $38,764 million of total value of shipments acquired over the period (98 percent). Of the remaining 656 plants, 93 plants were acquired by 93 single-unit firms, 134 plants were acquired by 132 non-manufacturing firms, and 431 plants were sold to 150 other nonmanufacturing multiunit firms.

For the nonacquiring group, we identified 17,409 firms that had at least one food manufacturing plant in 1977. Of the 17,409 firms, 15,067 were single-unit firms, 1,185 were nonmanufacturing firms having one food manufacturing plant, and 1,157 were multiunit manufacturing firms. These 1,157 firms owned 7,701 manufacturing plants (both food and nonfood plants) in 1977.

Thus our data cover the entire 1977 population of food-manufacturing firms in the United States. This population consists of 18,141 firms, of which 17,763 firms operated primarily in the food industry. The 18,141 firms owned 30,086 plants in 1977, of which 23,980 plants were owned by food firms and 6,106 plants were owned by nonfood firms.

6.3.2   Ownership Change: Concept and Measurement

Ownership and Control

"Ownership" refers to the person(s) that controls particular resources in the economy. Owners make the decisions about the use of these scarce resources. When resources change hands, the new owners typically change the way the resources are used. Therefore, ownership and ownership change are important aspects of economic growth and have important implications for economic policies. For example, antitrust authorities (the U.S. Department of Justice and the Federal Trade Commission) are concerned with the effects of ownership change on output and pricing decisions. The Securities and Exchange Commission protects minority shareholders' (owners') rights and protects the public

Table 6.1   **Acquiring and Nonacquiring Food-Producing Firms, 1977**

Firm	Number of Firms			Total Shipments (hundred thousand)	Total Employment	Average Employment	1977 Labor Productivity 1987 ($)
	Food[a]	Nonfood	Total				
Acquiring firms[b] 1977–82							
1. Single unit	62	31	93	1,381	14,694	158	73.94
2. Nonmanufacturing, one food plant	109	25	134	1,798	17,554	131	75.06
3. Nonmanufacturing, more than one food plant	103	47	150	9,623	75,600	504	86.73
4. Multiunit manufacturing	236	119	355	172,164	1,203,095	3,389	118.82
Total	510	222	732	184,967	1,278,695	1,747	97.75
Nonacquiring firms[b] 1977–82							
1. Single unit	15,067	–	15,067	26,124	286,273	19	67.20
2. Nonmanufacturing, one food plant	1,185	–	1,185	8,361	82,950	70	73.67
3. Multiunit[c]	1,001	156	1,157	129,466	1,253,031	1,083	89.42
Total	17,253	156	17,409	163,931	1,622,254	93	69.08

[a]Firms are allocated to food or nonfood industries based on the largest category of shipments.

[b]These firms had no acquisitions in the 1978–82 period but may have had acquisitions in the 1983–87 period.

[c]Includes multiunit firms with nonmanufacturing operations.

against securities fraud. These issues often become important when ownership shifts from one person or group to another. The Department of Labor is concerned with issues involving worker rights and working conditions that can change when ownership changes. Moreover, in the continuing debate on the relative roles of small and large firms in job creation and destruction, it is important to measure ownership and ownership change correctly.

None of the ownership concepts used in the databases underlying the studies considered in this paper (or any study) exactly match those needed for policy purposes. The key issue for policy is "control." Measuring control is particularly difficult for corporations. For corporations, the extent of ownership is determined by the proportion of the ownership shares held by an owner and the legal rules for exercising those shares. Roughly speaking, if a firm acquires more than 50 percent of the shares of another company, it obtains a majority of that firm and the ability to control it. It, of course, may decide not to exercise this right. But even without majority control, an owner may effectively control another company. The issue of who controls corporate assets has a long history. It was raised over 50 years ago by Berle and Means (1932) and is the subject of a large literature. For our purposes, we simply note that in some contexts criteria other than 50 percent ownership are used to approximate a level of ownership at which control is exerted. For example, for many securities transactions, a company is considered to be under the control of another if more than 10 percent of its stock is obtained by one investor.

Even if one settles on the conceptual issues and can precisely define "control," and thereby ownership, it is not simple to define ownership or measure ownership and ownership change in plant- and firm-level data sets like the LRD. These issues and a comparison of our methods for measuring ownership and ownership change with those of Lichtenberg and Siegel (1992a, 1992b) and Brown and Medoff (1988) are presented next.

Measuring Ownership and Ownership Change

Both Lichtenberg and Siegel's study and ours use the LRD as the source of the data set. The ownership concepts in the LRD reflect the LRD's roots in the Census Bureau's Standard Statistical Establishment List (SSEL), which is used as a sampling frame for most Census Bureau surveys of businesses with employment.[7] The SSEL contains current information on ownership, address, classification, employment, payroll, and operational status of each establishment. It also includes limited historical information. The SSEL is based on administrative information maintained in Internal Revenue Service (IRS), Social Security Administration, and (since 1990) Bureau of Labor Statistics re-

---

7. The SSEL is described in Bureau of the Census (1979), and its role in the Census Bureau's manufacturing establishment surveys is described in Cole, Petrik, and Struble (1995). The SSEL currently covers the following economic sectors: agriculture, mining, manufacturing, transportation and communication, wholesale, retail, finance, insurance, and real estate, services, and public administration.

cords. To facilitate the tracking of ownership at the plant level for the multiunit companies in the SSEL, the Census Bureau collects information from all multiunit companies in the economic censuses (every five years) and from a sample of companies in the Company Organization Survey (COS) in noncensus years. Moreover, ownership information on multiunit companies is often obtained from other ongoing Census Bureau surveys.

For the Census Bureau, a company (company A) owns another company (company B) if either of two basic criteria is met: (1) company A owns more than 50 percent of the voting stock of company B or (2) company A has the power to direct the management and policies of company B. Census Bureau data collection forms ask respondents whether they own or are owned by other companies. If the answer is yes, the forms request the name, address, and employer identification number (EIN) of the owned or owning companies. Each business with paid employees is required to obtain a nine-digit EIN from the IRS.

The IRS does not require an enterprise to obtain a unique EIN for each location (establishment) at which it operates—EINs are assigned to facilitate companies' tax reporting, and they can cover anything from a single establishment of a multiunit company up to the entire company. Therefore, the Census Bureau cannot assign a unique ID to each establishment from EINs alone. But it does use the EIN along with information from the COS in constructing its ID numbers. In the LRD, the ID numbers of particular plants can and do change over time. An ID change often indicates an ownership change, but it can indicate other things as well. The following describes the process we used to identify ownership changes and separate them from other types of ID changes.

To identify ownership changes in the LRD requires three steps: (1) Identify plants that change firm ID between two census years. (2) Within this set of plants, use certain codes in the LRD, called coverage codes (CC codes), to identify directly a subset of plants that change ownership for a particular reason. (3) From the remaining plants, identify further ownership changes indirectly.

In step 1 in identifying mergers, we observe the change in the firm ID numbers of each establishment in the period under study. A change in ID can mean any of the following:

1. The establishment was sold to another firm—a true ownership change (merger).
2. A multiunit firm (a firm that owns more than one plant) closed or sold all of its plants but one and became a single-unit firm (a firm with only one plant).
3. A single-unit firm became a multiunit firm by opening new plants or acquiring existing plants. (Note that the ID variable in the LRD for each plant of a multiunit firm incorporates a code for the firm to which the plant belongs.)
4. A multiunit or single-unit firm underwent a legal reorganization (e.g.,

partnership to corporation) that spurred a firm ID change without a change in actual ownership.

5. Errors—erroneous ID changes can occur.

To identify most true ownership changes (mergers or divestitures)—step 2—we need to use information available in the LRD in addition to the ID variable. The main additional information is in the census CC codes assigned to establishments in the census or Annual Survey of Manufactures (ASM). The CC codes are two-digit numbers indicating the status of the establishment in the survey. In particular, there is a CC code indicating that an establishment was acquired by another company. For a complete list of CC codes, see the LRD documentation (Bureau of the Census 1992).

Ideally, all new firm ID and CC codes would be recorded during the years that establishments change status (including ownership), so that it would be easy to identify mergers. In practice, this does not always happen. Except for a set of large ASM establishments, neither changes in ID nor proper CC codes are systematically recorded during the years of status change. In many cases, particularly for small establishments, a change in firm ID appears one or more years before the corresponding CC code change occurs to explain the reason for the ID change. The reverse is also possible: the CC code can indicate an ownership change before the ID changes. To mitigate these problems, we examined CC codes in the years before and after the ID change. However, these procedures have two problems. First, in ASM (noncensus) years, not all plants are in the data set, and in particular, when the ASM panel changes (in years ending in 4 and 9), the set of noncertainty cases (the smaller plants) turns over completely. Second, for a number of single-unit non-ASM establishments (in census years), proper CC codes are not assigned at all.

So, using CC codes allows us to identify only a portion of the establishments that have ID changes due to ownership changes. However, as table 6.2 indicates, this is a large portion. The table summarizes the results for plants that are classified in the food industry. We identified 2,010 establishments that changed ID between 1977 and 1982. The CC codes gave reasons for ID change for 85.7 percent (1,722) of these establishments—of these, 1,507 (75 percent) were acquired and 215 (10.7 percent) changed ID for other known reasons, such as reclassification, combined reports, firm reorganization, and so forth. The remaining 14.3 percent of establishments (288) were not assigned a CC code.

For the 288 plants with unexplained ID changes, we brought together initial and ending firm IDs for all plants that were owned by the firm in question. For example, suppose the LRD shows that plant A belonged to firm X in 1977 and to firm Y in 1982, but the 1982 CC code for plant A does not show this as an ownership change. Suppose, however, we know that firm Y also acquired at least one other plant from firm X between 1977 and 1982. In this case, it seems likely that firm Y bought plant A as well, and we code plant A accordingly. By

Table 6.2   Identifying Ownership Change in SIC 20 (Food), 1977–82

Reason for ID Change	Ownership Change Identified Using CC Codes Only			Ownership Change Identified Using CC Codes and Matching Techniques		
	Number of Plants	Percentage of Plants	Average Employment	Number of Plants	Percentage of Plants	Average Employment
Acquired	1,507	75.0	177.9	1,573	78.3	174.2
Converted	160	8.0	112.8	160	8.0	112.8
Duplicate	2	0.1	D	2	1.0	D
Error	4	0.2	D	4	0.2	D
Reclassified	18	0.9	60.8	18	0.9	60.8
Reorganized	22	1.0	124.8	22	1.0	124.8
Sold to nonmanufacturing firm	6	0.3	D	6	0.3	D
Split	3	0.1	D	3	0.1	D
Nonidentifiable	288	14.3	89.1	222	11.0	88.5
Total	2,010	100.0	158.0	2,010	100.0	158.0

Note: D = suppressed to prevent disclosure of confidential information on individual firms.

making such assumptions, we increase the number of plants identified as acquired by 66 to 1,573.[8]

Lichtenberg and Siegel (1992b) use two separate data sets for their studies. One data set is taken from the Census Bureau's auxiliary reports of the 1977 and 1982 economic censuses. This data set is used to study the effects of ownership change on central office employees. The other data set is a balanced panel extracted from the LRD. It contains 20,493 U.S. manufacturing plants that continuously operated during the period 1972–81. This sample is about 6 percent of the population of U.S. manufacturing establishments in 1977 (350,648 establishments), but it accounts for about 55 percent of total U.S. manufacturing employment in that year. Thus the establishments in the Lichtenberg and Siegel data set are very large. Specifically, 82 percent of the plants in this sample employ at least 250 workers, 28.8 percent employ between 250 and 499 workers, and 52.7 percent employ more than 500. The average number of workers per establishment is 501, almost 10 times as large as the population average (53 workers).

Lichtenberg and Siegel identify ownership changes using only CC codes (Lichtenberg and Siegel 1992a, 31). They do not take our last step of trying to identify ownership changes not indicated by CC codes.[9] However, their procedure probably presents few problems for accurately tracking ownership change of the plants included in their sample because they use only the balanced panel that contains the largest establishments in the LRD. These plants are generally included in the ASM and have CC codes. On the other hand, because their sample excludes all plants (both small and large) that entered or exited manufacturing after 1972, Lichtenberg and Siegel miss a significant number of plants entering manufacturing and changing owners after 1972 and those that had ownership change during 1972–80 and exited by or before 1981.[10] For the period 1972–81, they identify about 4,300 manufacturing plants changing ownership (21 percent of their sample of 20,500 continuous plants). In preliminary work for the entire manufacturing sector, McGuckin and Nguyen find 7,414 plants with at least one change during the period 1972–77 and 12,289 plants changing owners during 1977–82.

Lichtenberg and Siegel's data set has several disadvantages. First, because

8. Recall that section 6.3.1 indicates that the 1977–82 selling firms sold 1,573 food plants and 538 nonfood plants.

9. For their study of employment in auxiliary establishments, Lichtenberg and Siegel (1992a, 31–32) assume that ownership changes if and only if the ID of the auxiliary establishment changes. They recognize that "this procedure is subject to errors: Some nonmatches of the code may be due to coding errors, and certain ownership changes may not result in changes in the code" (Lichtenberg and Siegel 1992b, 49).

10. The ending date, 1981, of the Lichtenberg-Siegel sample period is unfortunate because it is just before the 1982 Census of Manufactures. This means that extensive revisions in the Census Bureau data files undertaken in preparation for each economic census were not available to help identify ownership change. This increases the possibility of mistakes in identifying ownership change. On the other hand, restriction of the sample to large plants, while raising selection bias issues, mitigates the source of this measurement error in their study.

their balanced panel contains only large, surviving plants, it is not representative of the entire distribution of plants. In fact, it excludes most acquisitions from consideration. Second, their sample requires continuous plants and, hence, excludes plants entering manufacturing after 1972 and subsequently acquired. Finally, their sample excludes closed plants, including plants acquired between 1973 and 1980 and closed by or before 1981.

Brown and Medoff (1988) use data on the employment and wages of firms in Michigan compiled from unemployment insurance (ES-202) records kept by the Michigan Employment Security Commission (MESC). The research database, constructed at the Institute for Social Research at the University of Michigan, covers over 200,000 firms located in the state of Michigan during the period 1978:3–1984:4, is described in Brown et al. (1990). The basic documentation is in Connor et al. (1984).

The MESC database contains data on all Michigan employers that are required to pay unemployment insurance taxes ("liable employers"). The MESC system assigns a six-digit unemployment insurance number to each firm. (The MESC data system also includes the EIN—so there is a link between the EIN and the unemployment insurance number—but the research file used by Brown and Medoff does not include the EIN.) MESC tracks ownership changes that affect the set of liable employers. In general, liable employers are those that had employees in each of a set of different weeks in a calendar year, had persons covered by unemployment insurance on their payrolls, or acquired another liable employer.[11] A business can acquire another business through "sale, foreclosure, lease, bankruptcy, or merger" (MESC 1995, 7). The new owner is known as the successor, and the process of acquiring an existing business is called successorship.[12]

The MESC data set allows Brown and Medoff (1988) to define three types of acquisitions: (1) "simple sales," (2) "asset-only sales," and (3) "mergers." They also define "reorganizations," which look like simple sales except that the type of business changes. Brown and Medoff recognize the difficulty in distinguishing between reorganizations and simple sales.

This data set contains firm-level data, in contrast to the plant-level data in the LRD. The MESC has two advantages over the LRD (used in Lichtenberg and Siegel study and ours): it is not limited to the manufacturing sector, and it has relatively complete coverage of firm activity within Michigan (at least

---

11. As of 1995, "generally, a liable employer is an employing unit that either (1) employed one or more employees in each of any 20 different weeks in a calendar year . . . ; or (2) paid $1,000 or more in payroll in a calendar year to employees covered by unemployment insurance; or (3) acquired the trade, organization (i.e., all employees), or business, or at least 75 percent of the assets of a liable employer" (MESC 1995, 2). There are different requirements for employers of agricultural or domestic workers.

12. As of 1995, "if a new or existing business acquires 75 percent or more of the assets of another business, and within 12 months either continues the previous or a similar business, or uses the trade name or good will of the previous business, then there is a mandatory transfer of the unemployment tax experience, or history, of the previous business" (MESC 1995, 7).

firms covered by unemployment insurance). However, the MESC data set exhibits certain weaknesses in identifying ownership changes. A major weakness—not shared by the LRD—stems from its coverage of only one state. Mergers between a Michigan firm and an out-of-state firm will look like a simple sale because there is no record of the out-of-state firm in the MESC data set. Also, when a Michigan firm acquires an out-of-state firm, there is no record of the acquisition at all (Brown and Medoff 1988, 12). "For instance, General Motors' acquisition of EDS and Hughes Aircraft would probably not be recorded in their data" (Carliner 1988, 27). Farber observed that "the central limitation of the data is that it deals explicitly with employment in Michigan. In particular, many firms have business . . . operations that span state boundaries, so that looking strictly at Michigan employment is likely to give a misleading picture of both the employment size distribution of firms involved in mergers and acquisitions and the employment effects of mergers and acquisition" (1988, 28–29).

Compared to Brown and Medoff's and Lichtenberg and Siegel's data sets, our sample has several advantages. First, our data cover the entire *population* of the food-manufacturing industry and includes all small, medium-size, and large establishments located anywhere in the United States. Second, our unbalanced panel includes both entering and exiting plants. This allows us to more accurately measure ownership change activities and hence the effects of ownership change on labor. Finally, our decomposition of individual firms into separate components (own plant, closed plant, and acquired plant, etc.) allows us to take a close look at individual components of the firm before and after ownership change.

While our data set has advantages, it also has several shortcomings. First, it includes only one two-digit SIC industry. Therefore, it is not representative of the entire U.S. manufacturing sector. Second, it does not contain data for central offices. This prevents us from examining the effect of ownership change on control management operations. Finally, as with the other two data sets, ours does not contain information on types of merger, for example, whether a takeover is hostile or friendly.

6.3.3   Unit of Analysis: Firm versus Plant

An important issue in studying the impact of ownership change on firms' activities is: What is the appropriate unit of analysis? Is the "firm" or "plant" the right unit of analysis? Because acquisition is part of a strategy to realign resources and operations of the firm—a strategy that may encompass acquisition, divestiture, and internal growth—the *composition effects* associated with the nature and timing of the transaction may be important in assessing the impact of particular transactions. Indeed, the components of a firm can and do change over time. In particular, the mix of plants of an acquiring firm before and after merger can differ substantially. Before merger, the firm owns a set of plants: some will be closed, some will be sold, and others will be retained by the firm. After merger, the structure of the firm may look much different from before: it now includes acquired plants and plants that are newly built in addition to its surviving own plants. Thus simply looking at the performance (e.g., employment, wage, and productivity growth) of the *whole* firm before and after merger may not be appropriate. A related issue involves the empirical flexibility and richness of models based on plant-level data.

For example, in their conclusions, Brown and Medoff point out that "the estimated effects of mergers are also subject to a composition effect. If the (relatively highly paid) head of the acquired firm leaves following the merger, average wages will fall. Given the small size of our typical firm, a nontrivial share of our estimated wage decline from merger may be due to such composition effects" (1988, 23). Lichtenberg and Siegel's results based on plant-level data provide strong evidence on this composition effect: ownership changes have a significant, negative effect on both employment and wage growth in central offices and little effect in production plants. The advantages of plant data are discussed further in McGuckin (1995).

6.3.4 Variable Measurement

The main variables used in this study are employment, wages, and productivity.

Employment and Wage Variables

Employment is measured by the total number of employees, which comprise production workers and nonproduction workers. Wages are defined as workers' annual salaries. We note that this measure of wages does not include nonwage costs associated with labor because separate data on these costs are not available for the two types of workers. In addition, Dunne and Roberts find that "non-wage costs are a poorly reported variable in the census data . . . many of the plants have this variable imputed" (1993, 7). Following Dunne and Roberts, we do not include nonwage costs in the wage measure used here. This is a potentially important measurement problem since the form of compensation can vary across firms and industries. Real wages are defined as nominal wages deflated by the consumer price index taken from the *Survey of Current Business* (September 1993).

Productivity Measurement

We use value of shipments as our measure of output in the productivity measure. Data on value added are not always available, particularly for small plants. In practice, productivity results using either measure are highly correlated. For example, the results in McGuckin and Nguyen (1994), which also use food industry data over this period, are unaffected by the choice of value added or shipments. (See also Baily et al. 1992; Baily et al. 1994.)

Productivity can be measured either for each single input such as labor (labor productivity, LP) or for all inputs (total factor productivity, TFP). Theoretically, TFP is the appropriate measure of productivity because it takes into account all inputs. In practice, LP is often used because data on inputs, such as capital, that are required for the measurement of TFP are not available. Because of data limitations, we base our analysis on LP.[13]

Plant LP is measured as value of shipments in current dollars divided by the total number of employees. While output prices and value of shipments vary across plants and over time because of price dispersion and inflation, deflating each plant's LP by its industry average LP produces a comparable productivity measure through time.[14] We call this adjusted LP measure relative labor productivity (RLP).[15]

Plant RLP provides a good measure of plant performance if all plants in the same industry have similar input-output ratios. If the production technology differs substantially among plants, RLP could be a misleading measure of performance. However, in our earlier work (McGuckin and Nguyen 1994), we estimate TFP for a number of large plants for which the required data are available. We then compare the TFP results to the RLP results and find that both measures lead to the same conclusions regarding plant performance.

While single-unit firms are classified in a single industry, multiunit firms often have plants operating in various industries. For multiunit firms, we calculate the productivity for each plant separately then obtain the firm productivity as a weighted sum of plant productivities. Thus we measure the RLP of the firm by

$$(1) \qquad \mathrm{RLP}_k^F = \sum_j w_{kj} \mathrm{RLP}_{kj},$$

where RLP_k^F is RLP of firm k, the weight w_{kj} is the ratio of plant j's employment to the total number of employees of firm k, and the summation is over the n plants of firm k.

6.4 Descriptive Statistics

6.4.1 Firm-Level Data

Table 6.3 presents 1977 and 1987 wages, productivity, and total employment for all firms operating in the food industry during the period under study. Since we only observe the manufacturing operations of each firm, we classify acquiring firms into four groups: (1) single-unit firms, (2) multiunit nonmanufacturing firms entering manufacturing by buying one food plant, (3) multiunit nonmanufacturing firms entering manufacturing by buying more than one food

---

13. McGuckin and Nguyen (1994) estimate both RLP and TFP using data for 3,800 continuous plants in the food industry. They then use these two productivity estimates in their regression analysis of ownership change and find that the two measures yield very similar results. They note, however, that the results based on data for continuous plants are subject to serious sample selection bias.

14. Industry is defined at the four-digit level throughout the paper.

15. For further justification on its use, see McGuckin and Nguyen (1994) and Christensen, Cumming, and Jorgenson (1981).

Table 6.3 Acquiring and Nonacquiring Food Manufacturing Firms 1977–87

Firm	Average Employment Size		No. of Firms		Wage Rate		Total Employment		1977 RLP[a]	
	1977	1987	1977	1987	1977	1987	1977	1987	1977	1987
Acquiring firms 1977–82										
1. Single unit										
Surviving by 1987	113	79	25	25	20,228	18,911	2,821	1,980	.82	.65
Sold by 1987	195	–	–	–	22,183	–	2,920	–	1.11	–
Exit by 1987	172	–	–	–	20,747	–	8,955	–	.98	–
Subtotal	158	79	25	25	20,839	18,911	14,696	1,980	.96	.65
2. Nonmanufacturing, one food plant										
Surviving by 1987	91	208	48	48	22,581	20,817	4,379	9,997	1.09	.98
Sold by 1987	225	–	33	–	19,708	–	7,425	–	.82	–
Exit by 1987	109	–	53	–	19,751	–	5,754	–	.93	–
Subtotal	131	208	134	48	20,754	20,817	17,558	9,997	.96	.96
3. Nonmanufacturing, more than one food plant										
Surviving by 1987	638	1,086	84	84	22,605	22,566	53,557	91,201	1.03	1.07
Sold by 1987	393	–	40	–	20,323	–	15,739	–	1.05	–
Exit by 1987	234	–	27	–	21,202	–	6,308	–	1.07	–
Subtotal	501	1,086	151	84	21,750	22,566	75,604	91,201	1.04	1.07

4. Multiunit manufacturing									
Surviving by 1987	3,649	5,011	268	268	22,352	23,360	977,878	1,343,051	1.14	1.08
Sold by 1987	2,407	–	65	–	22,202	–	221,430	–	1.03	–
Exit by 1987	157	–	22	–	24,200	–	3,463	–	1.07	–
Subtotal	3,338	5,011	355	268	22,439	23,360	1,202,734	1,343,051	1.11	1.08
Nonacquiring firms 1977–82[b]									
1. Single unit									
Surviving by 1987	25	32	5,162	5,162	19,849	16,222	129,050	163,864	.76	.69
Sold by 1987	60	–	436	–	20,266	–	26,160	–	.90	–
Exit by 1987	13	–	9,469	–	19,438	–	123,097	–	.78	–
Subtotal	18	32	15,067	5,162	19,603	16,222	278,307	163,864	.78	.69
2. Nonmanufacturing, one food plant									
Surviving by 1987	90	121	475	475	19,908	19,507	42,750	57,686	.88	.82
Sold by 1987	126	144	80	80	21,431	21,851	10,080	11,527	.96	–
Exit by 1987	48	–	630	–	19,467	–	30,240	–	.84	–
Subtotal	70	125	1,185	555	19,776	19,845	83,070	69,213	.87	.82
3. Multiunit manufacturing[c]									
Surviving by 1987	1,570	1,451	667	667	21,298	22,203	1,047,255	967,793	1.00	1.02
Sold by 1987	981	–	169	–	21,843	–	165,789	–	.96	–
Exit by 1987	124	–	321	–	19,735	–	39,804	–	.90	–
Subtotal	1,083	1,451	1,157	667	20,940	22,203	1,252,848	967,793	.97	1.02

[a]Multiunit firm productivity is based on the weighted average (labor weights) of plant productivity.

[b]Includes 120 firms that acquired properties in the 1983–87 period.

[c]Includes multiunit firms with nonmanufacturing operations.

plant, and (4) multiunit manufacturing acquiring firms. Using the same framework gives three groups for nonacquiring firms: (1) single-unit firms, (2) nonmanufacturing multiunit firms having only one plant operating in the food-manufacturing industry, and (3) multiunit manufacturing firms having at least one plant operating in the food-manufacturing industry.

While we report data by each grouping of firms, we focus our discussion on multiunit manufacturing firms because they account for most economic activity in the food industry, regardless of how economic activity is defined. For example, in both 1977 and 1987, multiunit manufacturing acquirers accounted for more than 91 percent of the total number of workers employed by all firms that acquired at least one food plant. Multiunit manufacturing firms also accounted for large fractions of total nonacquiring firm output, 77.6 and 80.0 percent in 1977 and 1987, respectively.

Table 6.3 shows a striking difference in employment growth between acquiring and nonacquiring surviving firms. The average size of multiunit manufacturing acquiring firms increased by 37.3 percent (from 3,649 employees in 1977 to 5,011 employees in 1987), whereas the average size of nonacquiring multiunit manufacturing firms declined by 7.6 percent during the same period (from 1,570 in 1977 to 1,451 employees in 1987). By 1987 the 268 surviving multiunit acquiring firms employed in total 1,343,051 workers, approximately 12 percent more than the total employment of the 1977 cohort of 355 acquiring firms (1,202,734 workers) and 37.3 percent more than the 977,878 workers they employed in 1977. In contrast, by 1987 the 667 surviving multiunit nonacquiring firms employed 967,793 workers, a 7.6 percent decline from their 1977 employment level and well below the 1,252,848 workers employed by the 1977 cohort of 1,157 firms that did not change owners during 1977–82.

Turning to wages, we find that, on average, multiunit firms paid the highest wages. Multiunit acquiring firms paid average wages of $22,439 (in 1987 dollars) per year in 1977 and $23,360 per year in 1987, a 3.6 percent increase in real wages. Multiunit nonacquiring firms paid average wages of $20,940 per year in 1977 and $22,203 in 1987, a 5.7 percent increase.

Regarding productivity, we find that firms having the highest initial productivity survived, while those with the lowest closed. Acquired firms had above average levels of productivity, but their productivity levels were well below those of surviving firms and above those of closed firms. Acquiring firms had higher productivity levels than nonacquiring firms in both 1977 and 1987. The 1977 and 1987 productivities of acquiring firms were 1.14 and 1.08, while those of nonacquiring firms were 1.00 and 1.02, respectively. Thus, although acquiring firms showed higher productivity levels at both the beginning and end of the 1977–87 period, they experienced a 56 percent decline in relative productivity over the period, while nonacquiring firms showed modest productivity improvement (2.0 percent).

Unfortunately, it is not clear from these results exactly how acquisition affects a firm's productivity, employment, and wages. For example, table 6.3

shows that acquiring firms increased their employment substantially during the 1977–87 period, but it is not clear whether this increase came from upsizing existing plants or acquired plants or simply from opening new plants. In a similar vein, the decline in productivity of acquiring firms could come from the diminishing productivity of old existing plants or acquisition of plants with productivity levels below those already a part of the firm, or it could come from a decline in productivity of acquired plants. It is imperative to turn to plant-level data and examine the performance of the different components of the firm to isolate the impacts of acquisition on observed firm-level results.

6.4.2 Plant-Level Data

Table 6.4 reports productivity, total employment, and wages for individual components of both acquiring and nonacquiring firms in 1977 and 1987. Columns (1) and (2) show that, except for plants purchased during 1983–87 by firms acquiring in both the 1977–82 and 1983–87 periods, all groups of purchased plants show improvement in relative productivity by 1987. Specifically, plants purchased during 1977–82 and kept by acquiring firms through 1987 increased their productivity by 4 percent (from 1.02 in 1977 to 1.06 in 1987). Plants purchased by (1977–82) nonacquirers during 1983–87 also increased their productivity by 2 percent (from 0.95 in 1977 to 0.97 in 1987).

In contrast, the relative productivity of plants initially owned and kept until 1987 by both acquirers and nonacquirers declined noticeably: a 6 percent decline for plants owned by acquirers (from 1.18 in 1977 to 1.11 in 1987) and a 5 percent decline for plants owned by nonacquirers (from 1.04 in 1977 to 0.99 in 1987). New plants opened by both acquirers and nonacquirers had 1987 productivity levels well above those of existing and purchased plants.

These results suggest two major sources for the observed decrease in the relative productivity of acquiring firms. The first is the decline in the *relative* efficiency of older plants initially owned by the acquiring firms. The second is the lower productivity of the plants purchased by acquirers: while acquired plants experienced a noticeable improvement in productivity, their 1987 productivity levels were still below those of old (1977 kept plants) and new plants. Inclusion of these "below average" plants lowers the average productivity of the firm.

New plants built by both acquirers and nonacquirers had the highest levels of productivity. For nonacquirers, these high-productivity new plants offset the decline in the relative efficiency of their older plants. However, in the case of acquiring firms, the high productivity of new plants could not compensate for the relative efficiency decline because acquired plants had lower levels of productivity than previously owned plants. Thus, even though acquired plants had above industry average productivity prior to acquisition and became more productive after acquisition, the firm-level relative productivity of acquiring firms fell.

Turning to employment, columns (3) and (4) show that both acquiring and

| | Table 6.4 | | Productivity, Employment, and Wages of Acquiring and Nonacquiring Multiunit Manufacturing Firms and Component Parts, 1977 and 1987 (simple means) | | | |

	Relative Productivity		Total Employment		Real Wage Rates	
Firm or Component	1977 (1)	1987 (2)	1977 (3)	1987 (4)	1977 (5)	1987 (6)
Acquiring firms 1977–82[a]						
Surviving to 1987	1.14	1.08	977,878	1,343,051	22,352	23,630
Sold by 1987	1.03	–	221,430	–	22,202	–
Exit by 1987	1.07	–	3,460	–	24,200	–
All firms	1.12	1.08	1,202,768	1,343,051	22,439	23,630
Components of surviving acquiring firms						
Plants owned in 1977						
Kept in 1987	1.18	1.11	647,486	662,300	22,554	23,793
Sold by 1987	1.11	–	139,643	–	22,645	–
Exit by 1987	1.04	–	190,749	–	21,628	–
All plants	1.12	1.11	977,878	662,300	21,806	23,793
Plants acquired 1977–82						
Kept in 1987	1.02	1.06	189,496	261,811	21,198	21,653
Sold by 1987	.95	–	75,234	–	21,265	–
Exit by 1987	.97	–	15,919	–	24,205	–
All plants	.98	1.06	280,649	261,811	21,629	21,653
New plants 1977–82	–	1.20	–	52,335	–	21,808
New plants 1983–87	–	1.16	–	67,687	–	23,034
Plants acquired 1983–87	1.01	.98	322,328	347,404	21,719	21,876
Nonacquiring firms 1977–82[a,b]						
Surviving to 1987	1.00	1.02	1,047,255	967,793	21,291	22,203
Sold by 1987	.96	–	165,789	–	21,843	–
Exit by 1987	.90	–	39,804	–	19,735	–
All firms	.97	1.02	1,252,848	967,793	21,422	22,203
Components of surviving nonacquiring firms						
Plants owned in 1977						
Kept in 1987	1.04	.99	639,377	595,662	21,515	22,184
Sold by 1987	1.05	–	127,241	–	22,616	–
Exit by 1987	.95	–	235,637	–	20,198	–
All plants	1.01	.99	1,047,255	595,662	21,136	22,184
New plants 1978–82	–	1.21	–	65,626	–	20,935
New plants 1983–87	–	1.15	–	100,145	–	22,305
Plants acquired 1983–87	.95	.97	183,752	206,360	22,157	22,376

[a]Firm productivity is based on the weighted average (labor weights) of plant productivity.

[b]Includes 120 firms that acquired plants in the 1983–87 period.

nonacquiring firms were very active in restructuring themselves. Each sold and built new plants and closed old plants. However, only acquirers also bought plants. Acquiring firms increased their employment, while nonacquiring firms showed decreases. The reason for this difference is that acquiring firms increased their employment by acquiring and building plants more than they decreased their employment by closing and selling plants. In contrast, nonacquiring firms closed and sold more plants than they built.

One of the reasons that the surviving acquiring firms show good job performance is that they include the employment of sold firms that they acquire. As shown in table 6.4, this source of growth for acquiring firms is substantial. But even taking this source of employment into account does not alter the conclusion that ownership change is associated with employment increases. Unlike acquirers that hired more workers for their existing plants, nonacquiring firms cut employment in their existing plants. Taken together, the net employment gain for plants purchased by acquirers during 1977–87 was 16,238 workers (from 602,977 workers in 1977 to 619,215 workers in 1987).

Finally, columns (5) and (6) report on annual wages. In general, plants owned by acquiring firms paid higher wages than those owned by nonacquiring firms. This is expected because, on average, acquirers' plants were bigger and more productive than nonacquirers' plants. Nonetheless, the differences between acquiring and nonacquiring firms are not large in either 1977 or 1987. While both surviving acquiring and nonacquiring firms show increases in real wages in all their components, the observed increases range from 2 to 7 percent over the 10-year interval.

These statistics suggest that ownership change had positive effects on both employment and productivity growth during the period under study. For wages, the difference in performance appears much smaller. However, conclusions based on simple averages like these can only be tentative because they do not control for the effects of factors other than ownership change. Among other things, such factors include the firm's size, technology, and the industry in which the firm operates. For this reason, we turn to a regression analysis. This allows us to assess the impact of ownership change on employment, wages, and productivity while controlling for possible effects of other factors. It also helps to clarify the important differences in experimental design associated with use of firm or plant as the unit of analysis.

6.5 Regression Analysis

In this section, we use the detailed microdata described above to estimate the effects of ownership change on employment, wage, and labor productivity growth. To control for the effects of factors other than ownership change, we estimate reduced-form regressions in which the growth rates of employment, wages, and productivity are the dependent variables. Ownership change and several predetermined variables are used as explanatory variables. We also perform probit regressions designed to assess the likelihood that ownership change is associated with plant closures. We note that most variables in our models are likely to be determined jointly, and without a structural model, including good instrumental variables, we are limited in what we can say about causality. Nonetheless, we think this exercise is an instructive first step in understanding the role of ownership change in labor markets.

We specify our wage and employment equations as

$$\ln X_{87} - \ln X_{77} = a_0 + a_1 OC_{77\text{-}82} + a_2 \ln W_{77} + a_3 \ln E_{77}$$
$$+ a_4 \Delta\text{TECH} + a_{12} OC_{77\text{-}82} * \ln E_{77},$$

(2)

where ln is natural logarithm; X denotes total employment (number of workers, E) or wages (Wage); OC is a dummy variable (OC = 1 if the firm or plant experienced ownership change; otherwise OC = 0); and ΔTECH denotes change in technology of the firm or plant. The ratio of machinery and equipment to capital stock provides a proxy for the level of technology of the firm— we assume that given the same level of capital stock, the firm that uses more equipment and machinery is more technologically advanced. This variable may also be viewed as an adjustment to account for the fact that, other things equal, labor productivities will be higher in capital-intensive plants.

The above wage and employment equations are similar to those used by Brown and Medoff (1988) and Lichtenberg and Siegel (1992b). They reflect specifications used in the literature analyzing the impact of training on workers' earnings and employment. The basic idea underlying the equations is to ask whether changes in ownership had significant effects on employment and wages controlling for initial conditions (i.e., initial employment and wages). Our specifications differ in that we also include the variable ΔTECH and an interaction term, $OC_{77\text{-}82} * \ln E_{77}$, to allow for interactions between OC and (employment) size. We do this because our data reveal that large firms (or plants) behave differently from small ones.

Similarly, our productivity change equation is specified as

$$\ln \text{RLP}_{87} - \ln \text{RLP}_{77} = b_0 + b_1 OC_{77\text{-}82} + b_2 \ln \text{RLP}_{77} + b_3 \ln E_{77}$$

(3)

$$+ b_4 \Delta\text{TECH} + a_{13} OC_{77\text{-}82} * \ln E_{77}$$

$$+ a_{23} \ln \text{RLP}_{77} * \ln E_{77},$$

where RLP denotes relative labor productivity. Other variables are defined as above.

The regression analysis outlined so far is based on *surviving* plants: each equation relates ownership change to changes in productivity, wages, and employment that are estimated using data on surviving plants. Thus it is important to address the issue of plant closing or exiting after ownership change. To do so, we run probit regressions in which plant closing (PC) is the dependent variable. Ownership change (OC) is specified as an explanatory variable. We include initial relative productivity (RLP_{77}) and employment (E_{77}) as control variables. For comparisons, we also include the variable $OWNPLT_{AF77}$, which identifies whether the plant was originally owned by an acquiring firm in 1977 (the omitted category is plants that were owed by nonacquiring firms in 1977). Finally, we allow for nonlinear effects of initial productivity and employment size on plant closure. Our probit regression is

(4)
$$PC_{87} = a_0 + a_1 OC_{77\text{-}87} + a_2 OWNPLT_{AF77} + a_3 RLP_{77} + a_4 \ln E_{77}$$
$$+ a_{13} OC_{77\text{-}87} * RLP_{77} + a_{14} OC_{77\text{-}87} * \ln E_{77}$$
$$+ a_{23} OWNPLT_{AF77} * \ln E_{77} + a_{33}(RLP_{77})^2$$
$$+ a_{44}(\ln E_{77})^2 + a_{34} RLP_{77} * \ln E_{77},$$

where PC_{87} equals one if the plant was closed by 1987 (zero otherwise), $OC_{77\text{-}87}$ equals one if the plant changed ownership during 1977–87 (zero otherwise), and $OWNPLT_{AF77}$ equals one if the plant was owned by an acquiring firm in 1977 (zero otherwise). The remaining variables are defined as before.

Before proceeding, we note that RLP_{77}, E_{77}, and W_{77} may reflect "transitory" rather than "initial" conditions of plants acquired during 1977–82. A better approach is to use data on these variables for several years before the plant is acquired to describe its initial condition. However, doing so requires continuous data, which in turn significantly reduces our sample size. Estimates based on such a truncated sample could lead to serious sample selection bias. Nevertheless, in preliminary work using data for the entire U.S. manufacturing sector, use of average values of 1972 and 1977 data as a proxies for initial conditions of acquired plants (e.g., initial $RLP = (RLP_{72} + RLP_{77})/2$) shows results very similar to those using 1977 values alone.

6.6   Regression Results

6.6.1   Firm-Level Results

Table 6.5 reports the firm-level results for the wage, employment, and productivity equations.[16] In each equation, the variable ACQUIRER equals one if the firm is an acquiring firm. FOOD is a zero-one dummy variable having a value of one if the firm is a primary food-producing firm. The variable ξ is the residual estimated from the productivity equation (3). This variable is included in the wage equation to capture the possible effect of productivity on wages. We use ξ instead of the explicit productivity variable to avoid a potential simultaneity problem. Inclusion of ξ, FOOD, and ΔTECH does not significantly affect the estimated coefficients of the key variable ACQUIRER.

---

16. In our preliminary work, we estimated various competing models for each equation. Here we report only the results of two models for each equation because other models yield very similar results.

Table 6.5   **Firm-Level Regressions**

Independent Variable	Wage Equation		Employment Equation		Productivity Equation	
	Model I (1)	Model II (2)	Model I (3)	Model II (4)	Model I (5)	Model II (6)
Intercept	1.094*	1.143*	.536	.390	.452*	.519*
	(12.6)	(13.8)	(1.6)	(1.1)	(3.8)	(4.0)
ACQUIRER	−.082	−.087	.459	.166	−.196	−.205
	(1.2)	(1.4)	(1.7)	(1.7)	(1.3)	(1.4)
$\ln E_{77}$	.046+	.012	−.262*	−.258*	−.022	−.024*
	(2.1)	(1.7)	(8.9)	(8.6)	(0.9)	(1.0)
$\ln W_{77}$	−.384*	−.374*	.234+	.241+		
	(14.5)	(15.5)	(2.3)	(2.1)		
$\ln RLP_{77}$					−.363*	−.358*
					(4.8)	(4.8)
$\ln E_{77}*$ACQUIRER	.010	.010	.067	.068	.031	.030
	(0.9)	(0.9)	(1.6)	(1.6)	(1.3)	(1.3)
$\ln E_{77}*\ln RLP_{77}$					.006	.006
					(0.4)	(1.4)
ΔTECH		.138*		.047		−.317*
		(2.5)		(0.2)		(2.4)
FOOD		−.076*		.115		−.069
		(3.8)		(1.3)		(1.4)
ξ		.188*				
		(12.5)				
R^2	.212	.353	.166	.166	.147	.154
n	804	804	804	804	804	804

Notes: Dependent variables of the wage, employment, and productivity equations are $\ln W_{87} - \ln W_{77}$, $\ln E_{87} - \ln E_{77}$, and $\ln RLP_{87} - \ln RLP_{77}$, respectively. Numbers in parentheses are t-ratios.
*Significant at the 1 percent level.
+Significant at the 5 percent level.

For the wage equation (cols. [1] and [2]), the ACQUIRER coefficient is about −0.08 and that for the interaction term, $\ln E_{77} *$ ACQUIRER, is 0.01. These estimates imply that the wage growth of a typical acquiring firm—a firm with average (log) employment of 5.65—is about 2.5 percent higher than that of a typical nonacquiring firm, but the result is not statistically significant. This estimate is consistent with the Brown and Medoff (1988) firm-level finding that the impact of acquisition on wages is small.

Columns (3) and (4) present estimated coefficients for the employment equations. The coefficient for ACQUIRER is 0.166 and that for $\ln E_{77} *$ ACQUIRER is 0.068 (col. [4]), indicating that, on average, the employment growth of acquiring firms is about 55.2 percent (= 0.166 + 0.068(5.65)) higher than that of nonacquiring firms. While this estimate is not statistically significant, it appears to be economically significant. Acquiring firms do not appear to reduce their workforces.

Finally, columns (5) and (6) show estimated coefficients for the productivity growth equations. The estimated coefficient for the ACQUIRER variable is about -0.200 and that for $\ln E_{77}$ * ACQUIRER is 0.006. These estimates imply labor productivity growth for an average acquiring firm about 16.5 percent lower than that for an average nonacquiring firm. While economically significant, the estimated coefficients are statistically insignificant. The negative coefficients for ACQUIRER are consistent with the figures reported in table 6.3 showing that the average relative labor productivity of multiunit acquiring firms declined from 1.14 in 1977 to 1.08 in 1987, while that of multiunit nonacquiring firms increased from 0.97 to 1.02. More generally, these results are consistent with many studies of mergers and acquisitions that suggest there has been little gain to acquiring firms after merger (see, e.g., Ravenscraft and Scherer 1987). Before drawing any conclusions we turn to analysis with the plant-level data. The figures in table 6.4 show vastly different performance among the various components of both acquiring and nonacquiring firms. The plant-level data allow us to directly model these differences and to isolate the effects of ownership change on the performance of acquiring firms.

6.6.2   Plant-Level Results

Wage Change Equation

Table 6.6 reports the coefficients for the wage equations estimated using plant-level data.[17] The variable OC has a value of one if a plant had ownership change in either the 1977–82 or the 1983–87 period. In addition, we introduce two variables: $OC_{77\text{-}82}$ equals one if a plant had ownership change between 1977 and 1982 and zero otherwise, and $OC_{82\text{-}87}$ equals one if it was purchased between 1982 and 1987 and zero otherwise. This specification allows us to isolate the impacts in each subperiod of the 1972–87 period. In the plant-level specifications, we also introduce a new variable, $OWNPLT_{AF}$, which equals one if a plant is initially owned by an acquiring firm in 1977 and operates through 1987 and zero otherwise. The omitted category is nonacquiring firms' own plants. Other variables are defined as before. Models II, IV, and VI use four-digit industry dummies as control variables, while models I, III, and V do not.[18]

Columns (1) and (2) of table 6.6 show estimated coefficients for the linear wage equation model. The coefficient for the OC variable is negative and insignificant (model I). It is only marginally significant when four-digit industry dummies are incorporated into the model (model II). With the nonlinear models (models III and IV), the coefficient for OC is positive and highly significant and that for $\ln E_{77}$ * OC is significantly negative. The significance of the inter-

17. Inclusion of non-food-manufacturing plants owned by food-manufacturing firms does not alter the results.
18. Because the dependent variables are in growth rates, the sample used in this regression analysis does not include closed plants and new plants.

Table 6.6   **Wage Change Equation: Food Plant Data**

Independent Variable	Model I (1)	Model II (2)	Model III (3)	Model IV (4)	Model V (5)	Model VI (6)
Intercept	.494*	.757*	.490*	.754*	.485*	.732*
	(14.8)	(20.4)	(14.8)	(20.4)	(19.6)	(19.6)
OC	−.012	−.020$^+$	.508*	.387*		
	(1.2)	(1.9)	(13.0)	(10.2)		
$OC_{77\text{-}82}$					.470*	.377*
					(8.3)	(7.0)
$OC_{83\text{-}87}$					.599*	.465*
					(11.3)	(9.1)
$OWNPLT_{AF}$					.403*	.278*
					(9.8)	(6.8)
$\ln E_{77}$	.125*	.132*	.134*	.138*	.140*	.144*
	(55.4)	(54.5)	(54.0)	(55.2)	(49.0)	(50.9)
$\ln W_{77}$	.374*	−.471*	−.373*	−.468*	−.379*	−.465*
	(34.2)	(40.4)	(34.6)	(40.4)	(35.1)	(40.1)
$\Delta TECH$	.085*	.074*	.046*	.035*	.048*	.035*
	(16.8)	(15.3)	(9.1)	(7.1)	(9.2)	(7.2)
$\ln E_{77}*OC$			−.113*	−.089*		
			(13.8)	(11.3)		
$\ln E_{77}*OC_{77\text{-}82}$					−.115*	−.095*
					(9.6)	(8.3)
$\ln E_{77}*OC_{83\text{-}87}$					−.127*	−.104*
					(11.7)	(9.9)
$\ln E_{77}*OWNPLT_{AF}$					−.083*	−.063*
					(9.5)	(7.2)
ξ	.262*	.272*	.262*	.273*	.259*	.271*
	(47.3)	(50.3)	(47.9)	(50.9)	(4.73)	(50.5)
Four-digit industry	No	Yes	No	Yes	No	Yes
R^2	.450	.576	.462	.523	.469	.526
n	8,955	8,955	8,955	8,955	8,955	8,955

Notes: Dependent variable is $\ln W_{87} - \ln W_{77}$. Numbers in parentheses are *t*-ratios.
*Significant at the 1 percent level.
$^+$Significant at the 5 percent level.

action term indicates that a nonlinear model is more appropriate than a linear model.

Models III and IV indicate that the wages of smaller plants increase more quickly if they have an ownership change. But larger plants increase wages faster if they do not undergo ownership change. More specifically, the estimate of 0.387 for OC and −0.089 for $\ln E_{77} * OC$ (with the mean of $\ln E_{77}$ equal to 3.00) implies that a typical acquired plant increased its workers' wages 12 percent (= 0.387 − 0.089(3)) faster than a plant owned by a nonacquiring firm.[19]

19. The exact size at which performance of nonacquirers exceeds acquirers is sensitive to the sample of plants and model specification. Nonetheless, the size cutoff is always well above the third quantile of the employment size distribution and usually falls in the top 10 to 20 percentiles.

While for many questions the behavior of a typical plant is a key issue, for many others the effect on a typical worker is of interest. We assess the latter using the (employment size) weighted average of the estimated effect of ownership change on the dependent variable (wage growth). We find this weighted average effect is positive, indicating that the wage growth of a typical worker in acquiring firms is 1.4 percent higher than that of a typical worker in nonacquiring firms. This figure is much smaller than that found for the typical acquired plant because a typical worker is more likely to work in a large plant than in a small plant. Thus the slower growth in wages at large plants affects more workers. Nevertheless, using either the unweighted or weighted figure, ownership change has a positive effect on wages.

A key question is whether this gain in wages for workers in acquired plants is achieved at the expense of workers in other plants of the firm. Columns (5) and (6) show estimates for models V and VI, which classify acquiring firms' plants into three groups: plants acquired between 1977 and 1982 (OC_{77-82}), plants acquired between 1982 and 1987 (OC_{82-87}), and acquiring firms' surviving plants ($OWNPLT_{AF}$). The coefficients for OC_{77-82} and OC_{82-87} are significantly positive, and the corresponding interaction terms are significantly negative. This is in accord with the estimate of ownership change discussed above: except for a subset of large plants, plants having ownership change tend to increase wages more quickly than plants that do not change ownership. Using the coefficients of model VI (col. [6]) and keeping employment fixed at the mean plant size, we find that typical plants acquired during 1977–82 and 1982–87 outperformed the corresponding nonacquiring firms' plants in terms of wage growth by 9.2 and 15.3 percent, respectively. The corresponding (employment) weighted figures are -2.2 percent and 2.9 percent, indicating that typical workers in plants acquired during 1977–82 were worse off, while typical workers in plants acquired during 1982–87 were better off, compared with workers in plants owned by nonacquiring firms.

Turning to the workers in acquiring firms' plants owned prior to acquisition, we estimate the coefficients for $OWNPLT_{AF}$ and $\ln E_{77} * OWNPLT_{AF}$ as 0.278 and -0.063, respectively. These coefficients indicate that wage growth in acquiring firms' own plants is about 9 percent higher than in plants of nonacquiring firms. The corresponding employment-weighted figure is 5.5 percent. Thus a typical worker in an acquiring firm's own plant also experiences wage gains relative to a typical worker in a nonacquiring firm.

Employment Change Equation

Columns (1) and (2) of table 6.7 report estimated coefficients for the linear employment models, while the remaining columns show estimated coefficients for nonlinear models. The estimated coefficients for OC in both linear and nonlinear models are significantly positive, indicating that acquired plants' employment grew faster than that of nonacquired plants. Using the estimates from model IV and fixing employment at mean plant size, we find that, on average, acquired plants increased employment faster than nonacquiring firms' plants

Table 6.7   **Employment Change Equation: Food Plant Data**

Independent Variable	Model I (1)	Model II (2)	Model III (3)	Model IV (4)	Model V (5)	Model VI (6)
Intercept	−.147*	−.480*	−.140⁺	.493*	−.057	−.412*
	(2.3)	(6.7)	(2.2)	(6.8)	(0.91)	(5.6)
OC	.114*	.119*	.033	.239*		
	(6.0)	(6.3)	(0.4)	(3.3)		
$OC_{77\text{-}82}$					−.150	.033
					(1.4)	(0.3)
$OC_{83\text{-}87}$					.067	.357*
					(0.7)	(3.6)
$OWNPLT_{AF}$					−.434*	−.004
					(5.6)	(0.1)
$\ln E_{77}$	−.155*	−.183*	−.156*	−.181*	−.181*	−.200*
	(31.5)	(36.1)	(30.1)	(33.9)	(29.5)	(32.5)
$\ln W_{77}$	.209*	.387*	.209*	.389*	.203*	.374*
	(18.3)	(17.3)	(10.3)	(17.3)	(10.0)	(16.7)
$\Delta TECH$	.351*	.354*	.351*	.353*	.351*	.355*
	(35.7)	(36.9)	(35.9)	(36.8)	(36.0)	(37.09)
$\ln E_{77}*OC$			.018	−.026		
			(1.1)	(1.7)		
$\ln E_{77}*OC_{77\text{-}82}$					.069*	.239
					(3.0)	(1.3)
$\ln E_{77}*OC_{83\text{-}87}$					.021	−.038⁺
					(1.0)	(1.9)
$\ln E_{77}*OWNPLT_{AF}$					.116*	.033⁺
					(7.0)	(2.0)
					(7.0)	(2.0)
Four-digit industry	No	Yes	No	Yes	No	Yes
R^2	.226	.286	.228	.288	.277	.293
n	8,955	8,955	8,955	8,955	8,955	8,955

Notes: Dependent variable is $\ln E_{87} - \ln E_{77}$. Numbers in parentheses are t-ratios.
*Significant at the 1 percent level.
⁺Significant at the 5 percent level.

by 16.1 percent (i.e., $0.239 - 0.026(3) = 0.161$). The employment-weighted figure is 13.0 percent.

When we split the OC variable into two variables, $OC_{77\text{-}82}$ and $OC_{82\text{-}87}$, the estimated coefficient for $OC_{77\text{-}82}$ is 0.033 and that for $\ln E_{77} * OC_{77\text{-}82}$ is 0.029, indicating that growth in a typical plant acquired between 1977 and 1982 is about 12 percent higher than that in a nonacquiring firm's plant. Weighting the estimates by employment, we find this effect to be even higher, about 15.5 percent. Note that, although these figures appear to be economically significant, they are not statistically significant. For the 1982–87 period, the estimated coefficients for $OC_{82\text{-}87}$ and $\ln E_{77} * OC_{82\text{-}87}$ are 0.357 and −0.038. Both are statistically significant. These estimates imply that a typical plant acquired during 1982–87 had an employment growth rate about 24 percent higher than that of a typical plant of a nonacquiring firm. The employment-weighted effect is about 20 percent.

Finally, the coefficient for $OWNPLT_{AF}$ is -0.004 and is not statistically significant, while that for $\ln E_{77} * OWNPLT_{AF}$ is 0.033 and is significant at the 5 percent level. These coefficients imply that a typical previously owned plant of an acquiring firm had an employment growth rate 9.5 percent higher than that of a typical plant of a nonacquiring firm. The weighted figure is even higher at 13.5 percent. These estimates suggest that the increase in employment at acquired plants did not come at the expense of workers in existing plants.

Productivity Change Equations

Table 6.8 reports results for the productivity equation. The coefficient for OC is negative in the linear models (cols. [1] and [2]). It, however, becomes significantly positive in the nonlinear models (cols. [3]–[6]). The coefficient for $\ln E_{77} * OC$ is also significant in the nonlinear models. Columns (5) and (6) show that the coefficients for OC_{77-82} are significantly positive, indicating that productivity grew faster for plants acquired during 1977–82 than for non-acquiring firms' plants. This result holds whether or not four-digit dummies are incorporated in the regressions. The coefficients for OC_{83-87} are negative and insignificant, indicating that plants changing ownership just before 1987 did not perform better than nonacquiring firms' plants. These results are consistent with the data, reported earlier in table 6.4, that showed that the productivity of plants purchased during 1977–82 grew 4.0 percent (from 1.02 in 1977 to 1.06 in 1987), while the productivity of plants acquired during 1982–87 declined by 3.0 percent (from 1.01 in 1977 to 0.98 in 1987). One explanation for this is that it takes some time for acquiring firms to integrate purchased plants into their operations. For this reason, and because preliminary work with other industries suggests the positive effect is robust, we give more credence to the results for ownership changes for the 1977–82 period.

Using the estimates of model VI and fixing employment at mean plant size, we find that productivity for a typical plant acquired during 1977–82 grew faster than that for a plant owned by a nonacquiring firm (by 16.2 percent [i.e., $0.459 - 0.099(3) = 0.162$]). This advantage for acquired plants diminishes as plant size increases. To be exact, when $\ln E = 4.64$ (i.e., $0.459/0.099 = 4.64$, the eightieth percentile value of the sample) the productivity of both types of plants grew at the same rate. Beyond this size—about twice the average size in our sample—the productivity of acquiring firms' plants grew more slowly than for nonacquired plants. The weighted estimates suggest that the plants acquired during 1977–82 had a 4.4 percent higher productivity growth rate than nonacquired plants.

The coefficients for $OWNPLT_{AF}$ and $\ln E_{77} * OWNPLT_{AF}$ are 0.580 and -0.115. Both are statistically significant at the 1 percent level. These estimates suggest that labor productivity for a typical existing plant is 23.5 percent

Table 6.8   Productivity Change Equation: Food Plant Data

Independent Variable	Model I (1)	Model II (2)	Model III (3)	Model IV (4)	Model V (5)	Model VI (6)
Intercept	−.239*	−.089*	−.251*	−.084+	−.268*	−.088*
	(13.0)		(10.2)	(2.3)	10.7)	(2.5)
OC	−.127*	−.123*	.194*	.104		
	(6.0)	(6.0)	(2.5)	(1.4)		
$OC_{77\text{-}82}$					.535*	.459*
					(4.8)	(4.3)
$OC_{83\text{-}87}$					−.084	−.167
					(0.8)	(1.5)
$OWNPLT_{AF}$					.617*	.580*
					(7.5)	(7.0)
$\ln RLP_{77}$	−.220*	−.205*	−.228*	−.227*	−.247*	−.243*
	(38.7)	(35.6)	(12.6)	(12.9)	(13.4)	(13.6)
$\ln E_{77}$	.086*	.101*	.091*	.100*	.096*	.099*
	(18.5)	(21.2)	(13.8)	(15.2)	(13.5)	(14.1)
ΔTECH	.142*	.169*	.141*	.168*	.141*	.167*
	(14.4)	(17.6)	(14.3)	(17.5)	(14.3)	(17.5)
$\ln E_{77}*OC$			−.069*	−.049*		
			(4.2)	(3.1)		
$\ln E_{77}*OC_{77\text{-}82}$					−.118*	−.099*
					(5.0)	(4.3)
$\ln E_{77}*OC_{83\text{-}87}$					−.041	−.020
					(1.8)	(.9)
$\ln E_{77}*OWNPLT_{AF}$					−.130*	−.115*
					(7.5)	(6.6)
$\ln E_{77}*\ln RLP_{77}$			.001	.005	.008	.011*
			(.3)	(1.2)	(1.6)	(2.5)
Four-digit industry	No	Yes	No	Yes	No	Yes
R^2	.191	.267	.193	.268	.203	.277
n	8,955	8,955	8,955	8,955	8,955	8,955

Notes: Dependent variables is $\ln E_{87} - \ln RLP_{77}$. Numbers in parentheses are t-ratios.
*Significant at the 1 percent level.
+Significant at the 5 percent level.

higher for an acquiring firm than for a nonacquiring firm. Using weighted estimates, we also find that productivity growth is higher in acquiring firms' own plants than in nonacquiring firms' plants by about 10 percent.

Plant Closing Equation

The probit regression results reported in table 6.9 show that the coefficients for $OC_{77\text{-}87}$ are negative and significant in all models. This indicates that plants experiencing ownership change are less likely to be closed than plants not changing owners. The coefficient for $OWNPLT_{AF}$ is negative and significant with the linear models (models I and II); however, this coefficient becomes significantly positive in the nonlinear models (models III and IV). The coeffi-

Table 6.9   **Probit Regressions of Plant Closure**

Independent Variable	Model I (1)	Model II (2)	Model III (3)	Model IV (4)
Intercept	.315*	.887*	.809*	.931*
	(.009)	(.017)	(.025)	(.032)
$OC_{77\text{-}87}$	−1.266*	−.926*	−1.520*	−1.372*
	(.025)	(.026)	(.089)	(.090)
$OWNPLT_{AF}$	−.428*	−.076*	.671*	.861*
	(.024)	(.026)	(.095)	(1.00)
$\ln E_{77}$		−.203*	−.186*	−.263*
		(.005)	(.008)	(.016)
$\ln RLP_{77}$		−.053*	−.045$^+$	−.029*
		(.009)	(.022)	(.028)
$\ln E_{77}^2$				.012*
				(.002)
$\ln RLP_{77}^2$				.006*
				(.001)
$OC_{77\text{-}78}*\ln E_{77}$			.139*	.113
			(.018)	(.018)
$OC_{77\text{-}87}*\ln RLP_{77}$			−.012	−.050$^+$
			(.027)	(.027)
$OWNPLT_{AF}*\ln E_{77}$			−.128*	−.166*
			(.019)	(.020)
$OWNLPT_{AF}*\ln RLP_{77}$			−.147*	−.169*
			(.023)	(.024)
$\ln E_{77}*\ln RLP_{77}$			−.022*	−.013
			(.007)	(.008)
n	28,236	28,236	28,236	28,236

Notes: Dependent variable is plant closure (equals one if the plant was closed by 1987, zero otherwise). Numbers in parentheses are standard errors.
*Significant at the 1 percent level.
$^+$Significant at the 5 percent level.

cients for the interaction terms $OWNPLT_{AF} * RLP_{77}$ and $OWNPLT_{AF} * \ln E_{77}$ are negative and significant. These estimates imply that small plants originally owned by acquirers are more likely to be closed than those owned by nonacquirers. However, for larger plants nonacquirers are more likely to close plants than acquirers. To better assess the probability of plant closure, we used the parameter estimates for a probit model reported in table 6.8 to estimate the probabilities of plant closure for plants that experienced ownership change and plants originally owned by acquirers and nonacquirers.

The results reported in table 6.10 show that plants owned by nonacquirers were most likely to be closed and plants that had ownership change are most likely to survive. The unconditional probability of closure (model I) for plants owned by nonacquirers is .62, while that for plants having ownership change is .17. The probability of closing for acquirers' own plants is .46. When con-

Table 6.10   Probabilities of Plant Closings

Plant Type	Model I	Model II	Model III	Model IV
Plant had ownership change	.1708	.1525	.1329	.1519
Acquirer's own plants	.4550	.4323	.3838	.4120
Nonacquirer's own plants	.6236	.6322	.6011	.6326

trolling for initial productivity and employment size and allowing nonlinearity, we find similar results. The evidence suggests that plants changing owners had a much greater chance to survive than plants not changing owners. Acquirers' own plants are less likely to be closed than those originally owned by nonacquirers.

6.7   Discussion

Our regression results can be summarized as follows. The firm-level results suggest that, on average, acquiring firms increased both employment and wages faster than nonacquiring firms. Using the firm-level specifications, the rate of increase for employment is 55 percent faster, while that for wages is in the 2.5–3.0 percent faster range. However, acquiring firms' labor productivity grew about 16.5 percent slower. While these estimates—especially those for employment and productivity—are large in magnitude, they are not statistically significant.

At first glance, these estimates, especially the 55 percent figure, seem to be economically significant; but they are misleading because comparing a *whole* firm before and after ownership change does not isolate the effects of ownership change on the firm. Ownership change is one of many changes in composition that typically occur in acquiring firms. The possibilities for misinterpretation of a firm-level change can be illustrated by considering, for example, a firm with 50 employees in 1977 that purchases another firm that also has 50 employees in 1977. If the acquiring firm has 90 workers in 1987, one might conclude that its employment increased by 80 percent, from 50 to 90 employees. However, the true effect of this acquisition is a 10 percent decline in total employment: the combined firm fell from 100 to 90 employees. (A more sophisticated way to estimate the impact of mergers might include projections of each plant's employment growth based on the average growth for plants classified in the same industry and then do the calculation.) The key issue is knowing what to hold constant in assessing the impact of mergers.

Using the plant-level specifications, we found a typical plant acquired during 1977–82 showed increases in wages, employment, and labor productivity of about 12, 16, and 16 percent, respectively, higher than for the typical plant of a nonacquiring firm. The growth rates of productivity and employment of the typical worker in plants acquired during 1977–82 were also higher, about 4.5 and 13 percent, respectively. However, the growth rate of wages for a typical worker in nonacquiring firms' plants was about 2 percent lower than that of a typical worker in acquired plants during this period. The results for the 1982–87 subperiod were similar except for productivity, for which we found insignificant effects. As we noted, we think this is because integration of acquired properties takes time and productivity gains probably lag labor force adjustments. The growth rates of employment, wages, and productivity at the typical acquiring firm's existing plant grew about 9, 9.5, and 23.5 percent, respectively, faster than those of a typical nonacquiring firm's plant. The typical worker in these plants also gained in wages, employment, and productivity growth, about 5.5, 13.5, and 10 percent, respectively, higher than the corresponding growth rates for a typical worker in nonacquiring firms' plants.

The above results show that ownership change had stronger positive effects on the typical plant than on the typical worker, particularly with respect to wages and productivity. For example, the growth rate of wages at a typical acquired plant was about 12 percent higher than that at a typical plant of an acquiring firm, whereas the typical worker in an acquired plant enjoyed wage growth only about 1.4 percent higher than that of a typical worker in a nonacquiring firm. Similarly, productivity growth in a typical plant acquired during 1977–82 increased about 16 percent more than that in a typical nonacquiring plant. In contrast, the typical worker employed in a plant acquired during 1977–82 worked in a plant with a productivity growth increase only about 4.0 percent higher than that of a plant that employed a typical nonacquiring firm worker. The reason for these differences is that wages and productivity grew more slowly in large acquired plants than in smaller plants. Because the large plants employed a substantial number of workers, weighting the effect of ownership change by employment reduces the measurement effect on a typical worker.

Comparing the plant-level results to those obtained using firm-level data, we find that both suggest ownership change has positive effects on employment and wages. But with respect to productivity, the firm-level results suggest a negative effect of ownership change, while the plant-level results show a positive effect of ownership change on labor productivity, especially for plants that were acquired during 1977–82. But all the estimates associated with ownership change in the firm-level regressions are statistically insignificant. In contrast, the plant-level results are generally significant and positive. As already discussed, while firm-level regressions fail to capture changes in the composition of the firm, plant-level specifications account for individual components of the firm. Thus they allow us to isolate the effects of ownership change.

The finding that wages of workers in the typical acquired plant grew faster than those in the typical nonacquiring firm's plant is striking and does not support the notion that acquisitions and mergers cut wages. This result holds for all plants undergoing ownership change in both the 1977–82 and 1982–87 periods, even after controlling for the effects of plant initial employment, size, wages, productivity, changes in technology, and (four-digit) industry. This result is inconsistent with both Brown and Medoff's (1988) and Lichtenberg and Siegel's (1992a) findings that wage changes associated with ownership change are relatively small. However, the Brown-Medoff evidence is based on firm-level data. In this regard, our results are not inconsistent with theirs. The difference between Lichtenberg and Siegel's results and ours needs to be explained because both studies use plant-level data.

As discussed before, Lichtenberg and Siegel use a sample of very large plants, but we think the difference is mainly due to the fact that they classify plants in their sample into only two categories: acquired plants and nonacquired plants. In contrast, we classify plants into four categories: plants acquired during 1977–82, plants acquired during 1982–87, acquiring firms' existing (own) plants, and nonacquiring firms' existing (own) plants. Lichtenberg and Siegel's categorization puts acquiring firms' existing own plants together with nonacquiring firms' own plants in one group and compares them with all acquired plants. Because employment, wages, and productivity of acquiring firms' existing own plants grew faster than those of nonacquiring firms' plants, grouping these plants together would bias the results.

Our finding that ownership change has a significant, positive effect on plants' employment growth is not consistent with the findings of either Lichtenberg and Siegel or Brown and Medoff. Again, we think that this difference is due to our explicit introduction of individual components of firms into the regression. Moreover, in contrast to Lichtenberg and Siegel, who use data for large plants, we include small-plant data in our sample. In view of our results that large acquired plants increase their employment relatively slowly, their finding of a negative (but small) effect of ownership change on employment is not surprising. Overall, we find no evidence supporting the hypothesis that ownership change destroys jobs by either reducing employment in surviving plants or increasing the probability of plants' closing. This, together with the result that acquired plants are less likely to be closed than nonacquiring firms' plants, provides strong evidence against the notion that mergers and acquisitions reduce employment.

Finally, when using the firm as the unit of analysis, we find no statistically significant effects of ownership change on productivity, wages, and employment.[20] This result is extremely important. It points to the fact that assessing the impact of ownership change (including mergers and acquisitions) on the structure and performance of firms requires a careful look at individual components—establishments—of the firms. Mueller (1993) correctly pointed out that "any *real* consequences of a merger must come about through changes in the development of one or both joining units that can be attributed to the merger in the following years" (emphasis in original). Our firm-level results

---

20. McGuckin and Nguyen (1995) use firm-level data to estimate productivity growth equations in which acquiring firms are classified into two groups: full mergers and divestitures. They obtain similar results for both groups.

demonstrate that simply looking at the performance of firms before and after ownership change fails to capture the effects of ownership change and the different factors at work.

Before concluding, we note that our data do not cover auxiliary establishments. Lichtenberg and Siegel (1992b) find that failure to account for auxiliary establishments leads to an underestimate of productivity gains associated with ownership change. However, this indicates that including auxiliary establishment data would strengthen, rather than weaken, our finding that ownership change improved productivity.

Regarding wages and employment, if ownership change results in reduced wages and employment in auxiliary establishments as indicated by the Lichtenberg-Siegel study, our estimates of employment and wage growth are likely to be biased upward. We note, however, that this bias is most likely to be serious in the case of large multiunit firms. For smaller firms, the bias may be less important; and it does not exist in the case of single-unit firms.

6.8 Concluding Remarks

A wide range of recent empirical work with establishment-level data finds within-industry differences between establishments to be the major source of variation in productivity, wages, and jobs. For example, Davis, Haltiwanger, and Schuh (1996) report a greater range of variation in job changes between plants in the steel industry than the range of difference between the average establishments in the steel and textile industries. Similarly, Davis and Haltiwanger (1992) and Bernard and Jensen (1994) show that most of the variation in wages occurs within industries. Moreover, Baily et al. (1992) demonstrate that the within-industry variation in productivity growth is primarily associated with movements between establishments. In the Baily et al. study it is gains in market share by high-productivity plants and the exit of low-productivity plants that drive industry-level changes in productivity. Entry plays a significant but much smaller role in productivity growth, according to these studies. Taken together, these studies convincingly demonstrate that between-plant variation is important for productivity, wages, and job reallocations.

The evidence developed in this study shows that, at least for food industry establishments, ownership change is associated with increased productivity and employment growth. For wages the impacts are very small. Acquiring firms are high-productivity firms that acquire plants with above average productivity and improve them. This suggests that ownership change is an important part of the process of reallocating resources from lower to higher valued plants found in these earlier plant-level studies. The result that ownership change is associated with productivity growth appears robust across the U.S. manufacturing sector for the period studied, the late 1970s and 1980s.[21] Thus,

---

21. Our preliminary results based on data for the entire manufacturing sector appear to be consistent with those based on data for the food industry.

ownership change fits well within a framework emphasizing productivity growth through reallocations of labor from lower to higher productivity firms. While the benefits associated with changing ownership—movement of resources from lower to higher valued uses—may be large, the costs also can be significant. The often expressed hostility toward mergers—by labor unions and the press—reflects the view that the costs are high. Typically cited effects of ownership change are closed plants and shifts of production to areas with low labor costs. The combination of high costs and benefits makes the study of ownership change a prime area for applied research.

While we think this work is in the right direction, the results obtained should be considered suggestive rather than conclusive. Several reasons for this have been discussed. First, we use data for only one industry, although it is one of the most active in terms of ownership change in the period we study. Second, we do not include data for central offices in the analysis. Third, our models do not take into account potential endogeneity of ownership change, and hence, the results may be subject to simultaneity biases. Finally, our data cover only the 1977–87 period, and therefore other merger waves are excluded from the analysis. Despite these shortcomings, we think the results strongly suggest that ownership change is an important avenue for enhancing productivity in job reallocation. Most important, we think that further examination of this issue must proceed with plant-level models.

In closing, we note that we plan to continue this line of research on several fronts. Our immediate plan is twofold: to extend the data set in time to account for more than one merger wave and to include other industries. We also plan to extend the data set to include data for auxiliary establishments such as central offices. Finally, rather than looking at total employment, further research should treat production workers and nonproduction workers separately. This would shed more light on the impact of ownership change on wages and shifts in the skill distribution of workers within the firm.

References

Baily, M. N., E. J. Bartelsman, and J. C. Haltiwanger. 1994. Downsizing and productivity growth: Myth or reality? Discussion Paper no. CES 94-4. Washington, D.C.: U.S. Bureau of the Census, Center for Economic Studies.

Baily, M. N., D. Campbell, and C. Hulten. 1992. Productivity dynamics in manufacturing plants. *Brookings Papers on Economic Activity: Microeconomics,* 187–249.

Baldwin, J. 1995. Turnover and productivity growth. In *The dynamics of industrial competition,* ed. J. Baldwin, 208–38. Cambridge: Cambridge University Press.

Berle, A. A., and G. C. Means. 1932. *The modern corporation of private property,* New York: Commerce Clearing House (rev. ed.; New York: Harcourt, Brace and Jovanovich, 1968).

Bernard, A. B., and J. B. Jensen. 1994. Exporters, skill-upgrading, and the wage gap.

Discussion Paper no. CES 94–13. Washington, D.C.: U.S. Bureau of the Census, Center for Economic Studies.

Brown, C., J. Connor, S. Heeringa, and J. Jackson. 1990. Studying (small) businesses with the Michigan Employment Security Commission longitudinal data base. *Small Business Economics* 2:261–77.

Brown, C., and J. L. Medoff. 1988. The impact of firm acquisition on labor. In *Corporate takeovers: Causes and consequences,* ed. Alan J. Auerbach, 9–25. Chicago: University of Chicago Press.

Carliner, G. 1988. The impact of acquisition on labor: Comment. In *Corporate takeovers: Causes and consequences,* ed. Alan J. Auerbach, 25–28. Chicago: University of Chicago Press.

Christensen, L. R., D. Cumming, and D. W. Jorgenson. 1981. Relative productivity levels, 1947–1973: An international comparison. *European Economics Review,* 16: 61–94.

Cole, S. J., J. Petrik, and R. E. Struble. 1995. The relation between the Standard Statistical Establishment List and Manufacturing Establishment Surveys. MCD Working Paper no. Census/MCD/WP-95/02. Washington, D.C.: U.S. Bureau of the Census, Manufacturing and Construction Division.

Connor, J. H., M. Converse, S. G. Heeringa, and J. E. Jackson. 1984. The Michigan Employment Security Commission longitudinal database of Michigan businesses. Ann Arbor: University of Michigan, Institute for Social Research, Survey Research Center.

Davis, S. J., and J. Haltiwanger. 1992. Gross job creation, gross job destruction, and employment reallocation. *Quarterly Journal of Economics* 107:819–63.

Davis, S. J., J. Haltiwanger, and S. Schuh. 1996. *Gross job flows in U.S. manufacturing.* Cambridge, Mass.: MIT Press.

Dunne, T., and M. J. Roberts. 1993. The long-run demand for labor: Estimates from census establishment data. Discussion Paper no. CES 93-13. Washington, D.C.: U.S. Bureau of the Census, Center for Economic Studies.

Farber, H. S. 1988. The impact of firm acquisition on labor: Comment. In *Corporate takeovers: Causes and consequences,* ed. Alan J. Auerbach, 28–31. Chicago: University of Chicago Press.

Jensen, M. C. 1993. Corporate control and the politics of finance. *Bank America Journal of Applied Corporate Finance* 4 (2): 13–33.

Jensen, M. C., and R. S. Ruback. 1983. The market for corporate control: The scientific evidence. *Journal of Financial Economics* 11:5–50.

Lichtenberg, F., ed. 1992. *Corporate takeovers and productivity.* Cambridge, Mass.: MIT Press.

Lichtenberg, F., and D. Siegel. 1992a. Productivity and changes in ownership of manufacturing plants. In *Corporate takeovers and productivity,* ed. F. Lichtenberg, 25–43. Cambridge, Mass.: MIT Press.

———. 1992b. Takeovers and corporate overhead. In *Corporate takeovers and productivity,* ed. F. Lichtenberg, 45–67. Cambridge, Mass.: MIT Press.

Matsusaka, J. G. 1993a. Takeover motives during the conglomerate merger wave. *Rand Journal of Economics* 24:357–79.

———. 1993b. Target profits and managerial discipline during the conglomerate merger wave. *Journal of Industrial Economics* 41:179–89.

McGuckin, R. H. 1995. Establishment microdata for economic research and policy analysis: Looking beyond the aggregates. *Journal of Business and Economic Statistics* 13 (1): 121–26.

McGuckin, R. H., and S. V. Nguyen. 1994. On productivity and plant ownership change: New evidence from the LRD. *Rand Journal of Economics* 26 (2): 257–76.

———. 1995. Exploring the role of acquisition in the performance of firms: Is the "firm" the right unit of analysis? Discussion Paper no. CES 95-13. Washington, D.C.: U.S. Bureau of the Census, Center for Economic Studies.

McGuckin, R. H., and G. Pascoe. 1988. The Longitudinal Research Database: Status and research possibilities. *Survey of Current Business* 68:30–37.

Michigan Employment Security Commission (MESC). 1995. Overview of unemployment insurance taxes. From the Internet: http://www/mesc.state.mi.us/mesc/empirhb/taxover1.htm.

Mueller, D. C. 1969. A theory of conglomerate mergers. *Quarterly Journal of Economics* 83:643–59.

————. 1993. Mergers: Theory and evidence. In *Mergers, markets, and public policy,* ed. Gallium Mussati. Dordrecht: Kluwer.

Ravenscraft, D. J., and F. M. Scherer. 1987. *Mergers, selloffs, and economic efficiency.* Washington, D.C.: Brookings Institution.

Shleifer, A., and R. W. Vishny. 1989. Management entrenchment: The case of manager-specific investments. *Journal of Financial Economics* 25:123–39.

U.S. Bureau of the Census. 1979. The Standard Statistical Establishment List program. Washington, D.C.: U.S. Department of Commerce.

————. 1992. Longitudinal Research Database technical documentation. Washington, D.C.: U.S. Department of Commerce.

Comment   Frank R. Lichtenberg

This paper represents a very useful extension and contribution to the literature on the "real" (ex post) effects of ownership change (as opposed to its effects on investor expectations, as measured in "event studies" of stock prices). The period studied in the paper (1977–87) is more recent than that studied in Lichtenberg and Siegel's (1987) analysis of 1972–81 ownership changes (although Lichtenberg and Siegel 1990a studied the effects of leveraged buyouts—a specific type of ownership change—that occurred through 1986). Hence, the authors' sample period includes most of the takeover wave of the 1980s. Their sample also includes a substantial number of small plants, whereas previous studies were based primarily on large plants.

On the other hand, they study a single industry—food manufacturing—whereas previous studies of ownership change have analyzed data for the entire manufacturing sector, if not also nonmanufacturing industries. (I have no particular reason to believe that the food industry is atypical with regard to the effects of ownership change, however.) Their sample also excludes central administrative offices and auxiliary establishments; Lichtenberg and Siegel (1990b) showed that the largest (most negative) employment and wage responses to ownership change often occur in these establishments and that these need to be accounted for to obtain accurate estimates of productivity effects.

Frank R. Lichtenberg is the Courtney C. Brown Professor of Business at the Columbia University Graduate School of Business and a research associate of the National Bureau of Economic Research.

Ownership change is a reasonably frequent event: about 10 to 15 percent of workers are employed in plants that will be acquired in the next five years, and 50 percent of workers are employed by firms that will engage in acquisitions in that period. The authors make a convincing case that using firm-level data to determine the effects of ownership change is far from optimal and may yield quite distorted estimates of these effects. This is not very surprising, since many changes in ownership involve only parts (often small parts) of firms; for example, a firm may decide to "spin off" one of its minor divisions.

I will therefore focus on their plant-level analysis of the effects of ownership change. The authors reexamine the question of whether it is relatively efficient (high productivity level) or inefficient plants that are most likely to subsequently undergo ownership change. The authors find that *among large plants* the correlation between initial productivity and ownership change is negative: inefficient plants are more likely to subsequently change owners. This is consistent with Lichtenberg and Siegel's (1987) findings, which were also based primarily on large plants.

However, when they include small as well as large plants in their sample, they reach the opposite conclusion: "It is high, not low, productivity establishments that are most likely to experience ownership change." Thus the negative correlation between initial productivity and ownership change (which is implied by the "managerial discipline theory" of ownership change) "only" applies to large plants. *But most people are employed, most wages are paid, and most output is produced in large plants.* In 1982, for example, there were 335,000 small establishments (less than 250 employees) and 13,000 large establishments (250 or more employees) in U.S. manufacturing, but large establishments employed more people and their aggregate value added and investment were respectively about 60 and 94 percent larger than those of small establishments.

The finding that there are significant differences between the ownership change behavior of small and large plants is certainly interesting and merits further study and explanation. But in their analysis of the full sample of plants, the authors implicitly give equal weight to large and small plants; since small plants are far more numerous, their overall estimates are dominated by these plants. This does not seem to be the appropriate way to determine the aggregate or (weighted) average effect of ownership change.

In the conclusion of the paper, the authors claim that "ownership change is associated with increased productivity and employment growth." But their estimates of the productivity change equation based on plant-level data (reported in table 6.8) do not seem to support this. These estimates are fairly unstable, and it is difficult to know what we can conclude from them. In the simplest models (I and II) of productivity change, the coefficient on ownership change is *negative* and significant. When the authors allow the effect of ownership change on productivity growth to depend on plant size by including an interaction term of ownership change with initial employment (models III and

IV), their results imply that ownership change has a positive effect on productivity growth only for very small plants (those with fewer than 20 employees). Again, the appropriateness of giving equal weight to small and large plants seems questionable, especially when the effect (sign as well as magnitude) of ownership change seems to be so size related.

The estimates also imply that the effect of ownership change on the rate of plant productivity growth between 1977 and 1987 depends crucially on when in that period the ownership change occurred. Only ownership changes during the first five years appeared to have a significant effect (table 6.8, models V and VI). (Also, ownership changes occurring during the 1983–87 period had a significant positive effect on employment growth, but those during 1977–82 did not.) The authors conjecture that this may be due to the fact that "it takes some time for acquiring firms to integrate with purchased plants." Indeed, Lichtenberg and Siegel (1987), who analyzed *annual* data on productivity and ownership change, found support for the gradual adjustment hypothesis. But the stark contrast between the estimated effects of "early" and "late" (and small plant and large plant) ownership changes is somewhat troubling to me. I think that additional empirical research (e.g., on other industries) is needed to assess whether these apparent differences reflect signal rather than noise. If these patterns are confirmed, they will constitute a new (and difficult!) set of stylized facts for future theorists of ownership change to explain.

References

Lichtenberg, Frank, and Donald Siegel. 1987. Productivity and changes in ownership of manufacturing plants. *Brookings Papers on Economic Activity,* no. 3: 643–73.
———. 1990a. The effect of leveraged buyouts on productivity and related aspects of firm behavior. *Journal of Financial Economics* 26:165–94.
———. 1990b. The effect of ownership changes on the employment and wages of central-office and other personnel. *Journal of Law and Economics* 33 (October): 383–408.

7 The CPS after the Redesign: Refocusing the Economic Lens

Anne E. Polivka and Stephen M. Miller

The Current Population Survey (CPS) is a major source of information about the American labor market. In addition to providing monthly estimates of unemployment and employment, economists, sociologists, and policy analysts use data from the CPS to examine broad societal and cyclical changes in economic activity over time. For example, data from the CPS have been used to investigate the declining rate of employment among men, especially older men (e.g., Peracchi and Welch 1994), the rising labor force participation rate of women since the 1960s (Smith and Ward 1985; Michael 1985), the changing demographic composition and number of the self-employed (Devine 1994a, 1994b; Aronson 1991), the fluctuations in the number of involuntary part-time workers over the business cycle (Blank 1990), the increase in wage inequality over time (Levy and Murnane 1992; Bound and Johnson 1992), and the relationship between unemployment and inflation (Tobin 1972; Murphy and Topel 1987).

In January 1994, the CPS underwent a major redesign both in the wording of the questionnaire and the methodology used to collect the data. The objective of the redesign was to improve the quality and expand the quantity of available data. However, the redesign also caused changes in the measurement of many of the estimates derived from the CPS. The major purpose of this paper is to estimate adjustment factors for various aggregate measures derived from the CPS in order to permit comparisons of estimates before and after the redesign. In addition, these adjustment factors will be analyzed to assess

Anne E. Polivka is a research economist in the Office of Employment Research and Program Development at the Bureau of Labor Statistics, U.S. Department of Labor. Stephen M. Miller is a mathematical statistician in the Office of Survey Methods Research at the Bureau of Labor Statistics, U.S. Department of Labor.

The views in this paper are those of the authors, and do not represent official Bureau of Labor Statistics policy.

the impact of the redesign on some of the key conclusions drawn from the CPS.[1]

The remainder of the paper is structured as follows. Section 7.1 briefly summarizes the reasons for the CPS redesign. Section 7.2 contains a description of the data and a discussion of the motivation for the methodology used in the empirical analysis. Section 7.3 presents the empirical model. The estimated adjustment factors, along with a discussion of possible causes and implications of the estimated changes, are presented in section 7.4. The paper concludes with a brief summary of the results and implications of the redesign.

7.1 Reasons for Redesigning the Current Population Survey

The redesigned CPS was the culmination of a massive eight-year collaborative effort between the Bureau of Labor Statistics (BLS) and the Bureau of the Census. The impetus for changing the CPS was fourfold. First, there were indications that some of the concepts and wording in the CPS were becoming dated. The last major revision to the wording of the CPS occurred in 1967. Since that time there have been many changes in the U.S. labor market. Women's labor force activity has increased dramatically. Service sector employment has grown. The proportion of the employed working in factory jobs has declined. Two-income households have become the norm in husband-wife households. Single-parent households have become more prevalent. The population has grown older, and minorities constitute a larger proportion of the labor force than previously. Given these societal changes, some of the wording of the CPS questions were inappropriate, and new situations had arisen that were not adequately covered by the survey.

For example, in the unrevised CPS, interviewers were instructed to tailor the wording of the first labor force question to the gender and age of the respondent. Specifically, if the respondent "appears to be a homemaker," the manual instructed interviewers to ask, "What were you doing most of last week—keeping house or something else?" If the respondent appeared to be relatively young, interviewers were supposed to ask, "What were you doing most of last week—going to school or something else?" For all other respondents, interviewers were instructed to ask, "What were you doing most of last week—working or something else?" The next question about work activities in the unrevised questionnaire included the phrase "not counting work around the house." Given the increased labor market activity of women and the rising prevalence of home offices or other work arrangements that involve individuals working from their homes, the wording of these questions could be both offensive and confusing (Polivka and Rothgeb 1993; Rothgeb 1994; Polivka 1994).

Other examples of the datedness of the CPS occurred with respect to the

---

1. The estimates presented in this paper are being provided only to aid individuals who use the CPS historically. The Bureau of Labor Statistics will not revise previously published official estimates.

recording of reasons why individuals were working part time or were absent from work. The unrevised CPS did not include the response categories of child care problems or maternity or paternity leave. In the mid-1960s, when the last redesign was implemented, dual-income households and women working outside of the home were not as prevalent. However, with the tremendous increase over the past quarter-century of women in the labor market, the lack of these response categories raised the probability of answers being inaccurately classified and reduced the usefulness of the data (Fracasso 1989).

Investigation also revealed that the meaning of several phrases and words in the CPS have changed over time. An important example of shifting meanings involves the measurement of individuals "on layoff." In the past, most people defined a layoff as a temporary spell of unemployment from which an individual expected to be recalled as soon as business conditions improved or retooling was completed. Research showed, however, that in the late 1980s and early 1990s, the majority of individuals used the word "layoff" to refer to permanent separations from which they did not expect to be recalled (Rothgeb 1982; Palmisano 1989).

A second motivation for the revisions is that changes previously recommended in the 1970s—most notably those from the National Commission on Employment and Unemployment Statistics—had not been fully implemented. Several recommendations were tested in the 1980s through the Methods Development Survey jointly developed by the BLS and the Bureau of the Census, but lack of funding for a large overlap sample to assess the effect of the changes precluded the implementation of these recommendations.

The changes that were occurring in survey methodology provided a third impetus for redesigning the CPS. In the early 1980s, the introduction of cognitive psychological theory and research methods provided a means for understanding and reducing measurement error in the survey process (Jabine et al. 1984). Two important aspects of the application of cognitive methodology were used in the redesign of the CPS. One was the development of a psychological model to relate psychological theory to how the questionnaire affects responses, and the other was the incorporation of laboratory techniques into the questionnaire design and testing process (Dippo et al. 1994).

A fourth reason for the revision was the advent of the ability to conduct surveys using laptop computers. The use of laptop computers made it possible to develop a completely computerized survey instrument. In turn, a computerized instrument permitted the methods and procedures used to conduct interviews to be altered. For example, use of a computer allows information from a previous interview to easily be inserted into the current interview and permits internal data consistency checks to be built into the survey.[2]

For these reasons, an effort to redesign the CPS was begun in 1986. From

2. For a more complete description of the general motivation for the CPS revision, see Bregger and Dippo (1993). For a discussion of the motivation of specific questionnaire changes, see Polivka and Rothgeb (1993). For a description of the use of computers in redesigning and administering the CPS, see Dippo et al. (1994).

1988 through 1991, a series of research projects was conducted to guide the development of the revised CPS. Included in this research were two large-scale tests of alternative versions of the questionnaire collected using centralized computer-assisted telephone interviewing with samples of households selected through random digit dialing. The result of these tests was a completely revised questionnaire designed to be collected with an entirely automated survey instrument.

7.2   The Data

As mentioned in the introduction, the major goal of this paper is to provide a set of adjustment factors that account for the redesign for application to aggregate estimates derived from the CPS. Initially, to assess the effect of the redesign, a parallel survey was conducted using the new automated collection procedure from July 1992 through December 1993. This parallel survey provided the BLS with its first estimates of the expected effect of the redesign. For example, based on the parallel survey it was estimated that the redesign would increase the overall unemployment rate 0.5 percentage points and that the increase would be larger for women than for men. The initial parallel survey estimates also indicated that the employment-to-population ratio would be 0.7 percentage points higher for women and 0.6 percentage points lower for men after implementation of the redesign.[3]

As an additional tool to assess the impact of the redesign, households in the sample used for the parallel survey were interviewed with the unrevised procedures from January 1994 through May 1994. The primary purpose of extending the parallel survey, while switching households to the old procedures, was to obtain an estimate of what the unemployment rate would have been under the old procedures. However, examination of the data from the extended parallel survey called into question the interpretation of some of the results of the initial parallel survey. Specifically, the unemployment rate, rather than being lower than in the CPS when the parallel survey was conducted with the old methodology, instead remained higher. As can be seen in figure 7.1, plots of parallel survey and CPS estimates of monthly unemployment rates do not cross as would be expected if the new methodology were increasing the rate.

The failure of the two plots to cross suggests that there may have been something specific to or distinct about the parallel survey. In other words, there may have been a "parallel survey effect." This parallel survey effect could exist even for estimates that appeared to perform as predicted by the initial parallel survey. For example, figure 7.2 indicates that monthly estimated employment-to-population ratios for women were, by and large, higher in the parallel survey

---

3. More detailed estimates of the effect of the redesign from the initial parallel survey can be found in Cohany, Polivka, and Rothgeb (1994).

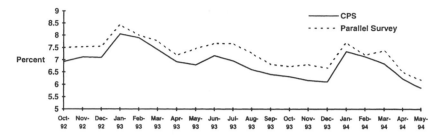

Fig. 7.1   Total national unemployment rates (not seasonally adjusted)

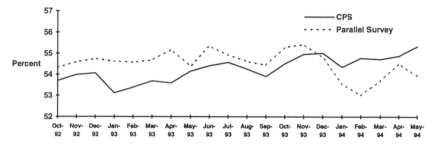

Fig. 7.2   Employment-to-population ratios for women (not seasonally adjusted)

than in the CPS prior to January 1994 and were lower in the parallel survey than in the CPS after January 1994. This crossing of the plots is consistent with there being a new method effect on women's estimated employment-to-population ratio. However, if there is a parallel survey effect in addition to a new method effect, the effect of the redesign on women's employment-to-population ratios would be different from what was observed prior to January 1994, since prior to January 1994 the two effects would be confounded.

A parallel survey effect could occur for a variety of reasons. For example, a parallel survey effect could be due to differences between the CPS sample and the sample used for the parallel surveys, differences in supervision of the interviewer staff between the CPS and the parallel surveys, or differences that arose just because respondents and interviewers knew that they were part of an experiment. The last effect is sometimes referred to as a "Hawthorne effect."

Given the graphical results and the possibility of a parallel survey effect, it is important to construct adjustment factors that control for a parallel survey effect. Consequently, data collected with the parallel surveys using the new procedures prior to January 1994 and the unrevised procedures from January through May 1994, along with data collected from the unrevised CPS prior to January 1994 and the revised CPS beginning in January 1994, will all be used in the estimation of adjustment factors. Throughout the remainder of this paper, estimates and data pertaining to the portion of the parallel survey test conducted prior to January 1994 will be referred to as "parallel survey prior to

January" estimates or data (PSpj). Estimates or data pertaining to the portion of the parallel survey conducted since January 1994, using the unrevised procedures, will be referred to as "parallel survey since January" estimates or data (PSsj). Estimates or data derived from the unrevised CPS will be referred to as "unrevised CPS," "old method," or "unrevised methodology" estimates or data. Estimates or data derived from the revised CPS after January 1994 will be referred to as "revised CPS" or "revised methodology" estimates or data.

To aid in subsequent discussion of the statistical modeling and to provide additional insight into why a parallel survey effect may exist, the sample design and procedures used in each of the surveys are described below.

7.2.1   Unrevised Current Population Survey (Old Method before January 1994)

The CPS includes 60,000 households monthly that are selected to represent the population in the nation and each state. The probability sample of housing units is drawn using a multistage stratification procedure. The largest metropolitan areas within each state are always included; the remaining areas of a state are sampled on a probability basis, with the probability of selection being proportionate to the population of the area. In an effort to balance respondent burden with improved estimates of change, households are interviewed for four consecutive months, not interviewed for the next eight consecutive months, and then interviewed for another four consecutive months. Each month, a new household panel of approximately one-eighth of the total monthly sample size is initiated, and the panel that received its eighth interview the previous month is dropped. Given this rotating panel structure, in any month one-eighth of the households will be receiving their first interviews, one-eighth will be receiving their second interviews, one-eighth will be receiving their third interviews, and so forth. This rotating panel structure means that three-quarters of the sample in a given month is retained in the sample the next month. This improves estimates of month-to-month change, but it also means that there is a great deal of correlation in the data month to month. The first interview in each of the four consecutive interview months is conducted through a personal visit. In subsequent months, the majority of interviews are conducted over the phone, either from interviewers' homes or from one of two centralized computer-assisted telephone interviewing (CATI) facilities. The majority of the unrevised CPS data were collected with a paper survey instrument, although approximately 9 percent of the data were collected by interviewers working in the two centralized CATI facilities.

7.2.2   Revised Current Population Survey (New Method since January 1994)

Starting in January 1994, the 60,000-household CPS sample was switched to the revised questionnaire and computerized collection procedure. The rotation pattern established prior to January 1994 was maintained; therefore, 88 percent of the households that received the revised CPS questionnaire and procedures in January 1994 had previously received the CPS using the unrevised questionnaire and procedures, with 75 percent of the households having experienced the unrevised CPS in December 1993. Except for staff turnover, all of the CPS interviewers in January 1994 had previous experience with the unrevised CPS. The revised CPS data were collected entirely with the new computerized instrument. Again, the majority of the households were interviewed in a decentralized manner, either through personal visits or by telephone from interviewers' homes. In January 1994, a little less than 13 percent of the data were collected from the centralized CATI facilities. By May 1994, the percentage of interviews conducted by CATI in the revised CPS had increased to 14.5 percent.

7.2.3   Parallel Survey prior to January (New Method before January 1994)

The parallel survey prior to January 1994 (PSpj) included 12,000 households that were interviewed monthly starting in July 1992. The sample design for the PSpj was that used by the National Crime Victimization Survey, which is conducted by the Bureau of the Census for the Bureau of Justice Statistics. Like the CPS, the PSpj sample was drawn using a multistage stratified design. Unlike the CPS's state-based design, geographic areas for the PSpj were selected only to be nationally representative. The PSpj had the same 4-8-4 interview rotation pattern as the CPS. However, since the PSpj was initiated in 1992 and it takes 16 months to phase in this type of rotation scheme, September 1993 was the first month in which the rotation scheme was fully in place.[4] As in the CPS, the first and fifth month-in-sample households in the PSpj were interviewed through personal visits. In subsequent months, the majority of interviews were conducted by telephone. In the PSpj, 82 percent of the data were collected by field representatives using laptop computers, either during personal visits or by telephone from their own homes. The remaining 18 percent of the data were collected using CATI by a separate staff of interviewers working in the same two centralized facilities used for the CPS. The interviewer

4. The rotation scheme was such that from October 1992 forward all of the households in month-in-sample 1 through 4 actually were interviewed for their first through fourth times. In October 1992, the month-in-sample 1 through 4 households constituted 50 percent of the sample. At the same time, half of the survey households were designated as month-in-sample 5 through 8. The majority of these households actually were having their first through fourth monthly interviews, where households designated as month-in-sample 5 were really month-in-sample 1, households designated as month-in-sample 6 were really month-in-sample 2, etc. Historically, changes in estimates for month-in-sample 5 through 8 have shown the same pattern as changes in estimates for month-in-sample 1 through 4. A small percentage of the month-in-sample 5 households in October 1992 had been previously interviewed in January 1992 as part of a large-scale operations test of the new instrument and collection procedures. Starting in January 1993, 30 percent of the households designated as month-in-sample 5 actually were being interviewed for the fifth time after having not been interviewed for eight months. The percentage of "true" month-in-sample 5 households increased to 63 percent in April 1993 and 100 percent in May 1993. The percentage of true month-in-sample 6 through 8 households followed a similar pattern to the month-in-sample 5 households lagged by one calendar month.

staff for the PSpj was drawn to reflect the experience of CPS interviewers in a given year. Fifty percent had experience on the unrevised CPS, 25 percent had experience on other Census Bureau surveys, and 25 percent were new hires. While the PSpj was being conducted, none of the PSpj interviewers conducted the unrevised CPS. The PSpj had a supervisory staff that was separate and independent from that for the unrevised CPS. For each supplement conducted in the CPS from July 1992 through December 1993, a computerized version was also administered in the PSpj. Due to factors related to the initialization of the new procedures and implementation of the revised questionnaire, only data from October 1992 to December 1993 will be used for analysis.

7.2.4   Parallel Survey since January (Old Method since January 1994)

Starting in January 1994, the sample used for the PSpj was switched to the unrevised CPS paper questionnaire. Given the rotation structure of the parallel survey sample, this meant that in January 1994, 88 percent of the respondents had previous experience with the revised computerized questionnaire and, for 75 percent of the sample, this experience had been in December 1993. By May 1994, the percentage of respondents who had previous experience with the revised CPS had decreased to 50 percent, with none of this experience having occurred in a contiguous month. In January 1994, approximately 16 percent of the households in the parallel survey since January (PSsj) were eligible to be interviewed through CATI. By May 1994, the percentage of interviews eligible to be conducted by CATI had been reduced to 9 percent. Twenty-six percent of the field interviewers for the PSsj had conducted interviews with the unrevised CPS using the paper instrument. The majority of the remaining field interviewers were newly hired to work on the PSsj. Approximately 6 percent of these new hires had received training on the new questionnaire and methodology. None of the CATI interviewers for the PSsj had experience with the old questionnaire. The PSsj had the same supervisory staff as did the PSpj. The PSsj did not have any of the supplements that were administered with the revised CPS in 1994. It is important to note that the switching of the same households from the PSpj to the PSsj permitted an estimate of the parallel survey effect.

7.3   Description of Statistical Modeling

7.3.1   Introduction

Let Y_{it} be a non–seasonally adjusted estimate for a particular labor force measure (e.g., total national unemployment rate) for the ith survey in month t. Here $i = 1$ refers to the CPS and $i = 2$ refers to the parallel survey. In addition, t ranges from 1 to 20, denoting the months October 1992 to May 1994, respectively.

We will consider two models, an *additive factor* model and a *multiplicative factor* model. The additive factor model is given by

$$(1) \qquad\qquad Y_{it} = \mu_t + \lambda_i + \sum_{j=1}^{4} \delta_{itj} m_j + e_{it},$$

where

μ_t = True mean for month t,

λ_1 = Effect due to CPS,

λ_2 = Effect due to parallel survey,

δ_{itj} = 1 if m_j occurs in month t and survey i (zero otherwise),

m_1 = Effect due to old method before January 1994,

m_2 = Effect due to new method before January 1994,

m_3 = Effect due to old method since January 1994,

m_4 = Effect due to new method since January 1994,

e_{it} = Sampling error for survey i and month t.

We make the assumption that the sampling errors are normally distributed with mean zero. In addition, the sampling errors are uncorrelated between the two surveys but are correlated within survey. This within-survey correlation is mainly caused by the rotating panel structure of the CPS, mimicked in the parallel survey, which creates a 75 percent overlap between sampled units one month apart and 50 percent overlap between units twelve months apart.

The multiplicative model is given by

$$(2) \qquad\qquad \log Y_{it} = \log \mu_t^* + \log \lambda_i^* + \sum_{j=1}^{4} \delta_{itj} \log m_j^* + u_{it},$$

where the parameters are defined analogously to those in equation (1) and the sampling error u_{it} is normally distributed with mean zero.

Our goal with the additive model is to estimate the effect of the new methodology, $\hat{m}_4$ say, in order to create a revised estimate $\hat{Y}_t^{(A)} = Y_{1t} + \hat{m}_4$ for any month before January 1994 that is comparable to data from the CPS since January 1994. Under the multiplicative model we estimate a new methodology effect, $\hat{m}_4^*$, in order to create the revised estimate $\hat{Y}_t^{(M)} = Y_{1t} \hat{m}_4^*$. Unfortunately, the parameters of the models in equations (1) and (2) are not fully identified, even though some linear combinations are identified. For example, if we look at months prior to January 1994 for the additive factor model we get

$$(3) \qquad\qquad E\{Y_{2t} - Y_{1t}\} = \lambda_2 - \lambda_1 + m_2 - m_1,$$

while since January 1994 for the additive factor model we get

$$(4) \qquad\qquad E\{Y_{2t} - Y_{1t}\} = \lambda_2 - \lambda_1 + m_3 - m_4.$$

The linear combinations in equations (3) and (4) are estimable, even though the individual parameters are not estimable. In order to make progress with respect to individual parameters, additional restrictions need to be imposed.

Basic Assumption

The basic assumption we used is to make everything relative to the CPS prior to January 1994:

(5)

$$\text{Additive factor:} \quad \lambda_1 = 0, \ m_1 = 0,$$

$$\text{Multiplicative factor:} \quad \lambda_1^* = 1, \ m_1^* = 1.$$

This brings us down to four free parameters plus twenty monthly mean parameters. Unfortunately, all of the parameters of the model still are not identified. There are several ways to further restrict the parameters, and we list three reasonable ones next.

Restriction 1

In addition to the basic restriction, we could assume that the new method had the same effect before January 1994 as from January 1994 on and that there is no parallel survey effect:

(6)

$$\text{Additive factor:} \quad \lambda_2 = 0, \ m_2 = m_4,$$

$$\text{Multiplicative factor:} \quad \lambda_2^* = 1, \ m_2^* = m_4^*.$$

This would allow us to estimate a new method effect and an effect due to the way in which the old methodology was applied from January 1994 forward.

Restriction 2

In addition to the basic restriction, we could assume that the old methodology had the same effect from January 1994 on as it did previously and that there is no parallel survey effect:

(7)

$$\text{Additive factor:} \quad \lambda_2 = 0, \ m_3 = 0,$$

$$\text{Multiplicative factor:} \quad \lambda_2^* = 1, \ m_1^* = m_3^* = 1.$$

This would allow us to estimate a new method effect before January 1994 and a new method effect from January 1994 forward.

Restriction 3

In addition to the basic restriction, we could assume that the new methodology had the same effect before January 1994 as it has had since January 1994 and that the old methodology has had the same effect since January 1994 as it had previously:

(8)

Additive factor: $m_2 = m_4$, $m_3 = 0$,

Multiplicative factor: $m_2^* = m_4^*$, $m_1^* = m_3^* = 1$.

This would allow us to estimate a new method effect and a parallel survey effect.

7.3.2   Specification Used in Our Analysis

For the purposes of our analysis we used the additive and multiplicative models in equations (1) and (2) along with the basic assumption (eq. [5]) and restriction 3 (eq. [8]). We chose this specification because it most closely fits our understanding of the data. Specifically, everything possible was done to ensure that the new methodology was applied in the same way in the PSpj and in the CPS since January 1994. In addition, all possible measures were undertaken to ensure that the old method was implemented in the PSsj in the same way it was in the CPS prior to January 1994. The measures taken to ensure that the old and new methods were implemented in 1994 as they had been previously mean that we can estimate one parameter for the new method effect. The addition of a parallel survey effect parameter allows us to use data from 1994 to disentangle the confounding effects of the parallel survey and the new method, which are present if one analyzes only data prior to January 1994.

A variety of evidence both empirical and qualitative also supports use of the specification with a parallel survey effect and a single new method effect. Empirically, as will be discussed below, for the unemployment rate our additive model specification yields an insignificant point estimate of 0.079 for the new method effect and a significant point estimate of 0.41 for the parallel survey effect. Modeling done with employment data from the monthly Current Employment Statistics and unemployment insurance claims data estimating what the national unemployment rate would have been with the unrevised CPS methodology during 1994 also indicates that there was approximately a 0.08 percentage point change in the unemployment rate due to a change in methodology and weights (Tiller and Welch 1994).

A qualitative explanation of why a parallel survey effect might exist, independent of sample design differences, was provided by CPS and parallel survey supervisors in focus groups where they discussed their recent experiences. In these focus groups, some supervisors volunteered that CPS interviewers had larger caseloads than those working on the parallel surveys. The larger CPS caseloads reduced the amount of time interviewers had to follow up on households that did not initially respond. Furthermore, members of the focus groups noted, the smaller caseloads of the parallel survey supervisors gave them more time to monitor the survey process and pursue field problems (Tucker 1994). Differences in following up on nonresponders and monitoring of potential problems between the CPS and the two parallel surveys might have contributed to a parallel survey effect.

There could be some concern that respondents who switched from the revised to the unrevised procedure and vice versa were contaminated by their previous experiences. It should be noted, however, that on average the difference in unemployment rates between surveys from January through May 1994 did not diminish or change signs as would be expected if contamination were affecting the estimates. Therefore, in order to maintain sample size and capture any effect that was peculiar to the households actually selected for the parallel survey prior to January 1994, a decision was made to use the entire sample for January through May 1994, rather than restricting the analysis to households with no previous experience with another methodology.

Finally, we would like to make two other points about the specification we chose. First, even though we are modeling non–seasonally adjusted data, the parameter estimates for the parallel survey effect and new method effect also can be applied to seasonally adjusted data in the following sense. For those data series that are additively seasonally adjusted, we would get the same parameter estimates, with the additive model, for the parallel survey effect and the new method effect if we had used seasonally adjusted or non–seasonally adjusted data (assuming the same variances and covariances were used in the general least squares estimation). This is because the true monthly mean in equation (1) for seasonally adjusted data is just the true mean for the non–seasonally adjusted data plus a unique additive monthly seasonal adjustment factor that can be absorbed into the definition of the mean. A similar situation occurs for series that are multiplicatively seasonally adjusted, if we use the multiplicative model. Again, this occurs because the seasonal adjustment is additive on the scale in which we are modeling (i.e., the seasonal adjustment is additive in the logarithmic scale).

The second point we want to make about the selected specification has to do with why we did not model the underlying true monthly means with some method other than just monthly dummies. For example, it would be possible to specify a polynomial time trend model for the underlying monthly means with splines in time. The specification of such a model would allow us to, in general, identify an additional parameter, for example, freeing up the parameters m_3 and m_3^* in restriction 3. We actually attempted to estimate such models but found the models were still "close" to being not identified in the sense that while we were able to obtain parameter estimates, their standard errors were large and multicollinearity inflated the variance estimates of the parallel survey and new method effects. Thus we chose to continue modeling the monthly means as main effects in the linear model for all of our analyses and gave up trying to identify an additional parameter. In addition, it was felt that using one specification for all of the analyses would help our analysis seem more objective, since we would not have to be engaged in fitting different models for the monthly means, which may have involved the use of additional explanatory variables apart from the CPS and the parallel surveys, such as employment data from the monthly establishment survey (Current Employment Statistics) to model nonagricultural employment.

7.3.3 Estimation

For the model specified above we estimated the remaining parameters by generalized least squares. We illustrate in detail the estimation for the additive model; the estimation for the multiplicative model is analogous. Let $\mathbf{Y}_{(1)}$ be the vector of size 20×1 that contains the consecutive months of data from the CPS from October 1992 to May 1994, let $\mathbf{Y}_{(2)}$ be the data from the parallel surveys, and let $\mathbf{Y}' = (\mathbf{Y}'_{(1)}, \mathbf{Y}'_{(2)})$. Let $\mathbf{X}$ be the 40×22 model matrix associated with the specified model, and let $\boldsymbol{\beta}$ be the 22×1 vector of free parameters. The 22 free parameters consist of 20 monthly means, a parallel survey effect, and a new method effect. Then we can write

$$(9) \qquad \mathbf{Y} = \mathbf{X}\boldsymbol{\beta} + \mathbf{e},$$

where $\mathbf{e} \sim \mathbf{N}_{40}(\mathbf{0}, \mathbf{V})$ and $\mathbf{V} = \text{Block}(\mathbf{V}_1, \mathbf{V}_2)$, where $\mathbf{V}_1$ is the 20×20 covariance matrix of the CPS data and $\mathbf{V}_2$ is the 20×20 covariance matrix of the parallel survey data. The matrices $\mathbf{V}_1$ and $\mathbf{V}_2$ are estimated by the method of generalized variances along with correlation estimates obtained from previous CPS research. We will condition on the covariance matrix $\mathbf{V}$ and treat it as known.[5]

The estimated parameters are given by

$$(10) \qquad \hat{\boldsymbol{\beta}} = (\mathbf{X}'\mathbf{V}^{-1}\mathbf{X})^{-1} \mathbf{X}'\mathbf{V}^{-1}\mathbf{Y},$$

and the estimated covariance matrix of the estimates is given by

$$\hat{\mathbf{V}}\{\hat{\boldsymbol{\beta}}\} = (\mathbf{X}'\mathbf{V}^{-1}\mathbf{X})^{-1}.$$

All of the estimations are done with uncomposited data using 1990 population weights. The 1990 population weights are used to obtain a pure estimate of a method effect.[6]

---

5. Frequently, researchers ignore the complex nature of the sample design for surveys such as the CPS. In practice this will tend to underestimate the variance of most statistics. An illustration of this can be constructed using the non–seasonally adjusted unemployment rate. The estimated standard error from a standard computer package, such as SAS, for the non–seasonally adjusted April 1996 unemployment rate of 5.4 percent was 0.075. In comparison, the estimated standard error from the generalized variance function, which accounts for the complex survey design, for the April 1996 unemployment rate was 0.107. In addition, when analyzing CPS data over time, it is important to account for autocorrelation in monthly estimates. These autocorrelations vary by characteristics. For example, the first-order autocorrelation for the level of unemployment for consecutive months was estimated to be 0.43, while the first-order autocorrelation for the level of employment for consecutive months was estimated to be 0.71.

6. The 1980 weights with modifications for projected growth were used for originally published estimates from 1985 through 1993. In January 1996, the BLS reissued estimates for January 1990 through December 1993 using 1990 weights. No adjustment to official BLS estimates will be made to account for the survey redesign. Appendix C presents the effects of using 1980 vs. 1990 weights for selected 1993 annual average estimates.

7.4   The Results

7.4.1   General

All of the adjustment factors presented in the tables were estimated using the linear model specified above, which includes a new method effect and a parallel survey effect. Standard errors are provided in parentheses below the adjustment factors. Adjustment factors that were significantly different from one for the multiplicative model or zero for the additive model at the 5 percent level are indicated with asterisks. Point estimates for adjustment factors that were not significant are also provided, although when adjustment factors are not significant, depending on the sensitivity of the analysis, one could historically compare data before and after January 1994 without adjustment. Annual averages for 1993 are also included in the tables as a point of reference.

The effect of using the adjustment factors is illustrated graphically for several of the characteristics. The data in these graphs were adjusted multiplicatively. For comparisons over long time periods, multiplicative factors are recommended, since adjustments using multiplicative factors will account for differences in the level of the characteristic at different points in time. It should be noted, however, that for multiplicatively adjusted data, changes over time will not be the same as the changes measured by the unadjusted series. In contrast, the additively adjusted series will change the level of the series while leaving the estimates of change unaffected.

7.4.2   Unemployment and Related Unemployment Estimates

Unemployment Rate

Table 7.1 presents adjustment factors for the unemployment rates for detailed demographic groups. Examination of the adjustment factors in table 7.1 indicates that, unlike what was expected from the PSpj, the new methodology *did not* have a significant effect on the overall unemployment rate, although the point estimate for the additive factor was 0.079 and the point estimate for the multiplicative factor was 1.009, which would be equivalent to an approximately 1 percent increase in the unemployment rate. As could be anticipated from figure 7.1, the parallel survey effect in the linear model for the overall unemployment rate was estimated to be 0.41, which was statistically significant at the 1 percent level.

Further examination of the adjustment factors for the unemployment rates for various demographic groups reveals that the new methodology did not cause a significantly higher unemployment rate for any demographic group except older Americans. Specifically, the adjustment factors for all individuals aged 55–64, all individuals aged 65 or older, men aged 65 or older, women aged 55–64, and women aged 65 or older are each statistically significant and indicate that the revised methodology raised their rates.

Table 7.1   **Unemployment Rate Adjustment Factors for 1994 Methodological Change**

Demographic Group	Multiplicative Factor	Additive Factor	1993 Annual Average
Total 16+	1.009	0.079	6.8
	(0.011)	(0.076)	
Men 16+	1.012	0.10	7.1
	(0.015)	(0.11)	
Women 16+	1.007	0.07	6.5
	(0.016)	(0.11)	
White men 16+	1.029	0.19	6.2
	(0.018)	(0.11)	
White women 16+	1.025	0.15	5.7
	(0.021)	(0.11)	
Black men 16+	0.971	−0.38	13.8
	(0.032)	(0.49)	
Black women 16+	0.965	−0.48	12.0
	(0.031)	(0.43)	
Teenagers (16–19)	1.035	0.65	19.0
	(0.027)	(0.51)	
20–24-year-olds	1.007	0.03	10.5
	(0.026)	(0.28)	
25–54-year-olds	0.985	−0.075	5.8
	(0.014)	(0.084)	
55–64-year-olds	1.121*	0.50*	4.7
	(0.053)	(0.21)	
65 years or older	1.52*	1.52*	3.2
	(0.16)	(0.31)	
Men 16–19 years old	1.029	0.71	20.4
	(0.033)	(0.66)	
Men 20–24 years old	1.024	0.16	11.3
	(0.035)	(0.40)	
Men 25–54 years old	0.985	−0.07	5.9
	(0.019)	(0.12)	
Men 55–64 years old	1.06	0.29	5.2
	(0.06)	(0.30)	
Men 65 years or older	1.69*	1.93*	3.2
	(0.25)	(0.42)	
Women 16–19 years old	1.029	0.58	17.4
	(0.040)	(0.69)	
Women 20–24 years old	0.980	−0.23	9.6
	(0.036)	(0.38)	
Women 25–54 years old	0.990	−0.05	5.6
	(0.020)	(0.12)	
Women 55–64 years old	1.232*	0.76*	4.0
	(0.096)	(0.26)	
Women 65 years or older	1.33*	0.85*	3.1
	(0.19)	(0.44)	
Adult men (20+)	1.005	0.04	6.4
	(0.016)	(0.11)	
Adult women (20+)	1.001	0.016	5.9
	(0.017)	(0.10)	

Note: Numbers in parentheses are standard errors.

*Significant at the 5 percent level.

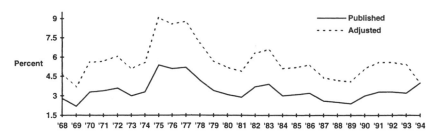

Fig. 7.3   Unemployment rate of men aged 65 or older (multiplicatively adjusted vs. published data)

The higher unemployment rates for older Americans are probably due to a combination of automation and rewording of the questionnaire. One of the most frequently heard complaints from respondents about the unrevised CPS was that it was burdensome and irritating for retired workers who had no attachment to the labor force. To alleviate this burden, the response category "retired" was added to each question about labor force activity. If individuals aged 50 or older volunteer that they are retired in answer to any of these questions, they are skipped directly to a specific question asking whether they currently want a job, either full or part time. Individuals who indicate that they want a job are asked the job search questions to establish if they have been looking for work in order to potentially classify them as unemployed. It could be that by reducing respondent irritation with the survey, directly asking older respondents if they currently want a job after they have said they are retired, and using the "part time" reference could prompt some older individuals to report that they have looked for work. In addition, a lower level of respondent irritation in combination with the automation of the survey could reduce the propensity for interviewers to make a personal assessment of older respondents and inappropriately lead them through the questionnaire.

The effect of applying the multiplicative adjustment factor for men aged 65 or older can be seen in figure 7.3. In addition to noting the dramatic shift in the graph for men aged 65 or older—the multiplicative factor increases the unemployment rate for older men as measured by the unrevised CPS 69 percent—it also is interesting to note that the redesign brings older men's unemployment rate closer to the unemployment rate for prime-aged males. Consequently, as the population ages, the redesign could have an effect on the overall unemployment rate independent of societal and economic changes that may occur.

Reasons for Unemployment

In addition to the unemployment rate, analysts frequently are interested in the reasons individuals are unemployed. The CPS allows unemployed individuals to be classified into one of five reasons for unemployment. Individuals

Table 7.2   **Reasons for Unemployment: Adjustment Factors for 1994
                            Methodological Change**

Reason for Unemployment	Multiplicative Factor	Additive Factor	1993 Annual Average
Total			
Laid off	0.975	−0.51	12.6
	(0.027)	(0.40)	
Other job losers	0.952*	−1.89*	42.0
	(0.014)	(0.56)	
Job leavers	0.866*	−1.39*	10.8
	(0.027)	(0.31)	
Reentrants to the job market	1.308*	7.79*	24.6
	(0.022)	(0.47)	
New entrants to the job market	0.622*	−4.01*	10.0
	(0.021)	(0.30)	
Men			
Laid off	0.932*	−1.30*	15.0
	(0.031)	(0.57)	
Other job losers	0.974	−1.02	47.7
	(0.017)	(0.76)	
Job leavers	0.910*	−0.88*	9.9
	(0.041)	(0.40)	
Reentrants to the job market	1.354*	6.80*	18.5
	(0.035)	(0.58)	
New entrants to the job market	0.592*	−3.74*	8.9
	(0.029)	(0.39)	
Women			
Laid off	1.068	0.43	9.6
	(0.053)	(0.53)	
Other job losers	0.914*	−2.84*	34.5
	(0.024)	(0.81)	
Job leavers	0.822*	−2.03*	12.0
	(0.037)	(0.49)	
Reentrants to the job market	1.266*	8.85*	32.4
	(0.027)	(0.76)	
New entrants to the job market	0.649*	−4.28*	11.5
	(0.030)	(0.48)	

Note: Numbers are percentages of total unemployed. Numbers in parentheses are standard errors.
*Significant at the 5 percent level.

could be unemployed because they were laid off from their jobs, lost their jobs for some other reason, voluntarily left their jobs, were reentrants into the job market, or were new entrants in the job market. Table 7.2 provides adjustment factors for these five reasons for being unemployed for all unemployed, unemployed men, and unemployed women, respectively.

Although the new methodology does not seem to have affected the overall unemployment rate, the adjustment factors in table 7.2 suggest that the new methodology did affect the overall composition of individuals' reasons for unemployment. For all unemployed, the adjustment factors indicate that the new methodology significantly increased the proportion of unemployed classified as reentrants and decreased the proportion of unemployed in the other four reason categories, with the proportions classified as "other job losers," "job leavers," and "new entrants" decreasing significantly. For men, the estimated adjustment factors also indicate that the new methodology significantly decreased the proportion classified as "laid off."

The estimated effect of the new methodology on reentrants is probably related to a combination of questionnaire wording and minor definitional changes. First, the wording of the question where the majority of unemployed provide their reasons for unemployment was changed from "At the time you started looking for work, was it because you lost or quit a job or was there some other reason?" in the unrevised CPS to "*Before* you started looking for work, what were you doing: working, going to school, or something else?" with the follow-up for those who said they were working "Did you lose or quit that job, or was it a temporary job that ended?" in the revised CPS. The wording of the unrevised question may have led those who had previously been employed to gloss over subsequent periods of time in which they were out of the labor market before searching for work. In that case, they would have been classified as job losers or job leavers in the unrevised CPS rather than as reentrants as is required by CPS definitions.[7]

Second, part of the new method effect on the estimate of reentrants can be attributed to a seemingly innocuous definitional change. In the unrevised CPS, individuals were asked when they had last worked full time for two weeks or longer. With this question only individuals who had worked full time were considered to have previous work experience and thus were classified as reentrants. Individuals whose entire work experience was part time or had lasted less than two weeks were classified as new entrants. The wording in the revised CPS was broadened to take into account any type of previous work experience, which should serve to reduce the proportion of unemployed classified as new entrants and increase the proportion classified as reentrants.

Finally, the proportion classified as reentrants could be affected by a change in the implementation of the on layoff concept. According to the official CPS definition, individuals must expect to be recalled to be classified as laid off. However, the unrevised CPS did not verify whether individuals who said they were laid off expected to be recalled. After asking a direct question about whether an individual is laid off, the revised CPS verifies whether individuals expect to be recalled through a series of two questions. Respondents are first asked if they were given a date to be recalled. If they say no, respondents are then asked if they expect to be recalled in the next six months. Only individuals

7. It should be noted that in the CPS information is collected on how long it has been since an individual last worked. However, according to the CPS definition, previously employed individuals should be classified as reentrants if there was a period during which they were out of the labor market, regardless of the duration of this period.

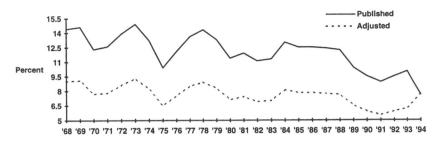

Fig. 7.4   New entrants as a percentage of unemployed (multiplicatively adjusted vs. published data)

who indicate either that they were given a recall date or that they expect to be recalled in the next six months are classified as laid off in the revised CPS. Those who do not meet the layoff criteria continue to the job search questions. Consequently, even those who do not expect to be recalled have an opportunity to be classified as unemployed in the revised CPS. For men, the adjustment factors indicate that the expectation of recall questions did screen respondents from being classified as laid off. However, the lack of significant adjustment factors for men's unemployment rates seems to indicate that the recall expectation questions did not have an effect on men's overall rate of unemployment.

Figure 7.4 plots adjusted and unadjusted series for new entrants.

Duration of Unemployment

The distribution of the length of time individuals have been unemployed is one indicator of the economy's relative position in a business cycle. In addition, economists examine the duration of unemployment spells to obtain a measure of economic hardship and to test alternative theories about the effects of unemployment insurance or reservation wages. Table 7.3 presents adjustment factors for the proportion of the unemployed who have been unemployed less than 5 weeks, 5 to 14 weeks, and 15 weeks or more.

Examination of the adjustment factors in table 7.3 reveals that the new methodology significantly increased the proportion of unemployed who had long spells of unemployment and significantly decreased the proportion of unemployed with spells of unemployment less than 5 weeks. The 17 percent change between the revised and unrevised questionnaire in the proportion of the unemployed reported to be without work 15 weeks or longer probably can be attributed to two methodological changes.

The first change involved the use of dependent interviewing. Previous research indicated that the duration of unemployment was not reported consistently for individuals who had been unemployed in consecutive months. (Polivka and Rothgeb 1993). Results collected using the unrevised CPS from November 1992 through December 1993 verified this previous research. Specifically, when unemployment durations were collected independently using

Table 7.3   **Duration of Unemployment: Adjustment Factors for 1994 Methodological Change**

Duration of Unemployment	Multiplicative Factor	Additive Factor	1993 Annual Average
Less than 5 weeks	0.830*	−6.32*	36.2
	(0.011)	(0.46)	
5–14 weeks	1.014	0.36	28.9
	(0.016)	(0.49)	
15 weeks and over	1.169*	5.58*	34.9
	(0.019)	(0.54)	

Note: Numbers are percentages of total unemployed. Numbers in parentheses are standard errors.
*Significant at the 5 percent level.

the unrevised procedures each month, only 26.1 percent of those unemployed in consecutive months increased their reported durations by four weeks plus or minus a week. Only 15.3 percent increased their length of unemployment by exactly four weeks. Approximately 46 percent of those unemployed in consecutive months reported a duration in the subsequent month that was less than three weeks greater than the duration reported in the previous month, and 28.5 percent reported a duration that was more than five weeks greater than the length of unemployment reported in the previous month.

In the revised CPS, these reporting inconsistencies were eliminated through the use of dependent interviewing and automatic updating. Rather than being asked each month how long they had been unemployed, individuals who were looking for work or laid off in consecutive months had their initially reported durations automatically increased by four or five weeks in the subsequent months.[8] The choice of adding four or five weeks was based on the number of weeks between surveys.

The second methodological change that probably influenced the reported duration of unemployment involved the reduction of response burden for the longer term unemployed. In the unrevised CPS, respondents were forced to report how long they had been looking for work or laid off in weeks. Research by Bowers and Horvath (1984) found that forcing respondents to report in weeks resulted in underreporting of durations for those with spells of unemployment lasting 26 weeks or longer. In the revised CPS, respondents are permitted to report their durations of joblessness in weeks, months, or years as they prefer. To incorporate this change the question wording was changed from "How many weeks have you been looking for work?" ("How many weeks ago were you laid off?") to "As of the end of *last week,* how long had you been

8. This methodology could smooth over short jobs held between monthly interviews. However, direct questioning conducted from July 1991 to October 1991 during the testing of the revised CPS indicated that only 3.2 percent of those who said they were looking for work in consecutive months had worked between interviews.

looking for work?" ("As of the end of *last week,* how long had you been on layoff?")

There is evidence that the choice of reporting periodicity and alternative wording in the revised questionnaire increased the reported durations of unemployment, independent of the effect of dependent interviewing. Specifically, the average duration of unemployment from November 1992 through December 1993 for those who were either in their first or fifth monthly interviews or not unemployed in consecutive months was 14.96 weeks for those who received the unrevised CPS and 17.19 weeks for those who received the revised procedures. In addition, in January 1994 when there was no dependent interviewing in the revised CPS, the proportion of unemployed whose durations were 15 weeks or longer was 34.23 percent for those who received the revised procedures in the CPS compared to 29.3 percent for those who received the unrevised procedures in the parallel survey.

Industry and Occupation of the Unemployed

In addition to variations in the measurement of unemployment in the aggregate and for various demographic groups, analysts are also interested in the cyclical behavior of unemployment within various industries and occupations. To facilitate comparisons after the redesign, table 7.4 presents adjustment factors for the proportion of unemployed with previous work experience in nine broad industry categories, and table 7.5 provides adjustment factors for the proportion of unemployed in six broad occupation groups.[9]

The adjustment factors in table 7.4 indicate that the new methodology significantly increased the proportion of unemployed with previous work experience who had worked in the agriculture and service industries and significantly decreased the proportion who had worked in the manufacturing sector. Figure 7.5 plots adjusted and unadjusted series for the proportion of unemployed with previous work experience in the manufacturing sector.

The almost 9 percent decrease in the proportion of unemployed who worked in the manufacturing sector documented in figure 7.5, along with the almost 9 percent increase in the proportion of unemployed who worked in the service sector, suggests that not accounting for the redesign could distort comparisons over time of slack demand within industries.

The adjustment factors for the occupations of the unemployed with previous work experience indicate that the new methodology increased the proportion classified as having worked in the farming, forestry, and fishing occupation by 19 percent. None of the other occupational adjustment factors were significant at the 5 percent level.

The changes between the new and old methodologies in the industry and occupation distributions of the unemployed with previous work experience are probably due to a combination of factors. As was previously noted, the new

---

9. Unemployed individuals who were classified as new entrants to the labor market or whose immediate work experience was in the military were excluded from the analysis.

Table 7.4 **Industry of the Unemployed: Adjustment Factors for 1994 Methodological Change**

Industry	Multiplicative Factor	Additive Factor	1993 Annual Average
Agriculture	1.264*	0.69*	3.0
	(0.088)	(0.19)	
Mining	0.79	−0.105	0.7
	(0.13)	(0.081)	
Construction	0.981	−0.26	12.3
	(0.029)	(0.37)	
Manufacturing	0.910*	−1.57*	19.1
	(0.023)	(0.46)	
Transportation and public utilities	0.979	−0.10	5.2
	(0.051)	(0.26)	
Wholesale and retail trade	0.980	−0.43	25.4
	(0.020)	(0.53)	
Finance, insurance, and real estate	0.941	−0.19	4.1
	(0.057)	(0.21)	
Services	1.089*	2.50*	27.9
	(0.020)	(0.54)	
Public administration	0.848*	−0.30	2.4
	(0.062)	(0.19)	

Note: Numbers are percentages of total unemployed who had previous work experience. Numbers in parentheses are standard errors.
*Significant at the 5 percent level.

Table 7.5 **Occupation of the Unemployed: Adjustment Factors for 1994 Methodological Change**

Occupation	Multiplicative Factor	Additive Factor	1993 Annual Average
Managerial and professional specialty	1.009	0.23	12.7
	(0.033)	(0.39)	
Technical, sales, and administrative support	0.986	−0.39	26.8
	(0.019)	(0.53)	
Service occupations	1.049	0.87	17.6
	(0.026)	(0.46)	
Precision production, craft, and repair	0.952	−0.72	14.8
	(0.028)	(0.42)	
Operators, fabricators, and laborers	0.973	−0.65	24.3
	(0.020)	(0.51)	
Farming, forestry, and fishing	1.190*	0.71*	3.8
	(0.071)	(0.22)	

Note: Numbers are percentages of total unemployed who had previous work experience. Numbers in parentheses are standard errors.
*Significant at the 5 percent level.

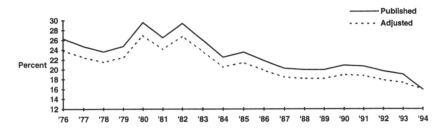

Fig. 7.5   Unemployed who had worked in manufacturing as a percentage of unemployed who had previous work experience (multiplicatively adjusted vs. published data)

methodology was estimated to cause a smaller proportion of the unemployed to be classified as new entrants. A decline in the proportion of unemployed classified as new entrants would cause an increase in the proportion of the unemployed classified as having previous work experience, which in turn could influence the industry and occupation distributions of the unemployed with previous work experience.

Other changes in the revised questionnaire such as an explicit probe about the existence of a family business or farm and the reordering of the questions asking unemployed individuals about the industry and occupation of their previous employment also could have affected the industry and occupation distributions of the unemployed.

7.4.3   Employment and Related Employment Estimates

Employment-to-Population Ratios

Table 7.6 presents adjustment factors for employment-to-population ratios for various demographic groups. Examination of the adjustment factors indicates that the new methodology significantly raised the overall employment-to-population ratio; however, the estimated adjustment factors also indicate that the overall effect masked differences by gender. Specifically, the multiplicative adjustment factors for all men, black men, and men aged 20–24 were significantly less than one at the 5 percent significance level, and the additive factors were negative and statistically different from zero at the 5 percent level. These results suggest that the new methodology significantly lowered the employment-to-population ratios for these groups. In contrast, the estimated adjustment factors indicate that the new method would significantly raise the employment-to-population ratios for women, white women, women aged 25–54, women aged 55–64, and women aged 65 or older. The only group that did not follow this pattern was men aged 65 or older. Using the estimated adjustment factor to account for the new methodology would significantly raise the employment-to-population ratio for these men.

Table 7.6　　　　**Employment-to-Population Ratio: Adjustment Factors for 1994 Methodological Change**

Demographic Group	Multiplicative Factor	Additive Factor	1993 Annual Average
Total 16+	1.0053*	0.33*	61.6
	(0.0017)	(0.10)	
Men 16+	0.9964*	−0.25*	69.9
	(0.0020)	(0.14)	
Women 16+	1.0156*	0.84*	54.1
	(0.0025)	(0.13)	
White men 16+	0.9967	−0.23	71.3
	(0.0025)	(0.18)	
White women 16+	1.0169*	0.92*	54.7
	(0.0030)	(0.16)	
Black men 16+	0.9831*	−1.02*	59.1
	(0.0089)	(0.53)	
Black women 16+	1.0093	0.48	50.5
	(0.0089)	(0.45)	
Teenagers (16–19)	1.005	0.21	41.7
	(0.011)	(0.45)	
20–24-year-olds	0.9920	−0.55	69.0
	(0.0056)	(0.38)	
25–54-year-olds	1.0035*	0.27	78.7
	(0.0018)	(0.14)	
55–64-year-olds	1.0124	0.65	53.8
	(0.0075)	(0.39)	
65 years or older	1.078*	0.84*	10.9
	(0.019)	(0.20)	
Men 16–19 years old	0.988	−0.41	42.2
	(0.014)	(0.60)	
Men 20–24 years old	0.9815*	−1.38*	73.8
	(0.0068)	(0.51)	
Men 25–54 years old	0.9969	−0.27	87.1
	(0.0019)	(0.16)	
Men 55–64 years old	0.9927	−0.44	63.1
	(0.0089)	(0.55)	
Men 65 years or older	1.062*	0.88*	15.1
	(0.025)	(0.36)	
Women 16–19 years old	1.025	0.97	41.2
	(0.017)	(0.68)	
Women 20–24 years old	1.0047	0.30	64.4
	(0.0079)	(0.50)	
Women 25–54 years old	1.0110*	0.77*	70.5
	(0.0027)	(0.19)	
Women 55–64 years old	1.032*	1.47*	45.4
	(0.011)	(0.47)	
Women 65 years or older	1.098*	0.77*	7.9
	(0.027)	(0.20)	
Adult men (20+)	0.9970	−0.21	72.0
	(0.0024)	(0.18)	
Adult women (20+)	1.0150*	0.83*	55.0
	(0.0029)	(0.16)	

Note: Numbers in parentheses are standard errors.

*Significant at the 5 percent level.

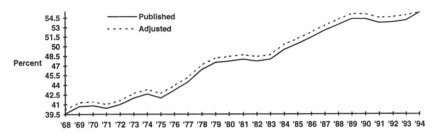

Fig. 7.6 Women's employment-to-population ratio (multiplicatively adjusted vs. published data)

The effect of the new methodology on women's and older workers' employment-to-population ratios probably is at least partially attributable to changes in wording of the questionnaire. These changes include the elimination of the opening labor force question inquiring about major activities last week, which may have caused some respondents to think that the CPS was not interested in more casual or intermittent work activity; the rephrasing of the questions asking about work activities last week to specifically refer to any work for pay and to remove the phrase "not counting work around the house"; and the addition of an explicit question about employment in family businesses.[10]

Figure 7.6 plots both adjusted and unadjusted employment-to-population ratios for women. The increase in women's employment-to-population ratio may not seem large; however, the increase implied by the multiplicative factor is equivalent to approximately 750,000 women.

Part-Time Workers and Workers Who Are Part Time for Economic Reasons

In addition to the proportion of the population employed, economists, sociologists, and policy analysts are also interested in the percentage of the employed who are working part time and the percentage of the employed who are part time for economic reasons such as poor business conditions or the inability to find full-time work. Table 7.7 provides adjustment factors to account for the effect of the new methodology on the number of part-time workers and workers who are part time for economic reasons.

The adjustment factors for part-time workers imply that the unrevised CPS either was not completely enumerating individuals who were working part time or was misclassifying them. Specifically, the multiplicative adjustment factors indicate that the unrevised CPS underestimated the proportion of employed who were working part time by 9.8 percent. The adjustment factors

10. See Cohany et al. (1994), Polivka (1994), and Rothgeb (1994) for a more detailed discussion of why women's employment-to-population ratios may be larger with the new methodology. See Martin and Polivka (1995) for a discussion of the difficulty of measuring work and employment in household surveys.

Table 7.7   **Part-Time Workers and Economic Part-Time Workers: Adjustment Factors for 1994 Methodological Change**

Demographic Group	Multiplicative Factor	Additive Factor	1993 Annual Average
Part-time workers			
Total	1.0983*	1.73*	17.5
	(0.0080)	(0.13)	
Adult men	1.074*	0.65*	8.5
	(0.016)	(0.13)	
Adult women	1.1246*	2.81*	22.8
	(0.0094)	(0.20)	
Teenagers	1.0329*	2.35*	67.7
	(0.0092)	(0.64)	
Part-time workers for economic reasons	0.806*	−1.003*	5.3
	(0.011)	(0.062)	

Note: Numbers are percentages of total employed. Numbers in parentheses are standard errors.
*Significant at the 5 percent level.

further indicate that this incomplete enumeration or misclassification occurred across various age and gender groups, since the multiplicative and additive factors for adult men, adult women, and teenagers all are significantly different from one and zero, respectively, at the 5 percent level.

Part of the estimated effect of the new methodology on the proportion of employed classified as part-time workers could be due to the elimination of a misclassification caused by the structure of the unrevised CPS. In the unrevised CPS, only individuals who actually worked less than 35 hours in the reference week were asked how many hours they usually worked. All individuals who were at work 35 hours or more were automatically classified as full time, regardless of the number of hours they usually worked. In the revised CPS, all respondents are first asked how many hours they usually work and then asked in subsequent questions about their actual hours. The new methodology could also increase the proportion of employed workers classified as part time if the additional workers measured in the revised CPS, as evidenced by the revised CPS's higher employment-to-population ratios, were disproportionately part-time workers.

At the same time that the adjustment factors imply that the new methodology increases the percentage of the employed working part time, they also indicate that the new methodology would decrease the proportion of the employed classified as part time for economic reasons by approximately 20 percent. The reduction in the proportion of the employed classified as part time for economic reasons most likely occurred because the unrevised CPS did not directly ask people if they wanted to and were available to work full time. Rather, individuals' desire and availability to work full time were assumed

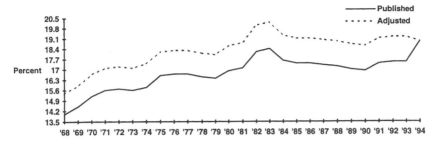

Fig. 7.7   Part-time workers as a percentage of employed (multiplicatively adjusted vs. published data)

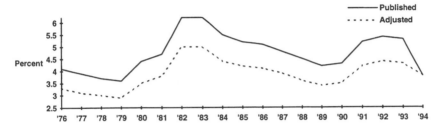

Fig. 7.8   Workers who are part time for economic reasons as a percentage of employed (multiplicatively adjusted vs. published data)

from the reasons they gave for working part time. In the revised CPS, individuals are asked directly if they want to and are available to work full time. In addition, part of the decrease in the proportion of employed working part time for economic reasons with the new methodology could be attributable to the more complete measurement of part-time workers in the revised CPS.

Figures 7.7 and 7.8 plot multiplicatively adjusted versus published data for part-time workers and workers who are part time for economic reasons, respectively. The sharp jumps in the unadjusted data highlight the importance of adjusting the CPS data for the redesign when making comparisons over time. Failure to adjust the data could cause analysts to reach improper policy conclusions about societal or economic changes that may or may not have occurred between the early 1990s and later years.

Class of Worker

Using the CPS data, employed individuals can be classified as wage and salary workers who work in the private sector, wage and salary workers who work for the government, self-employed incorporated, self-employed unincorporated, and unpaid family workers. Table 7.8 contains adjustment factors for these class-of-worker categories, along with factors for self-employed incorporated and self-employed unincorporated combined and for all wage and salary

Table 7.8 **Class of Worker: Adjustment Factors for 1994 Methodological Change**

Class of Worker	Multiplicative Factor	Additive Factor	1993 Annual Average
Total			
Wage and salary, private	0.9925*	−0.55*	72.6
	(0.0018)	(0.14)	
Wage and salary, government	0.9783*	−0.34*	15.5
	(0.0070)	(0.11)	
Self-employed incorporated	1.160*	0.462*	3.0
	(0.022)	(0.058)	
Self-employed unincorporated	1.062*	0.486*	8.7
	(0.012)	(0.091)	
Self-employed unincorporated and incorporated	1.088*	0.95*	11.7
	(0.011)	(0.11)	
Unpaid family workers	0.750*	−0.057*	0.3
	(0.062)	(0.015)	
Wage and salary and self-employed incorporated	0.99535*	−0.429*	91.1
	(0.00089)	(0.083)	
Men			
Wage and salary, private	0.9965	−0.26	71.7
	(0.0025)	(0.18)	
Wage and salary, government	0.986	−0.18	13.0
	(0.011)	(0.14)	
Self-employed incorporated	1.099*	0.401*	4.3
	(0.023)	(0.087)	
Self-employed unincorporated	1.004	0.03	10.9
	(0.013)	(0.13)	
Self-employed unincorporated and incorporated	1.031*	0.44*	15.2
	(0.011)	(0.15)	
Unpaid family workers	0.93	−0.007	0.1
	(0.13)	(0.013)	
Wage and salary and self-employed incorporated	0.9996	−0.04	89.0
	(0.0014)	(0.12)	
Women			
Wage and salary, private	0.9881*	−0.88*	73.6
	(0.0025)	(0.19)	
Wage and salary, government	0.9677*	−0.61*	18.5
	(0.0086)	(0.17)	
Self-employed incorporated	1.368*	0.547*	1.4
	(0.049)	(0.060)	
Self-employed unincorporated	1.184*	1.02*	6.0
	(0.022)	(0.11)	
Self-employed unincorporated and incorporated	1.22*	1.58*	7.5
	(0.02)	(0.12)	
Unpaid family workers	0.673*	−0.120*	0.4
	(0.058)	(0.024)	
Wage and salary and self-employed incorporated	0.9902*	−0.925*	93.5
	(0.0010)	(0.098)	

Note: Numbers are percentages of total employed. Numbers in parentheses are standard errors.
*Significant at the 5 percent level.

workers. In addition, since the BLS publishes estimates that classify the self-employed incorporated as wage and salary workers, adjustment factors for wage and salary workers and the self-employed incorporated combined are also provided.

The adjustment factors in table 7.8 indicate that under the new methodology, a significantly higher proportion of the total employed and employed women were classified as self-employed incorporated and self-employed unincorporated. At the same time a significantly smaller proportion were classified as wage and salary workers—either government or private—and unpaid family workers. The larger proportion of employed classified as self-employed incorporated and unincorporated with the new methodology is probably due to a combination of changes incorporated into the revised questionnaire. These include a direct question about household businesses at the beginning of the labor force questions, the reordering of the class-of-worker and industry and occupation questions to prevent interviewers from entering responses without asking all the appropriate questions, and the general changes in the measurement of employment embodied in the revised CPS.

Industry and Occupation of the Employed

In addition to determining whether individuals are wage and salary workers or self-employed, the CPS also collects information about the industry and occupation in which people work. Table 7.9 contains adjustment factors for the proportion of the employed who were classified as working in one of nine broad industry categories. Table 7.10 presents adjustment factors for the proportion of the employed who were reported as working in one of six major occupation groups.

Examination of the adjustment factors in table 7.9 indicates that the new methodology significantly increased the proportion of the employed classified as working in the agriculture, manufacturing, and finance, insurance, and real estate industries. The adjustment factors also indicate that at the 5 percent level, the new methodology significantly decreased the proportion of the employed classified as working in the construction and transportation and public utilities industries.

The adjustment factors for the proportion of the employed working in various occupations indicate that the new methodology significantly increased the proportion classified in the managerial and professional specialty group and significantly decreased the proportion of the employed classified as working as an operator, fabricator, or laborer.

Shifts between the revised and the unrevised CPS in the industry and occupation distributions of the employed are probably attributable to a combination of methodological differences. Again, as with the class-of-worker distribution, the industry and occupation distributions could be influenced by the different ordering of the class-of-worker and industry and occupation questions and by the inclusion of a direct probe about the existence of a household business

Table 7.9   **Industry of the Employed: Adjustment Factors for 1994 Methodological Change**

Industry	Multiplicative Factor	Additive Factor	1993 Annual Average
Agriculture	1.088*	0.195*	2.6
	(0.024)	(0.051)	
Mining	1.078	0.028	0.6
	(0.056)	(0.019)	
Construction	0.960*	−0.247*	6.1
	(0.013)	(0.081)	
Manufacturing	1.0197*	0.33*	16.4
	(0.0069)	(0.11)	
Transportation and public utilities	0.976*	−0.177*	7.1
	(0.011)	(0.079)	
Wholesale and retail trade	0.9925	−0.16	20.8
	(0.0059)	(0.12)	
Finance, insurance, and real estate	1.015	0.099	6.7
	(0.012)	(0.075)	
Services	0.9987	−0.05	35.1
	(0.0041)	(0.15)	
Public administration	0.991	−0.042	4.8
	(0.014)	(0.064)	

Note: Numbers are percentages of total employed. Numbers in parentheses are standard errors.
*Significant at the 5 percent level.

Table 7.10   **Occupation of the Employed: Adjustment Factors for 1994 Methodological Change**

Occupation	Multiplicative Factor	Additive Factor	1993 Annual Average
Managerial and professional specialty	1.0155*	0.42*	27.1
	(0.0050)	(0.14)	
Technical, sales, and administrative support	0.9947	−0.17	30.9
	(0.0048)	(0.15)	
Service occupations	0.9983	−0.02	13.8
	(0.0078)	(0.11)	
Precision production, craft, and repair	0.9837	−0.18	11.2
	(0.0089)	(0.10)	
Operators, fabricators, and laborers	0.9805*	−0.28*	14.3
	(0.0076)	(0.11)	
Farming, forestry, and fishing	1.082*	0.196*	2.8
	(0.026)	(0.058)	

Note: Numbers are percentages of total employed. Numbers in parentheses are standard errors.
*Significant at the 5 percent level.

or farm in the revised questionnaire. In addition, the industry and occupation distributions of the employed could be affected by the increase in work activity, particularly among women, measured in the revised questionnaire.

Another change in the industry and occupation questions is that after occupation information is collected in the first and fifth monthly personal interviews, in successive months individuals are asked if they work for the same employer and have the same job duties as they initially reported. Individuals who indicate that there were no changes simply are asked to verify the industry and occupation information they previously provided; the information is not collected anew. This dependent interviewing technique should have little effect on the level of employment within industries and occupations, but it will affect estimates of change, especially at the more detailed level. When information was collected independently each month in the unrevised CPS, in a test conducted from July 1991 to October 1991, it was estimated that at the three-digit level, 23 percent of respondents changed industry and 39 percent changed occupations month to month. Using the revised methodology it was estimated that during the same time period, 5 percent of individuals changed industries and 7 percent changed occupations. True measures of change generated for about the same time period were 3.8 to 4.2 percent for industry and 5.9 to 7.4 percent for occupation (Polivka and Rothgeb 1993).

7.4.4 Labor Force Participation and Discouraged Workers

Labor Force Participation Rates

Table 7.11 presents multiplicative and additive adjustment factors for the labor force participation rate—the proportion of the population that is either employed or unemployed—for various demographic groups. In general, the adjustment factors for the labor force participation rates follow the pattern one would expect after examining adjustment factors for both unemployment rates and employment-to-population ratios. The estimated factors indicated that the new methodology would significantly raise the labor force participation rates of all women, white women, and women in every age category except 20–24. In contrast, the adjustment factors suggest that the new methodology would significantly lower the labor force participation rates of men aged 20–24 and 25–54.

Discouraged Workers

In the unrevised CPS, individuals who were not in the labor force, wanted jobs, but had not looked for work in the prior month because they believed no jobs were available were defined as discouraged workers. Discouraged workers have been the focus of attention in the past as one indicator of the economy's health and as a group of individuals who may be suffering particular economic hardship. Nevertheless, the definition of discouraged workers in the unrevised CPS has frequently been criticized. The National Commission on Employment

Table 7.11   **Labor Force Participation Rate: Adjustment Factors for 1994 Methodological Change**

Demographic Group	Multiplicative Factor	Additive Factor	1993 Annual Average
Total 16+	1.0064*	0.423*	66.2
	(0.0014)	(0.093)	
Men 16+	0.9979	−0.16	75.2
	(0.0022)	(0.16)	
Women 16+	1.016*	0.95*	57.9
	(0.0027)	(0.15)	
White men 16+	0.9988	−0.08	76.1
	(0.0022)	(0.17)	
White women 16+	1.0194*	1.12*	58.0
	(0.0031)	(0.17)	
Black men 16+	0.9885	−0.83	68.6
	(0.0076)	(0.52)	
Black women 16+	0.9990	−0.04	57.4
	(0.0076)	(0.45)	
Teenagers (16–19)	1.0173*	0.90*	51.5
	(0.0090)	(0.44)	
20–24-year-olds	0.9941	−0.46	77.1
	(0.0044)	(0.34)	
25–54-year-olds	1.0024	0.20	83.5
	(0.0015)	(0.12)	
55–64-year-olds	1.0190*	1.04*	56.4
	(0.0071)	(0.38)	
65 years or older	1.094*	1.03*	11.3
	(0.019)	(0.20)	
Men 16–19 years old	1.004	0.24	53.1
	(0.012)	(0.60)	
Men 20–24 years old	0.9847*	−1.30*	83.1
	(0.0053)	(0.45)	
Men 25–54 years old	0.9960*	−0.37*	92.6
	(0.0015)	(0.14)	
Men 55–64 years old	0.9961	−0.25	66.5
	(0.0087)	(0.56)	
Men 65 years or older	1.084*	1.25*	15.6
	(0.026)	(0.38)	
Women 16–19 years old	1.033*	1.67*	49.9
	(0.014)	(0.65)	
Women 20–24 years old	1.0049	0.35	71.3
	(0.0066)	(0.46)	
Women 25–54 years old	1.0099*	0.74*	74.7
	(0.0024)	(0.18)	
Women 55–64 years old	1.043*	2.03*	47.3
	(0.01)	(0.47)	
Women 65 years or older	1.106*	0.85*	8.2
	(0.026)	(0.20)	
Adult men (20+)	0.9975	−0.20	76.9
	(0.0022)	(0.17)	
Adult women (20+)	1.0153*	0.90*	58.4
	(0.0027)	(0.16)	

Note: Numbers in parentheses are standard errors.

*Significant at the 5 percent level.

Table 7.12   **Discouraged Workers: Adjustment Factors for 1994**
                          Methodological Change

	Multiplicative Factor	Additive Factor	1993 Annual Average
Total	0.500*	−0.782*	1.72
	(0.011)	(0.025)	

Note: Numbers are percentages of those not in the labor force. Numbers in parentheses are standard errors.

*Significant at the 5 percent level.

and Unemployment Statistics faulted the definition for being too subjective because it was based primarily on individuals' desire for work rather than on more objective criteria such as recent job search. The definition in the unrevised CPS also has been criticized because individuals' information about availability for work was inferred from their reasons for not looking. To address the commission's concerns, two new requirements were added to the definition in the revised CPS questionnaire. To be classified as discouraged under the new methodology, individuals must have engaged in some job search within the past year (or since they last worked if they have worked within the past year) and must currently be available to take a job, in addition to the old criteria of currently wanting a job and having given up looking for reasons related to the economy.[11] The adjustment factors for discouraged workers, contained in table 7.12, indicate that the two additional criteria in the revised CPS decreased the proportion of those not in the labor force classified as discouraged workers by 50 percent.

7.5 Conclusion

The purpose of this paper was to provide adjustment factors in order that individuals could continue to use CPS data historically after the redesign. In addition, the adjustment factors were examined to provide insight into how the unrevised CPS might have been providing a distorted picture of the American economy. Overall, the adjustment factors suggest that the unrevised CPS was not mismeasuring individuals who were working full time in steady jobs or the vast majority of individuals looking for work—those in the center of the lens, so to speak. Rather, the adjustment factors indicate that the unrevised CPS was less in focus for those on the periphery of the labor market—those involved in more casual, intermittent, or marginal work activities, individuals who might have tentatively tested the labor market, and older workers. The adjustment

11. Also starting in January 1994, the series of questions that potentially classifies those not in the labor force as discouraged is asked of the entire CPS sample, rather than being limited to individuals in their fourth and eighth monthly interviews as was done in the past.

factors also imply that the unrevised CPS was not measuring as accurately as possible some of the characteristics of the employed and the unemployed. Specifically, the adjustment factors suggest that the unrevised CPS underestimated the proportion of employed who were part-time workers, overestimated the proportion of employed who were part time for economic reasons, and mismeasured individuals' reasons for being unemployed. By providing adjustment factors, it is hoped that a clearer picture of the economy through a redesigned CPS can be obtained without precluding comparisons of CPS estimates over time.

Appendix A
Note on Using the Adjustment Factors

Aggregation

The adjustment factors presented in tables 7.1 through 7.12 were estimated to be optimal for the statistic specified. In order to obtain a set of estimates that are consistent for both an overall statistic and mutually exclusive subgroups beneath the overall statistic (e.g., the total unemployment rate, adult men's unemployment rate, adult women's unemployment rate, and teenagers' unemployment rate), it would be necessary to subdivide the population into the lowest level of mutually exclusive subgroups for whom consistent estimates are desired and then adjust the component levels that are used for calculating the statistics for each of the subgroups (e.g., employment levels, unemployment levels, and, by subtraction from the population estimates, not in labor force levels). Once the adjusted levels for the subcategories have been obtained, consistent estimates for the statistics of interest for the subgroups and the aggregate could be derived. It is important to note, however, that enforcing consistency would not necessarily result in the same adjusted aggregate statistics as would be obtained if the aggregate statistic had been adjusted directly. The issues of aggregation surrounding the adjustment factors for the redesign are similar to those surrounding the aggregation and estimation of seasonally adjusted statistics. For statistics that the BLS seasonally adjusts, consistent estimates are obtained by first seasonally adjusting levels for subgroups and then aggregating. Adjustment factors for the 12 basic labor force series that are seasonally adjusted to obtain the seasonally adjusted total national unemployment rate are provided in appendix B. A comparison of what the annual unemployment rate would have been in 1992 if the multiplicative adjustment factor for the redesign had been applied directly as opposed to adjusting the subgroups first is also provided in appendix B. It should be noted that the estimates differ by only 0.03 percentage points.

Microdata Weighting

Our primary concern has been to develop adjustment factors, both additive and multiplicative, for aggregate series. Undoubtedly, some researchers will want "adjusted microdata weights" so that they can do analyses that are comparable before and after the redesign. A tempting way to do this is next described by example. First partition the population into men aged 16–19, men aged 20+, women aged 16–19, and women aged 20+ and cross these classifications with the labor force categories unemployed, employed in agriculture, employed in nonagricultural industries, and not in labor force. Multiplicative adjustment factors for 12 of these are given in appendix B. Implied adjustment factors for the remaining four not-in-labor-force categories could be obtained by taking the adjusted not-in-labor-force total (obtained by subtracting the adjusted labor force total from the unadjusted population count for each group) and dividing that by the unadjusted not-in-labor-force total. This ratio would be different for any given month (unlike the direct adjustment factors for unemployment and employment) because not in labor force is obtained indirectly by subtraction from the population total, which is assumed fixed and not subject to adjustment. Once the 16 multiplicative adjustment factors are obtained, they could be applied to the sampling weights for each of the respondents within each of the 16 groups, producing "adjusted microdata weights." Then the sum of all of the respondents within each of the 16 groups, using the adjusted microdata weights, would equal the multiplicatively adjusted aggregate total by the distributive law. While this may be tempting, we do not recommend using these microdata weights for any analyses other than constructing totals for each of those 16 groups since there is no guarantee that these weights would have any meaning if used in more complicated analyses.

Appendix B

Table 7B.1 below contains adjustment factors for the 12 series that are seasonally adjusted and then aggregated together to obtain a seasonally adjusted total national unemployment rate. Adjusted levels of those not in the labor force could be obtained by subtraction from the population estimates for the given characteristic.

The 1992 annual average unemployment rate obtained when the levels for the subgroups were adjusted and the unemployment rate was then calculated was 7.45 percent. The 1992 annual average unemployment rate when the multiplicative adjustment factors in table 7.1 were applied directly was 7.47 percent.

Table 7B.1   Unemployment and Employment Levels: Adjustment Factors for 1994 Methodology Change

Characteristic	Multiplicative Factor	Additive Factor
Unemployed teenage men	1.030	20,963
	(0.036)	(26,192)
Unemployed teenage women	1.063	44,656
	(0.044)	(25,338)
Unemployed adult men	1.0024	12,765
	(0.016)	(70,595)
Unemployed adult women	1.018	62,617
	(0.017)	(58,405)
Teenage men employed in agriculture	1.076	10,340
	(0.094)	(13,515)
Teenage women employed in agriculture	1.034	−1,799
	(0.18)	(6,861)
Adult men employed in agriculture	1.042	80,156
	(0.024)	(47,058)
Adult women employed in agriculture	1.326*	175,713*
	(0.057)	(24,904)
Teenage men employed in nonagriculture	0.986	−32,305
	(0.017)	(48,911)
Teenage women employed in nonagriculture	1.022	56,280
	(0.020)	(53,558)
Adult men employed in nonagriculture	0.9956*	−263,973*
	(0.0023)	(138,281)
Adult women employed in nonagriculture	1.012*	627,993*
	(0.0026)	(135,314)

Note: Numbers in parentheses are standard errors.
*Significant at the 5 percent level.

Appendix C

Table 7C.1 below contains differences in 1993 annual average CPS labor force estimates when 1990 versus 1980 census-based population controls were used. The differences are defined as the 1990 estimates minus the 1980 estimates.[12]

12. The proportion of the population within any subgroup may not remain constant when 1980 vs. 1990 population weights are used. For example, the percentage of women aged 25–54 when 1980 population weights were used was 55.8 percent. When 1990 population weights were used, the percentage was 71.7 percent. Since the proportion of the population within subgroups may not remain constant when different weights are used, the difference between estimates for an aggregate group (e.g., the labor force participation rate for all women) does not have to be bound by the differences for various subgroups (e.g., the labor force participation rates for women aged 16–19, 20–24, 25–54, 55–64, and 65 years or older).

Table 7C.1   Difference in 1993 Annual Average Labor Force Estimates Using 1990 versus 1980 Population Weights

Demographic Group	Unemployment Rate	Employment-to-Population Ratio	Labor Force Participation Rate
Total 16+	0.10	0.08	0.16
Men 16+	0.10	0.17	0.26
Women 16+	0.10	−0.02	0.04
White men 16+	0.09	0.07	0.15
White women 16+	0.06	−0.09	−0.06
Black men 16+	0.03	0.85	1.01
Black women 16+	0.13	0.38	0.52
Teenagers (16–19)	0.03	−0.04	−0.03
20–24-year-olds	0.06	−0.13	−0.09
25–54-year-olds	0.04	−0.10	−0.07
55–64-year-olds	−0.02	−0.02	−0.03
65 years or older	−0.01	−0.07	−0.08
Men 16–19 years old	−0.04	0.08	0.08
Men 20–24 years old	0.00	0.07	0.08
Men 25–54 years old	0.04	−0.08	−0.05
Men 55–64 years old	−0.03	0.04	0.02
Men 65 years or older	0.00	−0.05	−0.05
Women 16–19 years old	0.09	−0.16	−0.14
Women 20–24 years old	0.11	−0.42	−0.38
Women 25–54 years old	0.05	−0.14	−0.12
Women 55–64 years old	0.00	−0.09	−0.09
Women 65 years or older	−0.02	−0.03	−0.04
Adult men (20+)	0.07	0.28	0.36
Adult women (20+)	0.07	0.03	0.08

Note: Difference = 1990 − 1980.

References

Aronson, Robert. 1991. *Self-employment: A labor market perspective.* Ithaca, N.Y.: ILR.

Blank, Rebecca. 1990. Are part-time jobs bad jobs? In *A future of lousy jobs?* ed. Gary Burtless. Washington, D.C.: Brookings Institution.

Bound, John, and George Johnson. 1992. Changes in the structure of wages in the 1980s: An evaluation of alternative explanations. *American Economic Review* 82, no. 3 (June): 371–92.

Bowers, Norman, and Francis Horvath. 1984. Keeping time: An analysis of errors in the measurement of unemployment duration. *Journal of Business and Economic Statistics* 2, no. 2 (April): 140–49.

Bregger, John, and Cathryn Dippo. 1993. Overhauling the Current Population Survey: Why is it necessary to change? *Monthly Labor Review* 116, no. 9 (September): 3–9.

Cohany, Sharon, Anne Polivka, and Jennifer Rothgeb. 1994. Revisions in the Current Population Survey effective January 1994. *Employment and Earnings* 41, no. 2 (February): 13–37.

Devine, Theresa. 1994a. Changes in wage-and-salary returns to skill and the recent rise in female self-employment. *American Economic Review* 84, no. 2 (May): 108–19.

————. 1994b. Characteristics of self-employed women in the United States. *Monthly Labor Review* 117, no. 3 (March): 20–34.

Dippo, Cathryn, Anne Polivka, Kathleen Creighton, Donna Kostanich, and Jennifer Rothgeb. 1994. Redesigning a questionnaire for computer-assisted data collection: The Current Population Survey experience. Washington, D.C.: U.S. Department of Labor, Bureau of Labor Statistics. Unpublished manuscript.

Fracasso, M. P. 1989. Categorization of responses to the open-ended labor force questions in the Current Population Survey. In *Proceedings of the Section on Survey Research Methods*. Alexandria, Va.: American Statistical Association.

Jabine, Thomas, Miron Straf, Judith Tanur, and Roger Tourangeau. 1984. *Cognitive aspects of survey methodology: Building a bridge between disciplines*. Washington, D.C.: National Academy Press.

Levy, Frank, and Richard Murnane. 1992. U.S. earnings levels and earnings inequality: A review of recent trends and proposed explanations. *Journal of Economic Literature* 30, no. 3 (September): 1333–81.

Martin, Elizabeth, and Anne Polivka. 1995. Diagnostics for redesigning survey questionnaires: Measuring work in the Current Population Survey. *Public Opinion Quarterly* 59, no. 4 (winter): 547–67.

Michael, Robert. 1985. Consequences of the rise in female labor force participation rates: Questions and probes. *Journal of Labor Economics* 3, no. 1, pt. 2 (January): S117–S146.

Murphy, Kevin, and Robert Topel. 1987. The evolution of unemployment in the United States: 1968–1985. In *NBER macroeconomics annual*, ed. Stanley Fischer. Cambridge, Mass.: MIT Press.

Palmisano, Mark. 1989. Respondents' understanding of key labor force concepts used in the CPS. In *Proceedings of the Section on Survey Research Methods*. Alexandria, Va.: American Statistical Association.

Peracchi, Franco, and Finis Welch. 1994. Trends in labor force transitions of older men and women. *Journal of Labor Economics* 12, no. 2 (April): 210–41.

Polivka, Anne. 1994. *Comparisons of labor force estimates from the parallel survey and the CPS during 1993*. CPS Overlap Analysis Team Technical Report no. 1. Washington, D.C.: U.S. Department of Labor, Bureau of Labor Statistics.

Polivka, Anne, and Jennifer Rothgeb. 1993. Overhauling the Current Population Survey: Redesigning the questionnaire. *Monthly Labor Review* 116, no. 9 (September): 10–28.

Rothgeb, Jennifer. 1982. Summary report of July follow-up of the unemployed. Unpublished memorandum, 20 December. U.S. Bureau of the Census, Washington, D.C.

————. 1994. *Revisions to the CPS questionnaire: Effects on data quality*. CPS Overlap Analysis Team Technical Report no. 2. Washington, D.C.: U.S. Department of Labor, Bureau of Labor Statistics.

Smith, James, and Michael Ward. 1985. Time-series growth in the female labor force. *Journal of Labor Economics* 3, no. 1, pt. 2 (January): S59–S89.

Thompson, Jenny. 1994. *Mode effects analysis of labor force estimates*. CPS Overlap Analysis Team Technical Report no. 3. Washington, D.C.: U.S. Department of Labor, Bureau of Labor Statistics.

Tiller, Richard, and Michael Welch. 1994. *Predicting the national unemployment rate that the "old" CPS would have produced*. CPS Bridge Team Technical Report no. 2. Washington, D.C.: U.S. Department of Labor, Bureau of Labor Statistics.

Tobin, James. 1972. Inflation and unemployment. *American Economic Review* 62, no. 2 (March): 1–18.

Tucker, Clyde. 1994. Visit to the Census regional office in New York. Unpublished memorandum, 6 October. U.S. Bureau of Labor Statistics, Washington, D.C.

Comment   Gary Solon

This is a nicely crafted paper, and the evidence it provides about comparability of the Current Population Survey labor force statistics before and after the survey's 1994 redesign will be useful to researchers for many years to come.

Before saying a bit about the statistical work in the paper, I first want to applaud the authors for explaining why the redesign was necessary. I suspect the first reaction of many of us academic researchers to the overhaul of the CPS is to wonder why the statistical agencies are once again disrupting the continuity of our time-series data. Polivka and Miller answer this question well. They give some compelling examples of how survey questions that may have been clear and appropriate in the 1960s had become confusing or offensive by the 1990s. The point is that our way of life has changed, and even if the statistical agencies stuck to asking the same old questions, the way respondents interpret and react to the questions would change. As a result, perfect continuity in the data series is unattainable, and we are better off if the survey instrument is periodically brought up to date. In addition, the new survey takes advantage of technological advances, especially the advent of laptop computers. It would be a shame if, for the sake of continuity, the statistical agencies forever avoided the adoption of superior survey methods just because the methods used to be technologically infeasible.

Moving on to the statistical analysis, Polivka and Miller use a simple but sensible model for Y_{it}, the labor force statistic (e.g., the unemployment rate) from survey i in period t. Their model is

$$(1) \qquad Y_{it} = \mu_t + \lambda(i - 1) + \beta D_{it} + \varepsilon_{it},$$

where $i = 1, 2$ indexes respectively the CPS and the parallel survey and $t = 1, 2, \ldots, 20$ indexes the months from October 1992 to May 1994. The μ_t parameters represent time effects, λ is the effect of the parallel survey, ε_{it} is a zero mean error term arising mainly from sampling error, and the dummy variable D_{it} equals one if survey i used the new survey design in month t and equals zero otherwise. The new survey design was introduced into the CPS in January 1994 ($t = 16$), while the parallel survey used the new design *before* January 1994 and then switched to the old design. Thus

$$D_{it} = \begin{cases} 1 & \text{for } i = 1 \text{ and } t \geq 16, \\ 1 & \text{for } i = 2 \text{ and } t < 16, \\ 0 & \text{otherwise}. \end{cases}$$

The coefficient of D_{it}, β, is the parameter of main interest. It represents the effect of the new survey design and therefore is the amount we need to subtract

Gary Solon is professor of economics at the University of Michigan.

off the CPS series after January 1994 to make it comparable with the CPS series before January 1994.

Because of the sample rotation pattern used in the CPS and the parallel survey, Polivka and Miller expect ε_{it} to be serially correlated, so they estimate equation (1) by generalized least squares (GLS). This is a good idea, but I also want to propose a simpler alternative estimator of β. Although in principle my estimator suffers from a small statistical inefficiency, its simplicity clarifies what in the data generates the evidence on the magnitude of β.

To begin with, note that in the period before January 1994, $E(Y_{1t}) = \mu_t$ and $E(Y_{2t}) = \mu_t + \beta + \lambda$. Consequently, the sample mean over this period of the discrepancy between the two surveys, $\overline{Y}_2 - \overline{Y}_1$ has expected value $E(\overline{Y}_2 - \overline{Y}_1) = \beta + \lambda$. For the unemployment rate, the sample mean discrepancy before January 1994 was $7.405 - 6.931 = 0.474$. This discrepancy was initially viewed as evidence that the new survey design would raise the unemployment rate by about half a point, but as Polivka and Miller emphasize, this discrepancy is a biased estimate of β if $\lambda \neq 0$.

The key to correcting for the bias is to note that from January 1994 on, $E(Y_{1t}) = \mu_t + \beta$ and $E(Y_{2t}) = \mu_t + \lambda$, so that $E(\overline{Y}_1 - \overline{Y}_2) = \beta - \lambda$. For the unemployment rate, $\overline{Y}_1 - \overline{Y}_2$ over this later period was $6.681 - 6.993 = -0.312$. This discrepancy also is a biased estimate of β if $\lambda \neq 0$, but the bias is precisely equal in magnitude and opposite in sign to that of the other discrepancy. An obvious unbiased estimator, then, is the simple average of the two discrepancies. For the unemployment rate, the resulting estimate of β is $(0.474 - 0.312)/2 = 0.081$, quite close to the $\hat{\beta}_{GLS} = 0.079$ reported by Polivka and Miller. The small magnitude of these estimates suggests that for the overall unemployment rate, we need not lose sleep over the discontinuity caused by the new survey design.

As it happens, it is easy to show that my estimator is precisely the same as the estimator of β obtained by applying ordinary least squares (OLS) to the between-survey difference of equation (1):

$$(2) \qquad Y_{2t} - Y_{1t} = \lambda + \beta(D_{2t} - D_{1t}) + \varepsilon_{2t} - \varepsilon_{1t}.$$

Estimating equation (2) by OLS reproduces my $\hat{\beta} = 0.081$ with estimated standard error 0.044. It also produces $\hat{\lambda} = 0.393$ (with estimated standard error 0.044), quite close to Polivka and Miller's $\hat{\lambda}_{GLS} = 0.41$.

The one odd difference between my results and Polivka and Miller's is that they report a 0.076 standard error estimate for their $\hat{\beta}$, much larger than the 0.044 standard error estimate I get for my $\hat{\beta}$. At first, one might think this is because my standard error estimate is biased downward by my neglect of serial correlation in the equation (2) error term. In fact, however, the usual diagnostic statistics reveal very little serial correlation in $\varepsilon_{2t} - \varepsilon_{1t}$. My Durbin-Watson statistic is 1.89, suggesting a first-order autocorrelation of less than .1, and the higher order autocorrelations of the residuals also are small. This makes me wonder what "**V** matrix" Polivka and Miller use in their GLS estimation and whether it is consistent with the pattern of regression residuals. If they have used an inappropriate **V** matrix, their attempt at GLS estimation may be further away from true GLS estimation than OLS estimation is. In that case, the estimator I have proposed not only is simpler than theirs but may even be more efficient.

III Employee Compensation: Measurement and Impact

8   Divergent Trends in Alternative Wage Series

Katharine G. Abraham, James R. Spletzer, and
Jay C. Stewart

8.1   Introduction

The average wage level is a key aspect of economic well-being in a society. Several alternative wage measures based on official government statistics are available to analysts. Although there always have been differences among the various measures with respect to the implied average wage level, since the mid-1970s they have diverged markedly. The present paper has several goals: to describe the various available hourly wage series, to characterize the differences in behavior among them, and to explore alternative hypotheses concerning these differences.

Figure 8.1 graphs annual average values of selected hourly wage series, all converted to 1993 dollars.[1] Users who rely on national income accounts data

Katharine G. Abraham is commissioner of the Bureau of Labor Statistics, U.S. Department of Labor. James R. Spletzer and Jay C. Stewart are research economists in the Office of Employment Research and Program Development at the Bureau of Labor Statistics, U.S. Department of Labor.

This work has benefited from the assistance of many Bureau of Labor Statistics staff members, including Patricia Getz, Michael Roosma, Anne Polivka, John Stinson, and George Werking in the Office of Employment and Unemployment Statistics; Wayne Shelly and Donald Wood in the Office of Compensation and Working Conditions; Michael Harper and Phyllis Otto in the Office of Productivity and Technology; and Cheryl Kerr in the Office of the Commissioner. The authors also are indebted to Robert Parker of the Bureau of Economic Analysis and John Robinson of the University of Maryland, for assistance with data, and to John Haltiwanger, Daniel Hamermesh, Lawrence Katz, Marilyn Manser, Lawrence Mishel, and Jack Triplett, for their thoughtful comments on an earlier draft of the paper. Any remaining errors are, of course, the authors' own. The views expressed are those of the authors.

1. Two significant hourly compensation series are omitted from fig. 8.1: the BLS Office of Productivity and Technology's (OPT's) hourly compensation measure and the hourly compensation cost series produced by the BLS Employment Cost Index (ECI) program. The OPT measure is constructed in very much the same way as the series based on the NIPA shown in fig. 8.1 but is a total compensation rather than a wage and salary measure. The ECI is designed to capture changes in the employer cost of employing labor of a fixed type. Since 1987, the program also has produced hourly labor cost estimates that reflect the actual mix of employment at a point in time

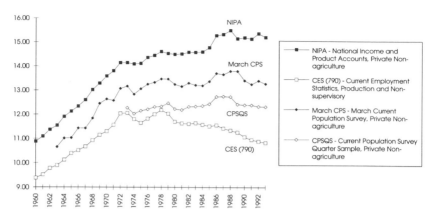

Fig. 8.1   Real hourly earnings (CPI-U-X1 adjusted dollars, 1993 = 100)

for other purposes seem likely to rely on the wage and hours information from the accounts for assessing the trend in the hourly wage. The National Income and Product Accounts (NIPA) series in figure 8.1 was constructed by dividing the (deflated) wages and salaries of private industry workers by total hours for the same group. To the extent that they are interested in current information regarding real wages, the business community and the press tend to focus on the average hourly earnings of production and nonsupervisory workers from the Bureau of Labor Statistics (BLS) monthly employer survey, the Current Employment Statistics (CES) series. In contrast, most of the academic literature on real wage trends has used data either from the March income supplements to the Current Population Survey (the March CPS series) or from the earnings questions asked of CPS outgoing rotation groups each month beginning in 1979 and, earlier, of all CPS respondents each May from 1973 through 1978 (the CPS quarter sample, or CPSQS, series); see, for example, Bound and Johnson (1992), Levy and Murnane (1992), Katz and Murphy (1992), Murphy and Welch (1992a, 1992b), Juhn, Murphy, and Pierce (1993), Buchinsky (1994).

These four series exhibit some significant differences in trend, particularly since the mid-1970s. Between 1973 and 1993, the NIPA real hourly wage measure rose by more than 7 percent, the March CPS and the CPSQS measures held roughly steady, and the CES measure fell by 10 percent. Although all three series that begin before 1973 show a significant slowdown in the rate of real wage growth starting in the mid-1970s, someone who looked at NIPA data

and thus conceptually are more comparable to the other series we consider. The available time series still is relatively short, and the historical rotation of sample units on an industry-by-industry basis complicates the interpretation of year-to-year changes in the hourly cost estimates.

nonetheless would have a very different picture of recent real wage trends than someone who looked at CPS data or, especially, CES data.

Because our primary interest here is to understand the significant differences in the trends implied by different sources of wage information, all of the series shown in figure 8.1 have been deflated using the same deflator, the CPI-U-X1, an experimental Consumer Price Index (CPI) series that measures inflation more consistently over time than the official CPI series.[2] Critics have argued that the CPI is an upward-biased measure of changes in living costs. Although the questions raised by these critics are important, they are not relevant to understanding the differences in growth rates among alternative wage series that are the focus of the present paper.

Both the NIPA series and the CES series are, in effect, hours-weighted average wages; for consistency, both of the CPS series shown in the graph also have been computed as hours-weighted averages. In addition, the CPS series have been adjusted for the top-coding of reported earnings in the survey.[3] All series cover the private sector exclusive of agriculture and private households. Although we have made every effort to report wages on a comparable basis, some differences remain. Earnings concepts differ across the four series, and the worker population covered by the CES series is less inclusive than that covered by the other data series.

The remainder of the paper is devoted to explaining the differences in the behavior of the four wage series shown in figure 8.1. All of these hourly wage measures are computed from reported annual or weekly earnings and a measure of weekly hours (further details are provided in the data appendix). Section 8.2 explores the relative contributions of earnings and hours to the behavior of the various hourly wage measures. The divergence of the CES hourly wage measure from other available wage measures reflects the very different behavior of the CES weekly earnings series. Possible reasons for that difference are examined in section 8.3. Understanding the different behavior of NIPA and CPS weekly hours turns out to be central to understanding the divergence of NIPA and CPS average hourly wages and thus is the focus of section 8.4. Concluding observations and our thoughts concerning directions for future research are offered in section 8.5.

2. Prior to 1983, the homeowners' housing component of the official CPI series was based on the cost of purchasing a home; in 1983, it was changed to reflect the value of rental services received by owners. The CPI-U-X1 uses available information to construct a "rental equivalence" measure of owners' housing costs for the pre-1983 period that is as consistent as possible with the measure for more recent years.

3. Our initial approach to adjusting for top-coding was to model the top-coded data for each year as the right-hand tail of a Pareto distribution. Although this approach generated mean earnings estimates that seemed sensible for individual years, the implied year-to-year changes in earnings, especially those surrounding the change in the CPSQS top-code from $999 in 1988 to $1,923 in 1989, were not sensible. Following Murphy and Welch (1992a), we therefore adopted the simpler expedient of multiplying all top-coded values by 1.50 prior to averaging. Others who have used a similar approach include Juhn et al. (1993) and Katz and Murphy (1992).

8.2   Trends in Weekly Earnings and Weekly Hours

One way to think about differences across the various available wage series just described is to ask whether they differ because the respondents to the underlying surveys are telling us different things about earnings or because they are telling us different things about hours of work. We begin to answer this question by looking at the trends in weekly earnings and weekly hours associated with each of the four hourly wage series. A relative increase in a particular hourly wage measure could reflect either a relative *rise* in the associated weekly earnings series or a relative *decline* in the associated weekly hours series. One complication is that, whereas both the NIPA and the CES data measure the average weekly earnings and hours associated with *jobs,* both the March CPS and the CPSQS data refer to the earnings and hours of *individuals.* In assessing the trends in the data, therefore, we include an assessment of the likely impact of these differences.

8.2.1   Weekly Earnings versus Weekly Hours Effects

One of the trend comparisons highlighted earlier was the decline in the CES hourly wage relative to the March CPS, the CPSQS, and, especially, the NIPA hourly wage. As can be seen in figure 8.2, CES weekly earnings have fallen sharply relative to all three of the other weekly earnings series. Between 1973 and 1993, CES real weekly earnings fell by 16.1 percent. Over the same period, each of the other three weekly earnings measures held relatively stable, with NIPA real weekly earnings rising by 1.8 percent, March CPS real weekly earnings falling by 0.7 percent, and CPSQS real weekly earnings rising by 0.4 percent. The decline in CES weekly earnings relative to the two CPS weekly earnings series is considerably more pronounced than the corresponding relative decline in CES hourly wages.[4]

Average weekly hours from all four sources are shown in figure 8.3. Not surprisingly given that the NIPA hours estimates are based principally on CES data, NIPA and CES hours have similar trends; between 1973 and 1993, average weekly NIPA hours dropped by 5.2 percent and average weekly CES hours by 6.5 percent.[5] In contrast, over the same period, March CPS hours fell by just 1.4 percent, and CPSQS hours were essentially unchanged. The relative decline in CES hourly earnings as compared to CPS hourly earnings caused by the relative decline in CES weekly earnings would have been larger but for the offsetting effect of the relative decline in CES weekly hours.

4. Between 1973 and 1993, the logarithm of the CES average hourly wage fell by 0.115 relative to the logarithm of the March CPS average hourly wage and by 0.111 relative to the logarithm of the CPSQS average hourly wage. Over the same period, the logarithm of the CES average *weekly* wage declined 0.168 relative to the corresponding March CPS series and 0.179 relative to the corresponding CPSQS series.
5. The levels of the CES and NIPA weekly hours series differ principally because the CES series employs an hours paid concept, whereas the NIPA series employs an hours worked concept. The main difference between hours paid and hours worked is that the latter excludes paid leave.

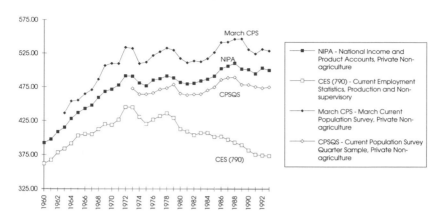

Fig. 8.2   Real weekly earnings (CPI-U-X1 adjusted dollars, 1993 = 100)

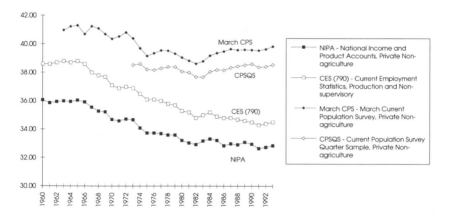

Fig. 8.3   Average weekly hours

One implication of these patterns is that any explanation for the divergence of the CES hourly wage from other available hourly wage series should focus on reported earnings rather than reported hours. A second implication is that understanding the growth in NIPA hourly earnings relative to March CPS and CPSQS hourly earnings requires that we understand the relative decline in reported NIPA weekly hours.

These conclusions are borne out by more formal decompositions of the differences between each of the various possible hourly wage series pairs into a weekly earnings piece and a weekly hours piece. Consider, for example, the log difference between the CES hourly wage and the NIPA hourly wage:

$$\ln(\text{CES hourly wage}) - \ln(\text{NIPA hourly wage})$$

$$= [\ln(\text{CES weekly earnings}) - \ln(\text{CES weekly hours})]$$

(1) $$- [\ln(\text{NIPA weekly earnings}) - \ln(\text{NIPA weekly hours})]$$

$$= [\ln(\text{CES weekly earnings}) - \ln(\text{NIPA weekly earnings})]$$

$$+ [\ln(\text{NIPA weekly hours}) - \ln(\text{CES weekly hours})].$$

The first term in brackets on the right-hand side of the second equal sign is the contribution of differences in weekly earnings derived from the two data sources to differences in the hourly wage; the second term in brackets is the contribution of differences in weekly hours. Similar decompositions of the differences between any wage series pair can be performed.

The log difference between the CES and the NIPA hourly wage, together with the contributions of weekly earnings and weekly hours to this difference, is graphed in figure 8.4A. The figure makes clear that the divergence between CES and NIPA hourly earnings is attributable entirely to the divergence in weekly earnings. As shown in figures 8.4B and 8.4C, the same is true of the divergence between CES and CPS hourly earnings, which would have been even larger but for the offsetting effect of the relative decline in average CES hours.

Another trend comparison highlighted in our earlier discussion was the growth in the NIPA hourly wage relative to both the March CPS and the CPSQS wage. Figure 8.4D focuses on the divergence between the NIPA and the March CPS hourly wage, and figure 8.4E offers a similar decomposition of the difference between the NIPA and the CPSQS hourly wage. In both cases, weekly earnings as measured by the NIPA versus the CPS have exhibited little trend relative to one another, and the trend divergence in the NIPA versus the CPS hourly wage principally reflects a trend divergence in the measures of weekly hours.[6]

For completeness, figure 8.4F decomposes the difference between the March CPS and CPSQS hourly wage over time. Although the two series do not move in lockstep, they also have exhibited no systematic divergence. The similarity in these two series' trends suggests that differences in earnings concepts are unlikely to explain the divergences between other hourly wage series pairs: the March CPS earnings concept is very inclusive, while the CPSQS earnings concept is relatively restrictive, yet the two earnings series have behaved similarly.

---

6. Between 1973 and 1993, the logarithm of the NIPA hourly wage rose by 0.064 relative to the logarithm of the March CPS hourly wage; 62 percent of this net relative growth was attributable to a decline in NIPA hours relative to March CPS hours. Over the same period, the logarithm of the NIPA hourly wage rose by 0.068 relative to the logarithm of the CPSQS hourly wage; 79 percent of this net relative growth was due to the relative decline in NIPA weekly hours.

8.2.2   Adjusting for Multiple Job Holding

A remaining question is whether the findings just summarized are affected by taking into account the fact that the CES and NIPA data are reported on a job basis, whereas the March CPS and CPSQS data are reported on a person basis. Because individuals may hold more than one job, the two are not equivalent. The incidence of multiple job holding has risen since the late 1970s, and multiple job holders generally earn less and work fewer hours on their second jobs than on their first jobs. These facts imply that weekly earnings and weekly hours per person likely have risen relative to their per job values, which in turn implies that the decompositions just reported could be misleading.

The most natural approach to assessing the importance of reporting on different bases is to convert the CES and NIPA data from a job basis to a person basis, or, alternatively, to convert the CPS series from a person basis to a job basis, and then repeat our decomposition analysis. Because the only available data on multiple job holding are CPS data, we have adopted the latter approach.

Questions about multiple job holding were asked on May CPS supplements in 1962–66, 1969–80, 1985, 1989, and 1991 and have been asked as part of the basic CPS in every month since January 1994. The May 1985 and May 1989 supplements also asked about individuals' earnings and hours on their second jobs.[7] With some interpolation, these data provide a reasonably good time series on the aggregate incidence of multiple job holding. After generally fluctuating between 4.5 and 5.2 percent from 1962 through 1980, the multiple job holding rate began to rise, growing from 4.9 percent in May 1980 to 6.2 percent in May 1989 and remaining at or above 6.0 percent in May of all years since that time for which data are available. The available information does not allow any strong conclusions about the trend in either second job earnings or second job hours.

Were we using March CPS earnings and hours data for all employed persons, conversion from a person to a job basis would be relatively straightforward. The March CPS earnings and hours information covers all jobs an individual may have held. Ignoring jobs beyond the second job, the total job count equals the number of employed persons times one plus the multiple job holding rate (hereafter MJH).[8] Conversion of the March CPS average weekly earnings and average weekly hours series from a person basis to a job basis then would require only that both be divided by $1 + MJH_t$.

Because we have restricted our March CPS universe to individuals whose primary employment was a private nonagricultural wage and salary job, the

---

7. The new CPS questionnaire provides information on multiple job holding in every month of the year, not just in May. Data for 1994, 1995, and 1996 suggest that multiple job holding in May is comparable to the average for the year as a whole.

8. Persons holding three or more jobs account for only a small share of all multiple job holders. In May 1994, e.g., just 7 percent of multiple job holders held three or more jobs.

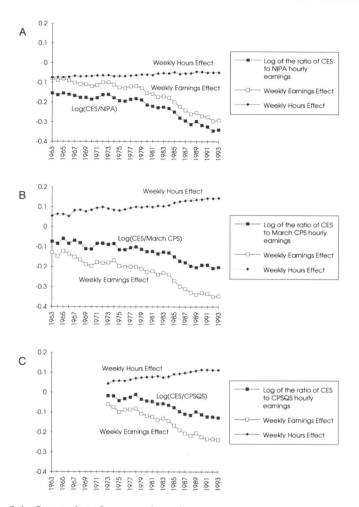

Fig. 8.4 Log ratios of wage series pairs
Note: (*A*) CES to NIPA hourly earnings; (*B*) CES to March CPS hourly earnings; (*C*) CES to CPS quarter sample hourly earnings; (*D*) NIPA to March CPS hourly earnings; (*E*) NIPA to CPS quarter sample hourly earnings; (*F*) March CPS to CPS quarter sample hourly earnings.

appropriate adjustment to the person-based data is a bit more complex. First, the multiple job holding rate among such individuals may differ from the overall rate. In addition, some of those whose primary job is a private sector nonagricultural wage and salary position may have a second job that is not; conversely, some of those whose primary job places them outside of our universe may have a second job that we would like to include.

Conversion of the CPSQS weekly earnings and weekly hours series from a person to a job basis raises similar issues. The CPSQS series covers only the

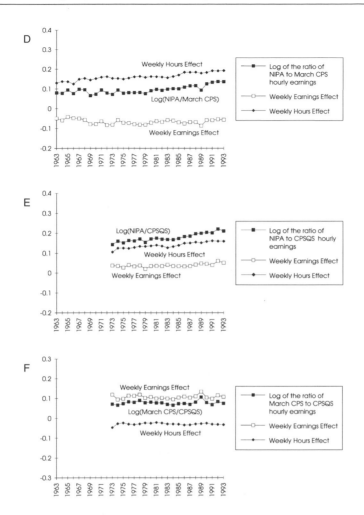

main job held by each respondent. Were we adjusting series that covered all employed persons, average per job weekly earnings could be expressed as

$$\text{MAINEARN}_t (1 + \text{MJH}_t * \text{RATIO}_t) / (1 + \text{MJH}_t),$$

where MAINEARN represents average weekly earnings on the main job, RATIO equals the ratio of average weekly earnings on the second job to average weekly earnings on the main job among the population of multiple job holders, and MJH is as before. Similarly, average per job weekly hours could be expressed as

$$(\text{MAINHRS}_t + \text{MJH}_t * \text{SECONDHRS}_t) / (1 + \text{MJH}_t),$$

where MAINHRS represents average weekly hours on the main job, SEC-ONDHRS represents average weekly hours on the second job among the population of multiple job holders, and MJH is as before. In this case, then, a conversion from person-based to job-based reporting would require year-by-year information not only on the multiple job holding rate but also on the earnings and hours associated with second jobs. In addition, as with the March CPS series, further complications arise as a consequence of the fact that we have restricted our CPSQS universe to individuals whose primary job is a private nonagricultural wage and salary position.

Available published information for May 1985, May 1989, May 1991, and May 1994 indicates that the multiple job holding rate for private sector nonagricultural wage and salary workers averaged about 0.33 percentage points less than the multiple job holding rate for all employed persons, with the discrepancy exhibiting no consistent trend. We subtract this amount from the published overall multiple job holding rate for all years to arrive at our estimate of the rate that applies to our samples. Based on data from the May 1985 and May 1989 supplements, we assume that earnings on the second job average 30 percent of earnings on the main job and that individuals holding second jobs work on them an average of 14 hours per week. In addition, absent published data that would allow us to do better, we assume that second jobs outside of the nonagricultural private sector wage and salary universe held by persons whose primary jobs fall within that universe are approximately offset by an equivalent number of otherwise similar second jobs that fall within the universe held by persons whose primary jobs are excluded.

By construction, conversion of the March CPS data from a person to a job basis does not affect our estimates of average hourly earnings. Conversion of the CPSQS data had a negligible effect, reflecting the assumed stability of the ratio of average second job earnings to average main job earnings and of average hours on the second job, together with the fact that reported average hours on the main job have not changed much over time.

After conversion to a job basis, both CPS weekly earnings series and both CPS weekly hours series decline slightly over time rather than holding more or less stable. Because CES weekly hours still decline more sharply than CPS weekly hours, the weekly earnings effect continues to explain more than fully the divergence of CES from CPS hourly earnings. With both series on a job basis, however, weekly earnings are somewhat more important, and weekly hours somewhat less important, in explaining the divergences between NIPA and CPS average hourly earnings. Using adjusted rather than unadjusted data, the share of the 1973–93 growth in the logarithm of the NIPA versus the March CPS hourly wages attributable to the relative decline in NIPA weekly hours falls from 62 to 47 percent (roughly a 3.0 percent hourly wage divergence), and the share of the 1973–93 growth in the logarithm of the NIPA versus the CPSQS hourly wage due to the relative decline in NIPA weekly hours falls from 79 to 70 percent (roughly a 4.8 percent hourly wage divergence).

In short, putting all of the data on a per job basis alters our estimates of the precise contributions of weekly earnings and weekly hours to observed hourly wage divergences. It does not, however, change either our conclusion that understanding the anomalous behavior of CES hourly earnings requires a focus on weekly earnings rather than weekly hours or our conclusion that understanding the quite different trends in employer-reported and worker-reported hours is critical to a full understanding of the divergence of the NIPA from the CPS hourly earnings measures.

8.3 Comparison of CES against NIPA and CPS Weekly Earnings

As was noted earlier, there are marked differences in trend between the CES and the other weekly earnings series. Between 1973 and 1993, CES real weekly earnings dropped by more than 16 percent. Over the same period, NIPA weekly earnings rose by 1.8 percent; even after conversion to a job basis, March CPS weekly earnings fell by just 1.6 percent and CPSQS weekly earnings by just 0.3 percent. Put slightly differently, CES weekly earnings have declined by about 14 to 18 percent relative to the other weekly earnings measures. The very different behavior of CES weekly earnings is responsible for the significant divergence of the CES from the other hourly earnings series. In this section, we consider three possible explanations for the differences between the trend in CES weekly earnings as compared with the trends in NIPA, March CPS, and CPSQS weekly earnings. These are (1) problems related to the underrepresentation of young establishments in the CES sample, (2) differences in the earnings concepts employed across data series, and (3) differences in the worker populations covered.

8.3.1 Underrepresentation of Young Establishments in
        the Current Employment Statistics Sample

One possible explanation for the divergence of the CES weekly earnings series from the other earnings series is that the underrepresentation of young establishments in the CES sample could have biased its trend downward. Although this soon will change as a consequence of a major redesign of the survey announced in June 1995, the CES sample historically was not rotated on any regular schedule. Establishments that agreed to participate often remained in the sample for many years.

Making use of establishment "birth dates" that are recorded in the unemployment insurance (UI) microdata files, we have used data from five states (Florida, Michigan, New Jersey, New York, and Pennsylvania) to assess the representativeness of the CES sample with respect to the distribution of establishment age. An establishment's birth date is the date of the last UI reporting change recorded for it, reflecting the date at which the establishment first became liable for UI tax payments or the date of any subsequent change in ownership or reporting configuration. Generally speaking, the recorded birth date should provide a fairly accurate indication of age for single establishments, though its interpretation is considerably more problematic for establishments that are part of larger enterprises. Comparing the CES sample to the UI universe in the five states shows that, as of the second quarter of 1993, establishments under four years old accounted for just 13 percent of the total employment of singles in the CES panel, compared with 26 percent of employment in the universe of singles covered by the UI system. Single establishments four to eight years of age also were somewhat underrepresented in the CES sample, accounting for 16 percent of singles' employment there as compared with 21 percent of singles' employment in the UI universe.[9]

These discrepancies could at least partially reflect lower CES sampling ratios in industry–establishment-size cells with a relatively large share of young establishments. Even when we weighted the CES data to account for differences in sampling ratios across industry–establishment-size cells, however, singles zero to three years old accounted for only 14 percent, and singles four to eight years old for just 17 percent, of the weighted total employment of singles in the CES panel (vs. 26 and 21 percent, respectively, of singles' employment in the UI universe).[10]

It long has been recognized that problems with the representativeness of the CES sample might affect the monthly employment estimates. Once each year, those estimates are benchmarked to data for the universe of UI-covered establishments (and other benchmark data for the small noncovered sector). Moreover, the monthly employment estimates as reported prior to benchmarking include a so-called bias adjustment, which is designed based on historical experience to account for the likely discrepancy between the sample-based employment trend and the employment trend for the universe of establishments. The CES earnings and hours data, however, are not benchmarked, as there is no suitable source of data available for that purpose, and, for the same reason, are not subject to bias adjustment, though the CES earnings and hours aggregates are affected by the benchmarking of the employment data used in constructing the earnings and hours weights.

The problems that sample unrepresentativeness causes for the monthly estimation of employment have been well documented (see U.S. Department of Labor 1994, 1995) and, indeed, have motivated the thoroughgoing redesign of the CES program in progress at this writing. The underrepresentation of young establishments in the CES panel appears to have been the principal source of these problems. Young establishments (those up to three years old) grow more

9. The shares of CES employment accounted for by establishments of different ages were calculated using UI records in conjunction with a "crosswalk file" that allowed us to identify establishments that were CES respondents as of the second quarter of 1994. Using the 1994:2 crosswalk file to identify the 1993:2 CES panel might have led to our including a few too many young establishments among those identified as CES respondents, but the proportions of CES employment accounted for by establishments of different ages were very similar in the 1994:2 sample.

10. For these calculations, we use two-digit industry classifications and establishment size categories of 0–49, 50–249, and 250+ employees.

rapidly, on average, than older establishments, so their underrepresentation in the CES panel has meant that, absent bias adjustment, estimated month-to-month employment growth would have been systematically understated.[11]

Problems with sample representativeness also have been cited as a potential source of bias in the CES earnings estimates (see, e.g., American Statistical Association Panel 1993; Bosworth and Perry 1994). Even if there are systematic differences in the level and growth rate of wages at younger versus older establishments, however, underrepresentation of young establishments need not bias the estimated wage trend. Consider, for example, a hypothetical situation in which wages at younger establishments start out below those paid by established firms and then catch up over time. In this scenario, wages at younger establishments will be lower and will grow faster than wages at older establishments. Unless, however, there are changes in the proportion by which new establishments' wages initially fall short of those paid by established concerns, in the length of time it takes for young establishments' wages to catch up, or in the shares of employment accounted for by establishments of different ages, a CES panel on which the underrepresentation of younger establishments was relatively consistent over time—even a panel that included *no* younger establishments—would provide a valid estimate of the trend growth in average earnings.

Problems could arise as a consequence of differences in wage levels for younger versus older establishments if the composition of the CES sample were to change significantly over time. Examination of the "link and taper" estimator used for CES weekly earnings and weekly hours estimation cells may help to make clear how this might happen. This estimator is

(2a) $$X_c = (0.9 \; X_p + 0.1 \; x_p) + (x_c - x_p),$$

which can be rewritten

(2b) $$X_c = [X_p + (x_c - x_p)] + 0.1 \; [x_p - X_p],$$

---

11. Another characteristic of the CES sample is that, by design, small establishments are less likely than large establishments to be included. For sample selection purposes, the universe of establishments is stratified by industry (generally at the four-digit level within manufacturing and the three-digit level outside of manufacturing) and size (generally into six employment size bands, consisting of establishments employing 0–9, 10–19, 20–49, 50–99, 100–249, and 250+ employees). As documented in U.S. Department of Labor (1989), sampling ratios for the survey vary significantly with establishment size. Sample establishments are not assigned weights that reflect these sampling ratios, but the cells used for estimation are stratified by industry and, in most cases outside of manufacturing, by establishment size. Use of the same size stratification bands for estimation as for sample selection would be equivalent to weighting establishments in inverse proportion to their probability of selection. Because the size stratification bands used for estimation are coarser than those used for sample selection, larger establishments within estimation size bands tend to receive disproportionate weight. In contrast to expanding the representation of young establishments in the sample, however, the use of finer vs. coarser firm size stratification bands for estimation purposes appears to have a relatively limited effect on the employment estimates (see U.S. Department of Labor 1994, 1995).

where X represents the published estimates, x represents the average value for the sample of matched establishments reporting in both the current month and the prior month, c denotes the current month, and p denotes the prior month. In the event of a change in sample composition that leads to a systematic divergence between the sample average value and the published estimate $(x - X)$, this estimator ensures that the published figures will move toward the sample average value over time (for additional details, see U.S. Department of Labor 1997). In consequence, shifts in the composition of the survey sample could affect the trend in the published estimates.

The CES sample grew from about 166,000 to about 330,000 establishments between 1980 and 1993; the increase was spread fairly evenly over that period. This expansion likely led to better representation of younger establishments, and especially small younger establishments, at least compared to their representation prior to 1980.[12] The best information on the relative earnings of workers employed by younger versus older establishments of which we are aware derives from the UI universe files in which establishments' birth dates are recorded. As already noted, the administrative context within which these dates are recorded makes them more suitable for determining the economic age of single establishments than of establishments that are part of larger enterprises. UI data for Florida, Michigan, New Jersey, New York, and Pennsylvania indicate that workers' earnings at young single establishments tend to be systematically lower than those paid at more established concerns. Factoring out differences in the two-digit industry and establishment size distribution of employment for establishments of different ages, monthly earnings at the youngest single establishments in the UI universe (those zero to three years old) averaged 11.8 percent lower, and monthly earnings at intermediate-aged singles in the same universe (those four to eight years old) averaged 6.4 percent lower, as of the second quarter of 1993 than those at the oldest single establishments (those nine or more years old).[13] Under the assumption that comparisons of weekly earnings for production and nonsupervisory workers (not available in the UI records) would have yielded similar differences by age of establishment, these figures suggest that, although likely improving the estimates of weekly wage levels, increased representation of young establishments in the CES sample could have contributed a downward bias to the estimated trend in those levels.

12. Representation of young establishments may not have increased over the period from 1980 forward, as young establishments brought into the sample at the beginning of the 1980s no longer would have been especially young by the early 1990s.

13. We use data for 1993:2 rather than annual average 1993 data because of concern that shifts in the timing of bonus payments across calendar years, from 1993:1 back to 1992:4, due to anticipated tax law changes, could have distorted the annual average figures. We control for industry and size of establishment in these calculations because the CES earnings estimates make use of UI employment weights associated with estimation cells defined by industry and establishment size, and an average difference between younger and older establishments' average earnings calculated on a similar, though somewhat cruder, basis thus seems most appropriate for our purposes.

Interestingly, when we repeated the calculations just described using monthly earnings data only for those singles that were part of the CES panel, but retaining employment weights for industry–establishment-size cells derived from the full universe of singles, we found that the difference in average earnings between singles zero to three years old and singles nine or more years old was only 70 percent as large as that based on earnings data for the full universe of singles. In other words, the earnings of workers at the youngest CES singles were somewhat closer to those of older singles' employees than those of the typical young single's employees. This does not, however, change the conclusion that increased representation of young establishments in the CES sample could have contributed a downward tilt to the CES earnings trend.

One still must ask how important this effect could have been. To attempt a rough answer to this question, we carried out a simple experiment. First, we estimated average monthly earnings in the CES sample using UI employment weights for industry–establishment-size cells and monthly earnings for the CES establishments in each cell. This simulates the CES estimator, which stratifies the sample by industry and size and then weights each cell's importance using employment figures that are benchmarked to the UI universe each year. The resulting estimate should provide a crude approximation to the estimate that would be obtained by the application of CES earnings estimation procedures in this sample (assuming, as discussed above, that estimated earnings move toward the weighted sample average). We then recomputed this average, first dropping all CES singles aged zero to three years, and then dropping all CES singles less than nine years old, from the computations. Our CES-like estimate of average monthly earnings is only 1.1 percent higher than the estimate excluding the youngest establishments, and only 2.5 percent higher than the estimate excluding all establishments under nine years old. Even the larger figure is only one-sixth as large as the relative decline in CES weekly earnings we seek to explain.

The actual shift in CES sample composition, moreover, undoubtedly was less marked than that we have simulated, as even the pre-1980 CES panel would have contained some younger establishments. In short, although we suspect that the CES sample expansion had some effect on the trend in CES average weekly earnings, that effect most likely was relatively modest, perhaps no more than a percentage point, though we are unable to provide a precise quantification.[14]

14. The fact that the data available on employment and relative earnings by age of establishment refer only to the population of singles means that all of the calculations just described should be viewed as illustrative. To assess whether our results could have been affected by imperfect identification of the 1993:2 CES panel using the 1994:2 crosswalk file, we repeated the calculations just described using data for 1994:2. None of our findings were materially affected.

The increase in CES sample size also led to an increase in the representation of small establishments in the panel, though, due to the lower sampling ratios for small establishments, they continue to account for a smaller share of panel employment than of total employment. Because the CES program long has made use of estimation cells stratified by establishment size, however, this

Table 8.1   **Items Included in Alternative Earnings Measures**

Item	NIPA	CES	March CPS	CPSQS
Gross wages and salaries, prior to deductions for such things as social security, tax withholding, insurance, and salary reduction plans	Yes	Yes	Yes	Yes
Commissions	Yes	Yes, if earned and paid at least monthly	Yes	Yes, if usual
Bonuses	Yes	Yes, if earned and paid each pay period	Yes	Yes, if usual
Tips	Yes	No	Yes	Yes, if usual
Payments in kind	Yes	No	No	No
Employer 401(k) contributions	Yes, in some states	No	No	No
Employer contributions for such things as social security, unemployment insurance, and other insurance	No	No	No	No

Note: NIPA = National Income and Product Accounts; CES = Current Employment Statistics survey; March CPS = March Current Population Survey; CPSQS = Current Population Survey quarter sample.

8.3.2   Narrower Definition of Earnings in the Current Employment Statistics

A second possible explanation for the slower growth in CES average weekly earnings relative to other weekly earnings measures is that payments excluded from the CES but included in other measures have grown in importance over time. Table 8.1 summarizes the differences in the earnings concepts underlying the different available measures; additional details are provided in the data appendix. The CES earnings concept is the most restrictive of the four shown in the table. In contrast to the NIPA and March CPS measures (but not the CPSQS measure), CES average weekly earnings exclude bonus payments unless they are earned and paid each pay period; excluded bonuses have become a larger share of total compensation in recent years. Tips are included in the other earnings series but are excluded from the CES data. In principle, earnings in all of the series are reported before deductions for 401(k) and other salary reduction plans; in practice, there is evidence that some proportion of employ-

---

increase in representation of smaller establishments need not have had any significant effect on estimated weekly earnings. Finer size stratification for estimation purposes was introduced for many retail trade and service industries in 1985, but this finer stratification had no obvious impact on the higher level aggregates in those sectors.

ers report earnings net of these deductions in their CES payroll reports. Because contributions to these plans have grown in importance over time, this underreporting conceivably also could have contributed to the relative decline of CES earnings, though only if one assumes that they are not similarly underreported in the NIPA and CPS data.[15]

Although the restrictiveness of the CES earnings concept may have contributed to the relative decline of CES weekly earnings, our back-of-the-envelope calculations suggest that the effect cannot have been very large. Consider first the potential impact of excluding from CES earnings bonuses not earned and paid routinely as part of workers' regular wages. The similar behavior of March CPS earnings (which include such bonuses) and CPSQS earnings (which do not) suggests that this exclusion does not explain the divergent behavior of CES earnings. Moreover, despite their rapid growth, such bonuses are still a small share of total earnings. According to BLS Employer Costs for Employee Compensation (ECEC) figures, so-called nonproduction bonuses and other lump-sum payments added 1.4 percent to earnings received in the form of wages and salaries, commissions, and other more routine incentive payments in March 1993, compared with 1.1 percent in March 1987.[16] Although published ECEC data are unavailable prior to 1987, ECI data suggest that, between 1980 and 1987, this category of payments grew no more rapidly than earnings overall.[17] The exclusion of nonproduction bonuses thus would appear to account for no more than about 0.3 percentage points of the very much larger relative decline in CES weekly earnings.

Any divergence between CES weekly earnings and the other weekly earnings series attributable to changes in the reporting of tip income similarly seems likely to have been modest. In the process of preparing the national accounts, the Bureau of Economic Analysis estimates both the dollar amount of tips included in reported earnings of UI-covered workers (reported tips) and the dollar amount of tips not reflected there (unreported tips). Published NIPA compensation estimates incorporate an adjustment for unreported tips. The Bureau of Economic Analysis's estimates of total tip income imply that tips contributed $4.49 to average weekly NIPA earnings of $499.99 in 1993, up from $2.79 contributed to real average weekly earnings of $491.17 in 1973. These figures suggest that the relative importance of tip income has grown over this period but that the growth has been modest: NIPA weekly earnings in 1993 would have been only about 0.3 percent lower had the share of tips in average weekly earnings remained at its 1973 level.

15. This assumption may be plausible at least with respect to the NIPA data, which are derived from reports filed for unemployment compensation administration purposes; employers may have some incentive to ensure that the amounts shown on these reports are accurate.

16. The share of production and nonsupervisory workers' compensation paid as bonuses is lower than that for all employees, but the increase in share in recent years has been of a comparable magnitude.

17. ECEC and ECI data are not strictly comparable, as the former reflect the effects of shifts in industry and occupation mix that are held constant in the latter.

Another possibility we considered is that the failure of some CES respondents to include employees' 401(k) and flexible spending account contributions in reported earnings could explain why CES earnings look so different. Insofar as similar reporting problems equally well might have affected other earnings measures, there is reason to doubt that this explains the facts in question. Nonetheless, we ask whether the growth in salary reduction plans has been sufficient to explain the large divergence between the CES and the other earnings measures. Interviews with 3,400 CES respondents conducted by telephone in fall 1994 as part of an informal effort designed to improve understanding of CES reporting indicated that about 10 percent of establishments that had such plans reported earnings net of 401(k) and flexible spending deductions. Data from various sources suggest that roughly 25 percent of the workforce participated in a 401(k) plan as of the end of 1993, with perhaps half that many participating in a flexible spending plan. Participants' 401(k) contributions appear to have averaged under 10 percent of earnings; we have no data on flexible spending plan contributions, but we guess that 5 percent of earnings might be a plausible average for participants' contributions.[18] Although they were written into law as part of the Revenue Act of 1978, Treasury Department regulations governing 401(k) and flexible spending plans were not issued until the early 1980s; contributions to such plans were negligible prior to that point. The impact of a 10 percent underreporting of such contributions would have been to reduce the cumulative decline of CES earnings by less than 0.3 percent between 1973 and 1993, a small fraction of the trend gap to be explained.

In sum, there are several types of payments that are at least partially excluded from CES earnings and that have become a more important part of the earnings captured in the other earnings series since the late 1970s. Although the exclusion from the CES of payments in each of these categories may have accounted for a small part of the divergence between CES weekly earnings and the other weekly earnings measures, the evidence we have examined suggests that, taken together, they account for no more than a small share—perhaps a percentage point—of the roughly 14 to 18 percentage point divergence over the period from 1973 to 1993 that we seek to explain.

8.3.3   Different Worker Coverage in the Current Employment Statistics

A final possibility is that the CES earnings series diverges from the NIPA and CPS earnings series because it covers different workers. The NIPA series and both of the CPS series cover workers in all occupations; in contrast, the CES series is defined to cover only production and nonsupervisory workers.

---

18. Estimated 401(k) participation and contribution rates and estimated flexible spending plan participation rates, based on the May 1988 and April 1993 CPS benefit supplements and Pension and Welfare Benefits Administration Form 5500 data, are reported in Employee Benefit Research Institute Issue Briefs nos. 141 (September 1993), 144 (December 1993), and 155 (November 1994) and Reno (1993).

The fact that the CES weekly earnings series lies below the others is not surprising in view of its more limited coverage: one would expect the average earnings of production and nonsupervisory workers to be lower than the overall average. For the difference in coverage to explain the divergent trend in CES earnings, however, either the production and nonsupervisory share of total employment must have fallen sharply over time, so that the gap between production and nonsupervisory and overall average earnings has grown, or the earnings of production and nonsupervisory workers must have fallen—indeed, fallen significantly—relative to the earnings of nonproduction and supervisory workers. CES data provide little if any evidence that a falling production and nonsupervisory share of employment has contributed to the divergent wage trend. The production and nonsupervisory share of employment fell from 82.8 percent in 1973 to 80.7 percent in 1982, but over the period since 1980 when the divergence between the CES and the other earnings series has been most pronounced, the production and nonsupervisory share of employment has hovered between 80.7 and 81.4 percent, exhibiting some cyclical variation but no trend.

Is there any evidence, then, that the earnings of production and nonsupervisory workers have risen less rapidly than the earnings of other workers? Or, to put the question somewhat differently, had the data from other sources been restricted to information for the CES production and nonsupervisory population, would average weekly earnings from those sources have looked more like the CES series? Given the well-documented and dramatic growth in the inequality of earnings during the 1980s, it seems reasonable to suppose that they might have.

As one approach to providing a more rigorous answer to this question, we attempted to identify those in the CPSQS whose reported occupations were consistent with their employers' classifying them as production or nonsupervisory; then we looked at the trend in those workers' earnings.[19] As shown in figure 8.5, individuals in this group (labeled "CES Replication 1") had lower wages than the average for all private nonagricultural wage and salary workers, but the trends in the two groups' earnings were very similar—and very different from the trend in actual CES earnings.[20]

A possible explanation for our failure to reproduce the trend in CES weekly

19. The classification scheme we used is essentially that underlying the ECI and ECEC series for production and nonsupervisory workers. Briefly, all who were reported to be employed as managers were excluded from the production and nonsupervisory group. Professional, technical, sales, and clerical workers were excluded if employed in mining, construction, or manufacturing, but included otherwise.

20. The ECI and the ECEC wage and salary series for production and nonsupervisory workers also have moved similarly to the corresponding series for all private sector workers. As we noted earlier, the ECEC data conceptually are more comparable than the ECI data to the series on which the present paper focuses. Over the period from 1987 forward, the ECI data exhibit a trend similar to that of the CPSQS data, and the ECEC data register real wage declines that are comparable in magnitude to those in the CES data. The behavior of the ECI and ECEC series is a subject that merits further study.

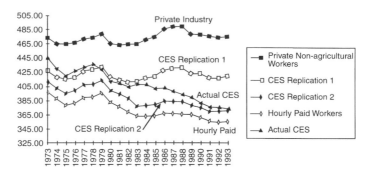

Fig. 8.5   Replication of CES weekly earnings using CPS quarter sample data

earnings using this first approach is that the employers who supply CES data commonly report for a group different than that called for by the CES definitions. Particularly outside of the goods-producing sector, the production and nonsupervisory classification is not one that employers would use for any other purpose. At least some employers might, for example, be supplying earnings data for hourly paid workers instead.[21] Interestingly, as can be seen in figure 8.5, average weekly earnings of CPS respondents paid on an hourly basis have tracked CES earnings more closely than those of the replication 1 group. Between 1973 and 1993, CES weekly earnings fell by 16.1 percent; over the same period, CPSQS weekly earnings for those paid by the hour fell by 10.5 percent. Hourly paid workers, however, account for only about 60 percent of total private nonagricultural wage and salary employment, whereas the CES production and nonsupervisory group accounts for about 80 percent.

Another possibility is that some employers are reporting the earnings of nonexempt workers, a larger group that includes hourly paid workers and, moreover, a group that they would need to be able to identify for other purposes. To assess this possibility, we attempted to identify those CPS respondents whom employers would classify as being nonexempt under the Fair Labor Standards Act, which is the law that established the minimum wage and governs eligibility for overtime payments.[22] As a check on whether this could be the group for whom employers were reporting, we compared the industry-by-industry

21. The best direct evidence on this comes from a response analysis survey of CES respondents conducted in 1981. Whether an employee was hourly paid or salaried was used by 18 percent of establishments to distinguish between production and nonsupervisory employees and other employees for CES reporting purposes. Fewer than half of establishments reported that their payroll records contained sufficient information to allow production and nonsupervisory status to be determined based on the nature of the work an employee performed. See U.S. Department of Labor (1983).

22. There are several important differences between our first production and nonsupervisory classification and this second nonexempt classification. First, we categorized everyone paid by the hour as nonexempt, regardless of their industry and occupation. Second, for those not paid by the hour, classification as nonexempt is based purely on occupation, rather than on industry and occupation. Outside of manufacturing, professionals generally were included in our synthetic nonsupervisory group but excluded from our synthetic nonexempt group.

proportions of employment both in our synthetic production and nonsupervisory group and in our synthetic nonexempt group with the actual CES production and nonsupervisory employment proportions. These comparisons suggested that, although goods-producing employers more likely were reporting data for production workers, employers outside the goods-producing sector could have been reporting for nonexempt rather than for nonsupervisory employees. We therefore proceeded to identify in the CPS data, as best we were able, production workers in the goods-producing sector and nonexempt workers outside of the goods-producing sector. As can be seen in figure 8.5, weekly earnings for this hybrid group (labeled "CES Replication 2") came closer to tracking actual CES weekly earnings than did earnings of our first synthetic CES group, falling by 9.9 percent over the 1973–93 period as compared with the 16.1 percent decline over the same period in the CES series.[23]

As already noted, both the expansion of the CES sample during the 1980s and the relative narrowness of the CES earnings concept likely have made modest contributions to the relative decline of CES weekly earnings. Taking all of the available evidence into account, however, the most important factor causing CES weekly earnings to diverge from the other available weekly earnings measures appears to have been that the CES earnings cover a different worker population, a population that has experienced substantial relative earnings declines, though perhaps not precisely the production and nonsupervisory group specified by the formal CES definitions.

8.4   Comparison of NIPA against CPS Weekly Hours

Between 1973 and 1993, the NIPA workweek fell from 34.7 to 32.9 hours, a decline of 1.8 hours. Over the same period, the March CPS workweek fell from 40.4 to 39.8 hours, and the CPSQS workweek held steady at about 38.5 hours. The fact that NIPA data are reported on a job basis and CPS data on a person basis explains part of the difference in trends. Even converted to a job basis, however, the March CPS workweek declined by only half as much as the NIPA workweek (0.9 hours), and the CPSQS workweek dropped by just 0.2 hour over the 1973–93 period.

Understanding why NIPA and CPS weekly hours have diverged is important for understanding why NIPA and CPS hourly earnings have trended differently. Several possible explanations can be suggested. The NIPA hours series rests on CES data, which are derived from employer payroll records. The CES data cover only production and nonsupervisory workers; in the construction of the NIPA series, it is assumed either that supervisors work a 40-hour workweek (within manufacturing) or that they work the same number of hours as nonsupervisory workers in their industry (outside of manufacturing). Problems with

---

23. Because the March supplements do not include a question about whether individuals were paid hourly, no similar calculations could be carried out using March CPS data.

the hours data reported by CES respondents or with the assumptions used in constructing an all-employee hours series from the CES data thus might account for the NIPA versus CPS discrepancies. Alternatively, the source of the discrepancies might lie with misreporting of CPS hours by household respondents.

We have little to say about potential problems with the CES hours data related to changes in the representativeness of the CES sample. As with CES earnings, the trend in CES hours could have been distorted by changes over time in the representation of young establishments in the CES panel, though there is no clear basis for having any particular prior expectation as to whether workers at younger establishments should work more or fewer hours than their counterparts at more established concerns. Unfortunately, we also know of no comprehensive alternative source of data on average hours at younger versus older establishments that would allow us to evaluate how important any distortion in the estimated CES hours trend attributable to changes in the composition of the CES sample conceivably might be. The fact that sample representativeness appears to explain so little with respect to CES earnings, however, suggests that it may be fair to suppose that it has not greatly affected the behavior of CES hours.

Another question to be considered is whether the hours recorded in employers' payroll records, which serve as the principal source for CES reporting, accurately reflect what actually occurs in the workplace. CES hours paid numbers are converted to an hours worked basis for use in the NIPA. The conversion of hours paid to hours worked uses information from the BLS Hours at Work Survey, which defines hours at work to be equal to hours paid minus hours of recorded paid leave. If, however, employees are expected to perform significant amounts of "off the clock" work, the NIPA series could be misleading. For the purpose of assessing wage trends, the resulting error would be unimportant so long as off-the-clock work had not become more or less important over time but would matter if it had grown or shrunk in importance. While there are some who believe that off-the-clock work increasingly has become expected of employees, we know of no hard evidence bearing on the level of such activity or, more important, on its trend.

The assumptions concerning nonproduction and supervisory hours as compared to production and nonsupervisory hours that underlie the NIPA hours series also could be questioned. Any upward trend in nonproduction workers' hours in manufacturing, or in supervisory hours relative to nonsupervisory hours outside of manufacturing, would be missed by the NIPA calculations. This could have led to a spurious downward drift in NIPA average weekly hours. A quick-and-dirty check on whether this might have occurred may be carried out by examining the trends in average weekly hours for workers categorized as production or nonexempt versus nonproduction or exempt using CPSQS data, where the former consists of the CES replication 2 group discussed in the previous section of the paper and the latter of its obverse.

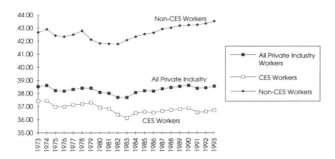

Fig. 8.6   Average weekly hours from the CPS quarter sample: CES replication 2

Figure 8.6 displays average weekly hours for these groups constructed using CPSQS data. For reference, the figure also plots overall CPSQS average weekly hours. The hours of non-CES individuals, as best we can identify them in the CPS, appear to have risen relative to the hours of those covered by the CES hours questions. Between 1973 and 1993, the average weekly hours of CPS production or nonexempt workers declined by 0.7 hours, while the average weekly hours of CPS nonproduction or exempt workers rose 0.9 hours.

Assuming that the discrepancies in the hours trends for workers reported on and not reported on by CES respondents are of a similar magnitude, the assumptions that underlie the NIPA hours calculations could impart a significant bias to the NIPA hours trend. We have carried out some simple calculations intended to give a rough idea of the possible magnitude of this bias. Our approach is to use the CPS data to replicate the NIPA hours calculations, imposing the assumptions that non-CES workers in manufacturing work 40 hours per week and that non-CES workers outside of manufacturing work the same hours as do CES workers in their one-digit industry, and then to compare the synthetic NIPA series to the actual CPSQS series. Over the period 1973–93, the synthetic NIPA average hours series fell from 37.2 to 36.8 hours per week, a decline of 0.4 hours. In contrast, overall CPSQS average weekly hours, reported comparably on a person basis, held steady at 38.5 hours. All of this assumes, of course, that workers' reporting of their hours is accurate. As we will discuss shortly, there is some evidence that individuals tend to overreport their hours of work, that this tendency may be more pronounced among exempt than among nonexempt workers, and that it may have worsened over time. If so, the NIPA assumptions may be more accurate than these calculations suggest. Still, our admittedly crude calculations suggest that problems with the underlying assumptions could have imparted a spurious downward drift to NIPA hours.

Could this fully explain the divergence between NIPA and CPS hours? Actual NIPA hours fell from 34.7 to 32.9 hours per week over the period 1973–93, a decline of 1.8 hours. Measured on a job basis, as is most appropriate for direct comparison with the NIPA series, the March CPS average hourly workweek declined by only 0.9 hours over the 1973–93 period and the CPSQS average hourly workweek declined by just 0.2 hours. The total divergence between the NIPA and the CPS hours series to be explained thus is about 0.9 hours for NIPA versus the March CPS and 1.6 hours for NIPA versus the CPSQS. Even taking our calculations regarding possible spurious drift in the NIPA measure at face value, problems with the assumptions used in its construction account for only a fraction of the 0.9 to 1.6 hour growth in the discrepancy between NIPA and CPS hours. We conclude, therefore, that this cannot be the whole story and turn to the possibility that the trend in CPS hours might be biased.

For some time, it has been recognized that there is considerable noise in CPS hours estimates.[24] Errors arise in the case of the March estimates because of imprecision both in the reporting of weeks worked per year and in the reporting of hours worked per week, and in the CPSQS because of imprecision in the reporting of usual weekly hours. In order for misreporting of CPS hours to explain the divergence between the NIPA/CES and CPS hours series, however, it would have to be the case that any such problems had become more serious over time. In particular, it would have to be the case that there had been an increasing tendency for CPS respondents to overreport their hours.

There are some reasons to think that overreporting of hours might indeed have worsened. Intuitively, it seems plausible that workers in factory or similarly structured jobs should be better able to report their hours accurately than workers on jobs where hours of work are more flexible or more variable. It also seems plausible that persons on jobs with less rigid and less stable schedules might be more likely to overreport their hours. An individual who typically arrived at work at 9:00 A.M. and left for home at 7:00 P.M., for example, might say that she worked a 50-hour workweek, even though she commonly ran errands or engaged in other personal business during that period of time. On certain types of jobs, there may be an ethic that says that good employees work more hours; persons in such jobs also may tend to overreport their hours. Changes in the occupational mix of employment, away from production jobs and toward managerial and professional jobs, or a shift toward greater flexibility in work-scheduling practices more generally, thus might have produced increased overreporting of hours.

There is some direct evidence that workers report working more hours than their employers say they work. Mellow and Sider (1983) examine data from a CPS sample matched with employer records so that individuals' answers to a question concerning their usual weekly hours could be compared to their employers' answers to the same question. On average, the CPS respondents report working 3.9 percent more hours than their employers say they work. Interestingly, this discrepancy varies across worker groups. Among workers

24. This is one reason why the BLS does not publish hourly wage estimates constructed using CPS annual or weekly earnings responses combined with information on hours of work.

paid by the hour, the hours reported by the individual and by the employer are very close. Among managers and professionals, however, worker-reported hours exceed employer-reported hours by nearly 11 percent. A question about these numbers, of course, is whether the worker-reported or the employer-reported numbers are more accurate.

Another source of evidence on biases in workers' reports of their hours comes from a comparison of worker-reported hours with time diary data. Hamermesh (1990) analyzes data for 1975 and 1981 from the University of Michigan Time Use Study. The data for each year consist of individuals' answers to a question about how many hours they worked last week, together with time diary data for four days—two weekdays, a Saturday, and a Sunday—collected at roughly three-month intervals. A group of about 310 employed individuals provided usable data in 1975; about 80 of these same people were reinterviewed and provided usable data in 1981. Hamermesh uses the diary data for each individual in each year to construct a synthetic workweek. He then compares reported weekly hours to the estimated hours based on the time diary data. His results are striking. First, respondents report working more hours (44.0 hours per week, on average, in 1975) than are recorded in their time diaries (42.5 hours per week, on average, again in 1975). Second, and more important, the data show a growing discrepancy between reported and recorded hours over time. By 1981, in answer to a CPS-like hours question, employed respondents in the reinterviewed subsample reported working an average of 43.3 hours; their time diaries, however, recorded only 39.7 hours of work, a discrepancy of 3.6 hours, more than twice as large as in the 1975 data.

Robinson and Bostrom (1994) report on the results of a similar study that reaches similar conclusions. The data that Robinson and Bostrom study were collected at three separate points in time: 1965, 1975, and 1985.[25] The main difference between the Robinson and Bostrom analysis and the Hamermesh analysis is that Robinson and Bostrom construct synthetic workweeks using data for all of the individuals reporting weekly hours in particular hours intervals (generally five hours in width), rather than pooling diary data for the same individual collected at different times. Robinson and Bostrom report several interesting findings. First, on average, workers appear to overreport their hours of work when answering questions similar to those asked on the CPS. Second, this overreporting is more serious for workers who work more hours than for workers who work fewer hours. Third, the tendency to overreport appears to have worsened over the time period studied by Robinson and Bostrom. Treating their time diary estimates as "truth," workers overreported their workweeks by an average of one hour in 1965, by an average of four hours in 1975, and by an average of seven hours in 1985.

Although neither set of estimates can be treated as definitive, both of the

25. The 1975 data analyzed by Robinson and Bostrom come from the same source as those used by Hamermesh.

studies just described provide evidence both that workers tend to overreport their hours and that the tendency to overreport may have worsened over time. If this conclusion is correct and if the trend toward overreporting continued during the late 1980s and early 1990s, it implies that the CPS data may *understate* the growth in hourly wages.

8.5 Conclusions

Real average hourly wage growth slowed dramatically during the early 1970s. This slowdown is evident in all four of the series we have analyzed here: the CES, the NIPA, and the two CPS wage measures. Since 1973, however, these series have diverged markedly. As shown in figure 8.1, between 1973 and 1993, the NIPA real hourly wage rose by 7 percent, the two CPS real hourly wage measures held roughly steady, and the CES hourly wage fell by 10 percent.

In an accounting sense, hourly earnings may rise (fall) either because weekly earnings have risen (fallen) or because weekly hours have fallen (risen). The relative decline of CES hourly wages as compared to the other three hourly wage series is due entirely to the relative decline of CES weekly earnings. In contrast, the relative increase in NIPA hourly earnings as compared to the two CPS series is due primarily to the relative decline in NIPA weekly hours.

We have considered several possible explanations for the relatively large decline in CES weekly earnings that underlies the divergence of the CES hourly wage. By leading to a better representation of younger establishments, the expansion of the CES sample during the 1980s may have imparted a downward drift to CES weekly earnings, but it does not appear that this effect could have been very large. Similarly, the exclusion from the CES of earnings components that are included in the other series (such as nonproduction bonuses and tips) can explain no more than a modest portion of the divergence of the CES from other earnings series. Our findings suggest that the principal explanation for the divergence of CES weekly earnings from the other measures is the restricted occupational coverage of the CES data: the CES earnings series is designed to cover only production or nonsupervisory workers, whereas both the NIPA and the CPS series cover almost all workers. This explanation is consistent with the large body of work on increasing income inequality by skill level. It also should be noted that, while we believe the CES provides an accurate picture of the trend in earnings of a certain population of workers, that group may well not conform to the production or nonsupervisory category specified by the formal CES definitions. In particular, outside of the goods-producing sector, there is some indication that CES respondents may be reporting wages for workers who are nonexempt from the Fair Labor Standards Act, rather than for the nonsupervisory workers called for by CES program guidelines.

We have less to say about the divergence of NIPA and CPS average weekly hours. There is some evidence that CPS hours worked are overreported, that this overreporting may have worsened over time, and that this increased overreporting accounts for a substantial share of the divergence between NIPA and CPS hourly earnings. Given the paucity of data on hours worked, we view our conclusions on this subject as suggestive rather than definitive. Nevertheless, any bias in the trend of weekly hours has important implications for our understanding of labor markets. For example, since productivity measures rely on hours worked as a measure of labor input, analysts should be careful when drawing inferences about productivity trends.

In view of the very different behavior of CES weekly earnings and the other weekly earnings measures, the BLS, working together with staff from the Bureau of Economic Analysis, has undertaken an evaluation of whether and how the CES might collect all-employee earnings, either instead of or in addition to production workers' weekly wages. Our findings indicate that better information on hours of work, and perhaps on time use more generally, also would be of value. One possible approach to producing such data would be to inaugurate a regular, periodic time use survey.

We conclude with two thoughts concerning future research. First, this paper has examined divergent trends in alternative real wage series only at the aggregate "topside" level. Although it currently is impossible to use establishment surveys to analyze wage trends for different demographic groups, we have not attempted a thorough investigation of any possible divergences that may exist at the industry level. This may be important, for example, for wage or other escalation contracts that are based on the trend in wages in an industry as measured by any one particular series. Second, and perhaps more important to labor economists, it would be fruitful to expand our analysis of divergences in hourly wage measures to study divergences in measures of hourly *compensation*. Benefits are a large and growing share of total compensation. Our preliminary explorations into this topic (not reported here) reveal that measures of various sorts of benefit expenditures differ considerably across data sources. Reconciling these different sources of information would be a valuable contribution. The BLS, in conjunction with the Bureau of Economic Analysis, recently formed a working group to analyze the concepts underlying published government benefits series; we look forward to that group's report.

Data Appendix

Two of the series we analyze are derived principally or wholly from employer-provided data (the NIPA and the CES series), whereas two are based on household reports collected as part of the CPS program (the March CPS and CPSQS series). Because CES data are used in constructing the NIPA figures, we turn first to a description of the CES program.

The Current Employment Statistics Program

The CES data come from a monthly survey of almost 400,000 nonagricultural establishments. Although the survey sample is very large and stratified in such a way as to include both large and small establishments in most industries, it is not a probability sample. Rather, the CES makes use of a quota sample stratified by industry (at the four-digit level within manufacturing and the three-digit level outside of manufacturing) and number of employees (0–9, 10–19, 20–49, 50–99, 100–249, or 250+). Once an establishment agrees to participate in the survey, it typically has remained in the sample indefinitely; as a rule, fresh units have been solicited for participation only as required to meet cell quotas.

The CES program collects data on the total number of employees, the number of female employees, the number of production workers (in manufacturing, mining, and construction) or nonsupervisory workers (in other industries), the production or nonsupervisory worker payroll, and the number of hours for which production or nonsupervisory workers are paid. Because the definitions of production workers and nonsupervisory workers differ, whether workers in a particular occupation are included in the group for which employers are asked to report depends on their industry. For example, accountants and salespersons are excluded if they work in a manufacturing industry but included if they work in a service industry.

Aggregate payrolls include pay before deductions for social security, unemployment insurance, group insurance, withholding tax, salary reduction plans, bonds, and union dues. The payroll figures also include shift premiums and pay for overtime, as well as pay for holidays, vacations, sick leave, and other leave paid directly by the employer to employees for the pay period reported. The payroll figures exclude bonuses (unless earned and paid regularly each pay period), commissions and other lump-sum payments (unless earned and paid at least monthly), and other pay not earned in the pay period. Tips and payments in kind are not included.

Total hours paid during the pay period include all hours worked (both straight time and overtime hours), hours paid for standby or reporting time, and hours for which employees received pay directly from the employer for holidays, vacations, sick leave, and other leave.

The CES data on weekly earnings, weekly hours, and hourly earnings that we use come directly from published sources and refer to the total private sector, exclusive of agriculture and private households. Average hourly earnings equal the ratio of total estimated payroll, summed over the 12 annual reporting periods, divided by total estimated hours, again summed over the 12 annual reporting periods.[26]

26. Most respondents (90 percent or more) provide data for payroll reporting periods that are shorter than a month (weekly, biweekly, or semimonthly) and thus do not span the entire year. Note also that, to the extent hours worked vary across reporting periods, the annual value for average hourly earnings need not equal the simple average of the 12 monthly values.

The National Income and Product Accounts Data

The NIPA data are constructed and published by the Bureau of Economic Analysis (BEA) of the Department of Commerce. The NIPA wage and salary disbursement estimates for private industry are based principally on earnings data from the BLS ES-202 program.[27] Total wages, for purposes of the ES-202 reports, include gross wages and salaries, bonuses, tips and other gratuities, and the value of meals and lodging where supplied. In certain states employer contributions to certain deferred compensation plans such as 401(k)s are included in total wages. Total wages do not include employer contributions to social security, health insurance, unemployment insurance, worker's compensation, or private pension and welfare funds. The BEA makes several additions to these wage and salary data to account for noncoverage or inadequate coverage; these additions account for about 5 percent of total estimated wages and salaries, a fraction that has not changed much over time, and are explained more fully in U.S. Department of Commerce (1989).

The NIPA hours data measure aggregate hours worked, defined as hours paid less vacation time, holidays, sick days, and other paid absences. The NIPA series is based principally on BLS data. For manufacturing industries, the production worker proportion of employment from the BLS CES program is multiplied by the BEA's measure of total employment (including both full-time and part-time employees), derived mainly from ES-202 data, to obtain counts of production and salaried worker employment. CES data are used to determine manufacturing production workers' paid weekly hours; salaried workers in manufacturing are assumed to be paid for 40 hours per week. In other sectors of the economy, the paid weekly hours of nonsupervisory employees are derived from the CES, and supervisory employees are assumed to have paid hours equal to those of nonsupervisory employees in the same one-digit industry. In all cases, the NIPA data are converted from an hours-paid to an hours-worked basis, using data from the BLS Hours at Work Survey.[28]

Our construction of the NIPA hourly wage makes use of annual NIPA data on wages and salaries, employment, and hours worked, all for private industry exclusive of agriculture. We compute average weekly earnings as total wages and salaries divided by average employment, further divided by 52, and average weekly hours as total hours worked divided by average employment, further divided by 52. Hourly earnings were computed as the ratio of weekly earnings to weekly hours.

27. The ES-202 program is a cooperative endeavor of the BLS and the employment security agencies of the 50 states, the District of Columbia, Puerto Rico, and the Virgin Islands. Each quarter, employers report on the employment and earnings of workers covered by state UI laws. The UI system covers approximately 95 percent of private sector wage and salary employment.

28. The BLS Hours at Work Survey indicates that, at least since 1981, the ratio of hours worked to hours paid has been very steady at about 0.93. For this purpose, hours worked are defined as hours paid minus leave hours.

Construction of Current Population Survey Earnings Series

In contrast to the NIPA and CES data we use, which come exclusively from published sources, our CPS series were constructed using CPS microdata files. Average hourly earnings from both CPS sources were computed as hours weighted means, to make them more comparable to the NIPA and CES figures. The March CPS weekly earnings estimates were computed as a weeks-weighted measure, again for comparability reasons. We also restricted our CPS samples to private wage and salary workers not employed either in agriculture or in a private household.

The March CPS collects information about earnings and weeks worked in the previous year, together with information on weekly hours while employed. The earnings concept employed encompasses bonuses, commissions, and tips in addition to ordinary wage and salary payments, all prior to any deductions. Payments in kind are excluded.

The March CPS hours series refers to hours worked, rather than hours paid. Between 1964 and 1975 (covering the years 1963–74), the March CPS did not collect information on hours per week, though from 1968 onward respondents were asked whether they had worked full time or part time. When possible, we imputed hours per week during the reference year using hours worked in the week prior to the interview. For those people who did not report any hours for the previous week, we assigned a 40-hour workweek (for those who said they had worked full time), the average hours of part-time workers with similar observable characteristics (for those who said they worked part time), or the average hours of all workers with similar characteristics (in years when individuals were not asked whether they had worked full time or part time). Prior to the 1976 survey, weeks worked in the previous year was recorded only in intervals. We computed average weeks for each interval using data from the March 1977 CPS and assigned respondents to the pre-1976 surveys the appropriate interval average.[29]

Because the March CPS weeks worked and hours per week questions refer to all employment a person may have experienced during the previous year, including any self-employment, we included self-employment income in earnings. Average hourly earnings equal aggregate annual earnings divided by aggregate annual hours. Average weekly earnings is computed analogously, as the ratio of aggregate annual earnings to aggregate annual weeks.[30]

In addition to the earnings and work experience questions asked on the

29. A more detailed description of the imputation process is available from the authors on request.

30. Aggregate annual earnings equals annual earnings multiplied by the March CPS sampling weight, summed over all observations. Aggregate annual hours equals hours per week times weeks worked last year times the sampling weight, summed over all observations. Aggregate annual weeks equals weeks worked in the previous year times the sampling weight, summed over all observations.

March CPS, questions about usual weekly earnings and usual weekly hours on the worker's main job last week have been asked each May from 1973 through 1978 of all households and, in each month since January 1979, of households in the outgoing rotation groups. The data pertain only to wage and salary workers, and in constructing a wage series based on these data, we excluded persons employed in either agriculture or a private household. Usual weekly earnings are defined to encompass any pay that is normally received, including tips and commissions but excluding payments in kind and irregular bonuses. It also is worth noting that, at least prior to 1994, a sizable fraction of respondents in the CPS reported net rather than gross earnings.[31] Our average hourly earnings figures were calculated by dividing estimated aggregate earnings by estimated aggregate hours. Average weekly earnings were computed similarly, as the ratio of aggregate earnings to aggregate employment.[32]

References

American Statistical Association Panel. 1993. A research agenda to guide and improve the Current Employment Statistics survey. Alexandria, Va.: American Statistical Association.

Bosworth, Barry, and George Perry. 1994. Productivity and real wages: Is there a puzzle? *Brookings Papers on Economic Activity,* no. 1: 317–43.

Bound, John, and George Johnson. 1992. Changes in the structure of wages in the 1980s: An evaluation of alternative explanations. *American Economic Review* 82 (3): 371–92.

Buchinsky, Moshe. 1994. Changes in the U.S. wage structure 1963–1987: Application of quantile regression. *Econometrica* 62 (2): 405–58.

Hamermesh, Daniel S. 1990. Shirking or productive schmoozing: Wages and the allocation of time at work. *Industrial and Labor Relations Review* 43 (3): 121S–133S.

Juhn, Chinhui, Kevin M. Murphy, and Brooks Pierce. 1993. Wage inequality and the rise in returns to skill. *Journal of Political Economy* 131 (3): 410–42.

Katz, Lawrence F., and Kevin M. Murphy. 1992. Changes in relative wages, 1963–1987: Supply and demand factors. *Quarterly Journal of Economics* 107 (1): 35–78.

Levy, Frank, and Richard J. Murnane. 1992. U.S. earnings levels and earnings inequality: A review of recent trends and proposed explanations. *Journal of Economic Literature* 30:1333–81.

Mellow, Wesley, and Hal Sider. 1983. Accuracy of response in labor market surveys: Evidence and implications. *Journal of Labor Economics* 1 (4): 331–44.

---

31. Testing associated with the development of the redesigned CPS questionnaire introduced in January 1994 indicated that about 30 percent of CPS respondents were reporting net earnings, rather than gross earnings. We have no way of knowing whether this number was constant over time. The redesign appears to have reduced the severity of this misreporting problem; testing indicates that only about 15 percent of those administered the new questionnaire report net earnings (see Polivka and Rothgeb 1993).

32. We computed aggregate earnings by multiplying usual weekly earnings by the earnings weight and summing over all observations. Aggregate hours were computed similarly. Aggregate employment equals the sum of the earnings weights.

Murphy, Kevin M., and Finis Welch. 1992a. Real wages, 1963–1990. Unicon Research Corporation Working Paper. Santa Monica, Calif.: Unicon Research Corporation.
———. 1992b. The structure of wages. *Quarterly Journal of Economics* 107 (1): 285–326.
Polivka, Anne E., and Jennifer M. Rothgeb. 1993. Redesigning the CPS questionnaire. *Monthly Labor Review* 116 (9): 10–28.
Reno, Virginia P. 1993. The role of pensions in retirement income. In *Pensions in a changing economy,* ed. Richard Burkhauser and Dallas Salisbury, 19–32. Washington, D.C.: Employee Benefit Research Institute.
Robinson, John, and Ann Bostrom. 1994. The overestimated workweek? What time-diary measures suggest. *Monthly Labor Review* 117 (8): 11–23.
U.S. Department of Commerce. Bureau of Economic Analysis. 1989. State personal income: 1929–87, Estimates and a statement of sources and methods. Washington, D.C.: Government Printing Office.
U.S. Department of Labor. Bureau of Labor Statistics. 1983. Employer records analysis survey of 1981. Final report. Washington, D.C.: U.S. Department of Labor, Bureau of Labor Statistics.
———. 1989. CES employment statistics manual. Washington, D.C.: U.S. Department of Labor, Bureau of Labor Statistics.
———. 1994. CES benchmark research: Measuring the impact of a non-probability CES sample on the 1993 state and national benchmarks. Washington, D.C.: U.S. Department of Labor, Bureau of Labor Statistics. Working paper.
———. 1995. Research results: March 1994 CES benchmark. Washington, D.C.: U.S. Department of Labor, Bureau of Labor Statistics. Briefing package.
———. 1997. *BLS handbook of methods.* BLS Bulletin no. 2490. Washington, D.C.: U.S. Department of Labor, Bureau of Labor Statistics.

Comment   Lawrence F. Katz

Katharine Abraham, James Spletzer, and Jay Stewart have produced a careful analysis of trends over the past three decades in four widely used alternative measures of average hourly wages for private sector, nonagricultural workers. The paper reflects much clever and compelling detective work.

In particular, the authors make four significant contributions in this study. First, they clearly explain the differences in earnings concepts and coverage of hourly wage series computed from the NIPA, the CES program, the March CPS, and the CPS outgoing rotation groups. Second, they document large divergences among these alternative hourly wage series starting at the end of the 1970s, with the CES series sharply declining relative to the others and the NIPA series showing the most rapid growth. Third, they convincingly show that the divergence between the NIPA series and series based on household data from the CPS arises largely from differences in trends in average weekly hours from establishment and household data. Finally, they show that the huge

Lawrence F. Katz is professor of economics at Harvard University and a research associate of the National Bureau of Economic Research.

relative decline in average hourly wages from the CES arises from the behavior of average weekly earnings in the CES. The authors convincingly demonstrate that the divergence of CES average weekly earnings from other series largely arises from its limited occupational coverage (only production and nonsupervisory workers) in a period of rising wage inequality and expanding wage differentials by skill and occupation.

This paper's findings have some potentially important implications for future data collection efforts and conceptual work. The divergence in average weekly hours series from the CPS series and the establishment-based series raises serious questions concerning the accuracy of our hours measures. The measurement of hours worked is integral not only to the measurement of hourly wages but also to the measurement of aggregate labor input, which is a key ingredient in estimates of labor productivity (output per hour) and total factor productivity. Hours measurement matters here both for understanding U.S. productivity growth trends and for making cross-country comparisons of output per hour, particularly given apparent large differences in hours worked per week between the United States and European nations. The conceptual and practical issues concerning the measurement of output and price deflators have received much attention lately, but the (less glamorous) issues arising from the measurement of hours of work has been much neglected. Larger, more representative, and more frequent time use surveys are necessary to better understand trends in hours of work reported in the CPS and recorded by employers. Interesting conceptual issues also require thought on what should count in hours worked when more individuals are employed in nontraditional jobs where the margins between work and leisure and work and home may be less clear than in the past.

The authors' documentation of substantial differences in wage trends over the 1980s between exempt and nonexempt workers raises the interesting question of whether this is fully explained by well-known increases in returns to education and skills. Alternatively, changes in wage-setting institutions and practices may differentially affect exempt and nonexempt workers in a manner not fully captured by differences in education and other measured skills. This is a topic worthy of further examination.

IV   Looking Inside the Firm

9   What Happens within Firms? A Survey of Empirical Evidence on Compensation Policies

Canice Prendergast

9.1   Introduction

The employment relation is perhaps the most important contractual relationship in the economy. The way in which this relationship translates worker preferences and capabilities into production affects the daily lives of all parties concerned. The organization of work and pay affects such diverse aspects of our lives as our education decisions, our social lives, and our effort choices. The objective of this paper is to offer some insight into the employment relationship by reviewing the available empirical work on how firms compensate their workers.

Following a long tradition from Mincer and Becker, labor economists have typically studied compensation by estimating earnings equations using individual data across a wide range of firms. The standard wage equation then identifies the reduced form mapping from worker characteristics to pay. This work has been particularly successful in understanding the effect of education, labor market experience, or training on earnings. This approach is generally associated with the human capital model of the labor market, where the regression coefficients on education, experience, and tenure typically reflect the market price of those attributes. Therefore, wages reflect contemporaneous marginal product.[1]

Canice Prendergast is professor of business economics at the University of Chicago Graduate School of Business and a faculty research fellow of the National Bureau of Economic Research.

Many thanks to George Akerlof, Judy Chevalier, Bob Gibbons, Mike Gibbs, Chip Heath, Nachum Sicherman, Bob Topel, and an anonymous referee for helpful comments. All errors are the author's.

1. Earnings equations typically include coefficients on demographic variables, which are more difficult to interpret. In particular, coefficients on gender and race variables may reflect preferences for discrimination rather than the marginal product of those groups. However, it is still fair to say that the standard approach to understanding earnings in the economy is firmly grounded in human capital theory.

The purpose of this paper is to show that factors beyond contemporaneous human capital also affect wage determination. Deviations from the human capital model will be described using two themes of the recent theoretical literature on compensation, namely, incentive theory and learning or matching theory. I begin by considering the effect of incentives on wages. There is a large theoretical literature on agency contracts, and there is empirical evidence on a wide array of workers showing how such agency considerations affect compensation. The literature has taken two conceptual approaches. Some work directly considers whether incentives matter by estimating the effect of incentive provisions on some measure of performance. A more indirect approach has been to test the importance of agency theory by checking whether observed contracts contain the incentive features predicted by the theory.

The second area of research surveyed examines how learning about the talents of workers affects the dynamics of wages. The purpose of this line of research is to better understand how careers develop within firms. For instance, are more able workers assigned to more suitable jobs and offered more training than their less able counterparts? If so, a considerable part of the returns to experience and tenure may be attributable to the assignment of workers to jobs, offering a social return to the information that firms collect on their workers. Related to this, another theme of the literature on careers has been the role of jobs in the careers of workers. For instance, how important is it that workers change position for advancement?

Section 9.3 provides a critical overview of how much has been learned from the existing studies. Two themes emerge. First, I argue that an empirical identification problem and a theoretical identification problem hamper our understanding of incentive compensation. The empirical identification problem arises from the fact that different contracts are not randomly assigned to different workers. For example, suppose that one contract is offered to better workers.[2] In this case, simply comparing productivity under different contracts could reflect these omitted variables rather than the effect of the contracts themselves. This is the standard *empirical identification* problem well known in the literature. However, section 9.3 also argues that it is difficult to distinguish between the theories at a conceptual level. For example, suppose that a researcher finds that individual wages rise with tenure in a firm. This finding is consistent with agency theory, learning theory, or human capital theory. To put this in more familiar terms, much of the empirical work clearly spells out its null hypothesis but leaves unspecified a plausible alternative hypothesis against which the theory is being compared. I call this issue *theoretical identification.* Many of the papers provide evidence that is compatible with a particular theory, but also with some other plausible alternatives. As a result, theoretical work that intends to inform empirical work is insufficiently oriented toward distinguishing between plausible alternatives.

---

2. Available evidence clearly points to such selection.

The second central theme of section 9.3 is to point out data needs in this field. There is a current sentiment that enormous advances in this field can be made by studying the personnel files of large companies. By doing so, researchers can develop a better understanding of work lives than is possible with aggregate data, which are often collected on workers across many firms. I share the enthusiasm for such data sets but believe that they will be capable of answering only a limited set of questions. I think that the greatest need in this field is to collect data on contracts themselves. Put simply, it is extremely difficult to make progress in understanding the effects of the employment contract if the contract itself cannot be observed. Some recent research in understanding the effect of incentives on performance, such as Knoeber and Thurman (1994), Chevalier and Ellison (1995), Lazear (1996), and Fernie and Metcalf (1996) has taken such a perspective with impressive results, and I conclude by arguing that more progress can be made in this manner.

9.2   Evidence on the Major Theories

Researchers use three major theories to analyze compensation within firms: human capital theory, incentive theory, and learning or matching theory. The purpose of this section is to identify the evidence on the relevance of these theories in the data.

9.2.1   Human Capital

Human capital theory argues that the primary source of variation in individual wages is the value of the individual's skills. Typically workers begin their careers at low wages, perhaps as they are paying for the cost of on-the-job training that they receive; ultimately they earn higher wages through the use of these skills. With some further restrictions on the model, human capital theory predicts a wage that is concave in experience or tenure, as observed in the typical earnings equation.

The basic earnings equation yields reasonable estimates of a return of 7 percent for a year of education and a return to labor market experience of up to 7 percent, though there is some dispute about the return to tenure within a firm (Topel 1991; Abraham and Farber 1987; Altonji and Shakotko 1987). Education and experience generate the most important differences in wages across workers, but other factors also affect how wages are determined and how they change throughout a worker's career. The papers reviewed below should be seen as evidence that factors beyond contemporaneous human capital affect wages.[3]

---

3. The tenor of the paper is that many factors other than human capital generate wages within firms. However, as an early antidote it is worth bearing in mind the findings of Brown (1989), who argues for the predominance of human capital theory in explaining wage dynamics. He argues that wage increases can be predicted only by human capital acquisition. Using data from the Panel Study of Income Dynamics, where workers are asked the amount of training it would take for a

9.2.2   Incentives

Incentives are generally argued to be the cornerstone of economics, yet there is surprisingly little clear-cut evidence that changing incentive provisions within firms affects worker behavior. The available literature has taken two conceptual approaches to identifying the importance of incentive concerns. First, a relatively small number of papers have addressed the direct question Do incentives matter? in cases where data on contracts and productivity measures are available. Second, most of the empirical work has tested for the importance of incentives by comparing the contracts that are observed with those that "should" arise if the theory is correct. Thus, if agency theory suggests that contract X should operate in some circumstances, then the existence of contract X implies that incentives must be relevant.

Do Incentives Matter?

The first approach taken in the literature is to directly relate productivity measures to contracts offered. Few papers have addressed this issue for employees within firms. This is largely due to data limitations. In order to carry out such an exercise, the researcher needs to collect data on both performance measures and the contracts offered to workers. Furthermore, the researcher must worry about the danger of selection in contracts offered. For example, if one worker is offered a piece rate and another is offered a salary, one must ask why this is the case. Could it be that better workers are observed receiving piece rates while their less able counterparts are paid salaries? If so, any estimate of productivity differences will overstate the true effect of piece rates. Despite these obstacles, a number of recent papers have successfully addressed these problems.[4]

Lazear (1996) uses data from a windshield fitting company to estimate the change in performance that occurred when the firm introduced piece rates. A change in management resulted in the introduction of piece rates, initially in selected areas but eventually to all employees. He finds that productivity rose on the order of 35 percent from the introduction of piece rates. However, he shows that almost half the increase occurred from a selection effect, where the most able workers were attracted to piece rates and the less able left, again as predicted by the theory. Paarsch and Shearer (1996) use data on tree planters in British Columbia, where in some instances piece rates are used but in others

---

replacement to be as competent as the respondent on his current job, Brown finds that individuals' wage increases can be closely approximated by the length of training time necessary on the job. After this reported training period, rewards do not increase. Brown's interpretation of this phenomenon is that without human capital acquisition, there is little room for wage growth.

4. It should be remembered that workers operate under implicit contracts, possibly in addition to explicit contracts. In the most prevalent form of implicit contract, poor performance will result in the worker's being fired. Such implicit contracts, which are never observed, surely affect worker behavior. As a result, we should be aware that the studies in this section (and throughout the paper) can only estimate the marginal effect of the explicit contracts given an unobserved set of implicit contracts.

there are fixed wages. Using a more structural approach than Lazear, they find incentive effects that account for between 6 and 35 percent increases in productivity due to the compensation scheme. Once again, they find evidence of the selection effects of piece rates, providing another warning about simply comparing the productivity of those on piece rates with those who are not. Fernie and Metcalf (1996) use data on the performance of British jockeys to illustrate that the use of bonuses attached to victories results in improved performance.[5] One of the most interesting discoveries of these recent papers has been the very large returns to pay-for-performance.

In most firms, it is almost impossible to obtain a comprehensive objective measure of a worker's performance. Kahn and Sherer (1990) proxy worker performance by performance evaluations provided by a superior. They find that managers with higher incentive provisions have higher subsequent performance levels than other managers.[6] Causality may be a concern here as there is a large literature illustrating that pay-for-performance can often *cause* high ratings, as supervisors realize that the cost of poor evaluations to workers is large.[7]

The performance of entire nations is sometimes attributed to the provision of incentives. Some recent work has addressed the effect of compensation in Japan and in Russia to understand the role of pay-for-performance contracts in explaining productivity. First, Jones and Kato (1995) use panel data on Japanese firms to estimate that the introduction of employee stock option plans (ESOPs) increases worker productivity by approximately 5 percent, though the full effects are felt only after about four years. It should be remembered here that this does not really provide much of a vindication of standard agency theory because in a large firm ESOPs should have little effect as the marginal effect of effort on wages is negligible. Second, Barberis, Boycko, and Shleifer (1996) have addressed the effect of equity ownership for managers on the performance of privatized shops in Russia. Their results suggest that this form of incentive provision has had little effect, though selection issues remain a concern here.

Another line of research has considered the effect of nonlinearities in rewards. For example, suppose that a worker is rewarded with a salary unless he sells more than $100 worth of output in a year, in which case he gets a bonus. Agency considerations suggest that the behavior of the worker changes as he gets close to selling $100. For example, we would expect the worker to have different incentives if he has sold $90 by 1 December than if he has sold $9. A

---

5. Marschke (1996) studies the effect of incentive provision in the context of a federal bureaucracy, where states offer incentives to the providers of publicly funded job training for welfare recipients. He shows that the providers of training offer more appropriate skills when they are rewarded based on employment rates for the trainees.

6. The identification strategy used here is that some plant locations offer different incentive packages than others.

7. Abowd (1990) uses the event study methodology (where changes in stock prices reflect the importance of "news") to illustrate the effect of new compensation plans on firm value. See also Putterman (1990) for an application to data on Chinese communes.

number of papers have addressed the effect of these nonlinearities on behavior. Chevalier and Ellison (1995) consider their effect on the risk-taking behavior of mutual fund managers. They show that mutual fund managers face nonlinear incentives because the "top" mutual funds tend to attract a particularly large inflow of funds and managers are rewarded according to fund size. Those managers close to the top have an incentive to take (inefficient) risks to gain such inflow. Chevalier and Ellison find that those managers who are found on the convex component of the reward schedule increase the riskiness of their portfolios, as predicted by agency theory.

Other attempts to identify the effects of nonlinearities in rewards have been made by estimating the impact of quotas on performance. Asch (1990) studies the behavior of navy recruiters who are rewarded on the basis of a quota of recruits at the end of the calendar year. As they approach the end-of-year deadline, the average quality of recruits falls, illustrating harmful incentives induced by the contract offered. Similar evidence is provided by Healy (1985) on the willingness of executives to hide earnings if they are rewarded on the basis of thresholds. In particular, many executives are rewarded on company earnings only if they lie within a certain range. Above some level, rewards are fixed, while there is also a lower bound to rewards if earnings are particularly poor. This gives rise to an incentive for executives to hide earnings until the following year if they are not within the range that generates returns. (This behavior is known among sales force workers as sandbagging.) Healy's empirical evidence supports this hypothesis. Finally, Oyer (1997) finds similar behavior by sales force workers and argues that business seasonality is likely to be partly generated by such incentives.[8]

Two remaining areas of incentive theory that have attracted attention are tournament theory and the behavior of teams. Following Lazear and Rosen (1981), many authors have considered competition between workers through the lens of tournaments, where agents compete for a fixed set of prizes, such as promotion. Tournament theory carries the following two testable implications: (i) larger marginal prizes should increase performance, and (ii) those who are behind (ahead) should take more (fewer) risks. Empirical evidence (largely from sports contests) shows that as the spread in prizes between ranks increases, performance improves. Ehrenberg and Bognanno (1990) find that golfers' performances appear to vary positively with the marginal return to effort, proxied by how prize money is allocated among finishers of different ranks. Becker and Huselid (1992) find similar behavior among professional auto drivers, but they also endorse another prediction of tournament theory, namely, that large prizes can give rise to dysfunctional behavior, as a greater return to a high placement results in more risky driving. Similar results have been found for the behavior of farmers raising chickens (who are rewarded relative to their peers by the broiler companies) in Knoeber (1989) and

8. For related work on the behavior of the providers of publicly funded job training schemes, see Courty and Marschke (1996).

Knoeber and Thurman (1994). Knoeber and Thurman also provide evidence on risk taking by the less able in these chicken-breeding tournaments.[9]

A particular area of incentive provision that remains largely untested is the behavior of individuals within teams. Some economists warn against the incentive effects of teams, as free riding is likely to harm performance. Others claim that peer pressure is likely to mitigate these problems. Gaynor and Pauly (1990) study productivity in medical practices of different sizes to illustrate the importance of free riding. The doctors were asked about their willingness to accept risky income, which was used as an instrument to predict the size of the practice.[10] Gaynor and Pauly illustrate how performance falls as medical practice groups get larger, endorsing the free rider problem. Newhouse (1973) also addresses the effect of group-based incentives in medical practices and shows that (i) overhead costs are higher in practices that share their costs and (ii) those doctors who share profits work less. Bailey (1970) finds similar results with data on medical practices, while Leibowitz and Tollison (1980) find evidence that cost control is poorer in large legal practices than in small practices. Each of these papers endorses the preeminence of free riding over any peer effects. On the other hand, Weiss (1987) is to my knowledge the only illustration of the effect of peer pressure in teams. He uses data from a manufacturing company to show that the introduction of team-based compensation increases the performance of the least able but decreases the performance of the most able, relative to outcomes that arise when workers are rewarded based on individual performance. A reasonable interpretation of this is that under team-based rewards, workers learn to conform to a common norm. Additionally, he shows that the piece rate system increases turnover among the least able and the most able but not among average workers. A reasonable interpretation of this is that the talented feel underrewarded and the least able feel excess pressure from the norms. In summary, then, the effect of incentives in teams seems to be largely dominated by free rider effects, so that any benefits to teams must be largely technological rather than based on incentives.

The Existence of Contracts

The data requirements for testing whether incentives matter are stringent. As a result, a second approach to testing agency theory has been to consider whether observed contracts accord with available theory.

Pay-for-performance contracts. The early literature on agency contracting has emphasized the trade-off of risk and incentives. From that perspective, incen-

---

9. Using Australian data, Drago and Garvey (1998) verify the hypothesis that greater returns to promotion will result in less cooperative behavior by workers. This accords with theoretical work by Lazear (1989) and Holmstrom and Milgrom (1992). Finally, Main, O'Reilly, and Wade (1993) endorse an implication of tournament theory by showing that the reward for becoming CEO is greater if there are more possible candidates for the job at the next level down.

10. Those who are less risk averse will work in smaller practices, as they are more willing to give up divestification to avoid free rider problems.

tive provision is muted by the desire to provide agents with a relatively smooth income stream. We would expect pay-for-performance to be lower in cases where either the environment is more risky or the agent is more risk averse. By contrast, those instances where the return to effort is large will imply higher pay-for-performance. The more recent literature (Holmstrom and Milgrom 1992) has also emphasized the possibility that agents are likely to substitute between activities if offered piece rates. The typical example of this trade-off, referred to as multitasking, is where an employee ignores quality considerations to maximize the quantity of output he produces under a piece rate.

Two approaches have been taken in the literature on estimating pay-for-performance, which for the most part has either been on executives or sales force workers. First, Murphy (1986), Jensen and Murphy (1990), and Kaplan (1994) have estimated the return to executives from improving various measures of performance, such as earnings, the stock price, and so on. On the basis of these estimates, the authors have drawn conclusions about the effectiveness of corporate governance. These papers have one potentially important drawback; it is extremely difficult to identify the "right" level of incentives predicted by the theory since many of the relevant variables (such as the cost of effort) are unobservable. Consequently, a second way of understanding the relevance of the theory is to consider whether pay-for-performance varies with the parameters identified above. Garen (1994), Shaefer (1994), Coughlin and Narasimhan (1992), John and Weitz (1989), and Kawasaki and McMillan (1987) provide evidence suggesting that contracts operate in the predicted way, though the results are rarely resounding.

Agency theory also predicts that when workers face common shocks to productivity, it is efficient to compare them to one another when deciding on rewards. In this setting, workers are rewarded when those similar do badly and punished when similar workers do well. This serves to filter out common risk. Using data on executives, Antle and Smith (1986) find little evidence of such relative performance evaluation. By contrast, Gibbons and Murphy (1990) find that firms tend to compare their senior managers' performance to stock market performance when determining rewards. Somewhat surprisingly, they are more likely to use the stock market as the relevant comparison than the performance of competitors.

It should be obvious that in some instances it is not necessary to provide workers with explicit incentives when they can develop reputations, if those reputations affect their wages. For instance, baseball players would continue to exert effort without rewards explicitly tied to measures of performance because there is a market for players. An important consideration for many firms is to optimally combine these implicit contracts with more explicit contracts, such as stock ownership. Gibbons and Murphy (1992) address this problem by considering how managerial tenure affects the combinations of implicit and explicit contracts. In particular, does agency contracting for executives seem to reflect such reputational concerns? On the one hand, such reputational concerns are likely to be more effective when executives are new to the job, both because little is known about them and because they potentially have a long time in the job to garner the fruits of a reputation. On the other hand, as they come close to retirement, they have less concern for reputation.[11]

An implication of agency theory is that managers close to retirement should be offered contracts with steeper incentive provisions, where rewards are directly tied to performance, as reputational concerns are not sufficient to provide incentives. Gibbons and Murphy find support for this proposition in their data, and more recent work by Gompers and Lerner (1994) on venture capitalists finds similar evidence.

Some recent theoretical contributions to the compensation literature stress that incentives are likely to be constrained by the fact that they will result in inefficient rent-seeking behavior: workers will waste valuable time and resources attempting to persuade their superiors of their talents rather than producing (Milgrom and Roberts 1990; Prendergast and Topel 1996). An implication of this literature is that firms may use institutional rules that constrain supervisors from rewarding those employees who are most able. Many authors have examined such bureaucracy in the employment relation, where many decisions are made by rule rather than by discretion. For example, Freeman and Medoff (1984) highlight the importance of seniority restrictions not only in layoff decisions but also in determining promotion. Similar data on bureaucratic restrictions in firms are provided by Spilerman (1986), who examines how firms doing similar things (e.g., policemen in Chicago vs. policemen in Philadelphia) often bureaucratically specify very different wage scales while leaving supervisors almost no room to maneuver.[12]

Agency theory focuses extensively on the effects of monitoring on the provision of contracts. Firms spend considerable time and resources identifying how best to monitor workers, but at an empirical level economists have done little to understand the costs and benefits of various forms of evaluation. Some workers are monitored on the basis of counted output, while others' performance is measured in a subjective fashion by a boss. This typically gives rise to certain problems, such as reluctance to offer bad evaluations (Larkey and Caulkins 1992) or accusations of favoritism (Bretz and Milkovitch 1989). Certain types of workers are monitored frequently, while others are monitored at most annually. Many individuals are monitored on their inputs, while in other occupations workers can come and go as they please. With the exception of

11. This arises because current performance is less informative about ability later in a career than when the worker begins and because workers have little time left in which to get the returns to a good reputation. Consequently, poor performance later in the career will be less costly to the worker than earlier. Chevalier and Ellison (1996) show that among mutual fund managers, the marginal effect of poor performance on the propensity for the manager to be fired is greater for older managers, as predicted by the theory.

12. The existing research on such bureaucratic constraints is mostly based on blue-collar work, often in unionized settings. It would be useful to know more about their prevalence. E.g., are such seniority restrictions less common the farther one ascends in the hierarchy?

Brown (1990) and Bishop (1987), there has been little descriptive work that could identify how evaluations occur. Work needs to be done here in devising a simple taxonomy of monitoring arrangements because this would provide useful information on how incentives are provided to workers who do not operate under explicit incentives.

Deferred compensation. A question that has received considerable attention from empirical researchers has been whether firms overpay older workers and underpay younger workers, which has been suggested as an optimal way of providing incentives (Lazear 1981) and reducing turnover. These tests suffer from one major difficulty: observing productivity. Indeed, there is little need for seniority wages in situations where productivity is easily observed; it is a more potent instrument where output is difficult to measure or becomes observed only after some time. The only cases where this policy will be used is where output cannot be observed, making tests difficult. Despite this, a number of ingenious ways of identifying productivity have been considered.

First, Medoff and Abraham (1981) use performance evaluations as a proxy for worker performance. In particular, they note that the wages of older workers are higher than their younger counterparts, despite equivalent performance ratings across age cohorts. To the extent that performance evaluations measure productivity (rather than, say, productivity relative to age-dependent expectations) this constitutes evidence in favor of deferred compensation.

Another way of estimating productivity would be to find a group of workers who do the same job as the workers in question but for whom there is no opportunity for backloading of wages. With this in mind, Lazear and Moore (1986) consider whether the wages of those in self-employment are as steeply sloped as those who work for organizations. Assuming that the jobs of the self-employed and employed are similar, any difference in slope between the two groups could be attributable to the desire of the firm to backload wages. The identifying assumption here is that the slope of the productivity profile is similar for the two types of workers. Lazear and Moore find that the wage profiles of the self-employed are less steeply sloped than those of the non-self-employed, which is consistent with deferred compensation being used.

The idea behind backloading wages is that workers when they are young pay into a trust fund that is returned later in life. This logic holds only if the worker has been with the firm for some time. For a worker who joins a firm late in life, opportunities for backloading are severely limited. Using this idea, Kotlikoff and Gokhale (1992) proxy productivity within firms by the wages of newcomers. For example, consider the wage of a worker who is in her final year of employment and who joined a firm in that year. Her wage should be a reasonable measure of her productivity. If matching issues and specific human capital are not important, this wage should also be a good measure of the productivity of a worker of that age who has been employed there for a longer time. Using this methodology, Kotlikoff and Gokhale compare the wages of newcomers and similar workers with more tenure and find that (i) the wages of office workers appear to be backloaded and (ii) those of salespeople are not. It should be remembered, however, that the identification restrictions (little specific human capital and little selection in late hires) are strong here.[13]

Alternative ways to identify the effect of seniority on pay come from directly considering rules in firms where wages or promotions increase with seniority independent of any productivity issues. As mentioned above, Freeman and Medoff (1984) and Spilerman (1986) illustrate the prevalence of rules relating tenure and wages independent of productivity.[14]

The importance of jobs. The standard labor problem cares little about the notion of a job, but it is clear that in many cases the primary route for advancement within a firm is through changing jobs, or at least through changing job titles. Should we care about this correlation? Is it not enough to know the reduced form mapping given by earnings equations? There are a number of reasons for understanding the role of tasks and job assignments. First, researchers interested in discrimination often describe the mechanism by which women and minorities are restricted in the labor market as a "glass ceiling," where certain jobs are restricted to favored groups. But if the sole route to career advancement is through changing jobs, there may be inefficiencies caused by certain jobs being "dead-end jobs." Similarly, if a particular individual has poor promotion prospects, he is likely to have few incentives in a world where wages are largely attached to jobs (Gibbs 1995; Gibbs and Hendricks 1996). Finally, jobs play a central role in tournament theory, so an understanding of the role of job changes in career advancement may also cast light on how firms provide incentives.

Many personnel files include data on wages and the history of jobs that an individual previously held within the firm, so that it is sometimes possible to identify the relationship between job changes and the evolution of wages. For example, using data from a single company Lazear (1991) finds that those workers who have experienced promotion in the past earn 21 percent higher

---

13. Furthermore, an auxiliary implication of the deferred compensation model is that mandatory retirement is also likely to be used in conjunction with deferred compensation, since overpaid older workers will be reluctant to leave. This has been addressed by Hutchens (1986), who shows that the existence of mandatory retirement can be predicted by the steepness of worker wage profiles.

14. As with many of the studies in this review, there is an alternative interpretation of the data. Some authors have argued that wages rise with seniority simply because workers like wages increasing the longer they stay on the job rather than because firms use this strategy to provide incentives. E.g., Loewenstein and Sicherman (1991) use survey data that illustrate that individuals seem to prefer such wage profiles, even when net present value considerations suggest otherwise. Another related effort is Frank and Hutchens (1993), who consider two occupations (bus driver and airline pilot) where productivity "should be" relatively flat after initial training and where monitoring concerns are not deemed to be important. They show that the wages of airline pilots and bus drivers continue to increase long after agency and productivity growth issues would suggest is warranted. They attribute this increase in wages to worker preferences.

wages than those individuals who have not. Baker, Gibbs, and Holmstrom (1994b) find that the immediate premium on promotion in the firm they study is on average 6 percent but that this difference underestimates (by a factor of about four) the difference in average wages across levels, as subsequent pay increases are higher for those promoted than for those passed over.[15] Furthermore, there is considerable overlap in wages across adjacent (in the hierarchical sense) jobs, so that some workers in "lower" jobs are earning more than others in "higher" jobs. This observation is important as it suggests that firms use many means of providing incentives, not just the prospect of promotion, because there is considerable variation in wages within job grades.

One of the most common bureaucratic rules within firms is that each job classification has a wage range that cannot be violated. For example, a job may have six grades; when a worker has reached grade six, there may be little the firm can do to increase the worker's wage other than to promote her to a different job. This phenomenon, known as "topping out," appears to be a concern of practitioners but has played little role in economic work on compensation. Some evidence on this phenomenon is provided in Baker et al. (1994b), who show that such limits seem to constrain wage growth. Gibbs and Hendricks (1996) illustrate that firms do not seem to provide other incentives for those workers. Spilerman and Petersen (1993) show that firms can partly overcome this problem by transferring workers to jobs that do not entail such constraints. They also show that such transfers are an imperfect mechanism and that workers who are at the top of their wage grades are generally impeded from future increases. Somewhat surprisingly, they find no evidence that exits from the firm are accelerated by being at the top of a wage grade.[16]

Doeringer and Piore (1971) argue that one of the defining characteristics of an internal labor market is limited ports of entry, where the most senior jobs are filled by insiders. In other words, working one's way through the system is an integral part of a career. However, the small amount of available data from personnel files on ports of entry (Lazear 1991; Baker, Gibbs, and Holmstrom 1994a) show little evidence of this; instead there is considerable hiring from outside at all levels of the firm. Further work on this issue seems necessary. For example, what are the characteristics of those jobs filled internally? Are they predominantly low-skill jobs?

Efficiency wages. Efficiency wage theory argues that workers will be offered rents in order to increase productivity. Some work testing the validity of these theories has revolved around studying interindustry wage differentials using large data sets to measure whether workers are earning rents in high-wage

---

15. Groshen (1991) also addresses the importance of job classifications in wage determination.
16. Lazear (1991) also points to the existence of considerable differences in promotion prospects across different jobs.

industries (Krueger and Summers 1988). An alternative test can be carried out using firm-level data, operating on the premise that firms will see supervision and wage premiums as substitutes for inducing effort. Since firms can induce effort either by wages or by monitoring, these instruments should be substitutes. Data testing this hypothesis have been analyzed by Leonard (1987), Groshen and Krueger (1990), and Cappelli and Chauvin (1991) with mixed results.[17]

9.2.3   Learning

The talents of workers are rarely known for sure when they join a firm; they are gradually revealed as the worker spends time there. Recent theoretical work has argued for the importance of learning about worker talent as an explanation of wage dynamics in the labor market (e.g., Holmstrom 1982). The starkest form of learning, called pure learning by Farber and Gibbons (1996), assumes that the productivity of an individual is determined by a time-invariant characteristic, ability, where ability is gradually revealed over time. In this world, perceptions of ability evolve according to a random walk.

Suppose that markets clear contemporaneously. Then the evolution of wages will map the arrival of information about the worker's talent. An immediate implication is that the variance of wages for a cohort of similar workers will increase over time as workers who were initially similar are revealed to be dissimilar.[18] Furthermore, wages in this environment will follow a martingale, as the law of iterated expectations implies that future innovations to wages cannot be predicted by previous innovations.[19]

This is a very stark form of learning as it allows no efficiency value to information on the worker's ability and suggests that there are few returns to allocating workers to suitable tasks or to allocating additional training to the most able. However, firms often devote considerable resources to identifying talent. This ability to assign workers on the basis of more precise information implies that wages no longer follow a martingale but instead follow a submartingale,

17. It should not be surprising that this work has not provided a clear result, as it is not obvious at a theoretical level whether supervision and wages are complements or substitutes. Would we expect supervisors and rents to be complements or substitutes in the data? This seems to depend critically on the source of variation across firms. On the one hand, if the source of variation across companies is the cost of supervisors, the two instruments probably will act as substitutes in the data where the high-cost-supervisor firms will use more wages and fewer supervisors to get effort exertion. On the other hand, if the variation across firms is primarily through the value of effort exertion, those firms that want more effort will probably use more of both instruments relative to those that do not value so much effort, so that supervision and wages will be complements in the data. Therefore, this does not seem as powerful a test as one might like.

18. See, e.g., data in Spurr and Barber (1994) on the evolution of baseball salaries reflecting the revelation of information on talent.

19. A further implication of this model is that the value of any attribute the worker holds when he joins the firm (such as race or education) will not change over time in an econometric regression predicting wages. See Farber and Gibbons (1996) for details.

where the expectation of next year's wage, given this year's information, exceeds this year's wage. To phrase this in more familiar terms, information is useful because workers can be better sorted to jobs that match their talents.

The role of learning in firms has often been analyzed by considering the serial correlation of changes in rewards. There have been studies on serial correlation in rewards using both personnel files and larger data sets. Many studies using personnel files find evidence of serial correlation in promotions; those who are promoted quickly are more likely to be promoted again than the slow movers (Rosenbaum 1979; Bruderl, Diekmann, and Preisendorfer 1991; Spilerman and Petersen 1993; Baker et al. 1994b; Spilerman and Ishida 1994). Baker et al. find similar evidence on wage changes (and residuals). However, the results from the more aggregate studies are mixed. For instance, Lillard and Weiss (1979) and Card and Hyslop (1995) find evidence of such serial correlation by observing a person-specific growth rate in wages. Farber and Gibbons (1996) also reject the assumption that wages can be modeled as a martingale, though not convincingly. On the other hand, Abowd and Card (1989), Topel (1991), and Topel and Ward (1992) find little evidence of correlation in wage changes.

Some literature on human capital can also be used to cast light on this issue. Correlation in wage changes or promotion would be expected if the more able were trained more intensively throughout their careers. Barron, Black, and Loewenstein (1989) and Ashenfelter and LaLonde (1997) illustrate such a complementarity between observed ability and on-the-job training. For example, college graduates get more training than high school graduates, who in turn get more training than high school dropouts. As a result, we would expect the wages of the more talented workers to increase at a more rapid rate than those of their less able counterparts.

It is difficult to know how to interpret these results. The firm-level studies suggest that talent is identified and talented workers are treated differently than their less able counterparts, through either extra training or more difficult assignments. At an intuitive level, this result is not surprising. More surprising is the lack of support for the idea in the aggregate data, even when restricting attention to workers who do not change firms, as in Topel (1991) and Topel and Ward (1992). One possible reason for this, suggested by Gibbons (1996), is that such person-specific growth rates are evident only in particularly skilled occupations, but this has yet to be tested.

One value of theoretical work should be to allow researchers to distinguish among various competing theories. A prime example of such an identification problem is the ability to distinguish between human capital theory and learning as an explanation for wage dynamics. Consider the problem of distinguishing between a model that views wages as evolving through learning about worker talents and another that identifies wage changes as being caused by human capital evolving throughout a worker's career. Suppose that there is a random component to skills, where the value of skills moves about each year subject to upward drift caused by skill collection. What does the learning model predict? First, the variance of wages will increase over time, and second, wages will follow a submartingale (if workers can be assigned to jobs based on differing talents). Can this theory be distinguished from a model of human capital acquisition, where the value of a worker's skills varies over time? A number of possible routes can be followed. First, Farber and Gibbons (1996) use a measure of talent that is available to the econometrician but not available to the firm to address whether wages are increasingly correlated with this measure over time.

This is a prediction of the learning model since wages should increasingly track ability over time, and the ability measure is by assumption privately observed by the econometrician. There are two necessary conditions for this to operate as a valid test of learning over purely human capital: (i) the worker cannot credibly transmit this information to the firm, and (ii) the innovations to skills are not correlated with this measure of ability (so that the human capital model has different predictions than the learning model). Using this methodology, Farber and Gibbons use aptitude test scores that suggest the importance of learning in the workplace.

A final route that might be considered is to compare the relationship between wage innovations and tenure. A plausible restriction on the learning model is that the value of information is greatest at the beginning of a worker's career and that ultimately new information is of little value. It is not as clear why a human capital model with random shocks to productivity should have this feature, particularly for negative shocks.[20] As a result, it may be possible to identify the effects of learning in the workplace by considering the innovations of old workers relative to newcomers who are otherwise observationally equivalent. See Baker et al. (1994a) for details.[21]

Learning and Insurance

Learning involves the revelation of information that may reduce the wages of workers. However, risk-averse workers may demand that wages be insured against variation in the price of their services, say through an economic down-

---

20. In most occupations, there is more opportunity to learn new skills when the worker is new to a job. However, there is little reason to expect that depreciation in skills should have this feature.

21. A final career issue studied by sociologists is how quickly individuals become differentiated from their peers. Is it the case that within a given cohort of entrants, firms identify and reward their high performers soon after they arrive, or do they try to minimize differentiation within a cohort? Anecdotally it appears that firms are often reluctant to differentiate among workers, perhaps for fear of discouraging workers who are "left behind." This aspect of career development has been addressed recently by Spilerman and Ishida (1994) using Japanese data. They show that for the first 10 years of a worker's career there is little differentiation, with most workers moving up the corporate hierarchy at roughly the same rate (only the very low quality are not promoted). However, after 10 to 15 years, there is much more noticeable differentiation of workers.

turn. One strategy for understanding the importance of such insurance would be to compare real wage changes with changes in productivity, although such productivity may be hard to measure.

A second approach, taken by Beaudry and Di Nardo (1991) and Baker et al. (1994b), has been to address the effect of starting wages on current wages. Consider a world where workers are risk averse and write long-term contracts when they join a firm. The optimal risk-sharing contract smooths consumption across time periods. Therefore, economic conditions when the worker joins the firm will predict future wages: those who join the firm when conditions are good will continue to get high wages in future years, even if conditions in those years are poor. Beaudry and Di Nardo show that a worker's wage can be predicted by his entry-level (market) wage, even after controlling for the entry wages of newcomers. Even if the wages of entry-level workers fall, the wages of existing workers will not change much. If the newcomers are similar in quality to the older workers, this evidence suggests an insurance motive for a deviation from marginal product.

Baker et al. (1994a) use firm-level data to illustrate the same phenomenon and can show in addition that despite differences in wages across entry cohorts, there is no difference in their promotion performance so it does not appear that these differences reflect talent differences. Therefore, there appears to be a contractual mechanism between existing workers and employers that does more than simply equate marginal revenue with the wage.

Another form of insurance that workers may desire applies to their ability. When workers join a firm, there is typically uncertainty about their talents. In some instances, workers will be worse than initially anticipated. Workers may demand insurance against such permanent changes in their human capital. This demand for insurance must be balanced against the possibility of the worker's leaving to get a better job. Harris and Holmstrom (1982) illustrate that the optimal solution to this problem is to offer workers a real wage that increases if the perception of the worker improves but cannot be reduced. A clever test of this model has been developed by Chiappori, Salanié, and Valentin (1996). They compare workers who started their careers similarly but whose paths diverged such that one employee had rapid wage increases followed by flat wages while another had a slow beginning but eventually caught up to the first worker. An implication of Harris and Holmstrom is that the latter worker will fare better in future because his wage is increasing, implying that he must at least have been better than his last year's impression. The most recent performance of the other worker was poor and so (in finance parlance) his option is likely to be "out of the money," in that marginal increases in his performance will have no effect on future wages. Chiappori et al. find this pattern in the data.

Learning and Turnover

Learning also plays a central role in the understanding of worker turnover, though in this case workers and employers typically learn about the aptitude of workers with particular employers. Matching theory provides another reason for wages to increase with tenure—those with long tenure will have found better matches than those who have recently arrived in jobs. Available empirical work has focused on the implications of tenure and demographic characteristics for job changing (see Farber 1994; Sicherman 1995; Mincer 1986). One way of identifying the effect of matching is to identify whether turnover predominantly comes from those who appear to be faring poorly within firms, indicating that they are poorly matched. Little work has been done on turnover using personnel files, but available evidence suggests little evidence of systematically more movement among the less able than among those whose performance is better than expected (Baker et al. 1994b).

9.3   Identification and Data Issues

9.3.1   Identification

The ultimate objective of empirical work on incentives should be to find out why firms use the compensation policies they do and to determine the impact of such policies on productivity or welfare. This involves two important identification problems. First, there is a need to develop empirical tests where productivity measures are related to compensation policies, where the source of the variation in such policies has been accounted for. This is the standard empirical identification problem. However, in many instances theories have not yet been sufficiently developed to distinguish among different plausible theories. The typical theoretical paper offers few empirical predictions: those that do so often offer suggestions about the data that are consistent with the theory, but unfortunately as yet we have few ways of distinguishing *between* theories, which I think is necessary to fully develop empirical testing of compensation policies.

Empirical Identification

Selection problems pervade economic analysis, as individuals frequently choose the treatments they undergo. In studies of the employment relation, a two-sided selection problem clouds identification of the effects of contracts. First, employers choose the contract that will be offered to workers; quite possibly different workers are offered different contracts. Second, workers are not bonded to their employers, so only certain workers may accept a given contract. Controlling for this problem is difficult, but without addressing it, there is little hope that the effects of contracts can be truly identified.

Both empirical and theoretical work emphasize the importance of such selection effects. For instance, Lazear (1996) estimates that approximately half of the effect of piece rates on productivity can be attributed to more able workers' being assigned to such contracts. Paarsch and Shearer (1996) find similar results from their study on Canadian tree planters. Given such selection issues, it is important to control appropriately for their effects in studying compensations. Various ingenious strategies have been followed to control for such selection.[22] Such identification assumptions play a particularly important role here because in many cases only imprecise information is available on other relevant data. For instance, in many studies either the contracts offered have to be inferred (from, say, the relation between performance evaluations and wages, as in Kahn and Sherer 1990) or the measures of the worker's performance are imprecise (e.g., the stock price as a measure of a CEO's performance). There is little room for maneuver if the instruments are weak. In some cases the weakness of the basic data has made some of the identification restrictions less reliable than we would like.

Theoretical Identification

Perhaps the primary objective of empirical research on organizations should be to understand why firms treat workers as they do. This requires that the available theoretical work be used to explain the data. Two approaches to making the theory data friendly can be followed. First, theoretical work can predict certain outcomes in the data, such as whether a particular outcome is compatible with the theory. For instance, to use the example earlier, incentive theory suggests that firms will sometimes backload wages. A failure to observe backloaded wages would negate the relevance of this theory. However, if we see that wages are indeed backloaded, this does not necessarily imply that firms

22. Among those used are the following:

(1) *Variation in risk tolerance.* Gaynor and Pauly (1990) use survey evidence on doctors that asks them about the importance of smoothness in their income. This variable is then used to predict contracts offered and their impact on the performance of medical practices. If risk tolerance is uncorrelated with ability and the instrument has reasonable power in predicting contract choices, this would be a reasonable instrument.

(2) *Variation across location.* Kahn and Sherer (1990) use variation across positions and locations in the firm in the sensitivity of pay-for-performance. Lazear (1996) uses the fact that contracts differ across plants as a means of identifying the effect of incentives. He uses worker fixed effects, so this identification strategy is reasonable as long as other (unobserved) management changes do not also differentially affect productivity in those locations.

(3) *Newcomers to the firm.* In any situation where workers are compensated over the long term, we would expect to observe a difference in the way newcomers are paid relative to observationally equivalent workers with long tenure in the firm. This approach has been taken by Kotlikoff and Gokhale (1992), Beaudry and Di Nardo (1991), and Baker et al. (1994a). One attraction of Baker et al. is that they illustrate that the quality of workers is similar across the various cohorts, thus alleviating fears of selection effects caused by ability differences across cohorts.

(4) *Age or tenure.* Age and tenure constitute a legitimate source of identification in a couple of settings. Models that rely on the importance of reputation typically depend on the worker's horizon, which obviously depends on how long they will work before retirement. Gibbons and Murphy (1992) use such theoretical constraints based on tenure to identify variation in the contracts offered to workers. As long as worker tenure is not correlated with other confounding effects, such as that the marginal return to effort is higher for older workers, this is a useful source of variation in the data that can be exploited. Tenure and age also play an important role in the identification of learning models, as plausible restrictions on learning models will imply that most learning about workers occurs early in the worker's career. This feature has been exploited in Farber and Gibbons (1996), Glaeser (1992), and Baker et al. (1994a).

do so for the reason posited; it could be for any other reason. A second approach, which is much more difficult, is to offer suggestions about how the data could help to distinguish among a number of plausible theories. In other words, offer a plausible alternative hypothesis against which to compare theoretical predictions. It is not the purpose of this paper to provide a menu of ways this could be done, but the following examples may be suggestive.[23]

Are wages backloaded? Assume that a researcher finds evidence that firms overpay older workers but underpay younger workers and would like to interpret her results. One interpretation is that firms find this the optimal way to provide incentives to workers. Another interpretation would be that they do so to offer a deterrent to quitting early, in which case firms will incur training or hiring costs. Finally, the data could simply reflect a preference among workers for wages that grow with age, say, as a way of forced saving.

As yet, researchers have not tried to disentangle these competing hypotheses. However, a deeper look at the theories may help us to make progress. Backloaded wages are likely to be a desirable means of inducing incentives when output is hard to observe, where it may take some time to determine performance. In cases where performance measures are easily available, there should be little need for such measures: instead, straight piece rates are likely to dominate. Next, consider the interpretation of the data that firms wish to backload wages to induce workers not to quit. Such inducements are likely to be greatest when firms pay significant training or turnover costs. It may be possible to disentangle these theories by considering whether the extent of backloading varies by occupation. Those occupations where output is hard to observe (or where training is intensive) are more likely to offer backloaded wages than are other occupations if the incentive (or turnover) story is true, which is unlikely to be the case if workers simply prefer wages that rise with age.[24]

The return to promotion. Wages rise as workers ascend a hierarchy. This is hardly surprising: more interesting is that the returns to promotion increase as one moves up the ranks of an organization. Hence, the increase in wages on becoming CEO is larger than the increase on becoming a senior executive and so on. There are a number of possible reasons why firms may choose to skew

---

23. An alternative approach to designing theories that carefully distinguish among plausible alternatives is to provide multiple predictions from a given theory. The idea here is that the combination of predictions is unlikely to replicate any other theory. See Gibbons and Waldman (1996) for such an approach.

24. Kotlikoff and Gokhale (1992) consider a firm including both office workers and sales force workers. Measurement of performance is easier with sales force workers, who are typically rewarded by piece rates. Kotlikoff and Gokhale find that backloading of wages occurs only for the office workers. This evidence suggests incentive concerns (or possible turnover issues if office workers have more training than sales force workers) rather than simply preferences for wages that increase with age, as there would be little reason for such preferences to be specific to office workers.

wages in this way. One is that workers are sorted to jobs on the basis of their talents (Rosen 1982), where the most able affect the productivity of many others, and so their marginal product in those jobs is large. From this perspective, wage increases are simply a reflection of marginal product. However, tournament theory suggests that firms may choose such skewed returns as a means of providing incentives (Rosen 1986). A useful analogy is a tennis tournament. Consider the incentives of a player in the first round of a tournament. His return from winning the game is not only the prize money from being a first-round winner but also the option associated with the possibility of winning future rounds. This implies that there is a reason for the organizers of the tennis tournament to increase prizes in the later rounds, providing incentives not only in the later rounds but also in the earlier rounds through the increased value of the option. Similar logic holds within firms, where the return to becoming a senior manager may act as an inducement not just to middle managers but also to those lower in the organization who believe they ultimately have a chance of becoming a senior manager.

Recent work on tournament theory, such as Eriksson (1996), has argued that increasing returns to promotion across ranks in a hierarchy constitutes evidence in favor of tournament theory. At one level, this is of course true, as a failure to find this would be a direct contradiction. However, it fails to distinguish tournament theory from the plausible alternative described above. As a result, it may be necessary once again to delve somewhat deeper to better understand the motivation of firms. One plausible way to do this is to directly estimate the value of the option that underlies the tennis tournament analogy. In other words, how much should workers value the prospect of future promotions? This is not a conceptually difficult exercise to carry out as future promotion prospects and returns can be estimated. By estimating this option value, we can then determine whether the observed differences in wages across ranks correspond closely to the value of this option. If they do not, some other explanation would be more plausible.

Learning and human capital. Wages typically rise as workers gain experience in the labor market. As described in the previous section, this could be caused by workers' collecting more skills or because information is learned about workers that improves matching. Distinguishing between these two competing explanations has been the focus of recent work by Farber and Gibbons (1996) and Baker et al. (1994b) and is an area where recent theory has been successful at providing a means of potentially distinguishing between the two theories. Two competing theories about wage dynamics are that (i) the value of a worker's skills varies over time and (ii) information is arriving on worker talents that allows better assignment of the worker to jobs. Either of these theories would predict wages that increase with tenure. However, the value of information on a worker is likely to be greatest at the beginning of a worker's career (or when he starts a new job); ultimately new information is of little value. It is not as clear why a human capital model with random shocks to productivity should have this feature, particularly for negative shocks. Baker et al. (1994a, 1994b) use this temporal dependence to argue for the importance of learning in explaining wage dynamics.

9.3.2 Data Needs

Tests of theories of compensation have been highly constrained by data limitations. To understand the effect of incentives on productivity, at the very least the researcher needs data on some reliable measure of output and the contracts under which workers operate. Given the difficulty in getting reliable measures of performance on workers, it is not surprising that much of the literature on agency contracting has been concerned with estimating the existence of contracts compatible with the theory, rather than their effects. It is also not surprising that most work on agency contracting has been done on either sales force workers or CEOs, for whom contracts are most likely to be available.

The greatest challenge to those studying the effect of compensation on performance is to understand how wages are determined for the typical worker who is not on a piece rate, whose output is subjectively determined by his boss, and for whom there are little data on the contractual environment. I would argue that this covers the majority of workers in the economy, yet we know little about the contractual environment in which they work. It is in this context that there is considerable enthusiasm about recent work on personnel files of the type studied by Lazear (1991), Baker et al. (1994a, 1994b), and Gibbs and Hendricks (1996). I believe that a great deal can be learned about compensation from such data archives. They may be even more useful as a means of describing the work lives and careers of workers than for either identifying how workers respond to incentives or understanding why firms carry out observed policies. Such personnel files typically contain voluminous information about jobs, wages, and benefits, and plenty of demographic data, but are bereft of information about contracts or performance. As a result, they may ultimately be more useful as a description of careers than anything else. While this is very valuable, a need for other types of data remains.[25]

Huge advances in our understanding could be made by a concerted effort to collect data on contracts. By and large, data on contracts are scant, with the exception of some work on executives and sports players. However, my sense

---

25. It would be useful to identify areas in which such data files can dominate the larger data sets commonly used by labor economists. What is it exactly about these data sets that distinguishes them from larger data sets with workers from many firms? To take one example, consider the issue of whether wage changes are serially correlated within firms. There is considerable work from the Panel Study of Income Dynamics data set on this issue, with mixed results. It is not yet clear how to evaluate the marginal product of work from personnel files that tackle the same issue. They clearly constitute a more restricted environment than the larger data sets, but all the observations are from one firm. What is the implication of this? Does the fact that the studies from personnel files suggest strong evidence of serial correlation mean that it is important to use other workers in the same firm as a benchmark?

is that the marginal return to collecting such data would be large, and some of the most interesting papers on compensation (Knoeber and Thurman 1994; Chevalier and Ellison 1995; Lazear 1996; Paarsch and Shearer 1996; Fernie and Metcalf 1996) have given preeminence to collecting such data. Without data on contracts, it is close to impossible to identify how incentives affect behavior. Therefore, I believe that perhaps the largest holes in our knowledge about the provision of incentives arise from ignorance on how workers are rewarded.

Only a limited number of workers are offered explicit contracts that relate wages to performance measures. The majority of workers operate in shadier territory where contracts are implicit, with the promise of a wage increase or promotion based on good performance. As I mentioned above, one data limitation for understanding such workers is that there is little information on how workers are evaluated. Having such information may be a second-best way of understanding the contractual environment in which they operate. This is not an easy task, as illustrated by the dearth of papers that seriously consider performance evaluation (Brown 1990 is a notable exception). However, I would recommend that data be collected on such issues as (i) whether workers are promoted by merit or seniority, (ii) whether they are given discretionary bonuses, (iii) how often they are formally evaluated, and (iv) whether evaluations are based on objective or subjective criteria. Such data would be very useful to researchers for understanding how incentives are provided within firms.

9.4   Conclusion

Empirical work on incentives and compensation policies within firms is still at an early stage. In truth, there are few areas where much is known with certainty, even at the level of the most basic question of all, Do incentives matter? The prime reason for this has been limitations on data. As a result, I feel that the most important advances in this field can be obtained by collecting more data on contracts and relating these to available measures of performance. This, of course, is easily said, but I believe that our understanding of the effect of incentives has been advanced enormously in just the past two years by a series of papers that have taken this approach with much success. Each of these papers has illustrated large effects attributable to the use of pay-for-performance, which needs to be further studied.

A second, and in my mind equally important, problem is that the available theoretical work has made too little progress in identifying the empirical implications of theories relative to some plausible alternatives. A recent paper by Baker and Holmstrom (1995), "Internal Labor Markets: Too Many Theories, Too Few Facts," summarizes their view of the prevailing state of knowledge in this field. I think that it is indeed true that we have far too few facts, but I also believe that there is need to carry out theoretical work that could take a more empirical approach, ultimately allowing data to answer the question Can we distinguish between two supposedly plausible theories? If we do not answer these conceptual questions, progress in this field may be severely limited.

References

Abowd, J. 1990. Does performance-based managerial compensation affect corporate performance? *Industrial and Labor Relations Review* 43:52–74.

Abowd, J., and D. Card. 1989. On the covariance of earnings and hours changes. *Econometrica* 57:411–45.

Abraham, K., and H. Farber. 1987. Job duration, seniority and earnings. *American Economic Review* 77:278–97.

Altonji, J., and R. Shakotko. 1987. Do wages rise with job seniority? *Review of Economic Studies* 54:437–60.

Antle, R., and A. Smith. 1986. An empirical investigation of the relative performance evaluation of corporate executives. *Journal of Accounting Research* 24:1–39.

Asch, B. 1990. Do incentives matter? The case of navy recruiters. *Industrial and Labor Relations Review* 43:89–107.

Ashenfelter, O., and R. LaLonde. 1997. The economics of training. In *Handbook of human resources,* ed. D. Lewin, D. Mitchell, and M. Zaidi. Greenwich, Conn.: JAI.

Bailey, R. 1970. Economies of scale in medical practice. In *Empirical studies in health economics,* ed. H. Klarman. Baltimore: Johns Hopkins University Press.

Baker, G., M. Gibbs, and B. Holmstrom. 1994a. The internal economics of a firm: Evidence from personnel data. *Quarterly Journal of Economics* 107:881–921.

———. 1994b. The wage policy of a firm. *Quarterly Journal of Economics* 107:921–57.

Baker, G., and B. Holmstrom. 1995. Internal labor markets: Too many theories, too few facts. *American Economic Review Papers and Proceedings* 85:255–59.

Barberis, N., M. Boycko, and A. Shleifer. 1996. How does privatization work? Evidence from Russian shops. *Journal of Political Economy* 104:764–91.

Barron, J., D. Black, and M. Loewenstein. 1989. Job matching and on-the-job training. *Journal of Labor Economics* 7:1–19.

Beaudry, P., and J. Di Nardo. 1991. The effect of implicit contracts on the movement of wages over the business cycle: Evidence from micro data. *Journal of Political Economy* 99:665–89.

Becker, B., and M. Huselid. 1992. The incentive effects of tournament compensation systems. *Administrative Science Quarterly* 37:336–50.

Bishop, J. 1987. The recognition and reward of employee performance. *Journal of Labor Economics* 5:36–56.

Bretz, R., and G. Milkovich. 1989. Performance appraisals in large organizations: Practice and research implications. Ithaca, N.Y.: Cornell University. Mimeograph.

Brown, C. 1990. Firms' choice of method of pay. *Industrial and Labor Relations Review* 43:165–83.

Brown, J. 1989. Why do wages increase with tenure? *American Economic Review* 79:971–92.

Bruderl, J., A. Diekmann, and P. Preisendorfer. 1991. Patterns of intraorganizational mobility. *Social Science Research* 20:197–216.

Cappelli, P., and K. Chauvin. 1991. An interplant test of the efficiency wage hypothesis. *Quarterly Journal of Economics* 106:769–87.

Card, D., and D. Hyslop. 1995. Does inflation "grease the wheels of the labor market"? Princeton, N.J.: Princeton University. Mimeograph.

Chevalier, J., and G. Ellison. 1995. Risk taking by mutual funds as a response to incentives. *Journal of Political Economy* 105:1167–1200.

———. 1996. Are some mutual fund managers better than others? Chicago: University of Chicago. Mimeograph.

Chiappori, P.-A., B. Salanié, and J. Valentin. 1996. Insurance, learning and career profiles: An empirical test. Paris: Institut National de la Statistique et des Etudes Economiques. Mimeograph.

Coughlin, A., and C. Narasimhan. 1992. An empirical analysis of sales-force compensation plans. *Journal of Business* 65:93–123.

Courty, P., and J. Marschke. 1996. Moral hazard under incentive systems: The case of a federal bureaucracy. *American Economic Review Papers and Proceedings* 87: 383–87.

Doeringer, P., and M. Piore. 1971. *Internal labor markets and manpower analysis.* Lexington, Mass.: Heath.

Drago, R., and G. Garvey. 1998. Incentives for helping on the job: Theory and evidence. *Journal of Labor Economics* 16:1–25.

Ehrenberg, R., and M. Bognanno. 1990. The incentive effects of tournaments revisited: Evidence from the European PGA tour. *Industrial and Labor Relations Review* 43:74–89.

Eriksson, T. 1996. Executive compensation and tournament theory: Empirical tests on Danish data. Aarhus, Denmark: Aarhus University. Mimeograph.

Farber, H. 1994. The analysis of interfirm worker mobility. *Journal of Labor Economics* 12 (4): 554–94.

Farber, H., and R. Gibbons. 1996. Learning and wage dynamics. *Quarterly Journal of Economics* 111:1007–49.

Fernie, S., and D. Metcalf. 1996. "It's not what you pay it's the way that you pay it and that's what gets results": Jockeys' pay and performance. London: London School of Economics. Mimeograph.

Frank, R., and R. Hutchens. 1993. Wages, seniority, and the demand for rising consumption profiles. *Journal of Economics, Behavior and Organization* 21:251–76.

Freeman, R., and J. Medoff. 1984. *What do unions do?* New York: Basic Books.

Garen, J. 1994. Executive compensation and principal-agent theory. *Journal of Political Economy* 102:1175–99.

Gaynor, M., and M. Pauly. 1990. Compensation and productive efficiency in partnerships: Evidence from medical group practice. *Journal of Political Economy* 98: 544–74.

Gibbons, R. 1996. Incentives and careers in organizations. NBER Working Paper no. 5705. Cambridge, Mass.: National Bureau of Economic Research.

Gibbons, R., and K. J. Murphy. 1990. Relative performance evaluation for chief executive officers. *Industrial and Labor Relations Review* 43:30–52.

———. 1992. Optimal incentive contracts in the presence of career concerns. *Journal of Political Economy* 100:468–506.

Gibbons, R., and M. Waldman. 1996. A theory of wages and promotion dynamics inside a firm. Ithaca, N.Y.: Cornell University. Mimeograph.

Gibbs, M. 1995. Incentive compensation in a corporate hierarchy. *Journal of Accounting and Economics* 19:247–77.

Gibbs, M., and W. Hendricks. 1996. Are administrative pay systems a veil? Urbana: University of Illinois. Mimeograph.

Glaeser, E. 1992. Who knows what about whom. Chicago: University of Chicago. Mimeograph.

Gompers, P., and J. Lerner. 1994. An analysis of compensation in the U.S. venture capital partnership. Cambridge, Mass.: Harvard Business School. Mimeograph.

Groshen, E. 1991. Sources of intra-industry wage dispersion. *Quarterly Journal of Economics* 106:869–85.

Groshen, E., and A. Krueger. 1990. The structure of supervision and pay in hospitals. *Industrial and Labor Relations Review* 43:S134–S147.

Harris, M., and B. Holmstrom. 1982. A theory of wage dynamics. *Review of Economic Studies* 49:315–33.

Healy, P. 1985. The effect of bonus schemes on accounting decisions. *Journal of Accounting and Economics* 7:85–107.

Holmstrom, B. 1982. Managerial incentive problems: A dynamic perspective. Evanston, Ill.: Northwestern University, Kellogg School of Management. Mimeograph.

Holmstrom, B., and P. Milgrom. 1992. Multi-task principal agent analyses: Linear contracts, asset ownership and job design. *Journal of Law, Economics, and Organization* 7:24–52.

Hutchens, R. 1986. Delayed payment contracts and a firm's propensity to hire older workers. *Journal of Labor Economics* 4:439–57.

Jensen, M., and K. J. Murphy. 1990. Performance pay and top management incentives. *Journal of Political Economy* 98:225–64.

John, G., and B. Weitz. 1989. Salesforce compensation: An empirical investigation of factors related to the use of salary versus incentive compensation. *Journal of Marketing Research* 26:1–14.

Jones, D., and T. Kato. 1995. The productivity effects of employee stock-ownership plans and bonuses. *American Economic Review* 85 (3): 391–415.

Kahn, L., and P. Sherer. 1990. Contingent pay and managerial performance. *Industrial and Labor Relations Review* 43:107–21.

Kaplan, S. 1994. Top executive rewards and firm performance: A comparison of Japan and the United States. *Journal of Political Economy* 102:510–46.

Kawasaki, S., and J. McMillan. 1987. The design of contracts: Evidence from Japanese subcontracting. *Journal of the Japanese and International Economies* 1:327–49.

Knoeber, C. 1989. A real game of chicken: Contracts, tournaments and the production of broilers. *Journal of Law, Economics, and Organization* 5 (2): 271–92.

Knoeber, C., and W. Thurman. 1994. Testing the theory of tournaments: An empirical analysis of broiler production. *Journal of Labor Economics* 12:155–79.

Kotlikoff, L., and J. Gokhale. 1992. Estimating a firm's age-productivity profile using the present value of workers' earnings. *Quarterly Journal of Economics* 107:1215–43.

Krueger, A., and L. Summers. 1988. Efficiency wages and the inter-industry wage structure. *Econometrica* 56:259–93.

Larkey, P., and J. Caulkins. 1992. All above average. Pittsburgh: Carnegie-Mellon University. Mimeograph.

Lazear, E. 1981. Agency, earnings profiles, productivity, and hours restrictions. *American Economics Review* 71:606–20.

———. 1989. Pay equality and industrial politics. *Journal of Political Economy* 97:561–80.

———. 1991. The job as a concept. Chicago: University of Chicago. Mimeograph.

———. 1996. Performance pay and productivity. NBER Working Paper no. 5672. Cambridge, Mass.: National Bureau of Economic Research.

Lazear, E., and R. Moore. 1986. Incentives, productivity and labor contracts. *Quarterly Journal of Economics* 99:275–96.

Lazear, E., and S. Rosen. 1981. Rank order tournaments as optimal labor contracts. *Journal of Political Economy* 89:841–64.

Leibowitz, A., and R. Tollison. 1980. Free riding, shirking and team production in legal partnerships. *Economic Inquiry* 18:380–94.

Leonard, J. 1987. Carrots and sticks: Pay, supervision, and turnover. *Journal of Labor Economics* 5:S136–S152.

Lillard, L., and Y. Weiss. 1979. Components of variation in panel data: American scientists 1960–70. *Econometrica* 47:437–54.

Loewenstein, G., and N. Sicherman. 1991. Do workers prefer increasing wage profiles? *Journal of Labor Economics* 9:67–84.

Main, B., C. O'Reilly, and J. Wade. 1993. Top executive pay: Tournament or teamwork? *Journal of Labor Economics* 11:606–28.

Marschke, J. 1996. Incentives in a government bureaucracy. Chicago: University of Chicago. Mimeograph.

Medoff, J., and K. Abraham. 1981. Are those paid more really more productive? The case of experience. *Journal of Human Resources* 16:186–216.

Milgrom, P., and J. Roberts. 1990. The efficiency of equity in organizational decision processes. *American Economic Review* 80:154–59.

Mincer, J. 1986. Wage changes in job changes. *Research in Labor Economics* 8:171–97.

Murphy, K. J. 1986. Incentives, learning and compensation: A theoretical and empirical investigation of managerial labor contracts. *Rand Journal of Economics* 17:59–76.

Newhouse, J. 1973. The economics of group practice. *Journal of Human Resources* 8:37–56.

Oyer, P. 1997. The effect of sales incentives on business seasonality. *Quarterly Journal of Economics* 113:149–86.

Paarsch, H., and B. Shearer. 1996. Fixed wages, piece rates, and incentive effects. Quebec: University of Laval. Mimeograph.

Prendergast, C., and R. Topel. 1996. Favoritism in organizations. *Journal of Political Economy* 104 (5): 958–78.

Putterman, L. 1990. Effort, productivity, and incentives in a 1970s Chinese people's commune. *Journal of Comparative Economics* 14:88–104.

Rosen, S. 1982. Authority, control, and the distribution of earnings. *Bell Journal of Economics* 13:311–23.

———. 1986. Prizes and incentives in elimination tournaments. *American Economic Review* 76:921–39.

Rosenbaum, J. 1979. Tournament mobility: Career patterns in a corporation. *Administrative Science Quarterly* 24:220–40.

Shaefer, S. 1994. The dependence of CEO pay-performance sensitivity on the value of the firm. Stanford, Calif.: Stanford University. Mimeograph.

Sicherman, N. 1995. Gender differences in departures from a large firm. *Industrial and Labor Relations Review* 49:484–505.

Spilerman, S. 1986. Organizational rules and the features of work careers. *Research in Social Stratification and Mobility* 5:41–102.

Spilerman, S., and H. Ishida. 1994. Stratification and attainment in large Japanese firms. New York: Columbia University. Mimeograph.

Spilerman, S., and T. Petersen. 1993. Organizational structure, determinants of promotion, and gender differences in attainment. New York: Columbia University. Mimeograph.

Spurr, S., and W. Barber. 1994. The effects of performance on a worker's career: Evidence from minor league baseball. *Industrial and Labor Relations Review* 47: 692–709.

Topel, R. 1991. Specific human capital, mobility and wages: Wages increase with job seniority. *Journal of Political Economy* 99:145–76.

Topel, R., and M. Ward. 1992. Job mobility and the careers of young men. *Quarterly Journal of Economics* 107:439–79.

Weiss, A. 1987. Incentives and worker behavior. In *Information, incentives and risk sharing,* ed. H. Nalbantian. New Jersey: Rowman and Littlefield.

Comment   George A. Akerlof

This interesting paper summarizes what we can learn from data on individual firms. It describes the ways in which compensation patterns might be used to test alternative theories of internal labor markets and the theoretical problems of interpretation of these tests.

The interest in this subject comes from the different implications the various theories have for economic policy. At one pole are theories of the labor market based on perfect competition. Although compensation may not equal the marginal product of each worker at each point in time, over the course of a worker's tenure the expected value of her discounted marginal product should be equal to the expected value of her discounted compensation. If employees get more or less their marginal product in this fashion and there is an almost perfectly competitive labor market for workers, interventionist microeconomic and macroeconomic policy will be counterproductive.

In contrast, if wages depend significantly on sociological considerations, if labor markets are noncompetitive, or if there are important forms of money illusion, interventionist policy can be effective in increasing welfare. If firms, for whatever reason, pay on average more than market-clearing wages, unemployment will develop. If, in addition, there is money illusion so that wages are sticky, monetary and fiscal policy will affect the level of aggregate employment.

This paper pays special attention to three theories that can be tested from firm data. The first of these is the specific human capital theory; the second is information or learning theory; the third is implicit contract theory. The author gives an excellent survey of the findings of various researchers in firm personnel records and the implications of those findings for the three theories. However, since all of the theories are at least partially correct and they are hard to identify, the empirical findings are not very surprising. I would have liked to have seen more attention paid in the paper to the testing and implications of sociological or money illusionist theories—partly because the testing of these theories has much more potential for surprise. Because only a handful of economists will give even the intellectual time of day to such theories, rejection of the null hypothesis—that a neoclassical model enriched by human capital theory, contract theory, and information theory explains all—will have important implications. A discovery that there is something beyond the neoclassical model would be unexpected by the economic orthodoxy. In addition, such a discovery should affect the construction of macroeconomic models. An outstanding example of research of this type is the examination of interindustry wage differentials by Dickens and Katz (1986, 1987) and Krueger and Summers (1987, 1988). The results in these papers on the nature of interindustry

George Akerlof is professor of economics at the University of California, Berkeley, and a senior fellow of the Brookings Institution.

wage differentials cannot be easily explained by efficient markets and efficient contracts and have been interpreted, although not without objections, as support for efficiency wage theories.

The theme of this conference is the potential collection of new data. The author has suggested that more data should be collected on the *nature* of labor contracts. That is a wonderful idea. The difficulties discussed in the paper in identifying the different theories occur because crude data is not sufficiently informative to allow acceptance or rejection of any of the different theories. Like the author, I believe that much of the real data we need from firms will not come in the form of numbers but instead will be qualitative descriptions of compensation and personnel practices. Such information can be obtained by firm-level questionnaires. Alternatively, participant-observers can watch people closely at the workplace and interpret the meaning of their actions.

A short time ago the Census Bureau contracted with anthropologists to study reactions to the census, in order to determine where there would be important biases. I can imagine that firm-level sociological studies on wages, prices, career paths, entry and exit from firms, and forms of contracts could be very helpful in understanding how participants interpret personnel practices. Many years ago such questionnaire-based and participant-observer studies were quite common. The names of Shultz, Myers, Bakke, Dunlop, and others stand out. With the identification problems discussed in this paper from examining only data on wages, such microstudies are likely to be the only way to assess the relative importance of different theories of internal labor markets. How else are we going to discover what managers *think* they are accomplishing with their wage and promotion structures? How else could we know about gift exchange in the workplace if Blau and Homans had not observed workers closely and discovered the social meaning of their actions? A return to the research methods of yesteryear could have a very large return in our understanding of labor markets.

References

Dickens, William, and Lawrence F. Katz. 1986. Industry wage patterns and theories of wage determination. Berkeley: University of California. Mimeograph.
————. 1987. Interindustry wage differences and industry characteristics. In *Unemployment and the structure of labor markets,* ed. Kevin Lang and Jonathan S. Leonard, 48–89. New York: Blackwell.
Krueger, Alan B., and Lawrence H. Summers. 1987. Reflections on the interindustry wage structure. In *Unemployment and the structure of labor markets,* ed. Kevin Lang and Jonathan S. Leonard, 17–47. New York: Blackwell.
————. 1988. Efficiency wages and the inter-industry wage structure. *Econometrica* 56 (March): 259–93.

10 Internal and External Labor Markets: An Analysis of Matched Longitudinal Employer-Employee Data

John M. Abowd and Francis Kramarz

10.1 Introduction

For more than three decades, since the publication of Gary Becker's classic treatise on human capital in 1964 and Jacob Mincer's fundamental empirical analysis of earnings in 1974, the study of wage determination has relied heavily on models of labor supply and the analysis of individual wage outcomes. The supply-based models considered the labor market as a whole, the external market, to represent essentially all of the economically important possibilities for the individual. Glenn Cain recognized in 1976 that the labor-supply-based analysis of earnings determination would have difficulty explaining the internal (to the firm) market phenomena that were then called the "segmented" labor markets. In 1986 both Sherwin Rosen and Robert Willis called for increased analysis of matched employer-employee data as a necessary part of the unification of the supply-side and demand-side models of compensation and employment outcomes. The external labor market represents a heterogeneous collection of employment opportunities that might be available as an alternative to any particular person's current job. The internal labor market represents a heterogeneous collection of compensation and human resource management policies that describe the career possibilities for an individual who does not change employers. There is now a general consensus within labor economics

John M. Abowd is professor of labor economics at Cornell University and a research associate of the National Bureau of Economic Research. Francis Kramarz is head of the Research Department CREST/CNRS at the Institut National de la Statistique et des Etudes Economiques (INSEE) in Paris, France.

The authors are grateful for research support in the United States by the National Science Foundation (grants SBR 91-11186 and SBR 93-21053) and in France by the Département de la Recherche in the Centre de Recherche en Economie et Statistique (CREST) at INSEE. The data used in this paper are confidential, but the authors' access is not exclusive. Other researchers interested in using these data should contact CREST, ENSAE, 15 bd Gabriel Péri, 92245 Malakoff Cedex, France.

that symmetric modeling of the employee and employer outcomes and detailed information on both the employer and employee are essential to distinguish internal and external labor market factors. More important, longitudinal data on employers and employees, data in which individuals are observed at multiple employers and a significant percentage of employees are observed within sampled firms, are required to identify the basic individual and firm effects that are at the heart of internal and external labor market models and descriptions.

We begin our analysis by supposing that real compensation costs per employee can be described as the sum of effects due to observable human capital investments by the individual, heterogeneous individual factors revealed to the labor market (but not to the statistician, except by inference), and heterogeneous employer factors. The internal labor market is modeled as factors specific to the employing firm. These include the firm effect in the compensation equation and also the firm's choices regarding the distribution of individual characteristics (including unobservable heterogeneity). The external labor market is the description of the opportunities available to a given individual at a given time. These include the returns to human capital and the returns to search among heterogeneous potential employers. Building on the analysis of Abowd, Kramarz, and Margolis (in press, AKM hereafter) we define a measure of an employee's external wage rate that depends on the worker's labor market characteristics and wage outcomes of other workers with the same characteristics (those observed at different employers). We also define an internal-external wage differential that we show depends only on the firm's compensation policy and the correlation of its human resource management policies with policies of other firms in the labor market. Our measure of the internal-external wage gap can only be identified using longitudinal data on employees and employers. We use estimates from AKM to assess the correlation among the observable human capital, individual heterogeneity, and firm heterogeneity components of compensation. We then use our sample estimates to examine the sources of interindustry wage differentials and firm size-wage differentials for French firms. For France, person and firm effects are positively but weakly correlated. The firm size-wage effect is due almost entirely to variation in the external wage rate (person effects). Ninety percent of the interindustry wage differential is due to variation in the external wage rate.

There are two major barriers to the statistical and economic analysis of models with unobservable personal and firm heterogeneity. First, one must be able to quantify the components of pay related to individual characteristics, individual heterogeneity, employer characteristics, and employer heterogeneity. In an imperfectly designed sample, one may not be able to distinguish among individual and firm effects and may, as a consequence, attribute too much of the empirical variation to one source. This purely statistical phenomenon places heavy demands on the data—demands that can only rarely be satisfied. Second, in the face of the measured heterogeneity of labor market outcomes among individuals and among employers, modeling the economic structure of the worker's "opportunity wage" or the firm's "internal compensation policy" is not straightforward, even if statistical components associated with the individual or the firm are estimable.

Section 10.2 presents a linear model of components of compensation based on a statistical decomposition of real annual compensation costs per employee. The relation between various sources of heterogeneity in wages and interindustry or firm size differentials is explained. Section 10.3 describes our analysis of a matched longitudinal sample of French employers and employees. Section 10.4 presents our results on the employer size-wage differential. Section 10.5 presents our results on the interindustry wage differential. Section 10.6 concludes.

10.2   A Model of Internal and External Wages

We begin with a straightforward model, taken directly from AKM, for the statistical structure of individual compensation:

$$(1) \qquad\qquad w_{it} = \theta_i + \psi_{J(i,t)} + x_{it}\beta + \varepsilon_{it},$$

where w_{it} is the natural logarithm of pay per unit of time for individual i in period t; θ_i is the part related to the individual, including observable non-time-varying characteristics; $\psi_{J(i,t)}$ is the part related to the firm;[1] $x_{it}\beta$ is the part related to individual and general time-varying characteristics; ε_{it} is the idiosyncratic part uncorrelated with θ, ψ, and $x\beta$; and the function $J(i,t)$ gives the identity of the employing firm. For a sample of N individuals followed over $t = 1, \ldots, T_i$ years, the general statistical structure of equation (1) is

$$(2) \qquad\qquad E\begin{bmatrix} \theta_i \\ \psi_{J(i,t)it} \\ x_{it}\beta \\ \varepsilon_{it} \end{bmatrix} = \begin{bmatrix} \mu \\ 0 \\ \bar{x}\beta \\ 0 \end{bmatrix},$$

$$(3) \qquad\qquad V\begin{bmatrix} \theta_i \\ \psi_{J(i,t)it} \\ x_{it}\beta \\ \varepsilon_{it} \end{bmatrix} = \begin{bmatrix} \sigma_{\theta\theta} & \sigma_{\theta\psi} & \Sigma_{\theta x}\beta & 0 \\ \sigma_{\psi\theta} & \sigma_{\psi\psi} & \Sigma_{\psi x}\beta & 0 \\ \beta'\Sigma_{x\theta} & \beta'\Sigma_{x\psi} & \beta'\Sigma_{xx}\beta & 0 \\ 0 & 0 & 0 & \sigma_{\varepsilon\varepsilon} \end{bmatrix},$$

where μ is the overall intercept of w, Σ is the covariance matrix for $[\theta, \psi, x]$, and σ represents elements of Σ. Using data for 1.1 million French workers

---

1. The firm effect may vary across individuals and over time because of individual-specific seniority effects, which we ignore in this discussion for simplicity.

Table 10.1   **Covariances and Correlations among Components of Real Compensation for a Sample of French Workers**

	Individual Effect	Firm Effect	Individual Characteristics
Individual effect θ	*0.1811*	*0.0027*	*0.0046*
Firm effect ψ	0.1079	*0.0042*	*0.0003*
Individual characteristics $x\beta$	0.0787	0.0325	*0.0192*

Source: Abowd, Kramarz, and Margolis (in press, table VI).

Note: Italic numbers (above the diagonal) are covariances; roman numbers (below the diagonal) are correlations. The correlations with the individual effect have been corrected for sampling variability (not required for the other correlations).

followed from 1976 to 1987, AKM estimated that the covariance matrix in equation (3) had the form shown in table 10.1.[2]

Equations (1), (2), and (3) can be used to construct direct measures of an individual's internal and external wage rates. Define the internal wage rate as the expected wage rate given employment in firm j:

$$(4) \qquad E[w_{it} \mid \theta_i, \ x_{it}, \ J(i,t) = j] = \theta_i + \psi_{jit} + x_{it}\beta.$$

Define the external wage rate, w^a, as the expected wage rate given alternative employment in a firm other than j:

$$(5) \qquad E[w_{it}^a \mid \theta_i, \ x_{it}, \ J(i,t) = j' \neq j] = \theta_i + E[\psi_{j'} \mid \theta_i, \ x_{it}] + x_{it}\beta.$$

The expectation in equation (5) is taken over all possible employers $j' \neq j$ according to the distribution of employer effects in the population of employees conditional on the individual effect and observable characteristics. We assume that the expectation on the right-hand side of equation (5) is zero. Hence, the expected difference between an individual's internal and external wage rates is given by

$$E[w_{it} - w_{it}^a \mid \theta_i, \ x_{it}, \ J(i,t) = j] = \psi_j \ .$$

In data where individual and firm characteristics are both observable for representative longitudinal samples of the relevant populations, a natural estimator of the gap between an individual's internal and external wage rates is given by the least squares estimator of equation (1) from the sample of individuals for the vector of firm effects $\hat{\psi}_j$ for $j = 1, \ldots, J$, where J is the total

---

2. AKM actually estimate a model in which the individual effect is decomposed into a part due to permanent (non-time-varying) individual characteristics and a part due to nonobservable (to the statistician) individual characteristics. The effect labeled θ in this paper is the full person effect from AKM. Similarly, the firm effect in AKM is decomposed into a part due to initial differences in firm compensation policies and a part due to differential slopes on seniority within the firm. The effect labeled ψ in this paper is the full firm effect from AKM.

number of firms in the sample. Similarly, a natural estimator for the individual-specific component of the wage rate is the least squares estimator of the person effects $\hat{\theta}_i$ for $i = 1, \ldots, N$. This leads to the natural least squares decomposition of equation (1). The statistical problem arises because the full least squares solution to equation (1) is difficult or impossible to compute for samples sufficiently large to permit estimation of a reasonable percentage of the firm effects. AKM propose a solution based on the use of a set of variables z_{it} that do not appear in the model (1) and for which they maintain the assumptions

$$\text{Cov}[\theta_i, \ \psi_{J(i,t)} | Z] = 0 \quad \text{and} \quad \text{Cov}[x_{it}, \ \psi_{J(i,t)} | Z] = 0$$

$$\text{for all } t = 1, \ldots, T_i \text{ and } i = 1, \ldots, N,$$

where Z is the matrix of all observations of the variables z_{it}. Under these maintained assumptions, there are a variety of potential estimators for the effects in equation (1). In this paper we focus on the implications of the estimator in which the person effects are estimated first and the firm effects are estimated second, conditional on z_{it}. The estimation formulas give the following statistical decomposition of equation (1):[3]

(6) $$w_{it} = \hat{\theta}_i + x_{it}\hat{\beta} + z_{it}\hat{\lambda} + \hat{u}_{it},$$

(7) $$\hat{u}_{it} = \hat{\psi}_{J(i,t)} + \hat{\varepsilon}_{it},$$

where the circumflex over the indicated effect means that it was estimated by least squares in the given equation, either equation (6) or (7). An individual's estimated internal wage rate is then

(8) $$\hat{w}_{it} = \hat{\theta}_i + \hat{\psi}_{J(i,t)} + x_{it}\hat{\beta},$$

and an individual's estimated external wage rate is

(9) $$\hat{w}_{it}^a = \hat{\theta}_i + x_{it}\hat{\beta},$$

An alternative to direct estimation of the internal-external wage difference is to use estimates of the person and firm effects to decompose conventional aggregated components of compensation, such as industry effects or firm size effects, into the part due to person and firm effects. Suppose that one considered the following model as an alternative to equation (1):

(10) $$w_{it} = \kappa_{K(i,t)} + x_{it}\beta + \varepsilon_{it},$$

where the effect κ measures the effect of some aggregation, say industry or firm size, and the function $K(i,t)$ classifies the individual into the aggregated

---

3. The estimator discussed here is called "order-dependent: persons first" by AKM. It is one of the two estimators they used for most of their analyses.

category k. AKM show that the least squares estimator of κ can be expressed as a properly weighted average of the average person and firm effects within the category k:[4]

$$(11) \qquad\qquad \hat{\kappa}_k = \overline{\theta}_k + \overline{\psi}_k ,$$

where $\overline{\theta}_k$ and $\overline{\psi}_k$ are the average firm and person effects, respectively, in category k, given the individual characteristics, x.[5] The interpretation of equation (11) is also straightforward: given the individual characteristics, x, the measured average effect of being in category k consists of the amount by which the external wage rate differs from the average $\overline{\theta}_k - \mu$ plus the amount by which the internal wage rate differs from the average $\overline{\psi}_k - 0$, in both cases given x.

10.3   Characteristics of the French Longitudinal Matched Employer-Employee Data

Our analysis sample is the same one used by AKM. The reader is invited to consult the data appendix therein for details on the construction of the employee and firm characteristics. We review only the variables used in the present analysis.

The longitudinal sample of employees is a 1/25th sample of all persons for whom employers filed the mandatory "Déclaration annuelle des salaires" (DAS), the French equivalent of the U.S. social security earnings report (see INSEE 1990c; Lollivier n.d.). A person is sampled if he or she was born in October of an even-numbered year. Once sampled, all data from 1976 until 1987 are available (except for the years 1981 and 1983 when the underlying administrative data were not sampled). We converted the reported net salaries of the sampled individuals into annual equivalent real total compensation cost using information on the days worked during the year and on the employer and employee payroll tax rates in effect each year.[6] From the DAS and supplemental sources, AKM were able to measure labor force experience, education, sex, region of employment, and seniority at the employing firm. These variables, as well as data year, were included in the statistical model for estimating the

---

4. The effect κ in this paper is called κ^{**} in AKM. The average person and firm effects within the category k are estimated conditional on the time-varying observable characteristics x and any observable non-time-varying personal characteristics (e.g., education and sex).

5. For simplicity we have not used the matrix weighting formulas to express the averages in eq. (9). If the variables x_{it} do not enter the equation, these are simple averages; otherwise, the formulas in AKM must be used.

6. The difference between net salary and gross salary in the French reporting system is employee payments for social benefits (health insurance, retirement income, unemployment insurance, workers' compensation, family support, etc.), which are collected through the imposition of a variable rate payroll tax. The difference between gross salary and total compensation costs is employer payments for these same social benefits, which are also collected through the imposition of a (different) variable rate payroll tax. We used the total compensation costs as our measure of the employee's wage rate.

Table 10.2   **Distribution of French Workers by Number of Employers and Years in Sample**

	Number of Employers			
Years in Sample	1	1a	2	3+
1	318,627	247,532		
2	75,299	57,411	51,066	
3+	298,572	254,105	203,710	219,031
Total	692,498	559,048	254,776	219,031

Source: Abowd, Kramarz, and Margolis (in press, table I).
Note: Individuals in column 1a had only one employer but worked for a company employing a mover. $N = 1,166,305$.

coefficients β in equation (1). The effect of observable characteristics was fully interacted in sex and included unrestricted individual and firm effects.[7] For the present paper, the internal-external wage differentials given in equations (7) and (8) for the DAS individuals were estimated using the AKM estimates of $x_{it}\hat{\beta}$.

Our sample of firms is also the same one used by AKM from the "Echantillon d'entreprises" (INSEE 1990a, 1990b). This sample of 21,642 firms is representative of private French industry. The agricultural and governmental sectors were not sampled. A firm (*entreprise*) is a business unit engaged in a principal economic activity that involves substantially all of the component establishments. For all firms, regardless of their presence in the "Echantillon d'entreprises," an estimate of the size of the firm is available based on the sampling method used for the DAS. The firm size measure, used below, is an estimate of average employment over the calendar year for all the sampled years that the firm appears in the DAS.

Table 10.2 summarizes the pattern of individual responses and employers in our analysis data set. An important consideration in the identification of the person and firm effects in equation (1) is the extent of within-sample mobility between firms. Column 1a of table 10.2 shows that a very large fraction of our single-employer individuals worked for a firm that employed a worker who also worked for another firm in the sample. This feature of large administrative databases is the reason why we are able to estimate person and firm effects for almost 90 percent of the observations.

10.4   Results of the Analysis of Firm Size-Wage Differentials

To study the extent to which the firm size-wage differential is related to our measure of the internal-external wage gap, we constructed an estimate of $\hat{\kappa}_k =$

---

7. See AKM (table III) for the full set of coefficients in this statistical analysis.

Table 10.3   **Analysis of the Importance of Internal and External Factors in the Firm Size-Wage Differential**

Firm Size	N (1)	Average Firm Size in Cell (2)	Raw Firm Size Effect (3)	Average Person Effect (4)	Average Firm Effect (5)
0–25	1,226,844	11.4	−0.092	−0.068	−0.016
26–50	614,604	34.4	−0.021	−0.011	−0.007
51–100	535,169	70.5	−0.015	−0.009	−0.006
101–200	449,723	142.7	−0.015	−0.012	−0.005
201–300	257,305	245.7	0.010	0.010	−0.004
301–400	164,426	346.6	0.014	0.015	−0.004
401–500	140,786	447.6	0.029	0.028	−0.003
501–600	110,075	548.1	0.023	0.023	−0.005
601–700	95,336	648.7	0.033	0.030	−0.002
701–800	91,048	747.5	0.053	0.050	−0.001
801–900	72,221	850.1	0.051	0.047	−0.002
901–1,000	56,384	947.4	0.038	0.034	−0.001
1,001–1,250	104,416	1,118.4	0.035	0.035	−0.004
1,251–1,500	90,103	1,362.1	0.063	0.058	0.000
1,501–1,750	68,537	1,621.9	0.048	0.041	−0.003
1,751–2,000	60,723	1,882.5	0.056	0.049	0.002
2,001–2,500	117,750	2,224.6	0.042	0.042	−0.005
2,501–3,000	83,316	2,728.7	0.075	0.068	−0.002
3,001–4,000	138,872	3,542.5	0.084	0.079	−0.001
4,001–5,000	102,670	4,427.4	0.054	0.047	−0.002
5,001–7,500	138,154	6,165.6	0.075	0.066	0.002
7,501–10,000	69,059	8,437.2	0.132	0.106	0.008
10,001–15,000	76,514	12,290.3	0.043	0.034	0.000
15,001–20,000	41,252	17,304.1	0.090	0.068	0.006
20,001 or more	399,821	101,444.2	0.111	0.032	0.081

Source: Abowd, Kramarz, and Margolis (in press, estimates related to table VIII).
Note: The maximum standard error for the raw firm size effect and the average person effect is 0.003, while the maximum standard error for the average firm effect is 0.0005.

$\overline{\theta}_k + \overline{\psi}_k$ in equation (11) for 25 firm size cells as shown in table 10.3. As is clear from the table, French firms display the same strong firm size-wage relation that Brown and Medoff (1989) found for American firms.[8] Column (3) shows the estimated differential for firms of that size as compared to zero, the arbitrary reference point, and is the estimated $\hat{\kappa}_k$, controlling for x. Column (4) shows the average, within the firm size cell, of the person effects, again con-

8. The reported results adjust for time-varying personal characteristics x and for measurable non-time-varying personal characteristics (e.g., education) so that person and firm effects reflect only nonobservable heterogeneity. The amount of the firm size-wage effect not related to differences in personal unobservable heterogeneity is much smaller in France than the amount reported by Brown and Medoff (1989, table 2) in their longitudinal analysis.

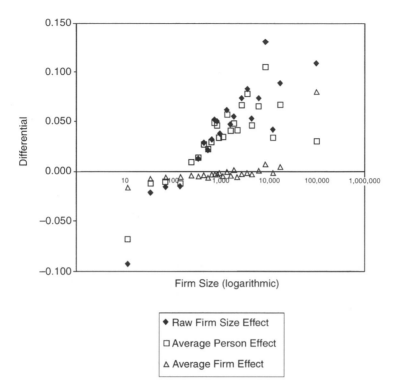

Fig. 10.1   Firm size-wage effects in France

trolling for x, and is the estimated $\bar{\theta}_k$. Finally, column (5) shows the average, within the firm size cell, of the firm effects, again controlling for x, and is the estimated $\bar{\psi}_k$. Figure 10.1 presents the results graphically. Except for the largest firm size, virtually all of the firm size-wage effect in France is explained by the average person effect in the firm size group. In France, the largest firms are almost all stock-based companies in which the government is the sole or majority shareholder. The presence of a firm size effect in the wage rates of the employees of these firms that is not due to a high average person effect could be interpreted as evidence of rent splitting between the government and the employees of these firms. Alternatively, these firms may also be the ones that use technologies most conducive to compensation plans that involve a distinction between the internal and external wage rates.

10.5   Results of the Analysis of Interindustry Wage Differentials

We also used our estimates of the internal-external wage differential to revisit the question of interindustry wage differentials in France. Table 10.4

Table 10.4   **Analysis of the Importance of Internal and External Factors in the Interindustry Wage Differential**

Industry[a]	N (1)	Raw Industry Effect (2)	Average Person Effect (3)	Average Firm Effect (4)
04 Coal mining	6,020	0.251	0.218	0.023
05 Crude petroleum and natural gas extraction	15,009	0.340	0.316	0.002
06 Electricity production and supply	52,017	0.188	0.084	0.109
08 Water and city heating supply	9,064	0.137	0.109	−0.001
09 Ferrous metal mining	88	0.056	0.048	−0.024
10 Iron and steel foundries	48,708	0.082	0.053	0.008
11 Primary metal manufacturing	18,385	−0.031	−0.051	−0.003
13 Primary nonmetallic manufacturing	23,694	0.107	0.079	0.003
14 Miscellaneous mineral production	2,622	0.036	0.008	0.002
15 Cement, stone, and concrete products	63,544	0.041	−0.061	−0.007
16 Glass and glass products	27,307	0.113	0.084	0.001
17 Basic chemical manufacture	52,526	0.193	0.166	0.002
18 Allied chemical products, soaps, and cosmetics	46,553	0.110	0.099	−0.001
19 Pharmaceuticals	27,691	0.170	0.151	0.007
20 Founderies and smelting works	30,673	−0.015	−0.040	0.001
21 Metal works	154,626	−0.002	−0.023	−0.007
22 Farm machinery and equipment	17,755	−0.025	−0.048	−0.004
23 Metalworking machinery manufacture	24,740	0.038	0.012	−0.004
24 Industrial machinery manufacture	100,679	0.044	0.020	−0.005
25 Material handling machines and equipment	28,277	0.052	0.022	0.000
26 Ordnance	3,073	0.110	0.075	0.000
27 Office and accounting machines	20,918	0.328	0.283	0.018
28 Electrical machinery equipment	82,859	0.025	−0.005	−0.001
29 Electronic computing equipment	101,851	0.058	0.026	0.001
30 Household appliances	21,367	−0.016	−0.049	−0.002
31 Motor vehicles, trains, and land transport manufacture	180,678	0.027	−0.014	0.024
32 Ship and boat building	20,145	0.101	0.065	0.007
33 Aircraft and parts manufacture	45,188	0.182	0.153	0.008
34 Professional and scientific equipment manufacture	34,121	0.017	−0.010	−0.006
35 Meat products	30,861	−0.003	−0.033	−0.004
36 Dairy products	27,123	0.061	0.023	0.005
37 Canned and preserved products	14,528	−0.004	−0.051	0.002
38 Bakery products	46,156	−0.067	−0.095	−0.012
39 Grain mill and cereal products	25,195	0.044	0.008	0.002
40 Miscellaneous food preparations	29,140	0.082	0.043	0.006
41 Beverage industries	21,277	0.118	0.083	0.007
42 Tobacco products manufacture	3,464	0.246	0.212	0.007
43 Knitting mills, threads, and artificial fibers	4,132	0.052	0.022	0.006

Table 10.4 (continued)

Industry[a]	N (1)	Raw Industry Effect (2)	Average Person Effect (3)	Average Firm Effect (4)
44 Textile products	112,839	−0.082	−0.099	−0.005
45 Leather products except footwear	14,004	−0.105	−0.120	−0.011
46 Footwear	26,097	−0.077	−0.097	−0.007
47 Apparel, clothing, and allied products	91,927	−0.098	−0.115	−0.007
48 Lumber mills	36,965	−0.111	−0.115	−0.009
49 Furniture and fixtures manufacture	42,245	−0.097	−0.098	−0.009
50 Pulp and paper mills and packaging products	49,447	0.065	0.037	−0.003
51 Printing and publishing	81,786	0.126	0.115	−0.004
52 Rubber products	39,252	0.026	−0.008	0.013
53 Plastic products	46,464	0.014	−0.015	−0.004
54 Miscellaneous manufacturing industries	43,463	−0.068	−0.077	−0.006
55 Construction	580,802	−0.119	−0.076	−0.012
56 Waste product management	8,978	−0.123	−0.090	−0.013
57 Wholesale food trade	94,773	−0.009	−0.004	−0.007
58 Wholesale nonfood trade	100,879	0.020	0.029	−0.008
59 Interindustry wholesale trade	139,851	0.061	0.068	−0.007
60 Commercial intermediaries	23,632	0.091	0.105	−0.013
61 Retail food and supermarkets	63,039	−0.037	−0.035	0.000
62 Retail specialty and neighborhood food trade	110,251	−0.103	−0.091	−0.008
63 Retail general merchandise and nonfood trade	30,734	−0.040	−0.033	−0.005
64 Retail specialty nonfood trade	202,973	−0.059	−0.043	−0.014
65 Automobile dealers, auto parts, and repair trade	131,469	−0.059	−0.023	−0.008
66 Miscellaneous repair services	7,733	−0.096	−0.056	−0.013
67 Hotels, motels, bars, and restaurants	171,703	−0.132	−0.103	−0.013
68 Railroad transportation	94,582	0.051	−0.135	0.207
69 Bus, taxicab, and other urban transit	105,248	−0.039	−0.029	−0.009
70 Inland water transportation	1,076	−0.011	−0.017	−0.001
71 Marine transport and coastal shipping	3,469	0.191	0.187	−0.001
72 Air transportation	18,400	0.269	0.256	0.018
73 Allied transportation and warehousing services	12,739	0.069	0.066	−0.003
74 Travel agencies	50,459	0.015	0.015	−0.005
75 Telecommunications and postal services	3,036	0.069	0.070	−0.008
76 Financial holding companies	4,457	0.299	0.301	0.004
77 Advertising and consulting services	275,102	0.038	0.070	−0.016
78 Brokers, credit agencies, and insurance sales	20,119	0.076	0.108	−0.005
79 Commercial real estate development and sales	38,615	−0.045	−0.007	−0.012

(*continued*)

Table 10.4   (continued)

Industry[a]	N (1)	Raw Industry Effect (2)	Average Person Effect (3)	Average Firm Effect (4)
80 Nonresidential goods rental services	14,453	0.031	0.057	−0.004
81 Real estate renting and leasing	28,879	−0.080	−0.048	−0.013
82 Commercial education services	7,141	−0.141	−0.092	−0.016
83 Commercial research services	3,837	0.165	0.182	−0.005
84 Commercial health services	368,696	0.064	0.089	−0.001
85 Commercial social services	35,987	−0.120	−0.094	−0.007
86 Commercial entertainment and recreation services	27,719	0.111	0.127	0.005
87 Miscellaneous commercial services	85,144	−0.246	−0.207	−0.023
88 Insurance carriers	53,292	0.099	0.124	−0.001
89 Banks and financial institutions	138,909	0.172	0.188	0.003
Weighted adjusted standard deviation		0.098	0.090	0.032

Source: Abowd, Kramarz, and Margolis (in press, table VII).

Notes: Standard errors available on request. Except for ferrous metal, the maximum standard error for the raw industry effect and the average person effect is 0.006 and for the average firm effect is 0.001. The weighted average standard deviation is based on the formula from Krueger and Summers (1988).

[a]Translation of the Nomenclature d'Activités Productives–100 to SIC two-digit.

shows the basic interindustry wage differentials at the two-digit level for the sample of French firms. These basic differentials are adjusted for time-varying individual characteristics, x, and non-time-varying characteristics so that they represent only the unobservable personal and firm-level heterogeneity. Column (2) is our estimate of $\hat{\kappa}_k = \bar{\theta}_k + \bar{\psi}_k$ for the two-digit industrial classification. The overall magnitude of the interindustry wage differentials in France is not as great as in the United States (compare our weighted standard deviation of 0.098 to the Krueger and Summers 1988 estimate of 0.160). Column (3) shows the part of the interindustry wage differential that is the average person effect within the industry, the estimated $\bar{\theta}_k$. The weighted adjusted standard deviation of this average person effect is 0.090, so it is clear that person effects represent the major part of the interindustry wage differential in France. Column (4) is the average firm effect within the industry, the estimated $\bar{\psi}_k$. The weighted adjusted standard deviation of the firm effect is only 0.032; thus firm effects account for only about 10 percent of the total interindustry wage differential in France.[9] Virtually all of the interindustry wage differential in France is due

9. The decomposition is not orthogonal because our method permits the average person and firm effects to be correlated across individuals, firms, and industries. Our estimates are not comparable to Groshen (1991) because she cannot control for individual heterogeneity except through an observable occupation effect.

to the tendency to employ individuals with high external wage rates (high θ_j). Evidently, accounting for the higher external wage rates of employees in high-wage industries is an important part of understanding the economic basis of these differentials.[10]

10.6   Conclusions

We have proposed a new measure of external wage rates that is identified in matched longitudinal individual-firm data. Using this measure, in conjunction with other firm and individual data, we have shown that virtually all of the firm size-wage effect (adjusted for individual characteristics) is due to the tendency of large firms to employ individuals with high external wage rates. Similarly, about 90 percent of the interindustry wage differential, again adjusted for individual characteristics, is due to the tendency of high-wage industries to employ individuals with high external wage rates. We believe that these calculations demonstrate, once again, the importance of matched individual-firm data, particularly longitudinal data, for understanding the structure of the labor market.

References

Abowd, John M., Francis Kramarz, and David Margolis. In press. High wage workers and high wage firms. *Econometrica.*

Becker, Gary S. (1964) 1993. *Human capital: A theoretical and empirical analysis with special reference to education,* 3d ed. Chicago: University of Chicago Press.

Brown, Charles, and James Medoff. 1989. The employer size-wage effect. *Journal of Political Economy* 97:1027–59.

Cain, Glenn. 1976. The challenge of segmented labor market theories to orthodox theory. *Journal of Economic Literature* 14 (December): 1215–57.

Groshen, Erica. 1991. Sources of the inter-industry wage structure. *Quarterly Journal of Economics* 106:869–84.

Institut National de la Statistique et des Etudes Economiques (INSEE). 1990a. Echantillon d'entreprises fichier de référence de l'échantillon, no. 06/G231. Paris: Institut National de la Statistique et des Etudes Economiques.

———. 1990b. Echantillon d'entreprises: Mise à disposition des données BIC, no. 64/G231. Paris: Institut National de la Statistique et des Etudes Economiques.

———. 1990c. Echantillon d'entreprises mise à disposition de données tirées des DADS, no. 73/G231. Paris: Institut National de la Statistique et des Etudes Economiques.

Krueger, Alan B., and Lawrence Summers. 1988. Efficiency wages and inter-industry wage structure. *Econometrica* 56 (March): 259–94.

10. It is interesting to note, especially in conjunction with the firm size-wage coefficient for the largest firm size category, that the estimated average person effect for the railroad transportation industry, a national monopoly called the SNCF, is large and negative while the average firm effect in this industry is large and positive. This again supports the rent-sharing interpretation we made above.

Lollivier, Stephan. n.d. *Le panel DAS de 1967 à 1982* (includes unpublished supplementary tables to 1987). Paris: Institut National de la Statistique et des Etudes Economiques.

Mincer, Jacob. 1974. *Schooling experience and earnings.* New York: Columbia University Press.

Rosen, Sherwin. 1986. The theory of equalizing differences. In *Handbook of labor economics,* ed. O. Ashenfelter and R. Layard. Amsterdam: North-Holland.

Willis, Robert. 1986. Wage determinants: A survey and reinterpretation of human capital earnings functions. In *Handbook of labor economics,* ed. O. Ashenfelter and R. Layard. Amsterdam: North-Holland.

11 The Worker-Establishment Characteristics Database

Kenneth R. Troske

11.1 Introduction

A data set combining information on the characteristics of both workers and their employers has long been a grail for labor economists. In his article in the *Handbook of Labor Economics* Sherwin Rosen writes: "On the empirical side of these questions the greatest potential for future progress rests in developing more suitable sources of data on the nature of selection and matching between workers and firms. Virtually no matched worker-firm records are available for empirical research, but obviously are crucial for the precise measurement of job and personal attributes required for empirical calculations" (1986, 688).[1]

The motivation behind the Rosen quote is that existing data sources have proved inadequate for understanding the matching of workers and employers in the labor market. Currently, almost all empirical work in labor economics relies on either worker surveys with little information about the characteristics of a worker's employer or establishment surveys with little information about the characteristics of workers in the establishment. Obviously, a more complete understanding of the sorting of workers and employers in the labor market is required before we will begin to understand a number of current puzzles in labor economics such as rising wage inequality or the establishment size-wage

Kenneth R. Troske is assistant professor of economics at the University of Missouri, Columbia. This work was conducted while the author was an economist at the Center for Economic Studies, U.S. Bureau of the Census.

The author thanks Will Carrington, Stacey Cole, Tim Dunne, Brian Greenberg, Erica Groshen, Robert McGuckin, Nash Monsour, Brian Richards, Richard Sigman, SuZanne Troske, and seminar participants at the Bureau of the Census for helpful comments. All remaining errors are the responsibility of the author. The opinions expressed herein are solely those of the author and do not reflect the opinions of the Bureau of the Census.

1. In another article in the *Handbook of Labor Economics* Robert Willis (1986) writes, "Future progress in this area will hinge critically on the development of data which links information on the individual characteristics of workers and their household with data on the firms who employ them."

premium. As the Rosen quote makes clear, further understanding of the matching of workers and employers will only come about through the use of employer-employee matched data.

Employer-employee matched data would also prove useful in a number of other fields in economics. For example, economists interested in estimating production functions at either the aggregate or plant level have long been concerned about possible biases resulting from treating labor as a unidimensional input in production (Griliches 1969, 1970). Estimating production functions with employer-employee matched data allows researchers to avoid this problem by enabling them to treat labor as a multidimensional input in the production function.

The Worker-Establishment Characteristics Database (WECD) represents just such an employer-employee matched data set. Containing 199,557 manufacturing workers matched to 16,144 manufacturing establishments, the WECD is the largest worker-firm matched data set available for the United States. The primary purpose of this paper is to describe the data set and to assess its quality. In addition, I explore some of the issues that can be investigated using employer-employee matched data and discuss preliminary plans for creating larger, more representative versions of the WECD.

The WECD is created from two data sources. The first is the Sample Detail File (SDF), which contains all individual responses to the 1990 decennial census one-in-six long form. The second is the 1990 Standard Statistical Establishment List (SSEL), which is a complete list of all establishments operating in the United States in 1990. The WECD is constructed by using detailed location and industry information available in both data sets to assign an establishment identifier to a subset of manufacturing worker records in the SDF. This identifier in turn enables the worker data to be matched to establishment data available in the Longitudinal Research Database (LRD).[2] Each linked record provides both cross-sectional demographic information for workers such as age, sex, race, marital status, and earnings and longitudinal information for workers' employers such as the total value of output, cost of materials, investment, and total employment.

I assess the quality of the data in three steps. First, I examine the accuracy of the employer-employee match. Second, I ask whether these data are representative of the underlying population of manufacturing workers and establishments. Third, I examine whether these data can replicate results obtained by previous researchers using alternative data sources.

Results from this analysis are somewhat mixed. On the positive side, several facts suggest that most WECD workers are matched to the correct establish-

---

2. The WECD is limited to manufacturing workers and plants for two reasons. First, preliminary analysis suggested that it would be impossible to match nonmanufacturing employers and employees given the limited place-of-work information, and second, the LRD only contains data for manufacturing plants. The availability of plant data depends on the year. In Census of Manufactures years (all years ending in a 2 or 7) data are available for all plants in existence. However, in all other years data are only available for plants included in the Annual Survey of Manufactures.

ments. First, the matching of worker and establishment data produces two estimates of average earnings for each establishment. The average difference between these two estimates is less than 5 percent, and the two estimates are positively and significantly correlated. Second, establishments in the WECD have on average 16 percent of their workforce matched, which is the expected match rate given the sampling frame of the SDF. Another positive finding is that parameter estimates from regressions of wages on worker or plant characteristics are almost identical to results from alternative data sets.

On the negative side, only 6 percent of manufacturing workers in the SDF and 5 percent of manufacturing plants in the SSEL appear in the WECD, and this match rate varies by industry, plant location, and plant size. In addition, the WECD is not a representative sample of either workers or plants. The WECD contains a larger proportion of white, male, married, production workers than the SDF, and relative to all plants in the SSEL, the WECD contains a larger proportion of large, old, urban establishments and establishments located in the northeastern and midwestern regions of the country. However, using weights based on the probability that a plant appears in the WECD, one can produce estimates of worker and plant characteristics that are very similar to estimates of these characteristics found using the SDF and SSEL data.

Because the WECD does not contain a representative sample of workers and employers and we only have indirect evidence on whether workers are being matched to the correct establishments, one needs to use these data with caution. As is the case with any new data source, the usefulness of these data can only be established by using them in empirical research and comparing the results found with these data to those obtained using alternative data sources. Nevertheless, the results from this analysis suggest that the WECD is appropriate for testing hypotheses about relationships between variables derived from theoretical models—relationships that should hold for any sample of plants or workers, not just a representative sample of these groups.[3] Of course, it must be recognized that results based on these data only apply to a select group of workers and plants and may not generalize to the entire population. However, even with these limitations, these data offer a unique opportunity to examine a number of previously intractable issues.

Apart from the concerns about the representativeness of these data, the primary limitation of the WECD is that it only contains information for manufacturing workers and employers. To try to address this problem, and to make the data more representative, future versions of the WECD will be created from data with much more detailed place-of-work information. While these data were originally collected for workers in the decennial census, they were destroyed prior to the start of this project. However, in the future, this more de-

---

3. E.g., the competitive model of wage determination says that a worker's wage should equal the worker's marginal product. This should be true for all workers—not just a representative sample of workers. Therefore, we should be able to test this hypothesis using any available sample of workers. However, to conclude that this theory is true for all workers in the labor market we would need to test this hypothesis on a random sample of workers.

tailed place-of-work information for workers will be saved, making it possible to create larger, more representative versions of the WECD that contain workers and employers from all sectors of the economy.

The rest of the paper proceeds as follows. Section 11.2 discusses the data sets used to match workers to establishments and outlines the matching process. Section 11.3 investigates the accuracy of the match. Section 11.4 presents examples of how these data can be used in empirical work to increase our understanding of the wage determination process. Section 11.5 summarizes and discusses preliminary plans for creating new versions of the WECD.

11.2   The Data and the Matching Algorithm

11.2.1   The Data

Matching workers to establishments is based on detailed location and industry information available for both groups. Information on the location and industry of a worker's employer comes from two questions asked on the one-in-six long form of the 1990 decennial census:[4] "At what location did this person work *last week?*" and "What kind of business or industry was this?"[5] The Census Bureau assigns geographic and industry codes to each person's record in the SDF based on the individual's response to these questions. Using these codes it is possible to assign each respondent to a unique industry-location cell. For this project I select all respondents who indicated that they worked in manufacturing and worked in the previous week. This file contains approximately 3.18 million individual records.[6]

Each plant record in the 1990 SSEL includes a four-digit SIC code indicating the establishment's primary industry and geographic codes showing its location.[7] This information allows each plant in the United States to be assigned to a unique industry-location cell. For this project all 342,471 manufacturing establishments are selected from the 1990 SSEL.[8]

---

4. For a more complete discussion of data available from the 1990 decennial census, along with a copy of the long form, see Bureau of the Census (1992b). The form is referred to as the "one-in-six" long form because it is sent to one in six households on average. However, this rate varies by location. In places with fewer than 2,500 people a form was sent to one in two households, while in tracts with more than 2,500 housing units it was sent to one in eight households.

5. One problem with these questions is that they refer to the business where a person worked last week, which is not necessarily a person's primary place of employment. Another problem is that these questions are only relevant if an individual was employed in the previous week.

6. The estimated manufacturing workforce based on the 1990 census is 20.5 million, so the SDF sample of 3.18 million represents approximately 16 percent of the population of manufacturing workers. While over 4.5 million workers indicated they worked in manufacturing, only 3.18 million of these worked in the previous week.

7. For a more complete description of the SSEL, see Bureau of the Census (1979).

8. The entire 1990 SSEL contains approximately 7.04 million nonagricultural establishments, of which 424,519 are manufacturing establishments. However, once I eliminate records for establishments that are closed, duplicate records, records for establishments with zero payroll or employment, and records for nonproduction unit establishments, I am left with 342,471 establishments.

11.2.2   The Matching Process

Assigning a unique establishment identifier to worker records proceeds in four steps:

1. Standardize the geographic and industry definitions in the two data sources.
2. Eliminate all establishments that are not unique in an industry-location cell.
3. Assign a unique establishment identifier to the records of all workers located in the same industry-location cell as a unique establishment.
4. Eliminate all matches based on imputed data.

First, I will briefly describe the geographic coding system of the U.S. Bureau of the Census as of 1990.[9] The Census Bureau divides the entire country into a hierarchy of geographic areas and assigns codes to each area. The most aggregated areas are the four census regions and the nine census divisions. For example, the first region is the Northeast region, which consists of the New England and Middle Atlantic divisions. The New England division consists of the states of Maine, New Hampshire, Vermont, Massachusetts, Connecticut, and Rhode Island. Each state is assigned a unique geographic code, as is each county within a state. Thus each county in the United States has a unique state-county code combination. Counties are further divided into incorporated and unincorporated areas, and each incorporated area with a population of over 2,500 is assigned a unique place code.[10] Finally, highly populated places are further subdivided, with each separate physical block in a place assigned a unique block code.[11] Thus, for addresses located in central cities, the Census Bureau assigns a unique code for the block, place, county, state, division, and region of the address.

The first step in matching workers to establishments is to standardize the geographic and industry codes across the two data sources. Originally, only place code information was available for establishments in the 1990 SSEL. I used the Census Bureau's 1990 Address Reference File (ARF) to assign block codes to 36 percent of the establishments in the 1990 SSEL.[12]

Industry codes must also be standardized since establishments in the 1990 SSEL are classified into industries using the SIC system, while workers in the

9. For a more complete description of geographic codes, see Bureau of the Census (1992b).
10. Portions of counties not in a qualifying place are assigned a place code of 9999.
11. In 1990 block codes were only available for addresses in Tape Address Register (TAR) areas. TAR areas roughly correspond to central cities or metropolitan statistical areas (MSAs).
12. The ARF is a file of address ranges with the corresponding geographic codes. Given a street address one can use the ARF to assign the appropriate geographic codes.
    The main reason why establishments in the 1990 SSEL do not have block codes is that in 1990 block code information is only available for establishments located in TARs. Data from the 1990 SSEL shows that 40 percent of manufacturing establishments are located in an MSA. Thus I am missing block codes for only 4 percent of the establishments.

SDF are classified into industries using census industry codes. To make the industry data for both workers and establishments compatible, the SIC codes in the 1990 SSEL are converted to census industry codes using a concordance table.[13]

The second step in the matching process is to eliminate nonunique establishments. To do this I first keep all establishments that are unique in an industry-block cell. However, because some plants have missing block codes, I only keep establishments that are unique in an industry-block cell when all establishments in the industry-place cell have valid block codes, or when an establishment is unique in an industry-place cell.[14] Eliminating nonunique establishments reduces the number of establishments available for matching from 342,471 to 63,949. Next, I assign workers and establishments to industry-location cells and match workers and establishments in the same cell. This is a two-step process. First, workers and establishments are assigned to industry-*block* cells and matched. Then all remaining workers and establishments are assigned to industry-*place* cells and matched.

Finally, to minimize the probability of incorrectly matching workers to establishments, I drop all worker-establishment matches based on imputed industry or geographic data.[15] In addition, I drop all matches where the total number of workers matched to a given establishment is greater than the establishment's reported employment.[16]

The resulting data set contains 199,557 worker records matched to 16,144

13. See Bureau of the Census (1992a). SIC codes are converted to census codes because the census codes are more aggregated than SIC codes.

14. Multiple establishments owned by the same firm that are in the same block or place cell are kept.

15. E.g., if I match a worker to an establishment using block code information and the worker's block code is imputed, I throw out the match. However, if I match a worker to an establishment using place code information and the place code is not imputed, I keep the match, whether or not the block code is imputed. I chose to eliminate imputed data after I matched workers and establishments to increase the number of successful matches. This way I keep matches based on place codes even when the block codes have been imputed. In the SDF 1,790,851 worker records have imputed block codes, 218,558 have imputed place codes, and 157,185 have imputed industry codes. Imputation of these items is done by cold decking. In this process, when information for an individual is missing the computer draws another individual at random from a distribution of individuals with similar characteristics. Then information from the selected record replaces the missing information in the original record. Obviously, using imputed data would increase the number of incorrect matches.

16. Dropping matches based on imputed geographic or industry codes eliminates 218,507 matches. Dropping matches where the number of workers matched to an establishment is greater than the establishment's reported employment eliminates 17,826 matches. There are a number of possible reasons why I matched more workers to an establishment than the establishment's reported employment. First, a worker's industry or geographic code could be misassigned. Second, an establishment's employment may have changed between the pay period including 12 March, which is when employment is recorded in the SSEL, and 1 April, the date of the census. Third, reported employment in the SSEL does not include the owner of an establishment, while the owner could be in the SDF. Matching the owner to the establishment may make it appear that more workers are matched to an establishment than the establishment's reported employment. The last two reasons are more likely to be problems with small establishments.

different plants.[17] The appendix provides a list of variables available for workers in the WECD and for establishments in the LRD.

11.3   Evaluating the Worker-Establishment Characteristics Database

11.3.1   Examining the Accuracy of the Match

One advantage to using the matching algorithm described above is that coding errors should be the primary reason for incorrectly assigning workers to establishments.[18] The matching algorithm only matches workers to establishments that are unique in an industry-location cell. Therefore, if workers and establishments have the correct geographic and industry codes, all workers in an industry-location cell that contains an establishment *must* work in that establishment. Furthermore, all workers in the same industry-location cell who filled out the long form in the census are matched to the same plant. This means that the WECD will contain a random sample of workers in the plant.[19]

In spite of these assurances, some tests of the match are desirable. To begin, table 11.1 presents statistics examining the quality of the match. One test of whether workers and establishments are correctly matched is to compare similar information from the worker and establishment data. This is done in rows 1–4 in table 11.1. Row 1 presents the cross-plant mean of worker earnings using data from the SSEL. Per worker earnings in a plant are estimated by dividing the 1990 annual payroll for the establishment by the plant's employment in the pay period including 12 March 1990. The number in row 1 is an average of this per worker earnings estimate across all plants in the data. I will refer to this number as SSEL worker earnings. Row 2 presents the cross-plant mean of worker earnings based on the worker data. Each worker in the SDF reports his or her total earnings in the previous year. Per worker earnings in a plant are estimated by taking the average earnings for all workers matched to the plant. The number in row 2 is then the average of this per worker earnings

17. While the matching algorithm results in 16,144 unique establishment-level identifiers being attached to the 199,557 worker records, detailed information is not available for all of these plants in all years. This is because detailed information on plant inputs and outputs comes from the LRD, which consists of the plant-level records contained in the various years of the Census of Manufactures and the Annual Survey of Manufactures. Therefore, the number of plants for which detailed data are available depends on the year (in particular, whether a survey or a census was conducted in a year). E.g., matching the worker file to 1989 LRD data (a survey year) results in a match of 152,987 worker records to 5,423 establishments. In contrast, matching the worker data to 1987 LRD data (a census year) results in 195,943 worker records matched to 15,557 establishments.

18. One large source for coding error is assigning an industry code to a worker's description of the primary industry of his or her employer. Another possible source of error is mismatching workers who work in new establishments that are not yet included in the SSEL to older establishments in the SSEL in the same industry-location cell.

19. This assumes that there is no systematic bias in response rates to the long form. See Bates, Fay, and Moore (1991) and Kulka et al. (1991) for a discussion of response rates to the 1990 decennial census.

Table 11.1   Comparing Matched Plant and Worker Data

	All Matched Workers and Plants (1)	Only Workers between Ages 18 and 65 Who Usually Worked 30–65 Hours a Week (2)	Only Plants with More than 10% of the Workforce Matched (3)
1. SSEL worker earnings	24,371.17	25,204.59	23,542.37
	(148.27)	(144.09)	(179.40)
2. SDF worker earnings	24,317.26	24,530.20	23,838.04
	(115.28)	(117.45)	(207.58)
3. Log difference (across plants)	−0.048	0.003	−0.006
	(0.005)	(0.005)	(0.008)
4. ρ (SSEL worker earnings, SDF worker earnings)	0.47	0.45	0.33
	(0.001)	(0.001)	(0.001)
5. Mean total employment in plants	151.43	156.29	105.74
	(4.32)	(4.48)	(4.70)
6. Mean proportion of workers matched to the plants	0.16	0.15	–
	(0.002)	(0.002)	
7. Number of plants	15,435	14,851	7,226

Note: Numbers in parentheses are standard errors except for row 4, where they are *p*-values.

estimate across all plants in the data. I will refer to this number as SDF worker earnings. Row 3 presents the cross-plant mean log difference between these two estimates of worker earnings, while row 4 presents the cross-plant correlation of these two estimates of worker earnings. Row 5 presents the cross-plant mean of total employment in the plants (based on SSEL data), while row 6 presents the average proportion of workers matched to the plant. Column (1) in table 11.1 presents numbers for all plants and workers in the WECD; column (2) presents numbers for workers, and plants that contain workers, who are between 18 and 65 years old and who usually worked between 30 and 65 hours a week in 1989; and column (3) presents numbers for plants with more than 10 percent of the workforce matched to the plant.

The numbers in table 11.1 suggest that workers are matched to the correct establishments. The numbers in rows 1 and 2 show that the estimates of worker earnings from the SSEL and SDF data are very similar. The numbers in row 3 show that for all plants and workers in the data the average plant-level difference between the two estimates is less than 5 percent.[20] Further, when we con-

20. There are a number of reasons why these two estimates might differ. First, the estimate of earnings per worker based on plant data is an estimate of earnings paid to a worker by the plant, while the estimate based on worker data is total earnings paid to a worker by all employers. If some workers in a plant hold multiple jobs, the estimate based on worker data will be larger. Second, worker earnings reflect total earnings of a worker in 1989, while the estimate based on plant data is the total amount paid in salary and wages by the plant to all workers in 1990 divided by the number of workers in the plant in the pay period including 12 March 1990. If the plant is growing over the year, the pay for workers added to the plant after 12 March will appear in the wage data but these workers will not appear in the employment figures. This will tend to make

sider the samples in columns (2) and (3), this difference falls to less than 1 percent and is statistically insignificant. The numbers in row 4 show that the SSEL and SDF worker earnings are positively and significantly correlated.[21] Finally, row 6 shows that on average 16 percent of a plant's workforce is matched to the plant. This is the exact rate one would expect given the one-in-six sampling frame of the SDF.

Table 11.2 breaks out the numbers in table 11.1, first by the size of the plant (panel A), and second by the nine census divisions (panel B). The numbers in table 11.2 are for workers who are between 18 and 65 years old and who usually worked between 30 and 65 hours a week in the previous year.[22]

The numbers in panel A reveal no systematic relationship between the difference between SSEL and SDF worker earnings and plant size. The largest difference, 14 percent, is found for plants with 1–9 employees, while the smallest difference, −0.1 percent, is found for plants with 10–24 employees. However, there is a strong negative relationship between plant size and the proportion of workers matched to the establishment, and a strong positive relationship between plant size and the correlation of the two measures of worker earnings. Plants with 1–9 employees average 40 percent of their workforce matched to the plant. However, the correlation between SSEL and SDF worker earnings in these plants is only .20. In contrast, plants with over 1,000 workers average 8 percent of their workforce matched to the plant, while the correlation between the two earnings measures is .78. The negative relationship between the proportion of workers matched and size is the result of an integer constraint. Plants must have at least one worker matched to the plant to appear in the data. For a plant with five employees this means that the minimum percentage matched will be 20 percent. Obviously, as a plant gets larger, this minimum approaches zero. The reason that the correlation between the two measures of worker wages increases with plant size is that as the size of a population increases it requires a smaller percentage of the population to have a representative sample. Thus, in plants with more than 1,000 employees, we are able to get a relatively accurate estimate of worker wages with only 8 percent of the workforce. Overall, while it appears that smaller plants have a much larger proportion of their workforce matched, larger plants appear to have a much more representative sample of workers matched.

SSEL worker earnings larger than SDF worker earnings. Also, if employment in a plant is seasonal and 12 March is a period of low (high) employment, SSEL earnings will appear higher (lower) than SDF earnings.

21. The reader should note that, because the SDF earnings estimates are based on a sample of workers in a plant, even if all workers are matched to the correct establishment the estimate of ρ will in general be less than one because of sampling error. Thus the fact that these correlations are significantly greater than zero is fairly strong evidence that workers are being matched to the correct establishments.

22. I focus on these workers for two reasons. First, these workers have the strongest labor market attachments and therefore should have the most reliable earnings and hours worked data. Second, the log difference across plants (table 11.1, row 3) is small and insignificant for these workers.

Table 11.2   **Comparing Matched Plant and Worker Data by Size and Region**

	SSEL Worker Earnings (1)	SDF Worker Earnings (2)	Log Difference (3)	ρ(SSEL Earnings, SDF Earnings) (4)	Proportion Matched (5)	Number of Plants (6)
A. Plant size (total employment)						
1–9	24,146.61	22,173.18	0.142	0.20	0.40	2,277
	(381.37)	(453.24)	(0.02)	(0.0001)	(0.006)	
10–24	24,955.41	23,803.62	–0.001	0.32	0.16	2,718
	(436.68)	(302.33)	(0.01)	(0.0001)	(0.003)	
25–49	25,252.59	24,286.80	–0.040	0.41	0.10	2,542
	(425.09)	(304.20)	(0.01)	(0.0001)	(0.002)	
50–99	24,628.26	24,205.75	–0.025	0.52	0.09	2,746
	(289.74)	(182.88)	(0.009)	(0.0001)	(0.002)	
100–249	25,185.07	25,068.49	–0.014	0.60	0.08	2,640
	(237.41)	(174.12)	(0.020)	(0.0001)	(0.001)	
250–499	25,408.95	25,908.63	–0.033	0.68	0.08	1,079
	(306.91)	(274.49)	(0.010)	(0.0001)	(0.002)	
500–999	27,881.66	25,950.63	–0.026	0.76	0.08	520
	(428.18)	(427.73)	(0.011)	(0.0001)	(0.003)	
1,000+	34,280.33	35,850.85	–0.036	0.78	0.08	329
	(531.51)	(576.57)	(0.013)	(0.0001)	(0.004)	

B. *Census division*

New England	27,432.81	26,314.58	0.032	0.41	0.12	1,429
	(520.59)	(496.30)	(0.015)	(0.0001)	(0.005)	
Middle Atlantic	26,446.22	25,092.65	0.009	0.46	0.14	3,391
	(357.98)	(231.26)	(0.010)	(0.0001)	(0.003)	
East–North Central	26,149.54	25,887.90	−0.012	0.44	0.14	4,224
	(268.08)	(208.37)	(0.009)	(0.0001)	(0.003)	
West–North Central	23,895.70	24,537.35	−0.037	0.46	0.16	1,198
	(434.34)	(438.11)	(0.018)	(0.0001)	(0.005)	
South Atlantic	23,132.80	22,138.76	0.020	0.43	0.14	1,732
	(323.94)	(310.25)	(0.014)	(0.0001)	(0.004)	
East–South Central	21,531.13	21,325.68	0.007	0.47	0.14	768
	(397.98)	(571.55)	(0.021)	(0.0001)	(0.006)	
West–South Central	21,570.96	21,555.19	−0.015	0.40	0.17	900
	(443.11)	(367.30)	(0.022)	(0.0001)	(0.007)	
Mountain	21,132.11	20,512.80	0.027	0.38	0.17	318
	(663.16)	(636.55)	(0.044)	(0.0001)	(0.011)	
Pacific	26,503.12	24,931.35	0.038	0.36	0.20	891
	(649.21)	(501.76)	(0.025)	(0.0001)	(0.009)	

Note: Numbers are for workers between ages 18 and 65 who usually worked 30–65 hours a week. Numbers in parentheses are standard errors except in column (4), where they are *p*-values.

The numbers in panel B show no systematic relationship between the difference in the two earnings measures and plant location. While the mean difference between the two earnings measures varies between −0.037 and 0.038, this difference is never significantly different from zero for plants in any census division. In addition, there is very little variation in either the proportion matched or in the correlation between the two earnings measures across plants in the various census divisions. The numbers in panel B suggest that the matching process works equally well for plants in all areas of the country.

Table 11.3 breaks out the numbers presented in table 11.1 by two-digit industry again for workers between 18 and 65 years old who usually worked between 30 and 65 hours a week in the previous year. Column (3) in table 11.3 shows that the log difference between the measures of worker earnings varies from a high of 0.24 for tobacco to a low of −0.13 for petroleum refining. However, of the 20 two-digit industries, 12 have an absolute difference of less than 0.05, and in 13 industries the difference is not significantly different from zero at the 1 percent significance level. Further, in all 20 industries there is a positive correlation between these two measures of workers earnings, and in 18 of the 20 industries the correlation is significantly different from zero at the 0.1 percent significance level. Viewed as a whole the numbers in tables 11.1, 11.2, and 11.3 suggest that workers are being matched to the correct establishments.

11.3.2   Examining the Representativeness of the Data

To begin examining whether the WECD data are representative of the underlying population of workers and plants, table 11.4 compares the number and annual earnings of workers in the SDF with workers in the WECD, for all workers (the total row) and by two-digit industry. Columns (1) and (2) present the number of workers in the SDF and WECD, respectively, while column (3) presents the proportion of workers in the industry matched to an establishment (col. [2]/col. [1]). Columns (4) and (5) present the industry mean of worker earnings in the SDF and WECD, respectively, while column (6) presents the cross-plant log difference in average worker earnings.

The total row in table 11.4 shows that of the 3,176,986 manufacturing workers in the SDF, 199,558 appear in the WECD, a match rate of 6 percent. The numbers in column (3) show that this match rate varies by industry. Tobacco, paper, leather, and primary metals all have match rates of 10 percent or greater, while lumber, instruments, and miscellaneous all have match rates of 3 percent. The numbers in column (6) show that matched workers average 10 percent higher wages than all SDF workers but that the size and sign of this difference varies by industry. In 3 two-digit industries matched workers average lower wages than workers in the SDF. In 15 two-digit industries the absolute difference in earnings is less than 10 percent.

Table 11.5 presents the number and average employment for all SSEL plants, unique plants, and WECD plants, for all plants in the data (the total row) and

Table 11.3   **Comparing Matched Plant and Worker Data by Industry**

Industry	SSEL Worker Earnings (1)	SDF Worker Earnings (2)	Log Difference (3)	ρ(SSEL Earnings, SDF Earnings) (4)	Proportion Matched (5)	Number of Plants (6)
Food	24,055.82	23,750.41	−0.01	0.48	0.12	1,665
	(347.16)	(421.18)	(0.01)	(0.0001)	(0.003)	
Tobacco	22,557.58	26,785.83	0.24	0.68	0.08	25
	(2502.03)	(2020.56)	(0.09)	(0.0002)	(0.01)	
Textile	20,419.94	20,618.58	−0.03	0.46	0.13	438
	(561.06)	(660.45)	(0.03)	(0.0001)	(0.01)	
Apparel	15,462.98	16,470.58	0.02	0.33	0.13	559
	(380.04)	(544.22)	(0.03)	(0.0001)	(0.01)	
Lumber	20,039.38	23,254.54	0.08	0.27	0.19	572
	(460.79)	(912.31)	(0.03)	(0.0001)	(0.01)	
Furniture	20,047.37	22,125.10	0.02	0.42	0.19	379
	(421.61)	(996.03)	(0.03)	(0.0001)	(0.01)	
Paper	26,981.37	27,280.02	−0.04	0.50	0.10	866
	(303.99)	(525.90)	(0.02)	(0.0001)	(0.004)	
Printing	19,348.33	21,666.39	0.09	0.44	0.16	1,228
	(313.51)	(362.91)	(0.02)	(0.0001)	(0.01)	
Chemicals	30,598.58	30,012.29	−0.03	0.28	0.17	1,165
	(641.66)	(501.74)	(0.02)	(0.0001)	(0.01)	
Petroleum refining	37,282.11	33,492.94	−0.13	0.07	0.17	161
	(1,434.79)	(1,502.55)	(0.05)	(0.38)	(0.02)	

(*continued*)

Table 11.3 (continued)

Industry	SSEL Worker Earnings (1)	SDF Worker Earnings (2)	Log Difference (3)	ρ(SSEL Earnings, SDF Earnings) (4)	Proportion Matched (5)	Number of Plants (6)
Rubber	23,691.93	24,052.27	−0.03	0.45	0.12	717
	(467.37)	(467.37)	(0.02)	(0.0001)	(0.01)	
Leather	16,662.93	17,503.39	0.05	0.46	0.14	178
	(754.53)	(777.90)	(0.05)	(0.0001)	(0.01)	
Stone	26,068.61	25,288.76	−0.06	0.41	0.14	853
	(409.75)	(528.45)	(0.02)	(0.0001)	(0.01)	
Primary metals	26,942.87	27,624.96	−0.02	0.45	0.12	898
	(372.66)	(702.90)	(0.02)	(0.0001)	(0.005)	
Fabricated metals	26,287.79	26,299.20	−0.04	0.33	0.14	1,490
	(500.68)	(484.06)	(0.02)	(0.0001)	(0.005)	
Machinery	27,216.31	28,512.74	0.02	0.34	0.19	1,421
	(324.71)	(576.73)	(0.02)	(0.0001)	(0.01)	
Electrical equipment	23,467.39	25,601.72	0.06	0.40	0.13	726
	(394.61)	(608.20)	(0.02)	(0.0001)	(0.01)	
Transportation	26,112.19	26,212.33	0.01	0.52	0.17	715
	(455.76)	(534.98)	(0.02)	(0.0001)	(0.01)	
Instruments	28,540.42	29,043.37	0.02	0.18	0.17	257
	(1,049.58)	(950.43)	(0.05)	(0.0041)	(0.02)	
Miscellaneous	20,423.02	22,959.16	0.07	0.26	0.17	538
	(427.49)	(696.47)	(0.03)	(0.0001)	(0.01)	

Note: Numbers are for workers between ages 18 and 65 who usually worked between 30–65 hours a week. Numbers in parentheses are standard errors, except in col. (4), where they are *p*-values.

Table 11.4 **Number and Mean Earnings of SDF and WECD Workers by Industry**

Industry	SDF Workers (1)	WECD Workers (2)	Proportion Matched (3)	Mean Earnings of SDF Workers (4)	Mean Earnings of WECD Workers (5)	Log Difference (6)
Food	231,420	20,597	0.09	22,131	23,619	0.07
Tobacco	7,393	1,379	0.19	35,899	35,890	0.00
Textile	121,159	6,485	0.05	18,307	19,228	0.05
Apparel	161,014	6,255	0.04	13,946	14,722	0.05
Lumber	134,031	3,856	0.03	18,214	26,448	0.37
Furniture	92,274	3,217	0.04	18,576	20,482	0.10
Paper	106,615	14,411	0.14	29,322	31,217	0.06
Printing	282,069	11,510	0.04	23,143	21,154	−0.09
Chemicals	176,282	12,089	0.07	33,342	33,183	0.00
Petroleum	27,194	1,913	0.07	36,301	37,633	0.04
Rubber	109,594	8,608	0.08	23,484	25,854	0.10
Leather	24,484	2,442	0.10	16,025	16,606	0.04
Stone	88,855	6,666	0.08	24,271	26,167	0.08
Primary metals	126,963	17,224	0.14	28,897	31,854	0.10
Fabricated metals	185,281	13,435	0.07	25,108	27,417	0.09
Machinery	373,079	17,313	0.05	28,804	31,515	0.09
Electrical equipment	281,519	14,633	0.05	27,810	25,342	−0.09
Transportation	379,002	30,622	0.08	32,035	35,379	0.10
Instrument	92,684	2,406	0.03	29,057	29,868	0.03
Miscellaneous	176,074	4,442	0.03	21,693	21,264	−0.02
Total	3,176,986	199,558	0.06	25,558	28,107	0.10

Table 11.5 Number, Proportion, and Average Total Employment of All, Unique, and Matched Plants by Industry

Industry	All SSEL Plants (1)	Unique Plants (2)	WECD Plants (3)	Proportion Unique (4)	Proportion Matched (5)	Average SSEL Plant Employment (6)	Average Unique Plant Employment (7)	Average WECD Plant Employment (8)
Food	19,117	6,598	1,801	0.35	0.09	75.6	89.9	143.4
Tobacco	134	75	25	0.56	0.19	297.4	417.5	844.0
Textile	5,838	1,804	466	0.31	0.08	112.0	124.4	161.4
Apparel	21,275	2,858	643	0.13	0.03	47.9	76.7	110.5
Lumber	31,573	3,845	657	0.12	0.02	22.2	31.3	52.5
Furniture	11,168	1,612	421	0.14	0.04	45.3	50.8	64.5
Paper	6,126	2,342	888	0.38	0.15	103.1	123.7	163.5
Printing	58,803	5,514	1,491	0.09	0.03	26.3	39.3	75.3
Chemicals	11,659	3,914	1,230	0.34	0.11	74.3	82.5	126.9
Petroleum refining	2,161	922	165	0.43	0.08	53.4	67.3	130.8
Rubber	14,435	2,884	752	0.20	0.05	60.8	93.1	155.0
Leather	1,897	767	198	0.40	0.10	62.2	76.0	118.1
Stone	15,245	4,368	931	0.29	0.06	34.2	44.4	80.0
Primary metals	6,548	2,843	934	0.43	0.14	109.7	130.9	222.1
Fabricated metals	35,513	6,742	1,580	0.19	0.04	41.7	61.3	121.6
Machinery	49,097	6,255	1,514	0.13	0.03	39.1	68.5	127.8
Electrical equipment	15,941	2,887	757	0.18	0.05	97.4	142.3	240.0
Transportation	10,002	3,170	762	0.32	0.08	180.7	241.9	448.4
Instrument	9,688	1,851	283	0.19	0.03	99.6	123.6	229.4
Miscellaneous	16,251	2,698	646	0.17	0.04	24.2	36.7	66.6
Total	342,471	63,949	16,144	0.19	0.05	52.2	84.5	146.3

by two-digit industry. Unique plants are plants that are unique in an industry-location cell. As mentioned earlier, only plants that are unique in an industry-location cell are matched to workers. Plants with workers matched to them are WECD plants. Columns (1), (2), and (3) present the number of SSEL plants, unique plants, and WECD plants, respectively. Column (4) presents the proportion of plants that are unique (col. [2]/col. [1]), while column (5) presents the proportion of plants in the WECD (col. [3]/col. [1]). Columns (6), (7), and (8) present the mean employment for all SSEL plants, unique plants, and WECD plants, respectively.

The total row in table 11.5 shows that of the 342,471 plants in the 1990 SSEL, 16,144 appear in the WECD, a match rate of 5 percent. This is almost identical to the match rate for workers. The numbers in column (5) show that this rate varies considerably across two-digit industries in a manner similar to the pattern seen in table 11.4. Tobacco, paper, leather, and primary metals have the highest match rates, while lumber, instruments, and miscellaneous have the lowest.

The numbers in column (4) show that being unique in an industry-location cell does not guarantee that a plant appears in the final data. Overall, almost 20 percent of plants in the SSEL are unique, but only 5 percent appear in the WECD. The numbers in columns (6), (7), and (8) show why this is the case. Comparing the average employment of unique plants with the average employment of all SSEL plants shows that unique plants are much larger than all SSEL plants. This is because it is much more likely that a large plant will be unique in an industry-location cell. Comparing the average employment of unique plants with the average employment of WECD plants shows that WECD plants are even larger than unique plants. This is the result of the sampling scheme of the decennial census long form. Since this form was sent to one in six households on average it is much more likely that a large establishment will contain a worker who received the form, and therefore, more likely that a large establishment will appear in the WECD.

The fact that WECD plants are larger than SSEL plants also explains why WECD workers have higher average wages than SDF workers. Previous research has found a positive correlation between plant size and worker wages (Brown and Medoff 1989; Troske, in press). Since WECD workers work in larger establishments than SDF workers they will in turn have higher average earnings.

Table 11.6 repeats the same analysis for workers found in table 11.4, this time broken out by census division. One thing to notice in table 11.6 is that the match rate is significantly lower in the Mountain and Pacific divisions. In the Pacific division only 2 percent of the workers in the SDF are matched to plants.

Table 11.7 repeats the same analysis for plants found in table 11.5, this time broken out by plant size (panel A) and census division (panel B). The numbers in panel A of table 11.7 confirm the fact that large plants are both more likely to be unique and more likely to appear in the WECD. Column (4) shows that

Table 11.6 **Number and Mean Earnings of SDF and WECD Workers by Census Division**

Census Division	Number of SDF Workers (1)	Number of WECD Workers (2)	Proportion Matched (3)	Mean Earnings of SDF Workers (4)	Mean Earnings of WECD Workers (5)	Log Difference (6)
New England	189,131	17,673	0.09	28,781.95	22,822.79	0.00
Middle Atlantic	469,899	37,820	0.08	27,559.07	27,151.79	0.01
East–North Central	772,079	69,986	0.09	27,362.52	30,617.08	−0.05
West–North Central	276,567	18,682	0.07	23,049.96	26,582.73	−0.06
South Atlantic	479,648	20,263	0.04	22,508.84	25,788.60	−0.06
East–South Central	234,695	11,066	0.05	20,469.50	23,810.22	−0.07
West–South Central	293,049	12,234	0.04	23,764.57	23,212.54	0.01
Mountain	105,588	3,408	0.03	24,224.02	23,400.80	0.02
Pacific	356,322	8,426	0.02	28,571.62	33,644.64	−0.07

Table 11.7 Number, Proportion, and Average Total Employment of SDF, Unique, and Matched Plants by Plant Size and Census Division

	All SSEL Plants (1)	Unique Plants (2)	WECD Plants (3)	Proportion Unique (4)	Proportion Matched (5)	Average SSEL Plant Employment (6)	Average Unique Plant Employment (7)	Average WECD Plant Employment (8)
A. Plant size (total employment)								
1–9	161,192	24,765	2,924	0.15	0.02	4.1	4.1	5.0
10–24	74,981	12,944	3,088	0.17	0.04	15.5	15.7	16.2
25–49	41,796	8,415	2,687	0.20	0.06	34.9	35.2	35.9
50–99	28,877	7,014	2,821	0.24	0.10	70.1	70.8	71.2
100–249	22,599	6,401	2,673	0.28	0.12	154.2	155.8	156.3
250–499	7,973	2,259	1,091	0.28	0.14	345.8	347.9	346.5
500–999	3,378	1,197	526	0.35	0.16	679.3	680.2	683.3
1,000+	1,675	654	334	0.39	0.20	2,411.6	2,450.2	2,527.3
B. Census division								
New England	23,616	5,416	1,560	0.23	0.07	48.8	67.8	153.2
Middle Atlantic	54,657	12,063	3,667	0.22	0.07	46.4	70.4	116.2
East–North Central	65,381	13,629	4,526	0.21	0.07	59.3	95.6	165.8
West–North Central	23,252	5,478	1,308	0.24	0.06	56.2	84.7	153.5
South Atlantic	50,336	8,013	1,866	0.16	0.04	58.9	108.5	178.6
East–South Central	19,235	3,847	815	0.20	0.04	69.9	113.9	169.9
West–South Central	34,872	5,831	1,025	0.17	0.03	47.4	72.9	123.2
Mountain	15,868	2,553	385	0.16	0.02	38.6	63.7	111.7
Pacific	55,254	7,119	992	0.13	0.02	44.1	73.6	104.5

as plant size increases the probability that a plant is unique in an industry-location cell rises, from 0.15 for plants with 1–9 employees to 0.39 for plants with 1,000 or more employees. However, column (5) shows an even greater increase with size, rising from 0.02 in the smallest plants to 0.20 in the largest plants. In fact, the probability that a plant appears in the WECD, conditional on the plant's being unique, rises from 0.12 for plants with 1–9 employees to 0.51 for plants with 1,000 or more employees (not in table).[23]

Similar to table 11.6, the numbers in panel B show that the match rate for plants is significantly lower in the Mountain and Pacific divisions. While part of this is because plants in these divisions are less likely to be unique, this is not a complete explanation. Even conditional on being unique, plants in the Mountain and Pacific divisions are much less likely to appear in the WECD. The figures in columns (6), (7), and (8) suggest one explanation for why this is the case. Plants in these divisions are smaller on average than plants in other divisions. As is shown in panel A, small plants are not only less likely to be unique, they are also less likely to include workers who received a one-in-six long form in the decennial census.[24]

Tables 11.4 through 11.7 show that the success of the matching procedure varies by the industry and location of plants and workers and by the size of the plant. Since the characteristics of workers and plants are not distributed randomly across industry, location, and plant size, this affects the representativeness of the WECD. In addition, work at the Census Bureau and elsewhere (Bates et al. 1991; Kulka et al. 1991) shows that the probability that a household responded to the 1990 decennial census was correlated with the income and race of the household, the age and education of the head of the household, and whether the household contained related persons. Since the WECD only contains workers with nonimputed data this will also affect the representativeness of the WECD data.

These effects can be seen in table 11.8 and figure 11.1. Table 11.8 presents characteristics for all manufacturing workers in the SDF (col. [1]), for all manufacturing workers in the May 1988 Current Population Survey (CPS; col. [2]), and for all WECD workers (col. [3]). Figure 11.1 presents the educational distribution for SDF and WECD workers.[25] The numbers in table 11.8 show that workers in the WECD are not a representative sample of the entire population of manufacturing workers. A larger percentage of workers in the WECD are white, male, married, production workers than in either the SDF or the CPS.

---

23. This is computed as WECD plants/unique plants (col. [3]/col. [2]).

24. An alternative explanation could be that workers in these divisions are more likely to have imputed industry and location information. However, this is not the case. In fact, workers in the Mountain division are less likely to have imputed data than workers in the other divisions.

25. Respondents to the CPS report the number of years of education completed. Respondents to the decennial census report the highest degree completed. Since these are not completely analogous concepts I do not include CPS workers in fig. 11.1.

Table 11.8   **Comparing the Characteristics of SDF, CPS, and WECD Workers**

Characteristic	SDF Workers (1)	1988 May CPS Workers, Manufacturing (2)	WECD Workers (3)	WECD Workers Weighted (4)
Percentage male	66.9	65.4	70.1	66.9
Percentage non-Hispanic white	85.2	88.8	89.6	88.3
Percentage now married	67.3	66.7	71.0	67.7
Percentage in occupation				
Manager and professional	18.2	18.6	16.4	19.2
Technical, clerical, and sales	21.6	20.8	19.7	21.4
Production worker	60.2	60.6	64.0	59.4
Percentage in region				
Northeast	20.8	27.6	27.9	19.9
Midwest	33.0	28.4	44.5	33.3
South	31.7	32.5	21.8	33.8
West	14.5	11.5	5.9	11.8
Mean age	38.9	38.3	39.9	38.8
	(37)	(37)	(39)	(39)
Mean number of weeks worked[a]	47.5	–	48.9	48.2
	(52)		(52)	(52)
Mean usual hours worked per week[a]	41.2	41.0	41.7	41.3
	(40)	(40)	(40)	(40)
Mean wage or salary income[a]	25,558.1	–	28,106.7	25,676.8
	(21,000)		(25,000)	(25,000)
Mean hourly wage[a,b]	13.25	10.30	13.87	12.90
	(10.58)	(9.08)	(11.96)	(11.96)
N	3,176,986	4,757	199,558	1,639,556.2

Note: Numbers in parentheses are the medians of the distribution.

[a]Reference period is the previous year (1989) for SDF and WECD workers and the previous week for the CPS workers.

[b]For the SDF and WECD workers, hourly wage is estimated as: (wage or salary income / number of weeks worked) / usual hours worked per week.

Workers in the WECD are slightly older than workers in the SDF or the CPS and are more likely to be located in the Northeast and Midwest regions of the country. Table 11.8 also shows that, relative to workers in the SDF or the CPS, workers in the WECD worked more weeks, usually worked more hours per week, and averaged higher earnings and hourly wages. Finally, figure 11.1 shows that, relative to workers in the SDF, workers in the WECD are more likely to have a high school diploma and are less likely to have less than a high school diploma, a bachelor's degree, or an advanced degree. All of these results are very similar to the findings of Bates et al. (1991) and Kulka et al. (1991) and are exactly what we would expect given that large plants are overrepresented in the WECD.

To make estimates of characteristics based on the data in the WECD more

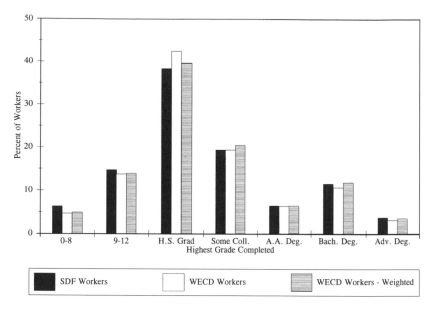

Figure 11.1   Educational distribution of SDF and WECD workers

closely match estimates of characteristics based on the SDF data, I produce weighted estimates of these characteristics using weights based on the conditional probability that a plant appears in the data. First, I will discuss how I construct these weights.

As the discussion in section 11.2 shows, the probability that a plant appears in the data is a function of whether the plant is unique in an industry-location cell and of whether the plant contains a worker who received and responded to the one-in-six long form in the 1990 decennial census. I assume that these two probabilities are independent and estimate the probability of the two events separately. The product of the two probabilities will then be an estimate of the conditional probability that a plant appears in the data.

The probability that a plant is unique is given by

(1) $$P(u) = \mathbf{X}'\beta + u,$$

where $P(u)$ is the probability that a plant is unique in an industry-location cell, $\mathbf{X}$ is a vector of plant characteristics, and u is a normally distributed random error term. Results from tables 11.4 through 11.7 show that the probability that a plant is unique is related to plant size, industry, and location. Therefore, $\mathbf{X}$ includes controls for (the log of) plant employment, two-digit industry, and census division. In addition, since the geographic detail of a plant's location is related to whether the plant is located in an urban area, $\mathbf{X}$ includes controls for whether the plant is located in a valid place (has a place code other than 9999) and the total population and the population per square mile for the county where a plant is located.[26] Since I cannot directly observe $P(u)$ but instead only observe $P^*(u)$, where

(2)
$$P^*(u) = \begin{cases} 1 & \text{if a plant is unique,} \\ 0 & \text{otherwise,} \end{cases}$$

equation (1) is estimated using a probit model. Results from this estimation are available from the author.

The probability that a plant is matched, conditional on being unique, is given by

(3)
$$P(m \mid u) = \mathbf{Y}'\gamma + \varepsilon,$$

where $P(m \mid u)$ is the probability that, conditional on being unique, a plant appears in the WECD, $\mathbf{Y}$ is a vector of plant characteristics, and ε is a normally distributed random error term. The results in tables 11.4 through 11.7 show that plant size also affects whether a plant contains matched workers. Therefore, (the log of) plant employment is included in $\mathbf{Y}$. Since the sampling frame of the SDF varied with the population of an area, $\mathbf{Y}$ includes controls for the population per square mile and the total population for a plant's county. County-level measures of median age, median education of individuals over age 25 and its square, density of nonminority whites, and density of family households are also included in $\mathbf{Y}$ to control for variation in response rates with age, education, and household type. To control for the fact that more detailed geographic information is available for workers in urban areas, $\mathbf{Y}$ includes a control for whether the plant is located in a valid place. Finally, $\mathbf{Y}$ includes controls for census division and two-digit industry. Again, since I do not directly observe $P(m \mid u)$ but instead observe $P^*(m \mid u)$, where

(4)
$$P^*(m \mid u) = \begin{cases} 1 & \text{if a plant is matched,} \\ 0 & \text{otherwise,} \end{cases}$$

equation (3) is estimated using a probit model. Results from this estimation are available from the author.

Column (4) in table 11.8 presents estimates of the characteristics of workers in the WECD weighted by the inverse of the estimated probability that a worker's plant appears in the data. Figure 11.1 includes the weighted educational distribution for WECD workers. The numbers in table 11.8 show that weighted estimates of worker characteristics are much closer to estimates of these characteristics based on the SDF data. The weighted cross-worker means of age, sex, race, marital status, occupation, and location are all much closer to the cross-worker means of these characteristics found in the SDF. The weighted means of number of weeks worked, usual hours worked last year, wage or

---

26. The latter two numbers are based on the 1980 decennial census.

Table 11.9   Characteristics of SSEL Plants, Unique Plants, and WECD Plants

Characteristic	All SSEL Plants (1)	Unique Plants (2)	Unique Plants Weighted (3)	WECD Plants (4)	WECD Plants Weighted (5)
Mean employment	52.2	84.5	60.2	146.3	63.3
	(11)	(16)	(16)	(43)	(43)
Mean annual payroll	1,414,237	2,377,177	1,688,294	4,411,189	1,731,777
	(199,000)	(312,000)	(312,000)	(943,000)	(943,000)
Average earnings	21,496	21,917	21,819	24,088	22,540
	(18,686)	(19,500)	(19,500)	(22,531)	(22,531)
Percentage in place	74.1	87.7	61.1	89.1	61.1
Percentage multiunit	20.0	31.1	20.1	44.3	22.7
Plant age					
0–4	26.8	19.4	21.4	5.9	8.8
5–9	18.5	22.7	25.4	20.8	27.3
10–14	23.3	30.2	24.7	41.5	29.3
15+	26.9	27.8	28.5	31.9	34.6
Percentage in region					
Northeast	22.9	27.4	22.0	32.4	23.4
Midwest	25.9	29.9	24.3	36.1	25.9
South	30.5	27.6	31.2	22.9	33.3
West	20.5	15.1	12.6	8.5	17.3
N	342,524	63,949	381,309.22	16,144	317,440.76

Note: Numbers in parentheses are medians of the distribution.

salary income, and hourly wage are also much closer to the values found in the SDF. Finally, figure 11.1 shows that the weighted educational distribution for WECD workers is quite similar to the educational distribution for SDF workers.

To examine how representative plants in the WECD are of the entire population of plants, table 11.9 presents various characteristics for all manufacturing plants in the SSEL (col. [1]), unique plants (col. [2]), unique plants weighted by the inverse of the estimated probability of being unique (col. [3]), all plants in the WECD (col. [4]), and all WECD plants weighted by the inverse of the estimated probability that they appear in the WECD (col. [5]). The unweighted numbers show that neither unique nor WECD plants are representative of the entire population of manufacturing plants. As shown in previous tables, unique plants and WECD plants are much larger and are more likely to be located in the Northeast and Midwest regions. The plant age variable shows that a much larger percentage of unique and WECD plants are more than 10 years old, while the place and multiunit variables show that unique and WECD plants are more likely to be located in a place and to be part of a multiestablishment firm. However, columns (3) and (5) show that the weighted cross-plant means of these characteristics more closely resemble the means for all manufacturing plants in the SSEL.

11.3.3   Replicating Previous Findings

While the results in tables 11.8 and 11.9 are encouraging, they are in some ways incomplete. Given that the primary use of these data is to study relationships in a regression framework, a more complete test of these data involves examining whether regression results using these data can replicate results found in the original data and results found by previous researchers using alternative data sources. This is what is done in tables 11.10 and 11.11. Table 11.10 presents the results from regressions of (log) worker wages on a standard set of worker characteristics. Column (1) presents results based on all workers in the SDF controlling for whether a worker is matched to a plant. Column (2) presents the results from the identical regression excluding this control. Column (3) presents the results for the identical regression in column (2) using only data for workers in the WECD, while column (4) presents the results from the same regression where the WECD data are weighted by the estimated probability that a worker appears in the matched data.

The coefficient on the match variable shows that workers matched to plants earn 3 percent higher wages than nonmatched workers. However, comparing the coefficients on the rest of the variables across the four columns shows that there is almost no difference in the relationship between these characteristics and the wages of matched and nonmatched workers. The only major difference among the four columns is the relationship between education and wages. The coefficients on the education variables in column (2) show a much stronger relationship between education and wages than the coefficients on education in either column (3) or (4). However, all four regressions show a very strong positive relationship between education and wages. The most likely explanation for this finding, and the positive coefficient on the match variable in column (1), is that the matched workers work in larger plants than the nonmatched workers. Results in Troske (in press) show that workers in large establishments earn higher wages and that part of the observed education premium is the result of more educated workers working in larger establishments.[27]

The estimated relationships seen in table 11.10 are similar to previously reported relationships between experience, sex, marital status, race, education, and wages (Cain 1986; Korenman and Neumark 1991; Mincer 1974). For example, the coefficients on the female, black, and married variables and the female-married and female-black interactions show that women earn 17 percent less than men, black men earn 4 to 6 percent less than nonblack men, married men earn 13 percent more than single men, married women earn about the same as single women, and black women earn about the same as white women.

Table 11.11 presents the results from regressions of (log) average annual earnings in a plant on various plant characteristics, for all plants in the SSEL

---

27. Further evidence that this is true is given by the fact that the coefficients on the education variables are the only coefficients to change significantly between cols. (3) and (4).

Table 11.10   **Regression of Worker Wages for SDF and WECD Workers**

	SDF Workers with Match (1)	SDF Workers without Match (2)	WECD Workers (3)	WECD Workers Weighted (4)
Intercept	1.55	1.55	1.41	1.34
	(0.008)	(0.008)	(0.031)	(0.02)
Experience	0.06	0.06	0.06	0.07
	(0.001)	(0.001)	(0.002)	(0.002)
Exp^2*10	−0.02	−0.02	−0.02	−0.03
	(0.001)	(0.001)	(0.001)	(0.001)
Exp^3*1000	0.05	0.05	0.05	0.07
	(0.002)	(0.002)	(0.004)	(0.004)
$Exp^4*10000$	−0.05	−0.05	−0.04	−0.06
	(0.002)	(0.002)	(0.004)	(0.004)
Female	−0.17	−0.17	−0.17	−0.18
	(0.002)	(0.002)	(0.004)	(0.004)
Married	0.13	0.13	0.12	0.13
	(0.001)	(0.001)	(0.002)	(0.003)
Black	−0.06	−0.06	−0.04	−0.05
	(0.002)	(0.002)	(0.004)	(0.005)
Female*Married	−0.14	−0.14	−0.13	−0.14
	(0.002)	(0.002)	(0.004)	(0.004)
Female*Black	0.08	0.08	0.07	0.08
	(0.004)	(0.004)	(0.007)	(0.008)
Educ1				
Educ2	0.13	0.13	0.10	0.12
	(0.001)	(0.001)	(0.002)	(0.003)
Educ3	0.21	0.21	0.17	0.18
	(0.002)	(0.002)	(0.003)	(0.003)
Educ4	0.41	0.41	0.36	0.39
	(0.002)	(0.002)	(0.004)	(0.004)
Educ5	0.55	0.55	0.49	0.47
	(0.003)	(0.003)	(0.006)	(0.006)
Match	0.03			
	(0.002)			
Adjusted R^2	0.50	0.50	0.51	0.47
N	704,373	704,373	185,186	185,007

Notes: These regressions only include workers who are between ages 18 and 65, who usually work 30–65 hours a week, and who have average wages between $2.50 and $100.00 an hour. Numbers in parentheses are standard errors.

(col. [1]), unique plants (col. [2]), unique plants weighted by the probability of being unique (col. [3]), WECD plants (col. [4]), and WECD plants weighted by the probability of appearing in the WECD (col. [5]). As in table 11.10, the coefficients on the various variables in table 11.11 are similar across the five regressions. The major differences occur for the location variables. The coefficient on place in column (1) is positive while the coefficients on place in the other four regressions are all negative (although never significantly different

Table 11.11   **Plant-Level Regression of Log Average Earnings in the Plant**

	SSEL Plants (1)	Unique Plants (2)	Unique Plants Weighted (3)	WECD Plants (4)	WECD Plants Weighted (5)
Intercept	2.34	2.46	2.35	2.51	2.25
	(0.017)	(0.04)	(0.035)	(0.114)	(0.082)
Log employment	0.18	0.15	0.17	0.13	0.23
	(0.003)	(0.005)	(0.005)	(0.010)	(0.010)
Log employment squared	−0.02	−0.01	−0.01	−0.01	−0.02
	(0.000)	(0.001)	(0.001)	(0.001)	(0.002)
Place	0.03	−0.10	−0.07	−0.18	−0.10
	(0.013)	(0.036)	(0.025)	(0.082)	(0.056)
Multiunit	0.16	0.16	0.14	0.13	0.13
	(0.004)	(0.008)	(0.009)	(0.011)	(0.015)
Plant age					
0–4	−0.19	−0.19	−0.17	−0.18	−0.18
	(0.004)	(0.009)	(0.009)	(0.015)	(0.015)
5–9	−0.10	−0.11	−0.11	−0.10	−0.08
	(0.003)	(0.007)	(0.008)	(0.012)	(0.013)
10–14	−0.05	−0.06	−0.04	−0.06	−0.07
	(0.004)	(0.008)	(0.008)	(0.011)	(0.013)
15+					
Region					
Northeast	0.13	0.14	0.22	0.08	0.32
	(0.012)	(0.036)	(0.020)	(0.103)	(0.051)
Midwest	−0.01	0.05	0.10	0.005	0.15
	(0.012)	(0.036)	(0.021)	(0.103)	(0.051)
South	−0.02	0.05	0.15	−0.02	0.19
	(0.012)	(0.036)	(0.020)	(0.103)	(0.050)
West					
Adjusted R^2	0.23	0.26	0.23	0.32	0.31
N	234,694	49,735	49,698	15,138	15,137

Note: Numbers in parentheses are standard errors.

from zero). The coefficients on the three region variables also vary in sign and magnitude across the five regressions (although in all five regressions plants in the Northeast region pay the highest wages). The most likely explanation for these differences is that almost all unique plants and WECD plants are located in a place, and very few of these plants are located in the West region.[28]

28. The fact that only the coefficients on the size and location variables change between the weighted and unweighted regressions provides further evidence that these characteristics are significant determinants of whether a plant appears in the WECD. Obviously, given that I am controlling for these characteristics in the unweighted regressions, the coefficients on the other variables should be unbiased estimates of the effect of these characteristics on wages and therefore will not change when estimating the weighted regression (assuming that they are uncorrelated with size or location).

The estimated relationships seen in table 11.11 are also similar to previously reported relationships between plant characteristics and average wages. The coefficient on log plant employment shows that large employers pay higher average wages (Brown and Medoff 1989; Dunne and Schmitz 1995), while the coefficients on the plant age variables show that older plants also pay higher wages (Brown and Medoff 1995; Dunne and Roberts 1990).

The results in tables 11.8 and 11.9 show that, while the unweighted data are not a representative sample of either the underlying population of workers and plants, it is possible to use weights based on the probability that a plant appears in the data to produce estimates of characteristics that are similar to estimates from the SDF and SSEL data. Even more encouraging, the results in tables 11.10 and 11.11 show that these data are capable of replicating both the relationships found in data for the underlying population and the relationships found by previous researchers using alternative data sources. Thus it appears that these data are useful for addressing certain empirical questions. Just what some of these questions are is what I turn to next.

11.4   What Can We Learn from the Worker-Establishment Characteristics Database?

11.4.1   The Establishment Size-Wage Premium

One question that has long interested labor economists is why large employers pay higher wages than small employers—what is referred to as the employer size-wage premium.[29] Despite this long interest, previous attempts to account for the employer size-wage premium in terms of observable worker or employer characteristics have met with limited success. The reason for this lack of success is that, while most theoretical explanations for the employer size-wage premium stress the matching of workers and employers (e.g., Oi 1983, 1990; Hamermesh 1980, 1993; Dunne and Schmitz 1995), previous empirical work has relied on either worker surveys with little information about the characteristics of a worker's employer or establishment surveys with little information about the characteristics of workers in a plant. Obviously the WECD, which contains information for both workers and employers, is an ideal source for investigating the employer size-wage premium.

Consider the results in Troske (in press). Using the WECD data this paper examines a number of possible explanations for the employer size-wage premium. The main conclusion is that, while a significant portion of the size-wage premium is reduced once the fact that large plants are more capital intensive and employ more skilled workers has been controlled for, a majority of the premium remains unexplained. However, the primary importance of these results is that they represent the first attempt to account for the establishment size-wage premium in terms of both worker and employer characteristics.

---

29. For a complete discussion of the issues in this section, see Troske (in press).

11.4.2   Wages, Productivity, and Worker Characteristics

Models of wage determination such as life cycle wage models, models of race or sex discrimination, returns to education, productivity effects of marriage, models of job-specific human capital accumulation, industry rents, and the like, all hinge on the relationship between wages, productivity, and worker characteristics.[30] However, direct measures of worker productivity are hard to obtain, so economists usually must rely on proxies for worker productivity when conducting empirical research. The problem with this approach is that whether these proxies reflect productivity differences is always in doubt, making it difficult to distinguish between competing models. However, data such as the WECD, by combining worker and plant data, avoid these difficulties by allowing researchers to directly compare estimates of the relative wages of workers with estimates of workers' relative marginal productivity.

As an example, consider Hellerstein et al. (in press). This paper uses a production function approach, where workers with different characteristics are treated as substitute labor inputs in the plant, to directly estimate the marginal product of workers. These estimates are then compared with estimated wage differentials among groups of workers. This analysis represents a departure from most of the existing empirical literature on wage determination because the authors directly compare estimates of workers' relative wages with estimates of workers' marginal products. Two of the findings from this analysis are that (1) there is no significant difference in the marginal product and marginal wages of married workers and (2) the marginal wages of women appear to be significantly less than their marginal product. Although these results are tentative, they suggest two things. First, explanations for the observed marriage premium should focus on whether marriage is a signal for inherent productivity differences between married and single men or whether marriage in some way makes men more productive. Second, explanations for the gender wage gap should focus on why women receive lower wages than men and not on why women are less productive than men. However, the primary importance of these results is again the new insight into the wage determination process that we gain using employer-employee matched data.

11.4.3   Technology Use and Worker Wages

While there has been growing interest among both economists and policy-makers regarding the importance of skill-biased technical change in determining both the rate of return to education and the increasing wage differential between skilled and unskilled workers, there have been few microlevel studies that contain direct evidence on the effects of technical change on worker wages.[31] One of the principal reasons for this is the lack of data linking

---

30. For a complete discussion of the analysis discussed in this section, see Hellerstein, Neumark, and Troske (in press).

31. For a complete discussion of the issues in the section, see Doms, Dunne, and Troske (1997).

a plant's use of advanced technology and the plant's demand for skilled labor. Linking the WECD with the plant-level data from the Census Bureau's Survey of Manufacturing Technology, which asks manufacturers about their use of advanced manufacturing technology in the plant, creates a data set that contains direct measures of a plant's use of technology, along with information on the characteristics of workers in the plant. These data can then be used to examine the effect of technology use on the wages and skill mix of workers in the plant.

As an example of this, consider Doms et al. (1997). Results in this paper show that plants that use advanced technology capital in production pay workers higher wages. However, these authors also show that a significant portion of this premium is accounted for once they control for cross-plant differences in worker skill. These results are consistent with the hypothesis that much of the recent increase in the dispersion of wages is the result of skill-biased technical change. However, these results also represent one of the first successful attempts to show that worker skill varies systematically with employer characteristics.

11.5   Summary and Concluding Remarks

Results from examining the quality of the WECD are mixed. The results from section 11.3 show that, while a rather small percentage of workers and plants appear in the WECD, it does seem that workers are being matched to the correct establishments. The results from tables 11.8 and 11.9 show that, while the WECD data is not a representative sample of the underlying population of workers and plants, it is possible to construct weights so that estimates of characteristics using these data more closely resemble estimates of these characteristics from data on the underlying population. Even more important, the results in table 11.10 show that these data are capable of replicating relationships found in both the original data and in previous research based on alternative data sources. The latter finding in particular suggests that these data allow investigation of hypothesized relationships between worker and plant characteristics that are derived from theoretical models. Evidence on this point is found in section 11.4, where I present examples of how these data have been used to investigate hypotheses regarding the determination of worker wages. I should point out, however, that these data will offer only limited support for theories. They can show whether the hypothesized relationships are present in a select sample of workers and plants—they may not generalize to the entire population. However, given the uniqueness of these data, even with these limitations they should prove to be a valuable research tool.

One of the strongest conclusions that emerges from this analysis is that creating employer-employee matched databases requires very detailed information on which to base the match. The two major weaknesses of the WECD, the fact that it is a nonrandom sample and the fact that it only contains data for manufacturing workers and employers, are a direct result of not having detailed place-of-work information. Obviously, if we hope to produce larger, more representative employer-employee matched databases containing workers and employers from all sectors of the economy, we will need more detailed information to link workers to employers.

While more detailed name and address information for both workers and employers was collected, it was not possible to use this information when constructing the WECD because the name and address information for workers' employers was destroyed prior to starting the WECD project. However, in the future this information will be saved and made available to researchers at the Census Bureau. This more detailed information, in conjunction with business name and address matching algorithms, should allow us to construct larger, more representative employer-employee matched databases and to extend these databases to nonmanufacturing workers and employers.

Appendix

Worker Variables Available from the Worker-Establishment Characteristics Database

Place of residence: state code
Place of residence: county code
Place of residence: place code
Place of residence: block code
Sex
Detailed race code (three-digit race code)
Age
Marital status
Person weight
Place of birth
Citizenship
Year of entry
School enrollment
Highest degree completed
Ancestry (six-digit code)
Mobility status (where lived on 1 April, 1985)
Language other than English at home
English ability
Military service
Work limitation status
Mobility limitation
Personal care limitation

Number of children ever born
Hours worked last week
Principal means of transportation to work
Time of departure for work
Travel time to work
Occupation (three-digit code)
Class of worker
Worked last year (1989)
Weeks worked last year (1989)
Usual hours worked last year (1989)
Wage or salary income (1989)
Nonfarm self-employment income (1989)
Farm self-employment Income (1989)
Interest, dividends, and net rental income (1989)
Social security income (1989)
Public assistance income (1989)
Retirement income (1989)
All other income (1989)

Establishment Variables Available in the Longitudinal Research Database

Total value of shipments
Four-digit SIC code
Establishment state code
Establishment county code
Establishment place code
Value added
Value of resales
Receipts for contract work
Miscellaneous receipts
Total employment
Total employment: production workers
Total production worker man-hours
Total salary and wages
Total production worker wages
Total supplemental labor costs
Legally required supplemental labor costs
Cost of materials
Cost of resales
Cost of fuels
Cost of purchased electricity
Cost of contract work
Beginning-of-year inventory: finished goods
Beginning-of-year inventory: work-in-progress

Beginning-of-year inventory: materials
Beginning-of-year inventory: total
End-of-year inventory: finished goods
End-of-year inventory: work-in-progress
End-of-year inventory: materials
End-of-year inventory: total
New building expenditure
New machinery expenditures
Used capital expenditures
Beginning of year: building assets
Beginning of year: machinery assets
End of year: building assets
End of year: machinery assets
Building depreciation
Machinery depreciation
Building retirements
Machinery retirements
Material code
Product code

References

Bates, Nancy, Robert E. Fay, and Jeffery C. Moore. 1991. Lower mail response in the 1990 census: A preliminary interpretation. In *1991 Annual research conference proceedings.* Washington, D.C.: U.S. Bureau of the Census.

Brown, Charles, and James Medoff. 1989. The employer size-wage effect. *Journal of Political Economy* 97 (November): 1027–59.

———. 1995. Firm age and wages. Ann Arbor, University of Michigan, March. Unpublished paper.

Cain, Glen. 1986. The economic analysis of labor market discrimination: A survey. In *Handbook of labor economics,* ed. Orley C. Ashenfelter and Richard Layard. Amsterdam: North-Holland.

Doms, Mark, Timothy Dunne, and Kenneth R. Troske. 1997. Workers, wages, and technology. *Quarterly Journal of Economics* 112 (February): 253–90.

Dunne, Timothy, and Mark Roberts. 1990. Plant, firm and industry wage variation. Norman: University of Oklahoma, December. Unpublished paper.

Dunne, Timothy, and James A. Schmitz. 1995. Wages, employment structure and employer size-wage premia: Their relationship to advanced-technology usage at U.S. manufacturing establishments. *Economica* 62:89–107.

Griliches, Zvi. 1969. Capital-skill complementarity. *Review of Economics and Statistics* 51:465–68.

———. 1970. Notes on the role of education in production functions and growth accounting. In *Education, income, and human capital,* ed. W. Lee Hansen. New York: Columbia University Press.

Hamermesh, Daniel S. 1980. Commentary. In *The economics of firm size, market structure and social performance,* ed. John J. Siegfried. Washington, D.C.: Federal Trade Commission.

————. 1993. *Labor demand*. Princeton, N.J.: Princeton University Press.

Hellerstein, Judith K., David Neumark, and Kenneth R. Troske. In press. Wages, productivity, and worker characteristics: Evidence from plant-level production functions and wage equations. *Journal of Labor Economics.*

Korenman, Sanders, and David Neumark. 1991. Does marriage really make men more productive? *Journal of Human Resources* 26 (2): 282–307.

Kulka, Richard A., Nicholas A. Holt, Woody Carter, and Kathryn L. Dowd. 1991. Self-reports of time pressures, concerns for privacy, and participation in the 1990 mail census. In *1991 Annual research conference proceedings*. Washington, D.C.: U.S. Bureau of the Census.

Mincer, Jacob. 1974. *Schooling, experience, and earnings*. New York: Columbia University Press.

Oi, Walter Y. 1983. The fixed employment costs of specialized labor. In *The measurement of labor costs,* ed. Jack E. Triplett. Chicago: University of Chicago Press.

————. 1990. Employment relations in dual labor markets ("It's nice work if you can get it"). *Journal of Labor Economics* 8 (January): S124–S149.

Rosen, Sherwin. 1986. The theory of equalizing differences. In *Handbook of labor economics,* ed. Orley C. Ashenfelter and Richard Layard. Amsterdam: North-Holland.

Troske, Kenneth R. In press. Evidence on the employer size-wage premium from worker-establishment matched data. *Review of Economics and Statistics.*

U.S. Bureau of the Census. 1979. The Standard Statistical Establishment List program. Bureau of the Census Technical Paper no. 44. Washington, D.C.: U.S. Bureau of the Census.

————. 1992a. 1990 Census of Population and Housing—Classified index of industries and occupations. Washington, D.C.: U.S. Bureau of the Census.

————. 1992b. 1990 Census of Population and Housing—Guide part A. Text. Washington, D.C.: U.S. Bureau of the Census.

Willis, Robert. 1986. Wage determinants: A survey and reinterpretation of human capital earnings functions. In *Handbook of labor economics,* ed. Orley C. Ashenfelter and Richard Layard. Amsterdam: North-Holland.

12 A Needs Analysis of Training Data: What Do We Want, What Do We Have, Can We Ever Get It?

Lisa M. Lynch

12.1 Introduction

The marked acceleration of changes in the nature of work over the past two decades has generated a growing interest in the process of skill accumulation. In the past, most human capital research focused on skills acquired in schools and the impact of formal education on earnings. However, issues such as the impact of trade and technology on incumbent and dislocated workers, welfare reform, and the transition from school to work have created the need for a better understanding of how workers cope with changing skill demands once they leave the formal education system. In spite of this demand for information, the supply is quite limited. For example, policymakers are faced with the challenge of reforming the welfare system with little or no documentation of the skills gap of welfare recipients and no system in place to monitor the role of training in facilitating the transition from welfare to work. Businesses that choose between "making or buying" skills have relatively little information on the impact of different training programs on productivity. Incumbent and dislocated workers who find their jobs dramatically redefined by new technology do not always know how to determine the best source of training for their new skill needs.

Although there has been a great deal written about the measurement issues associated with formal education, there has been relatively little analysis of the existing sources of postschool training. While progress has been made in recent years to improve the quantity and quality of information available on private sector training, current data sources are quite primitive when contrasted

Lisa M. Lynch, formerly chief economist at the U.S. Department of Labor, is the William L. Clayton Professor of International Economic Affairs at the Fletcher School of Law and Diplomacy, Tufts University, and a research associate of the National Bureau of Economic Research.

The author thanks Jack Barron for comments on an earlier draft of this paper.

with data on education. For example, there is no annual time series of expenditures on postschool training similar to what we have on annual expenditures for education. We have no aggregate measure of the stock of postschool training in the economy that parallels the information we have on the average educational attainment of workers by demographic group. While much of the recent empirical work on the returns to education has focused on the role of the quality of education, this issue has barely begun to be addressed in the training arena. Therefore, this chapter tries to summarize what training information we would like to have, what information we have at the moment, and whether we can ever get all the information we actually need.

12.2   What Do We Want?

Substantial investments in human capital are made every year in the United States. For example, during the period 1990–91 more than $248 billion was spent by federal, state, and local governments on public and private K–12 education and $166 billion was spent on public and private higher education (Department of Education 1993). Unfortunately, estimates of the expenditures on postschool training are harder to come by, and the few estimates that do exist differ greatly. For example, Carnevale, Gainer, and Villet (1990) estimated that in the 1980s more than $30 billion was spent annually on firm-provided training in the United States. At the same time Ann Bartel (1989) estimated that $55 billion was spent on firm-provided training in 1987, and Jacob Mincer, using Panel Study of Income Dynamics data from 1976 and interpolating to 1987, estimated that $148 billion was spent on formal private sector training. Including informal training expenditures in Mincer's calculations would boost his estimate to $296 billion in 1987. More recently, the American Society of Training and Development reported that in 1995 businesses spent $55 billion on training.

So depending on which estimate we believe, we can conclude that real training expenditures have risen or fallen over the past 10 years, while per capita training expenditures seem to have decreased. The main reason for this variance of estimates is that there is no longitudinal database of firms and their training expenditures. Even if there were such a database, there is no agreed upon accounting method by which to calculate training expenditures. Companies are not required to separately report in a common fashion direct training expenditures and would never report the largest indirect cost—wages and salaries of trainees. Until we resolve the rather serious measurement issues associated with these types of training expenditures, we will not be able to determine which of the current estimates of training expenditures is most accurate.

The measurement discussion on postschool training investments, however, is not just about how to come up with a better estimate of the amount spent on training. Much of the current interest in firm-provided training has been driven by the perception that the current system of education and training does not

Table 12.1   **Literacy Skills of U.S. Young Adults Aged 21–25, 1985**

Education	Prose Literacy[a]	Document Literacy[b]	Quantitative Literacy[c]
High school dropout	24.1	18.8	20.6
High school graduate	45.1	46.2	45.2
Some postsecondary	67.0	68.0	66.8
College graduate	84.3	85.6	84.2

Source: Department of Education (1989).

[a]Percentage able to locate information in a newspaper or almanac.

[b]Percentage able to follow directions to travel from one location to another using a map.

[c]Percentage able to enter deposits and checks and balance a checkbook.

seem to be working as well as it once did. Some have argued that over the past 20 years educational quality has declined in the United States and, consequently, new entrants are not as well prepared as they were in the past to meet employer skill needs. As a result, employers find that they have to "top up" the skills of new entrants.

Some evidence on the degree of topping up is presented in table 12.1 using data from a literacy survey of young adults in 1985 conducted by the Department of Education. The percentage of young adult high school graduates or dropouts who were able to perform relatively straightforward tasks such as locating information in a newspaper or balancing a checkbook is quite low (20 to 25 percent of high school dropouts and only 45 percent of high school graduates). Almost as disturbing are the 15 percent of college graduates who are unable to complete these tasks.

While many of us may have some sympathy with the difficulties of balancing a checkbook, the empirical evidence on the rising wage gap (for a recent survey of this literature, see Freeman and Katz 1994) suggests a dramatic change in the demand for those workers without a college degree relative to those who have completed college. For those with a high school degree, the old system of "learning by doing" does not seem to be as efficient a way to develop their human capital as it once was. Employers are looking for workers who have broad and deep general education to be able to adjust to the changing skill requirements associated with changing technology and workplace practices such as job rotation and cross-training. Skills such as team work, problem solving, communication, and quality control do not seem to be easy to learn informally on the job. It would be useful to have a longitudinal survey of firms and their employment practices to capture this shift from informal learning by doing to more formal skill development. Unfortunately, we do not have any time-series information on the incidence, content, or delivery of training of a sample of representative firms to document this phenomenon.

Currently, the only source of information on some of the changes in the use of formal and informal training is the supplements to the Current Population

Table 12.2   **Percentage of Workers Receiving Training on the Job**

Type of Worker	Formal On-the-Job Training		Informal On-the-Job Training	
	1983	1991	1983	1991
All	12.0	16.8	15.2	16.2
Men	13.8	18.3	15.5	15.9
Women	9.9	15.0	14.7	15.9
Age				
16–19	1.9	2.8	13.6	13.3
20–24	7.7	9.9	15.2	15.0
25–34	14.0	17.5	16.3	16.4
35–44	15.4	20.9	16.0	18.0
45–54	13.8	20.1	15.0	16.7
55+	9.3	13.8	12.3	13.8
Education				
Dropout	3.8	5.2	11.7	10.8
High school	10.5	13.9	15.9	15.6
Some college	15.1	20.4	17.2	18.9
College	20.5	26.1	16.7	18.7
College+	16.7	23.4	12.6	16.8

Source: January 1983 and January 1991 Current Population Survey from Bowers and Swaim (1994).

Survey in 1983 and 1991 that collected information on the percentage of workers ever receiving formal or informal training in their current employment. Table 12.2 shows that the incidence of formal training has risen between 1983 and 1991 from 12 percent to almost 17 percent of workers. The rise has been especially sharp for workers aged 45–54 and those with more than a high school education. Therefore, a second training data need is to find a way to better document the changing pattern of formal and informal training over time.

The apparent switch from informal to formal on-the-job training is not sufficient to explain the current interest of many policymakers in identifying ways to augment firm-provided training. There is concern that while skill needs have changed and a greater premium is being paid for those with more education and skills, the marketplace is not delivering a sufficient supply of more skilled workers. In other words, as discussed in Bishop (1994) and Lynch (1994), there is a potential market failure in the provision of more general training. Possible reasons for a market failure in the provision of more general training include higher training costs for smaller firms than for larger firms, capital market imperfections, and other institutional barriers. This means that when measuring training we need to also capture training that is not occurring and why this investment is not being made. The reason may be that some firms are concerned about raiding by other firms of their trained workers or that employee turnover is high. In both cases, the firm may not be able to fully capture its training investment.

But improving the measurement of the incidence and types of training that workers are receiving is not our only training data need. The continuing debate on rising wage inequality and competitiveness requires an increased understanding of the role training plays for wage determination and firm competitiveness. During the 1960s and 1970s, empirical studies on the impact of postschool training on wages that built on the fundamental contributions of Becker (1962, 1964) and Mincer (1974) had to infer this impact by what the wage profile looked like over an individual's work experience. This was necessary because while we had relatively good information on workers' wages and tenures with firms, we had little information on postschool training investments. Apart from the fact that this was not a terrific way to test human capital theory, there were other theories developed in the 1970s and 1980s that generated upward-sloping wage profiles that had little to do with human capital investment. Fortunately, during the 1980s, researchers were able to use an increasing supply of microbased databases that included information on the incidence of both education and firm-provided training. As a result, we are finally able to begin examining both the returns to investments in education and the varying impact of different types of postschool training on wages of workers.

The impact of training on wages is not the only outcome of interest to policymakers. Much of the current debate on training was originally motivated by the perception that U.S. workers' skills lagged behind those of workers in other countries. This skills gap in turn may be partly responsible for a decline in the competitiveness of U.S. firms, especially in manufacturing. Some recent data collection efforts on training have included attempts to measure its impact on the productivity of firms, as well as its impact on wages, by doing surveys of establishments that include questions on their training practices and outcomes.

In sum, better training data are needed to document how much is currently invested in postschool training and how the nature of this training has switched from informal to formal. Measuring the incidence of training and expenditures on training is only a very small part of the measurement needs. However, much of the current policy debate is motivated by who is not getting training rather than who is. Therefore, documentation is needed on who are the individuals (firms) receiving (providing) training and what are possible barriers to the provision or receipt of training. In order to understand the changes in training over time, one also needs to understand the possible sources of the increased demand for training—declining school quality, increasing international competition, changing technology, and changing work organization. Therefore, measuring the incidence of training within a firm or for workers without seeing how they are also affected by these external factors provides a limited picture. Finally, much of the current policy debate is about how training can affect wages of workers and productivity of firms. This suggests that measuring the impact of training on wages and productivity is at least as important as measuring its incidence.

The rest of this chapter summarizes what is currently available on postschool training investments and highlights the ability of these data to provide insights into the outcomes of training. The paper discusses the current measurement needs for training data and outlines issues associated with closing the gap between current data sources on training and our needs.

12.3   Sources of Training Data

The following summarizes the current information on training contained in a variety of household, employer, and matched employer-employee surveys in the United States. In addition, representative studies using data from these surveys are summarized in table 12.3. Since the general characteristics of most of the houschold surveys listed here have already been summarized by Manser (chap. 1 in this volume), I only discuss the specific training questions asked in each of the surveys. In particular, I summarize whether the survey can be used to distinguish between informal and formal training, whether it includes duration measures, whether the content of the training program be determined, and whether the timing of training spells can be identified. The description of the establishments surveys details differences in target respondent, response rates, types of training questions collected, and other data that the training questions can be matched with. Finally, the description of matched employer-employee surveys describes alternative strategies for generating this type of matched information.

12.3.1   Household-Based Surveys

In general, all of the following surveys allow one to estimate the impact of postschool training on the wages of workers controlling for a wealth of demographic characteristics including education, race, gender, and work experience. There is usually little information on firm characteristics in these surveys other than industry and, occasionally, firm size. As a result, none of these surveys can be used to examine how training affects productivity or how training is linked to other firm practices.

Current Population Survey (CPS), 1983 and 1991. Although this is not a longitudinal survey, the CPS is currently the best source of information on how the incidence of training has changed over the past 10 years for the workforce as a whole. Training questions were asked in just two years—1983 and 1991, when a training supplement was added to the January CPS (for studies using these data, see Carey 1985; Pergamit and Shack-Marquez 1987; Lillard and Tan 1986; Bowers and Swaim 1994; Hollenbeck and Wilkie 1985). A variety of questions on training are asked, such as "What training was needed to get the current or last job, and what training was needed to improve skills on the cur-

Table 12.3   Data Sources for Private Sector Training

Survey	Representative Studies Using Data
Household	
Current Population Survey (CPS) 1983 and 1991	Carey 1985; Pergamit and Shack-Marquez 1987; Lillard and Tan 1986; Bowers and Swaim 1994; Hollenbeck and Wilkie 1985
Employment Opportunities Pilot Project (EOPP) individual survey, 1979–80	
High School and Beyond (HS&B), 1986	
Panel Study of Income Dynamics (PSID), 1976–80	Duncan and Hoffman 1978; Brown 1989; Lillard and Tan 1986
National Longitudinal Survey (NLS) young men and women cohorts	Lillard and Tan 1986
National Longitudinal Survey of Youth (NLSY)	Lynch 1992b; Veum 1994; Loewenstein and Spletzer 1994
National Longitudinal Study of the Class of 1972 (NLS72)	Lillard and Tan 1986; Altonji and Spletzer 1991
Survey of Income Participation and Program (SIPP), 1984, 1986, and 1987	
Employer based	
Bartel (1983 and 1986 data)	Bartel 1992
Columbia human resource management survey, 1985	Bartel 1989
Department of Labor training surveys, 1993 and 1995	
EOPP–National Center for Research in Vocational Education (NCRVE), 1982	Barron, Black, and Lowenstein 1987, 1989; Bishop 1994
Educational Quality of the Workforce (EQW) National Employers' Survey (NES), 1994	
National Federation of Independent Business (NFIB), 1987	Bishop 1994
Training Magazine	October issues
Small Business Administration (SBA), 1992	Barron, Berger, and Black 1997
Spencer Foundation, 1992	Osterman 1995
Southport Institute	Bassi 1994
Matched employer-employee surveys	
BLS White Collar Pay Survey (WCP), 1989 and 1990	Bronars and Famulari, chap. 13 in this volume
National Organization Survey (NOS)	Knoke and Kalleberg 1994
Upjohn, 1993	Barron, Berger, and Black 1994

rent job?" It is possible to distinguish between formal and informal training and between training received on the current job and training received prior to the current job. Information on the duration of training spells is not available, and there may have been some underreporting of the incidence of training if workers only reported training spells that were associated with changing jobs or obtaining a promotion. It is not possible to determine the timing of the training spells.

Panel Study of Income Dynamics (PSID), 1976–80. The training data available in the PSID cannot be classified into formal or informal training, or on-site or off-site training. This is because the question the PSID asked—"On a job like yours how long does it take the average person to become fully qualified?"—does not reveal where the training occurred or the nature of the training. Duration of training spells can be calculated with this question, but unfortunately the question refers to the average person not the actual respondent (for studies using these data, see Duncan and Hoffman 1978; Brown 1989; Lillard and Tan, 1986). It is also not possible to determine the timing or intensity of the training with this question. There is even the possibility that some respondents may refer to training that took place before employment with the current employer. The primary advantage of this question is that it is more likely to pick up both formal and informal training. There is a second question that could be used to capture the degree of portability of training. This question is: "Are you learning skills on the current job which could lead to a better job or promotion?" This survey can be used to examine how the incidence of training and its impact varied over certain periods of time for the workforce as a whole. Nachum Sicherman (1990) has done an interesting study on the training questions in the PSID in which he compares training measures in the PSID with those listed in the *Dictionary of Occupational Titles* (DOT). The DOT data are not self-reports. Rather, they are obtained by detailed site visits of jobs. Sicherman (1990) finds that the PSID appears to underreport training duration when compared to what is listed in DOT for the same occupation.

Survey of Income and Program Participation (SIPP), 1984 (wave 3), 1986 (wave 2), and 1987 (wave 2). All workers in the household aged 22–65 who reported earnings are asked, "Has . . . ever received training designed to help find a job, improve job skills, or learn a new job?" But the questions do not measure duration or timing or identify who provided the training—for example, firms, schools, or government. The incidence measure on this training variable is much lower than the incidence measure from the CPS 1983 and 1991 training supplements. Zemsky and Shapiro (1994) have suggested that one reason why the incidence rate is lower in the SIPP than in the CPS is that these questions follow a sequence of questions probing about difficulties in the labor market. Training therefore is asked in the context of labor market difficulties, not general labor market experience.

Employment Opportunities Pilot Project (EOPP) individual survey. This Department of Labor survey administered in 1980 targeted workers employed in low-wage labor markets. Therefore, it is not representative of the labor force, and it is not a longitudinal survey. It does have detailed training questions such as "Describe up to four training events occurring between 1/1/79 and the interview date in 1980."

National Longitudinal Survey (NLS) young men, young women, and older men cohorts. These cohort surveys include training questions that can be matched with employment and wage histories of respondents (for a comprehensive study using data from various NLS cohorts, see Lillard and Tan 1986). Questions on training include "Do you receive or use additional training (other than schooling training) on your job?" and "What was the longest type of training you have had since the last interview?" Therefore, there is some information on timing, duration, and content of training programs. A primary disadvantage of these questions is that they are specific to a particular age cohort. In addition, it is not possible to distinguish between formal and informal training, and some previously acquired training could be captured as current training given the wording of the question.

National Longitudinal Survey of Youth (NLSY). Currently, the NLSY represents the most detailed individual survey on training available in the United States (see studies that use data from this longitudinal survey by Lynch 1992b; Veum 1994; Loewenstein and Spletzer 1994). From 1979–86 the following are some of the training questions asked of all respondents: "In addition to your schooling, military and government sponsored training programs, did you receive any other types of training for more than one month?" and "Which of the following categories best describes where you received this training?" (up to three spells per interview). Cost information has been collected periodically, and intensity of training (hours) and starting and ending month of training spells are collected so that it is possible to determine source, timing, intensity, and duration of training. Specifically, it is possible to distinguish between on-the-job training and off-the-job training.

These data can be linked to detailed weekly employment histories so that researchers can observe the impact of current completed or interrupted training on wages and labor mobility as well as the impact of past training spells on current labor market outcomes. From 1988 onward there was no restriction on the duration of the training spell. This appears to have greatly increased the incidence of reported on-the-job training spells that are usually less than one month in duration. In 1993, questions on informal training were added (see Loewenstein and Spletzer 1994) so that both formal and informal training spells can now be distinguished. While the 1993 survey provides informal training information, inadvertently not all workers were asked about informal training. This error will be corrected in the 1996 survey. The primary weakness of this survey is that the training information is specific to a particular cohort. However, since a great deal of human capital accumulation occurs early in a career, this is a cohort of importance for national trends in postschool training investments.

National Longitudinal Study of the Class of 1972 (NLS72). In the 1986 survey, a series of questions about employer-provided training were asked relative to respondents' current jobs (for a discussion of this survey, see Altonji and Spletzer 1991). Training information is gathered on formal on-site training, off-site training, and informal training. In addition, there is information on the duration (number of hours) of the training spells.

High School and Beyond (HS&B), 1986. This data set has a similar survey design to the NLS72. This survey was targeted at high school seniors and sophomores in 1980. The questions mimic the questions in NLS72.

12.3.2 Employer-Based Surveys

The following summarizes training data available in employer-based surveys. More specifically, I outline how representative each survey's sample is of establishments nationally, the type of survey instrument used (telephone or mailed), response rates to the survey, and the nature of the training measures (including cost estimates, incidence of training by occupational category, content of training, and duration or intensity measures). The following also identifies whether the data can be used to examine the impact of training on wages or productivity. A common dilemma faced in all of these surveys is identifying the target workers that the training questions will refer to. It is time consuming and expensive to ask detailed training questions about every type of worker in an establishment. Therefore, in order to get employers to provide higher quality data on employee training, many of the following surveys have opted to identify certain types of employees for whom to ask about specific training incidents rather than asking about all training spells for all employees in the establishment. This strategy is followed in the hope that it will improve the quality of the training data, but it clearly weakens the representativeness of the training data for the workforce as a whole.

Columbia human resource management (HRM) survey, 1985. This is a 1985 mailed national survey of establishments done by the Human Resource Management group at Columbia's Business School (see Bartel 1989). Data are obtained on approximately 600 establishments, but unfortunately the survey had only a 6 percent response rate. The survey includes comprehensive questions on HRM practices beyond training so that it is possible to see how training is combined with other HRM practices of the firm. Expenditures on training and incidence of training by occupation class are available in this survey. The data can also be linked to Compustat to obtain information on productivity and financial performance. However, for multiple establishments, the Compustat data refer to lines of business rather than to specific establishments. This clearly limits the productivity analysis. The very low response rate has limited the analysis of this survey.

Department of Labor training surveys, 1993 and 1995. The Department of Labor has conducted two recent surveys of employers and their training activities.

The first (DOL93) was a mailed questionnaire sent to approximately 8,000 establishments (70 percent response rate) surveying their formal training practices during 1993. No information on any dimension of informal training was gathered in this survey. Limited information on other HRM practices was collected in this survey, but wage and productivity measures were not collected. This survey can be used to determine the incidence of formal training across establishment size and industry, and there are detailed questions on the types of training provided—for example, occupational health and safety, orientation, and formal job skills training. The incidence of formal training by seven occupational groupings is also available, but it is not possible to determine how many workers actually received training during the reference period, 1993. This is because the respondents are only asked to check off whether they had any employees in that occupational category and, if yes, whether anyone got training. There are no duration measures, and it is not possible to use this survey to estimate the percentage of annual payroll devoted to training expenditures.

In 1996 the BLS released a second study on employer-provided training (DOL95) using information collected in a survey conducted by the BLS of establishments with 50 or more workers on their training activities from May through October 1995. This survey focused on the intensity of training efforts of firms. It also included some questions on direct costs of training but did not solicit information on the wage and salary value of time employees spent in training or other training costs such as equipment, space, or travel. Therefore, it is not possible to calculate total expenditures on training from this survey alone.

EOPP–National Center for Research in Vocational Education (NCRVE) employer survey, 1982. The second wave of the EOPP survey included a telephone survey in 1982 of employers that asked a series of questions about workers hired prior to August 1981. The survey included 3,411 establishments and had a response rate of 62 percent (for applications of this survey, see Barron, Black, and Loewenstein 1987, 1989; Bishop 1994). The survey also included retrospective information on 659 establishments about training and productivity of two recent hires. The training questions refer to training activities that occurred in the first three months of a new hire's tenure with the firm. Training is divided into formal and informal training, with data collected on the duration and intensity of training, starting wages, starting productivity, current wages, and current productivity. The survey includes a productivity measure where employers are asked to rate the productivity of the most recent hire at the start of their job and currently on a scale from 0 to 100 (where 100 equals the maximum productivity rating any employee in a defined position could attain).

This is not a nationally representative sample of employers, and the questions refer to the most recent new hires and not all incumbent workers in the establishment. Because the questionnaire refers to a specific newly hired employee, it is possible to ask for worker-specific information on race, gender, tenure on the job, relevant work experience, and wages. Therefore, even though this is not a "matched employer-employee" survey, employee-specific information can be determined. However, by focusing just on newly hired employees, the survey oversamples workers in high-turnover jobs. A priori we would expect that these jobs would have less training attached to them.

Educational Quality of the Workforce (EQW) National Employers' Survey (NES), 1994. This is a recently completed 1994 telephone interview of more than 3,200 private for-profit nonagricultural establishments in manufacturing and nonmanufacturing with 20 employees or more (73 percent overall response rate; for the questionnaire and a brief summary of the survey objectives and background, see Lynch and Zemsky 1994). The sample frame is the Census Bureau Standard Statistical Establishment List database. This nationally representative survey is designed so that the 1,700 manufacturing establishments can be matched with the Census Bureau's Annual Survey of Manufactures to obtain longitudinal data on output, materials, capital stock, and employment. A follow-up survey is planned that would contact approximately 20 workers per establishment in 500 of the manufacturing establishments for more detailed information on their current and past employment and training experience.

The survey is designed to elicit information on both formal and informal training, including the number of workers receiving training in 1993, how that number has changed relative to three years earlier, the hours and duration of training, the incidence of training by occupational category, and the content of the training. Future training needs are also measured, as is the percentage of total annual labor costs spent on training. Additional financial information on recent technological investments and other capital improvements, sales, competitive product strategy, age of the capital stock, and R&D has been collected so that determinants of productivity can be analyzed. Information on human resource practices, including employee involvement in decision making, the structure of compensation (including average wages by occupational category), recruitment and selection, and average educational level by occupational category, allow this survey to examine how training is linked to other HRM strategies. For example, this survey will allow researchers to distinguish between firms that train workers and firms that recruit already skilled employees. In addition, the survey can be used to see how training is bundled with other HRM practices and what its impact is on both wages and productivity in establishments.

National Federation of Independent Business (NFIB) survey, 1987. This was a mailed questionnaire in 1987 with 2,599 responses (approximately 25 percent response rate) of employers that were members of the NFIB and that hired someone in the past three years (for a complete discussion of the survey design, see Bishop 1994). This survey focused on the hiring and training of workers in the job in the firm that had the highest employee turnover. The survey design is similar to the EOPP survey except that questions concerning formal and informal training were merged into a single question: "How many hours did you or an employee spend training or closely supervising employee A or B?" An additional question is asked about informal training: "How many additional hours (beyond training and close supervision) did A/B spend learning the job by watching others rather than doing it?" The productivity measure used in this survey is similar to that in the EOPP survey. Since information is also gathered on starting and current wages of recent hires, it is also possible to estimate the impact of training on wages for recent hires in high-turnover positions.

Small Business Administration (SBA) survey, 1992. This is a 1992 telephone interview of 1,288 establishments (50 percent response rate; for a complete discussion of this survey, see Barron, Berger, and Black 1997). The sampling frame comes from Survey Sampling of Fairfield, Connecticut, and their Comprehensive Database. The survey is constructed to mimic much of the EOPP survey design, but in this survey it is possible to distinguish between on-site and off-site formal training, which was not possible in the EOPP survey. As in the EOPP, the training questions only refer to the last hired permanent employee. This is a nationally representative sample, but establishments in agriculture, forestry, fisheries, and public administration were excluded. One weakness of this and the EOPP survey is that both data sets truncate the training duration measures at three months. This may be a serious issue since there are a significant number of employees who report training spells of at least 12 weeks in duration.

Spencer Foundation employer survey, 1992. This is a telephone interview conducted in 1992 of 875 establishments with 50 or more employees (65.5 percent response rate; for a description of this survey and its training question, see Osterman 1995). Formal training information is gathered with reference to "core" employees only. This group is defined as the largest group of nonmanagerial workers directly involved in making the product or in providing the service at the location. This survey includes detailed information on a broad array of HRM practices but has no productivity measures. The focus on core employees appears to underrepresent employees who are women and minorities.

Training Magazine survey. This is a mailed survey of members of the American Society for Training and Development begun in 1981. Response rates vary around 15 percent. Over the years the sampling frame has changed, and it now refers to establishments with more than 100 employees. Because of changes in the year-to-year sampling frame, it is not appropriate to link survey years to obtain time-series information on the incidence of training. It is also likely that the survey oversamples corporate headquarters relative to actual production facilities. Training expenditure data and distribution of training by industry and occupation are available in this survey, but it is not possible to link these data to wage or productivity information.

As in the household-based surveys, it is difficult to compare training measures across any of these surveys. For employer-based surveys the difficulties in comparability are mainly due to the fact that each survey refers to a very different set of workers. However, given survey design, it is possible to make some comparison between the SBA, NFIB, and EOPP surveys on the one hand, and the Department of Labor and EQW surveys on the other. The SBA, NFIB, and EOPP surveys are especially good for identifying the training experience of new hires into a firm, and the Department of Labor and EQW surveys give a broader overview of the incidence and types of training across firms of varying sizes and industries.

12.3.3   Matched Employer-Employee Surveys

One way to resolve the problem of getting employers to provide high-quality data on the employment experience of different types of workers in the establishment is to do matched employer-employee surveys. In the employer survey, information on training, workplace practices, average wages, and productivity could be obtained by broad occupational categories, and then more detailed information on specific employee experiences in the establishment could be obtained with a simultaneous survey of employees. The quality of the data in this type of survey could be further enhanced if employers were willing to provide administrative records on employment and wages of employees. The matched survey would allow researchers and policymakers to see how diffuse reported workplace practices such as training and employee participation in decision making actually are in the workplace.

While this type of survey seems to be the ideal, there are some drawbacks. First, there may be substantial variation between the perceptions of employers and employees of the exact same practices. For example, a supervisor's close supervision of an employee may be regarded by the firm as employee training, while the worker may report it not as training but as monitoring. If the establishment is the frame of reference, when an employee leaves the establishment we lose information on what happens to this individual. If instead the worker is the frame of reference and we follow him or her through various employers, we may not be able to obtain sufficient information on the variation of the employment experience of other employees within the establishment. In addition, if the employee leaves the establishment, we lose the establishment from the survey. The following briefly describes some new surveys that have tried to match employees with employers.

BLS White Collar Pay Survey (WCP), 1989 and 1990. In 1989 and 1990, 354 establishments were asked by the Department of Labor about the demographic characteristics of a random sample of their white-collar employees. Three hundred establishments provided some information on more than 1,700 workers; however, after deleting cases with missing data the final sample only includes 601 full-time white-collar employees in 124 establishments. See Bronars and Famulari (chap. 13 in this volume) for a more complete description of this survey and its findings.

National Organization Survey (NOS). The sample frame was the 1991 General Social Survey of 1,517 respondents (see Knoke and Kalleberg 1994 for a detailed discussion of this survey and the June 1994 issue of *American Behavioral Scientist*). Each respondent was asked to identify his or her employer, and a telephone interview was attempted with the employer (1,427 establishments). Interviews were completed in establishments for 727 respondents, representing approximately a 50 percent response rate. The employer's survey included information on training, employment, fringe benefits, earnings, recruitment practices, and a subjective measure of productivity (a scale from 1 to 4 on whether current performance in producing the main product is better or worse than one year ago and three years ago).

Upjohn survey, 1993. This is a telephone survey of 305 establishments and their employees (20 percent response rate) conducted in spring 1993 (see Barron, Berger, and Black 1994 for a complete description of this survey). The sampling frame strategy is similar to the SBA survey and excludes establishments in agriculture, forestry, fisheries, and public administration. The survey is restricted to establishments with 100 or more employees that had hired someone in the past 10 days or expected to hire shortly. Training questions refer to training that occurred during the first month on the job and are based on the EOPP and SBA surveys. Productivity is a subjective measure of the new hire's productivity relative to a fully trained worker. In an attempt to improve the recall ability of employers and employees, the respondents (employers and employees) were contacted once after two weeks of employment and a second time after four weeks of employment. This is a unique feature in matched employee-employer surveys and something that hopefully will be repeated in future surveys.

DOL95 employer-employee training survey. As part of the BLS 1995 employer training survey, a matched employee survey was conducted in tandem of two employees in each of the businesses surveyed. There was a questionnaire that focused on demographic characteristics and a training log that collected detailed information on all training and learning activities the employee participated in over a 10-day period. The response rate for the employee survey was 35.3 percent. From this matched employer-employee survey the BLS concluded that an estimated total of $37 billion was spent on the indirect wage and salary costs of training during May–October 1995. Of this amount $13 billion, or 35 percent, was for formal training and the remaining $24 billion, or 65 percent, for informal training. The estimates in the BLS matched survey for indirect training costs are higher than those used by the American Society for Training and Development when it reported that employers spent $55 billion in 1995 on formal training.

The bottom line is that there have been very few matched employer-employee surveys. They are very expensive, response rates can be low, and there are large confidentiality issues for both respondents. Even drawing the sampling frame is difficult because it is not always clear whether one would want to start with a representative survey of employees or of employers.

12.4   The Training Gap: What Is It and How Could We Close It?

Table 12.4 summarizes how one can use the various surveys described above for analysis of training incidence and its impact on outcomes such as wages and productivity. As documented in several recent papers (Lynch 1992c; Zemsky and Shapiro 1994; Barron et al. 1997; Loewenstein and Spletzer 1994; Sicherman 1990) there is no consensus on the estimates of the incidence of formal and informal training across surveys, especially household-based surveys. This appears to be due to the questions used, who the questions refer to, the nature of the survey instrument, and when in the business cycle the surveys were done. As Zemsky and Shapiro (1994), Barron et al. (1997), and Loewenstein and Spletzer (1994) discuss, it does not seem possible to reconcile the different estimates on the incidence of training. Therefore, measuring the incidence of formal and informal training represents one gap in our training data.

In addition to the inconsistencies across surveys in how postschool training is defined, there is relatively limited work on the impact of training on productivity. Even though table 12.4 lists several studies that have examined the impact of training on productivity, most of these surveys use a subjective measure of productivity (e.g., "How has your productivity changed over the last year" on a scale of 1 to 4), rather than output divided by employment, total factor productivity, or value added. If output or sales are used, they are often data from the firm and not the establishment (e.g., the Columbia survey). The main problem with subjective measures of productivity is that these measures are not comparable across firms or even within firms over time. They also do not allow one to estimate rates of return to training versus other human resource practices. So far, only the EQW-NES will allow us to begin to look at the impact of training on more objective measures of productivity.

The recent Department of Labor surveys of establishments and their training practices highlight another gap in the collection of information on training. The Department of Labor training survey done by the BLS found that more than 70 percent of establishments in the United States offer some type of for-

Table 12.4   **Where to Go for Information on Training and Outcomes of Training**

Formal Training	Informal Training	Wages and Growth	Productivity	Changes Over Time
Household Surveys				
CPS	CPS	CPS		CPS
EOPP[a]	EOPP[a]	EOPP[a]		
HS&B	HS&B	HS&B		
NLS		NLS		NLS
NLSY	NLSY	NLSY		NLSY
NLS72	NLS72	NLS72		
PSID		PSID		
SIPP		SIPP		
Employer Surveys				
Columbia		Columbia	Columbia	
DOL93	DOL95			
EOPP[b]	EOPP[b]	EOPP[b]	EOPP[b]	
EQW-NES	EQW-NES	EQW-NES	EQW-NES	EQW-NES
NFIB		NFIB	NFIB	
SBA	SBA	SBA	SBA	
Spencer				
Matched Employer-Employee Surveys				
BSL-WCP		BLS-WCP		
NOS		NOS	NOS	
Upjohn	Upjohn	Upjohn	Upjohn	
DOL95	DOL95			

[a] Individual survey.
[b] Employer survey.

mal training. Fifty percent of establishments offered formal skills training, while the remaining establishments offered formal training in programs such as new hire orientation and occupational health and safety. At the same time, as shown in table 12.2, only 16 percent of workers in 1991 said they had ever received any type of training from their current employer. So we are left with an apparent paradox: most firms state that they are offering training while few workers seem to be getting it! A possible solution may be that while most firms offer training, only a small percentage of their workers actually receive it. Therefore, this paradox may be resolved with better matched information on firms and their employees.

Surveys that focus on identifying which firms are training and what is happening to their employees' wages and productivity may be problematic if they measure training at one point in time. From human capital theory we would expect workers' wages to be lower during periods of more general training as they share costs of training with their employers. Therefore, looking at a firm at a point in time and observing that those firms that are training have workers with lower wages than those firms that do not train, does not mean that the returns to training are low for workers. What is required instead are measurements of how training has changed over time and the corresponding changes in wages. At the same time, firms that train most heavily may also be the firms with lower productivity. Bartel (1992) shows that what training programs deliver in terms of productivity gains is often not seen until two or three years later. Training and productivity are potentially endogenous. This gap in the dynamics of training and productivity could be addressed with longitudinal data on training and productivity. Longitudinal information on training and productivity would also allow us to examine the depreciation of human capital investments.

In sum, the current training gap includes discrepancies in the measurement of formal and informal training, who provides the training, what training costs, how training investments vary over tenure within a firm and work experience in general, how training varies with demographic characteristics, what impact training has on establishment productivity, what are the dynamics of training investments and their impact on wages, wage growth, productivity and productivity growth, and what are the linkages between training and other HRM practices such as recruitment and selection, compensation, new technology, and changing work organization.

Much of the current training gap could be narrowed by the creation of a large, nationally representative, longitudinal matched employer-employee survey. This would allow us to see who gets training and when and then to observe the impact of this training on wages and productivity. This survey should be longitudinal so that we can see how firms vary their training practices over time in the face of changing product demand, technology, and work organization. Finally, the data should be collected in such a way that we are able to measure the skills workers bring to firms from previous employers, previous training spells, and education. Only by collecting information on preexisting skills can we hope to distinguish between firms that decide to hire relatively unskilled workers and train them and firms that hire already trained employees. By collecting information on both workers and firms we could observe the relative contribution of worker characteristics versus firm management practices and product market conditions on outcomes of interest. In addition, in order to understand the forces that drive the training needs of a business and the bundling of training with other workplace practices, the survey needs to go beyond just measuring different types of training in the workplace. It should document the menu of establishment practices to identify which practices or combinations of practices best improve the standard of living of workers and the productivity of firms.

One problem, however, in designing this type of longitudinal survey is selecting the optimal way to generate the sample. Many of the employer-based surveys described in section 12.3 relied on databases such as the Yellow Pages, Dun and Bradstreet, or other firm databases collected by opinion research firms. These listings tend to overrepresent corporate headquarters and are updated with varying frequency. This can lead to a bias in underrepresenting newly created establishments. The most comprehensive and up-to-date sampling frames for establishments currently reside in the Census Bureau and BLS. The ability of government agencies such as the Census Bureau and the BLS to gather data from establishments, especially on sensitive items such as profitability and productivity, has been shown to be quite high (see the reported response rates to the BLS and EQW training surveys). Unfortunately, due to confidentiality requirements, using establishment data from either the BLS or the Census Bureau generally restricts researchers' access to the data.

There is also a marked difference between a sample that is representative of establishments and one that is representative of establishments where workers are employed. More than 50 percent of all establishments in the United States employ fewer than 5 workers, while almost 50 percent of all workers are employed in establishments with 100 employees or more. Yet establishments with 100 employees or more represent less than 3 percent of all establishments. The researchers involved with the NOS chose to use a representative household survey to obtain their matched sample of employers. Unfortunately, there are very few firms for which there is more than one respondent working in an establishment to match individual data with firm characteristics. The Upjohn survey pursued an alternative strategy and contacted firms first and then workers in the firm. Due to budgetary constraints the Upjohn survey focused on new hires, which means that we are not able to determine what kind of training incumbent workers received.

So the researcher is left in a quandary over whether to go for more employees in fewer firms or to sample a few workers in a broader array of firms. The first strategy makes it difficult to infer what is happening to firms in general, and the second strategy means that we will have less information about variation in the employment experiences of similar individuals within and between firms. Even if we had a longitudinal survey of establishments, we would miss information on previous employment experience or postemployment experience of workers passing through the firm. Some of these issues might be resolved by pooling resources across government agencies such as the BLS, Department of Education, and Census Bureau and the greater use of administrative matches (e.g., Abowd and Kramarz, chap. 10; Troske, chap. 11 in this volume).

12.5 Conclusions

We are not alone in our problems with measuring training. A recent survey by the Organization for Economic Cooperation and Development (1991) on private sector training across member countries highlights the difficulty in coming up with measures within a country that could also be used for cross-country comparisons. The 1980s and early 1990s have seen an explosion of studies aimed at gathering more information on training and its impact on productivity and wages. Unfortunately, the studies on training's relationship with productivity are few. Most of the few studies that measure productivity use subjective measures or refer only to the productivity of recently hired employees—for example, the NFIB, SBA, and Upjohn surveys.

Currently we do not have in the United States a longitudinal database of individuals and firms and their training experiences and outcomes. This lack of matched employer-employee data is especially problematic in the study of training since there are two agents that are involved in the training investment—workers and firms. Obtaining data on just one of these two agents does not provide sufficient information on the incidence, constraints, and outcomes of training investments.

Response rates of employer-based surveys suggest that having a government agency collect information, especially on sensitive data such as profitability and actual measures of productivity or value added, would enhance data response quality. No matter who eventually fields a matched employer-employee survey, we should keep in mind that the current policy debate on training is motivated by two concerns—how to maintain and improve the standard of living of workers and how to improve the productivity and competitiveness of U.S. firms. Therefore, collecting information on training needs to go beyond just measuring its incidence.

References

Altonji, J., and J. Spletzer. 1991. Worker characteristics, job characteristics, and the receipt of on-the-job training. *Industrial and Labor Relations Review* 45 (1): 58–79.

Barron, J., M. Berger, and D. Black. 1994. New evidence on the measurement of training: Matched employee and employer responses. West Lafayette, Ind.: Purdue University; Lexington: University of Kentucky. Mimeograph.

———. 1997. How well do we measure training? *Journal of Labor Economics* 15 (3): 507–28.

Barron, J., D. Black, and M. Loewenstein. 1987. Employer size: The implications for search, training, capital investment, starting wages, and wage growth. *Journal of Labor Economics* 5 (January): 76–89.

———. 1989. Job matching and on-the-job training. *Journal of Labor Economics* 7 (1): 1–19.

Bartel, Ann. 1989. Formal employee training programs and their impact on labor productivity: Evidence from a human resource survey. NBER Working Paper no. 3026. Cambridge, Mass.: National Bureau of Economic Research.

———. 1992. Productivity gains from the implementation of employee training programs. NBER Working Paper no. 3893. Cambridge, Mass.: National Bureau of Economic Research.

Bassi, Laurie. 1994. Workplace education for hourly workers. *Journal of Policy Analysis and Management* 13:55–75.

Becker, Gary. 1962. Investments in human capital: A theoretical analysis. *Journal of Political Economy* 70, no. 5, pt. 2 (October): 9–49.

————. 1964. *Human Capital: A theoretical and empirical analysis with special reference to education.* New York: National Bureau of Economic Research.

Bishop, John. 1994. The impact of previous training on productivity and wages. In *Training and the private sector: International comparisons,* ed. L. Lynch. Chicago: University of Chicago Press.

Bowers, Norman, and Paul Swaim. 1994. Recent trends in employment-related training and wages. *Contemporary Policy Issues* 12:79–88.

Brown, James. 1989. Why do wages increase with tenure? *American Economic Review* 79 (December): 971–99.

Carey, M. L. 1985. *How workers get their training.* Bureau of Labor Statistics Bulletin no. 2226. Washington, D.C.: Government Printing Office.

Carnevale, Anthony, Leila J. Gainer, and Janice Villet. 1990. *Training in America: The organization and strategic role of training.* San Francisco: Jossey-Bass.

Duncan, Greg, and Saul D. Hoffman. 1978. Training and earnings. In *Five thousand American families: Pattern and progress,* ed. G. Duncan and J. Morgan, vol. 6. Ann Arbor: University of Michigan Press.

Freeman, Richard, and Lawrence Katz. 1994. Rising wage inequality: The United States vs. other advanced countries. In *Working under different rules,* ed. R. Freeman. New York: Russell Sage.

Hollenbeck, K., and R. Wilkie. 1985. The nature and impact of training: Evidence from the Current Population Survey. In *Training and human capital,* ed. J. Bishop. Columbus: Ohio State University, National Center for Research in Vocational Education.

Knoke, David, and Arne Kalleberg. 1994. Job training in U.S. organizations. *American Sociological Review* 59:537–46.

Lillard, Lee, and Hong Tan. 1986. Private sector training: Who gets its and what are its effects? Rand Monograph no. R-3331-DOL/RC. Santa Monica, Calif.: Rand Corporation.

Loewenstein, M., and J. Spletzer. 1994. Informal training: A review of existing data and some new evidence. BLS Working Paper no. 254. Washington, D.C.: U.S. Department of Labor, Bureau of Labor Statistics.

Lynch, Lisa. 1991. The role of off-the-job vs. on-the-job training for the mobility of women workers. *American Economic Review* 81 (May): 151–56.

————. 1992a. Differential effects of post-school training on early career mobility. NBER Working Paper no. 4034. Cambridge, Mass.: National Bureau of Economic Research.

————. 1992b. Private-sector training and the earnings of young workers. *American Economic Review* 82 (1): 299–312.

————. 1992c. Young people's pathways into work: Utilization of postsecondary education and training. Report prepared for the National Academy of Science, Washington, D.C., March.

————, ed. 1994. *Training and the private sector: International comparisons.* Chicago: University of Chicago Press.

Lynch, Lisa M., and Robert Zemsky. 1994. The EQW National Employers' Survey. Philadelphia: University of Pennsylvania, U.S. Department of Education National Center on the Educational Quality of the Workforce.

Mincer, Jacob. 1974. *Schooling, experience, and training.* New York: Columbia University Press.

Organization for Economic Cooperation and Development. 1991. *Employment outlook.* Paris: Organization for Economic Cooperation and Development.

Osterman, P. 1995. Skill, training, and work organization in American establishments. *Industrial Relations* 34 (2): 125–46.

Pergamit, M., and J. Shack-Marquez. 1987. Earnings and different types of training.

BLS Working Paper no. 165. Washington, D.C.: U.S. Department of Labor, Bureau of Labor Statistics.

Sicherman, Nachum. 1990. The measurement of on-the-job training. *Journal of Economic and Social Measurement* 16:221–30.

U.S. Department of Education. National Center for Education Statistics. 1989. *Young adult literacy and schooling.* Washington, D.C.: U.S. Department of Education.

———. 1993. *Digest of education statistics: 1993.* Washington, D.C.: Government Printing Office.

Veum, J. 1994. Sources of training and their impact on wages. *Industrial and Labor Relations Review* 47:812–26.

Zemsky, Robert, and Daniel Shapiro. 1994. On measuring a mirage: Why U.S. training numbers don't add up. EQW Working Paper no. 20. Philadelphia: University of Pennsylvania, U.S. Department of Education National Center for the Educational Quality of the Workforce.

Comment   John M. Barron

In the past 15 years, there have been numerous surveys that contained questions aimed at directly measuring the extent of on-the-job training. An important contribution of Lynch's paper is to highlight the key differences across these various surveys with respect to the measurement of on-the-job training. As such, it is of great value to researchers interested in the extent and effects of on-the-job training.

Lynch's review of available data sets on on-the-job training indicates that training measures have at least four potential dimensions:

1. The distinction between formal versus informal training. Data sets such as the 1982 EOPP and the 1992 SBA define formal training as training that involves self-paced learning programs or classes designed by specially trained personnel. Informal training is defined as the time spent by management and supervisors away from other activities giving employees informal individualized training or extra supervision, time spent by coworkers who were not supervisors away from their normal work giving individualized training or extra supervision, and time spent by the employee observing coworkers in order to learn skills required for the position.

2. The distinction between the incidence, intensity, and the duration of training. Some surveys measure only whether training has been given (e.g., the 1991 CPS). Some include a measure of the intensity of training such as the number of hours each week devoted to training during the first three months of employment (e.g., the 1993 Upjohn). Others measure only the duration of training for

John M. Barron is professor of economics at Purdue University and visiting professor of economics at the University of London, Royal Holloway.

a particular position in terms of number of weeks or months until a worker is fully trained (e.g., the NLSY).

3. The distinction between the training of new workers and ongoing training. Some surveys, for instance, the 1982 EOPP and the 1992 SBA, focus on the training of new hires, as such data provide a natural test for on-the-job training theories. Other surveys encompass all employees (e.g., DOL) and thus de facto focus on measuring the extent of training involved in maintaining or upgrading the capabilities of existing employees.

4. The distinction between employer-based and employee-based surveys to generate training measures. Surveys such as the 1991 CPS are worker based, while others such as the 1982 EOPP ask the employer to provide measures of various training activities. The recent 1993 Upjohn survey asks both employers and employees; a planned follow-up employee survey to the 1994 EQW employer-based survey and a proposed Department of Labor survey may also provide matched data from employers and employees.

Given the above four dimensions to training measures, it follows that the ideal survey would capture all four. That is, the ideal survey would contain questions concerning both informal and formal training activity; have questions that measured the incidence, intensity, and duration of each type of training; ask training questions for a sample that includes a sufficient number of new hires; and ask training questions of both the employer and the employee (generate a "matched" data set). In addition, the survey would obtain information on how the initial matching of a worker to a position at a firm occurs (e.g., employer and employee prior search activities), the wages and other key contractual provisions of the employment relationship, relevant characteristics of employees (e.g., past education, experience, age, and gender), relevant characteristics of the employer (e.g., size of establishment, the capital-labor ratio, and financial statistics), and changes in the employment relationship that follow the initial training, including the experience of worker at subsequent employers.

As Lynch's paper makes clear, such an ideal survey does not currently exist. But by indicating precisely what is missing from each of the available surveys, Lynch provides the necessary information for future surveys to be constructed that fill in the missing pieces with respect to the measurement of on-the-job training. Lynch suggests that one focus of future surveys should be time-series data to document a possible movement away from informal toward formal training. Such a movement clearly has important policy implications given the substantial role that government might play in providing formal training programs. However, Lynch's paper contains at least two other important messages. First, in order to test on-the-job theories against alternative theories arising from learning and job-matching models (e.g., Jovanovic 1979) or incentive-based compensation models (e.g., Lazear 1981), future surveys would be well advised to adopt sampling procedures that focus on obtaining information concerning the training of new hires. Second, future surveys should not neglect, and in fact should emphasize, the measurement of informal training.

One might argue that a focus on informal training seems misplaced given the growing importance of formal training. Lynch cites an increase from 12 to 17 percent in the incidence of formal training across all worker indicated by a comparison of the CPS surveys of 1983 and 1991. A comparison of employers' responses to the 1982 EOPP survey with their answers to similar questions in the 1992 SBA survey indicates an even more dramatic increase, with the incidence of formal training rising from 15 percent to close to 30 percent of new hires. Note that these results hold even adjusting for the fact that the EOPP sample is weighted toward smaller employers. However, formal training still is not widespread among workers. In contrast, virtually all new employees received some informal training. Further, the extent of informal training is substantial, and has increased as well during this period. In addition, both the 1982 EOPP employer survey and 1992 SBA employer survey indicate that a new worker spends close to one-fourth of her time in various informal training activities during the first three months of employment, versus less than one-twentieth of her time in formal training activities.

One might instead object to a survey that focuses on informal training by claiming that measures of informal training are inherently less precise than those of formal training. However, if the extent of training is to be used as a basis for deciding government subsidies to particular employers or employees, then it is important not to neglect survey measures of the type of training—informal—that employers appear to favor. In addition, preliminary work by Barron, Berger, and Black (1997b) that uses the 1993 Upjohn matched employer-employee survey suggests that aggregate measures of informal training may not be less precise than measures of formal training.

In sum, new surveys on training measures should not adopt the DOL training survey strategy of asking a random sample of workers only questions about formal training. Of value instead are surveys that focus on measuring both formal and informal training and surveys that focus on sampling new hires, for here the predictions of on-the-job training theories can be clearly tested. In this regard, one important puzzle to resolve is the issue of who initially pays for on-the-job training, especially if the government is to be involved in subsidizing such training. Preliminary work by Barron, Berger, and Black (in press) based primarily on the 1992 SBA survey raises the possibility that most training costs are initially borne by the employer.

Lynch is quite right that future training surveys should also consider a matched survey, as there is evidence that each side of the employment agreement can provide useful information. For instance, there is evidence that some activities identified by employers as periods of training are perceived by workers as periods of monitoring instead. Employers can provide key information concerning the matching of workers and positions, such as the extent of employer search to fill the position. Barron, Berger, and Black (1997a) document that employers search more when filling high-training positions, suggesting that part of the return to training may reflect differences in the quality of the employment match. On the other hand, workers can provide more complete information on such activities as their prior job search and prior on-the-job training.

References

Barron, John M., Mark C. Berger, and Dan A. Black. 1997a. Employer search, training, and vacancy duration. *Economic Inquiry* 35 (January): 167–92.

———. 1997b. How well do we measure training? *Journal of Labor Economics* 15 (July): 507–28.

———. In press. Does on-the-job training lower the starting wage? *Journal of Human Resources.*

Jovanovic, Boyan. 1979. Job matching and the theory of turnover. *Journal of Political Economy* 87, no. 5, pt. 1 (October): 972–90.

Lazear, Edward P. 1981. Agency, earnings profiles, productivity and hours restrictions. *American Economic Review* 71, no. 4 (September): 606–20.

13 Employer-Provided Training, Wages, and Capital Investment

Stephen G. Bronars and Melissa Famulari

13.1 Introduction

The returns to labor market skills have risen in the past two decades, prompting renewed interest in public and private sector training programs. Employer-provided training, which includes both formal training programs and informal on-the-job training, appears to be an important source of human capital acquisition. National Longitudinal Survey of Youth (NLSY) data indicate that 38 percent of young adults in the United States participated in formal training programs such as company training programs, courses in vocational and technical institutes, business school courses, seminars, or apprenticeship programs between 1986 and 1991 (Veum 1993). Despite the prevalence of these private sector formal training programs, few empirical studies have analyzed the employer characteristics or types of companies that are associated with the provision of employee training.

The existing empirical literature on formal training has focused on the relationship between worker characteristics, the likelihood of participating in a formal training program, and subsequent wage growth (see, e.g., Altonji and Spletzer 1991; Barron, Black, and Loewenstein 1993; Duncan and Hoffman 1978; Krueger and Rouse 1994; Lillard and Tan 1992; Lynch 1992; Veum 1994). In these empirical studies, establishment size and industry dummy variables are the employer characteristics that are typically related to the incidence and effectiveness of training programs (see Bishop 1982a, 1982b, 1985; Bar-

Stephen G. Bronars is professor of economics at the University of Texas at Austin. Melissa Famulari is senior lecturer and research associate at the University of Texas at Austin.

The authors thank preconference and conference participants for helpful comments. In particular, L. Lynch, M. Manser, and C. C. Rouse provided useful comments. Preliminary research on this project was conducted while Bronars was an ASA/NSF/BLS fellow and Famulari was at the Bureau of Labor Statistics, U.S. Department of Labor.

ron, Black, and Loewenstein 1989). Research on private sector training has been limited by the availability of data sets that report firm characteristics, such as profitability and capital investment, as well as information about training programs and worker demographic characteristics. For example, Bartel's (1994) recent study of formal training programs uses an employer survey with extensive data on firm behavior and performance but no information about worker characteristics, such as education, experience, tenure, race, or sex. In contrast, many empirical studies of training have utilized the NLSY data set, which provides comprehensive information about worker characteristics, wage growth, and the type and duration of training programs but no information about employers' investment behavior or profitability.

It is widely accepted in the labor demand literature that skilled labor and capital are complements in production: more capital-intensive firms are expected to hire more skilled labor (Hamermesh 1993). The implied empirical relationship between a firm's capital or R&D investments and its provision of formal training is less clear. Firms that demand skilled workers may either provide their own training programs or hire workers who have been trained by previous employers or in school. The specificity of skills determines the substitution possibilities between workers trained on the current job and previously trained workers. In addition, we expect training to occur in firms where output and training tend to be complementary and the forgone output from training is lowest.

In this paper, we use a unique cross-sectional sample of white-collar workers from a Bureau of Labor Statistics (BLS) establishment survey to analyze the incidence of employer-provided training programs and their impact on wage-tenure profiles. In addition, we match a subset of these data on individual worker wages, tenure, and participation in a formal training program, with firm-level data on profitability and investment behavior from the Compustat database. Using these matched data, we provide evidence on the empirical relationship between firm profitability, firm investments in capital equipment and R&D, the provision of formal training programs, and the returns to training.

A second goal of this paper is to evaluate the feasibility of gathering worker-level wage, tenure, training, and demographic data in an establishment or employer survey. This data issue is important because there appears to be considerable demand for employer-employee matched data sets (in this volume, see Abowd and Kramarz, chap. 10; Prendergast, chap. 9; Troske, chap. 11). We examine establishments' responses to a pilot BLS survey, conducted in 1989 and 1990, which tested the feasibility of collecting worker demographic data from establishments. We analyze response rates to this pilot survey and compare our establishment-reported data to data for white-collar workers in two household surveys: the NLSY and the Current Population Survey (CPS). Although we find some significant differences in worker characteristics across all three surveys, we conclude that matched worker-employer data sets, based on

BLS establishment surveys, can provide useful information about internal and external labor market behavior.

A matched worker-employer data set has some advantages over household panel data sets, such as the NLSY, in analyzing employer-provided training programs. First, we observe multiple workers per establishment so that employer-specific effects can be included in models of the incidence of training and wage growth. Empirical models based on household data must ignore these employer-specific wage and training effects. Second, as noted above, our matched data set allows us to link individual worker wage, tenure, and training information with employer characteristics such as profitability, capital/labor ratio, and expenditures on R&D, for the subsample of workers employed by publicly traded firms.

There are also some caveats to our data set and empirical approach. First, our sample size is small by conventional labor economics standards, and we have retrospective data for starting wages rather than panel data. Second, the training variable we use is dichotomous—we do not observe the type or duration of the training that was provided. Third, our data set is not based on experimental data. The training programs we observe are endogenously determined, and we do not observe instrumental variables for the incidence of training programs. Unobserved heterogeneity in productivity growth across workers and firms may bias our estimates of the effects of training on wage growth.

13.2 Data

13.2.1 White Collar Pay Survey

The data set used in this study is derived from a subsample of the BLS White Collar Pay Survey (WCP), which is collected to determine the wages of private sector employees in white-collar occupations that match occupations in the federal government.[1] The WCP collects the straight-time salary and detailed occupation of full-time workers (who work between 37.5 and 40 hours per week) from a nationwide sample of private sector employers. The survey samples goods-producing establishments in even-numbered years and service-producing establishments in odd-numbered years. The probability that an establishment is sampled is approximately proportional to its employment.

Our data set is based on a supplement to the WCP conducted in 1989 and

---

1. The WCP occupations are accountants, chief accountants, auditors, public accountants, personnel specialists, personnel supervisors/managers, directors of personnel, attorneys, buyers, computer programmers, computer systems analysts, computer systems analysts supervisor/manager, chemists, engineers, tax collectors, registered nurses, licensed practical nurses, nursing assistants, medical machine operating technicians, civil engineering technicians, engineering technicians, drafters, computer operators, photographers, accounting clerks, file clerks, key entry operators, messengers, secretaries, typists, personnel clerks/assistants, purchasing clerks/assistants, and general clerks.

1990. In this test survey, 354 establishments were asked questions about a random sample of their employees in "matched" white-collar occupations.[2] The employer was asked to report the worker's current and starting pay, age, race, sex, years of education, highest educational degree obtained, and tenure with the employer. In addition, the employer was asked whether the worker received "formal training (specific course work or a training program) within or outside the establishment which was paid for wholly or in part by the establishment."

Three hundred establishments provided information on current pay, tenure, and standard demographic characteristics for 1,727 workers between the ages of 18 and 64.[3] Employers were least likely to respond to questions about workers' starting pay and formal training.[4] Moreover, when either training or starting wage is not reported for one worker in an establishment, it tends to be missing for all workers in the establishment. Training is not reported for 28.6 percent of the 1,727 workers, and over 90 percent of the workers with missing values for training are employed in establishments that did not report training for any worker. Starting pay information is not reported for 55.7 percent of the workers in the 1,727 sample, and over 86 percent of the workers with missing values for starting pay are employed in establishments that did not report starting pay for any worker. There are 1,234 workers with valid responses to the training question in our sample, and starting wages are also reported for 601 of these 1,234 workers.

Our primary concern is that an employer's decision to report training may be correlated with unobserved variables that also influence wages and the costs and benefits of training. We check for possible patterns in nonresponse behavior across establishments by estimating a probit model where the dependent variable is one if the establishment did not report training for any worker and zero otherwise. Unfortunately, we do not observe any variables that are valid instruments for the incidence of training. Hence we do not attempt to correct for selection bias in our sample due to nonresponses but merely examine patterns of establishment nonresponses in the data.

Table 13.1 reports the estimated coefficients for a probit model of nonre-

---

2. Establishments were asked to report demographic data for a random sample of 2,386 workers. The mean wage and occupational distribution of these 2,386 workers is not significantly different from the mean wage and occupational distribution of the entire WCP sample from these 354 establishments. The sample sizes per establishment range from 1 to 33 workers, with more workers sampled in the larger establishments. Almost 80 percent of the sample was collected in 1990 when goods-producing industries were surveyed.

3. We excluded observations from the sample of 2,386 workers in 354 establishments for the following reasons: 362 for missing age, 25 because age was less than 18 or greater than 64, 17 for missing race, 17 for missing tenure, 208 for missing education, 16 because age minus tenure was less than 16 years, 1 because age minus education minus 6 was less than zero, and 13 because education was less than 12 years. This leaves a total of 1,727 workers in 300 establishments.

4. We had the least success in obtaining information about the duration of training programs from employers. Only 13 percent of our sample has valid information about the length of training programs. The mean duration across these 231 workers is 5.18 weeks, with a median duration of 1.4 weeks.

Table 13.1   **Probit Models of Training and Starting Wage Nonresponse by Establishments**

Independent Variable	Equals One if Training Not Reported (1)		Equals One if Starting Wage Not Reported (2)	
Education	.1153	(.1210)	−.0819	(.1025)
Experience	.0286	(.0227)	.0165	(.0181)
Tenure	.0168	(.0283)	.0057	(.0249)
Female	−.7035	(.5357)	−.2135	(.4127)
Black	−.0100	(.7798)	.0694	(.6583)
Log wage	−.9638*	(.5671)	.3012	(.4728)
Region				
Midwest	.3063	(.2645)	.4319*	(.2303)
South	−.4981*	(.2948)	.7616**	(.2391)
West	−.1810	(.3296)	.8719**	(.2882)
Industry				
Durable goods	−.4411*	(.2634)	.2502	(.2134)
Trade and finance	−.2327	(.4232)	−.4245	(.3896)
Services	−.3442	(.3949)	.1829	(.3151)
Mining and construction	.0504	(.3676)	.4564	(.3228)
MSA size				
Below 1 million	.1188	(.3246)	.0660	(.2553)
1–5 million	.5204*	(.3043)	.0433	(.2537)
Above 5 million	.5914	(.3779)	−.0330	(.3172)
Establishment size				
500–1,000 employees	1.0536**	(.2943)	.1354	(.2396)
Over 1,000 employees	1.2359**	(.2437)	.3061	(.1899)
Constant	3.9549	(3.8994)	−2.2987	(3.0784)
Sample size	300		300	

Notes: The omitted category is a nondurable-goods-manufacturing firm located in the Northeast outside of a metropolitan statistical area. Each observation is weighted by the number of surveyed workers in the establishment. Numbers in parentheses are standard errors.
*Significant at the 10 percent level.
**Significant at the 5 percent level.

sponse to the training question. We find that nonreporting establishments have more employees and are more likely to be located in larger metropolitan areas in the Northeast or Midwest, on average, than the reporting establishments. Relatively low wage employers are slightly less likely to respond to the training question. The mean wage in nonresponding establishments is about 3 percent lower, all else equal, than the mean wage in establishments that report training. There is no significant relationship between the probability of reporting training and the average education, experience, tenure, or the fraction of female or black workers in an establishment.

As noted above, nonresponse problems are more substantial for a worker's starting wage. We check for possible patterns in nonresponse to the starting wage question across establishments by estimating a probit model where the dependent variable is one if the establishment did not report starting pay for any worker and zero otherwise. Column (2) of table 13.1 reports the estimated coefficients for this probit model. We find that reporting establishments are more likely to be located in the Northeast than the nonreporting establishments. No other establishment characteristic and no worker characteristics are significantly related to the probability of nonresponse.

Throughout the paper we focus our analysis on two samples of the WCP: a sample of 1,234 workers with nonmissing training data and a sample of 601 workers with nonmissing training and starting wage data. In our larger sample we impute starting wages, using starting experience and interactions of starting experience as instrumental variables.[5] In general, as demonstrated below, we find similar empirical results across samples. These findings, in addition to the absence of a significant relationship (except for regional dummy variables) between worker and employer characteristics and employer nonresponse to the starting wage question, suggest that restricting the sample to workers with nonmissing starting wages does not result in serious sample selection bias.

Table 13.2 reports means and standard deviations of the variables in our two samples. The key variables in our analysis are the formal training dummy variable, the logarithm of the current monthly wage (measured in 1989 dollars), the logarithm of the starting monthly wage (also measured in 1989 dollars), and job tenure.[6] Approximately 30 percent of the workers in each sample received formal training from their employers. Mean tenure is substantially shorter and the current real wage is somewhat lower for workers with reported starting pay.

13.2.2   Comparison with the Current Population Survey

We first compare our data set to a sample of private sector white-collar workers in the outgoing rotation groups of the 1989 CPS employed in occupations that match those in the WCP. The CPS sample contains 15,784 private sector, nonagricultural workers between the ages of 18 and 64 who typically work between 37.5 and 40 hours per week. Table 13.3 presents sample statistics by

---

5. The 601 sample is a subset of our 1,234 sample. We use imputed, rather than actual, starting wages for all 1,234 workers. Our starting wage regression includes starting experience and its square, education, an education and starting experience interaction, female, female interactions with starting experience and its square, and dummy variables for race, two-digit SIC industry, region, metropolitan statistical area (MSA) size, and establishment size.

6. We converted all current reported wages into 1989 dollars, using the December 1989 to December 1990 average change in the Employment Cost Index (ECI) for wages and salaries of workers in goods-producing industries. We deflated nominal starting pay by the average hourly earnings of workers in the United States to obtain real starting wages because the ECI is not available for all starting years. All workers with less than 18 months of tenure were assigned one year of tenure, and workers with at least 18 months of tenure were assigned the nearest integer year of tenure.

Table 13.2   **Variable Means and Standard Deviations**

Variable	Actual Starting Wage Sample		Predicted Starting Wage Sample	
Real monthly wage	2,469.71	(1,146.04)	2,587.46	(1,197.88)
Log real wage	7.710	(.452)	7.755	(.460)
Real starting monthly wage	1,968.67	(965.80)		
Log real start wage	7.476	(.465)		
Predicted log real start wage			7.483	(.363)
Wage growth	.234	(.302)		
Tenure	6.494	(6.208)	8.224	(7.784)
Train	.280	(.449)	.303	(.460)
Education	14.403	(2.140)	14.396	(2.118)
Starting potential experience	10.311	(8.815)	9.983	(9.018)
Female	.521	(.500)	.487	(.500)
Black	.070	(.255)	.063	(.243)
Industry				
Nondurable goods	.186	(.390)	.216	(.412)
Durable goods	.509	(.500)	.496	(.500)
Trade and finance	.078	(.269)	.064	(.245)
Services	.163	(.370)	.132	(.339)
Mining and construction	.063	(.244)	.092	(.289)
MSA size				
Not an MSA	.165	(.371)	.212	(.409)
Below 1 million	.255	(.436)	.253	(.435)
1–5 million	.399	(.490)	.371	(.483)
Above 5 million	.181	(.386)	.165	(.370)
Region				
Northeast	.333	(.472)	.239	(.427)
Midwest	.295	(.456)	.281	(.450)
South	.271	(.445)	.355	(.479)
West	.101	(.302)	.125	(.331)
Establishment size				
Under 500 employees	.546	(.498)	.508	(.500)
500–1,000 employees	.155	(.362)	.160	(.367)
Over 1,000 employees	.300	(.458)	.331	(.471)
Sample size	601		1,234	

Note: Numbers in parentheses are standard deviations.

broad industry group (manufacturing; trade, finance, and services; and mining and construction) for the CPS and WCP data sets. We focus on within-industry comparisons because of the rather large differences in industry composition across data sets (the preponderance of the WCP data were collected from establishments in goods-producing industries).

    Workers in the WCP earn higher pay than full-time white-collar workers in the CPS, especially in nonmanufacturing industries. Some of this large pay differential is due to the fact that workers in the WCP are more experienced,

Table 13.3 **Comparison of Full-Time White-Collar Workers from the CPS and the WCP**

Manufacturing	CPS	(N = 3,405)	WCP	(N = 879)
Monthly wage	2,340.04	(1,183.03)	2,583.25	(1,187.36)
Education	14.13	(2.02)	14.46	(2.10)
Experience	16.80	(11.07)	18.08	(10.22)
Female	.52	(.50)	.46	(.50)
Black	.05	(.22)	.04	(.21)
Northeast	.31	(.46)	.24	(.43)
Midwest	.17	(.37)	.27	(.44)
South	.26	(.44)	.39	(.49)
West	.26	(.44)	.10	(.30)
Not an MSA	.20	(.40)	.27	(.44)
Below 1 million	.26	(.44)	.31	(.46)
1–5 million	.31	(.46)	.28	(.45)
Above 5 million	.23	(.42)	.14	(.35)

Trade, Finance, and Services	CPS	(N = 11,958)	WCP	(N = 242)
Monthly wage	1,815.08	(970.42)	2,411.59	(1,163.67)
Education	13.77	(1.88)	14.21	(2.17)
Experience	15.77	(10.92)	17.85	(10.96)
Female	.79	(.41)	.61	(.49)
Black	.10	(.30)	.14	(.34)
Northeast	.27	(.44)	.31	(.47)
Midwest	.19	(.39)	.38	(.49)
South	.30	(.46)	.20	(.40)
West	.25	(.44)	.11	(.32)
Not an MSA	.22	(.42)	0	
Below 1 million	.26	(.44)	.03	(.16)
1–5 million	.31	(.46)	.75	(.44)
Above 5 million	.20	(.40)	.23	(.42)

Mining and Construction	CPS	(N = 472)	WCP	(N = 113)
Monthly wage	2,017.30	(1,323.72)	2,996.85	(1,262.90)
Education	13.73	(1.88)	14.33	(2.13)
Experience	17.49	(11.07)	19.98	(10.94)
Female	.72	(.45)	.47	(.50)
Black	.03	(.18)	.05	(.23)
Northeast	.18	(.38)	.07	(.26)
Midwest	.25	(.43)	.18	(.38)
South	.39	(.49)	.42	(.50)
West	.18	(.39)	.33	(.47)
Not an MSA	.31	(.46)	.20	(.40)
Below 1 million	.28	(.45)	.31	(.46)
1–5 million	.28	(.45)	.29	(.46)
Above 5 million	.14	(.34)	.19	(.40)

Note: Numbers in parentheses are standard deviations.

more educated, and less likely to be female than workers in the CPS. In addition, wages in the CPS are likely to be underreported; a recent study found that 30 percent of CPS respondents report after-tax rather than gross pay (see Polivka and Rothgeb 1993). We also find that worker demographic characteristics account for 57 percent of the variation in log wages in the WCP; the same worker demographic characteristics account for less than 36 percent of the variation in log wages in our CPS data. In Bronars and Famulari (1997) we present a more complete comparison of the CPS and WCP data sets and provide some evidence that the difference in unexplained variation in log wages across samples is due to greater measurement error in CPS reported wages.

13.2.3 Comparison with the National Longitudinal Survey of Youth

We also compare our data to a sample of full-time white-collar workers from the NLSY in occupations that match the WCP. There are 779 white-collar workers in these occupations in the NLSY, for whom we observe wages in 1989, starting wages, and training. The oldest workers in the NLSY are aged 32 in 1989. Table 13.4 compares means and standard deviations of variables in this NLSY data set to sample statistics for workers under age 33 in our WCP data set and the CPS. Because of the substantial differences in industry composition across data sets, we again present comparisons of means within broad industry groups.[7] First, note that only about one-third of our WCP sample and 40 percent of the CPS sample are as young as the NLSY respondents. In addition, less than one-fifth of the NLSY sample is employed in the manufacturing sector, where most of the WCP data were collected. Despite these caveats, all three samples are reasonably similar with respect to education, experience, tenure, race, and sex in the manufacturing sector. In trade, finance, and services, WCP workers are more educated and less likely to be female than either NLSY or CPS workers. Average current wages are significantly higher in the NLSY in the manufacturing sector, and significantly higher in the WCP in trade, finance, and services. Wage growth appears to be substantially higher in the NLSY than in the WCP subsample, primarily because starting wages are much lower and have a much higher standard deviation in the NLSY.[8]

We find that 23 percent of white-collar NLSY workers and 28 percent of young WCP workers participated in training programs that were paid for by their employers. Note that we use information in the NLSY on participation in training programs that were explicitly paid for by the employer, which is only available from 1986 to 1989. We therefore underestimate participation in

---

7. We present comparisons only for manufacturing industries and finance, trade, and services because sample sizes for both the NLSY and the WCP (age 32 and under) are quite small in mining and construction industries.

8. We also find that worker demographic characteristics account for 61 percent of the variation in young workers' log wages in the WCP; the same worker demographic characteristics account for less than 35 percent of the variation in log wages in our NLSY data set.

Table 13.4 Comparison of Full-Time White-Collar Workers under Age 33 from the NLSY, the WCP, and the CPS

Manufacturing	NLSY	(N = 127)	WCP	(N = 283)	CPS	(N = 1,414)
Current monthly wage	2,207.23	(949.06)	2,022.75	(815.98)	2,030.17	(904.39)
Starting monthly wage[a]	1,476.92	(911.52)	1,678.17	(538.02)		
Training[b]	.30	(.46)	.23	(.42)		
Tenure	3.34	(2.62)	3.22	(2.49)		
Education	14.39	(2.08)	14.27	(1.94)	14.20	(1.92)
Experience	7.63	(3.15)	7.06	(3.06)	6.64	(3.82)
Female	.53	(.50)	.50	(.50)	.55	(.50)
Black	.05	(.21)	.04	(.20)	.05	(.22)
Northeast	.20	(.40)	.24	(.43)	.29	(.45)
Midwest	.35	(.48)	.28	(.45)	.17	(.37)
South	.31	(.46)	.37	(.48)	.28	(.45)
West	.14	(.35)	.11	(.32)	.27	(.44)
Under 500 employees	.45	(.50)	.55	(.50)		
500–1,000 employees	.11	(.31)	.19	(.40)		
Over 1,000 employees	.44	(.50)	.26	(.44)		
Not an MSA	.12	(.33)	.28	(.45)	.18	(.38)
Below 1 million	.27	(.45)	.31	(.46)	.25	(.43)
1–5 million	.36	(.48)	.28	(.45)	.32	(.47)
Above 5 million	.24	(.43)	.14	(.35)	.25	(.43)

Trade, Finance, and Services	NLSY	(N = 637)	WCP	(N = 88)	CPS	(N = 5,541)
Current monthly wage	1,620.88	(696.63)	1,996.37	(783.27)	1,626.32	(778.64)
Starting monthly wage[a]	1,180.89	(614.28)	1,682.83	(549.68)		
Training[b]	.23	(.42)	.36	(.48)		
Tenure	3.14	(2.51)	2.86	(2.27)		
Education	13.74	(1.94)	14.40	(2.10)	13.84	(1.83)
Experience	8.02	(3.00)	7.39	(3.26)	6.50	(3.81)
Female	.77	(.42)	.63	(.49)	.79	(.41)
Black	.13	(.34)	.07	(.25)	.10	(.30)
Northeast	.18	(.38)	.34	(.48)	.26	(.44)
Midwest	.28	(.45)	.38	(.49)	.17	(.40)
South	.37	(.48)	.23	(.42)	.30	(.46)
West	.16	(.37)	.06	(.23)	.26	(.44)
Under 500 employees	.74	(.44)	.74	(.44)		
500–1,000 employees	.08	(.27)	.02	(.15)		
Over 1,000 employees	.18	(.39)	.24	(.43)		
Not an MSA	.15	(.35)	0		.21	(.41)
Below 1 million	.33	(.47)	.02	(.15)	.27	(.44)
1–5 million	.30	(.46)	.83	(.38)	.32	(.47)
Above 5 million	.22	(.41)	.15	(.36)	.20	(.40)

Note: Numbers in parentheses are standard deviations.

[a]Predicted starting wage for the WCP sample.

[b]Training in the NLSY is employer-paid training since 1986 or beginning of job, whichever came last.

employer-provided training programs for workers with tenure of more than three years in the NLSY sample.[9]

The NLSY also contains information about the type and duration of training programs that can be used to augment the training information in our data set. Among workers in the NLSY who received employer-provided training, the median duration of their training is 2 weeks, with a mean of 7.33 weeks and standard deviation of 27.4 weeks. For workers age 32 and under in the WCP data set with nonmissing training duration data, the median duration of training is 1.7 weeks, with a mean of 8.03 weeks and standard deviation of 24.7 weeks. Despite the fact that responses to the training duration question are missing for a large portion of our sample, we are reassured by the remarkable similarity in the distribution of training episodes across the NLSY and WCP data sets.

Although we do not observe information about the type of training programs provided by employers in the WCP, this information is collected in the NLSY. Over 41 percent of the employer-provided training programs for white-collar workers (in matched WCP occupations) in the NLSY were classified as "formal company training programs run by the employer," over 25 percent were "seminars or training programs outside of work," and over 21 percent were classified as "seminars or training programs at work, not run by the employer." Given the other similarities in the two data sets, it is likely that workers in the WCP are also participating in the same types of training programs.

We conclude that our sample of WCP workers in manufacturing are reasonably representative of the population of white-collar workers in manufacturing. This is especially true for younger workers. The smaller sample of WCP workers in nonmanufacturing is less representative of the population: WCP workers are more likely to be male, highly educated, and highly paid. In empirical results not reported here, we find that standard demographic variables explain a much higher fraction of variation in pay across workers in the WCP than in either the CPS or the NLSY. These results are consistent with the hypothesis that wages in the WCP are measured with considerably less error than wages in the CPS or NLSY.

13.3   The Incidence of Training

13.3.1   Empirical Framework

We examine the relationship between participation in a formal training program and worker and employer characteristics by estimating the following regression:

---

9. We exclude the training information available in the NLSY prior to 1986 because it does not indicate whether the employer paid for the training program. Lynch (1992) shows that formal training programs are more likely to occur after the worker has completed one year on the job, which suggests that our conservative approach to measuring employer-provided training should underestimate actual training by a small amount: less than one-fourth of the NLSY sample has more than four years of job tenure.

(1) $\Pr(\text{Train}_{ij} = 1) = X_{ij}\theta_0 + Z_j\lambda_0 + (X_{ij}\theta_1 + Z_j\lambda_1)T_{ij} + \varepsilon_{ij},$

where i indexes workers and j indexes employers, $\text{Train}_{ij} = 1$ if the worker was trained by her employer, X_{ij} is a vector of worker demographic characteristics (including starting pay at the current employer), T_{ij} is job tenure, and Z_j is a vector of employer characteristics. Equation (1) includes interactions between job tenure and worker and employer characteristics to account for variation in the incidence of training due to differences in length of service with an employer. The error term in equation (1) is assumed to have the following form: $\varepsilon_{ij} = \mu_j + \nu_{ij}$, where μ_j is an employer-specific component of ε_{ij} and ν_{ij} is assumed to be identically independently distributed.

If workers share in the costs and benefits of formal training programs, trained workers receive lower starting wages and experience higher wage growth, ceteris paribus. Human capital models predict that workers face a trade-off between starting wages and training opportunities and the more general the training program, the higher the share of costs borne by the worker. Thus we expect the coefficient on starting wages in equation (1) to be negative, and it should be the most negative for workers acquiring the most general skills.

Starting pay may also be related to the incidence of training in equation (1) because starting pay may proxy for unobserved productivity differences across workers. Starting pay is correlated with the amount of skills acquired by a worker prior to the current job and consequently with a worker's productivity in human capital acquisition. Although it is plausible that workers with fewer skills at the start of a job are more likely to receive training, all else equal, these workers may also be the least productive in acquiring human capital. If the marginal productivity of human capital investment differs substantially across workers, relatively less productive workers may have lower starting wages (due to fewer previous investments) and be less likely to receive training from their current employers. In contrast, relatively more productive workers may have both higher starting wages and be more likely to receive training on the current job. Therefore, within-firm heterogeneity across workers implies an ambiguous empirical relationship between a worker's starting wage and the probability of training in equation (1).

13.3.2   Empirical Results

Comparisons to the National Longitudinal Survey of Youth

We first present estimates of equation (1) that ignore the employer-specific component of the error term. We consider this "pooled" specification because training studies based on household surveys do not have multiple observations per employer and therefore must ignore the employer-specific error component. We then compare our estimates to those obtained from the NLSY subsample in WCP-matched occupations. We use race, sex, education, tenure, and log starting pay as worker demographic characteristics, X_{ij}, and dummy variables for broad SIC industry group and establishment size as employer-specific characteristics, Z_j.

Column (1) of table 13.5 presents these pooled results for the 224 workers under age 33 in our WCP sample with reported starting pay. Few explanatory variables have a significant impact on the probability of receiving training. We find a significant positive coefficient on education and starting pay and a significant negative coefficient on the education and starting pay interaction. These results indicate that the workers most likely to receive training are relatively less educated workers with high starting wages and relatively more educated workers with low starting wages.

Column (2) presents regression results from the NLSY for the same specification of equation (1). The patterns of training incidence across NLSY workers and young workers in the WCP are reasonably similar. In both data sets we find that the workers most likely to receive training are relatively less educated workers with high starting wages and relatively more educated workers with low starting wages. Formal training programs appear to complement schooling for workers with low labor market experience and low starting wages, but employer-provided training programs may substitute for formal schooling for less educated workers with more labor market experience and higher starting wages. In the NLSY, we also find a significant relationship between tenure and the likelihood of receiving training, especially for workers with low starting wages, and significant differences in the incidence of training across establishment size categories and regions.

Random Effects Estimates of the Incidence of Training

In this section we use the WCP samples described in table 13.2 to estimate equation (1) and test for the presence of employer-specific effects in the error term.[10] In each case we strongly reject the null hypothesis that the variance of μ_j equals zero using a Breusch-Pagan Lagrange multiplier test. It is not surprising that we find an employer-specific component to the provision of training. In our sample of 1,234 workers with imputed starting pay, 148 establishments did not provide training to any of their 640 workers, 51 establishments provided training to all 197 of their workers, and 57 establishments with 397 workers exhibit some within-employer variation in the provision of training. A similar pattern is found in the sample of 601 workers with actual starting wages: 65 establishments did not provide training for any of their 297 employees, 25 establishments provided training for all 88 of their workers, and 34 establishments exhibit some within-employer variation in the provision of training to their 216 workers.

We test the hypothesis that μ_j is uncorrelated with the independent variables in our model using a Hausman specification test and fail to reject the null

---

10. We obtain similar results if we restrict the sample to the 224 workers under age 33 (comparable to the NLSY) in the WCP and use imputed starting wages.

Table 13.5   **Training Incidence: Full-Time White-Collar Workers under Age 33**

Variable	WCP (1)	(N = 224)	NLSY (2)	(N = 779)
Education	.7362**	(.2990)	.3517**	(.1050)
Tenure	−.4002	(.3521)	.1621*	(.0869)
Female	−.1322	(.1232)	−.0093	(.0583)
Black	.1807	(.2371)	−.1386*	(.0752)
Log starting wage	1.1113*	(.6321)	.8275**	(.2187)
Education*Log starting wage	−.0944**	(.0406)	−.0490**	(.0144)
Tenure*Education	−.0106	(.0115)	−.0001	(.0039)
Tenure*Female	.0348	(.0337)	−.0129	(.0162)
Tenure*Black	−.0330	(.0763)	.0219	(.0203)
Tenure*Log starting wage	.0929	(.0596)	−.0203**	(.0099)
Durable goods	−.0136	(.1732)	.0044	(.1181)
Trade and finance	−.4315*	(.2407)	.0724	(.1120)
Services	−.1845	(.2230)	.0531	(.1009)
Mining and construction	−.1985	(.2826)	−.1126	(.2025)
500–1,000 employees	−.0740	(.1752)	.1480*	(.0882)
Over 1,000 employees	.0210	(.1343)	.1612**	(.0660)
Below 1 million	.1685	(.1786)	.0585	(.0760)
1–5 million	.3246	(.2004)	−.0003	(.0775)
Above 5 million	.1831	(.2278)	.0711	(.0934)
Midwest	.1788	(.1562)	.0542	(.0844)
South	.1563	(.1535)	.0220	(.0870)
West	.1576	(.2193)	−.0835	(.0884)
Tenure*Industry				
Durable goods	−.0513	(.0488)	−.0170	(.0285)
Trade and finance	−.0267	(.0631)	−.0358	(.0268)
Services	−.0032	(.0662)	−.0251	(.0235)
Mining and construction	−.1107	(.1033)	−.0256	(.0525)
Tenure*Establishment size				
500–1,000 employees	−.0611	(.0524)	−.0191	(.0226)
Over 1,000 employees	−.0267	(.0390)	−.0205	(.0154)
Tenure*MSA size				
Below 1 million	−.0733	(.0541)	.0111	(.0183)
1–5 million	−.0663	(.0608)	.0338*	(.0183)
Above 5 million	−.0759	(.0697)	.0158	(.0238)
Tenure*Region				
Midwest	−.0185	(.0442)	.0258	(.0201)
South	−.0561	(.0436)	.0351*	(.0205)
West	.0127	(.0618)	.0646**	(.0233)
Constant	−8.6385*	(4.4977)	−5.8703**	(1.5739)
R^2	.2235		.1173	

Note: Numbers in parentheses are standard errors.

*Significant at the 10 percent level.

**Significant at the 5 percent level.

hypothesis of zero correlation in each WCP data set. The significant differences in training propensities across employers documented above are insignificantly correlated with observed worker characteristics in these establishments. Therefore, we account for the employer-specific component of training incidence by estimating equation (1) using employer random effects and present these results in table 13.6. Column (1) presents estimates based on the sample of 601 workers with reported starting wages, and column (2) presents estimates based on the sample of 1,234 workers with imputed starting wages.

We find that a one-year increase in tenure, evaluated at sample means, significantly raises the likelihood of training by 0.46 to 0.80 percentage points. We find no evidence of significant differences in the incidence of training by race or sex, evaluated at mean tenure. In both samples, workers in MSAs with populations of 1 to 5 million and workers in the West are significantly more likely to receive training, evaluated at mean tenure. In the smaller sample with reported starting wages, workers in mining and construction industries are significantly less likely to receive training, and workers in the Midwest are significantly more likely to receive training, evaluated at mean tenure.

We include interactions between a worker's starting wage and demographic characteristics to account for differences in the relationship between starting wages and the incidence of company training across workers. As in the previous section, we find significant positive coefficients on both education and starting pay and a significant negative coefficient on their interaction term in equation (1) using either sample. Estimated coefficients on interactions between a worker's starting pay and other demographic characteristics were insignificantly different from zero in all model specifications.[11]

Table 13.7 presents differences in the probability of training across low starting wage (10th percentile), medium starting wage (median), and high starting wage (90th percentile) workers across four education groups: 12, 13 to 15, 16, and more than 16 years of education. The coefficients in table 13.7 are the differences between the estimated training probability for each type of worker and the estimated probability that a low-starting-wage high school graduate received company training, evaluated at sample means.[12] We find that the incidence of training is highest for a low-starting-wage worker with a college degree. Training is least likely for a high-starting-wage worker with a graduate degree and a low-starting-wage worker with a high school diploma.

11. Across the two samples in table 13.6, we find no evidence of significant coefficients on the interactions between starting pay and either tenure, starting experience, or female.

12. Table 13.7 compares workers across education groups at the same *relative position* in the starting wage distribution, and not with the same starting wage; e.g., a "high" starting wage is defined as the 90th percentile of the starting wage distribution for a particular education group. To put these relative comparisons in perspective, the 90th percentile of the log starting wage distribution for workers with a high school diploma equals the median log starting wage for workers with a college degree (7.68).

Table 13.6   **Random Effects Estimates of Training Incidence among White-Collar Workers**

Variable	Actual Starting Wage Sample (1)		Predicted Starting Wage Sample (2)	
Education	.2895**	(.1053)	.2195**	(.0940)
Tenure	.0277	(.0451)	.0232	(.0412)
Female	.0394	(.0448)	.0285	(.0340)
Black	−.0808	(.0739)	−1.075*	(.0552)
Log starting wage	.4950**	(.2158)	.4236**	(.2018)
Education*Log starting wage	−.0361**	(.0139)	−.0285**	(.0124)
Tenure*Education	−.0016	(.0013)	−.0003	(.0009)
Tenure*Female	−.0011	(.0056)	.0015	(.0029)
Tenure*Black	.0221	(.0085)	.0181	(.0053)
Tenure*Log starting wage	−.0002	(.0062)	−.0011	(.0068)
Industry				
Durable goods	−.0989	(.0942)	−.0099	(.0667)
Trade and finance	−.5038**	(.1834)	−.2257*	(.1304)
Services	−.0652	(.1326)	.1692*	(.0954)
Mining and construction	−.3847**	(.1549)	−.1188	(.1088)
MSA size				
Below 1 million	.1399	(.1126)	.0919	(.0804)
1–5 million	.2827**	(.1181)	.2328**	(.0814)
Above 5 million	.1292	(.1342)	.1251	(.0978)
Region				
Midwest	.1915**	(.0968)	.0846	(.0759)
South	.1015	(.1014)	.0952	(.0787)
West	.1861	(.1310)	−.2023**	(.0920)
Establishment size				
500–1,000 employees	−.1956*	(.1141)	−.0718	(.0829)
Over 1,000 employees	−.0774	(.0941)	−.0105	(.0667)
Tenure*Industry				
Durable goods	.0011	(.0066)	−.0039	(.0034)
Trade and finance	.0429**	(.0126)	.0232**	(.0060)
Services	−.0099	(.0110)	−.0100	(.1226)
Mining and construction	−.0092	(.0098)	−.0005	(.0045)
Tenure*MSA size				
Below 1 million	−.0039	(.0079)	−.0010	(.0038)
1–5 million	.0023	(.0081)	−.0030	(.0035)
Above 5 million	.0045	(.0093)	.0009	(.0049)
Tenure*Region				
Midwest	.0034	(.0068)	−.0052	(.0036)
South	−.0131*	(.0072)	−.0102**	(.0039)
West	.0075	(.0098)	.0014	(.0055)
Tenure*Establishment size				
500–1,000 employees	.0134*	(.0079)	.0004	(.0049)
Over 1,000 employees	.0051	(.0059)	.0009	(.0029)
Constant	−3.8238**	(1.5938)	−3.186**	(1.471)
Sample size	601		1,234	

Notes: The omitted category is a nondurable-goods-manufacturing firm located in the Northeast outside of a metropolitan statistical area with less than 500 employees. Numbers in parentheses are standard errors.

*Significant at the 10 percent level.

**Significant at the 5 percent level.

Table 13.7   **Training Probabilities by Education and Starting Wage Group**

Starting Wage	Education			
	12 Years	13 to 15 Years	16 Years	More than 16 Years
Actual Starting Wage Sample (N = 601)				
Low (10th percentile)	.0000	.0745**	.1020**	.0962*
Median (50th percentile)	.0232	.0692**	.0662	.0229
High (90th percentile)	.0579	.0599	.0254	−.0413
Predicted Starting Wage Sample (N = 1,234)				
Low (10th percentile)	.0000	.0493**	.0643**	.0504
Median (50th percentile)	.0210	.0536	.0545	.0250
High (90th percentile)	.0433	.0583	.0407	−.0014

Note: Reported numbers are differences between estimated probability of training for a given worker and a low-starting-wage worker with a high school education.

*Significant at the 10 percent level.

**Significant at the 5 percent level.

13.4   Training and Wage Growth

13.4.1   Empirical Framework

Ideally, we would estimate the impact of training on wage growth in a panel data set by relating changes in workers' log wages over time to their investments in training. Our cross-sectional data set reports a worker's starting pay and training at an employer retrospectively. We therefore estimate a wage regression of the following form:

$$(2) \qquad \log W_{ij} = X_{ij}\beta_0 + Z_j\gamma_0 + (X_{ij}\beta_1 + Z_j\gamma_1)T_{ij} + \alpha_0\text{Train}_{ij}$$
$$+ \alpha_1\text{Train}_{ij}T_{ij} + \alpha_2\text{Train}_{ij}\log(SW_{ij})T_{ij} + u_{ij},$$

where $\log W_{ij}$ is a worker's current wage and the vector of worker characteristics, X_{ij}, includes a worker's starting pay. The coefficients on X_{ij}, Z_j, T_{ij}, and Train_{ij} represent the impact of worker characteristics, employer characteristics, job tenure, and training on a worker's current pay, conditional on starting pay. Thus equation (2) models variation in wage growth across workers, and interactions between X_{ij} and Z_j and job tenure account for differences in rates of wage growth by worker and employer characteristics. We hypothesize that the error term in equation (2) has an employer-specific component: $u_{ij} = \eta_j + e_{ij}$, where η_j is the employer-specific effect and e_{ij} is an independently identically distributed error.

Differences across the wage profiles of trained and untrained workers in our specification are determined by the parameters α_0, α_1, and α_2. The human capital model predicts that the returns to training, that is, wage growth, should be highest for workers who bear the highest fraction of training costs. Workers who receive more general company training and relatively lower starting pay are expected to experience more rapid wage growth. In other words, the human capital model suggests that the coefficient α_1 should be significantly positive and α_2 should be significantly negative in equation (2).[13]

13.4.2   Empirical Results

Comparison to the National Longitudinal Survey of Youth

Using the same subsamples of the WCP and NLSY as in table 13.5, we estimate the relationship between current wages, starting wages, and tenure in equation (2). We were unable to detect significant differences in the slopes of wage-tenure profiles across trained and untrained workers in either sample (estimates of α_1 and α_2 were insignificantly different from zero). We attribute this result to the small variation in job tenure across workers and our relatively small sample sizes. We therefore focus our attention on empirical models that estimate a common training effect across all workers (i.e., that restrict α_1 and α_2 to be zero).

Table 13.8 presents coefficient estimates for the wage growth model in equation (2) for the WCP data set; results for the NLSY are presented in column (2). We find large significant returns to tenure in both samples, but substantially more regression toward the mean in wage growth in the NLSY. Females experience significantly slower wage growth in the NLSY, and more educated workers have significantly faster wage growth in the WCP. For most worker and employer characteristics, the pattern of regression coefficients are similar across samples. We find a significant positive relationship between training and wage growth in both samples, but the effects are significantly larger in the NLSY. The mean trained worker in the NLSY earns wages 8.8 percent higher than a similar untrained worker, while the mean trained worker in the WCP earns wages that are 3.9 percent higher than a similar untrained worker, conditional on starting pay.

Random Effects Estimates of Wage Growth

Using the WCP samples described in table 13.2, we test for the presence of employer-specific effects in equation (2) and reject the null hypothesis that the variance of η_j equals zero. We then test the hypothesis that η_j is uncorrelated with the independent variables in our model using a Hausman specification test. In each WCP data set we fail to reject the null hypothesis of zero correlation. In other words, we find evidence of significant differences across employers in their average rates of wage growth, but these differences appear to be uncorrelated with observable worker characteristics. Therefore, we report ran-

---

13. Human capital models make few sharp predictions about the shape of wage profiles for trained workers relative to untrained workers. The "predictions" we outline here are conditional on the linear quadratic log(wage)-tenure relationship specified in eq. (2).

Table 13.8   OLS Wage Regressions: Full-Time White-Collar Workers under Age 33

Variable	WCP (1)		NLSY (2)	
Tenure	.5236**	(.1137)	.6057**	(.0655)
Tenure squared	−.0009	(.0016)	−.0118**	(.0018)
Log starting wage	.9590**	(.0663)	.5436**	(.0362)
(Log starting wage)*Tenure	−.0921**	(.0185)	−.0667**	(.0068)
Female	−.0350	(.0382)	.0150	(.0386)
Female*Tenure	.0005	(.0105)	−.0377**	(.0108)
Education	−.0085	(.0134)	.0564**	(.0090)
Education*Tenure	.0125**	(.0037)	.0036	(.0025)
Black	−.0300	(.0747)	−.0341	(.0500)
Black*Tenure	−.0158	(.0242)	−.0247*	(.0134)
Train	.0394*	(.0222)	.0880**	(.0241)
Industry				
Durable goods	.0322	(.0534)	.0560	(.0782)
Trade and finance	−.0004	(.0756)	−.0102	(.0744)
Services	.1500**	(.0712)	−.0398	(.0669)
Mining and construction	−.0090	(.0873)	.0793	(.1342)
MSA size				
Below 1 million	.0075	(.0556)	.0191	(.0504)
1–5 million	−.0311	(.0642)	.0635	(.0514)
Above 5 million	−.0503	(.0708)	.1444**	(.0619)
Region				
Midwest	−.1272**	(.0482)	−.0999*	(.0559)
South	−.0269	(.0473)	−.0406	(.0577)
West	−.0415	(.0673)	−.0484	(.0586)
Establishment size				
500–1,000 employees	.0739	(.0543)	.1134**	(.0586)
Over 1,000 employees	.0704	(.0427)	.0972**	(.0440)
Tenure*Industry				
Durable goods	−.0030	(.0151)	−.0165	(.0189)
Trade and finance	.0208	(.0198)	−.0304*	(.0179)
Services	−.0378*	(.0215)	−.0132	(.0156)
Mining and construction	.0247	(.0320)	−.0167	(.0348)
Tenure*MSA size				
Below 1 million	.0159	(.0169)	.0126	(.0121)
1–5 million	.0470**	(.0195)	.0230**	(.0121)
Above 5 million	.0549**	(.0216)	.0143	(.0157)
Tenure*Region				
Midwest	.0316**	(.0138)	.0108	(.0133)
South	.0122	(.0136)	−.0043	(.0136)
West	.0076	(.0189)	.0095	(.0155)
Tenure*Establishment size				
500–1,000 employees	−.0155	(.0164)	−.0123	(.0150)
Over 1,000 employees	−.0209	(.0128)	−.0047	(.0102)
Constant	.4198	(.3923)	2.3985**	(.2712)
Sample size	224		779	
R^2	.9046		.6289	

Notes: The omitted category is a nondurable-goods-manufacturing firm located in the Northeast outside of a metropolitan statistical area with less than 500 employees. Numbers in parentheses are standard errors.

*Significant at the 10 percent level.

**Significant at the 5 percent level.

dom effects estimates of equation (2) in table 13.9. Column (1) reports results for the 601 workers with reported starting wages, and column (2) reports results for the entire sample of 1,234 workers using imputed starting wages.[14]

The results in table 13.9 indicate that an additional year of tenure, holding constant starting wages, is associated with 4.3 percent higher current wages in column (1) and 3.5 percent higher current wages in column (2), evaluated at sample means. This difference in mean returns to tenure across samples is primarily due to the quadratic relationship between wages and tenure and the fact that the mean worker with nonmissing starting pay has about two years less tenure than the average worker with missing starting pay. The coefficient on the tenure–starting wage interaction is significantly negative, suggesting that wages exhibit moderate regression toward the mean over time.

Our estimates of α_1 and α_2 in table 13.9 are consistent with the predictions of the human capital model: low-starting-wage workers have the highest wage growth and therefore the highest returns to training. This result holds whether we use predicted or actual starting wages. We also find that wage growth is statistically significantly higher for whites, males, more educated workers, workers in trade and finance industries, and workers in the western region of the United States. Holding constant workers' starting wages in column (1), current wages are 7.9 percent lower for women, 6.8 percent lower for blacks, and 2.7 percent higher for workers with an additional year of education, evaluated at sample means. The race, gender, and education wage differentials in column (2) are similar in magnitude.

Table 13.10 presents estimates of average training effects for workers at the 10th, 50th, and the 90th percentiles of the starting wage distribution, evaluated at mean tenure. Female workers who received company training and earned low starting wages earn 5.5 to 10.2 percent higher wages than similar untrained workers in our samples. Trained female workers with the median starting wage receive 3.3 to 7.1 percent significantly higher current wages than similar untrained female workers. The current pay of trained female workers with high starting wages is insignificantly higher than the current wages of similar untrained female workers. The evidence of training effects for males is somewhat weaker; trained male workers with low starting wages currently earn 3.5 to 6.3 percent significantly higher wages than similar untrained male workers. The training effects for male workers with median and high starting wages are insignificantly different from zero in both samples.[15]

The evidence in table 13.10 suggests that employer-provided training has a

14. The specification differs from that in the previous section because it includes tenure squared, which is insignificant in eq. (1), and excludes the starting wage–education interaction, which is insignificant in eq. (2). Including tenure squared in eq. (1) or the starting wage–education interaction in eq. (2) does not substantially affect either set of results.

15. Note that we find larger and more significant effects for women than for men for the simple reason that women's average starting wage is lower than men's (there is no female–tenure–starting wage interaction in the regression). Thus, e.g., we would find a similar pattern for less educated compared to highly educated workers.

Table 13.9   **Random Effects Wage Regressions**

Variable	Actual Starting Wage Sample (1)		Predicted Starting Wage Sample (2)	
Tenure	.2413**	(.0274)	.1389**	(.0406)
Tenure squared	−.0011**	(.0002)	−.0009**	(.0001)
Log (starting wage)	.8413**	(.0341)	.6100**	(.0657)
(Log starting wage)*Tenure	−.0272**	(.0037)	−.0135**	(.0063)
Female	−.0054	(.0260)	−.0336	(.0302)
Female*Tenure	−.0126**	(.0033)	−.0079**	(.0028)
Education	.0196**	(.0070)	.0501**	(.0091)
Education*Tenure	.0011	(.0008)	.0002	(.0008)
Black	−.0219	(.0428)	−.0244	(.0475)
Black*Tenure	−.0068	(.0049)	−.0056	(.0046)
Train	.0373	(.0268)	.0528*	(.0278)
Train*Tenure	.0609*	(.0325)	.1104**	(.0332)
Train*Tenure*Log starting wage	−.0085*	(.0044)	−.0150**	(.0045)
Industry				
Durable goods	.0212	(.0309)	−.0168	(.0362)
Trade and finance	−.0140	(.0546)	−.0355	(.0675)
Services	.0467	(.0420)	−.0843*	(.0507)
Mining and construction	−.0039	(.0522)	−.0003	(.0575)
MSA size				
Below 1 million	.0174	(.0371)	.0739*	(.0424)
1–5 million	.0023	(.0395)	.1190**	(.0426)
Above 5 million	−.0053	(.0446)	.2065**	(.0519)
Region				
Midwest	−.0554*	(.0316)	−.0659*	(.0398)
South	−.0334	(.0329)	−.0247	(.0408)
West	−.0563	(.0413)	−.0555	(.0489)
Establishment size				
500–1,000 employees	−.0059	(.0349)	−.0098	(.0418)
Over 1,000 employees	−.0086	(.0276)	.0380	(.0339)
Tenure*Industry				
Durable goods	−.0099**	(.0035)	.0005	(.0028)
Trade and finance	.0162**	(.0069)	.0114**	(.0049)
Services	−.0111*	(.0058)	.0011	(.0051)
Mining and construction	−.0074	(.0055)	.0041	(.0038)
Tenure*MSA size				
Below 1 million	.0174	(.0371)	.0031	(.0032)
1–5 million	.0023	(.0395)	.0060*	(.0031)
Above 5 million	−.0053	(.0446)	−.0021	(.0041)
Tenure*Region				
Midwest	.0012	(.0037)	.0009	(.0029)
South	.0004	(.0039)	.0011	(.0032)
West	.0148	(.0056)	.0058	(.0047)
Tenure*Establishment size				
500–1,000 employees	−.0048	(.0043)	.0006	(.0032)
Over 1,000 employees	.0012	(.0031)	.0026	(.0025)
Constant	−.9032**	(.2217)	2.1627**	(.4074)
Sample size	601		1,234	

Notes: The omitted category is a nondurable-goods-manufacturing firm located in the Northeast outside of a metropolitan statistical area with less than 500 employees. Numbers in parentheses are standard errors.

*Significant at the 10 percent level.

**Significant at the 5 percent level.

Table 13.10   **Predicted Wage Growth of Trained Workers by Starting Wage Group**

Starting Wage	Actual Starting Wage Sample		Predicted Starting Wage Sample	
	Female	Male	Female	Male
Low (10th percentile)	.1018**	.0629**	.0545**	.0354*
	(.0270)	(.0221)	(.0250)	(.0209)
Median (50th percentile)	.0710**	.0094	.0331*	.0018
	(.0224)	(.0235)	(.0195)	(.0581)
High (90th percentile)	.0327	−.0464	.0064	−.0322
	(.0220)	(.0345)	(.0201)	(.0325)

Note: Numbers in parentheses are standard errors.
*Significant at the 10 percent level.
**Significant at the 5 percent level.

significant effect on wage growth for workers with relatively low starting wages. This effect is much less significant among workers with median to high starting wages. These results are consistent with human capital models that predict that workers receive returns to investments in training (experience more rapid wage growth) if they pay for the training through a lower starting wage. Workers who earned a relatively high starting wage and received training did not experience more rapid wage growth than untrained workers with relatively high starting wages in our sample. These differences may be due to differences in the specificity, duration, or intensity of training across workers with high and low starting wages.

13.5   Matching WCP Data with Firm Characteristics from Compustat and CRSP

One of the main contributions of this paper is to examine the relationship between company training and firm characteristics in greater detail than previous studies. In order to accomplish this, we matched establishments in our larger WCP sample to their publicly traded parent corporations in the Compustat database, which includes all firms traded on the New York Stock Exchange (NYSE), American Stock Exchange (AMSE), and NASDAQ exchange. (The Compustat data are compiled by Standard and Poor's from a firm's annual reports, financial statements, and 10K reports.) Many establishments in the WCP survey are not owned by these large publicly traded corporations, but there are 84 establishments owned by 69 different corporations that report valid current wage, demographic, and training data for 471 of their workers. We use this subsample of the WCP in our analysis of training and firm-specific characteristics. The Compustat database reports a firm's market value of equity, the value of its physical capital stock (plant and equipment) net of depreciation, R&D

expenditures, annual sales, and employment, in addition to a number of other financial variables. We were also able to match 61 firms and 420 workers to Center for Research in Security Prices (CRSP) data. CRSP data provide monthly (NYSE) or daily (AMSE and NASDAQ) stock market data for each of these firms. We determine each firm's annual stock market return in the year prior to the WCP survey.

The four firm characteristics that we use in our analysis are firm size (the logarithm of a firm's market value of equity), capital intensity (the logarithm of a firm's capital/labor ratio), R&D intensity (R&D/sales ratio),[16] and firm profitability (the firm's return on equity in the year prior to the WCP survey). Table 13.11 reports firm averages of the key variables in our analysis, and the number of corporations for which each variable is reported. Note that some variables, especially R&D, are not reported by some publicly traded corporations. Given our small sample sizes, we do not exclude these firms from our analysis. Instead, we replace all missing values with zeros and include a set of four "missing" dummy variables in our wage and training models. Each missing dummy variable equals one if the corresponding firm characteristic is not reported, and zero otherwise. As a result, we use all 69 firms and 471 workers throughout our analysis.

Table 13.11 presents means and standard deviations of worker characteristics for this subsample. Given our relatively small sample size we only report results for our sample of workers with imputed starting wages.[17] Note that the workers in the Compustat sample have 9.5 percent higher current wages, have 1.4 more years of tenure, and are less likely to be female than in our previous sample of workers with imputed starting wages. Employees in these large publicly traded firms are more likely to be employed in establishments in the South, more likely to have more than 1,000 employees, less likely to be in an MSA, and less likely to be in a service industry.

13.5.1   The Incidence of Training and Firm Characteristics

In estimating the probability of training in equation (1), we use the same explanatory variables as in table 13.6, with two exceptions. First, we measure employer size as the logarithm of a firm's market value of equity and exclude establishment size dummy variables from the regression. We also include the logarithm of a firm's capital/labor ratio, the ratio of a firm's R&D expenditures to its annual sales, and the firm's annual real stock market return (adjusted for dividends) in the previous year as employer characteristics, Z_j.

We find no evidence that worker characteristics are significantly related to the incidence of training across workers: we fail to reject the null hypothesis

---

16. All the Compustat variables we use in the analysis are real dollar averages compiled over the five-year period preceding the WCP survey. We do not use the logarithm of R&D as an explanatory variable, because R&D is zero for a number of firms, and instead consider the ratio of R&D to annual sales.

17. Of the 471 workers in Compustat firms, we have reported starting wages for 220 workers.

Table 13.11   Sample Statistics for Publicly Traded Firms and Their Employees

Variable	Observations	Mean (Standard Deviation)	
I. Means by 69 Firms			
Capital stock (billion $)	69	1,807.9	(6.070.7)
Capital/labor (thousand $ per worker)	66	53.48	(102.96)
Log (capital/labor)	66	3.177	(1.132)
Market value	67	2,635.8	(7,380.0)
Log (market value)	67	6.373	(1.893)
Sales	69	4,551.6	(9,962.0)
R&D	45	125.12	(218.93)
R&D/sales	45	.0225	(.0231)
Real annual return, previous year	61	.0102	9.3623)
II. Means by 471 Workers			
Real monthly wage	471	2,822.85	(1,240.65)
Log (real wage)	471	7.8496	(.4458)
Predicted log start wage	471	7.5551	(.3683)
Tenure	471	9.5881	(8.2242)
Train	471	.3376	(.4734)
Education	471	14.5074	(2.1407)
Starting potential experience	471	8.9130	(8.3467)
Female	471	.4331	(.4960)
Black	471	.0552	(.2286)
Nondurable goods	471	.2696	(.4442)
Durable goods	471	.5520	(.4978)
Trade and finance	471	.0318	(.1758)
Services	471	.0149	(.1211)
Mining and construction	471	.1316	(.3385)
Not an MSA	471	.2994	(.4585)
Below 1 million	471	.2803	(.4496)
1–5 million	471	.3142	(.4647)
Above 5 million	471	.0162	(.3084)
Northeast	471	.1592	(.3663)
Midwest	471	.2760	(.4475)
South	471	.4713	(.4997)
West	471	.0934	(.2913)

that the coefficients on X_{ij}, $X_{ij}T_{ij}$, and Z_jT_{ij} are all equal to zero.[18] It is surprising that we do not find a significant effect of years of tenure on the probability of training. Employer characteristics are significantly related to the incidence of training, but these regressors vary only across employers and not workers. Therefore, we present estimates of equation (1) that rely only on firm average data, where our dependent variable is the fraction of workers trained in the company.

18. We find similar coefficient estimates on worker characteristics in this smaller Compustat sample when using the same Z_j vector as in table 13.3. The finding that coefficients on starting wage, education, the starting wage–education interaction, and tenure are insignificant is attributable to the smaller sample size and the inclusion of a firm's market value of equity, log capital/labor ratio, R&D/sales ratio, and stock return in the Z_j vector.

Table 13.12   **Training Incidence: Linear Probability Model Results across 69 Firms**

Variable	Coefficient (1)	Coefficient (2)
Log (market value)		.0844**
		(.0382)
R&D/sales		−7.4675**
		(2.7944)
Log capital/labor		.0637
		(.0638)
Stock return		−.2264
		(.1713)
Industry		
Durable goods	−.1481	−.0674
	(.1122)	(.1157)
Trade and finance	−.4341	−.4051
	(.2956)	(.9085)
Services	.2249	.2235
	(.3897)	(.3637)
Mining and construction	.0481	−.2385
	(.1501)	(.1713)
MSA size		
Below 1 million	.5201**	.4302**
	(.1137)	(.1212)
1–5 million	.2515*	.2620
	(.1398)	(.1545)
Above 5 million	.2692	.0873
	(.1776)	(.1742)
Region		
Midwest	.1885	.0771
	(.1567)	(.1779)
South	−.1584	.4061**
	(.1514)	(.1217)
West	.0362	.3090
	(.1842)	(.1725)
Constant	.1494	.2281
	(.1650)	(.2565)

Notes: The omitted category is a nondurable-goods-manufacturing firm located in the Northeast outside of a metropolitan statistical area. We also include dummy variables in the model for missing R&D, capital/labor ratio, market value, and stock market return data. Numbers in parentheses are standard errors.

*Significant at the 10 percent level.

**Significant at the 5 percent level.

Column (1) of table 13.12 presents the results of a regression model weighted by the number of workers per firm including only industry, MSA size, and region dummy variables as explanatory variables. Column (2) includes these variables as well as the firm size, capital intensity, R&D intensity, and stock return variables calculated from Compustat and CRSP. We find that larger firms train a greater fraction of their workers. A 10 percent increase in the market value of equity, evaluated at sample means, increases the fraction of workers trained in a firm by 0.844 percentage points. Conditional on firm size, firms with higher R&D/sales ratios train a significantly smaller fraction of their workers. A 10 percent increase in the ratio of R&D to sales, evaluated at sample means (i.e., an increase of 0.00239) is associated with a 1.78 percentage point decline in the fraction of workers trained by a firm. Finally, we find that a firm's capital/labor ratio is unrelated to its likelihood of providing employee training.

Our empirical results that capital intensity and R&D intensity are not positively related to the incidence of formal training contrasts with the well-known empirical result that capital and skilled labor tend to be complements in production. Our results suggest that even though capital-intensive and R&D-intensive firms may employ more highly skilled labor, their workers are more likely to have obtained these skills in school, through previous employers, or through informal on-the-job training. Our results suggest that the costs of offering formal training programs are relatively lower in large corporations but appear relatively higher in companies that make large investments in R&D.

13.5.2 Wages, Training, and Firm Characteristics

We now consider the relationship between wage growth, training, and firm characteristics. We estimate equation (2) using ordinary least squares and cannot reject the null hypothesis of zero within-employer correlation in the error term u_{ij}. We therefore present OLS estimates of equation (2) in table 13.13. In table 13.9 above, we found strong evidence of an employer-specific component of the error term in equation (2). Much of the across-employer variation in wage growth appears to be accounted for by the inclusion of the capital intensity, stock market return, R&D intensity, and market value variables in the regression.

There have been few empirical studies of individual worker pay and firm profitability, capital intensity, and R&D intensity, other than studies of CEO and top executive pay (Troske 1993) is one of the few empirical studies that analyzes the relationship between individual worker pay and a plant's capital stock). Therefore, in column (1) of table 13.13 we present a standard wage regression that includes these firm characteristics but excludes training and starting wage variables. We find that capital intensity is much more important than firm size in explaining wage variation across employers.[19] A 10 percent increase in the capital/labor ratio is associated with 1.07 percent higher wages. Wages are also significantly higher in firms that spend relatively more on R&D; a 10 percent increase in the ratio of R&D to sales is associated with a

---

19. Troske (1993; chap. 11 in this volume) finds a similar result for wages and an establishment's capital stock. Conditional on capital intensity wages are insignificantly related to firm size measured by market value, employment, or sales.

Table 13.13   OLS Log Wage Regression: Workers in Publicly Traded Firms

Variable	Adding Compustat and CRSP to Standard OLS Wage Regression (1)		Wage Regression with CRSP, Compustat, and Starting Pay (2)	
Tenure	.0672**	(.0150)	.1740**	(.0857)
Tenure squared	−.0006**	(.0002)	−.0006**	(.0002)
Female	−.1141**	(.0416)	.0440	(.0537)
Female*Tenure	−.0046**	(.0036)	−.0114**	(.0047)
Black	−.0176	(.0932)	.0195	(.0923)
Black*Tenure	−.0047	(.0076)	−.0054	(.0076)
Education	.1273**	(.0100)	.0439**	(.0215)
Education*Tenure	−.0025**	(.0008)	−.0011	(.0018)
R&D/sales	1.6851**	(.7284)	1.0176	(.8244)
Log capital/labor	.1072**	(.0183)	.1014**	(.0244)
Log market value	.0103	(.0098)	−.0026	(.0119)
Stock return	.1144**	(.0475)	.1684**	(.0562)
Predicted starting wage			.6575**	(.1537)
Tenure*Log predicted starting wage			−.0208	(.0144)
Train			−.2940	(.1937)
Train*Tenure			.1271**	(.0488)
Train*(Log predicted starting wage) *Tenure			−.0168**	(.0065)
(Log capital/labor)*Train			.0722*	(.0413)
(R&D/sales)*Train			6.2008**	(2.7026)
(Log market value)*Train			−.0062	(.0025)
(Stock return)*Train			−.1377	(.1142)
Constant	5.3865**	(.1638)	1.7622**	(.9027)
R^2	.6991		.7248	

Notes: We also include dummy variables for SIC industry, region, and whether in an MSA, and these dummy variables interacted with tenure. We include dummy variables for missing R&D, capital/labor ratio, market value, and stock return data, and interactions between these four variables and Train. Numbers in parentheses are standard errors.

*Significant at the 10 percent level.

**Significant at the 5 percent level.

0.40 percent increase in wages. These empirical results suggest that capital-intensive and R&D-intensive firms employ workers with greater unobserved labor market skills, ceteris paribus. Thus our regression results support the hypothesis that skilled labor and capital, and skilled labor and R&D, are complements in production. Finally, note that a 10 percent increase in a firm's stock market return is associated with 1.14 percent higher wages.

In column (2) of table 13.13 we present estimates of the wage growth model in equation (2). We allow the returns to training to vary across companies by interacting training with capital intensity, stock market return, R&D intensity, and log market value. The average trained worker in our sample has 5.7 percent higher wages than the average untrained worker, though this difference is not statistically significant. As in table 13.7, we find a significant training effect for workers with relatively low starting wages.

The results in table 13.13 indicate that wage growth for trained workers is significantly higher in more capital-intensive and R&D-intensive firms. A 10 percent increase in the ratio of R&D to sales significantly increases the return to training by 1.48 percentage points. A 10 percent increase in the capital/labor ratio raises the return to training by 0.72 percentage points. Given the large variation in log capital/labor and R&D/sales in our sample, it appears that much of the variation in returns to training across workers is attributable to differences in firms' investments in capital equipment and R&D.[20]

The combined results of tables 13.12 and 13.13 indicate that (i) large employers are significantly more likely to provide training to their workers, (ii) conditional on firm size, a firm's capital/labor ratio is unrelated to its propensity to provide formal training to its workers, (iii) conditional on firm size, R&D-intensive firms are significantly less likely to provide formal training to their workers, (iv) both R&D- and capital-intensive firms employ relatively more skilled workers, and (v) when training is provided by capital- and R&D-intensive firms, their trained workers exhibit significantly faster wage growth than similar untrained workers. These results suggest that skilled labor is complementary to capital and R&D but R&D- and capital-intensive firms face higher costs of providing these skills through formal training programs.

13.6 Conclusions

In this paper we use a unique microdata set of white-collar workers that (i) has multiple observations per employer and (ii) allows us to match workers to their publicly traded employers in the CRSP and Compustat databases. Our data set is representative of the population of white-collar workers in manufacturing, based on CPS and NLSY samples, but overrepresents highly educated, high-wage, male workers outside of manufacturing. Patterns in the incidence and duration of training programs between young workers in our sample and white-collar workers in the NLSY are remarkably similar. There appears to be substantially less measurement error in wages in our sample than in either the NLSY or the CPS. The human capital and demographic variables used in standard wage regressions account for a much higher fraction of the variation in establishment-reported wages than household-reported wages for similar workers. Thus our empirical results suggest that matched worker-employer data sets based on BLS establishment surveys, such as the one analyzed here, can provide useful information about labor market behavior.

Company-provided formal training has a substantial employer-specific com-

---

20. E.g., a one standard deviation increase in R&D/sales results in a 14.3 percentage point increase in the return to training. A one standard deviation increase in log capital/labor results in an 8.2 percentage point increase in the effect of training on wage growth.

ponent: most firms trained either all or none of their white-collar workers in our sample. We consistently find that college graduates with low starting wages and high school graduates with high starting wages are the most likely to receive employer-provided training. This suggests that employee training programs complement formal schooling for college graduates with little work experience but substitute for formal schooling for workers with substantial experience and high school diplomas.

We find significant returns to training, but these returns are somewhat smaller for young workers in the WCP than for similar white-collar workers in the NLSY. Low-starting-wage workers receive the highest returns to training, earning 3.5 to 10.2 percent higher current pay than untrained workers with the same starting pay. These results confirm the implication of human capital models. Workers who pay a greater share of their training costs through lower starting wages experience faster wage growth.

In our subsample of workers in publicly traded firms, employer-provided training occurs significantly more frequently in large companies. Conditional on firm size, training programs occur relatively more often in firms that invest less in R&D, but the propensity for training is unrelated to capital intensity (conditional on firm size). We find strong evidence that the returns to training are higher in companies that invest in either R&D or capital equipment. In conclusion, our empirical results provide mixed evidence on the complementarity between training and investment in either R&D or capital equipment. Although the returns to training appear highest in companies that make investments in R&D or capital equipment, the incidence of training is somewhat lower in R&D-intensive companies. Higher returns to employer-provided training in large, capital-intensive, and R&D-intensive firms may occur for several reasons: (i) the typical duration of training programs in these firms may exceed the mean duration in other firms, (ii) the content, intensity, and opportunity cost of training programs may differ across firms, and (iii) unobserved skill differences across trained and untrained workers may vary across firms and be related to firm size and capital intensity. Additional empirical work, using matched worker and employer data, can aid in distinguishing between these competing hypotheses for interfirm differences in the returns to training.

References

Altonji, Joseph G., and James R. Spletzer. 1991. Worker characteristics, job characteristics, and the receipt of on-the-job training. *Industrial and Labor Relations Review* 45 (1): 58–79.

Barron, John M., Dan A. Black, and Mark A. Loewenstein. 1989. Job matching and on-the-job training. *Journal of Labor Economics* 7 (1): 1–19.

———. 1993. Gender differences in training, capital, and wages. *Journal of Human Resources* 28 (2): 341–62.

Bartel, Ann P. 1994. Productivity gains from the implementation of employee training programs. *Industrial Relations* 33 (4): 411–25.

Bishop, John H. 1982a. The social payoff from occupationally specific training: The employer's point of view. Columbus: Ohio State University, National Center for Research in Vocational Education.

———. 1982b. Subsidizing on-the-job training: An analysis of a national survey of employers. Columbus: Ohio State University, National Center for Research in Vocational Education.

———. 1985. The magnitudes and determinants of on-the-job training. In *Training and human capital formation,* ed. John H. Bishop et al. Columbus: Ohio State University, National Center for Research in Vocational Education.

Bronars, Stephen G., and Melissa Famulari. 1997. Wage, tenure, and wage growth variation within and across establishments. *Journal of Labor Economics* 15:285–317.

Duncan, Greg J., and Saul Hoffman. 1978. Training and earnings. In *Five thousand American families: Pattern and progress,* ed. Greg Duncan and James Morgan, 6:105–50. Ann Arbor: University of Michigan Press.

Hamermesh, Daniel. 1993. *Labor demand.* Princeton, N.J.: Princeton University Press.

Krueger, Alan, and Cecilia Rouse. 1994. New evidence on workplace education. NBER Working Paper no. 4931. Cambridge, Mass.: National Bureau of Economic Research.

Lillard, Lee A., and Hong W. Tan. 1992. Private sector training: Who gets it and what are its effects? *Research in Labor Economics* 13:1–62.

Lynch, Lisa M. 1992. Private-sector training and the earnings of young workers. *American Economic Review* 82 (1): 299–312.

Polivka, Anne, and Jennifer Rothgeb. 1993. Redesigning the CPS questionnaire. *Monthly Labor Review* 116 (9): 10–28.

Troske, Kenneth R. 1993. Evidence on the employer size-wage premia from worker establishment matched data. Bureau of the Census Working Paper. Washington, D.C.: U.S. Bureau of the Census.

Veum, Jonathan R. 1993. Training among young adults: What, what, and for how long? *Monthly Labor Review* 116 (8): 27–32.

———. 1994. Training, wages, and the human capital model. BLS Working Paper. Washington, D.C.: U.S. Department of Labor, Bureau of Labor Statistics, October.

Contributors

John M. Abowd
School of Industrial Relations
259 Ives Hall
Cornell University
Ithaca, NY 14853

Katharine G. Abraham
Bureau of Labor Statistics
2 Massachusetts Avenue NE
Suite 4040
Washington, DC 20212

George A. Akerlof
Brookings Institution
1775 Massachusetts Avenue NW
Washington, DC 20036

John M. Barron
Department of Economics
Purdue University
West Lafayette, IN 47907

Stephen G. Bronars
University of Texas at Austin
Department of Economics
Austin, TX 78712

Charles Brown
Department of Economics
University of Michigan
Ann Arbor, MI 48109

Steven J. Davis
Graduate School of Business
University of Chicago
1101 East 58th Street
Chicago, IL 60637

Melissa Famulari
University of Texas at Austin
Department of Economics
Austin, TX 78712

Henry S. Farber
Industrial Relations Section
Firestone Library
Princeton University
Princeton, NJ 08544

John Haltiwanger
Department of Economics
University of Maryland
College Park, MD 20742

Stephen R. G. Jones
Department of Economics
McMaster University
1280 Main Street West
Hamilton, ON L8S 4M4 Canada

Lawrence F. Katz
National Bureau of Economic Research
1050 Massachusetts Avenue
Cambridge, MA 02138

Francis Kramarz
Département Recherche
INSEE, P.O. Box 100
25, Boulevard Gabriel Peri
92244 Malakoff France

Thomas Lemieux
Department of Economics
University of Montreal
P.O. Box 6128, Station Downtown
Montreal, PQ H3C 3J7 Canada

Frank R. Lichtenberg
Graduate School of Business
726 Uris Hall
Columbia University
New York, NY 10027

Lisa M. Lynch
Fletcher School of Law and Diplomacy
Tufts University
Medford, MA 02155

Marilyn E. Manser
Bureau of Labor Statistics
Office of Employment Research and
   Program Development
2 Massachusetts Avenue NE
Suite 4945
Washington, DC 20212

Robert H. McGuckin
The Conference Board
845 Third Avenue
New York, NY 10022

Bruce D. Meyer
Department of Economics
Northwestern University
2003 Sheridan Road
Evanston, IL 60208

Stephen M. Miller
Bureau of Labor Statistics
Office of Research and Evaluation
2 Massachusetts Avenue NE
Suite 4915
Washington, DC 20212

Derek Neal
Department of Economics
University of Wisconsin
1180 Observatory Drive
Madison, WI 53706

Sang V. Nguyen
Center for Economic Studies
Bureau of the Census
Washington, DC 20233

Anne E. Polivka
Bureau of Labor Statistics
Office of Economic Research
2 Massachusetts Avenue NE
Suite 4915
Washington, DC 20212

Canice Prendergast
Graduate School of Business
University of Chicago
1101 East 58th Street
Chicago, IL 60637

Arnold P. Reznek
Center for Economic Studies
Bureau of the Census
Washington, DC 20233

W. Craig Riddell
Department of Economics
University of British Columbia
2075 Westbrook Mall
Vancouver, BC V6T 1Z1 Canada

Gary Solon
Department of Economics
University of Michigan
Ann Arbor, MI 48109

James R. Spletzer
Bureau of Labor Statistics
Office of Economic Research
2 Massachusetts Avenue NE
Suite 4915
Washington, DC 20212

Frank P. Stafford
Department of Economics
University of Michigan
Ann Arbor, MI 48109

Jay C. Stewart
Bureau of Labor Statistics
Office of Economic Research
2 Massachusetts Avenue NE
Washington, DC 20212

Robert Topel
Graduate School of Business
University of Chicago
1101 East 58th Street
Chicago, IL 60637

Kenneth R. Troske
Department of Economics
University of Missouri, Columbia
118 Professional Bldg.
Columbia, MO 65203

Author Index

467

Subject Index